International Refugee Law and Socio-Economic Rights

A range of emerging refugee claims is beginning to challenge the boundaries of the Refugee Convention regime and question traditional distinctions between 'economic migrants' and 'political refugees'. This book identifies the conceptual and analytical challenges presented by claims based on socio-economic deprivation, and assesses the extent to which these challenges may be overcome by a creative interpretation of the Refugee Convention, consistent with correct principles of international treaty interpretation. The central argument is that, notwithstanding the dichotomy between 'economic migrants' and 'political refugees', the Refugee Convention is capable of accommodating a more complex analysis which recognizes that many claims based on socio-economic deprivation are indeed properly considered within its purview. This, the first book to consider these issues, will be of great interest to refugee law scholars, advocates, decision-makers and non-governmental organizations.

MICHELLE FOSTER is a Senior Lecturer and Director of the Research Programme in International Refugee Law at the Institute for International Law and the Humanities, University of Melbourne Law School.

Cambridge Studies in International and Comparative Law

Established in 1946, this series produces high quality scholarship in the fields of public and private international law and comparative law. Although these are distinct legal sub-disciplines, developments since 1946 confirm their interrelation.

Comparative law is increasingly used as a tool in the making of law at national, regional and international levels. Private international law is now often affected by international conventions, and the issues faced by classical conflicts rules are frequently dealt with by substantive harmonisation of law under international auspices. Mixed international arbitrations, especially those involving state economic activity, raise mixed questions of public and private international law, while in many fields (such as the protection of human rights and democratic standards, investment guarantees and international criminal law) international and national systems interact. National constitutional arrangements relating to 'foreign affairs', and to the implementation of international norms, are a focus of attention.

The Board welcomes works of a theoretical or interdisciplinary character, and those focusing on the new approaches to international or comparative law or conflicts of law. Studies of particular institutions or problems are equally welcome, as are translations of the best work published in other languages.

General Editors	James Crawford SC FBA
	Whewell Professor of International Law, Faculty of Law,
	and Director, Lauterpacht Research Centre for
	International Law, University of Cambridge
	John S. Bell FBA
	Professor of Law, Faculty of Law, University of Cambridge
Editorial Board	Professor Hilary Charlesworth *Australian National University*
	Professor Lori Damrosch *Columbia University Law School*
	Professor John Dugard *Universiteit Leiden*
	Professor Mary-Ann Glendon *Harvard Law School*
	Professor Christopher Greenwood *London School of Economics*
	Professor David Johnston *University of Edinburgh*
	Professor Hein Kötz *Max-Planck-Institut, Hamburg*
	Professor Donald McRae *University of Ottawa*
	Professor Onuma Yasuaki *University of Tokyo*
	Professor Reinhard Zimmermann *Universität Regensburg*
Advisory Committee	Professor D. W. Bowett QC
	Judge Rosalyn Higgins QC
	Professor J. A. Jolowicz QC
	Professor Sir Elihu Lauterpacht CBE QC
	Professor Kurt Lipstein
	Judge Stephen Schwebel

A list of books in the series can be found at the end of this volume.

International Refugee Law and Socio-Economic Rights

Refuge from Deprivation

Michelle Foster

CAMBRIDGE
UNIVERSITY PRESS

University Printing House, Cambridge CB2 8BS, United Kingdom

Cambridge University Press is part of the University of Cambridge.

It furthers the University's mission by disseminating knowledge in the pursuit of education, learning and research at the highest international levels of excellence.

www.cambridge.org
Information on this title: www.cambridge.org/9780521870177

© Michelle Foster 2007

This publication is in copyright. Subject to statutory exception and to the provisions of relevant collective licensing agreements, no reproduction of any part may take place without the written permission of Cambridge University Press.

First published 2007
First paperback edition 2009

A catalogue record for this publication is available from the British Library

Library of Congress Cataloguing in Publication data

Foster, Michelle, 1972-
International refugee law and socio-economic rights : refuge from deprivation / Michelle Foster.
 p. cm. – (Cambridge studies in international and comparative law)
ISBN-13: 978-0-521-87017-7 (hardback)
ISBN-10: 0-521-87017-8 (hardback)
 1. Refugees–Legal status, laws, etc. 2. Asylum, Right of. 3. Human rights. 4. Convention Relating to the Status of Refugees (1951) 5. Migrant labor–Legal status, laws, etc. I. Title. II. Series.
K3230.R45F67 2007
342.08'3–dc22   2006102051

ISBN 978-0-521-87017-7 Hardback
ISBN 978-0-521-13336-4 Paperback

Cambridge University Press has no responsibility for the persistence or accuracy of URLs for external or third-party internet websites referred to in this publication, and does not guarantee that any content on such websites is, or will remain, accurate or appropriate.

Contents

Acknowledgements	page ix
Table of cases	xiii
Table of treaties and other international instruments	xliii
List of abbreviations	xlv

1 Introduction — 1
Background — 2
The key conceptual challenge: economic migrants versus refugees — 5
Challenging the simplistic dichotomy — 11
Organization and methodology of analysis — 21

2 A human rights framework for interpreting the refugee convention — 27
Part one: the developing human rights framework — 27
Part two: justification of the human rights framework — 36
The need for a universal and objective standard — 36
Human rights as the standard: object and purpose — 40
The human rights approach confirmed by context — 49
Other rules of international law: promoting coherence — 51
Part three: possible objections to the human rights approach — 75
Concerns about the legitimacy of the human rights approach — 75
Concerns about the workability of the human rights approach — 85
Conclusion — 86

3	**Persecution and socio-economic deprivation in refugee law**	**87**
	Introduction	87
	Socio-economic rights and persecution: an overview	90
	Conceptual approaches to socio-economic rights and persecution	111
	Problems and difficulties in the current approach	123
	Conclusion	154
4	**Rethinking the conceptual approach to socio-economic claims**	**156**
	Introduction	156
	Part one: the current approach to persecution in light of international human rights law	156
	The legitimacy of a normative hierarchy in human rights	157
	The merits of a categorical approach based on state obligation	168
	The interdependence of human rights	181
	Conclusion on hierarchies and models in refugee law	190
	Part two: revisiting violations of socio-economic rights and persecution	201
	The core obligations approach: general considerations	201
	Right to education and persecution	214
	Right to health and persecution	226
	Conclusion	235
5	**Economic deprivation as the reason for being persecuted**	**236**
	Introduction	236
	When is persecution for a Convention reason? The particular challenge of socio-economic claims	237
	The desire for a 'better life': economic migrants versus political refugees	238
	The causal connection to a refugee convention ground	247
	The meaning of the nexus clause: is intention required?	263
	Evidentiary issues: singling out versus group-based harm	286
	Conclusion	289
6	**Economic disadvantage and the Refugee Convention grounds**	**291**
	Introduction	291

	Interpreting the social group ground: conceptual approaches	292
	Particular social groups	304
	Economic class	304
	Occupation	313
	Disabled and ill persons	318
	Women	324
	Children	329
	Conclusion	339
7	**Conclusions**	**341**
	Bibliography	356
	Index	379

Acknowledgements

This book is based largely on my doctoral thesis, undertaken for the SJD degree at the University of Michigan Law School, under the supervision of James C. Hathaway. It would not have been possible without the encouragement, stimulation and support of Jim Hathaway. His inspiring teaching during my LLM studies at Michigan enlivened my passion for refugee law, and his encouragement and belief that I could and should enroll in the SJD programme is the reason that this project was begun. In addition to providing a provocative 'sounding board' for my ideas, he also carefully read and commented upon various drafts of my dissertation chapters, and then continued to provide feedback as I undertook the task of revising the thesis for publication. This book has undoubtedly benefited from his careful scrutiny and I am indebted to him for his involvement with this project.

I was extremely fortunate to have a wonderful SJD committee comprising also Christine Chinkin and Brian Simpson. They each read and commented upon various drafts and provided sharp insight into and critique of many fundamental issues. They were both willing to listen to my ideas and problems and helped shape the organization of the book and strengthened important arguments. Pene Mathew read and provided very thoughtful and detailed comments on some early draft chapters. I also benefited greatly from numerous challenging conversations in respect of various aspects of my work with many people I met at the University of Michigan including Christine Breining-Kauffman, Rodger Haines, Rob Howse, Christopher McCrudden, Karen Musalo, Luis Peral, Catherine Phuong and Bruno Simma. In addition to talking with me on a number of occasions about my work, Rodger Haines also referred me to many helpful sources, and I am very grateful for his engagement with my project.

I also benefited from participation in the Community of Scholars programme run by the University of Michigan's Institute for Research on Women and Gender in May–June 2003, the University of California San Diego's CCIS summer programme on International Migration Studies in June 2003, and the LSA Graduate Workshop and Annual Conference in May 2004, all of which provided helpful feedback on my work, particularly from a multi-disciplinary perspective.

I owe a huge thanks to all the library staff at the University of Michigan Law Library, in particular Beatrice Tice and Sandy Zeff. In addition, I am extremely grateful for the assistance in tracking down difficult to obtain tribunal decisions from Michael Simperingham and Rodger Haines of the New Zealand RSAA, Nicole Robinson of the Australian RRT, Rebecca Cooper of the UK IAT, Mark Symes (barrister, UK), Stephen Knight and Karen Musalo of the Centre for Gender and Refugee Studies (USA) and Theresa Smith and Chantal Ippersiel of the Canadian Immigration and Review Board. I am also very grateful to Hugo Storey (of the UK IAT) and Les Mugridge and John Dean (of the UK Electronic Immigration Network) for arranging free access to the EIN's database of UK decisions, which proved essential to my research.

I am enormously appreciative of the generous financial assistance I received from the University of Michigan Law School over four years, both for the LLM and SJD degrees. In addition, I am very grateful for the constant support and encouragement of Dean Virginia Gordan throughout my residence at Michigan. I am also indebted to the Skye International Foundation, which primarily funded my LLM studies and thus allowed me to go to the USA in the first place.

The University of Melbourne Law School has also been very supportive of this project and I am extremely grateful to Michael Crommelin and Jenny Morgan for allowing me to take leave from teaching in order to work on this book, and for their general encouragement and support. I am also very grateful to Melbourne Law School for awarding me Research Support Funds in order to employ Luke Raffin – an undergraduate Melbourne student whose excellent work was crucial in finalizing the manuscript for publication.

I would not have been able to complete this book without the friendship of a number of people, many of whom suffered the trials and tribulations of the SJD process alongside me. The community of international students at Michigan became my family and I am especially grateful for the support of Patrick Blatter, Mona Dimalanta, Laura Huomo, Zdenek and Eva Kuhn, Sagit Leviner, Barbara Miltner,

Louise Moor, Ivana Radicici, Carolyn Risk, Goran Selanec, Gitit Shriqui, Ninee Supornpaibul, Yofi Tirosh and Larissa Wakim. I was also extremely fortunate to have had the support of my friends from home, who, despite the considerable challenges presented by the distance from Australia, continued to provide support and love throughout my stay overseas, especially Rai Small and Tanya Segelov. In addition to her constant support, in particular Rai Small provided invaluable editing assistance when I needed it most.

I am, as always, grateful to my family for their constant love and encouragement, especially my mother and grandparents. Most importantly I am forever indebted to my partner Brad, who has been my best friend and most loyal and constant source of support during this challenging period. I will always be grateful for his wisdom, patience and belief in me.

Michelle Foster
Melbourne, June 2006

The law is stated as at 31 December 2005, although later developments have been incorporated where possible.

Table of cases

I. International Decisions

International Court of Justice

Aegean Sea Continental Shelf Case (Greece v. Turkey) 1978 ICJ Rep 3. 62
Application of the Convention on the Prevention and Punishment of the Crime of Genocide [1996] ICJ Rep 595. 47
Case Concerning the Gabcikovo-Nagymaros Project (Hungary/Slovakia) [1997] ICJ Rep 7. 52, 60
Legal Consequences of the Construction of a Wall in the Occupied Palestinian Territory, Advisory Opinion (I.C.J. July 9, 2004), 43 I.L.M. 1009 (2004) 177, 183
Maritime Delimitation and Territorial Questions between Qatar and Bahrain (Jurisdiction and Admissibility) [1995] ICJ Rep 6. 40
Namibia (Legal Consequences) Advisory Opinion (1971) ICJ Rep 31. 59
Reservations to the Convention on the Prevention and Punishment of the Crime of Genocide [1951] ICJ Rep 15. 47
Territorial Dispute (Libyan Arab Jamahiriya/Chad) [1994] ICJ Rep 6. 40

UN Human Rights Committee

ARJ v. Australia (Communication No. 692/1996, 11 August 1997) 353
Communication No. 458/1991: Cameroon 10/08/94, CCPR/C/51/D/458/1991. 185
F.H. Zwaan-de Vries v. the Netherlands (Communication No. 182/1984) U.N. Doc. hCCPR/C/29/D/182/1984 (16 April 1987). 186
L.G. Danning v. the Netherlands (Communication No. 180/1984), U.N. Doc. CCPR/C/29/D180/1984 (16 April 1987). 185

xiii

xiv   TABLE OF CASES

S.W.M. Broeks v. the Netherlands (Communication No. 172/1984),
U.N. Doc. CCPR/C/29/D/172/1984 (16 April 1987).   185

World Trade Organization

Dispute Regarding United States - Standards for Reformulated and
Conventional Gasoline, Appellate Body Report, adopted 20 May 1996
(WT/DS2/AB/R).
EC-Measures Affecting the Approval and Marketing of Biotech Products
(29 September 2006) WT/DS291-293 (WTO Panel).   55
Japan — Taxes on Alcoholic Beverages, WTO Doc AB-1996-2 (1996) s. D
(Report of the Appellate Body).   40
United States — Import Prohibition of Certain Shrimp and Shrimp Products, WTO
Doc. WT/DS58/AB/R (1998) (Report of the Appellate Body).   42, 76

II. Regional Decisions

African Commission on Human and Peoples' Rights

Decision Regarding Communication No. 155/96, African Commission on
Human and Peoples' Rights, ACHPR/COMM/A044/1, 27 May 2002.
174

European Court of Human Rights

Akdivar v. Turkey (1996) Eur. Court HR, Case No. 99/1995/605/693,
30 August 1996.   187
Aylor-Davis v. France Case No. 22742/93, 20 January 1994.   352
Berrehab v. The Netherlands (1988) 11 EHRR 322.   351
Bilgin v. Turkey (2000) Eur. Court HR, Case No. 23819/94,
16 November 2000.   187
Case of Airey v. Ireland (1979) Eur. Court HR, Application No. 6289/73,
9 October 1979.   187
Case of Bensaid v. United Kingdom (2001) 33 EHRR 10.   351
Case of Drozd and Janousek v. France and Spain Case No. 21/1991/273/344,
26 June 1992.   352
Chahal v. United Kingdom (1996) 23 EHRR 413.   348
Costello-Roberts v. United Kingdom (1993) 247-C Eur. Court HR (ser A).   76
Cyprus v. Turkey (2001) Eur. Court HR, Case No. 25781/94, 10 May 2001.   187

D v. the United Kingdom (1997), Eur. Court HR, Case No. 146/1996/767/964, 21 April 1997.   187, 188, 350
D v. United Kingdom, European Court of Human Rights, 42 BMLR 149, 2 May 1997.   21
Deumeland v. Germany (1986), Eur. Court HR, Case No. 9384/81, 29 May 1986.   187
Dulas v. Turkey (2001) Eur. Court HR, Case No. 25801/94, 3 January 2001.   187
Feldbrugge v. The Netherlands (1986) Eur. Court HR, Case No. 8562/79, 29 May 1986.   187
Gaygusuz v. Austria (1996) Eur. Court HR, Case No. 39/1995/545/631, 16 September 1996.   187
Golder v. United Kingdom (1975) Eur. Court HR (ser A); (1979) 1 EHRR 524.   42
Lopez Ostra v. Spain (1994) Eur. Court HR, Case No. 41/1993/436/515, 9 December 1994.   187
Mohamed Dougoz v. Greece Application No. 40907/98, 8 February 2000.   352
Pellegrini v. Italy Case No. 30882/96, 20 July 2001.   352
Salesi v. Italy (1993) Eur. Court HR, Case No. 11/1992/356/430, 26 February 1993.   187
Schuler-Zgraggen v. Switzerland (1993) Eur. Court HR, Case No. 17/1992/362/436, 24 June 1993.   187
Selçuk and Asker v. Turkey (1998) Eur. Court HR, Case No. 12/1997/796/998–9, 24 April 1998.   187
Sigurdur A Sijurjónsson v. Iceland, No. 24/1992/369/443, 24 June 1993.
Soering Case Case No. 1/1989/161/217.   352

Inter-American Court on Human Rights

Advisory Opinion on the Interpretation of the American Declaration of Rights and Duties of Man within the Framework of Article 64 of the American Convention on Human Rights (1990) 29 ILM 379, 14 July 1989.   60
Other Treaties Subject to the Consultative Jurisdiction of the Court, Advisory Opinion No. OC-1/82, Inter-American Court of Human Rights, 24 September 1982, reprinted in (1982) 3 *Human Rights Law Journal* 140   42
The Effect of Reservations on the Entry into Force of the American Convention, Advisory Opinion No. OC-2/82 (Inter-American Court of Human

Rights, 24 September 1982), reprinted in (1982) 3 *Human Rights Law Journal* 153 (1982).   42, 47

III. National Decisions

Australia

A v. *Minister for Immigration and Multicultural Affairs* [2002] FCA 238 (French, Lindgren and Stone JJ, 27 February 2002).   34

Ahmadi v. *Minister for Immigration and Multicultural Affairs* [2001] FCA 1070 (Wilcox J, 8 August 2001).   100

Amanyar v. *Minister for Immigration and Ethnic Affairs* (1995) 63 FCR 194.

Appellant S395/2002 v. *Minister for Immigration and Multicultural Affairs* (2003) 216 CLR 473.   29

Applicant A and Another v. *Minister for Immigration and Ethnic Affairs and Another* (1996) 190 CLR 225.   37

Applicant A v. *Minister for Immigration and Ethnic Affairs* (1997) 142 ALR 331.

Applicant in V488 of 2000 v. *Minister for Immigration and Multicultural Affairs* [2001] FCA 1815 (Unreported, Ryan J, 19 December 2001).   258

Applicant S v. *Minister for Immigration & Multicultural Affairs* (2004) 217 CLR 387   298

Applicant S61 of 2002 v. *Refugee Review Tribunal* [2003] FCA 1274 (Unreported, Lindgren J, 11 November 2003).   304

Applicant S469 of 2002 v. *Minister for Immigration and Multicultural and Indigenous Affairs* [2004] FCA 64 (Unreported, Bennett J, 6 February 2004).   325

Applicant VEAZ of 2002 v. *Minister for Immigration and Multicultural Affairs* [2003] FCA 1033 (Unreported, Gray J, 2 October 2003).   279

Chan Yee Kin v. *Minister for Immigration and Multicultural Affairs* (1989) 169 CLR 379.   224

Chen Ru Mei v. *Minister of Immigration and Ethnic Affairs* (1995) 130 ALR 405.   105

Chen Shi Hai (an infant) by his next friend Chen Ren Bing v. *Minister for Immigration and Multicultural Affairs* [1998] 622 FCA (French J, 5 June 1998).   48

Chen Shi Hai v. *Minister for Immigration and Multicultural Affairs* (2000) 201 CLR 293.   45, 264

Chokov v. *Minister for Immigration and Multicultural Affairs* [1999] FCA 823 (Unreported, Einfeld J, 25 June 1999).   256

Farajvand v. *Minister for Immigration and Multicultural Affairs* [2001] FCA 795 (Allsop J, 20 June 2001). 34

Gunaseelan v. *Minister for Immigration and Multicultural Affairs* (1997) 49 ALD 594. 225

Hagi-Mohamed v. *Minister for Immigration and Multicultural Affairs* [2001] FCA 1156 (Wilcox, Weinberg and Hely JJ, 23 August 2001). 259

Hapuarachchige v. *Minister for Immigration and Ethnic Affairs* (1997) 46 ALD 496. 224

Harirchi v. *Minister for Immigration and Multicultural Affairs* [2001] FCA 1576 (Sackville, Kiefel and Hely JJ, 7 November 2001). 224

IW v. *City of Perth* (1996) 191 CLR 1. 57

Jahazi v. *Minister for Immigration and Ethnic Affairs* (1995) 133 ALR 437.

Ji Kil Soon v. *Minister for Immigration, Local Government and Ethnic Affairs and the RRT* (1994) 37 ALD 609. 100

Kuthyar v. *Minister for Immigration and Multicultural Affairs* [2000] FCA 110 (Einfeld J, 11 February 2000). 227, 321

Li Shi Ping and Anor v. *Minister for Immigration, Local Government and Ethnic Affairs* (1995) 35 ALD 557. 98

Liu v. *Minister for Immigration and Multicultural Affairs* (2001) 113 FCR 541. 29

Liu v. *Minister for Immigration and Multicultural Affairs* [2001] FCA 257 (Cooper J, 16 March 2001). 85

Lo v. *Minister for Immigration and Ethnic Affairs* (1995) 61 FCR 221. 321

Minister for Immigration and Multicultural Affairs v. *Abdi* (1999) 162 ALR 105. 247

Minister for Immigration and Multicultural Affairs v. *Applicant S* (2002) 124 FCR 256. 292

Minister for Immigration and Multicultural Affairs v. *Cali* [2000] FCA 1026 (North J, 3 August 2000). 326

Minister for Immigration and Multicultural Affairs v. *Ibrahim* (2000) 204 CLR 1. 59, 127

Minister for Immigration and Multicultural Affairs v. *Khawar* (2002) 210 CLR 1. 29, 264

Minister for Immigration and Multicultural Affairs v. *Mohammed* (2000) 98 FCR 405. 43

Minister for Immigration and Multicultural Affairs v. *Ndege* [1999] FCA 783 (Weinberg J, 11 June 1999). 326

Minister for Immigration and Multicultural Affairs v. *Respondents S152/2003* (2004) 205 ALR 487. 29

Minister for Immigration and Multicultural Affairs v. *Sarrazola (No. 2)* (2001) 107 FCR 184.   28

Minister for Immigration and Multicultural Affairs v. *Savvin & Ors* (2000) 98 FCR 168.   41

Minister for Immigration and Multicultural Affairs v. *Wang* (2003) 215 CLR 518.   34

Minister for Immigration and Multicultural Affairs v. *Zamora* (1998) 84 FCR 458.   315

Minister for Immigration and Multicultural and Indigenous Affairs v. *Kord* [2002] FCA 334 (Heerey, Marshall and Dowsett JJ, 28 March 2002).   273

Minister for Immigration, Local Government and Ethnic Affairs v. *Che Guang Xiang* (Federal Court of Australia, Jenkinson, Spender and Lee JJ, 12 August 1994).   105

MMM v. *Minister for Immigration and Multicultural Affairs* (1998) 90 FCR 324.   44

Morato v. *Minister of Immigration* (1992) 39 FCR 401.   305

NACM of 2002 v. *Minister for Immigration and Multicultural and Indigenous Affairs* (2003) 134 FCR 550.   29

NACR of 2002 v. *Minister for Immigration & Multicultural & Indigenous Affairs* [2002] FCAFC 318   94

NAGV and NAGW of 2002 v. *Minister for Immigration and Multicultural and Indigenous Affairs* (2005) 213 ALR 668.   46

NASB v. *Minister for Immigration & Multicultural & Indigenous Affairs* [2003] FCA 1046 (Beaumont, Lindgren and Tamberlin JJ, 2 October 2003).   130

NBFP v. *Minister for Immigration and Multicultural and Indigenous Affairs* [2005] FCAFC 95 (Kiefel, Weinberg and Edmonds JJ, 31 May 2005).   130

Nouredine v. *Minister for Immigration and Multicultural Affairs* (1999) 91 FCR 138.   315

Okere v. *Minister for Immigration and Multicultural Affairs* (1998) 157 ALR 678.   271

Prahastono v. *Minister for Immigration and Multicultural Affairs* (1997) 77 FCR 260.   94

Premalal v. *Minister for Immigration, Local Government and Ethnic Affairs* (1993) 41 FCR 117.   28-29

Rajaratnam v. *Minister for Immigration and Multicultural Affairs* [2000] FCA 1111 (Moore, Finn and Dowsett JJ, 10 August 2000).   253

Ram v. Minister for Immigration (1995) 57 FCR 565.   264
Re Minister for Immigration and Multicultural Affairs, ex parte PT (2001)
    178 ALR 497.   252
Reference N01/37224, RRT, 12 August 2002.   304
Reference N01/38085, RRT, 18 February 2002.   223
Reference N01/38920, RRT, 11 July 2002.   86, 153
Reference N01/39111, RRT, 15 March 2002.   144
Reference N01/39925, RRT, 18 April 2002.   144
Reference N01/40604, RRT, 14 December 2001.
Reference N02/42226, RRT, 30 June 2003.   246, 339
Reference N02/43084, RRT, 5 September 2002.   130
Reference N02/43487, RRT, 29 September 2003.   233
Reference N02/43938, RRT, 1 July 2003.   260
Reference N02/44244, RRT, 1 October 2003.   282
Reference N03/45504, RRT, 1 July 2003.   227, 321, 322
Reference N03/45573, RRT, 24 February 2003.   282
Reference N03/45756, RRT, 28 January 2004.   303
Reference N03/46492, RRT, 24 July 2003.   225
Reference N03/46534, RRT, 17 July 2003.   192, 218, 219, 223, 226
Reference N03/46893, RRT, 5 December 2003.   225
Reference N03/47996, RRT, 10 February 2004.   219
Reference N93/02256, RRT, 20 May 1994.   119, 137
Reference N94/4731, RRT, 17 October 1994.   74
Reference N94/04178, RRT, 10 June 1994.   227, 321, 322
Reference N95/08165, RRT, 6 June 1997.   227
Reference N95/08624, RRT, 27 March 1997.   119, 125
Reference N96/11195, RRT, 10 September 1996.   73, 119, 137, 138, 139
Reference N97/13974, RRT, 10 July 1997.   144, 148
Reference N97/17592, RRT, 5 August 1997.   262
Reference N97/19558, RRT, 22 April 1999.   230
Reference N98/21471, RRT, 21 September 1998.   321
Reference N98/24000, RRT, 13 January 2000.   266
Reference V00/11003, RRT, 29 September 2003.   266
Reference V01/12621, RRT, 19 May 2002.   86, 153
Reference V01/12813, RRT, 1 December 2003.   270
Reference V01/13062, RRT, 16 March 2004.   326
Reference V01/13122, RRT, 19 August 2003.   222
Reference V01/13868, RRT, 6 September 2002.   266
Reference V02/14674, RRT, 13 February 2004.   282
Reference V5/03396, RRT, 29 November 1995.   231, 321

Reference V93/01176, RRT, 26 August 1994.   28
Reference V94/01570, RRT, 28 February 1995.   37
Reference V94/02084, RRT, 23 February 1996.   228, 321
Reference V94/02820, RRT, 6 October 1995.   28, 98
Reference V95/03256, RRT, 9 October 1995.   210, 216, 228, 230, 321, 322
Reference V95/03786, RRT, 3 May 1996.   28
Reference V98/08951, RRT, 11 March 1999.   28
Reference V98/09164, RRT, 12 January 2001.   216, 220
Reference N98/22948, RRT, 20 November 2000.   312
Rocklea Spinning Mills Pty Ltd v. Anti-Dumping Authority (1995) 56 FCR 406.
Salem Subramaniam and Ors v. Minister for Immigration and Multicultural Affairs [1998] 483 FCA (Davies J, 4 May 1998).   304
Sarrazola v. Minister for Immigration and Multicultural Affairs (No. 3) [2000] FCA 919 (Madgwick J, 23 August 2000).   50
Sarrazola v. Minister for Immigration and Multicultural Affairs [1999] FCA 101 (Hely J, 17 February 1999).   324
SBAS v. Minister for Immigration & Multicultural Affairs [2003] FCA 528 (Cooper J, 30 May 2003).   104
SBBA v. Minister for Immigration and Multicultural and Indigenous Affairs [2002] FCA 1401 (Mansfield J, 15 November 2002).   130
SCAT v. Minister for Immigration and Multicultural and Indigenous Affairs [2002] FCA 962 (Von Doussa J, 6 August 2002).   130
SCAT v. Minister for Immigration and Multicultural and Indigenous Affairs (2003) 76 ALD 625.   93
Seo v. Minister for Immigration and Multicultural Affairs [2001] FCA 1258 (Spender J, 7 September 2001).   98
SGBB v. Minister for Immigration and Multicultural and Indigenous Affairs [2003] FCA 709 (Selway J, 16 July 2003).   333
SGKB v. Minister for Immigration and Multicultural Affairs & Indigenous Affairs (2004) 76 ALD 381.   98
Sithamparapillai v. Minister for Immigration & Multicultural Affairs [2000] FCA 897 (Goldberg J, 5 July 2000).   148
Subermani Gounder v. Minister for Immigration and Multicultural Affairs (1998) 87 FCR 1.   321
SZAFS v. Minister for Immigration and Multicultural and Indigenous Affairs [2004] FCA 112 (Lindgren J, 20 February 2004).   327
SZBQJ v. Minister for Immigration and Multicultural and Indigenous Affairs [2005] FCA 143 (Tamberlin J, 28 February 2005).   130
Thalary v. Minister for Immigration and Ethnic Affairs (1997) 50 ALD 349.   98

Vam v. *Minister for Immigration and Multicultural Affairs* [2002] FCAFC 125 (Black CJ, Drummond and Kenny JJ, 10 May 2002).   316

VTAO v. *Minister for Immigration and Multicultural and Indigenous Affairs* (2005) 81 ALD 332.   105

VTAO v. *Minister for Immigration and Multicultural and Indigenous Affairs* [2004] FCA 927 (Merkel J, 19 July 2004).   130

WAEW of 2002 v. *Minister for Immigration and Multicultural and Indigenous Affairs* [2002] FCAFC 260 (Marshall, Weinberg and Jacobson JJ, 22 August 2002).   99

WAKZ v. *Minister for Immigration* [2005] FCA 1965 (2 August 2005)   260

Wang v. *Minister for Immigration and Multicultural Affairs* (2000) 105 FCR 548.   29, 279

Waters v. *Public Transport Corporation* (1992) 173 CLR 349.   277

Ye Hong v. *Minister for Immigration and Multicultural Affairs* [1998] 1356 FCA (Tamberlin J, 2 October 1998).   96

Yousefi v. *Minister for Immigration and Multicultural Affairs* [2000] FCA 1352 (Carr J, 22 September 2000).   144

Canada

AFW (Re), No. V99-03532 [2001] CRDD No. 215, 12 October 2001.   244, 267, 331

Ahmed v. *Canada (Minister of Citizenship & Immigration)* (2002) 7 Imm LR (3d) 286.   352

Akhter v. *Canada (Minister of Citizenship and Immigration)* [2000] FCJ No. 1125.   208

Ali v. *Canada (Minister of Citizenship and Immigration)* [1997] 1 FCD 26; 1996 FCD LEXIS 592.   103, 326

ANK (Re), No. TA1-19010 [2002] CRDD No. 172, 26 August 2002.   308

AWC (Re), No. AA1-01391 [2003] RPDD No. 71, 27 May 2003.   145

B (TD) (Re), Nos. T91-01497, T91-01498 [1994] CRDD No. 391, 9 August 1994.   326, 331

BNY (Re), Nos. TA1-03656, TA1-03657, TA1-03658 [2002] RPDD No. 223, 19 December 2002.   211, 218

BOG (Re), No. VA0-03441 [2001] CRDD No. 121, 16 July 2001.

Bougai v. *Canada (Minister of Citizenship and Immigration)* [1995] 3 FC D 32; 1995 FCTD LEXIS 211.   125

C(UY) (Re), Nos. T94-00416, T94-00418 and T94-00419 [1994] CRDD No. 389, 25 August 1994.   282
Cabarcas v. Minister of Citizenship and Immigration, 2002 FCT 297, 19 March 2002.   258
Cabello v. Canada (Minister of Citizenship and Immigration) [1995] FCJ No. 630.   100
Canada (Attorney-General) v. Ward [1993] 2 SCR 689.   29, 77
Canada (Minister of Citizenship and Immigration) v. Li [2001] FCJ No. 620.   331
Canada (Minister of Citizenship and Immigration) v. Smith [1998] FCJ No. 1613; [1999] 1 FC 310.   336
Chan v. Canada (Minister for Employment and Immigration) (1995) 128 DLR (4th) 213.   29
Chan v. Canada (Minister of Employment and Immigration) [1993] 3 FC 675, 20 Imm. LR (2d) 181.   234
Chan v. Canada (Minister of Employment and Immigration) [1995] 3 SCR 593.   40
Chen v. Canada (Minister of Citizenship and Immigration) [1995] FCJ No. 189.   109
Cheung v. Canada (Minister of Employment and Immigration) [1993] FCJ No. 309.   334
CSE (Re), No. VA0-00566, [2001] CRDD No. 29, 9 March 2001.   326
DJP (Re), No. T98-06446 [1999] CRDD No. 155, 3 August 1999.   267
DUR (Re), No. U96-03325 [1996] CRDD No. 243, 16 December 1996.   211, 334
EKD (Re), Nos. MA1-02054, MA1-02055, MA1-02056, [2001] CRDD No. 174, 21 December 2001.   334
END (Re), No. VA1-01344 [2002] CRDD No. 22, 3 January 2002.   244
ESO (Re), No. U96-04191 [1997] CRDD No. 27, 21 January 1997.   211, 334
Flores v. Canada (Minister of Citizenship and Immigration), 2002 ACWSJ LEXIS 5953; 2002 ACWSJ 8570; 116 ACWS (3d) 420.   279
FOO (Re), Nos. MA1-11675, MA1-11676, MA1-11677 [2003] CRDD No. 83, 16 June 2003.   337
FOS (Re), Nos. TA0-01421, TA0-01422, TA0-01423, TA0-01424 [2001] CRDD No. 262, 16 May 2001.   239
Freiberg v. Canada (Secretary of State) 78 FTR 283 (1994).   216
FYM (Re), Nos. V97-00708, V97-00709, V97-00710, V97-00711 [1998] CRDD No. 153, 11 August 1998.   211, 337
G (BB) (Re), Nos. T93-09636, T93-09638 and T93-09639 [1994] CRDD No. 307, 26 January 1994.   282

GAF (Re), No. V99-02929 [2000] CRDD No. 48, 21 February 2000.   272, 284, 331
GCH (Re), Nos. T99-00524, T99-00525 [2000] CRDD No. 12, 12 January 2000.   226
GIY (Re), No. T95-02172, [1996] CRDD No. 64, 25 July 1996.   306
Gonzalez v. Canada (Minister of Citizenship and Immigration), 2002 ACWSJ LEXIS 1317; 2002 ACWSJ 1921; 113 ACWS (3d) 126.   324
GPE (Re), No. U96-02717, [1997] CRDD No. 215, 16 September 1997.   319
GRF (Re), Nos. AA0-01454, AA0-01462 and AA0-01463 [2001] CRDD No. 88, 12 July 2001.   117, 133, 214
GVP (Re), No. T98-06186 [1999] CRDD No. 298, 2 November 1999.   245, 268
HDO (Re), T98-17677 [1999] CRDD No. 116, 26 May 1999.   244
Holloway [1983] 4 CHRR D/1454.   256
HQT (Re), Nos. T96-03054 and T96-03055, [1997] CRDD No. 149, 8 July 1997.   125
ICR (Re), Nos. V99-03509, V99-03511, V99-03532, V99-03536, V99-03540, V99-03544, V99-03547, V99-03548 [2000] CRDD No. 199, 14 February 2000.   244
IPJ (Re), No. A99-01121, [2000] CRDD No. 141, 29 August 2000.   73, 229
ITU (Re), Nos. T99-11540, T99-11541, [2001] CRDD No. 95, 31 May 2001.   336
IVV (Re), No. TA2-00027 [2003] CRDD No. 64, 26 May 2003.   279
J (RC) (Re), No. U93-04549, [1994] CRDD No. 265, 14 January 1994.   30
JDJ (Re), No. A95-00633 [1998] CRDD No. 12, 28 January 1998.   203, 204, 333
JLD (Re), No. T95-00305, [1996] CRDD No. 291, 9 April 1996.   106
KBA (Re), Nos. T98-03163, T98-03164, T98-03165 [2001] CRDD No. 56, 7 May 2001.   206, 210
KCS (Re), No. MA1-03477 [2002] CRDD No. 5, 16 January 2002.   213
KNA (Re), No. T97-05827 [1998] CRDD No. 148, 16 July 1998.   211
KRQ (Re), Nos. T95-01828, T95-01829 [1996] CRDD No. 232, 1 October 1996.   208
KWB (Re), Nos. A99-00789, A99-00790, A99-00791, A99-00792, A99-00793, [2002] CRDD No. 50, 8 April 2002.   336
L (HX) (Re), Nos. T93-05935, T93-05936 [1993] CRDD No. 259, 31 December 1996.   282
L (LL) (Re), Nos. A93-81751, A93-81752 and A93-81753 [1994] CRDD No. 368, 16 August 1994.   336
L (YO) (Re), No. V93-02851, [1995] CRDD No. 50, 3 October 1995.   336
Li v. Canada (Minister of Citizenship and Immigration) [1994] FCJ No. 1745.   95

TABLE OF CASES

Li v. *Canada (Minister of Citizenship and Immigration)* [2000] FCJ No. 2037. 245

Ling, Che Kueung v. *Minister of Employment and Immigration* (FCTD, Case No. 92-A-6555, Muldoon J, 20 May 1993). 191

Litvinov v. *Canada (Secretary of State)* [1994] FCJ No. 1061. 327

LXC (Re), No. TAO-05472, CRRD No. 96, 30 May 2001. 318

Madelat v. *Canada (Minister of Employment and Immigration)* [1991] FCJ No. 49. 104

Mare v. *Canada (Minister of Citizenship and Immigration)* [2001] FCJ No. 712. 152

MCK (Re), No. U97-00412 [1997] CRDD No. 156, 2 July 1997. 211, 334

MGG (Re), No. T99-10153 [2000] CRDD No. 191, 5 September 2000. 284

Mirzabeglui v. *Canada (Minister of Employment and Immigration)* [1991] FCJ No. 50. 103

MMS (Re), Nos. M95-02275, M95-02276, [1996] CRDD No. 162, 8 October 1996. 304

MOQ (Re), No. VA2-03015, 6 August 2003. 337

MYS (Re), Nos. V97-00156, V97-00962 [1998] CRDD No. 149, 23 July 1998. 330, 338

MZJ (Re), No. V97-03500 [1999] CRDD No. 118, 31 May 1999. 331, 333

NCM (Re), Nos. U94-04870, U94-04871, U94-04872 and U94-04873 [1996] CRDD No. 147, 19 July 1996. 336

Nejad, Hossein Hamedi v. *Minister of Citizenship and Immigration*, 1997 ACWSJ LEXIS 159001; 1997 ACWSJ 419632; 73 ACWS (3d) 1017. 275

NWX (Re), No. T99-01434 [1999] CRDD No. 183, 25 August 1999. 267

O (QB) (Re), No. U93-04790 [1993] CRDD No. 283, 8 December 1993. 211, 334

ODO (Re), Nos. VA1-03231, VA1-03232, VA1-03233 [2003] RPDD No. 66, 12 March 2003. 103, 216

OGW (Re), No. MA1-08719 [2002] CRDD No. 53, 16 April 2002. 227, 229

OPK (Re), No. U95-04575 [1996] CRDD No. 88, 24 May 1996. 232, 319

OQU (Re), No. T98-09064 [1999] CRDD No. 157, 19 July 1999. 29

ORL (Re), No. MAO-06253 [2001] CRDD No. 2, 18 January 2001. 313

OXJ (Re), No. U96-03098 [1997] CRDD No. 224, 15 July 1997. 211, 334

Oyarzo v. *Canada (Minister of Employment and Immigration)* [1982] 2 FC 779. 93, 224

PEF (Re), No. VA0-00091 [2000] CRDD No. 110, 29 May 2000. 245, 337, 338

PFH (Re), Nos. T96-00266, T96-00267, T96-00269, [1997] CRDD No. 327, 3 February 1997. 96

PKH (Re), No. T96-01209 [1996] CRDD No. 216, 17 December 1996. 149

PKM (Re), No. V98-00452 [1998] CRDD No. 179, 11 September 1998.   211, 334

Pushpanathan v. *Canada (Minister of Citizenship and Immigration)* [1998] 1 SCR 982.   43

PYM (Re), No. U98-01933 [1999] CRDD No. 163, 3 June 1999.   244

QDS (Re), Nos. A99-00215, A99-00256, A99-00258 [1999] CRDD No. 235, 30 September 1999.   209, 212, 334, 336

QJQ (Re), Nos. V97-01419, V97-01420, V97-01421, V98-02335, V98-02345, V98-02346 [1999] CRDD No. 189, 9 August 1999.   334

QJV (Re), No. U97-01267 [1997] CRDD No. 249, 8 October 1997.   211, 334

QQX (Re), No. T95-00479 [1996] CRDD No. 52, 5 July 1996.   210, 333

QWY (Re), No. T98-07956 [1999] CRDD No. 271, 29 November 1999.   336

R v. *Sharpe*, 2001 SCCDJ 42; 2001 SCCDJ LEXIS 2.   196

Ramirez v. *Canada (Solicitor General)* [1994] FCJ No. 1888.   109

RGC (Re), Nos. MA1-03752, MA1-03753 [2002] CRDD No. 23, 4 January 2002.   337

RJR-MacDonald Inc. v. *Canada (Attorney General)*, 1995 Can. Sup. Ct. LEXIS 69.   196

RMK (Re), No. TA1-06365 [2002] CRDD No. 300, 16 May 2002.   126, 127

RRF (Re), No. T99-00210 [1999] CRDD No. 220, 21 September 1999.   210, 262

S (ZD) (Re), No. T94-02002 [1995] CRDD No. 75, 20 June 1995.   263, 326

SBO (Re), Nos. VA1-02828, VA1-02826, VA1-02827, VA1-02829 [2003] RPDD No. 17, 27 February 2003.   218, 219, 221

SCK (Re), No. MA1-00356, [2001] CRDD No. 401, 15 November 2001.   93

SCP (Re), No. A95-00837, [1996] CRDD No. 244, 3 May 1996.   326

Serrano v. *Canada (Minister of Citizenship and Immigration)*, 1999 FTR LEXIS 745; 166 FTR 227.   324

Shahiraj, 2001 Fed Ct Trial LEXIS 443; 2001 FCT 453.   258, 275, 279

Shao Mei He v. *Minister of Employment and Immigration* [1994] FCJ No. 1243.   95, 100

Sinora v. *Minister of Employment and Immigration* [1993] FCJ No. 725.   306

SLH (Re), No. T95-07396 [1997] CRDD No. 121, 27 May 1997.   336

SNJ, No. V99-03818 [2000] CRDD No. 119, 8 June 2000.   244

STI (Re), No. T98-00366 [1999] CRDD No. 11, 18 January 1999.   211

Sulaiman, Hussaine Hassan v. *MCI* (FCTD, Case No. IMM-525-94, Mackay J, 22 March 1996).   191

Suresh v. *Canada (Minister of Citizenship and Immigration)* 2002 SCCDJ 8052.   63

SWE (Re), Nos. T99-04041, T99-04042, T99-04043, T99-04044, T99-06333, T99-06363, T99-04047, T99-04048, T99-06334, [2000] CRDD No. 45, 1 March 2000. 87
T (LR) (Re), No. V93-01037, [1994] CRDD No. 406, 29 March 1994. 312–13
TCV (Re), Nos. U95-00646, U95-00647 and U95-00648, [1997] CRDD No. 5, 15 January 1997. 336
TEK (Re), No. V99-03528 [2000] CRDD No. 21, 27 January 2000. 244
THK (Re), No. VA0-02635, [2001] CRDD No. 30, 22 March 2001. 330, 331
TNL (Re), No. T95-07647, [1997] CRDD No. 251, 23 October 1997. 319
TZU, No. TAO-03660 [2000] CRDD No. 249, 20 October 2000. 244
U (NX) (Re), Nos. T93-12579 and T93-12586 [1995] CRDD No. 74, 25 July 1995. 208, 210
UCR (Re), Nos. M99-07094, M99-07096 and M99-07098 [2001] CRDD No. 94, 31 May 2001. 337
UKS (Re), No. T96-02313, [1997] CRDD No. 223, 9 May 1997. 307
UKT (Re), No. T99-10465 [2000] CRDD No. 129, 12 July 2000. 211, 334
United States of America v. *Cotrobi* [1989] 1 SCR 1469. 196
UNN (Re), No. V95-00138, [1997] CRDD No. 12, 16 January 1997. 306
UWB (Re), Nos. MA0-10528, MA0-10529 [2001] CRDD No. 212, 15 November 2001. 337
UZG (Re), Nos. T96-06291 and T96-06292, [1997] CRDD No. 209, 2 September 1997. 334
V (HY) (Re), No. V91-00998, [1991] CRDD No. 746, 15 November 1991. 334
V (OZ) Re, No. M93-04717, [1993] CRDD No. 164, 10 June 1993. 106
VBJ (Re), No. T98-09801 [1999] CRDD No. 62, 30 April 1999. 211, 334
WBT (Re), No. V98-00787, [1997] CRDD No. 119, 4 June 1999. 306
WDK (Re), No. T96-04645 [1997] CRDD No. 187, 25 August 1997. 284
WMI (Re), Nos. T96-02166 and T96-02168 [1997] CRDD No. 113, 14 May 1997. 208, 333
WRH (Re), Nos. T97-05485, T97-05486, T97-05487, T97-05488, T97-05489, [1999] CRDD No. 112, 31 March 1999. 122
Xiao v. *Canada (Minister of Citizenship and Immigration)* [2001] FCJ No. 349. 331
Xie v. *Canada* [1994] FCJ No. 286. 95
XUG (Re), No. TAO-02066 [2000] CRDD No. 248, 20 October 2000. 285
Y (QH) Re, No. V93-02093 [1994] CRDD No. 203, 4 May 1994. 208
YCK (Re), No. V95-02904 [1997] CRDD No. 261, 26 November 1997. 285, 306, 339
YDJ (Re), Nos. V99-02955, V99-02956, V99-02953, V99-02914, V99-02933, V99-02912, V99-02951, V99-02913, V99-02960, V99-02927, V99-02931, V99-

02919, V99-02928, V99-02949, V99-02923, V99-02961 [2000] CRDD No. 401, 9 May 2000.   244
YHI (Re), No. T95-07066, [1996] CRDD No. 65, 16 August 1996.   323
YSC (Re), Nos. T97-00096, T97-00097, T97-00098 [1998] CRDD No. 26, 22 January 1998.   219
ZAJ (Re), Nos. T96-04022, T96-04023, T96-04024, T96-04025, T96-04026 and T96-04027 [1997] CRDD No. 205, 15 September 1997.   217
Zheng v. Canada (Minister of Citizenship and Immigration) [2002] FCJ No. 580.   244
Zhu v. Canada (Minister for Citizenship and Immigration) [1994] FCJ No. 80.   258
Zhu v. Canada (Minister of Citizenship and Immigration) [2001] FCJ No. 1251.   331
ZOI (Re), Nos. V99-02926, V99-02950, V99-02926, V99-02950 [2000] CRDD No. 91, 9 May 2000.   245, 338
ZWB (Re), Nos. T98-03011, T98-03012, T98-03013, T98-03014, T98-03015, T98-03016, T98-03017, T98-07280, T98-09201, T98-09202, T98-09203, [1999] CRDD No. 211, 27 September 1999.   117, 122

New Zealand

Butler v AG (1999) NZAR 205   62
DG v Refugee Status Appeals Authority (Unreported, High Court of New Zealand, Chisholm J, 5 June 2001).   31
H v. Chief Executive of the Department of Labour (Unreported, High Court of New Zealand, Case No. 183/00, 20 March 2001).   94, 191
K v Refugee Status Appeals Authority [2005] NZAR 441.   31
Q v. Refugee Status Appeals Authority [2001] NZAR 472.   191
Refugee Appeal No. 1/92, RSAA, 30 April 1992.   122
Refugee Appeal No. 3/91, RSAA, 20 October 1992.   294, 296, 305
Refugee Appeal No. 17/92, RSAA, 9 July 1992.   324
Refugee Appeal No. 24/91, RSAA, 9 June 1992.   305
Refugee Appeal No. 59/91, RSAA, 19 May 1992.   71
Refugee Appeal No. 61/92, RSAA, 22 July 1992.   314
Refugee Appeal No. 135/92, RSAA, 19 June 1993.   247
Refugee Appeal No. 547/92, RSAA, 2 June 1994.   324
Refugee Appeal No. 732/92, RSAA, 5 August 1994.   105, 122, 124, 137, 144
Refugee Appeal No. 1039/93, RSAA, 13 February 1995.   122, 132

xxviii TABLE OF CASES

Refugee Appeal No. 1312/93, RSAA, 30 August 1995.   296, 297, 299
Refugee Appeal No. 2039/93, RSAA, 12 February 1996.   39, 93, 117, 118, 122, 127,191, 192
Refugee Appeal No. 2217/94, RSAA, 12 September 1996.   106, 107, 289
Refugee Appeal No. 70366/96, RSAA, 22 September 1997.   41
Refugee Appeal No. 70597/97, RSAA, 1 September 1997.   99
Refugee Appeal No. 70618/97, RSAA, 30 June 1998.   261
Refugee Appeal No. 70651/97, RSAA, 27 November 1997.   144
Refugee Appeal No. 70667/97, RSAA, 18 September 1997.   99
Refugee Appeal No. 70846/98, RSAA, 28 May 1998.   225
Refugee Appeal No. 70863/98, RSAA, 13 August 1998.   95, 97, 102
Refugee Appeal No. 71018/98, RSAA, 30 October 1998.   261
Refugee Appeal No. 71145/98, RSAA, 28 May 1999.   324
Refugee Appeal 71163/98, RSAA, 31 March 1999.   191
Refugee Appeal No. 71193/98, RSAA, 9 September 1999.   108, 242
Refugee Appeal No. 71336/99, RSAA, 4 May 2000.   109, 208, 289
Refugee Appeal No. 71404/99, RSAA, 29 October 1999.   94, 191
Refugee Appeal No. 71427/99, RSAA, 16 August 2000.   31, 39, 48, 77, 94, 103, 108, 117, 118, 127, 136, 178, 190, 191, 192, 202, 269, 293, 296, 325
Refugee Appeal No. 71509/99, RSAA, 20 January 2000.   304, 305
Refugee Appeal No. 71605/99, RSAA, 16 December 1999.   99, 105, 124, 125, 260
Refugee Appeal No. 71606/99, RSAA, 31 March 2000.   117
Refugee Appeal No. 72024/2000, RSAA, 13 July 2000.   261
Refugee Appeal Nos. 72179/2000, 72180/2000, 72181/2000, RSAA, 31 August 2000.   310
Refugee Appeal No. 72189/2000, RSAA, 17 August 2000.   310
Refugee Appeal Nos. 72558/01 and 72559/01, RSAA, 19 November 2002.   31, 68, 82, 86, 147, 191
Refugee Appeal No. 72635/01, RSAA, 6 September 2002.   256, 258, 259, 274, 275
Refugee Appeal No. 72668/01, RSAA, 5 April 2002.   31, 41
Refugee Appeal No. 73361/02, RSAA, 19 June 2003.   259
Refugee Appeal No. 73378, RSAA, 11 December 2003.   272
Refugee Appeal No. 73607, RSAA, 26 February 2004.   134
Refugee Appeal No. 73952, RSAA, 26 May 2005.   147
Refugee Appeal No. 74395, RSAA, 21 January 2004.   106
Refugee Appeal No. 74665/03, RSAA, 22 July 2003.   80

Refugee Appeal No. 74665/03, RSAA, 7 July 2004.   25, 31, 37, 39, 40, 41, 48, 54, 68, 81, 82, 117, 118, 122, 274
Refugee Appeals Nos. 74754, 74755, RSAA, 7 January 2004.   118, 137
Refugee Appeal No. 74880, RSAA, 29 September 2005.   107, 292
Refugee Appeal No. 75221, 23 September 2005   84
Refugee Appeal 75233, 1 February 2005.   326

South Africa

Minister of Health v. Treatment Action Campaign (2002) (5) SA 721 (CC).   230

Minister of Home Affairs and Ors v. Watchenuka and Anor, 2004 (2) BCLR 120 (SCA) at 127.   102

National Coalition for Gay and Lesbian Equality and Anor v. Minister of Justice and Others (1998) (12) BCLR 1517 (CC), 1998 SACLR LEXIS 26, 9 October 1998.   182

Phillips and Anor v. Director of Public Prosecutions (Witwatersrand Local Division) and Others (2003) (4) BCLR 357 (CC).   200

Refugee Appeal Board, Appeal No. 53/2005, 30 November 2004.   102

S v. Makwanyane and Anor (1995) (6) BCLR 665 (CC).   196

Van der Walt v. Metcash Trading Limited (2002) (5) BCLR 454 (CC).   200

United Kindgom

Adan v. Secretary of State for the Home Department [1997] 2 All ER 723.

Amare v. Secretary of State for the Home Department [2005] All ER (D) 300.   29, 79, 191

Ameen v. Secretary of State for the Home Department [2002] UKIAT 07246.   259

Bukasa v. Secretary of State for the Home Department (Unreported, IAT, Appeal No. HX/60692/96, 24 June 1997).   243

Demirkaya v. Secretary of State for the Home Department [1999] Imm AR 498.   25

Devaseelan v. Secretary of State for the Home Department [2002] IAT 702.   352

Doymus v. Secretary of State for the Home Department (Unreported, IAT, Appeal No. HX/80112/99, 19 July 2000).   30

El Deaibes v. *Secretary of State for the Home Department* [2002] UKIAT 02582. 124

Ferdowsa Ismail Beldeq [2002] UKIAT 06753. 305

Filiusina v. *Secretary of State for the Home Department* (Unreported, IAT, Appeal No. HX/65188/2000, CC/13395/2000, 3 December 2001). 146

G (Somalia) [2003] UKIAT 00011. 206

Gashi and Nikshiqi v. *Secretary of State for the Home Department* [1997] INLR 96. 29

Gjoni v. *Secretary of State for the Home Department* [2002] UKIAT 06307. 270

Glowacka v. *Secretary of State for the Home Department* (Unreported, IAT, Appeal No. 18928, 9 July 1999). 214

Grahovac (Unreported, IAT, Case No. 11761, 9 January 1995). 93

Grecu (Unreported, IAT, Appeal No. HX/64793/96, 8 January 1998). 100, 146

Gudja (Unreported, IAT, CC/59626/97, 5 August 1999). 105

He v. *Secretary of State for the Home Department* [2002] EWCA 1150, [2002] Imm AR 590. 94

Horvath v. *Secretary of State for the Home Department* [2000] 3 All ER 577. 29

Horvath v. *Secretary of State for the Home Department* [2000] Imm AR 205. 37

HS [2005] UKIAT 00120. 116

Islam and Others v. *Secretary of State for the Home Department* (Unreported, Asylum and Immigration Tribunal, 2 October 1996). 39

Jain v. *Secretary of State for the Home Department* [2000] Imm AR 76. 69

Jakitay v. *Secretary of State for the Home Department* (Unreported, IAT, Appeal No. 12658, 15 November 1995). 207, 330

James v. *Eastleigh Borough Council* [1990] 2 AC 751. 277

Judgment of K [2003] UKIAT 00023, 7 July 2003. 269

Kagema v. *Secretary of State for the Home Department* [1997] Imm AR 137. 139

Karickova v. *Secretary of State for the Home Department* [2002] UKIAT 05813. 116

Koffi v. *Secretary of State for the Home Department* (Unreported, IAT, Appeal No. 18227, HX/60314/96, 17 September 1999). 146

Korca v. *Secretary of State for the Home Department* (Unreported, IAT, Appeal No. HX-360001-2001, 29 May 2002). 189

Kovac (Unreported, IAT, Appeal No. CC3034497, 28 April 2000). 292

Krayem v. *Secretary of State for the Home Department* [2003] EWCA Civ. 649. 117

Latheef v. *Secretary of State for the Home Department* (Unreported, IAT, 7 March 2002). 207

Macura, Ljiljana, Maletic v. *Secretary of State for the Home Department* (Unreported, IAT, Appeal No. HX-61441-00, 11 September 2001). 116, 122, 134

Majkic v. *Secretary of State for the Home Department* (Unreported, IAT, Appeal No. CC/12867/01, 10 December 2001). 134

Maksimovic v. *Secretary of State for the Home Department* (Unreported, IAT, Case No. 01TH00432, 16 May 2001). 272

Maksimovic v. *Secretary of State for the Home Department* [2004] EWHC 1026. 93, 105

Mandali v. *Secretary of State for the Home Department* (Unreported, IAT, Appeal No. HX16991-02, 27 March 2003). 188

Mandali v. *Secretary of State for the Home Department* [2002] UKIAT 0741. 351

Matthews v. *Ministry of Defence* [2003] All ER (D) 173.

Mohamad v. *Secretary of State for the Home Department* (Unreported, IAT, Appeal No. HX/74489/94, 21 October 1996). 241

Mohamud Osman Amin v. *Secretary of State for the Home Department* [2002] UKIAT 04084. 262

Montoya v. *Secretary of State for the Home Department* [2002] EWCA Civ. 620. 277, 305

Montoya v. *Secretary of State for the Home Department* [2002] INLR 399. 296

Moro v. *Secretary of State for the Home Department* [2001] EWCA Civ. 1680. 97

Moro v. *The Secretary of State for the Home Department* (Unreported, IAT, Appeal No. HX-72022-98, 11 September 2000). 97

NS Afghanistan CG [2004] UKIAT 00328, 30 December 2004 328

Ogbeide v. *Secretary of State for the Home Department* (Unreported, IAT, Appeal No. HX/08391/2002, 10 May 2002). 285, 307

Omoruyi v. *Secretary of State for the Home Department* [2001] Imm AR 175. 271

Paul Owen v. *Secretary of State for the Home Department* [2002] UKIAT 03285. 188

Peco (Unreported, IAT, Appeal No. HX-74935-94, 12 November 1996). 106, 116, 241, 292

Popik (Unreported, IAT, Case No. HX/70116/98, 20 May 1999). 223

Puzova v. *Secretary of State for the Home Department* [2001] UKAIT 00001. 121

Quijano v. *Secretary of State for the Home Department* [1997] Imm AR 227. 300

R (on the application of Adan) v. *Secretary of State for the Home Department* [2001] 2 AC 477. 36

R (on the Application of Altin Vallaj) v. *Special Adjudicator* [2001] INLR 455.
21, 63

R (on the application of C) v. *Immigration Appeal Tribunal* [2003] EQHC 883 (Admin), 9 April 2003. 270

R (on the application of Hoxha) v. *Special Adjudicator* [2005] 4 All ER 580. 43

R (on the application of Okere) v. *Immigration Appeal Tribunal* (Queen's Bench Division, Administrative Court, Scott Baker J, CO/5067/1999, 9 November 2000). 117

R (on the application of Razgar) v. *Secretary of State for the Home Department* [2004] All ER (D) 169. 351

R (on the Application of Secretary of State for the Home Department) v. *Immigration Appeal Tribunal* (Queen's Bench Division (Administrative Court), CO/593/1999, 21 November 2000), at para. 26. 101, 135

R (on the application of Sivakumar) v. *Secretary of State for the Home Department* [2003] 2 All ER 1097. 258

R (on the application of Ullah) v. *Special Adjudicator; Do* v. *Secretary of State for the Home Department* [2004] 3 All ER 785. 29, 352

R (on the application of Vuckovic) v. *Special Adjudicator and anor* (Queens's Bench Division (Administrative Court), CO/3021/2000, 18 December 2000). 242

R v. *Home Secretary, ex parte Sivakumaran* [1988] AC 958, [1988] 1 All ER 193. 77

R v. *Immigration Appeal Tribunal, ex parte Daniel Boahin Jonah* [1985] Imm AR 7. 30

R v. *Immigration Appeal Tribunal, ex parte De Melo and De Araujo* [1997] Imm AR 43. 324

R v. *Immigration Appeal Tribunal, ex parte Bolanus* [1999] Imm AR 350. 324

R v. *Immigration Appeal Tribunal, ex parte De Melo and Anor* (Unreported, IAT, Appeal No. CO/1866/96, 19 July 1996). 277

R v. *Immigration Appeal Tribunal, ex parte Sandralingham and Another; R* v. *Immigration Appeal Tribunal and Another, ex parte Rajendrakumar* [1996] Imm AR 97. 29

R v. *Immigration Appeal Tribunal and Secretary of State for the Home Department; ex parte Shah* (Queen's Bench Division, CO 4330/95, 12 November 1996). 301, 354

R v. *Immigration Appeal Tribunal and Secretary of State for the Home Department, ex parte Syeda Khatoon Shah* [1997] Imm AR 148. 21

R v. *Immigration Appeal Tribunal and Another, ex parte Shah* [1998] 4 All ER 30. 36

R v. *Immigration Appeal Tribunal, ex parte Shah* [1999] 2 AC 629.   29, 269

R v. *Secretary of State for Social Security; ex parte Joint Council for the Welfare of Immigrants*; R v. *Secretary of State for Social Security, ex parte B* [1996] 4 All ER 385.

R v. *Secretary of State for the Home Department, ex parte Adan, Subaskaran and Aitseguer* [1999] 4 All ER 774.   42

R v. *Secretary of State for the Home Department, ex parte Blanusa* (Court of Appeal, Civil Division, Henry, Ward and Schiemann LJJ, 18 May 1999).   117, 192

R v. *Secretary of State for the Home Department, ex parte Jeyakumaran* [1994] Imm AR 45.   344

R v. *Secretary of State for the Home Department ex parte Kebbeh* (Queen's Bench Division, Crown Office List, Case No. CO/1269/98, 30 April 1999).   189

R v. *Secretary of State for the Home Department, ex parte Osungo* (Unreported, English Court of Appeal (Civil Division), Buxton LJ, 21 August 2000).   36

R v. *Secretary of State for the Home Department, ex parte Ouanes* [1998] 1 WLR 218.   314

R v. *Secretary of State for the Home Department, ex parte Ravichandran* [1996] Imm AR 97.   117

R v. *Secretary of State for the Home Department, ex parte Robinson* [1998] QB 929, [1997] 4 All ER 210.   37

R v. *Secretary of State for the Home Department, ex parte Sasitharan* [1998] Imm AR 487.   93

R v. *Uxbridge Magistrates' Court and another, ex parte Adimi* [1999] Imm AR 560.   71

Ravichandran v. Secretary of State for the Home Department [1996] Imm AR 97.   152

Secretary of State for the Home Department v. Baglan (Unreported, IAT, Appeal No. HX-71045-94, 23 October 1995).   94

Secretary of State for the Home Department v. Chiver [1997] INLR 212.   94

Secretary of State for the Home Department v. Gudja (Unreported, IAT, Case No. CC/59626/97, 5 August 1999).   213

Secretary of State for the Home Department v. Dzhygun (Unreported, IAT, Appeal No. 00TH00728, 13 April 2000).   339

Secretary of State for the Home Department v. Kacaj (Unreported, IAT, Appeal No. 23044/2000, 19 July 2001).   351

Secretary of State for the Home Department v. *Kircicek* [2002] UKIAT 05491. 303

Secretary of State for the Home Department v. *Kondratiev* [2002] UKIAT 08283. 106

Secretary of State for the Home Department v. *Muchomba* [2002] UKIAT 1348. 328

Secretary of State for the Home Department v. *Padhu* (Unreported, IAT, Appeal No. HX 74530-94, 14 July 1995). 105

Secretary of State for the Home Department v. *Rakas* [2002] UKIAT 06426. 134

Secretary of State for the Home Department v. *Sijakovic* (Unreported, IAT, Appeal No. HX-58113-2000, 1 May 2001). 92

Secretary of State for the Home Department v. *SK (Appellant SK)* [2002] UKIAT 05613. 134

Secretary of State for the Home Department v. *Vujatovic* [2002] UKIAT 02474. 106

Sepet v. *Secretary of State for the Home Department* [2001] EWCA Civ. 681. 36

Sepet and Anor v. *Secretary of State for the Home Department* [2003] 3 All ER 304. 25

Skenderaj v. *Secretary of State for the Home Department* [2002] EWCA Civ. 567, [2002] 4 All ER 555. 302

Suarez v. *Secretary of State for the Home Department* [2002] 1 WLR 2663. 258

Svazas v. *Secretary of State for the Home Department* [2002] EWCA Civ. 74; [2002] 1 WLR 1891. 25

T v. *Secretary of State for the Home Department* [1996] 2 All ER 865. 36

Tam Thi Dao v. *Secretary of State for the Home Department* (Unreported, IAT, Appeal No. HX/28801/2003, 1 September 2003). 282

The Queen on the Application of Secretary of State for the Home Department v. *The IAT, re Oto Koncek* (Unreported, High Court of Justice, CO-593-99, 21 November 2000). 260

Todorovici v. *Immigration Appeal Tribunal* (Queen's Bench Division, Administrative Court, Jackson J, CO/4263/2000, 23 March 2001). 239

Tong v. *Secretary of State for the Home Department* [2002] UKIAT 08062. 335

VD (Trafficking) Albania CG [2004] UKIAT 00115 (26 May 2004) 270

Woldesmaet v. *Secretary of State for the Home Department* (Unreported, IAT, Case No. 12892, 9 January 1995). 132

YS and HA Somalia CG [2005] UKIAT 00088, 22 April 2005. 305

United States

Abay and Amare v. *Ashcroft*, 368 F 3d 634 (6th Cir. 2004). 93
Abdel-Masieh v. *Immigration and Naturalization Service*, 73 F 3d 579 (5th Cir. 1996). 119
Agbuya v. *Immigration and Naturalization Service*, 1999 US App. LEXIS 21091 (9th Cir. 1999). 119
Aguirre-Cervantes v. *Immigration and Naturalization Service*, 242 F 3d 1169 (9th Cir. 2001). 337
Ahmed v. *Ashcroft*, 341 F 3d 214 (3rd Cir. 2003). 292
Ali v. *Ashcroft* 394 F. 3d 780 (9th Cir. 2005). 258, 305
Alla Konstantinova Pitcherskaia v. *Immigration and Naturalization Service*, 118 F 3d 641 (9th Cir. 1997). 30
Alvarez-Montiel v. *Immigration and Naturalization Service*, 1996 US App. LEXIS 4802 (9th Cir. 1996). 130
Ambati v. *Reno; Immigration and Naturalization Service*, 233 F 3d 1054 (7th Cir. 2000). 109
Arout Melkonian v. *Ashcroft*, 320 F 3d 1061 (9th Cir. 2003). 248
Auriga v. *Immigration and Naturalization Service*, 1993 US App. LEXIS 6775 (9th Cir. 1993). 101
Baballah v. *Immigration and Naturalization Service*, 335 F 3d 981 (9th Cir. 2003). 97
Baballah v. *John Ashcroft*, 367 F 3d 1067 (9th Cir. 2003). 96
Baka v. *Immigration and Naturalization Service*, 963 F 2d 1376 (10th Cir. 1992). 96
Barreto-Clara v. *US Attorney General; Immigration and Naturalization Service*, 275 F 3d 1334 (11th Cir. 2001). 100
Basova v. *Immigration and Naturalization Service*, 185 F 3d 873 (10th Cir. 1999). 265
Begzatowski v. *Immigration and Naturalization Service*, 278 F 3d 665 (7th Cir. 2002). 38
Benevides v. *Immigration and Naturalization Service*, 1996 US App. LEXIS 8623 (9th Cir. 1996). 199
Bereza v. *Immigration and Naturalization Service*, 115 F 3d 468 (7th Cir. 1997).
Bhupendra Bhai Patel v. *Immigration and Naturalization Service* (1999) US App. Lexis 30517 (9th Cir. 1999).
Blanco-Herrera v. *Immigration and Naturalization Service*, 1996 US App. LEXIS 15280 (9th Cir. 1996).

Borca v. Immigration and Naturalization Service, 77 F 3d 210 (7th Cir. 1996). 100

Borja v. Immigration and Naturalization Service, 175 F 3d 732 (9th Cir. 1999). 249

Briones v. Immigration and Naturalization Service, 175 F 3d 727 (9th Cir. 1999). 258

Bucur v. Immigration and Naturalization Service, 109 F 3d 399 (7th Cir. 1997). 213

Cardoza-Fonseca v. INS, 480 U.S. 421 (1987). 71

Castellano-Chacon v. Immigration and Naturalization Service, 341 F 3d 533 (6th Cir. 2003). 23

Castillo-Ponce v. Immigration and Naturalization Service, 1995 US App. LEXIS 27058 (9th Cir. 1995). 95

Chand v. Immigration and Naturalization Service, 222 F 3d 1066 (9th Cir. 2000). 110, 288

Chen v. Ashcroft, 113 Fed. Appx. 135; 2004 US App. LEXIS 22942 (6th Cir. 2004). 224

Chen v. Gonzales, 2006 US App. LEXIS 2741 (2nd Cir. 2006) 224

Chen v. Immigration and Naturalization Service, 195 F 3d 198 (4th Cir. 1999). 109, 288

Damko v. Immigration and Naturalization Service, 430 F 3d 626 (2nd Cir. 2005). 128

De Souza v. Immigration and Naturalization Service, 999 F 2d 1156 (7th Cir. 1993). 38

Desir v. Ilchert, 840 F 2d 723 (9th Cir. 1998). 95

Dunat v. Hurney, 297 F 2d 744 (3rd Cir. 1961). 92

Deqa Ahmad Haji Ali v. Ashcroft, 394 F 3d 780 (9th Cir. 2005). 305

El Himri v. Ashcroft, 378 F 3d 932 (9th Cir. 2004). 107

El-Hewie v. Immigration and Naturalization Service, 1994 US App. LEXIS 34660 (9th Cir. 1994) 97

Escobar v. Gonzales, 417 F 3d 363 (3rd Cir. 2005) 310, 332

Escobar-Chavez v. Immigration and Naturalization Service, 1996 US App. LEXIS 17795 (9th Cir. 1996). 199

Faddoul v. Immigration and Naturalization Service, 37 F 3d 185 (5th Cir. 1994). 38

Fatin v. Immigration and Naturalization Service, 12 F 3d 1233 (3rd Cir. 1993). 93

Fisher v. Immigration and Naturalization Service, 37 F 3d 1371 (9th Cir. 1994). 93

Florante de Leon v. Immigration and Naturalization Service, 1995 US App. LEXIS 3690.   239
Gafoor v. Immigration and Naturalization Service (2000) 231 F 3d 645 (9th Cir. 2000).   255
Garcia-Martinez v. Ashcroft 371 F 3d 1066 (9th Cir. 2004)   258
Garcia-Ramos v. Immigration and Naturalization Service, 775 F 2d 1370 (1985).   248
Gheorghe v. Immigration and Naturalization Service, 1998 US App. LEXIS 14989 (9th Cir. 1998).   128
Gomez v. Immigration and Naturalization Service, 947 F 2d 660 (3rd Cir. 1991).   297
Gonzalez v. Immigration and Naturalization Service, 82 F 3d 903 (9th Cir. 1996).   105
Gonzalez-Alvarado v. Immigration and Naturalization Service, 1996 US App. LEXIS 16488 (9th Cir. 1996).   131
Gormley v. Ashcroft, 364 F 3d 1172 (9th Cir. 2004).   128
Haitian Legal Center v. Smith, 676 F 2d 1023 (5th Cir. 1982).   2
Haitian Refugee Center v. Smith, 503 F Supp 442 (1980).   310
Hekmat Wadih Mikhael v. Immigration and Naturalization Service, 115 F 3d 299 (5th Cir. 1997).   119, 264
Hernandez-Montiel v. Immigration and Naturalization Service, 225 F 3d 1084 (9th Cir. 2000).   294
Immigration and Naturalization Service v. Jairo Jonathan Elias-Zacarias 502 US 478 (1992).   58
In Re R-A-, BIA, 2001 BIA LEXIS 1; 22 I & N Dec. 906, 11 June 1999.   265
In Re S-P-, BIA, 1996 BIA LEXIS 25; 21 I & N Dec. 486, 18 June 1996.   258
In Re T-M-B-, BIA, 1997 BIA LEXIS 7; 21 I & N Dec. 775, 778, 20 February 1997.   255, 258
In the Matter of Juan, BIA, IJ Burkhart, 12 March 1998.   335
Jaars v. Gonzales, 148 Fed. Appx. 310; 2005 US App. LEXIS 15069 (6th Cir. 2005).   128
Jian Chen v. Ashcroft, 289 F 3d 1113 (9th Cir. 2002).   324
Kahssai v. Immigration and Naturalization Service, 16 F 3d 323 (9th Cir. 1994).   212
Karouni v. Gonzales, 399 F 3d 1163 (9th Cir. 2005)   323
Korablina v. Immigration and Naturalization Service, 158 F 3d 1038 (9th Cir. 1998).   37
Kornetskyi v. Gonzales, 129 Fed. Appx. 254; 2005 US App. LEXIS 7457 (6th Cir. 2005).   96

Korniejew v. Ashcroft, 371 F 3d 377 (7th Cir. 2004). 224
Kovac v. Immigration and Naturalization Service, 407 F 2d 102 (9th Cir. 1969). 119
Krastev v. Immigration and Naturalization Service, 101 F 3d 1213 (7th Cir. 1996). 100
Largaespada-Castellanos v. Immigration and Naturalization Service, 1995 US App. LEXIS 22919 (9th Cir. 1995). 128
Largaespada-Galo v. Immigration and Naturalization Service, 1996 US App. LEXIS 13267 (9th Cir. 1996). 99
Leticia Bartolome Vicente v. Immigration and Naturalization Service, 2000 US App. LEXIS 29893. 314-315
Levitskaya v. Immigration and Naturalization Service, 43 Fed. Appx. 38; 2002 US App. LEXIS 15799 (9th Cir. 2002). 106
Li v. Immigration and Naturalization Service, 92 F 3d 985 (9th Cir. 1996). 38, 307
Lim v. Immigration and Naturalization Service, 224 F 3d 929 (9th Cir. 2000). 258
Ljuljdjurovic v. Gonzales, 132 Fed. Appx. 607; 2005 US App. LEXIS 9644 (6th Cir. 2005). 101
Lukban v. Immigration and Naturalization Service, 1998 US App. LEXIS 10854 (7th Cir. 1998). 119, 264
Lukwago v. Ashcroft, 329 F 3d 157 (3rd Cir. 2003). 128, 332
Ly Ying Sayaxing v. Immigration and Naturalization Service, 179 F 3d 515 (7th Cir. 1999). 96
Mansour v. Ashcroft, 390 F 3d 667 (9th Cir. 2004). 207
Martinez v. Immigration and Naturalization Service, 1995 US App. LEXIS 27361 (9th Cir. 1995). 129
Matter of Acosta, BIA, 1985 BIA LEXIS 2, 19 I & N Dec. 211, 1 March 1985. 295, 314, 315, 316
Matter of Janus and Janek, BIA, 1968 BIA LEXIS 99, 12 I & N Dec. 866, 25 July 1968.
Matter of Kasinga, BIA, 1996 BIA LEXIS 15; 21 I & N Dec. 357. 327
Matter of Laipenieks, BIA, 1983 BIA LEXIS 16; 18 I & N Dec. 433, 8 September 1983. 264
Maya Avetova-Elisseva v. Immigration and Naturalization Service, 213 F 2d 1192 (9th Cir. 2000). 204
Minwalla v. Immigration and Naturalization Service, 706 F 2d 831 (8th Cir. 1983). 99
Mohammed v. Gonzales 400 F 3d 785 (9th Cir. 2005). 30, 71, 282, 328

Mohan v. Immigration and Naturalization Service, 1997 US App. LEXIS 6721 (9th Cir. 1997).   251
Molinares v. Immigration and Naturalization Service, 1995 US App. LEXIS 36930 (9th Cir. 1995).   287
Ms M, Immigration Judge, 3 December 1996; upheld on appeal to the BIA, 30 March 2001.   281
Nagoulko v. Immigration and Naturalization Service, 333 F 3d 1012 (9th Cir. 2003).   37
Navas v. Immigration and Naturalization Service, 217 F 3d 646 (9th Cir. 2000).   258
Nelson v. Immigration and Naturalization Service, 232 F 3d 258 (1st Cir. 2000).   238
Ni v. Immigration and Naturalization Service, 54 Fed. Appx. 212, 2002 US App. LEXIS 27189 (6th Cir. 2002).   97
Obando-Rocha v. Immigration and Naturalization Service, 1996 US App. LEXIS 8222 (9th Cir. 1996).   129
Okado v. Attorney-General of the United States, 2005 US App. LEXIS 24989 (3rd Cir. 2005)   323
Ontunez-Tursios v. Ashcroft, 303 F 3d 341 (5th Cir. 2002).   250
Osaghae v. Immigration and Naturalization Service, 942 F 2d 1160 (7th Cir. 1991).   39
Osorio v. Immigration and Naturalization Service, 18 F 3d 1017 (2nd Cir. 1994).   249
Ouda v. Immigration and Naturalization Service, 324 F 3d 445 (6th Cir. 2003).   30
Petkov and Tritchkova v. Immigration and Naturalization Service, 114 F 3d 1192 (7th Cir. 1997).   38
Pitcherskaia v. Immigration and Naturalization Service, 118 F 3d 641 (9th Cir. 1997).   30
Popova v. Immigration and Naturalization Service, 273 F 3d 1251 (9th Cir. 2001).   258
Raffington v. Immigration and Naturalization Service, 340 F 3d 720 (8th Cir. 2003).   322
Ram v. Immigration and Naturalization Service, 2000 US App. LEXIS 6811 (9th Cir. 2000).   99
Raudez-Hurtada v. Immigration and Naturalization Service, 1994 US App. LEXIS 28409 (9th Cir. 1994).   199,
Re Chang, No. A-2720715, BIA, 1989.   30
Rivera v. Immigration and Naturalization Service, 100 F 3d 964 (7th Cir. 1997).   131

Ruiz v. *Immigration and Naturalization Service*, 1996 US App. LEXIS 14687 (9th Cir. 1996).   100
Saballo-Cortez v. *Immigration and Naturalization Service*, 761 F 2d 1259 (9th Cir. 1984).   129
Sale v. *Haitian Centers Council Inc* (1994) 113 S Ct 2549.   347
Samimi v. *Immigration and Naturalization Service*, 714 F 2d 992 (9th Cir. 1983).   110
Sanchez-Trujillo v. *Immigration and Naturalization Service*, 801 F 2d 1571 (9th Cir. 1986).   294
Singh v. *Immigration and Naturalization Service*, 1999 US App. LEXIS 33649 (9th Cir. 1999).   110
Sizov v. *Ashcroft*, 70 Fed. Appx. 374, 2003 US App. LEXIS 13524 (7th Cir. 2003).   93
Sofinet v. *Immigration and Naturalization Service*, 196 F 3d 742 (7th Cir. 1999).   97
Suarez v. *Secretary of State for the Home Department* [2002] 1 WLR 2663.   258
Subramaniam v. *Immigration and Naturalization Service*, 724 F Supp 799 (9th Cir. 1989). 288
Tamas-Mercea v. *Reno*, 222 F 3d 417 (7th Cir. 2000).   37
Tarubac v. *Immigration and Naturalization Service*, 182 F 3d 1114 (9th Cir. 1999).   249
Tchoukhrova v. *Gonzales*, 404 F 3d 1181 (9th Cir. 2005).   104, 141, 322
Tecun-Florian v. *Immigration and Naturalization Service*, 207 F 3d 1107 (9th Cir. 2000).   265
Tesfu v. *Ashcroft*, 322 F 3d 477 (7th Cir. 2003).   37, 272
Tchoukhrova v. *Gonzales*, 404 F 3d 1181 (9th Cir. 2005).   104, 141, 322
Thomas v. *Gonzales*, 409 F 3d 1177 at 1187 (9th Cir. 2005)   294, 295, 307, 323
Ubau-Marenco v. *Immigration and Naturalization Service*, 67 F 3d 750 (9th Cir. 1995).   110
Urukov v. *Immigration and Naturalization Service*, 55 F 3d 222 (7th Cir. 1995).   97
Vega-Garcia v. *Immigration and Naturalization Service*, 1996 US App. LEXIS 10881 (9th Cir. 1996).   130
Villasenor v. *Immigration and Naturalization Service*, 2000 US App. LEXIS 781 (9th Cir. 2000).   249
Vura v. *Immigration and Naturalization Service*, 1998 US App. LEXIS 10755 (7th Cir. 1998).   119
Wang v. *US Department of Justice*, 2003 US App. LEXIS 11198 (2nd Cir. 2003).   131

Zalega v. Immigration and Naturalization Service, 916 F 2d 1257
  (7th Cir. 1990).   240
Zhang v. Gonzales, 408 F 3d 1239 (9th Cir. 2005).   223, 240
*Zhen Hua Li v. Attorney General of the United States; Immigration and
  Naturalization Service*, 400 F 3d 157 (3rd Cir. 2005).   95

Legislation

Migration Act 1958 (Cth).   129, 257, 324, 347
Migration Legislation Amendment Act (No. 6) 2001 (Cth).   257, 324
Racial Discrimination Act 1975 (Cth).   257

Table of treaties and other international instruments

1947 General Agreement on Tariffs and Trade, Geneva, 30 October 1947, in force 1 January 1948, 55 UNTS 187.   60
1948 Universal Declaration of Human Rights UNGA Resolution 217A (III). Dec. 10   16, 27-85
1950 European Convention for the Protection of Human Rights and Fundamental Freedoms, Rome, 4 November 1950, in force 3 September 1953, 213 UNTS 221.   21, 67-70, 186-9
1951 Convention Relating to the Status of Refugees, Geneva, 28 July 1951, in force 22 April 1954, 189 UNTS 150.   1-355
1966 Convention on the Elimination of All Forms of Racial Discrimination, New York, 7 March 1966, in force 4 January 1969, 660 UNTS 195.   64
International Covenant on Civil and Political Rights, New York, 16 December 1966, in force 23 March 1976, 993 UNTS 171.   21, 160-201
1967 International Covenant on Economic, Social and Cultural Rights, New York, 16 December 1966, in force, 3 January 1976, 993 UNTS 3; (1967) 6 ILM 360.   17, 27, 64, 83-4, 95-6, 107, 115, 122, 137, 141-7, 153, 156-235, 313-20
Protocol Relating to the Status of Refugees (Jan. 31) 606 UNTS 8791.   62
1969 American Convention on Human Rights, San Jose, 22 November 1969, in force 18 July 1978, 1144 UNTS 123.   67
OAU Convention Governing the Specific Aspects of Refugee Problems in Africa, Addis Ababa, 10 September 1969, in force 20 June 1974, 1001 UNTS 14691.   67
Vienna Convention on the Law of Treaties, Vienna, 23 May 1969, in force 27 January 1988, 1155 UNTS 331; (1969) 8 ILM 679.   27-86

1971 Declaration on the Rights of Mentally Retarded Persons, UNGA Resolution 2856 (XXVI), UN GAOR, 2027th mtg, UN Doc. 2856 (XXVI) (1971).   73
1975 Declaration on the Rights of Disabled Persons, UNGA Resolution 3447 (XXX), UN GAOR, 2433rd mtg, UN Doc. 3447 (XXX) (1975).   73, 320
1979 Convention on the Elimination of All Forms of Discrimination Against Women, New York, 18 December 1979, in force 3 September 1981, 1249 UNTS 13.   64, 143, 150–3
1982 African Charter on Human and Peoples' Rights, Banjul, The Gambia, 27 June 1981, in force 21 October 1986, (1982) 21 ILM 58.   67
1984 Convention against Torture and Other Cruel, Inhuman or Degrading Treatment or Punishment, New York, 10 December 1984, in force 26 June 1987, 1465 UNTS 85.   21
Cartagena Declaration on Refugees (OAS). (Nov. 19–22)   22
1989 Convention on the Rights of the Child, New York, 20 November 1989, in force 2 September 1990, 1577 UNTS 3.   64, 103, 143, 178, 189, 207, 208, 212–15, 329–30
1990 International Convention on the Protection of the Rights of All Migrant Workers and Members of Their Families, (Dec. 8) UNGA Resolution 45/158.   183
1994 Marrakesh Agreement Establishing the World Trade Organization, Marrakesh, 15 April 1994, in force 1 January 1995, 1867 UNTS 3.
1998 Rome Statute of the International Criminal Court, Rome, 17 July 1998, in force 1 July 2002, 2187 UNTS 90.   58
2004 Council Directive 2004/83/EC on Minimum Standards for the Qualification and Status of Third Country Nationals or Stateless Persons as Refugees or as Persons who Otherwise Need International Protection and the Content of the Protection Granted, (Apr. 29) OJ L 304, 30/09/2004 P. 0012–0023.   31, 67

List of Abbreviations

AC	Appeal Cases
ALD	Administrative Law Decisions (Australia)
All ER	All England law Reports
ALR	Australian Law Reports
BIA	Board of Immigration Appeals (USA)
BCLR	Butterworths Constitutional law Reports (South Africa)
CAT	Convention Against Torture and Other Cruel, Inhuman or Degrading Treatment or Punishment
CEDAW	Convention on the Elimination of All Forms of Discrimination Against Women
CERD	International Convention on the Elimination of All Forms of Racial Discrimination
CLR	Commonwealth Law Reports (Australia)
CRC	Convention on the Rights of the Child
CRDD	Convention Refugee Determination Division (Canada)
DLR	Dominion Law Reports (Canada)
ECHR	European Court of Human Rights
Economic Committee	Committee on Economic, Social and Cultural Rights
ECRE	European Council on Refugees and Exiles
EHRR	European Human Rights Reports
European Convention	European Convention for the Protection of Human Rights and Fundamental Freedoms
EWCA	England and Wales Court of Appeal
ExCOM	Executive Committee of UNHCR

FCA	Federal Court of Australia
FCAFC	Federal Court of Australia Full Court
FCJ	Federal Court of Justice (Canada)
FCR	Federal Court Reports (Australia)
FCTD	Federal Court Trial Division (Canada)
FLR	Federal Law Reports (Australia)
F Supp	Federal Supplement (US)
F 2d	Federal Reporter, 2nd Series (US)
F 3d	Federal Reporter, 3rd Series (US)
GA	General Assembly (UN)
GAOR	General Assembly Official Records
HRC	UN Human Rights Committee
HRW	Human Rights Watch
IAT	Immigration Appeal Tribunal (UK)
IBR	International Bill of Rights
ICC	International Criminal Court
ICCPR	International Covenant on Civil and Political Rights
ICESCR	International Covenant on Economic, Social and Cultural Rights
ICJ	International Court of Justice
IJ	Immigration Judge (US)
ILC	International Law Commission
ILM	International Legal Materials
ILO	International Labour Organization
Imm AR	Immigration Appeal Reports (UK)
INLR	Immigration and National Law Review (UK)
MPSG	Membership of a particular social group
NGO	Non-governmental organisation
NZAR	New Zealand Administrative Reports
NZ RSAA	New Zealand Refugee Status Appeals Authority
OAU	Organization of African Unity
PSG	Particular social group
Refugee Convention	Convention Relating to the Status of Refugees
RPD	Refugee Protection Division (Immigration and Review Board Canada)
RPDD	Refugee Protection Division Decision (Canada)
RRT	Refugee Review Tribunal (Australia)
SCR	Supreme Court Reports (Canada)
UDHR	Universal Declaration of Human Rights

UNHCR	Office of the High Commissioner for Refugees
UNTS	United Nations Treaty Series
US	United States Supreme Court Reports
VCLT	Vienna Convention on the Law of Treaties
WLR	Weekly Law Reports (UK)
WTO	World Trade Organization

1 Introduction

The phenomenon of flight from poverty, economic degradation and disadvantage poses a range of difficult ethical, legal and policy challenges for decision-makers and policy-makers alike. How should states that receive such persons respond to claims based on economic and social deprivation? In particular, what international legal principles operate to constrain the decision-making authority of states receiving such persons, and what rights are provided in international law for those wishing to avoid repatriation to a situation in which they will be subject to economic deprivation?

This book explores the legal challenges created by the phenomenon of migration caused by the deprivation of economic and social rights. In particular, it directly engages with the question whether the 1951 Convention Relating to the Status of Refugees ('Refugee Convention')[1] — the key instrument in international law for the protection of refugees — is capable of encompassing claims based on economic destitution. In exploring this question, the book identifies the conceptual and analytical challenges presented by such claims and assesses the extent to which these challenges may be resolved or overcome by a creative interpretation of the Refugee Convention consistent with correct principles of international treaty interpretation. The hypothesis is that, notwithstanding the dichotomy between 'economic migrants' and 'genuine' refugees which pervades both the refugee and migration literature and refugee determination, the Refugee Convention is capable of accommodating a more complex and nuanced analysis that recognizes that many types of claims with an economic element are properly considered within the purview of the Refugee Convention.

---

[1] Geneva, 28 July 1951, in force 22 April 1954, 189 UNTS 150.

Background

In considering international legal approaches to the problem of involuntary economic migration, the traditional position has been to construct a dichotomy between 'economic migrants' and 'political refugees', with the former falling outside the terms of the Refugee Convention. This distinction has been particularly evident at the political and rhetorical level of state policy and has underpinned the rejection of entire classes of applicants on the basis that their claims are clearly those of economic migrants rather than refugees.[2] Well-known examples include the US policy of interdiction in respect of Haitian refugees in the early 1980s, justified by the fact that Haitians were labelled as economic and not political refugees,[3] and the forcible repatriation of Vietnamese refugees by Hong Kong in the late 1980s based on a similar presumption.[4] In more recent times, the distinction has been relied upon by China as an explanation and justification for its decision to return thousands of North Koreans each year under bilateral diplomatic agreements with North Korea.[5] It has also been used extensively in the media in Western refugee-receiving states, often as a

---

[2] See, for example, the description of the UK's treatment of Roma asylum applicants in Dallal Stevens, 'Roma Asylum Applicants in the United Kingdom: "Scroungers" or "Scapegoats"', in Joanne van Selm et al. (eds.), *The Refugee Convention at Fifty: A View from Forced Migrations Studies* (Maryland: Lexington Books, 2003), pp. 145–60, where she explains that the perception of Roma as 'economic migrants' and 'street criminals' has led to the dismissal of many claims as 'manifestly unfounded': p. 154. The characterization of a vast number of asylum applicants as 'economic migrants' has also led to other state initiatives, such as the removal or reduction of welfare benefits for asylum seekers.

[3] This was the case even though US sanctions had exacerbated economic destitution: see Tom Farer, 'How the International System Copes with Involuntary Migration: Norms, Institutions and State Practice' (1995) 17 *Human Rights Quarterly* 72. For the history and background to the practice, see Janice D. Villiers, 'Closed Borders, Closed Ports: The Flight of Haitians Seeking Political Asylum in the United States' (1994) 60 *Brooklyn Law Review* 841. For judicial consideration of the practice see *Haitian Legal Center* v. *Smith*, 676 F 2d 1023 (5th Cir. 1982).

[4] For the background to this issue and practice, see Janelle M. Diller, *In Search of Asylum: Vietnamese Boat People in Hong Kong* (Washington: Indochina Resource Center, 1988).

[5] See generally Eric Yong-Joong Lee, 'National and International Legal Concerns regarding Recent North Korean Escapees' (2001) 13 *International Journal of Refugee Law* 142. Human Rights Watch explains that the Chinese Government 'maintains that no North Koreans are refugees, and that its primary obligation lies under a 1986 agreement with North Korea on the repatriation of refugees. Accordingly, China arrests and expels North Koreans without the opportunity to seek asylum': see Human Rights Watch, *The Invisible Exodus: North Koreans in the People's Republic of China* (2002) <http://www.hrw.org/reports/2002/northkorea/norkor1102.pdf> at 31 May 2006.

justification in support of the call for 'tougher' measures in respect of asylum-seekers.[6]

While the dichotomy is most clearly evident in these well-known and highly publicized examples of state practice, it is in fact an endemic and perennial problem that continues to challenge states presented with 'economic' claims, and to which there remains no satisfactory framework of analysis. The extent to which the dichotomy is entrenched in state practice is indicated in a study of refugee decision-making in the Netherlands, which concluded that 'the opposition between "economic" and "political" refugees is so strong and so total in the context of refugee law that anything related to the economic is assumed to be non-political'.[7] Moreover, the same study suggests that the distinction is 'so ingrained in the asylum procedure that interview officials are scarcely aware of it' and thus effortlessly reduce flight motives to economic ones.[8] Indeed, the terms 'economic refugees' and 'economic migrants' continue to pervade contemporary refugee jurisprudence.

In addition to state practice reflecting a rather simplistic analysis of such claims, policy-makers and refugee and migration scholars have, in the main, tended to accept the distinction. While it is acknowledged in the literature that there are claims that challenge the simplistic dichotomy and suggest that the lines are not as clear as might be asserted in the rhetoric of states, it is nonetheless frequently assumed that the key international treaties – and in particular the Refugee Convention – are not able to encompass such claims and thus appropriate policy and legal responses lie elsewhere.[9] For this

---

[6] For example, Dummett describes the use of this term in the United Kingdom, explaining that '[a] favourite propaganda device' of government employees 'is to repeat incessantly that most of the asylum seekers are mere "economic migrants"'. He argues that '[t]his phrase has the benefit of blurring the distinction between refugees and immigrants: it also serves to convey that the motives of those claiming asylum are trivial and unworthy': Michael Dummett, *On Immigration and Refugees* (London: Routledge, 2001), pp. 44–5. See also Tony Kushner and Katharine Knox, 'The Kurds: A Moment of Humanity in an Era of Restriction?' in Tony Kushner and Katharine Knox, *Refugees in an Age of Genocide: Global, National and Local Perspectives during the Twentieth Century* (London: Frank Cass, 1999), pp. 335–54.

[7] Thomas Spijkerboer, *Gender and Refugee Studies* (Aldershot: Ashgate, 2000), p. 76.

[8] *Ibid.*, pp. 76–7.

[9] For example, in Katharina Rohl's paper, 'Fleeing Violence and Poverty: Non-refoulement Obligations under the European Convention of Human Rights' (UNHCR, New Issues in Refugee Research, Working Paper No. 111, January 2005), she asserts that, 'the refugee definition in the 1951 Convention "almost completely exclud[es] the violation of economic and social rights from the concept of persecution", and thus immediately

reason, the debate within international refugee law is drastically underdeveloped.[10]

However, while the conceptual problems raised by the simplistic distinction between political (and therefore 'genuine') Convention refugees and 'economic migrants' are not new, they are rapidly becoming impossible to avoid as a range of emerging refugee claims challenges traditional distinctions between economic migrants and political refugees. For example, is a child born outside the parameters of China's one-child policy, and thus subject to deprivations of economic and social rights, such as education and health care, an 'economic migrant' or a refugee? What about a woman who 'voluntarily' agrees to be smuggled into a foreign country as part of a prostitution trafficking operation, because it is the only option for her survival, and who risks serious harm from traffickers if returned to her home country? Is a Roma man from the Czech Republic, who suffers extensive discrimination in education and employment, an 'economic migrant' or a refugee? What about a street child in the Democratic Republic of Congo whose government fails to provide him or her with the basic tools of survival, such as food and shelter? Or women who leave their country in order to earn a living when the major forces causing them to leave are 'their educational disadvantage, their inability to inherit land under customary law, and their exclusion from serious involvement in coffee production'?[11]

> moves to the consideration of remedies under other treaties' (p. 3, citations omitted). See also Peter Penz, 'Economic Refugees and Political Migrants: An Ethical Analysis of "Forced Migration"' (paper presented at the 7th International Conference of the International Research and Advisory Panel ('IRAP') of the International Association for the Study of Forced Migration, South Africa, 2001) (on file with author), p. 1; HRH Crown Prince El Hassan Bin Talal, 'Refugee Law: Protection for the Minority' (1993) 6 *Journal of Refugee Studies* 1 at 5 and R.J. Vincent, 'Political and Economic Refugees: Problems of Migration, Asylum and Resettlement' (1989) 2 *Journal of Refugee Studies* 504.
> [10] Even the UNHCR tends to accept the dichotomy to a certain extent, apparently assuming that refugees fleeing because of severe economic conditions are outside the bounds of the Refugee Convention. For example, in a recent consideration of the refugee–migration connection, the UNHCR appeared to treat separately the issues of 'serious human rights violations or armed conflict' from 'economic marginalization and poverty': see UNHCR, *Global Consultations on International Protection, Refugee Protection and Migration Control: Perspectives From UNHCR and IOM*, UN Doc. EC/GC/01/11 (2001), at para. 5. For an earlier example, see UNHCR, *Composite Flows and the Relationship to Refugee Outflows, Including Return of Persons not in Need of International Protection as Well as Facilitation of Return in its Global Dimension*, UN Doc. EC/48/SC/CRP.29 (1998), at para. 5.
> [11] Charles David Smith, 'Women Migrants of Kagera Region, Tanzania: The Need for Empowerment' in Doreen Indra (ed.), *Engendering Forced Migration: Theory and Practice*

These are just some examples of the types of claims that can be and indeed are being made at present under the auspices of the Refugee Convention regime. They raise controversial and difficult questions about different elements of the Refugee Convention definition, but all implicitly challenge the neat distinction inherent in the orthodox view. In particular, they indicate that there is a need for debate and analysis within the confines of international refugee law and that existing approaches, which treat claims involving economic deprivation as a point of departure from the refugee regime, ignore the fact that there is a grey area between the two extreme categories, which requires further exploration.[12]

The key conceptual challenge: economic migrants versus refugees

The primary challenge in attempting to deal with this emerging type of claim is the strong tradition of distinguishing between economic migrants or refugees and 'genuine' political refugees. Given that this distinction permeates many levels of decision-making, one might expect the definition of the term 'economic migrants' to be well established, and for the distinction between economic migrants or economic refugees and Refugee Convention refugees to be clear. However, one of the striking things that an investigation into the application of such labels reveals is that their meaning is seldom explained, nor are the distinctions between them made apparent. This is highlighted by the fact that the terms 'economic migrants' and 'economic refugees' are often used interchangeably, apparently under the assumption that their meaning is self-evident.

(New York: Berghahn Books, 1999), p. 162, discussing the situation of women in the Kagera region in Tanzania.

[12] The scope for development in this area has been noted in recent literature, particularly 'as the value of certain economic and social rights is increasingly accepted': Guy Goodwin-Gill, *The Refugee in International Law* (Oxford: Clarendon Press, 1996), p. 79. There is a view emerging in the most recent literature that an analysis which implicates economic and social rights is the 'next- or current-stage' in the development of refugee law: see Deborah Anker, 'Boundaries in the Field of Human Rights: Refugee Law, Gender and the Human Rights Paradigm' (2002) 15 *Harvard Human Rights Journal* 133 at 149.

While the reasons for the clear and straightforward separation between the categories economic migrants/refugees and political refugees are seldom explicitly made clear, it is possible to separate out the implicit assumptions at work. Before analysing the various strands inherent in the dichotomy, it is important to emphasize that there are different rationales underlying the distinction and there are different levels at which the differentiation operates. On one hand, there is a distinction that might be deemed rhetorical, rather than based on fine legal analysis. As Tuitt explains, the distinction between economic migrants and refugees is often 'not perceived as the honest conflict between refugees and a narrow legal definition, but that which arises between genuine humanitarian refugees and fraudulent economic migrants. Synonymous with the notion of the new asylum seeker is the idea of the bogus asylum seeker who manipulates the rules governing domestic immigration'.[13] The rhetorical invocation of these labels in respect of groups of asylum-seekers is widespread and has sometimes proven to be a convenient method for governments to justify minimizing their obligations under the Refugee Convention.[14]

However, on a different level, there are perceived underlying conceptual challenges to characterizing claims involving economic elements within the traditional refugee framework. First, underlying the lack of sympathy (and often hostility) towards persons deemed 'economic migrants' is a sense that they leave their home countries *voluntarily*, merely to attain a 'better life' in the destination state, and therefore have no legitimate reason for seeking protection.

---

[13] Patricia Tuitt, *False Images: Law's Construction of the Refugee* (London: Pluto Press, 1996), p. 70. Erika Feller, Director of the Department of International Protection in the UNHCR, has recently explained that a 'third assumption [underpinning waning public support for refugees and a harder line by governments] is that unsuccessful asylum seekers are all bogus': Erika Feller, 'The Evolution of the International Refugee Protection Regime' (2001a) 5 *Washington University Journal of Law and Policy* 129 at 137.

[14] For example, Goodwin-Gill explains in a recent article that '[o]ver the last twenty or so years, governments throughout the world have tried to avoid dealing with the difficult questions raised by refugee and related movements. One method is to seek to redefine the problem as one not involving obligation or responsibility'. He cites 'illegal migrants' and 'boat people' as examples of the terms engaged, but the term 'economic migrants' is used just as frequently: see Guy Goodwin-Gill, 'Refugees and Responsibility in the Twenty-First Century: More Lessons learned from the South Pacific' (2003) 12 *Pacific Rim Law and Policy Journal* 23 at 26-7. For a specific case study, see Stevens, 'Roma Asylum Applicants in the United Kingdom: "Scroungers" or "Scapegoats"', pp. 145-60.

These concerns reveal an underlying distinction between forced or involuntary migrants responding to the 'push' factors of persecution (and thus deserving of protection) and voluntary migrants primarily influenced by the 'pull' factors of the attractions present in the receiving state (therefore undeserving of protection).[15] As Zolberg, Suhrke and Aguayo have explained, the distinction is neatly encapsulated in the following simplistic formula: 'voluntary economic = migrants' and 'involuntary political = refugees'.[16]

The reliance on *voluntariness* may not, at first glance, seem surprising since one would not expect that a woman who left her country because she was able to earn a higher salary as a doctor in a second country – the classic definition of an economic migrant – should need or deserve international protection. However, this fairly obvious and intuitive distinction between voluntary and involuntary migration becomes less apparent once one moves beyond obvious examples and attempts to apply it to more complex situations. For example, is it truly accurate to argue that while a political dissident who leaves her country fearing imprisonment and torture is an 'involuntary' migrant, a woman who leaves her country due to severe discrimination based on her HIV-positive status, which renders her unable to provide her family with food, is a 'voluntary' migrant? Moreover, is it not true that in both cases the applicants are, at least to some degree, seeking 'a better life'?

Indeed, while migration theorists sometimes attempt to explain the phenomenon of migration according to a typology that is based, at least to some degree, on a distinction between voluntary and involuntary migration, they also acknowledge that making a binary distinction between the two categories is problematic, as it tends to mask

---

[15] Anthony H. Richmond, 'Reactive Migration: Sociological Perspectives on Refugee Movements' (1993) 6 *Journal of Refugee Studies* 7 at 7. See also Penz, 'Economic Refugees and Political Migrants: an Ethical Analysis of "Forced Migration"'. For a discussion of the 'push–pull' issue in the context of economic migration, see Bimal Ghosh, *Huddled Masses and Uncertain Shores: Insights into Irregular Migration* (The Hague: Martinus Nijhoff Publishers, 1998), pp. 34–43.

[16] Aristide R. Zolberg, Astri Suhrke and Sergio Aguayo, *Escape from Violence: Conflict and the Refugee Crisis in the Developing World* (New York: Oxford University Press, 1989), p. 30. See also Cecilia Menjívar, 'History, Economy and Politics: Macro and Micro Level Factors in Recent Salvadorean Migration to the US' (1993) 6 *Journal of Refugee Studies* 350. See also Susan F. Martin, *New Issues in Refugee Research: Global Migration Trends and Asylum* (2001) UNHCR <http://www.unhcr.org/cgi-bin/texis/vtx/research/opendoc.pdf?tbl=RESEARCH&id=3af66ccc4> at 31 May 2006.

complexities and subtleties in motivations for flight.[17] On one level, it might be said that the only true involuntary or forced migrants/refugees are those subject to expulsion by their own governments or forcibly removed from a country as part of a trade in trafficking humans (such as a slave trade).[18] In other words, even those fleeing the traditional forms of political persecution could be characterized as voluntary migrants to some degree. As Richmond explains, '[h]uman agency implies an element of choice and ensures that some degree of uncertainty is always present, even when the choices in question are severely constrained by external considerations'.[19]

Moreover, there is a 'voluntary' aspect to some kinds of traditional refugee claims. This is made explicit by Zolberg, Suhrke and Aguayo when they note that there is a category of 'traditional' refugees that challenges the voluntary/involuntary distinction, namely political and religious 'dissenters'. Responding to the suggestion by Vernant that refugees are distinguished from other migrants on the basis that a refugee is 'the victim of events for which, at least as an individual, he cannot be held responsible',[20] they point out that those who reject the alternative provided to them by their government of living within certain religious and political parameters make a choice to do so. They explain that 'it is precisely because dissent does entail the exercise of personal choice that those who engage in it are admirable'.[21] Modern examples include those who live an openly homosexual life or openly practice prohibited elements of their religion, a category of claim that has raised this precise tension.[22]

---

[17] See, for example, Sally E. Findley, 'Compelled to Move: the Rise of Forced Migration in Sub-Saharan Africa', in M. A. B. Siddique (ed.), *International Migration into the 21st Century* (Cheltenham: Edward Elgar, 2001), p. 279.

[18] Richmond, 'Reactive Migration', at 7.

[19] *Ibid.*, at 9. See also Charles B. Keely, 'Demography and International Migration' in Caroline B. Brettell and James F. Hollifield (eds.), *Migration Theory: Talking across Disciplines* (New York: Routledge, 2000), where the author states that '[t]he problem [with the distinction between voluntary and involuntary migrants] is that all migration includes elements of choice and pressure. Not all people in groups targeted for persecution leave a country. Not all economic migration is without some coercion on the migrant's decision making. It is also clear that refugee flows are quickly followed by some returns. Why do some people return quickly, while others take longer or even struggle against ever returning?': p. 50.

[20] Zolberg, Suhrke and Aguayo, *Escape from Violence*, p. 31.   [21] *Ibid.*

[22] See Rodger P. G. Haines, James C. Hathaway and Michelle Foster, 'Claims to Refugee Status Based on Voluntary but Protected Actions' (2003) 15(3) *International Journal of Refugee Law* 430.

Acknowledging these problems, Richmond concludes that 'a distinction between voluntary and involuntary movements is ... untenable'.[23] The richness and subtleties in the distinctions between different categories are reflected in his alternative method of distinguishing motives for flight. He constructs a typology of what he terms 'reactive migration' which comprises 25 categories of those 'whose degrees of freedom are severely constrained'.[24] Zolberg, Suhrke and Aguayo similarly reject the simplistic distinction between voluntary and involuntary migrants, concluding that the determination of whether movement is voluntary or involuntary must refer to 'some doctrine of rights'.[25]

A second key conceptual challenge relates to the issue of intent. Specifically, it is assumed that there is a fundamental and clear distinction between those suffering economic hardship and 'traditional' refugees in that, while the situation to which a person is required to return may be unfortunate, persons fleeing economic degradation are not 'deserving' of protection since they are not obviously fleeing a single and identifiable aggressor, but rather indiscriminate hardship or natural disasters. As Jeremy Harding has explained:

> In the past, refugees have won greater international sympathy than economic migrants. Theirs has been the more identifiable grievance: at its source there is often an identifiable persecutor. Yet the order of economic difficulty that prevails in some parts of the world is akin to persecution. No consensus exists about the identity of the tormentor, and so those who try to put it behind them are more easily reviled than others fleeing the attentions of secret police or state militias.[26]

This points to the tendency to assume that persons fleeing situations in which they do not have access to basic economic and social rights do not need or deserve protection because their position is a result of natural conditions (for example, an ecological disaster, famine or insufficient resources to provide basic health care) and not the result of a positive act on the part of the government or any other person. The prevalence of this distinction is highlighted in a submission made on behalf of a number of non-government organizations to a conference conducted under the auspices of the Office of the United Nations High Commissioner for

---

[23] Anthony H. Richmond, *Global Apartheid: Refugees, Racism, and the New World Order* (Toronto: Oxford University Press, 1994), p. 58.
[24] Richmond, 'Reactive Migration', at 10; see at 19–21 for his typology of forced migration.
[25] Zolberg, Suhrke and Aguayo, *Escape from Violence*, p. 31.
[26] Jeremy Harding, *The Uninvited: Refugees at the Rich Man's Gate* (London: Profile Books, 2000), p. 122.

Refugees ('UNHCR') Global Consultations on International Protection, in which it was noted that:

People leaving their home countries because of violations of their economic and social rights have generally not been granted the same level of protection as those fleeing violations of their civil and political rights. The denial of civil and political rights is considered as a 'violation', while the denial of economic and social rights is generally viewed as an 'injustice'.[27]

However, one might question how cogent and reliable this distinction is in assessing the category into which different claimants may fit. For example, it begins to break down in situations where a government uses starvation as a political tool, 'inducing famine by destroying crops or poisoning water in order to break the will of insurgency groups'.[28] Or in the situation where local warlords in civil conflicts withhold food from populations under their control in order to attract relief from international donors, which will then be sold in order to buy arms.[29]

The quotation from Harding above also points to a third conceptual distinction which often underlies objections to economic claims, namely that the individual claimant is not in a unique position, but rather is in the same position as an entire class of persons within his or her society, and thus does not fit within the conception of a refugee as a person who

---

[27] Human Rights Watch, International Catholic Migration Committee and the World Council of Churches, *NGO Background Paper on the Refugee and Migration Interface* (paper presented to the UNHCR Global Consultations on International Protection, Geneva, 28–29 June 2001a) (on file with author).

[28] Susanne Schmeidl, 'Conflict and Forced Migration: A Quantitative Review, 1964–1995', in Aristide R. Zolberg and Peter M. Benda (eds.), *Global Migrants, Global Refugees: Problems and Solutions* (New York: Berghahn Books, 2001), pp. 82–3. Schmeidl argues that such tactics were used by Nigeria during the Biafra conflict and by Ethiopia during its conflict with Eritrea. See also David Marcus, 'Famine Crimes in International Law' (2003) 97 *American Journal of International Law* 245.

[29] See Myron Weiner, 'The Clash of Norms: Dilemmas in Refugee Policies' (1998) 11 *Journal of Refugee Studies* 433 at 437. The author says that this was the strategy of warlords in the civil conflict in Liberia in 1996 and 1997 (citing David Breyer and Edmund Cairns, 'For Better? For Worse? Humanitarian Aid in Conflict' (1997) 7(4) *Development in Practice* 363–74). In addition, Weiner says that the government of Iraq reportedly withheld food and medical supplies from civilians in order to force the United Nations to end its embargo: at 437. A more recent example is the situation in North Korea, where it has been suggested the severe food shortage is at least partly caused (and exacerbated) by the North Korean government: see Marcus, 'Famine Crimes in International Law', at 259–62;
Eric Yong-Joong Lee, 'National and International Legal Concerns regarding Recent North Korean Escapees', at 143; see also Amnesty International, *Starved of Rights: Human Rights and the Food Crisis in the Democratic People's Republic of Korea (North Korea)* (2004b) <http://web.amnesty.org/library/index/engasa240032004> at 31 May 2006.

has been 'singled out' or individually targeted by an oppressor. However, the cogency of this rationale for dismissing economic claims is open to question on the basis that the system of international refugee protection was designed initially to accommodate extremely large groups of refugees such as Jews fleeing Nazi Germany.[30] Moreover, modern refugee doctrine has largely abandoned this 'singling out' requirement in the course of accommodating refugees fleeing civil war and other situations in which identification as a member of an at-risk group has proven sufficient to qualify for refugee status.[31]

Challenging the simplistic dichotomy

Given the artificial quality of the distinction between economic refugees and political refugees, it is not surprising that commentators and scholars have questioned the wisdom of insisting on these neat categories.[32] The awkwardness of the economic/political distinction has not been ignored by those involved in the application of the Refugee Convention regime. Rather, it is recognized in the early attempt by the UNHCR, in its authoritative 1979 Handbook, to distinguish

---

[30] This is made explicit in the instruments that pre-dated the Refugee Convention. For example, Goodwin-Gill explains that in 1926 a Russian refugee was defined to include 'any person of Russian origin who does not enjoy or who no longer enjoys the protection of the Government of the Union of Socialist Soviet Republics and who has not acquired another nationality': Goodwin-Gill, *The Refugee in International Law*, p. 2. He explains that a 'similar approach was adopted in 1936 arrangements in respect of those fleeing Germany, which were later developed by Article 1 of the 1938 Convention, to cover: "(a) Persons possessing or having possessed German nationality and not possessing any other nationality who are proved not to enjoy, in law or fact, the protection of the German Government" ': p. 3. Further, the constitution of the International Refugee Organization 'specified certain categories to be assisted', including 'victims of the Nazi, Fascist, or Quisling regimes which had opposed the United Nations, certain persons of Jewish origin, or foreigners or stateless persons who had been victims of Nazi persecution': p. 4.
[31] See generally Chapter 5, below.
[32] As a Justice of the Federal Court of Australia has noted (extra-curially) in relation to the phrase 'economic refugees', 'there is no such term in international or domestic law': His Honour Justice Marcus Einfeld, 'Is There a Role for Compassion in Refugee Policy?' (2000) 23(3) *University of New South Wales Law Journal* 303 at 312. This echoes a concern expressed by Grahl-Madsen, at a much earlier stage of the Refugee Convention's history, when he opined that the term 'economic refugees' is 'a misnomer' which 'should be avoided': Atle Grahl-Madsen, *The Status of Refugees in International Law* (Leyden: A. W. Sijthoff, 1966), vol. I, p. 76.

between economic migrants and refugees. The Handbook introduces the distinction by stating:

A migrant is a person who, for reasons other than those contained in the definition, voluntarily leaves his country in order to take up residence elsewhere. He may be moved by the desire for change or adventure, or by family or other reasons of a personal nature. If he is moved exclusively by economic considerations, he is an economic migrant and not a refugee.[33]

However, it immediately seeks to acknowledge the overly simplistic nature of the dichotomy by adding the following qualification:

The distinction between an economic migrant and a refugee is, however, sometimes blurred in the same way as the distinction between economic and political measures in an applicant's country of origin is not always clear. Behind economic measures affecting a person's livelihood there may be racial, religious or political aims or intentions directed against a particular group.[34]

The UNHCR's analysis suggests at least two ways in which the dichotomy between political and economic claims breaks down in refugee analysis. First, the use of the word 'exclusively' in relation to economic motives acknowledges that those fleeing their home country may have mixed motives for flight. Thus the fact that part of the motivation for a person's flight is 'economic' does not preclude a refugee claim, assuming the person is also fleeing traditional 'political' persecution.[35] This is the argument made, for example, by those who criticize the labelling of refugees from certain Central American countries as 'economic migrants'

---

[33] UNHCR, *Handbook on Procedures and Criteria for Determining Refugee Status under the 1951 Convention and the 1967 Protocol Relating to the Status of Refugees* (1992), para. 51 <http://www.unhcr.org/cgi-bin/texis/vtx/home/opendoc.pdf?tbl=PUBL&id=3d58e13b4> at 31 May 2006 ('UNHCR Handbook'). The reference to personal motivation likely reflects the origin of the persecution standard, which is said to have evolved from the concern expressed in the 1938 Convention concerning the Status of Refugees to exclude those persons leaving their country 'for reasons of purely personal convenience': Ivor Jackson, 'The 1951 Convention Relating to the Status of Refugees: A Universal Basis for Protection' (1991) 3 *International Journal of Refugee Law* 403 at 405–6.

[34] UNHCR Handbook, para. 64. In a much more recent exposition, the UNHCR observed: 'It should also be kept in mind that behind economic conditions affecting a person's livelihood, there are often in play the forces of nationalism, ethic intolerance, widespread violations of human rights and undemocratic government. According to some studies, no fewer than 250 million people live in a dozen countries where the whole population is subject to the most severe repression by the regime, the armed opposition or both. These are by and large the same countries that also produce "economic migrants"': UNHCR, *Discussion Paper: Reconciling Migration Control and Refugee Protection in the European Union: A UNHCR Perspective* (Geneva, 2000), para. 10 (on file with author).

[35] These causation issues are further discussed in Chapter 5, below.

on the basis that government reports have in fact indicated that people 'driven by political forces from their countries [follow] the familiar paths of an already established pattern of economic migration'.[36] In other words, political and economic elements are not mutually exclusive and the fact that the destination country is chosen partly because of its socio-economic status does not automatically preclude a refugee claim.

The second and more fundamental point is that political persecution can take the form of economic punishment or deprivation, a position that was accepted from the earliest days of the Refugee Convention's operation.[37] The UNHCR Handbook makes this meaning clear where it states that:

Where economic measures destroy the economic existence of a particular section of the population (e.g. withdrawal of trading rights from, or discriminatory or excessive taxation of, a specific ethnic or religious group), the victims may according to the circumstances become refugees on leaving the country.[38]

Thus, although there may well be cases in which it appears that citizens are leaving their home country because of general conditions of poverty, or general inability to obtain access to economic and social benefits, a closer analysis may reveal that the economic situation has been caused or worsened by a repressive regime and may reflect a wide-scale abuse of fundamental human rights, including economic, social and cultural rights, connected to political power and repression.[39] In other words, it may not be a coincidence that these so-called 'economic refugees' are fleeing repressive regimes.

This more complex analysis also resonates with the migration theory literature in which the simplistic distinction between economic and political factors has been questioned for decades.[40] Zolberg, Suhrke

---

[36] Milton H. Jamail and Chandler Stolp, 'Central Americans on the Run: Political Refugees or Economic Migrants?' (1985) 31(3) *Public Affairs Comment* 1 at 2.
[37] This issue is discussed in detail in Chapter 3, below.
[38] UNHCR Handbook, at para. 63.
[39] A similar approach was suggested by Justice Einfeld of the Federal Court of Australia when he voiced the concern (extra-curially) that the political/economic distinction is artificial because 'the economic turmoil which the people suffer is, more often than not, a direct consequence of the effect of foreign military intervention or internal political oppression often fed, or not helped, by the industrialized countries': Einfeld, 'Is There a Role for Compassion in Refugee Policy?', at 312. See also 'Political Legitimacy in the Law of Political Asylum' (1985) 99 *Harvard Law Review* 450.
[40] See for example, Tony Kushner and Katharine Knox, 'Refugees from Indo-China: A Media-Driven Resettlement Scheme?', in Kushner and Knox, *Refugees in an Age of Genocide*, pp. 306–31. See also Kushner and Knox, 'Refugees from the

and Aguayo note that the difficulty of distinguishing between political and economic migration-inducing events is 'hardly new', citing the example of the Irish during the Great Hunger of the late 1840s as an obvious example of the integral relationship between economic and political factors.[41] Numerous studies that have been undertaken in an attempt to challenge the 'political refugees versus economic migrants' distinction provide empirical evidence that political and economic factors are inextricably linked, and that it is artificial to distinguish between political and economic refugees in many circumstances.[42]

We can thus perceive 'cracks' in the orthodox veneer of the political versus economic distinction; however, openness to recognizing the complexity of the issues in the context of refugee law remains at a very preliminary stage. This book does not attempt to support the numerous studies that reveal the complex interplay between economic and political factors with further empirical evidence, but explores why, in the face of such evidence, we continue to insist on simplistic categories? It examines the way in which the key international

---

Former Zaïre: the Context of Colour' in Kushner and Knox, *Refugees in an Age of Genocide*, pp. 383–4, where the authors discuss the difficulties in separating political and economic factors for refugees from Zaïre. See also Joe Oloka-Onyango, 'Human Rights, The OAU Convention and the Refugee Crisis in Africa: Forty Years after Geneva' (1991) 3 *International Journal of Refugee Law* 452, where he notes that it is 'impossible to distinguish' between economic and political factors in the case of many refugees from Africa, leading him to conclude that 'the intransigence of refugee law on this matter is clearly not justifiable in all cases and at all times, especially when the social and economic ramifications of political measures become all the more apparent': at 458. See also Tandeka Nkiwane Muzenda, 'The Role of Social and Economic Factors and Natural Disasters in Forced Population Displacements in Africa' (1995) 7 *International Journal of Refugee Law* 46, where the author notes that 'the line once drawn between a refugee and an economic migrant, or what some have termed "political" versus "economic" refugee status is becoming finer and finer': at 47. In addition, important work has been undertaken by economists in this field, the most well-known being Amartya Sen, *Development as Freedom* (New York: Knopf, 1999).

[41] Zolberg, Suhrke and Aguayo, *Escape from Violence*, p. 31.

[42] Menjívar cites many studies to establish that there is empirical evidence which questions the political-economic distinction: 'History, Economy and Politics', pp. 350–1. See also Richmond, *Global Apartheid*, p. 52, where he quotes Dowty: 'So-called economic migrants are often responding as much to political repression as to material deprivation.' Richmond says: 'He gives examples of refugees from Ethiopia where political pressures and war combine with famine to cause massive flight, Haiti where political repression and economic underdevelopment go together, and El Salvador where would-be refugees have been returned because they are regarded as "victims of generalized violence" rather than individual persecution.' Dowty states that '[i]n such circumstances, the distinction between "economic" and "political" refugees becomes meaningless': p. 52.

instrument – the Refugee Convention – has responded to these challenges and analyses the question of how it should respond. What factors might explain the maintenance of the traditional distinction in refugee law? Is the conflict inherent in the refugee paradigm? Or rather, does it reflect a lack of legal creativity in reconceptualizing the traditional model in light of contemporary developments? Is it necessary to reconsider traditional approaches in order to ensure that refugee law remains meaningful and relevant?

On the one hand, it may be that the definition contained in art. 1A(2) of the Refugee Convention precludes an adequate exploration of these tensions and issues, given that it defines a refugee as:

[Any person who] owing to a well-founded fear of being persecuted for reasons of race, religion, nationality, membership of a particular social group or political opinion, is outside the country of his nationality and is unable or, owing to such fear, is unwilling to avail himself of the protection of that country.

In particular, the Cold War context in which the Convention was drafted,[43] and the resulting adoption of the notion of persecution as a key determinant of the refugee definition, has traditionally been relied upon to justify the exclusion of refugee claims based on the violation of socio-economic rights.

On the other hand, it may be that, notwithstanding the Convention's origins, the definition does not necessarily dictate such a clear dichotomy and that the reluctance of many courts to embrace such claims reflects the failure of advocates to link developments in the wider field of international law relating to economic and social rights to the refugee definition, in the same way that they have been able to do so, with much success, in the area of women's human rights.[44] This may have been exacerbated by the international community's historical focus on violations of civil and political rights at the expense of economic and social rights. In other words, it may be that the protective potential of the Refugee Convention has been unduly constrained by

---

[43] See, for example, James C. Hathaway, 'A Reconsideration of the Underlying Premise of Refugee Law' (1990) 31 *Harvard International Law Journal* 129.

[44] Developments in respect of refugee claims by women are discussed in detail in Chapters 3 and 4, below. Jacqueline Bhabha is one of the only refugee law scholars who has addressed the economic claims issue in refugee law. In her article, 'Boundaries in the Field of Human Rights: Internationalist Gatekeepers?: The Tension Between Asylum Advocacy and Human Rights' (2002) 15 *Harvard Human Rights Journal* 155, she argues that advocates need to take up these claims more vigorously and creatively.

an inadequate understanding of the equal importance and seriousness of violations of economic, social and cultural rights rather than because it is inherently incapable of responding to some of the challenging predicaments. This is not to say that there may not be fundamental limitations in the existing regime that are not capable of being expanded; but the Refugee Convention may be more flexible and open to creative application to economic claims than previously assumed.

In light of these insights, it is a particularly important time to be exploring these issues for two key reasons. First, some of the issues regarding the interpretation of the Refugee Convention raised by these types of claims are areas in which significant advances have been made in refugee law jurisprudence over the past decade. In particular, the notion that the Refugee Convention is a relic of the Cold War has not prevented it from undergoing a sophisticated evolution in jurisprudential terms, as decision-makers have increasingly accepted the integral connections between refugee law and human rights law – a development that has significantly expanded the definition to accommodate types of claims previously thought to fall outside the Refugee Convention regime. Despite the debate in the literature about the need for a new instrument, it has proven to be remarkably responsive.[45] In this regard, the advent of a human rights framework as a barometer of the question of whether harm amounts to persecution has had the most significant impact on refugee jurisprudence. This has provided the basis for the incorporation of many types of harm specific to women, including domestic violence and female genital mutilation, into understandings of 'being persecuted'. This interpretative move has often been justified by the reference to the Universal Declaration of Human Rights ('UDHR') in the Preamble to the Refugee Convention.[46] Given that this Declaration sets out both civil and political rights, and economic and

---

[45] Spijkerboer says that 10 years ago it was very difficult to make a successful claim based on gender, but now the situation has changed dramatically with the advent of gender guidelines in many states, and the acceptance of women as a particular social group in many jurisdictions: *Gender and Refugee Studies*, p. 177. Anker argues that '[r]efugee law has matured and evolved over the past decade. Gender has reflected and been part of – perhaps a key impetus or ingredient of – that maturation': see Deborah Anker, 'Refugee Status and Violence against Women in the "Domestic" Sphere: The Non-State Actor Question' (2001) 15 *Georgetown Immigration Law Journal* 391 at 393.
[46] GA Res. 217A, UN GAOR, 183rd mtg, UN Doc. A/Res/217A (1948).

social rights, and in light of the general position in international law regarding the indivisibility of the two sets of rights, this development holds considerable potential for extending the application of the Refugee Convention to claims based on deprivations of economic and social rights.

The second rationale for undertaking the present study is that these developments in the interpretation of the Refugee Convention coincide with a significant development in international human rights law regarding the equal value and importance of economic, social and cultural rights. In recent years there have been marked advances, both theoretical and practical, in giving content and meaning to economic, social and cultural rights, in order to consolidate the theoretical position of the 'universality, indivisibility, interdependence and interrelatedness of all human rights'.[47] Most significantly, the Committee on Economic and Social Rights (the committee vested with responsibility for monitoring the implementation of the most important source of socio-economic rights obligations – the International Covenant on Economic, Social and Cultural Rights)[48] has undertaken the task of elucidating the content of states' obligations with respect to the key treaty on socio-economic rights.[49] In addition, other important UN initiatives, such as the Commission on Human Rights' appointment of Special Rapporteurs on education,[50]

---

[47] See *Vienna Declaration and Programme of Action*, UN Doc. A/CONF.157/23 (1993). See also UN Commission on Human Rights, *Question of the Realization in All Countries of the Economic, Social and Cultural Rights Contained in the Universal Declaration of Human Rights and in the International Covenant on Economic, Social and Cultural Rights, and Study of Special Problems which the Developing Countries Face in their Efforts to Achieve these Human Rights*, UN Doc. E/CN.4/RES/ 2000/9 (2000a). For an excellent overview of the developments in the field of socio-economic rights, see Magdalena Sepulveda, *The Nature of the Obligations under the International Covenant on Economic, Social and Cultural Rights* (New York: Intersentia, 2003), pp. 45–71.

[48] New York, 16 December 1966, in force, 3 January 1976, 993 UNTS 3; (1967) 6 ILM 360 ('ICESCR').

[49] See the discussion in Chapters 3 and 4. This has most obviously been achieved via the issuance of General Comments on both general obligations and on a range of individual obligations.

[50] The Commission on Human Rights established the mandate of the Special Rapporteur on the right to education: Commission on Human Rights, *Question of the Realization in All Countries of the Economic, Social and Cultural Rights Contained in the Universal Declaration of Human Rights and in the International Covenant on Economic, Social and Cultural Rights, and Study of Special Problems which the Developing Countries Face in their Efforts to Achieve these Human Rights*, UN Doc. E/CN.4/RES/1998/33 (1998). For the most recent report, see Commission on Human Rights, *The Right to Education: Report Submitted by the Special Rapporteur on the Right to Education*, UN Doc. E/CN.4/2005/50 (2004b).

housing,[51] food[52] and health,[53] have highlighted the fundamental importance and binding content of socio-economic rights obligations as a matter of international law. There is an increasing sophistication in understanding the link between poverty and violations of economic, social and cultural obligations, which is occurring at many levels throughout the international legal order.[54] Both international and regional tribunals and adjudicatory panels are displaying an increasing willingness to hold governments responsible for practices that involve a breach of those rights, including projects undertaken in the name of development.[55] In the evolution of this jurisprudence, the connection

---

[51] The Commission on Human Rights established the mandate of the Special Rapporteur on adequate housing as a component of the right to an adequate standard of living: Commission on Human Rights, *Question of the Realization in All Countries of the Economic, Social and Cultural Rights Contained in the Universal Declaration of Human Rights and in the International Covenant on Economic, Social and Cultural Rights, and Study of Special Problems which the Developing Countries Face in their Efforts to Achieve these Human Rights*, UN Doc. E/CN.4/RES/2000/9 (2000). For the latest report, see Commission on Human Rights, *Report of the Special Rapporteur on Adequate Housing as a Component of the Right to an Adequate Standard of Living*, UN Doc. E/CN.4/2005/48 (2005a).

[52] The Commission on Human Rights established the mandate of the Special Rapporteur on the Right to Food: Commission on Human Rights, *The Right to Food*, UN Doc. E/CN.4/RES/2000/10 (2000b). For the latest report, see Commission on Human Rights, *The Right to Food: Note by the Secretary-General*, GA Res. A/60/350, UN GAOR, 60th sess., Agenda Item 73(b), UN Doc. A/60/350 (2005).

[53] The Commission on Human Rights established the mandate of the Special Rapporteur on the right of everyone to the enjoyment of the highest attainable standard of physical and mental health: Commission on Human Rights, *The Right of Everyone to the Enjoyment of the Highest Attainable Standard of Physical and Mental Health*, UN Doc. E/CN.4/RES/2002/31 (2002). For the latest report, see Commission on Human Rights, *Report of the Special Rapporteur on the Right of Everyone to the Enjoyment of the Highest Attainable Standard of Physical and Mental Health*, UN Doc. E/CN.4/2005/51 (2005b).

[54] For example, the Special Rapporteur of the Commission on Human Rights on the right to food has noted that, 'Hunger and famine are not inevitable. They are a violation of human rights': *The Right to Food: Note by the Secretary-General*, GA Res. A/60/350, UN GAOR, 60th sess., Agenda Item 73(b), UN Doc. A/60/350 (2005), para. 5.

[55] One of the most significant decisions is that of the African Commission on Human Rights and Peoples' Rights which found that Nigeria had violated a range of rights related to the right of health, including, inter alia, the right to food of the Ogoni people by facilitating and condoning the actions of an oil consortium which exploited oil reserves in Ogoniland 'with no regard for the health or environment of the local communities, disposing toxic wastes into the environment and local waterways': see African Commission on Human and Peoples' Rights, *Decision Regarding Communication No. 155/96*, ACHPR/COMM/A044/1, 27 May 2002, at para. 44. This is discussed further in Chapter 4. Other examples are provided in the Special Rapporteur's report: see Commission on Human Rights, *The Right of Everyone to the Enjoyment of the Highest Attainable Standard of Physical and Mental Health*, UN Doc. E/CN.4/2003/58 (2003), at paras. 18–19.

and inter-relationship between traditional civil and political rights and economic and social rights is being recognized and reiterated. In addition, analyses of poverty that reveal gender and other biases in its impact are challenging the view that poverty and lack of access to economic and social services are beyond the control of governments and (more importantly) that they affect all sectors of the population equally.[56] In other words, the simple distinction between political persecution, which is traditionally thought to involve positive action by an entity targeted at a particular individual or group, and economic degradation, which has traditionally been thought to be uncontrollable, inevitable, and just a sad fact of life, is being eroded. This is not to say that distinctions do not remain, but they are not as clear as may traditionally have been assumed.

These 'jurisprudential' or interpretive developments have been increasingly supported in important ways by civil society.[57] For example, two leading human rights organizations, Amnesty International and Human Rights Watch, whose work has long been central to refugee adjudication, have recently expanded their respective terms of reference into the field of economic and social rights, acknowledging the 'relative neglect' of this area by the international human rights movement.[58] This is an important factor in light of practical

---

[56] See, for example, Commission on Human Rights, *Report Submitted by the Special Rapporteur on the Right to Education*, UN Doc. E/CN.4/2005/50 (2004a), at paras. 73–84, where the 'worldwide gender gap in current primary school enrolment rates' is discussed. See also Human Rights Watch, *Failing Our Children: Barriers to the Right to Education* (2005a) <http://hrw.org/reports/2005/education0905/education0905.pdf> at 31 May 2006.

[57] Chisanga Puta-Chekwe and Nora Flood note that the interest and participation of NGOs in the issue of economic and social rights has increased significantly in the past decade: 'From Division to Integration: Economic, Social and Cultural Rights as Basic Human Rights', in Isfahan Merali and Valerie Oostervedl (eds.), *Giving Meaning to Economic, Social and Cultural Rights* (Philadelphia: University of Pennsylvania Press, 2001), p. 49.

[58] See Pierre Sané, Amnesty International Secretary General, *Globalisation: AI and Socio-Economic Rights* (2001) Amnesty International <http://web.amnesty.org> at 31 May 2006; Amnesty International, *Change in the Air for AI* (2001) <http://web.amnesty.org/wire/October2001/ICM> at 31 May 2006. In its most recent report, Amnesty has noted that '[s]ince the end of the Cold War, the role of economic, social and cultural factors as contributory causes of conflict and flight has become more and more evident': Amnesty International, *Amnesty International Report 2004 – Building an International Human Rights Agenda: Upholding the Rights of Refugees and Migrants* (2004) <http://web.amnesty.org/report2004/hragenda-8-eng> at 31 May 2006. See also Human Rights Watch, *Economic, Social and Cultural Rights* <http://hrw.org/esc/> at 31 May 2006.

concerns regarding the difficulty for decision-makers in refugee-receiving states to make factual assessments regarding economic and social rights, as it ensures that more sophisticated studies and information will be available to assist decision-makers to adjudicate these new types of claims in the future.[59]

In light of these developments, it may well be that the Refugee Convention is capable of responding to the new types of claims that are emerging in a more sensitive manner than the orthodox separation between the economic and political may suggest. This book does not, therefore, engage in an analysis of whether the Refugee Convention definition should be amended or reformulated to accommodate 'economic' refugees, or a broader category of 'forced migrants',[60] but explores the extent to which the definition in its existing form is capable of responding to the phenomenon of migration based on economic and social rights deprivations by addressing the salient conceptual challenges inherent in this question. The underlying hypothesis is that contemporary developments in the interpretation of the Refugee Convention by state parties, in conjunction with other important developments in international human rights law and theory, enable the Refugee Convention to respond in a more sophisticated manner to

---

Human Rights Watch 'considers that economic, social, and cultural rights are an integral part of the body of international human rights law, with the same character and standing as civil and political rights. We conduct research and advocacy on economic, social, and cultural rights using the same methodology that we use with respect to civil and political rights and subject to the same criteria, namely, the ability to identify a rights violation, a violator, and a remedy to address the violation'.
See also Kenneth Roth, 'Defending Economic, Social and Cultural Rights: Practical Issues Faced by an International Human Rights Organization' (2004) 24 *Human Rights Quarterly* 63.

[59] For some practical examples of the expansion of civil society into this arena, see Amnesty International, *Lebanon: Economic and Social Rights of Palestinian Refugees* (2003c) <http://web.amnesty.org/library/index/ENGMDE180172003> at 31 May 2006; Amnesty International, *Israel and the Occupied Territories Surviving under Siege: The Impact of Movement Restrictions on the Right to Work* (2003a) <http://web.amnesty.org/library/index/ENGMDE150012003> at 31 May 2006. See also Human Rights Watch, *Not Eligible: The Politicization of Food in Zimbabwe* (2003c) <http://www.hrw.org/reports/2003/zimbabwe1003/zimbabwe1003.pdf> at 31 May 2006; and Human Rights Watch, *Double Standards: Women's Property Rights Violations in Kenya* (2003b) <http://hrw.org/reports/2003/kenya0303/> at 31 May 2006.

[60] See, for example, Arthur C. Helton and Eliana Jones, 'What is Forced Migration?' (1999) 13 *Georgetown Immigration Law Journal* 521, proposing the formulation of a new category of 'forced migrant': at 526.

the claims of persons fleeing economic and social deprivation, which goes well beyond the simple division between 'economic migrants' and political refugees. This is not merely a theoretical aspiration, as there is an emerging jurisprudence in both senior common law courts and administrative tribunals regarding these issues. This jurisprudence is nascent but nonetheless significant, as it reveals the capacity of decision-makers to explore the logical limits of the definition in order to ensure that the Refugee Convention 'is seen as a living thing, adopted by civilized countries for a humanitarian end which is constant in motive but mutable in form'.[61]

Organization and methodology of analysis

Against this background, this book undertakes a detailed analysis of the key elements in the refugee definition most relevant to economic claims, drawing upon corresponding developments in international human rights law, in order to assess the logical parameters of the Refugee Convention definition in respect of claims involving deprivations of social and economic rights.

The primary focus of the book is on the Refugee Convention. Although it is now clear that the Refugee Convention is not the only international treaty which imposes *non-refoulement* obligations on states,[62] and that in some cases these prohibitions on removal have extended to a situation in which a person fears subjection to cruel and degrading treatment arising from violations of socio-economic rights,[63] the Refugee Convention

---

[61] R v. *Immigration Appeal Tribunal and Secretary of State for the Home Department, ex parte Syeda Khatoon Shah* [1997] Imm AR 148 at 152. See also *R on the Application of Altin Vallaj v. A Special Adjudicator* [2001] INLR 455, in which the court stated: 'it is common ground that the Convention should be construed as a living instrument, and that it should be interpreted in the light of current international circumstances': at para. 25.

[62] See International Covenant on Civil and Political Rights, New York, 16 December 1966, in force 23 March 1976, 993 UNTS 171; (1967) 6 ILM 368, art. 7 ('ICCPR'); Convention against Torture and Other Cruel, Inhuman or Degrading Treatment or Punishment, New York, 10 December 1984, in force 26 June 1987, 1465 UNTS 85, art. 3 ('CAT'); European Convention for the Protection of Human Rights and Fundamental Freedoms, Rome, 4 November 1950, in force 3 September 1953, 213 UNTS 221 ('*European Convention*').

[63] See *D v. United Kingdom*, European Court of Human Rights, 42 BMLR 149, 2 May 1997. See Katharina Röhl, *Fleeing Violence and Poverty: Non-Refoulement Obligations under the European Convention on Human Rights* (2005) <http://www.unhcr.org/cgi-bin/texis/vtx/research/opendoc.pdf?tbl=RESEARCH&id=41f8ef4f2> at 31 May 2006.

continues, in the words of the UNHCR, to 'serve as the cornerstone of the international refugee protection regime'.[64] The Refugee Convention has 147 state parties and remains the key universally applicable instrument in international law for the protection of refugees.[65] Moreover, the Refugee Convention deals not only with the definition of a refugee, but sets out a range of rights which attach to refugee status.[66] For this reason, while 'complementary' forms of protection will be referred to throughout the book, the primary analysis is focused on the Refugee Convention regime.

In considering the correct interpretation of the Refugee Convention, the jurisprudence analysed is primarily derived from all levels of decision-making (including executive and judicial) in five common law jurisdictions. Refugee law jurisprudence has traditionally been comparative, given that it is interpreted by domestic courts, cognizant of its status as an international treaty, and thus, in the main, concerned to ensure some degree of consistency in interpretation. In recent years, refugee decision-makers have displayed an increased willingness to consider jurisprudence from other jurisdictions. However, it should be noted that these 'comparative judicial conversations'[67] have primarily been carried out in the refugee context amongst the leading common law jurisdictions, namely Australia, Canada, New Zealand,

---

[64] Executive Committee of the High Commissioner's Programme ('ExCom'), *Conclusion on the Provision on International Protection Including Through Complementary Forms of Protection* (2005) <http://www.unhcr.org/cgi-bin/texis/vtx/excom/opendoc.htm?tbl=EXCOM&id=43576e292> at 31 May 2006.

[65] As of 1 December 2006, 147 states are party to either the 1951 Convention, 1967 Protocol or both: see <http://www.unhcr.org/cgi-bin/texis/vtx/protect/opendoc.pdf?tbl=PROTECTION&id=3b73b0d63> at 31 December 2006. There have been important developments in international law post-dating the Refugee Convention; however, these remain relevant at a regional level only: see for example, the *OAU Convention Governing the Specific Aspects of the Refugee Problem in Africa* 1969, AHSG, CAB/LEG/24.3 (discussed in Rachel Murray, *Human Rights in Africa* (Cambridge: CUP, 2004), Chapter 7) and the Cartagena Declaration, adopted by 10 Latin American states in 1984 (discussed in James C. Hathaway, *The Law of Refugee Status* (Toronto: Butterworths, 1991), pp. 19–21).

[66] See generally, James C. Hathaway, *The Rights of Refugees under International Law* (Cambridge: Cambridge University Press, 2005). By contrast, regional instruments, such as the OAU Convention, do not deal with the rights of refugees: see Murray, *Human Rights in Africa*, p. 189. Similarly, where a *non-refoulement* obligation is derived from general international human rights treaties, it is not clear what rights pertain to persons recognized under these regimes.

[67] See Laurence R. Helfer and Anne-Marie Slaughter, 'Toward a Theory of Effective Supranational Adjudication' (1997) 107 *Yale Law Journal* 273 at 372.

the United Kingdom and the United States.[68] While civil law courts are showing an increased willingness to join in the conversation, it remains the case that the most comprehensive analysis is undertaken in these leading jurisdictions. To a large extent, this reflects the inherent openness and appropriateness of the common law method of decision-making to such analysis. In other words, the level of detail and analysis required by common law reasoning makes it a particularly helpful vehicle for exploring the logical parameters of the refugee definition. For this reason, primary analysis of judicial reasoning will be confined to these jurisdictions. Reference to relevant findings or analysis by civil law jurisdictions will occasionally be made throughout the book, although this will primarily rely on secondary sources.

This book is organized as follows. Before turning to an analysis of each of the most pertinent elements, it is necessary first to consider the appropriate approach to an interpretation of the Refugee Convention. Chapter 2, therefore, reviews the growing acceptance of an approach that links the various elements of the Refugee Convention definition with developments in human rights law, and grapples with the issues of treaty interpretation that this development entails. In particular, it explores whether this approach is justified and what principles should guide courts in making reference to standards set out in other human rights treaties. The chapter considers this issue in the context of wider developments in international treaty interpretation.

Chapter 3 then analyses the key definitional requirement in refugee law, namely when harm is considered to amount to 'being persecuted'. The chapter provides an overview of the current treatment of socio-economic claims in refugee law, before considering some of the key problems in the jurisprudence to date. The analysis reveals that while

---

[68] Although with respect to one notable jurisdiction, namely the US, the conversations tend to be one-way – that is, the US courts traditionally have not tended to take notice of the development of jurisprudence in other jurisdictions. However, this does appear to be changing. For example in *Castellano-Chacon* v. *Immigration and Naturalization Service*, 341 F 3d 533 (6th Cir. 2003), the Sixth Circuit considered which conceptual approach it should adopt in interpreting the phrase 'membership of a particular social group' in the Refugee Convention definition. In the course of considering this question, it reviewed not only the position taken in the other US Circuit Courts of Appeal, but also in other jurisdictions, for example Canada, and also developments at the international level, for example, those emerging from the UNHCR Global Consultations process: at 540–1.

decision-makers have accepted a range of claims involving socio-economic deprivation as falling within the auspices of the Refugee Convention, some important issues remain unresolved, such as the place of socio-economic rights in a hierarchical model and the normative content of these rights. Chapter 4 continues this analysis by exploring the theoretical question of the place of economic and social rights in a human rights framework and, in particular, the extent to which refugee decision-makers should take a hierarchical approach to these questions. The chapter then addresses the question of when a breach of economic or social rights amounts to persecution, by applying developments in human rights theory and practice to refugee cases which suggest the logic of an approach based on core violations of fundamental human rights.

Chapter 5 considers the second key definitional element: the question of when a well-founded fear of being persecuted can be considered to be 'for reasons of' a Refugee Convention ground, that is, the meaning of the nexus clause. This issue often presents the biggest conceptual hurdle to economic claims because it is sometimes said to require discrimination (or singling out), an individual approach that is often not suitable to encompass economic claims. The chapter assesses whether, in light of contemporary developments in interpretation, the nexus issue is truly as large a barrier as might have been traditionally thought. In addition to developments in principle, the chapter considers the extent to which courts have been willing (and should be willing) to look to the wider context of an individual claim in order to find a connection to a Refugee Convention ground. Chapter 6 then completes the Refugee Convention inquiry by analysing the various Refugee Convention grounds and their relevance to economic and social claims. While all five grounds are considered potentially relevant, the primary focus is on 'membership of a particular social group' as the ground most likely to provide the basis for the application of the Refugee Convention to such claims. The chapter applies contemporary interpretative developments to a variety of relevant categories, including women and children, people in poverty, and people who have physical or intellectual disabilities.

Having explored the boundaries of the Refugee Convention, Chapter 7 reflects on the conclusions reached in the book. These conclusions give rise to unavoidable ethical, practical and policy questions which must be acknowledged and addressed. In the process of reflecting on the implications, the final chapter briefly considers other *non-refoulement* remedies available in international and regional law, particularly those relevant to violations of economic and social rights.

As decision-makers have sometimes observed, there is a certain element of artificiality in analysing the various elements of the Refugee Convention definition separately.[69] However, there are a number of important reasons why it is nonetheless important to do so. First, it is essential for the purposes of a study such as the present one to draw out the key issues in each element of the definition in order to assess the cogency of traditional objections to economic claims and to suggest more principled methods of assessing such claims. Second, and more important, as a number of senior courts have recognized, to adopt a 'holistic' approach,[70] which seeks to assess a refugee claim 'in the round', rather than by assessing each element separately, raises the risk of masking error. The point was well expressed by Lord Justice Sedley in *Svazas* v. *Secretary of State for the Home Department*:

experience shows that adjudicators and tribunals give better reasoned and more lucid decisions if they go step by step rather than follow a recital of the facts and arguments with a single laconic assessment which others then have to unpick, deducing or guessing at its elements rather than reading them off the page.[71]

This is supported by the analysis in this book. It will become evident that a 'holistic' approach is susceptible to the dismissal of claims on broad findings that the applicant is an 'economic migrant' or 'voluntary migrant', whereas a requirement to analyse a claim

---

[69] See, for example, *Demirkaya* v. *Secretary of State for the Home Department* [1999] Imm AR 498 (Stuart-Smith LJ) ('*Demirkaya*').
[70] UNHCR mentions the holistic approach: see 'The International Protection of Refugees: Interpreting Article 1 of the 1951 Convention Relating to the Status of Refugees' (2001) 20(3) *Refugee Survey Quarterly* 77 at 82.
[71] [2002] EWCA Civ. 74; [2002] 1 WLR 1891 at para. 30. See also *Sepet and Anor* v. *Secretary of State for the Home Department* [2003] 3 All ER 304 at para. 7 (Lord Bingham of Cornhill): 'analysis requires consideration of the constituent elements of the definition'. See also the comments by the New Zealand RSAA in *Refugee Appeal No. 74665/03*, RSAA, 7 July 2004, which, although accepting that one must take a 'holistic' interpretive approach, cautioned that this 'does not deny the necessity to analyse each constituent element or to examine the relationship of the elements to each other. It is essential to ensure that one element is not inadvertently given a function or meaning which more properly belongs to another': at para. 48.

systematically within the terms of the definition may well dictate the conclusion that the applicant is, in fact, a Convention refugee. The book thus proceeds on the basis that a principled assessment of the issues raised by socio-economic claims must be undertaken in light of the key elements of the Refugee definition.

2 A human rights framework for interpreting the Refugee Convention

PART ONE: THE DEVELOPING HUMAN RIGHTS FRAMEWORK

One of the most significant developments in refugee law jurisprudence in recent years has been the well-documented move towards an understanding of 'being persecuted', as well as other elements of the definition, that is informed and understood in the context of international human rights standards. This approach to interpretation was advocated as early as 1953, when Vernant suggested that 'persecution' should be equated 'with severe sanctions and measures of an arbitrary nature, incompatible with the principles set forth in the Universal Declaration of Human Rights'.[1] However its widespread acceptance is undoubtedly a result of the ground-breaking analysis produced by Hathaway in 1991, in which he proposed that persecution is best understood as the 'sustained or systemic violation of basic human rights demonstrative of a failure of state protection'.[2] Hathaway proposed that the treaties comprising the 'International Bill of Rights' ('IBR') – the UDHR, the ICCPR and the ICESCR – could provide a framework for measuring whether the nature and seriousness of harm in a specific case amounts to 'being persecuted'.[3] This development has been extremely significant in a number of ways and has been central to the ability of the Refugee Convention to be interpreted in a progressive manner in order to encompass claims involving, for example, gender-based persecution.[4]

---

[1] Grahl-Madsen, *The Status of Refugees in International Law*, p. 193.
[2] James C. Hathaway, *The Law of Refugee Status* (Toronto: Butterworths, 1991), pp. 104–5.
[3] Hathaway, *The Law of Refugee Status*, pp. 104–5. Note that the specific content of his framework is analysed in detail in Chapter 3.
[4] It is arguable that it has been the advent of a sensitivity to gender issues that has pioneered the human rights approach. See Anker, 'Boundaries in the Field of Human Rights', at 138 and Bhabha, 'Boundaries in the Field of Human Rights', at 157.

It is particularly important in light of the central thesis of this book, in that the inclusion of socio-economic rights in both the UDHR and ICESCR provides persuasive authority for the view that violations of socio-economic rights may amount to persecution.

Despite the fact that human rights standards were initially invoked in respect of the 'being persecuted' analysis, their relevance has not been confined to this inquiry, as they are often said to inform many other aspects of the refugee definition, including the parameters and meaning of the Refugee Convention grounds, particularly membership of a particular social group;[5] the question whether voluntary acts on the part of the applicant may nonetheless give rise to a well-founded fear of being persecuted;[6] and the availability and sufficiency of state protection, including the availability of an internal protection alternative for the applicant in his or her home country.[7]

While the human rights approach to interpreting the Refugee Convention has increasingly been adopted in domestic jurisdictions, it is important to note that it is not universally accepted. Further, when attempting to provide an overview of the degree of acceptance by different state parties, it is important to be cognisant of the inconsistencies that can exist within, but particularly between, jurisdictions. For example, inconsistencies can arise within a jurisdiction because the most superior court has not provided a coherent framework of analysis, thus leaving the specialist tribunals and lower courts to adopt a patchwork jurisprudence.[8] Conversely, in some jurisdictions it appears

---

[5] See *Minister for Immigration and Multicultural Affairs v. Sarrazola (No. 2)* (2001) 107 FCR 184 ('*Sarrazola*'), in which the Federal Court of Australia considered art. 16(3) of the UDHR in relation to a family-based membership of a particular social group claim: at 193–4.
For further analysis of the general approach of courts to this issue, see James C. Hathaway and Michelle Foster, 'Membership of a Particular Social Group' (2003) 15(3) *International Journal of Refugee Law* 477.

[6] See Haines, Hathaway and Foster, 'Claims to Refugee Status Based on Voluntary but Protected Actions'.

[7] See Hugo Storey, 'The Internal Flight Alternative Test: The Jurisprudence Re-Examined' (1998) 10(3) *International Journal of Refugee Law* 499 at 528–31; James C. Hathaway and Michelle Foster, 'Internal Protection/Relocation/Flight Alternative as an Aspect of Refugee Status Determination', in Erika Feller, Volker Türk and Frances Nicholson (eds.), *Refugee Protection in International Law: UNHCR's Global Consultations on International Protection* (Cambridge: Cambridge University Press, 2003a), pp. 353–413.

[8] Australia is a good example of this phenomenon. The human rights method of interpretation is enjoying increasing acceptance in Australia, being regularly invoked at the Refugee Review Tribunal level (see, for example, *Reference V94/02820*, RRT, 6 October 1995, at 6; *Reference V93/01176*, RRT, 26 August 1994, at 7–8; *Reference V95/03786*, RRT, 3 May 1996, at 5–9; *Reference V98/08951*, RRT, 11 March 1999) and at the Federal Court level (see, for example, *Premalal v. Minister for Immigration, Local Government and Ethnic Affairs*

that, although the highest courts have advocated a human rights-based approach, such as in Canada[9] and the United Kingdom,[10] lower-level

---

(1993) 41 FCR 117 at 138 ('*Premalal*'); *NACM of 2002* v. *Minister for Immigration and Multicultural and Indigenous Affairs* (2003) 134 FCR 550; *Liu* v. *Minister for Immigration and Multicultural Affairs* (2001) 113 FCR 541 and *Wang* v. *Minister for Immigration and Multicultural Affairs* (2000) 105 FCR 548 ('*Wang*')). It is also clearly advocated in the 'Guidelines on Gender issues for Decision-Makers' produced by the Department of Immigration and Multicultural Affairs ('DIMA'): see DIMA, *Guidelines on Gender Issues for Decision-Makers* (1996) <http://www.immi.gov.au> at 31 May 2006 ('Australian Gender Guidelines'). See particularly at para. 4.4–para. 4.5. However, the High Court of Australia has not embraced the human rights framework in explicit terms, although its analysis often suggests implicit acceptance: see for example *Minister for Immigration and Multicultural Affairs* v. *Khawar* (2002) 210 CLR 1, at 26; *Appellant S395/2002* v. *Minister for Immigration and Multicultural Affairs* (2003) 216 CLR 473 ('*S395/2002*'), at 491 (McHugh and Kirby JJ) and *Minister for Immigration and Multicultural Affairs* v. *Respondents S152/2003* (2004) 205 ALR 487 ('*S152/2003*'), at 492–3 (Gleeson CJ, Hayne and Heydon JJ).

[9] The most important case is *Canada (Attorney-General)* v. *Ward* [1993] 2 SCR 689 at 712–13 ('*Ward*'). See also *Chan* v. *Canada (Minister for Employment and Immigration)* (1995) 128 DLR (4th) 213. The Canadian Immigration and Review Board's Refugee Protection Division ('RPD') takes this approach: '[p]ersecution occurs when an individual's fundamental human rights are violated': *OQU (Re)*, No. T98-09064 [1999] CRDD No. 157, 19 July 1999, at para. 19. [Prior to 2003, the Refugee Determination Division of the Canadian Immigration and Review Board was called the Convention Refugee Determination Division ('CRDD'); this has now been renamed the RPD. For the purposes of consistency, the tribunal will be called RPD throughout this book, although all citations prior to 2003 will continue to refer to the CRDD.] The approach pertains to all aspects of the refugee definition, including the question of 'membership of a particular social group': see, for example, Krista Daley and Ninette Kelley, 'Particular Social Group: A Human Rights Based Approach in Canadian Jurisprudence' (2000) 12(2) *International Journal of Refugee Law* 148.

[10] The human rights approach was first clearly explored and adopted by the UK Immigration Appeal Tribunal ('IAT') in *Gashi and Nikshiqi* v. *Secretary of State for the Home Department* [1997] INLR 96 ('*Gashi and Nikshiqi*'), wherein it stated that: 'the principles of an internationally shared surrogate protection, rooted in fundamental human rights constitutes the basic approach to interpreting the word 'persecution': at 111. [In the UK, the Asylum and Immigration Tribunal ('AIT') is the successor to the IAT. The AIT was established under the Asylum and Immigration (Treatment of Claimants etc) Act 2004, and commenced operation on 4 April 2005.] This has now been adopted by the Court of Appeal (see *R* v. *Immigration Appeal Tribunal, ex parte Sandralingham and Another*; *R* v. *Immigration Appeal Tribunal and Another, ex parte Rajendrakumar* [1996] Imm AR 97 at 107 and *Amare* v. *Secretary of State for the Home Department* [2005] All ER (D) 300); and the House of Lords (see *R* v. *Immigration Appeal Tribunal, ex parte Shah* [1999] 2 AC 629; 644B-H, 648B, 651A, 652C, 653F, 658H (Lords Steyn, Hoffmann and Hutton) ('*Shah*'); *Horvath* v. *Secretary of State for the Home Department* [2000] 3 All ER 577; [2000] 3 WLR 379, 383B-H, 389A, 404F (Lords Hope, Browne-Wilkinson, Clyde and Hobhouse) ('*Horvath*') and *R (on the application of Ullah)* v. *Special Adjudicator; Do* v. *Secretary of State for the Home Department* [2004] 3 All ER 785 at para. 32). The approach is also clearly advocated in the UK Immigration Appellate Authority, *Asylum Gender Guidelines* (2000) <http://www.asylumsupport.info/publications/iaa/gender.pdf> at 31 May 2006 ('UK Gender Guidelines').

tribunals occasionally revert to earlier approaches.[11] In general, common law jurisdictions are more likely to refer explicitly to international human rights instruments in following a human rights approach,[12] whereas the human rights approach in civil law countries tends to be implicit, with explicit reference to other international instruments being rare.[13] Notwithstanding these

---

[11] This sometimes includes the dictionary approach. Curiously, in Canada, these lower-level decisions often rely both on a dictionary approach and the human rights method advocated by the Supreme Court: see, for example, the RPD decision in *J (RC) (Re)*, No. U93-04549 [1994] CRDD No. 265, 14 January 1994. The RPD's decision was apparently unaware of the potential inconsistency of this technique. In the UK, post-*Horvath*, it is arguably incorrect to use the dictionary approach, which was formerly advocated in *R v. Immigration Appeal Tribunal ex parte Daniel Boahin Jonah* [1985] Imm AR 7. Indeed, this was recognized by the IAT in *Doymus v. Secretary of State for the Home Department* (Unreported, IAT, Appeal No. HX/80112/99, 19 July 2000), at para. 19 ('*Doymus*'), where it noted that although 'in current UK case law it would appear that the dictionary definition approach and the more purposive approach are viewed as interchangeable ... it is the purposive approach that would prevail, based on House of Lords authority'.

[12] Reference to human rights treaties is – generally – much more prevalent in the reasoning of common law courts and tribunals. The key common law exception is the USA: reference to human rights principles in refugee adjudication in the USA has mixed support. It appears to be uncontroversial at the level of INS guidelines. (It should be noted that the INS is now the US Citizenship and Immigration Services, part of the Department of Homeland Security: see http://www.dhs.gov/dhspublic/.) The INS *Basic Law Manual* instructs Asylum Officers that '[o]ne must determine whether the conduct alleged to be persecution violates a basic human right, protected under international law': p. 24, quoted in Deborah E. Anker, *Law of Asylum in the United States* (Boston, MA: Refugee Law Center, 1999), p. 174. See also US Department of Justice, Immigration and Naturalization Service, *Guidelines for Children's Asylum Claims* (1998) pp. 2–4 <http://uscis.gov/graphics/lawsregs/handbook/10a_ChldrnGdlns.pdf> at 31 May 2006 ('US Children's Guidelines'). The human rights approach also has some support at the Board of Immigration Appeals ('BIA'): see *Re Chang*, No. A-2720715, BIA, 1989, and at the federal court level, see *Alla Konstantinova Pitcherskaia v. Immigration and Naturalization Service*, 118 F 3d 641 (9th Cir. 1997), at 648 ('*Pitcherskaia*'); *Ouda v. Immigration and Naturalization Service*, 324 F 3d 445 (6th Cir. 2003); *Abay and Amare v. Ashcroft* 368 F 3d 634 (6th Cir. 2004), at 639, and *Mohammed v. Gonzales* 400 F 3d 785 (9th Cir. 2005), at 795. However, it is rarely explicitly adopted as the basis of reasoning in court and tribunal decisions.

[13] The analysis of Dirk Vanheule supports the thesis that civil law countries tend not to refer to international instruments: Dirk Vanheule, 'A Comparison of the Judicial Interpretations of the Notion of Refugee', in Jean-Yves Carlier and Dirk Vanheule (eds.), *Europe and Refugees: A Challenge?* (The Hague: Kluwer Law International, 1997), pp. 98–103. Rather, an International Association of Refugee Law Judges ('IARLJ') study suggests that in many civil law (European) countries the human rights approach is primarily employed in the determination of a secondary or complementary status, such as 'B' status,

inconsistencies, the human rights approach is generally agreed to be 'the dominant view'.[14]

although this is because the secondary determinations often rely explicitly on obligations under human rights treaties, such as art. 3 of the European Convention: see James C. Simeon, *Background Paper: The Human Rights Paradigm and the 1951 Refugee Convention* (London: Human Rights Nexus Working Party, 1998), p. 2 (on file with author). There is evidence that in cases involving difficult questions related to the legitimacy of government action, civil law courts and tribunals have on occasion sought guidance from international human rights law. Dirk Vanheule provides a number of examples: see Vanheule, 'A Comparison of the Judicial Interpretations of the Notion of Refugee', p. 99, citing *ARR v. S*, 30 September 1982, RV1982 at 8 and *ARR v. S*, 19 July 1990, RV, 1990 at 3. The reasoning of courts and tribunals is often implicitly based upon notions of human rights principles and standards, particularly in cases involving religious freedom, notwithstanding that specific reference is rarely made to international instruments: Inter-Conference Working Parties: Human Rights Nexus Working Party, *Human Rights Conference Report* (IARLJ Annual Conference, Ottawa, 12–17 October 1998) (on file with author). More explicit reference to human rights standards may occur in future, in light of the fact that the technique of referring to human rights standards is supported by the recently enacted Council of the European Union's *Directive on Minimum Standards for the Qualification and Status of Third Country Nationals and Stateless Persons as Refugees or as Persons who Otherwise Need International Protection and the Content of the Protection Granted*, in which 'persecution' is defined to require 'severe violation of basic human rights': Council of the European Union, *Directive on Minimum Standards for the Qualification and Status of Third Country Nationals and Stateless Persons as Refugees or as Persons who Otherwise Need International Protection and the Content of the Protection Granted*, 29 April 2004, 2004/83/EC, art. 9(1)(a) ('EU Directive on a Common Asylum Policy').

[14] UNHCR Division of International Protection, 'Gender-Related Persecution: An Analysis of Recent Trends' (1997) 9 *International Journal of Refugee Law* 79 at 82. According to Symes, '[t]he dominant trend of the authorities is to accept the human rights approach': Mark Symes, *Caselaw on the Refugee Convention: The United Kingdom's Interpretation in the Light of the International Authorities* (London: Refugee Legal Centre, 2000), p. 70. This is borne out by an analysis conducted by a team of researchers at the Faculties of Law of the Universities of Namur and Antwerp, which was a comparative research project on the judicial interpretation of the refugee definition in 13 European states, Canada and the USA – a study that involved 5000 cases. In relation to the meaning of 'persecution', the study found that 'the only essential criterion applied, either expressly or implicitly, by the courts appears to be the disproportional or discriminatory violation of basic human rights for one of the reasons mentioned in the Geneva Convention': Vanheule, 'A Comparison of the Judicial Interpretations of the Notion of Refugee', p. 99. The New Zealand authorities review the general trend, especially in common law jurisprudence: see *Refugee Appeal No. 71427/99*, RSAA, 16 August 2000, para. 51; *Refugee Appeal No. 72668/01*, RSAA, 5 April 2002, paras. 155–9; *Refugee Appeal Nos. 72558/01 and 72559/01*, RSAA, 19 November 2002, para. 87; *Refugee Appeal No. 74665/03*, RSAA, 7 July 2004. The human rights approach of the RSAA was approved by the NZ High Court in *DG v. Refugee Status Appeals Authority* (Unreported, High Court of New Zealand, Chisholm J, 5 June 2001), at paras. 19 and 22 ('*DG*') and in *K v. Refugee Status Appeals Authority* [2005] NZAR 441 (2004).

The UNHCR has displayed strong support for this approach, in its authoritative Handbook,[15] Executive Committee ('ExCom') Conclusions,[16] Guidelines on International Protection[17] and interventions in domestic proceedings.[18] It considers an interpretation of the Refugee Convention definition that is 'informed by related bodies of law, including appropriate human rights principles', not only to be 'best practice',[19] but has said that this approach should apply 'as a matter of law'.[20] Indeed, the Director of International Protection has pressed a conference of international refugee law judges on the importance of the notion that 'human rights law should and must provide the broad and objective indicators against which the term "persecution" can

---

[15] The UNHCR Handbook adverts to the link between persecution and breach of human rights: for example, in discussing one particular aspect of interpreting the Refugee Convention, namely persecution versus punishment, the UNHCR Handbook suggests that 'recourse may usefully be had to the principles set out in the various international instruments relating to human rights, in particular the International Covenants on Human Rights, which contain binding commitments for the States parties and are instruments to which many States parties to the 1951 Convention have acceded': UNHCR Handbook (1992) <http://www.unhcr.org/cgi-bin/texis/vtx/home/opendoc.pdf?tbl=PUBL&id=3d58e13b4> at 31 May 2006 (at para. 60; see also para. 51).

[16] See UNHCR Executive Committee ('ExCom'), General Conclusion on International Protection (1993b) <http://www.unhcr.org/cgi-bin/texis/vtx/excom/opendoc.htm?tbl=EXCOM&id=3ae68c6814> at 31 May 2006; UNHCR Executive Committee, Conclusion on International Protection (1998) <http://www.unhcr.org/cgi-bin/texis/vtx/excom/opendoc.htm?tbl=EXCOM&id=3ae68c6e30> at 31 May 2006.

[17] See, for example, Guidelines on International Protection: Religion-Based Refugee Claims under Article 1A(2) of the 1951 Convention and/or the 1967 Protocol relating to the Status of Refugees, HCR/GIP/04/06, 28 April 2004, particularly at paras. 2 and 11.

[18] See, for example, the UNHCR submission to the UK IAT in Gashi and Nikshiqi [1997] INLR 96 at 104–5.

[19] UNHCR, 'Note on International Protection' (2001) 20(3) Refugee Survey Quarterly 34 at 58, aims to set out selected developments termed 'best practices' whose replication is promoted. See also UNHCR, Agenda for Protection, third edition (2003) <http://www.unhcr.org/cgi-bin/texis/vtx/protect/opendoc.pdf?tbl=PROTECTION&id=3e637b194> at 31 May 2006 ('Agenda for Protection'); UNHCR, 'The International Protection of Refugees: Interpreting Article 1 of the 1951 Convention Relating to the Status of Refugees' (2001) 20(3) Refugee Survey Quarterly 77 at 82.

[20] In Horvath, the UNHCR made the following submissions to the UK IAT: 'without reference to these fundamental rights standards, the assessment of persecution may take place in somewhat of a legal vacuum. In UNHCR's opinion this linkage exists as a matter of law and not only for the subjective convenience of the decision-maker in any particular case' (Unreported, IAT, Case No. CC/59978/97 (17338), 4 December 1998), at para. 37.

be interpreted'.[21] The human rights-based approach is also accepted by most commentators, as a perusal of recent literature in the field readily reveals,[22] and the scholarly trend appears to be in favour of an expansion of the refugee definition in light of human rights principles, as well as evolving standards of humanitarian law.[23]

However, a number of issues concerning the operation of the human rights framework remain to be resolved. For example, how do we decide which human rights treaties or other sources of international law are applicable? Does the answer depend on whether the home state or asylum state is a party to the relevant treaty? How do refugee decision-makers go about interpreting international human rights standards? Are they bound by the interpretation undertaken by international treaty bodies, or may they engage in their own interpretation? What is the relevance of decisions of regional human rights bodies? What are the benefits of such an approach?

These are not merely hypothetical or academic inquiries. Rather, it is crucial that such questions be considered because a failure to do so

---

[21] Erika Feller, 'Address to the Conference of the International Association of Refugee Law Judges' (2000–2001) 15 *Georgetown Immigration Law Journal* 381 at 383.

[22] See Goodwin-Gill, *The Refugee in International Law*, p. 67; C.J. Harvey, 'Review Essay: Gender, Refugee Law and the Politics of Interpretation' (2001) 12(4) *International Journal of Refugee Law* 680 at 686; Bhabha, 'Boundaries in the Field of Human Rights', p. 165; Helene Lambert, 'The Conceptualisation of "Persecution" by the House of Lords: *Horvath v. Secretary of State for the Home Department*' (2001) 13 *International Journal of Refugee Law* 19; Karen Musalo and Stephen Knight, 'Steps Forward and Steps Back: Uneven Progress in the Law of Social Group and Gender-Based Claims in the United States' (2001) 13 *International Journal of Refugee Law* 51 at 61. It also enjoys support from non-governmental refugee organizations such as the European Council on Refugees and Exile and Amnesty International: see European Council on Refugees and Exile, *Position on the Interpretation of Article 1 of the Refugee Convention* (2000) para. 44 <http://www.ecre.org/positions/csrinter.shtml> at 31 May 2006. In addition, drawing upon all of the above developments, the human rights approach has been endorsed in a paper produced under the auspices of the IARLJ Conference: Inter-Conference Working Parties: Human Rights Nexus Working Party, *Human Rights Conference Report*, p. 15. Accordingly, the IARLJ passed a resolution at its 1998 conference encouraging refugee law judges and decision-makers 'to utilize international human rights instruments to interpret the term persecution': Simeon, *The Human Rights Paradigm and the 1951 Refugee Convention*.

[23] See, for example, Hugo Storey and Rebecca Wallace, 'War and Peace in Refugee Law Jurisprudence' (2001) 95 *American Journal of International Law* 349; Mark R. von Sternberg, *The Grounds of Refugee Protection in the Context of International Human Rights and Humanitarian Law: Canadian and United States Case Law Compared* (The Hague: M Nijhoff Publishers, 2002), pp. 298–311.

gives rise to the possibility that decision-makers will reject this important development on the basis that it is unorthodox, unprincipled or even illegitimate.[24] Indeed, failure to provide a coherent and persuasive rationale could explain the reluctance of some courts to embrace this development and the tendency of those that accept the conceptual relevance of human rights standards to question the logical extent of its application because of the difficult (and as yet unanswered) questions that such an approach produces. Since terms such as 'persecution' and 'membership of a particular social group' do not appear in human rights instruments,[25] some may question whether the reference is as self-evident as is often assumed.

The importance of considering the issues in a principled fashion is highlighted by the fact that, in the absence of a coherent rationale, the selection of some treaties over others, or reference to treaties but not to other sources of international law, may seem arbitrary and selective. It is vital that this practice be undertaken in light of an appreciation of the different sources of international law, so that informed decisions can be made about which standards are appropriate to be referenced.

The continuing uncertainty regarding aspects of this interpretative approach, including the fundamental issue of its legitimacy,

---

[24] For example, in *Wang*, Wilcox J of the Federal Court of Australia expressed a reservation in relation to the question of the 'relevance of other international instruments to the interpretation of the Convention', noting that it 'is an issue of general importance' which 'may be critical to the determination of other cases': (2000) 105 FCR 548 at para. 4 [appeal to High Court allowed, but not in relation to this point: *Minister for Immigration and Multicultural Affairs* v. *Wang* (2003) 215 CLR 518]. In subsequent cases, the Federal Court and the RRT have continued to use the human rights approach, although some judges have also expressed uncertainty: see, for example, *Farajvand* v. *Minister for Immigration and Multicultural Affairs* [2001] FCA 795 (Allsop J, 20 June 2001), at para. 22; *A* v. *Minister for Immigration and Multicultural Affairs* [2002] FCA 238 (French, Lindgren and Stone JJ, 27 February 2002). Erika Feller has pointed to the reasons why judges may be reluctant to embrace this approach: 'Judges may be reluctant to embrace standards that have no clear legal authority in their own national laws. They may be cautious not to encroach too far into the realm of executive action and may wish to avoid any impression of judicial law-making': Feller, 'Address to the Conference of the International Association of Refugee Law Judges', at 388.

[25] However, the word 'persecution' appears in international criminal law: see below, notes 118–19.

is in part explained by the fact that the human rights–refugee link was not initially formulated as the logical outcome of the application of the rules of treaty interpretation, as expressed in the Vienna Convention on the Law of Treaties. While many decision-makers 'intuitively understood'[26] the connection, they did not initially attempt to justify it as a matter of international law. This trend has been observed in a report prepared for the International Law Commission ('ILC') vis-à-vis treaty interpretation in international law more generally: 'Reference to other rules of international law in the course of interpreting a treaty is an everyday, often unconscious part of the interpretation process.'[27] However, as that Report notes, 'it may be necessary to invoke an express justification for looking outside the four corners of a particular treaty to its place in the broader framework of international law'.[28] This book is based on the supposition that international human rights law is an appropriate reference for interpreting various aspects of the refugee definition, and moreover that, in interpreting such international human rights standards, refugee decision-makers must ensure coherence and consistency between their analysis and the understanding of those standards by the relevant authoritative treaty bodies. It is therefore important to begin by considering the justification for this approach by reference to the rules of treaty interpretation in international law.

---

[26] The IARLJ concludes that significantly more work on this topic is required if movement is to be made from an intuitive understanding to a working application of human rights principles: Inter-Conference Working Parties: Human Rights Nexus Working Party, *Human Rights Conference Report*.

[27] Mansfield, 'The Interpretation of Treaties in the Light of any Relevant Rules of International Law Applicable in the Relations between the Parties (Article 31(3)(c) of the Vienna Convention on the Law of Treaties), in the Context of General Developments in International Law and Concerns of the International Community' [quoted in ILC, *Report of the International Law Commission: Fifty-Seventh Session*, UN Doc. A/60/10 (2005), p. 214], at p. 4 (on file with the author). See also International Law Commission, *Fragmentation of International Law: Difficulties Arising from the Diversification and Expansion of International Law*, Report of the Study Group of the International Law Commission by Martti Koskenniemi (A/CN.4/L.682, 4 April 2006), at 175 ('Koskenniemi, Fragmentation of International Law').

[28] Mansfield, 'The Interpretation of Treaties' at p. 4. See also Campbell McLachlan, 'The Principle of Systemic Integration and Article 31(3)(c) of the Vienna Convention' (2005) 54 *International and Comparative Law Quarterly* 279 at 281.

PART TWO: JUSTIFICATION OF THE HUMAN RIGHTS FRAMEWORK

The need for a universal and objective standard

The first question which follows from the above description of the developing human rights framework is what is the principled reason for adopting such an external standard for interpreting key definitional elements of the Refugee Convention? The overwhelming response in the jurisprudence is that an international treaty, although interpreted and applied in domestic legal systems, must be interpreted as consistently and uniformly as possible.[29] As a member of the English Court of Appeal has explained, the assessment must be based on objective standards: 'However wide the canvas facing the judge's brush, the image he makes has to be firmly based on some conception of objective principle which is recognized as a legitimate source of law.'[30] This reflects the key concern that an international human rights treaty designed to provide protection to those falling within the relevant definition must operate so as to provide the same level of protection to individuals regardless of their nationality and regardless of the nature of the state party in which they seek refuge. It could hardly be consistent with the non-derogable nature of art. 1A(2) for domestic courts to undertake subjective and idiosyncratic interpretations,[31] according to their own notions of the kinds of applicants deemed worthy to receive protection under the Refugee Convention scheme. The need for consistency or, as sometimes expressed, for an 'international meaning',[32] has been repeatedly emphasized in

---

[29] See, for example, *R (on the application of Adan) v. Secretary of State for the Home Department* [2001] 2 AC 477, [2001] 1 All ER 593 at 517 where, referring to the meaning of the Refugee Convention, Lord Steyn said: 'In practice it is left to national courts, faced with material disagreement on an issue of interpretation, to resolve it. But in so doing it must search, untrammelled by notions of its national legal culture, for the true autonomous and international meaning of the treaty. And there can only be one true meaning.' See also *T v. Secretary of State for the Home Department* [1996] 2 All ER 865; [1996] 2 WLR 766; *R v. Immigration Appeal Tribunal and Another, ex parte Shah* [1998] 4 All ER 30, [1998] 1 WLR 74, [1997] Imm AR 584 ('*Shah*').

[30] *Sepet v. Secretary of State for the Home Department* [2001] EWCA Civ. 681 at para. 66 ('*Sepet*').

[31] Article 1 is one of the provisions to which no reservation may be made: see art. 42(1) of the Refugee Convention.

[32] See, for example, *R v. Secretary of State for the Home Department, ex parte Osungo* (English Court of Appeal (Civil Division), Buxton LJ, 21 August 2000), noting the 'importance now placed by this court on the international meaning of the Convention': at para. 9.

the case law[33] and by the UNHCR[34] and is manifested in the comparative approach to interpretation adopted by most common law countries.[35]

This need for an objective standard is arguably borne out by the approach taken in the US jurisprudence which, in the main, eschews an objective external barometer of persecution and adopts instead the approach that persecution is understood as 'the infliction of suffering or harm upon those who differ (in race, religion or political opinion) *in a way regarded as offensive*',[36] 'punishment' or 'infliction of harm' for political, religious or other illegitimate reasons 'that rises above the level of mere harassment',[37] and 'punishment or the infliction of harm for political, religious or other reasons *that this country does not recognize*

---

[33] According to the RRT, it is 'important that so far as possible decision-makers adhere to objective concepts capable of universal application and susceptible to the jurisprudence of international bodies, so that uniformity can be applied and applicants are able to have a better idea of whether their claims are likely to succeed': *Reference V94/01570*, RRT, 28 February 1995 at 4. See also *R v. Secretary of State for the Home Department, ex parte Robinson* [1998] QB 929, [1997] 4 All ER 210, [1997] 1 WLR 1162, [1997] Imm AR 568 ('*Robinson*'); *Horvath v. Secretary of State for the Home Department* [2000] Imm AR 205 (Ward LJ); *Applicant A and Another v. Minister for Immigration and Ethnic Affairs and Another* (1996) 190 CLR 225 (Kirby J) ('*Applicant A*'); *Refugee Appeal No. 74665/03*, RSAA, 7 July 2004, at para. 38.

[34] The High Commissioner has stated that 'the UNHCR has constantly sought to bring about a certain measure of uniformity in the elaboration of eligibility criteria with a view to ensuring that all applicants are treated according to the same standards': UNHCR, *Report on International Protection*, UN Doc. A/AC.96/527 (1996). See also UNHCR Executive Committee, *General Conclusion on International Protection* (1993) <http://www.unhcr.org/cgi-bin/texis/vtx/excom/opendoc.htm?tbl=EXCOM&id=3ae68c6814> at 31 May 2006. Indeed, in its *Agenda for Protection*, the UNHCR affirmed the 'importance of promoting universal adherence to the 1951 Convention': p. 26. It went on to state that '[m]ore harmonized approaches to refugee status determination, as well as to the interpretation of the 1951 Convention and to the use of complementary forms of protection, are also called for': p. 31.

[35] The establishment of a working party on 'Consistency in Judgments or Decisions in Asylum Matters' within the auspices of the IARLJ confirms the widespread recognition of the importance of this issue. According to the IARLJ Conference, '[t]he value of the achievement of a certain level of uniformity in the application of law at both the international and national levels is appreciated. Certainly it is valuable to have a certain degree of consistency among judgements and decisions made in different jurisdictions': *The Realities of Refugee Determination on the Eve of a New Millennium: The Role of the Judiciary* (Haarlem, The Netherlands: International Association of Refugee Law Judges, 1999), p. 336.

[36] *Nagoulko v. Immigration and Naturalization Service*, 333 F 3d 1012 (9th Cir. 2003), at 1015 ('*Nagoulko*'), citing *Korablina v. Immigration and Naturalization Service*, 158 F 3d 1038 (9th Cir. 1998), at 1043 (emphasis added) ('*Korablina*').

[37] *Tesfu v. Ashcroft*, 322 F 3d 477 (7th Cir. 2003), at 477, citing *Tamas-Mercea v. Reno*, 222 F 3d 417 (7th Cir. 2000), at 424.

as legitimate'.[38] As a result of the adoption of such vague and subjective notions as 'offensiveness', analysis often appears to be undertaken in a vacuum, according to the subjective assessments of judges in individual cases, rather than by reference to any principled or objective model.[39] Evidence of the dangers of a subjective approach, based on what the decision-maker regards as 'reasonable', abounds in the contemporary case law.[40] The risk of subjectivity is particularly acute in cases involving gender-related persecution, where decision-makers in many jurisdictions have shown a greater propensity to dismiss claims based on the view that discrimination against women is justified by culture, religion or

---

[38] *Begzatowski* v. *Immigration and Naturalization Service*, 278 F 3d 665 (7th Cir. 2002), at 668 (emphasis added).

[39] The deficiency in this approach is well illustrated in the decision of the Ninth Circuit in *Bhupendra Bhai Patel* v. *Immigration and Naturalization Service* (1999) US App. Lexis 30517 (9th Cir. 1999) ('*Patel*'). In that case the applicant for asylum had submitted that if he returned to Fiji he would be denied education, employment and the opportunity to lease or purchase property because of his ethnicity and political affiliations. The Court's entire analysis of this submission was: 'General concerns such as these, although understandable, are insufficient to establish eligibility for asylum.' The Court's judgment is troubling for its complete failure to consider the nature of the deprivations and their relationship to states' obligations under international law. This problem is particularly exemplified in US cases concerning claims based in whole or in part on denial of the right to education, in which courts have assessed the claims according to a subjective view about what is considered a 'right' and what is not. For example, the US Court of Appeals for the Fifth and Ninth Circuits have reiterated in a number of cases (including in relation to high school education) that '[e]ducation, although undeniably important, is a matter of government policy rather than a fundamental right': *Faddoul* v. *Immigration and Naturalization Service*, 37 F 3d 185 (5th Cir. 1994), at 188 ('*Faddoul*'); *Li* v. *Immigration and Naturalization Service*, 92 F 3d 985 (9th Cir. 1996), at 987 ('*Li*'). Consequently, 'the government could provide education for all people, some people or no people, without persecuting them': at 188. The corollary appears to be that denial of education, even for a Convention reason, is a relatively trivial matter. In one case, the Seventh Circuit described the applicant's daughters' denial of access to university as mere 'frustration of some opportunities for his children': *Petkov and Tritchkova* v. *Immigration and Naturalization Service*, 114 F 3d 1192 (7th Cir. 1997), at 11 ('*Petkov and Tritchkova*'). In another case, the same Court characterized the applicant's claim based on travel, living and educational restrictions (including exclusion from public high school) as 'border[ing] on frivolity': *De Souza* v. *Immigration and Naturalization Service*, 999 F 2d 1156 (7th Cir. 1993), at 1158 ('*De Souza*'). This case was cited with approval and followed in *Faddoul*, 37 F 3d 185 (5th Cir. 1994), at 188.

[40] In addition to those noted above, examples include cases where tribunals and courts have denied refugee status to homosexual applicants on the basis that they should hide their sexuality or exercise 'discretion' in their home countries in order to avoid persecution, an outcome inconsistent with the jurisprudence of the UN Human Rights Committee ('UNHRC'): see Haines, Hathaway and Foster, 'Claims to Refugee Status'.

social norms.[41] In this regard, reference to a uniform standard, such as that provided by international human rights principles, would assist in ensuring that refugee decision-makers do not dismiss cases based solely on their own subjective notions of cultural sensitivity, without sufficient regard to the rights of the individual applicant.

In addition, interpretation of key terms such as 'being persecuted' by reference to what '*our country [the state of asylum] does not recognise as legitimate*'[42] raises the possibility that doctrines and principles developed in the domestic context will govern the interpretation of the Refugee Convention, thus resulting in different interpretations of key provisions as amongst state parties.[43] Implicitly acknowledging these concerns, a Justice of the Supreme Court of Canada has explained, '[t]hese basic human rights [relevant to the Refugee Convention] are not to be considered from the subjective perspective of one country ... By very

---

[41] There is ample evidence in the case law of these dangers, particularly at the lower decision-making level. For example, in *Matter of Johnson*, a US Immigration Judge ('IJ') rejected the claim of a woman who feared that her daughters would be subject to female genital mutilation, noting that, 'while some cultures view [female genital mutilation ('FGM')] as abhorrent and/or even barbaric, others do not': *Matter of Johnson*, No. A72 370 565, 28 April 1995, at 3, 12, as cited in Stephen H. Legomsky, *Immigration and Refugee Law and Policy*, third edition (New York: Foundation Press, 2002), p. 952. Similarly, in the UK Immigration Appeal Tribunal's decision in the *Shah and Islam Case* (in which refugee status was ultimately granted by the House of Lords), the tribunal stated that 'we do not think that the purpose of the Convention is to award refugee status because of disapproval of social mores or conventions in non-western societies': *Islam and Others* v. *Secretary of State for the Home Department* (Unreported, Asylum and Immigration Tribunal, 2 October 1996) ('*Shah and Islam Case*'), cited in Heaven Crawley, *Refugees and Gender: Law and Process* (Bristol: Jordan Publishing, 2001), p. 48. See also Crawley, pp. 10–12, 180–5. This tends to confirm the view of the New Zealand RSAA that applying the domestic standards of the country of asylum rather than an international standard 'simultaneously allows too easily the intrusion of ideology and also the implication of censure of the state of origin': *Refugee Appeal No 2039/93*, RSAA, 12 February 1996, pp. 19–20. See also *Refugee Appeal No. 74665/03*, RSAA, 7 July 2004, para. 38; *Refugee Appeal No.71427/99*, RSAA, 16 August 2000, para. 52; Karen Musalo and Stephen Knight, 'Unequal Protection', *Bulletin of the Atomic Scientists*, November/December 2002, pp. 57–61.

[42] *Osaghae* v. *Immigration and Naturalization Service*, 942 F 2d 1160 (7th Cir. 1991), at 1163 (emphasis added), cited in Thomas Alexander Aleinikoff, David A. Martin and Hiroshi Motomura, *Immigration and Citizenship: Process and Policy* (St Paul, MN: West Group, 1998), p. 1060.

[43] In addition to the risk that individual domestic courts would engage in restrictive reasoning (inconsistent with the broad humanitarian aims of the Refugee Convention), there is also the risk that reasoning based on domestic principles will be rejected by other state parties and will thus undermine the aim of attaining an 'international meaning' of the Convention's terms.

definition, such rights transcend subjective and parochial perspectives and extend beyond national boundaries'.[44]

While the need for an objective and uniform standard appears to be well accepted, it does not necessarily follow that international human rights principles should constitute that standard. The following analysis therefore turns to consider why the correct interpretation of the Refugee Convention, consistent with principles of treaty interpretation, leads to the conclusion that international human rights law should constitute a guiding set of principles in refugee adjudication.

Human rights as the standard: object and purpose

The Vienna Convention on the Law of Treaties ('VCLT')[45] provides the authoritative guide to the interpretation of treaties. Although it does not technically apply to an interpretation of the Refugee Convention,[46] it is widely agreed that the VCLT encapsulates customary international law in relation to treaty interpretation,[47] and to that extent is applicable and

---

[44] *Chan v. Canada (Minister of Employment and Immigration)* [1995] 3 SCR 593, 635 (La Forest J). Although in dissent as to the outcome, La Forest's judgment is the one most often referred to in subsequent cases and in the literature. See also the decision in *Refugee Appeal No. 74665/03*, RSAA, 7 July 2004, para. 38. Similarly, the Director of International Protection for the UNHCR has said that '[t]he scope of the 1951 Convention refugee definition is a matter of international law and its interpretation should not be subject to variations deriving from idiosyncratic, legal, cultural or political determinants in any one State': Erika Feller, 'Challenges to the 1951 Convention in its 50th Anniversary Year' (Speech delivered at the Seminar on International Protection within One Single Asylum Procedure, Norrkoping, Sweden, 23–24 April 2001b). Indeed, this approach is arguably dictated by the spirit – if not the text – of art. 27 of the Vienna Convention on the Law of Treaties, which provides that a party may not invoke the provisions of its internal law as justification for its failure to perform a treaty: Vienna, 23 May 1969, in force 27 January 1988, 1155 UNTS 331; (1969) 8 ILM 679.

[45] *Ibid.*

[46] This is because both the 1951 Convention and the 1967 Protocol predate the VCLT (the VCLT entered into force on 27 January 1988) and art. 4 of the VCLT provides that 'the Convention applies only to treaties which are concluded by States after the entry into force of the present Convention'.

[47] See *Territorial Dispute (Libyan Arab Jamahiriya/Chad)* [1994] ICJ Rep 6 at 21, reaffirmed in *Maritime Delimitation and Territorial Questions between Qatar and Bahrain (Jurisdiction and Admissibility)* [1995] ICJ Rep 6 at 21. This view is also reflected in the decisions of the WTO Appellate Body: see, for example, *Japan – Taxes on Alcoholic Beverages*, WTO Doc AB-1996-2 (1996) s. D (Report of the Appellate Body).

authoritative.[48] The primary rule of interpretation is contained in art. 31 of the VCLT, entitled 'General Rule of Interpretation', and provides that '[a] treaty shall be interpreted in good faith in accordance with the ordinary meaning to be given to the terms of the treaty in their context and in the light of its object and purpose'.

It is well established that the use of the singular heading– 'general rule of interpretation'– indicates that art. 31 is to be interpreted 'in a holistic manner'[49] or, as one refugee tribunal has stated it, interpretation is a 'single combined operation'.[50] In other words, priority is given neither to a purely textual or literal approach, nor to one that focuses only on context or purpose. Rather, 'the determination of the ordinary meaning cannot be done in the abstract, only in the *context* of the treaty and in the light of its *object and purpose*'.[51] As Lord Lloyd of the British House of Lords has emphasized, given the nature of an international treaty and the process of negotiation and compromise that precedes agreement on the final text, '[o]ne cannot expect to find the same precision of

---

[48] This is so notwithstanding the fact that the Refugee Convention is primarily interpreted by domestic courts, since most domestic courts take the view that in interpreting a statute that transposes the text of a provision of a treaty, 'the rules applicable to the interpretation of treaties must be applied to the transposed text and rules generally applicable to the interpretation of domestic statutes give way': *Applicant A* (1996) 190 CLR 225 at 230–1 (Brennan CJ) (ultimately in dissent, but not as to this point). See also at 239 (Dawson J); at 251–2 (McHugh J); and at 292 (Kirby J). For explicit support for the relevance of the VCLT to the Refugee Convention, see *Minister for Immigration and Multicultural Affairs v. Savvin & Ors* (2000) 98 FCR 168; *Refugee Appeal No. 74665/03*, RSAA, 7 July 2004.

[49] According to Aust, 'Article 31 is entitled "General *rule* of interpretation". The singular noun emphasises that the article contains only one rule, that set out in paragraph 1': Anthony Aust, *Modern Treaty Law and Practice* (Cambridge: Cambridge University Press, 2000), p. 186 (emphasis in original). See also Sir Arthur Watts, *The International Law Commission, 1949–1998*, 2 vols. (Oxford: Oxford University Press, 1999), vol. II, p. 685. In the refugee context, see *Applicant A* (1996) 190 CLR 225 at 254 (McHugh J) and references cited therein.

[50] *Refugee Appeal No. 70366/96*, RSAA, 22 September 1997, p. 24. The dominant view in the common law world is that a holistic approach to refugee interpretation is required by the VCLT: see *Refugee Appeal No. 72668/01*, RSAA, 5 April 2002, para. 157, and the discussion in James C. Hathaway, *The Rights of Refugees under International Law* (Cambridge: Cambridge University Press, 2005), pp. 49–51.

[51] Aust, *Modern Treaty Law*, p. 188 (emphasis in original). In the refugee context, see *Applicant A* (1996) 190 CLR 225 at 253 (McHugh J): 'the ordinary meaning of the words is not to be determined in a vacuum removed from the context of the treaty or its object and purpose'. According to Ress, '[t]he ordinary meaning of a term can only be determined by looking at the context in which it is used': George Ress, 'The Interpretation of the Charter', in Bruno Simma et al. (eds.), *The Charter of the United Nations: A Commentary*, second edition (Oxford: Oxford University Press, 2002), p. 21.

language as one does in an Act of Parliament'.[52] For this reason, 'one is more likely to arrive at the true construction of Article 1A(2) by seeking a meaning which makes sense in the light of the Convention as a whole, and the purposes which the framers of the Convention were seeking to achieve, rather than by concentrating exclusively on the language'.[53]

The question then arises as to whether we can ascertain one key object and purpose of the Refugee Convention, or are there different or conflicting objects and purposes? While scholars observe that the task of ascertaining the 'object and purpose' of a treaty is not always straightforward,[54] reference to the Preamble appears to be the predominant method of ascertaining the object and purpose of a treaty, particularly in the human rights field.[55]

Reference to the Preamble of the Refugee Convention, however, could produce conflicting views as to its object and purpose. One perspective is that the aim of the Refugee Convention is fundamentally to pursue a social and human rights inspired purpose, namely to provide for the international protection of those individuals falling within the refugee

---

[52] *R v. Secretary of State for the Home Department, ex parte Adan, Subaskaran and Aitseguer* [1999] 4 All ER 774; [1999] 3 WLR 1274, [1999] Imm AR 521 (*'Adan, Subaskaran and Aitseguer'*).

[53] *Ibid.*

[54] In particular, see UNHRC, *General Comment No. 24: Issues relating to Reservations Made upon Ratification or Accession to the Covenant or the Optional Protocols thereto, or in relation to Declarations under Article 41 of the Covenant*, UN Doc. CCPR/C/21/Rev.1/Add.6 (1994a).
A number of scholars point out that while the concept of object and purpose is central to many aspects of the VCLT, there is little authoritative guidance regarding methods of divining the object and purpose of a treaty: Jan Klabbers, 'Some Problems regarding the Object and Purpose of Treaties' (1997) 8 *The Finnish Yearbook of International Law* 138 at 144–8. See also Isabelle Buffard and Karl Zemanek, 'The "Object and Purpose" of a Treaty: an Enigma?' (1998) 3 *American Review of International and European Law* 311.

[55] The preamble to human rights treaties frequently reveals their object and purpose. Accordingly, the ECHR has emphasized that 'the preamble is generally very useful for the determination of the "object" and "purpose" of the instrument to be construed': *Golder* v. *United Kingdom* (1975) Eur Court HR (ser A); (1979) 1 EHRR 524 at para. 34 (*'Golder'*).
A similar approach has been adopted by the Inter-American Court of Human Rights (see *Other Treaties Subject to the Consultative Jurisdiction of the Court*, Advisory Opinion No. OC-1/82, Inter-American Court of Human Rights, 24 September 1982), reprinted in (1982) 3 *Human Rights Law Journal* 140; *The Effect of Reservations on the Entry into Force of the American Convention*, Advisory Opinion No. OC-2/82 (Inter-American Court of Human Rights, 24 September 1982), reprinted in (1982) 3 *Human Rights Law Journal* 153) and, more recently, in a different context by the Appellate Body of the World Trade Organization: see, for example, *United States – Import Prohibition of Certain Shrimp and Shrimp Products*, WTO Doc. WT/DS58/AB/R (1998) paras. 127–34 (Report of the Appellate Body).

definition. This is said to be revealed in the Preamble to the Refugee Convention which provides (relevantly):

CONSIDERING that the Charter of the United Nations and the Universal Declaration of Human Rights approved on 10 December 1948 by the General Assembly have affirmed the principle that human beings shall enjoy fundamental rights and freedoms without discrimination,
CONSIDERING that the United Nations has, on various occasions, manifested its profound concern for refugees and endeavoured to assure refugees the widest possible exercise of these fundamental rights and freedoms.

The leading courts in common law jurisdictions have highlighted the significance of the Preamble for the human rights-based approach to an interpretation of the Refugee Convention, emphasizing that the Refugee Convention is understood to have been 'written against the background of international human rights law';[56] that the preamble expressly shows 'that a premise of the Convention was that all human beings shall enjoy fundamental rights and freedoms';[57] and that it 'places the Convention among the international instruments that have as their object and purpose the protection of the equal enjoyment by every person of fundamental rights and freedoms'.[58] In light of the preamble, it has been said that '[n]owhere are considerations of international instruments of human rights more important than in the area of refugees'.[59] Accordingly, common law courts have repeatedly recognized and reiterated that '[t]his overarching and clear human rights object and purpose is the background against which interpretation of individual provisions must take place'.[60]

In contrast to this view of the object and purpose of the Refugee Convention which focuses on its aim to provide protection to individuals

---

[56] *Applicant A* (1996) 190 CLR 225 at 296-7 (Kirby J). See also *Wang* (2000) 105 FCR 548 at paras. 74-81 (Merkel J); *Minister for Immigration and Multicultural Affairs v. Mohammed* (2000) 98 FCR 405 at 421.
[57] *Shah* [1999] 2 AC 629 at 639 (Lord Steyn).
[58] *Applicant A* (1996) 190 CLR 225 at 231-2 (Brennan CJ).
[59] *Premalal* (1993) 41 FCR 117 at 138.
[60] *Pushpanathan v. Canada (Minister of Citizenship and Immigration)* [1998] 1 SCR 982 at 1024 (Bastarache J). In *R (on the application of Hoxha) v. Special Adjudicator* [2005] 4 All ER 580 ('*Hoxha*'), Lord Hope of Craighead stated that '[t]he social and humanitarian nature of the problem of refugees was expressly recognised in the preamble to the convention': at para. 6. Moreover, the 'social and humanitarian nature' of the Refugee Convention has been confirmed by the UNHCR Executive Committee. For example, in its *Agenda for Protection*, it reaffirmed State parties' commitment to implementing the Refugee Convention obligations 'fully and effectively in accordance with the [humanitarian] object and purpose' of the Refugee Convention: paras. 1-3.

inspired by humanitarian principles, there is an alternative view that perceives the Refugee Convention's aim as being to resolve a difficult and inconvenient problem of mutual concern to state parties, and thus more clearly concerned with providing assistance to states than with conferring rights on individuals. This argument has, on occasion, been implicitly voiced by courts that have alluded to the fact that the Preamble also contains the following reference:

> Considering that the grant of asylum may place unduly heavy burdens on certain countries and that a satisfactory solution of a problem of which the United Nations has recognized the international scope and nature cannot therefore be achieved without international co-operation.[61]

This has sometimes been relied upon to suggest that circumspection should be exercised in interpreting the Refugee Convention too widely.[62] However, the reference to the concept of 'heavy burdens' does not undermine the humanitarian and human rights purpose of the Refugee Convention; rather the emphasis is on the need for co-operation in order adequately to deal with the humanitarian problem, as the following sentences, also in the Preamble, reveal:

> Expressing the wish that all States, *recognising the social and humanitarian nature of the problem of refugees*, will do everything within their power to prevent this problem from becoming a cause of tension between States,
>
> Noting that the United Nations High Commissioner for Refugees is charged with the task of supervising international conventions providing for the protection of refugees, and recognising that the effective co-ordination of measures taken to deal with this problem will depend upon co-operation of States with the High Commissioner [emphasis added].

Rather than suggesting a restrictive interpretation, these statements highlight the need for parties fully to uphold their obligations

---

[61] In *Applicant A* (1996) 190 CLR 225, Dawson J stated that '[o]n the other hand, the fourth preamble recognises that "the grant of asylum may place unduly heavy burdens on certain countries" and the need for international cooperation, whilst the fifth preamble implores all States to recognise "the social and humanitarian nature of the problem of refugees" and "do everything within their power to prevent this problem from becoming a cause of tension between States". By including in its operative provisions the requirement that a refugee fear persecution, the Convention limits its humanitarian scope and does not afford universal protection to asylum seekers': at 247–8. See also *MMM v. Minister for Immigration and Multicultural Affairs* (1998) 90 FCR 324.

[62] See, for example, *Applicant A* (1996) 190 CLR 225 at 247–8 (Dawson J), although His Honour essentially just acknowledges that the 'humanitarian scope' is limited by the nexus clause. See also *Khawar* (2002) 210 CLR 1 at para. 47 (McHugh and Gummow JJ).

in order to prevent the issue becoming a source of tension between states. While it is true that states were motivated to formulate an international refugee regime by the need to deal with a difficult problem of mutual concern, that 'problem' was conceived in humanitarian terms, as the following exposition by Kirby J of the High Court of Australia reveals:

> Whilst courts of law, tribunals and officials must uphold the law, they must approach the meaning of the law relating to refugees with its humanitarian purpose in mind. The convention was adopted by the international community, and passed into Australian domestic law, to prevent the repetition of the affronts to humanity that occurred in the middle of the twentieth century and earlier. At that time Australia, like most other like countries, substantially closed its doors against refugees. The Convention and the municipal law giving it effect, are designed to ensure that this mistake is not repeated.[63]

In addition to the Preamble providing a source of guidance, the text may shed light on the object and purpose of a treaty. Klabbers proposes that if most of a treaty's substantive provisions deal with a certain topic, 'one may well surmise that dealing with this topic constitutes the object and purpose of the treaty concerned'.[64] An application of this analysis to the text of the Refugee Convention reveals its overriding human rights purpose. Articles 2–34 are concerned with the clarification of the rights to which those falling within the definition are entitled.[65] While it is clear that there is no 'right to asylum' per se in international law,[66] the Refugee Convention imposes a *non-refoulement* obligation

---

[63] *Chen Shi Hai v. Minister for Immigration and Multicultural Affairs* (2000) 201 CLR 293 at 308 (Kirby J) ('*Chen Shi Hai*').

[64] Klabbers, 'Some Problems regarding the Object and Purpose of Treaties', p. 157. This appears to be borne out by the approach of human rights adjudicatory bodies in assessing the object and purpose of human rights treaties: see, for example, UNHRC, *General Comment No. 24: Issues relating to Reservations Made upon Ratification or Accession to the Covenant or the Optional Protocols thereto, or in relation to Declarations under Article 41 of the Covenant*, UN Doc. CCPR/C/21/Rev.1/Add.6 (1994a), para. 7.

[65] Although most of the relevant provisions are phrased in terms of obligations upon the state rather than rights to the individual, it does not change the fact that it – in effect – provides rights of minimum treatment of refugees. See generally, Hathaway, *The Rights of Refugees under International Law*.

[66] The UDHR speaks only of a right to *seek* asylum (art. 14) and the Refugee Convention does not provide a substantive right to be provided asylum. Rather, the salient obligation on State parties is to protect against *refoulement* (art. 33).

on states parties[67] and provides guarantees of non-discrimination in respect of a range of both civil and political rights and economic and social rights to those falling within the definition of 'refugee'.[68] Indeed, the key purpose of the Refugee Convention was not so much to define who constitutes a refugee but to provide for the rights and entitlements that follow from such recognition. As has been said, '[the Refugee Convention] provides a concrete human rights remedy for particular human rights violations, that is to say, it gives persons meeting the Convention definition the opportunity to live with greater freedom and dignity than in their country of origin'.[69] Thus, while the Refugee Convention has some of the hallmarks of more traditional multilateral treaties, in that some reciprocity of obligation as between state parties is inherent,[70] it is overwhelmingly concerned with the 'endowment of individuals

---

[67] Article 33. Aleinikoff notes that although it does not include monitoring provisions found in later human rights instruments, and does not extend status to all victims of human rights abuses, the Convention has important human rights features: '[m]ost significant, of course, is the protection against non-refoulement. The document also provides wide-ranging non-discrimination norms for persons recognised as refugees': Thomas Alexander Aleinikoff, 'The Refugee Convention at Forty: Reflections on the IJRL Colloquium' (1991) 3 *International Journal of Refugee Law* 617 at 625.

[68] The rights include those relating to non-discrimination (art. 3), religion (art. 4), rights of association (art. 15), access to courts (art. 16), employment (art. 17), welfare (Chapter IV) and freedom of movement (art. 26).

[69] Justice A. M. North and Nehal Bhuta, 'The Future of Protection – the Role of the Judge' (2001) 15 *Georgetown Immigration Law Journal* 479 at 486. See also *NAGV and NAGW of 2002 v. Minister for Immigration and Multicultural and Indigenous Affairs* (2005) 213 ALR 668 at 672. As the UNHCR has explained, the Refugee Convention 'provides the most comprehensive codification of the right of refugees yet attempted on the international level. It lays down basic minimum standards for the treatment of refugees . . . [and] is to be applied without discrimination as to race, religion or country of origin, and contains various safeguards against the expulsion of refugees': Office of the UN High Commissioner for Refugees, *Introductory Note to the Convention and Protocol Relating to the Status of Refugees* (1996) p. 5 <http://www.unhcr.org/cgi-bin/texis/vtx/protect/opendoc.pdf?tbl=PROTECTION&id=3b66c2aa10> at 31 May 2006. See also Jackson, 'The 1951 Convention Relating to the Status of Refugees', at 403–4.

[70] While the global refugee regime does contain an underlying principle of reciprocity in the sense that today nations are concerned with burden-sharing, it remains the case that the Refugee Convention is far more akin to a law-making or normative treaty than a contractual one. In terms it sets out the standards by which states are to treat those falling within the definition in art. 1A(2) and, following the adoption of the 1967 Protocol relating to the Status of Refugees, its commitments are open-ended and designed to govern the position of refugees indefinitely. See also Goodwin-Gill, 'Refugees and

with rights',[71] such that '[i]n concluding these human rights treaties, the States can be deemed to submit themselves to a legal order within which they, for the common good, assume various obligations, not in relation to other States, but towards all [refugees] within their jurisdiction'.[72]

Identification of the human rights objectives of the Refugee Convention has underpinned the growing preference for many common law courts and tribunals to eschew reliance on dictionary meanings of Refugee Convention terms.[73] Although many early cases relied on dictionary definitions, presumably in an attempt to discern the 'ordinary meaning' of the Refugee Convention terms, this approach is increasingly giving way to scepticism about the appropriateness of this method of interpretation in light of the human rights context and object of the Refugee Convention.[74] The key objection expressed by the courts to the use of dictionary definitions is a principled concern that reliance on a dictionary can lead a decision-maker to adopt an interpretation

---

Responsibility in the Twenty-First Century', at 24–5; Nicholas Sitaropoulos, *Judicial Interpretation of Refugee Status: In Search of a Principled Methodology Based on a Critical Comparative Analysis, with Special Reference to Contemporary British, French, and German Jurisprudence* (Athens: Sakkoulas, 1999), p. 96.

[71] UNHRC, *Issues relating to Reservations Made upon Ratification or Accession to the Covenant or the Optional Protocols thereto, or in relation to Declarations under Article 41 of the Covenant*, UN Doc. No CCPR/C/21/Rev.1/Add.6 (1994a) para. 17. The UN HRC was distinguishing human rights treaties from those which are 'a web of inter-State exchanges of mutual obligations'.

[72] *The Effect of Reservations on the Entry into Force of the American Convention*, Advisory Opinion No. OC-2/82 (Inter-American Court of Human Rights, 24 September 1982), reprinted in (1982) 3 *Human Rights Law Journal* 153, para. 30. The original quote states: 'all individuals within their jurisdiction'. These insights by the Inter-American Court of Human Rights are derived from the decision of the International Court of Justice ('ICJ') in *Reservations to the Convention on the Prevention and Punishment of the Crime of Genocide* [1951] ICJ Rep. 15 at 23. See also the separate opinion of Judge Weeramantry in *Application of the Convention on the Prevention and Punishment of the Crime of Genocide* [1996] ICJ Rep 595 at 645.

[73] This rejection of a dictionary approach to interpretation is consistent with that adopted by other human rights adjudicating bodies, such as the UNHRC: see *Van Duzen v. Canada*, Human Rights Committee, No R.12/50, 7 April 1982, cited in Dominic McGoldrick, *The Human Rights Committee: Its Role in the Development of the International Covenant on Civil and Political Rights* (Oxford: Clarendon Press, 1991), p. 159. In addition, the ECHR has held that many of the terms in the European Convention have 'a special, autonomous meaning': see Pieter van Dijk, G. J. H. van Hoof and A. W. Heringa, *Theory and Practice of the European Convention on Human Rights* (The Hague: Kluwer Law International, 1998), p. 77.

[74] In the decision of *Chen Shi Hai* (2000) 201 CLR 293, Kirby J reflected that he was, 'inclined to see more clearly than before the dangers in the use of the dictionary definitions of the word "persecuted" in the Convention definition', at para. 108.

inconsistent with the treaty's object and purpose.[75] One of the examples provided by the New Zealand Refugee Status Appeals Authority ('RSAA') as illustrative of the erroneousness of the dictionary method of treaty interpretation is the initial approach of the Australian courts which, relying on dictionary definitions that define persecution as involving enmity and malignity, rejected claims where such enmity on the part of the persecutor could not be established.[76] This approach was later rejected by the High Court of Australia (and other common law appellate courts) on the basis that it inappropriately focuses the attention of the decision-maker on the intent of the persecutor and ignores the fact that 'some persecution is performed by people who think that they are doing their victims a favour',[77] well exemplified in cases involving female genital mutilation, where the procedure may be perceived as benefiting the woman by initiating her into adulthood and societal inclusion, and the subjection of Russian homosexual women to involuntary psychiatric treatment in order to 'help' them.[78] Since the object of the Refugee

---

[75] The New Zealand RSAA has explained that 'it is neither appropriate nor possible to distil the meaning of persecution by having resort to English and Australian dictionaries. This can only lead to a sterile and mistaken interpretation of persecution': *Refugee Appeal No. 71427/99*, RSAA, 16 August 2000, para. 46. See also *Refugee Appeal No. 74665/03*, RSAA, 7 July 2004, para. 39. Another objection to the dictionary approach is based upon a rather obvious practical problem, namely that multilateral treaties, such as the Refugee Convention, are often produced in different languages, each version being equally authoritative. The two official languages of the Refugee Convention are English and French. The VCLT provides that the versions are equally authoritative: art. 33(1). As Steiner and Alston note, reliance on dictionaries, 'would seem particularly unwise when dictionaries in several languages (and in different legal systems according different meanings to linguistically similar terms) must be resorted to'. Henry J. Steiner and Philip Alston, *International Human Rights in Context*, second edition (Oxford: Oxford University Press, 2000), p. 109. This is borne out by Carlier's explanation of the meaning of 'persecution' in different language dictionaries. His perusal of English, French, German, Dutch and Spanish definitions of 'persecution' fails to yield a consistent approach to an understanding of the term as a matter of ordinary usage: Jean-Yves Carlier, Dirk Vanheule, Carlos Peña Galiano and Klaus Hullman (eds.), *Who is a Refugee? A Comparative Case Law Study* (The Hague: Kluwer Law International, 1997), p. 702. However, it should be noted that the authors appear to be advocating, rather than critiquing, a dictionary approach.

[76] See, for example, *Chen Shi Hai (an infant) by his next friend Chen Ren Bing v. Minister for Immigration and Multicultural Affairs* [1998] 622 FCA (Unreported, French J, 5 June 1998), later overturned by the High Court in *Chen Shi Hai* (2000) 201 CLR 293.

[77] *Khawar* (2002) 210 CLR 1 at para. 108.

[78] See *Pitcherskaia*, 118 F 3d 641 (9th Cir. 1997), at 645.

Convention is to provide protection, rather than to punish the perpetrators of harm, the imposition of a requirement to establish malignant intent is difficult to reconcile to the object and purpose of the Convention.

Rather than relying on dictionaries to provide the objective common indicator of the meaning of key Convention terms such as 'being persecuted', the dominant approach is that, in light of the human rights object and purpose of the Refugee Convention, the refugee definition is appropriately measured by reference to developing norms of international human rights law. As the UNHCR has explained, the 'strong human rights language' in the preamble indicates that, 'the aim of the drafters [was] to incorporate human rights values in the identification and treatment of refugees, thereby providing helpful guidance for the interpretation, in harmony with the Vienna Treaty Convention, of the provisions of the 1951 Convention'.[79]

The human rights approach confirmed by context

As explained above, the primary rule of interpretation of the VCLT also requires the text to be read according to its ordinary meaning *in context*. An examination of the context of the Refugee Convention further supports the adoption of international human rights standards as an appropriate source of guidance in interpreting the Refugee Convention. Article 31(2) of the VCLT sets out the permissible sources that may provide the context of a treaty; of those listed, the Preamble is the most relevant to an interpretation of the Refugee Convention.

In light of the reference in the Preamble to the UDHR, it is arguable that the Refugee Convention could be placed within the context of the developing body of international human rights law.[80] Underlying the exposition of the 'human rights as context' view is a growing recognition that the Refugee Convention should be interpreted in the context that it constitutes 'part of the total international human rights movement that began at the mid-point of the 20th century and has grown

---

[79] UNHCR, 'The International Protection of Refugees', at 78.
[80] After referring to the Preamble, Bhabha notes that 'it appears that refugee law and human rights law intersected from the outset': Jacqueline Bhabha, 'Boundaries in the Field of Human Rights: Internationalist Gatekeepers?', at 165. See also Karen Musalo, Jennifer Moore and Richard Boswell, *Refugee Law and Policy: Cases and Materials* (Durham, NC: Carolina Academic Press, 1997), p. 233.

exponentially since then'.[81] Thus, rather than being a self-contained, *sui generis* instrument, analysed in isolation from the 'increasingly sophisticated body of international law on human rights generally',[82] it should be considered part of the wider corpus of international human rights law.[83]

It is true that the implementation of the Refugee Convention took place in 'splendid isolation' from the developing corpus of international human rights law for much of its early life.[84] This was true of the

---

[81] Simeon, *The Human Rights Paradigm and the 1951 Refugee Convention*, p. 2. After referring to the Preamble, the UNHCR says that the 'human rights base of the Convention roots it quite directly in the broader framework of human rights instruments of which it is an integral part, albeit with a particular focus': UNHCR, 'Note on International Protection', at 35. Further, North J of the Federal Court of Australia took this view in an extra-curial exposition of the correct approach to an interpretation of the Convention: 'The 1951 Convention coincided with the birth of the modern human rights movement and encoded its nascent principles; fifty years on, the interpretation of protection obligations should reflect the advances in human rights consciousness that have occurred, consistently with the text, object and purpose of the 1951 treaty': North and Bhuta, 'The Future of Protection', p. 485.

[82] See the UNHCR submission in *Gashi and Nikshiqi* [1997] INLR 96 at 104–5, in which it was submitted that '[t]he term "persecution" cannot be seen in isolation from the increasingly sophisticated body of international law on human rights generally. In recognition of the adaptable nature of the refugee definition to meet the ever-changing needs of protection UNHCR recognises an important linkage between persecution and the violation of fundamental human rights.' Clark and Crêpeau also argue that '[f]or too long, the 1951 Convention relating to the Status of Refugees has been treated as a piece of international legislation that could only be interpreted according to its own internal logic and objectives in isolation from international human rights law': Tom Clark and Francois Crêpeau, 'Mainstreaming Refugee Rights: the 1951 Refugee Convention and International Human Rights Law' (1999) 17(4) *Netherlands Quarterly of Human Rights* 389.

[83] In *Sarrazola* (2001) 107 FCR 184, the Full Court (Merkel J, Heerey and Sundberg JJ agreeing) indicated that the major international human rights instruments, the 'International Bill of Rights' as they are often called, were part of the context of the Convention. See also the decision at first instance: *Sarrazola v. Minister for Immigration and Multicultural Affairs (No. 3)* [2000] FCA 919 (Unreported, Madgwick J, 23 August 2000), and the statement by Sadaka Ogata, then UN High Commissioner for Refugees, that 'the system of refugee protection fits into, supports and is indeed an indispensable part of the global human rights regime': cited in Tim Wichert, 'Human Rights, Refugees and Displaced Persons: the 1997 UN Commission on Human Rights' (1997) 9 *International Journal of Refugee Law* 500 at 500–1.

[84] This phrase is borrowed from Thomas Cottier, who argues that trade and human rights 'evolved in splendid isolation': Thomas Cottier, 'Trade and Human Rights: a Relationship to Discover' (2002) 5(1) *Journal of International Economic Law* 111 at 112. See also IARLJ Inter-Conference Working Parties: Human Rights Nexus Working Party, *Human Rights Conference Report*, which states: '[d]espite their almost concurrent inception, the 1951 Convention on Refugees ... and the Universal Declaration on Human Rights ... developed along parallel but separate trajectories': p. 15.

manner in which the UNHCR carried out its functions as well as the way in which the Refugee Convention was implemented in domestic jurisdictions.[85] However, the increasing convergence between the refugee regime and the wider context of international human rights law has been a significant feature of recent decades. The UNHCR's practice in recent years reflects a growing realization and acceptance of the role of refugee law in the broader framework of human rights and humanitarian law.[86] On a practical level, the Office is working more closely with various international human rights bodies and has strengthened collaboration with regional human rights bodies in order to 'raise awareness and illustrate the strong inter-linkages between legal regimes'.[87] Moreover, as outlined above, the UNHCR increasingly supports the interpretation of the Refugee Convention definition in line with evolving standards in international human rights law. To this extent, regardless of the original conception of the place of refugee law, it is clear that the context has now evolved to the point where the Refugee Convention is perceived as forming part of the wider body of international human rights law. Accordingly, it should be interpreted in a way that takes account of, and is consistent with, developing international human rights standards.

Other rules of international law: promoting coherence

Article 31(3)(c) of the VCLT requires an interpreter to take into account, together with the context, 'any relevant rules of international law

---

[85] For example, in 1997 a former High Commissioner explained that 'not until 1990 did a High Commissioner for Refugees ever address the Human Rights Commission, such was the perceived divide between human rights and humanitarianism': Sadako Ogata, 'Human Rights, Humanitarian Law and Refugee Protection', in Daniel Warner (ed.), *Human Rights and Humanitarian Law: The Quest for Universality* (The Hague: Martinus Nijhoff, 1997), p. 135.

[86] See the discussion of this issue in UNHCR, *'General Briefing Note: UNHCR, Human Rights and Refugee Protection'*, REFWORLD, July 1997, p. 1. This is a new phenomenon because the 'non-political' and 'humanitarian' nature of UNHCR's work was 'seen as requiring the Office to concern itself with the immediate needs of the refugees and not why they were forced to flee': Ogata, 'Human Rights', p. 135.

[87] See UNHCR, 'Note on International Protection', at 20–1. The UNHCR states: 'Recognizing the broader dimensions of refugee protection beyond the context of refugee law, UNHCR has continued to strengthen linkages between refugee law, human rights law and international humanitarian law, so that they can be better used for the protection of refugees and other persons of concern to UNHCR': at 20–1. See also UNHCR Executive Committee, *Conclusion on the Civilian and Humanitarian Character of Asylum* (2002) <http://www.unhcr.org/cgi-bin/texis/vtx/excom/opendoc.htm?tbl=EXCOM&id=3dafdd7c4> at 31 May 2006.

applicable in the relations between the parties'.[88] Although this provision has rarely been applied in the refugee context (or in international law more generally),[89] it provides an even clearer justification for the use of 'comparative treaty interpretation' as a method to ascertain the correct interpretation of key terms in the refugee definition. In particular, since this provision is said to express the general principle of 'systematic integration' of the international law system,[90] essential for ensuring that international obligations 'are interpreted by reference to their normative environment',[91] it provides a further principled foundation for the argument of this book that refugee decision-makers must ensure their understanding of the content and scope of international human rights law, especially socio-economic rights, is consistent with principles of international human rights law.

Art. 31(3)(c) embodies the principle that international obligations must be interpreted by reference to the broader framework of international law, and it also provides guidance as to how an interpreter may undertake such an exercise. In particular, as an ILC background study has observed, the phrase 'relevant rules of international law applicable in the relations between the parties' refers to the rules of

---

[88] Unlike art. 32 of the VCLT, which is a 'supplementary' means of interpretation, art. 31(3) forms a 'mandatory part of the interpretation process': McLachlan, 'The Principle of Systemic Integration', p. 290.

[89] Article 31(3)(c) is a relatively overlooked provision of the VCLT, perhaps in part due to the view that it 'offers very little guidance' and 'scarcely covers [the issue of comparative treaty interpretation] with the degree of clarity requisite to so important a matter': *Case Concerning the Gabcikovo-Nagymaros Project (Hungary/Slovakia)* [1997] ICJ Rep 7 at 114 (Separate Opinion of Vice-President Weeramantry). In addition, the difficulties in interpreting and applying 31(3)(c) are exacerbated by the fact that, as Sands points out, 'it appears to have been expressly relied upon only very occasionally in judicial practice. It also seems to have attracted little academic comment. There appears to be a general reluctance to refer to Article 31(3)(c)': Philippe Sands, 'Treaty, Custom and the Cross-Fertilization of International Law' (1998) 1 *Yale Human Rights and Development Law Journal* 85 at 94. However, it has been increasingly relied upon by international adjudicatory bodies in recent years, and promises to attain further significance in light of the ILC's work in this area as an aspect of the broader project on fragmentation in international law: see generally Koskenniemi, 'Fragmentation of International Law'. For recent academic consideration of Article 31(3)(c) see McLachlan, 'The Principle of Systemic Integration' and Duncan French, 'Treaty Interpretation and the Incorporation of Extraneous Legal Rules' (2006) 55 *International and Comparative Law Quarterly* 281.

[90] See Koskenniemi, 'Fragmentation of International Law', p. 175.

[91] Ibid. As Sands notes, it 'appears to be the only tool available under international law to construct a general international law by reconciling norms arising in treaty and custom across different subject matter areas': Sands, 'Treaty, Custom and the Cross-Fertilization of International Law', p. 87.

international law in general; thus '[t]he words are apt to include all of the sources of international law, including custom, general principles, and, where applicable, other treaties'.[92] Whether each of these sources is applicable and *relevant* in the context of refugee adjudication will now be examined.

Customary international law

Customary international law constitutes 'a field of reference of potential assistance in treaty interpretation' pursuant to art. 31(3)(c),[93] and is most often invoked where a treaty provision is ambiguous, the terms employed in the treaty have a recognized meaning in customary international law, or the terms of the treaty 'are by their nature open-textured' and the rules of custom 'will assist in giving content to the rule'.[94] Of course, if a customary rule represents a *jus cogens* norm, it will override the treaty provision.[95]

In the refugee adjudication context, reference to custom is potentially most useful in giving content to the 'open-textured' phrase 'being persecuted'. Courts have recognized the relevance of customary international law in assessing whether potential harm constitutes a violation of international law (and thus persecution).[96] However, the usefulness of custom in the refugee context is open to question, given that it can involve 'extensive investigation of sources outside the treaty in order to

---

[92] Mansfield, 'The Interpretation of Treaties', p. 13. See also Koskenniemi, 'Fragmentation of International Law', p. 180.
[93] Mansfield, 'The Interpretation of Treaties', p. 25. See also Sir Robert Jennings and Sir Arthur Watts (eds.), *Oppenheim's International Law*, ninth edition (Boston: Addison-Wesley, 1997), vol. I, p. 1275, fn 21, citing *The Reparations Case* [1949] ICJ Rep 174 at 182. For recent consideration of this issue in the wider literature, see Sands, 'Treaty, Custom and the Cross-Fertilization of International Law', p. 102; Gabrielle Marceau, 'A Call for Coherence in International Law' (1999) 33(5) *Journal of World Trade* 87 at 115–17.
[94] Mansfield, 'The Interpretation of Treaties', p. 27.
[95] Article 53 of the VCLT provides that a treaty is void if, at the time of its conclusion, it conflicts with a peremptory norm of general international law. Further, art. 64 of the VCLT provides that if a new peremptory norm of general international law emerges, any existing treaty which is in conflict with that norm becomes void and terminates.
[96] For example, in *Sepet*, the UK Court of Appeal considered at length whether the right to conscientious objection to compulsory military service had attained the status of customary international law, in the course of assessing the refugee claim: *Sepet* [2001] EWCA Civ 681. The Court of Appeal's conclusion that no such right has been established was upheld by the House of Lords: *Sepet* [2003] 3 All ER 304.

determine the content of the applicable rule of custom',[97] and determining that content 'may be the subject of contention and disagreement'.[98] As is the case with respect to *jus cogens* norms, only a limited number of human rights are clearly recognized to be protected by custom, thus suggesting that 'there is substantial doubt whether custom really is an adequate means of identifying fundamental human rights for the purpose of interpreting the inclusion clause of the Refugee Convention'.[99] In light of these concerns, reference to treaty obligations, which are clearly articulated and subject to interpretation by supervisory bodies, has a far greater potential to provide interpretative assistance in the refugee context.[100]

Treaties

Notwithstanding the relevance of other sources, where refugee decision-makers have referred to other rules of international law in the interpretation of the Refugee Convention, they have

---

[97] Mansfield, 'The Interpretation of Treaties', p. 28. This is supported by the litigation in *Sepet*, in which the court was asked 'to consider a mass of material illustrating the movement of international opinion among those concerned with human rights and refugees' with respect to the question of the customary status of conscientious objection: [2003] 3 All ER 304 at para. 11 (Lord Bingham of Cornhill).

[98] Mansfield, 'The Interpretation of Treaties', p. 28. This has been acknowledged in the refugee context by the NZ RSAA, which has observed that 'customary law is of limited assistance primarily due to the difficulty in establishing the two essential elements, namely state practice and *opinio juris*': *Refugee Appeal No. 74665/03*, RSAA, 7 July 2004, para. 63.

[99] *Refugee Appeal No. 74665/03*, RSAA, 7 July 2004, para. 63. One of the difficulties with peremptory norms is that the question of what norms and principles are properly characterized as 'peremptory' is vexed and difficult. There is considerable controversy as to the exact content of this category. Indeed, the difficult task of achieving the 'authoritative elaboration' of *jus cogens* norms for the purpose of ensuring 'objectivity, transparency and predictability' is currently a topic before the ILC as part of its study on 'Fragmentation in International Law': see ILC, *Report of the International Law Commission: Fifty-Fifth Session*, UN Doc. A/CN.4/537 (2004), at para. 237(51) which indicates the complexity and scope of the controversy. For the latest consideration of this question in the context of the ILC study, see Koskenniemi, 'Fragmentation of International Law', pp. 158–60.

[100] It should also be noted that 'general principles of law recognized by civilized nations' (arts. 38(1)(b) and (c) of the *Statute of the International Court of Justice*) is a possible source of assistance in the interpretation of a treaty: see, for example, *Golder* (1975) Eur Court HR (ser A); (1979) 1 EHRR 524; Gabrielle Marceau, 'WTO Dispute Settlement and Human Rights' (2002) 13 *European Journal of International Law* 753 at 780. However, they are not likely to be very pertinent to the concepts to be adjudicated in the refugee context.

overwhelmingly referred to other international human rights treaties. However, little attention has been directed to which kinds of treaties should be referred to, and, in particular, when can it be said that the other treaty is 'applicable in the relations between the parties'?

At one extreme is the requirement that in order for a second treaty to be taken into account it must have attained perfect co-extensive membership with the treaty to be interpreted.[101] However, if identical membership were required, the consequence would be that no additional treaty could be considered relevant to an interpretation of the Refugee Convention (or indeed any other Convention) because few, if any, treaties have co-extensive membership.[102] As an ILC Report concludes, this approach would thus have 'the ironic effect that the more membership of a particular multilateral treaty ... expanded, the more those treaties would be cut off from the rest of international law'.[103]

An alternative approach has been to argue that 'between the parties' refers to the parties to the dispute, so that, in interpreting a multilateral convention, a tribunal may seek guidance from those treaties to which the states involved in the extant dispute are also parties.[104] However, this approach is difficult to justify. The VCLT defines 'party' as 'a State which has consented to be bound by the treaty and for which the treaty is in force',[105] and there is little justification for adopting a different meaning of 'party' merely for the purposes of art. 31(3)(c). In addition, it is clear that the VCLT is designed to provide principles of interpretation to guide the application and implementation of treaties on a day-to-day basis,

---

[101] This is the approach taken in a recent decision of the WTO Panel in *EC-Measures Affecting the Approval and Marketing of Biotech Products* (29 September 2006) WT/DS291-293, pp. 332–34.

[102] This point is also made by Marceau, who argues that such an approach is problematic because few international agreements, if any, will have identical membership: Marceau, 'A Call for Coherence', p. 124. For example, even in the case of the two key international covenants that comprise (together with the UDHR) the International Bill of Rights, the membership is not coextensive with that of the Refugee Convention: of the 140 parties to both the 1951 Refugee Convention and 1967 Protocol, 12 have not ratified the ICCPR and 15 have not ratified the ICESCR: see further discussion of this point below at note 141.

[103] Koskenniemi, 'Fragmentation of International Law', p. 200. Marceau also makes this point: Marceau, 'WTO Dispute Settlement and Human Rights', p. 781.

[104] See Marceau, 'A Call for Coherence', p. 125, referring to the argument made by David Palmeter and Petros Mavroidis, 'The WTO Legal System: Sources of Law' (1998) 93(3) *American Journal of International Law* 398. See also Koskenniemi, 'Fragmentation of International Law', p. 200.

[105] VCLT, art. 2.

not solely in the context of a formal dispute. Moreover, such an approach would result in different interpretations of the relevant treaty provisions depending on which parties are 'disputing', a particular problem in the context of human rights treaties (including the Refugee Convention) which are intended to provide universal definitions of rights.[106] Most importantly, this approach encounters difficulties in application to the context of refugee and other human rights conventions, since the 'parties' in 'dispute' are, in the main, not states but rather a state and an individual who is asserting a right vis-à-vis the state.[107]

A third approach is that account must be taken of rules (including other treaties) that reflect the 'common intention' of the parties to the treaty under consideration.[108] This is said to require the interpreter to ascertain whether another treaty 'can be said to be at least implicitly accepted or tolerated ... in the sense that it can reasonably be considered to express the common intentions or understanding of all members as to the meaning of the ... term concerned'.[109] This approach has been adopted in some decisions of international adjudicatory bodies and is advocated by the ILC.[110] Although not framed in terms of art. 31(3)(c), it is at least an implicit justification for Hathaway's initial reference to the International Bill of Rights as an instructive tool for ascertaining the meaning of 'being persecuted'. He argues that it is necessary that the other treaty has attained acceptance by a super-majority of parties to the treaty to be interpreted.[111] Indeed, it could be argued that where

---

[106] This is also recognized by Mansfield, who asserts that 'it would run the risk of potentially inconsistent interpretation decisions dependent upon the happenstance of the particular treaty partners in dispute': Mansfield, 'The Interpretation of Treaties', p. 29 and in the most recent ILC report: see Koskenniemi, 'Fragmentation of International Law', p. 200.

[107] Whilst one signatory state may challenge the action of another in the ICJ pursuant to art. 38 of the Refugee Convention, this has never been invoked by a State party. Therefore interpretation is usually undertaken in the context of an individual challenging the action of a State party.

[108] Joost Pauwelyn, 'The Role of Public International Law in the WTO: How Far Can We Go?' (2001) 95 *American Journal of International Law* 535 at 578.

[109] *Ibid.*, p. 579.

[110] Koskenniemi, 'Fragmentation of International Law', p. 201, citing decisions of the Appellate Body of the WTO at note 669. It should be noted that the ILC Study Group appears to suggest that this approach be used in conjunction with the second outlined above: see at 200–1.

[111] James C. Hathaway, 'The Relationship between Human Rights and Refugee Law: What Refugee Judges Can Contribute', in *The Realities of Refugee Determination on the Eve of a New Millennium: The Role of the Judiciary* (Haarlem, The Netherlands: International Association of Refugee Law Judges, 1999), p. 85.

a treaty that sets out 'how states themselves have defined unacceptable infringements of human dignity' has been ratified by a super-majority of parties to the Refugee Convention,[112] it can 'reasonably be considered to express the common intentions or understanding' as to the meaning of the term 'being persecuted'.[113] Whether or not all (or a majority) of states comply with these obligations is not relevant. As Lord Hoffmann of the British House of Lords has observed, 'even if many state parties in practice disregard them', 'the instruments show recognition that such rights ought to exist'.[114]

In considering the issue of which treaties should be taken into account it is also important to focus on the reference in art. 31(3)(c) to any *relevant* rules of international law applicable between the parties.[115] Not every treaty which has attained the support of a super-majority of state parties to the Refugee Convention will be *relevant* to its interpretation. Rather, there is a need for caution in accepting without reservation the notion that, where a term has been defined in one area of international law, that definition can necessarily provide assistance to an interpretation in another area.[116] Since different aims and policy objectives inform different areas of the law, there is a danger in transplanting approaches developed in an area with one set of objectives into a field that has quite different policy aims.[117] In particular, these concerns should be kept in

---

[112] *Ibid.*, p. 85.
[113] Lauterpacht and Bethlehem also implicitly rely on art. 31(3)(c) in arguing that principles derived from human rights law – although not of themselves 'determinative of the interpretation of ... the 1951 Convention' – are of 'considerable importance [because] the law on human rights which has emerged since the conclusion of the 1951 Convention is an essential part of the framework of the legal system that must, by reference to the ICJ's observations in the Namibia case, be taken into account for the purposes of interpretation': Sir Elihu Lauterpacht and Daniel Bethlehem, 'The Scope and Content of the Principle of Non-Refoulement', in Feller, Türk and Nicholson, *Refugee Protection in International Law*, p. 113.
[114] *Sepet* [2003] 3 All ER 304 at para. 41. His Lordship goes on to note that '[t]he delinquent states do not normally deny this; they usually pretend they comply'.
[115] Koskenniemi, 'Fragmentation of International Law', p. 181.
[116] The background report of the ILC on art. 31(3)(c) states: '[a]s the International Tribunal for the Law of the Sea observed in another decision in the *Max Plant* litigation, considerations of context and object may well lead to the same term having a different meaning and application in different treaties': Mansfield, 'The Interpretation of Treaties', p. 26.
[117] This has long been recognized in domestic adjudication, where courts have warned against the use of 'inapplicable analogies': see *IW* v. *City of Perth* (1996) 191 CLR 1 at 66 (Kirby J); Michelle Foster, 'Causation in Context: Interpreting the Nexus Clause in the Refugee Convention' (2002) 23(2) *Michigan Journal of International Law* 265 at 291–6.

mind when engaging in a comparison between the notion of 'being persecuted' in the refugee field and the concept of 'persecution' in the field of international criminal law,[118] given that the object of the criminal justice system is to provide a fair trial for those accused of criminal offences in order to *ascertain responsibility* and *attribute guilt* for certain offences. By contrast, the refugee regime is not at all concerned with adjudicating guilt or allocating blame, but rather with providing international protection for those who satisfy the definition. As the UNHCR has observed, '[t]he legal regime of refugee protection ... is centred on the grant of a humanitarian benefit, not on the punishment of persecutors'.[119] Thus, requirements such as the necessity to prove intent in the criminal field may not be transferable to the refugee field.

By contrast, the focus on relevance supports the notion that international human rights standards are appropriate reference tools for ascertaining the meaning of key terms in a treaty with a human rights object and purpose, such as the Refugee Convention.[120] For example, in terms of the 'being persecuted' inquiry, Hathaway has explained that it makes sense to consider '*how states themselves* have defined unacceptable infringements of human dignity if we want to know which harms they

---

[118] The Rome Statute of the International Criminal Court defines 'persecution' as 'the intentional and severe deprivation of fundamental rights contrary to international law by reason of the identity of the group or collectivity': Rome, 17 July 1998, in force 1 July 2002, 2187 UNTS 90; (1998) 37 ILM 999, art. 7(1)(g).

[119] Brief of Amicus Curiae of the Office of the UNHCR in Support of Respondent in *Immigration and Naturalization Service v. Jairo Jonathan Elias-Zacarias* 502 US 478 (1992). See also Ulrike Davy, 'Refugees from Bosnia and Herzegovina: Are They Genuine?' (1995) 18 *Suffolk Transnational Law Review* 53 at 107; Foster, 'Causation in Context', p. 294 and Volker Türk and Frances Nicholson, 'Refugee Protection in International Law: An Overall Perspective', in Feller, Türk and Nicholson, *Refugee Protection in International Law*, p. 38.

[120] The practice of international adjudicatory bodies supports this argument, since international human rights tribunals and committees are displaying a greater willingness to consider the interpretations adopted by other treaty bodies in relation to similar concepts, in recognition of the similar purposes of the key international human rights treaties and also perhaps in recognition of the unsatisfactory situation that could result if similar concepts were accorded different meanings by different treaty bodies. Indeed, there is evidence that many of the treaty monitoring bodies refer to the standards and interpretation of such standards set out in other treaties when developing their own general comments: see Eric Tistounet, 'The Problem of Overlapping among Different Treaty Bodies', in Philip Alston and James Crawford (eds.), *The Future of UN Human Rights Treaty Monitoring* (Cambridge: Cambridge University Press, 2000), p. 395. See also Rosalyn Higgins, 'The United Nations: Still a Force for Peace' (1989) 52 *The Modern Law Review* 1 at 8; Bruno Simma, 'International Human Rights and General International Law: A Comparative Analysis' in *Collected Courses of the Academy of European Law* (Oxford: Oxford University Press, 1993), vol. IV, book II, pp. 193–5.

are truly committed to defining as impermissible'.[121] As he has explained, '[h]uman rights law is precisely the means by which states have undertaken that task'.[122]

Having determined that those human rights treaties which have attained widespread membership are relevant 'rules of international law' to which refugee decision-makers should have regard, we must now turn to consider which treaties should be relied upon in practice. One pressing issue is whether reference may be made to evolving developments, or whether decision-makers are restricted to those human rights standards in existence at the adoption of the Refugee Convention.

The debate concerning the appropriateness of an evolutionary approach to treaty interpretation is not a new phenomenon.[123] Nor is the practice limited to refugee law; it is well entrenched in the jurisprudence of human rights adjudicatory bodies. While it is most conspicuous in that of the European Court of Human Rights ('ECHR'),[124] other supervisory bodies have adopted the theory that relevant instruments must be examined from a contemporary perspective, rather

---

[121] Hathaway, 'The Relationship between Human Rights and Refugee Law', p. 86. A common approach to the 'being persecuted' question is to emphasize that it is action or conduct which 'constitutes an interference with the basic human rights or dignity of that person or the persons in the group': *Minister for Immigration and Multicultural Affairs* v. *Ibrahim* (2000) 204 CLR 1 at 21 (McHugh J) ('*Ibrahim*'); and *Refugee Appeal No. 1312/93 Re GJ*, RSAA, 30 August 1995, at 32. The emphasis on an infringement of human dignity points to the logic of reference to human rights standards, since human dignity is arguably the bedrock principle of human rights instruments: see Anker, *Law of Asylum in the United States*, p. 173. For example, the first sentence in the Preamble to the UDHR recognizes the 'inherent dignity' and 'the equal and inalienable rights of all members of the human family'.

[122] Hathaway, 'The Relationship between Human Rights and Refugee Law', p. 85.

[123] Ress, 'The Interpretation of the Charter', p. 24. In 1971, the ICJ explained that where concepts embodied in a treaty are 'by definition, evolutionary', then '[i]nterpretation cannot remain unaffected by the subsequent development of law ... Moreover, an international instrument has to be interpreted and applied within the framework of the entire legal system prevailing at the time of the interpretation, *Namibia (Legal Consequences) Advisory Opinion* (1971) ICJ Rep 31 ('*Namibia Case*').

[124] Although the evolutionary doctrine initially provoked dissent (see Sir Gerald Fitzmaurice's dissent in *Golder* (1975) Eur Court HR (ser A); (1979) 1 EHRR 524 at paras. 37–9), it is now well established that the ECHR is 'a living instrument' to be interpreted 'in light of present day conditions': *Bankovic and Others* v. *Belgium and 16 Other Contracting States* (2001) XII Eur Court HR 435 at para. 64. Indeed, it is the practice of the ECHR that has inspired some English courts to implement the dynamic approach in the refugee context: see, for example, *Adan, Subaskaran and Aitseguer* [1999] 4 All ER 774, [1999] 3 WLR 1274, [1999] Imm AR 521 at 530.

than by reference only to 'the normative value and significance which th[e] [relevant] instrument was believed to have had [at formation]'.[125] Moreover, it is increasingly being applied to other areas of international law, including international trade law.[126]

The issue of inter-temporality was explicitly considered by the drafters of the VCLT in the context of art. 31(3)(c). As the ILC commentary on the final draft articles (preceding the VCLT) reveals, the text of art. 31(3)(c) originally stated that a treaty was to be interpreted 'in the light of the general rules of international law *in force at the time of its conclusion*'.[127] The commentary explains that the italicized phrase was a reflection of the general principle of inter-temporality. However, when the provision

---

[125] *Inter-American Court of Human Rights: Advisory Opinion on the Interpretation of the American Declaration of Rights and Duties of Man within the Framework of Article 64 of the American Convention on Human Rights* (1990) 29 ILM 379, 14 July 1989, at 387. The HRC is similarly said to invoke an evolutionary or dynamic approach to interpretation, although it has not been as explicit in describing its interpretative method: see Sarah Joseph, Jenny Schultz and Melissa Castan, *The International Covenant on Civil and Political Rights: Cases, Materials, and Commentary* (Oxford: Oxford University Press, 2000), p. 19, where the authors describe the fact that the Committee has been willing to diverge from previous interpretations and conclude that this is 'a sign that the ICCPR is a living instrument capable of dynamic development'. See also David Harris, 'The ICCPR and the UK: An Introduction', in David Harris and Sarah Joseph (eds.), *The International Covenant on Civil and Political Rights and United Kingdom Law* (Oxford: Clarendon Press, 1995). An example is the UNHRC's *General Comment No. 28: Equality of Rights between Men and Women*, UN Doc. CCPR/C/21/Rev.1/Add.10 (2000) ('*General Comment No. 28*'), which is a comprehensive and far-reaching exposition of state obligations in relation to equality. *General Comment No. 28* begins by noting that the Committee has decided to update its general comment on art. 3 and to replace general comment 4 'in the light of the experience it has gathered in its activities over the last 20 years': para. 1. See also Elizabeth Evatt, 'The Impact of International Human Rights on Domestic Law', in Grant Huscroft and Paul Rishworth (eds.), *Litigating Rights: Perspectives from Domestic and International Law* (Oxford: Hart Publishing, 2002), p. 297; Manfred Nowak, *Introduction to the International Human Rights Regime* (Leiden: Martinus Nijhoff Publishers, 2003), p. 66.

[126] For example, in the *Shrimp Case*, the WTO Appellate Body was presented with the question of the meaning of the phrase 'exhaustible natural resources' in art. XX(g) of the *General Agreement on Tariffs and Trade*, Geneva, 30 October 1947, in force 1 January 1948, 55 UNTS 187. Noting that the words comprising this phrase 'were actually crafted more than 50 years ago', the AB emphasized the need for an interpreter to read them '*in the light of contemporary concerns of the community of nations about the protection and conservation of the environment*': *Shrimp Case*, at para. 129 (emphasis added). A similar approach to 'other treaties' has also been adopted in recent decisions of the ICJ. For example, the ICJ employed this technique in the *Case Concerning the Gabcikovo-Nagymaros Project (Hungary/Slovakia)* [1997] ICJ Rep 7, at 68–9.

[127] Sir Arthur Wattts, *The International Law Commission, 1949–1998* (Oxford: Oxford University Press, 1999), vol. II, p. 690 (emphasis in original).

was discussed, 'some members suggested that it failed to deal with the problem of the effect of an evolution of the law on the interpretation of legal terms in a treaty and was therefore inadequate'.[128] On reflection, the Commission decided to remove the italicized phrase since it considered that

> the relevance of rules of international law for the interpretation of treaties in any given case was *dependent on the intentions of the parties*, and that to attempt to formulate a rule covering comprehensively the temporal element would present difficulties. It further considered that correct application of the temporal element would normally be indicated by interpretation of the term in good faith.[129]

This suggests that determining whether an evolutionary approach to interpretation is appropriate in any given context depends on the *nature* of the treaty in question. The key is whether the treaty *evinces an intention* to allow for an evolutionary approach; in the words of the International Court of Justice ('ICJ') whether relevant terms are 'by definition, evolutionary'.[130] If so, the parties are taken to have consented to an evolutionary approach to the interpretation of their obligations from the beginning of the treaty's operation.[131] However, as the ILC has recently explained, in order to reach this conclusion, the interpreter must find 'concrete evidence' of the parties' intentions 'in the terms themselves; the context; the object and purpose of the treaty; and, where necessary, the *travaux*'.[132]

In terms of the text of a treaty the ICJ has explained that, where it is established that an expression or phrase was used in an international instrument as a generic term, 'the presumption necessarily arises that its meaning was intended to follow the evolution of the law and to

---

[128] *Ibid.*, p. 690. See also Shabtai Rosenne, *Developments in the Law of Treaties, 1945–1986* (Cambridge: Cambridge University Press, 1989), pp. 76–9.
[129] Watts, *The International Law Commission*, p. 690 (emphasis added).
[130] *Namibia Case* (1971) ICJ Rep 31.
[131] In *Namibia Case*, the Court considered itself 'bound to take into account the fact that the concepts embodied in art. 22 of the Covenant – "the strenuous conditions of the modern world" and "the well-being and development" of the peoples concerned – were not static, but were by definition evolutionary, as also, was the concept of the "sacred trust". *The parties to the Covenant must consequently be deemed to have accepted them as such*': (1971) ICJ Rep 31 at paras. 31–2 (emphasis added).
[132] ILC, *Report of the International Law Commission: Fifty-Seventh Session*, UN Doc. A/60/10 (2005), p. 219. See also Koskenniemi, 'Fragmentation of International Law', pp. 203–4.

correspond with the meaning attached to the expression by the law in force at any given time'.[133]

This approach invokes an implied or presumed intention, based on the text of the treaty under examination.[134] In this vein, interpreters of the Refugee Convention have noted that 'the fact that the Convention does not legally define persecution is a strong indication that, on the basis of the experience of the past, the drafters intended that all future types of persecution should be encompassed by the term'.[135]

A more specific justification is found in the history of the Refugee Convention itself and in particular in the fact that, following the adoption of the 1967 Protocol, which removed the geographic and temporal limitations contained in the original 1951 definition, it is clear that the Refugee Convention is 'intended to have application to a variety of countries and situations and for the indefinite future'.[136]

Another method of discerning whether a concept is 'by definition evolutionary' is by reference to the object and purpose of the treaty. For example, it is not difficult to imagine that the object and purpose of a human rights treaty could be undermined by a static interpretation that confined the meaning of key terms to the understanding that prevailed at the time of its formulation. As Simma notes, '[w]ere a human rights convention to be interpreted statically, it would soon prove to be an

---

[133] *Aegean Sea Continental Shelf Case (Greece v. Turkey)* 1978 ICJ Rep 3 at 33. Simma argues that '[w]hen a treaty lays down the basic rules of state behaviour and is meant to remain in force for a long time then an evolutionary interpretation is surely more appropriate than in the case of an agreement of short duration or providing for mechanisms facilitating adjustment to changed conditions': Bruno Simma, 'Consent: Strains in the Treaty System', in R. St. J. MacDonald and Douglas M. Johnston (eds.), *The Structure and Process of International Law: Essays in Legal Philosophy, Doctrine and Theory* (The Hague: Martinus Nijhoff Publishers, 1983), p. 496.

[134] See also Francis G. Jacobs and Robin C. A. White, *The European Convention on Human Rights*, second edition (Oxford: Clarendon Press, 1996), p. 32; Rosenne, *Developments in the Law of Treaties*, p. 77.

[135] UNHCR, 'Interpreting Article 1', p. 5. In *Adan* [1997] 2 All ER 723; [1997] 1 WLR 1107 (Court of Appeal), Laws LJ stated that '[i]t is clear that the signatory states intended that the Convention should afford continuing protection for refugees in the changing circumstances of the present and future world. In our view the Convention has to be regarded as a living instrument': at 1121. In *Sepet*, the House of Lords endorsed these views: [2003] 3 All ER 304. See also Türk and Nicholson, 'Refugee Protection in International Law', p. 39.

[136] *Applicant A* (1996) 190 CLR 225 at 292 (Kirby J). See also *Hoxha* [2005] 4 All ER 580 at para. 6 (Lord Hope of Craighead); *Chen Shi Hai* (2000) 201 CLR 293 at 312 (Kirby J); *Butler v. AG* (1999) NZAR 205 at 217.

impediment to the achievement of its own aims'.[137] It may be that this is an area in which the different nature of human rights treaties, vis-à-vis other types of bilateral and multilateral treaties, takes on particular significance, in the sense that it may be argued that all human rights treaties are by nature dynamic.[138]

In this manner domestic courts have emphasized the vital need for an evolutionary approach to the Refugee Convention. As a Justice of the English Court of Appeal has noted:

> Unless it is seen as a living thing, adopted by civilised countries for a humanitarian end which is constant in motive but mutable in form, the Convention will eventually become an anachronism.[139]

Accordingly, refugee status adjudication should properly take into account evolving developments in human rights law. Given the vast array of modern international treaties dealing with human rights issues, it is important to delineate clearly those which are appropriately referred to in refugee adjudication. Interestingly, state practice in the refugee context reveals not only that decision-makers take into account contemporary developments in human rights law, but also that they do not consider only those treaties that have been ratified by all or even a

---

[137] Bruno Simma, 'Consent: Strains in the Treaty System', p. 497.

[138] As a former judge of the ECHR has argued, '[t]he subject of human rights is not static. It is essentially dynamic in nature': Ganshof van der Meersch quoted in Andrew Drzemczewski, 'The Sui Generis Nature of the European Convention on Human Rights' (1980) 29 *International and Comparative Law Quarterly* 60 at 70.

[139] *Shah* [1998] 4 All ER 30, [1998] 1 WLR 74, [1997] Imm AR 584 at 152. This was approved in *Sepet* [2003] 3 All ER 304 at para. [6]. See also *R on the Application of Altin Vallaj v. A Special Adjudicator* [2001] INLR 455 at para. 25; *Suresh v. Canada (Minister of Citizenship and Immigration)* 2002 SCCDJ 8052 at para. 87; *Hoxha* [2005] 4 All ER 580 at para. 7 (Lord Hope of Craighead). The Executive Committee of the UNHCR has taken a similar approach: see UNHCR Executive Committee, *Note on International Protection* (1990) <http://www.unhcr.org/cgi-bin/texis/vtx/excom/opendoc.htm?tbl=EXCOM&id=3ae68c6114> at 31 May 2006. In its most recent exposition, ExCom recognized that 'refugee law is a dynamic body of law based on the obligations of State Parties to the 1951 Convention and its 1967 Protocol and, where applicable, on regional refugee protection instruments, and which is informed by the object and purpose of these instruments and by developments in related areas of international law, such as human rights and international humanitarian law bearing directly on refugee protection': *Conclusion on the Provision of International Protection Including Through Complementary Forms of Protection* (2005), para. (c) <http://www.unhcr.org/cgi-bin/texis/vtx/excom/opendoc.htm?tbl=EXCOM&id=43576e292> at 31 May 2006.

majority of the parties to the Refugee Convention to be relevant.[140] In practice, however, reference is most often made to the UDHR, ICCPR and ICESCR, a phenomenon which can be justified given the widespread membership of the ICCPR and the ICESCR, and the significant overlap between membership of those treaties and the Refugee Convention.[141]

Although he initially advocated reliance on the ICCPR and ICESCR alone, Hathaway has more recently acknowledged that similarly widely accepted treaties, such as the Convention on the Elimination of All Forms of Discrimination Against Women ('CEDAW'),[142] the Convention on the Rights of the Child ('CRC')[143] and the Convention on the Elimination of All Forms of Racial Discrimination ('CERD'),[144] may also provide insight into the question whether certain behaviour constitutes persecution.[145] Given that they each enjoy widespread support by an overwhelming majority of

---

[140] For example, the UK Gender Guidelines refer to the Convention on the Suppression of the Traffic in Persons and of the Exploitation of the Prostitution of Others, a treaty which has attracted 14 signatories and 74 parties, with the UK itself neither party nor signatory: p. 58. In addition, the Guidelines refer to the Supplementary Convention on the Abolition of Slavery, a treaty with 119 parties: p. 58. Both the UK and Australian Gender Guidelines refer to the Convention on Consent to Marriage, Minimum Age for Marriage and Registration of Marriages, a treaty with only 49 parties: p. 58 and p. 4 respectively. In addition, the Canadian Gender Guidelines reference the Convention on the Political Rights of Women, which has 115 parties: see United Nations International Research and Training Institute for the Advancement of Women, *International Agreements* (2006) <http://www.un-instraw.org/en/index.php?option=content&task=blogcategory&id=178&Itemid=239> at 31 May 2006. Both the Canadian and Australian Gender guidelines refer to the Convention on the Nationality of Married Women, a treaty with only 70 parties. See Australian Gender Guidelines; Immigration and Review Board Canada, *Women Refugee Claimants Fearing Gender-Related Persecution: Guidelines Issued by the Chairperson Pursuant to Section 65(3) of the* Immigration Act (1996) <http://www.cisr-irb.gc.ca/en/about/guidelines/women_e.htm> at 31 May 2006 ('Canadian Gender Guidelines').

[141] As of 31 May 2006, the ICCPR had 155 parties: <http://www.ohchr.org/english/countries/ratification/4.htm>. There were 140 State parties to both the 1951 Refugee Convention and 1967 Protocol: <http://www.unhcr.ch/cgi-bin/texis/vtx/protect/opendoc.pdf?tbl=PROTECTION&id=3b73b0d63>. Of the 140 states, only 12 had not also acceded to the ICCPR, and of those 12, four had at least signed the ICCPR (China, Guinea-Bissau, Kazakhstan and São Tomé and Principe). There were 152 State parties to the ICESCR: <http://www.ohchr.org/english/countries/ratification/3.htm>. Of the 140 State parties to both the 1951 Refugee Convention and 1967 Protocol, only 15 had not also acceded to the ICESCR, and of those 15, five had at least signed the ICESCR (Belize, Kazakhstan, São Tomé and Principe, South Africa and the USA).

[142] New York, 18 December 1979, in force 3 September 1981, 1249 UNTS 13.

[143] New York, 20 November 1989, in force 2 September 1990, 1577 UNTS 3.

[144] New York, 7 March 1966, in force 4 January 1969, 660 UNTS 195.

[145] Hathaway, 'The Relationship between Human Rights and Refugee Law', p. 87.

state parties to the Refugee Convention,[146] they can properly be said to reflect the 'common intentions' of the parties with respect to fundamental rights. This is important because, while it may be true that many cases that have relied explicitly on the CEDAW and other specific conventions could, in retrospect, have been justified by reference to the 'mainstream' human rights treaties,[147] it remains the fact that it is the advent of specific human rights conventions that has brought the particular needs of women and children to the fore and assisted decision-makers in understanding the ways in which women's and children's experiences of 'torture' and 'degrading treatment', while different from that experienced by men, are nonetheless incidences of persecution. Indeed, it is reliance on the more specific conventions, such as the CEDAW and the CRC, which has been instrumental in ensuring recognition of refugee status in cases involving a wide range of issues including female genital mutilation, reproductive rights and sexual abuse.[148]

There is no question that the specific conventions do make significant contributions to a more complex understanding of equality, which go considerably beyond the IBR. For example, the CEDAW contributes to a more complex understanding of the problems inherent in the traditional distinction between private and public harm, by focusing explicitly on the obligations of the state to eradicate private harm inflicted by non-state actors, as well as merely preventing state

---

[146] As at 31 May 2006, the CRC had 192 State parties: <http://www.ohchr.org/english/countries/ratification/11.htm>. Of the 140 State parties to both the 1951 Refugee Convention and 1967 Protocol, only two parties have not ratified the CRC: Somalia and the USA (although both parties have at least signed the CRC). There were 182 State parties to the CEDAW: <http://www.un.org/womenwatch/daw/cedaw/states.htm>. Of the 140 State parties to both the 1951 Refugee Convention and 1967 Protocol, only five were not also parties to the CEDAW (Holy See, Iran, Somalia, Sudan and the USA). However, the USA had at least signed the CEDAW. Finally, the CERD had 170 State parties: <http://www.ohchr.org/english/countries/ratification/2.htm>. Of the 140 State parties to both the 1951 Refugee Convention and 1967 Protocol, only eight had not also signed the CERD, although Guinea-Bissau and São Tomé and Principe had at least signed the CERD.
[147] According to Hathaway, '[n]o specialised conventions, declarations, or other standards are required to justify the recognition of the harms [specific to women] as sufficiently serious to fall within the scope of conduct adjudged persecutory': Hathaway, 'The Relationship between Human Rights and Refugee Law', p. 89. This argument is strengthened now that the HRC has issued such a progressive interpretation of the ICCPR in its *General Comment No. 28*, which is a comprehensive and far-reaching exposition of state obligations in relation to equality.
[148] See generally, Anker, 'Boundaries in the Field of Human Rights'.

discrimination.[149] This is particularly important in the refugee context where Coker et al. point out that 'the abuse of women often continues not to seem an international matter because the abusers of women are not direct representatives of the state'.[150]

In addition, reference to the more specific treaties is vital in responding to the tendency of courts, discussed above, to invoke cultural relativity arguments in respect of gender-based claims. In this regard, the specific conventions provide direct and relevant guidance in resolving these issues. For example, art. 5(a) of the CEDAW obliges state parties to take 'all appropriate measures to modify the social and cultural patterns of conduct of men and women, with a view to achieving the elimination of prejudices and customary and all other practices which are based on the idea of the inferiority or superiority of either of the sexes or on stereotyped roles for men and women'.[151] Similarly, art. 24(3) of the CRC states that 'States parties shall take all effective and appropriate measures with a view to abolishing traditional practices prejudicial to the health of children'.

Further, reliance on the CEDAW highlights the integral relationship between economic and social rights and equality for women in a way that is not as readily apparent by reference to the IBR alone. For example, the Preamble to the CEDAW sets out the states parties' concerns that 'in situations of poverty women have the least access to food, health, education, training and opportunities for employment and other needs' and the text of the Convention emphasizes both socio-economic rights and civil and political rights as vital to the achievement of equality for women.[152] This is particularly relevant in discussing hierarchies of rights, an issue that will be considered in detail in the following chapters.

This analysis underlines the importance of going beyond the IBR to refer to other international human rights treaties which have attained the support of a super-majority of state parties to the Refugee Convention. However, in order to ensure the legitimacy of the human rights

---

[149] See, for example, the CEDAW art. 2 compared with ICCPR art. 2.
[150] Jane Coker, Heaven Crawley and Alison Stanley, 'A Gender Perspective on the Human Rights Paradigm' (paper presented at the IARLJ Human Rights Nexus Working Party, London, 12 May 1998), p. 3 (on file with author).
[151] This article was specifically referred to by Baroness Hale of Richmond in *Hoxha* [2005] 4 All ER 580 at para. 38.
[152] See, for example, arts. 10, 11, 12, 13 and 14 of the CEDAW.

approach, reliance should not be placed upon treaties that have not yet attained the requisite level of support.

This leads into the final issue to be determined with respect to the relevance of 'other treaties' in refugee status determination, that is, the extent to which it is legitimate for parties to the Refugee Convention to make reference to regional, as well as universal, standards in interpreting the Refugee Convention terms. There is no doubt that in states that are also members of the Council of Europe (and therefore parties to the European Convention), reference is sometimes made to the European Convention in assessing claims for refugee status.[153] This issue could also arise in the context of countries that are parties to other regional human rights instruments such as the American Convention on Human Rights[154] or the African [Banjul] Charter on Human and Peoples' Rights.[155]

In considering the legitimacy of this practice, it is arguably logical for a court to turn in the first instance to a regional instrument, particularly when, as is the case with respect to the European Convention, it is incorporated in many domestic legal systems and there is a well-established and comprehensive body of case law emanating from the regional court (in the case of the European Convention, as a result of the compulsory individual complaints procedure). Notwithstanding this, there are potential problems with such an approach, as is well encapsulated in the following question posed by an IARLJ

---

[153] For example, the UK Gender Guidelines specifically list the European Convention as an appropriate reference point in assessing refugee claims involving gender issues: p. 58. Further, Vanheule provides some specific case examples in which European courts have referred to the European Convention in assessing refugee claims: Vanheule, 'A Comparison of the Judicial Interpretations of the Notion of Refugee', p. 99. It is also important to note that in the recently enacted EU *Directive on Minimum Standards for the Qualification and Status of Third Country Nationals and Stateless Persons as Refugees or as Persons who Otherwise Need International Protection and the Content of the Protection Granted*, 29 April 2004, 2004/83/EC, Article 9(1)(a) provides that '[a]cts of persecution ... must be sufficiently serious by their nature or repetition as to constitute a severe violation of basic human rights, in particular the rights from which derogation cannot be made under Article 15(2) of the European Convention for the Protection of Fundamental Rights and Freedoms'.

[154] American Convention on Human Rights, San Jose, 22 November 1969, in force 18 July 1978, 1144 UNTS 123.

[155] African Charter on Human and Peoples' Rights, Banjul, The Gambia, 27 June 1981, in force 21 October 1986, (1982) 21 ILM 58. However, there is a regional refugee agreement in Africa which provides wider protection than the 1951 Convention — OAU Convention Governing the Specific Aspects of Refugee Problems in Africa, Addis Ababa, 10 September 1969, in force 20 June 1974, 1001 UNTS 14691. For a discussion of that Convention, see Hathaway, *Law of Refugee Status*, pp. 16–19.

working party: 'What implications does this have on the overall fairness and consistency of the international asylum system?'[156]

There are a number of reasons why consistency problems can arise in this context and caution should be exercised in making reference to regional instruments.[157] The first point to note is that the international covenants, particularly the ICCPR, may provide a more comprehensive range of rights than do regional instruments such as the European Convention.[158] In addition, Jacobs and White point out that the standards adopted for interpreting the European Convention 'may sometimes differ from those applicable to other international instruments'.[159] This is said to be because the interpretation of the European Convention may 'legitimately be based on a common tradition of constitutional law and a large measure of legal tradition common to the Member States of the Council of Europe'.[160] An example of a key difference in interpretation is the fact that, at the European level, the Court accords a 'margin of appreciation' to state parties, thus providing a measure of flexibility in the manner in which they comply with their European Convention obligations.[161] Such a notion has not thus far been explicitly adopted by the HRC in relation to the ICCPR,[162] and caution should be exercised in importing such a doctrine into refugee law. This is particularly relevant in cases involving 'moral' or cultural issues where there is a concrete

[156] IARLJ, 'The Application of Human Rights Standards to the 1951 Refugee Convention: The Definition of Persecution' (paper presented by the Human Rights Nexus Working Party, 24 April 2001) (on file with author).
[157] This has been observed by the NZ RSAA: 'However, the European and inter-American systems differ in many ways from each other and from that provided for in the international human rights instruments referred to. Caution must be exercised in applying the jurisprudence of these regional organisations outside their proper context': *Refugee Appeal Nos. 72558/01 and 72559/01*, RSAA, 19 November 2002, at para. 119; *Refugee Appeal No. 74665/03*, RSAA, 7 July 2004.
[158] For example, Higgins notes that the ICCPR has a larger list of rights that may not be derogated from, even in times of national emergency, than the European Convention, and contains some rights that are not found in the European Convention at all: Rosalyn Higgins, 'Ten Years on the UN Human Rights Committee: Some Thoughts upon Parting' (1996) *European Human Rights Law Review* 572 at 573. She cites minority rights, rights of aliens, rights relating to the family and the child as examples of the latter point. Moreover, some rights that appear in both covenants 'are articulated in considerably more detail in the [ICCPR]': at 574, citing the right to a fair trial as an example.
[159] Jacobs and White, *The European Convention on Human Rights*, p. 32.
[160] Ibid.   [161] Ibid.
[162] See Joseph, Schultz and Castan, *The International Covenant on Civil and Political Rights*, p. 17. See also Harris, 'The ICCPR and the UK: An Introduction', p. 13.

danger that reliance on the concept of a 'margin of appreciation' could result in a rejection of refugee claims based on the notion that the state has discretion in regulating such issues.[163] Such a doctrine has no place in refugee law, where the focus is on the rights and protection needs of applicants, rather than the right of the home state to regulate social mores.

In light of these reservations, there is a question as to whether there can be any room for reference to the jurisprudence of regional bodies. In providing an answer to this question, it is important that a distinction be made between standards and an interpretation of those standards. Where the standards set out in a regional agreement correspond with an international standard, the jurisprudence of a regional body may well be relevant to an interpretation of the universal instrument (keeping in mind the reservation regarding the margin of appreciation issue). This is particularly so in the case of the Inter-American Court of Human Rights which has specific jurisdiction to interpret international covenants to which member states are also party.[164] However, even apart from this exceptional jurisdiction, reference to the decisions of regional courts may be justified on the basis that the international courts and decision-making bodies themselves have displayed a willingness to consider the way in which the same or similar rights have been interpreted by other international and regional bodies in interpreting human rights provisions, especially in exploring the parameters of rights and their application to novel factual circumstances. This phenomenon of 'judicial conversations' across jurisdictions is well documented in the literature and is occurring at all levels of judicial decision-making – international, regional and domestic.[165] Indeed, a former member of the HRC has publicly conceded that the jurisprudence of the

---

[163] Such a rationale could well have underpinned the IAT's statement in *Jain* v. *Secretary of State for the Home Department* [2000] Imm AR 76 (Schiemann LJ). The Tribunal warned that 'to deny a country its right to adhere to mores, to cultural attitudes and to laws different from one's own and which make up its inherent being cannot be acceptable if the [Refugee] Convention is to have any truly international acceptability': at 78. The dangers of relying on this doctrine in the context of refugee claims by homosexual men and women is highlighted in Catherine Dauvergne and Jenni Millbank, 'Before the High Court: Applicants S396/2002 and S395/2002, A Gay Refugee Couple from Bangladesh' (2003) 25 *Sydney Law Review* 97 at 111.

[164] See Mary Caroline Parker, '"Other Treaties": The Inter-American Court of Human Rights Defines its Advisory Jurisdiction' (1982) 33 *American University Law Review* 211 at 227.

[165] See generally Helfer and Slaughter, 'Towards a Theory of Effective *Supra*national Adjudication'.

European Court is considered by the HRC, even if the relevant cases are not explicitly discussed in the HRC case law. Higgins explains that '[t]he jurisprudence of the Covenant and of the European Convention are mutually reinforcing'.[166] As she explains, the language and concept of human rights 'encourages very similar legal reasoning between those who sit on regional courts and those who sit on universal bodies'.[167] This is particularly important in light of the fact that human rights law is constantly evolving and it is clear that developments at both regional and international levels influence this evolution.

Thus, in many refugee cases, reference to the principles enunciated in universal treaties will prove sufficient. However, in a case involving the application of a universal human right, where the relevant adjudicatory body has not yet considered the application of the specific right to the factual circumstances of the case, refugee decision-makers may well obtain guidance from the way in which the issue has been dealt with at a regional level.

Soft law

In light of the approach taken above to the method of selection of 'other treaties' in interpreting an international treaty, one would assume that if only treaties which enjoy a super-majority of international support may properly inform the interpretation of a treaty, soft law may not be directly relied upon in interpreting a treaty. Accordingly, Hathaway emphasizes, after acknowledging that the bright line as to what constitutes an appropriate reference point is difficult to draw, that:

> At a minimum, though, it seems to me that a commitment to legal positivism requires, first, that we focus on legal standards – primarily treaties – not on so-called 'soft law', which simply doesn't yet bespeak a sufficient normative consensus. While we can logically resort to these evolving standards as a means to contextualize and elaborate the substantive content of genuine legal standards, they should not, in my view, be treated as authoritative in and of themselves.[168]

As this passage suggests, even those scholars who maintain the positivist view that soft law is not per se a source of international law, acknowledge that the distinction between 'hard' and 'soft' law is not as

---

[166] Higgins, 'Ten Years on the Human Rights Committee', p. 574.
[167] Ibid.   [168] Hathaway, 'The Relationship between Human Rights and Refugee Law', p. 86.

clinical as the terminology may suggest and concede that 'soft law' can have a role in assisting in treaty interpretation.

First, as Simma notes, soft law will always play a role in the supervision of performance of human rights treaties and thus is vital in providing authoritative guidance as to the correct interpretation and meaning of treaty obligations.[169] In the refugee context, art. 35 of the Refugee Convention requires states to co-operate with the office of the UNHCR in order to facilitate the exercise of its functions, in particular, 'its duty of supervising the application of the provisions of this Convention'. Various documents produced by the UNHCR have thus been accorded significance by states in interpreting the Refugee Convention. The 1979 Handbook has been frequently relied upon by courts,[170] and has been described as providing 'significant guidance' in construing the Convention.[171] In addition, guidelines produced by the UNHCR have been 'accorded considerable weight' by some courts,[172] as have ExCom resolutions.[173] Describing the latter source, the New Zealand RSAA has explained: 'the Conclusions represent collective international expertise in refugee matters including legal expertise'.[174] While it has been suggested that

---

[169] Simma, 'Consent: Strains in the Treaty System', p. 234. Boyle also argues that soft law instruments are used 'as mechanisms for authoritative interpretation ... of the terms of a treaty': Allan Boyle, 'Some Reflections on the Relationship of Treaties and Soft Law', in Vera Gowlland-Debbas (ed.), *Multilateral Treaty Making, The Current Status of Challenges to and Reforms Needed in the International Legislative Process* (The Hague; Boston: M. Nijhoff, 2000), p. 29.

[170] See for example, *Adan, Subaskaran and Aitseguer* [1999] 4 All ER 774, [1999] 3 WLR 1274, [1999] Imm AR 521 (Laws LJ and Sullivan J); *Robinson* [1998] QB 929, [1997] 4 All ER 210, [1997] 1 WLR 1162, [1997] Imm AR 568.

[171] *Cardoza-Fonseca* v. *INS*, 480 U.S. 421, 439 (1987).

[172] In *Adimi*, Simon Brown LJ said, in relation to the UNHCR's Guidelines with regard to the detention of asylum seekers, '[h]aving regard to Article 35(1) of the Convention, it seems to me that such Guidelines should be accorded considerable weight': *R* v. *Uxbridge Magistrates' Court and another, ex parte Adimi* [1999] Imm AR 560, [1999] 4 All ER 520 at 530. In *Mohammed* v. *Gonzales* 400 F 3d 785 (9th Cir. 2005), the US Court of Appeals for the 9th Circuit noted that the UNHCR, Guidelines on International Protection: Membership of a Particular Social Group (HCR/GIP/02/02, 7 May 2002) provide 'significant guidance for issues of refugee law': at 798.

[173] For example, Brandl considers the impact of ExCom conclusions and resolutions on state practice: Ulrike Brandl, 'Soft Law as a Source of International and European Refugee Law', in Carlier and Vanheule (eds.), *Europe and Refugees*, pp. 214–15. For a general consideration of the history, use and purpose of ExCom conclusions as well as their status in international law, see Jerzy Sztucki, 'The Conclusions on the International Protection of Refugees Adopted by the Executive Committee of the UNHCR Programme' (1989) 1(3) *International Journal of Refugee Law* 285.

[174] *Re R, Refugee Appeal No. 59/91*, RSAA, 19 May 1992, at 20.

the Handbook and the UNHCR's Executive Committee Resolutions 'are to be taken into account as evidence of "subsequent agreement between the parties" on the meaning of the treaty', pursuant to art. 31(3)(a) of the VCLT,[175] it is questionable whether documents produced by the UNHCR alone (in the case of the Handbook)[176] or a limited number of state parties (in the case of the ExCom Conclusions)[177] could be said to constitute agreement between the parties for the purpose of art. 31(3)(a).[178] It is also unlikely that such documents could be considered 'state practice' for the purposes of art. 31(3)(b).[179] However, this does not detract from their status as a persuasive interpretative guide to the Convention, particularly given the propensity for reliance on such documents to aid in producing consistent interpretation between state parties, which, as explained above, assists in upholding the human rights objects of the Convention.

The second important way in which soft law instruments may be relevant to treaty interpretation is that they may explicate or amplify existing obligations.[180] To provide a relevant example in the refugee context, the CEDAW's General Recommendation Number 19 on Violence Against Women, together with the *Declaration on the Elimination of Violence Against Women*,[181] amplify the obligation to eliminate discrimination against women which states have undertaken in a number of human

---

[175] Hathaway, *The Rights of Refugees under International Law*, p. 54.

[176] Various guidelines and policy statements produced by UNHCR are not always discussed with State parties prior to formulation: Brandl, 'Soft Law as a Source of International and European Refugee Law', p. 215.

[177] Not all parties to the Convention participate in formulating Executive Committee conclusions. ExCom is composed of only 70 countries. For a full list of member countries see UNHCR, *Executive Committee of the High Commissioner's Programme*, UN Doc. A/AC.96/1020/Rev.1 (2005).

[178] Given that a subsequent agreement as to interpretation can effectively amount to a modification or even amendment of the treaty terms, it is assumed that all of the parties would be required to agree: see Aust, *Modern Treaty Law and Practice*, pp. 191–3. This also explains why the EU Joint Position and now EU Directive on a Common Asylum Policy is not a subsequent agreement, given that it applies to a limited number of State parties.

[179] The UK Court of Appeal has held that the Handbook constitutes state practice for these purposes: see *Adan, Subaskaran and Aitseguer* [1999] 4 All ER 774, [1999] 3 WLR 1274 at 1296F (appeal dismissed by House of Lords, with no comment on this point). However, it is not clear how 'state practice' is manifested in the context of a human rights treaty: Simma, 'Consent: Strains in the Treaty System', pp. 187–8. In any case, it is not clear that reliance on these documents is sufficiently 'concordant, common and consistent', 'sufficient to establish a discernable pattern implying the agreement of the parties regarding its interpretation': Sir Ian Sinclair, *The Vienna Convention on the Law of Treaties*, second edition (Manchester: Manchester University Press, 1984), p. 137.

[180] Boyle, 'Some Reflections on the Relationship of Treaties and Soft Law', p. 30.

[181] Declaration on the Elimination of Violence against Women, GA Res. 48/104, UN GAOR, 85th mtg, UN Doc. No A/RES/48/104 (1993).

rights conventions, and which can be central to refugee status determination.[182] This amplification role can be particularly important in the context of persons who may have particular needs but in respect of which there is no specific international human rights convention. Decision-makers in at least one jurisdiction – the Australian Refugee Review Tribunal ('RRT') – are encouraged to refer to soft law instruments when there is no relevant standard in conventions or treaties applicable to a particular case.[183] An example of the way in which this may be relevant pertains to the fact that there is no specific covenant dealing with persons with a disability.[184] However, a number of nonbinding international instruments may provide assistance to a refugee decision-maker in understanding the way in which rights contained in the general covenants may apply to the particular needs of mentally and physically disabled persons. Indeed, decision-makers have referred both to the 1971 *Declaration on the Rights of Mentally Retarded Persons* and the 1975 *Declaration on the Rights of Disabled Persons* in the refugee context.[185] Future decisions might benefit from reference to more recent instruments, such as the Montreal Declaration on Intellectual Disability.[186] By highlighting the special needs of disabled persons, such instruments can assist in understanding how the impact of a specific form of harm may be particularly severe on the disabled (possibly amounting to persecution), in a way that may be quite different from able-bodied persons.[187]

[182] These include: the ICCPR; the ICESCR; and the CEDAW.
[183] See RRT, *Legal Issues Research Paper No. 6*, p. 11, cited in Simeon, *The Human Rights Paradigm and the 1951 Refugee Convention*, p. 18.
[184] In December 2001, the United Nations General Assembly adopted a resolution titled *Comprehensive and Integral International Convention to Promote and Protect the Rights and Identity of Persons with Disabilities*, GA Res. 56/168, UN GAOR, 3rd Comm, 56th sess., 88th mtg, Agenda Item 119(b), UN Doc. A/RES/56/168 (2001). See Gerard Quinn and Theresia Degener, *Human Rights and Disability: The Current Use and Future Potential of United Nations Human Rights Instruments in the Context of Disability* (2002) <http://www.unhchr.ch/html/menu6/2/disability.doc> at 31 May 2006. The Convention on the Rights of Persons with Disabilities was opened for signature on 30 March 2007: see http://www.un.org/disabilities/convention
[185] 1971 Declaration: GA Res. 2856 (XXVI), UN GAOR, 2027th mtg, UN Doc. 2856 (XXVI) (1971) referred to by the RPD in *IPJ (Re)*, No. A99-01121 [2000] CRDD No. 141, 29 August 2000. 1975 Declaration: GA Res. 3447 (XXX), UN GAOR, 2433rd mtg, UN Doc. 3447 (XXX) (1975) referred to in *Reference N96/11195*, RRT, 10 September 1996.
[186] Adopted 6 October 2004 (Pan-American Health Organization/World Health Organization Conference on Intellectual Disability). See generally: Paul Hunt and Judith Mesquita, 'Mental disabilities and the human right to the highest attainable standard of health' (2006) 28 *Human Rights Quarterly* 332.
[187] The ExCom has recently emphasized the importance of states exercising sensitivity towards the special needs of persons with disabilities in undertaking individual asylum procedures: see UNHCR, *Agenda for Protection*, p. 32.

Accordingly, soft law documents are frequently relied upon as sources of interpretative guidance in the refugee context, both in administrative guidelines and in the case law. This is exemplified in the willingness of decision-makers to refer to soft law documents such as the *Declaration on Violence Against Women*,[188] and the *Declaration on the Protection of Women and Children in Emergency and Armed Conflict*;[189] as well as reports and guidelines developed by experts in the field of international human rights law.[190] Reliance on these sources has proven extremely helpful to refugee decision-makers in understanding the scope and parameters of international human rights treaty provisions, their application to specific groups and circumstances, and evolving notions of rights and corresponding obligations on the part of the state.

The key difficulty with 'soft law' sources arises when decision-makers misunderstand the status of a soft law instrument and attribute to it a status that it does not properly enjoy. This is both unsatisfactory in principle and runs the risk of undermining the cogency of the 'human rights as interpretative guide' approach.[191] This underlines the importance

---

[188] Referred to in: Canadian Gender Guidelines; Australian Gender Guidelines; US Gender Guidelines; UK Gender Guidelines; Swedish Migration Board, *Gender-Based Persecution: Guidelines for Investigation and Evaluation of the Needs of Women for Protection* (2001) <www.migrationsverket.se> at 31 May 2006. The UNHCR also supports reference to this document: UNHCR Division of International Protection, 'Gender-Related Persecution', at 81–2.

[189] General Assembly Resolution 3318 (XXIX) of 14 December 1974, referred to in Australian Gender Guidelines.

[190] For example in *Zheng v. Canada (Minister for Citizenship and Immigration)*, 2002 ACWSJ 2334, the Federal Court of Canada referred to the Report from the Roundtable on the meaning of 'Trafficking in Persons' and the Human Rights standards for the treatment of trafficked persons in relation to the question whether minors can consent to be trafficked: at para. 23.

[191] For example, in *Reference N94/4731*, RRT, 17 October 1994, the RRT relied on art. 16 of the *Proclamation of Teheran* (1968) which provides that parents 'have a basic human right to determine freely and responsibly the number and the spacing of their children' in adjudicating a case involving the one-child policy in China. The RRT concluded that this could be 'looked upon as elucidating the UDHR and the two together are a part of customary international law. There is therefore a clear international statement of the parent's right to control fertility and the right to control the number and spacing of children'. However, this is controversial and the ease with which the RRT came to this conclusion, particularly in relation to customary international law, based only on a 'soft law' document runs the risk of undermining the human rights approach (on the basis for example that it is too 'easy' to find a human right in international law). See generally Philip Alston, 'Conjuring Up New Human Rights: A Proposal for Quality Control' (1984) 78 *American Journal of International Law* 607.

of maintaining conceptual clarity as to sources of international human rights law and the important, although more limited, role that soft law can legitimately play.

In sum, it is vital that decision-makers focus initially on the standards set out in the widely accepted international treaties and the interpretation accorded such provisions by the relevant specific treaty bodies. In light of this, soft law sources may provide vital additional guidance, but cannot be used in lieu of, or to contradict, the standards themselves.

PART THREE: POSSIBLE OBJECTIONS TO THE HUMAN RIGHTS APPROACH

As explained above, the human rights framework for interpreting key aspects of the refugee definition is the dominant approach in refugee status determination, and is advocated by both the UNHCR and scholars. The analysis in this chapter has established the justification for this approach by reference to accepted principles of treaty interpretation. However, some lingering doubts remain in the literature concerning both the legitimacy and workability of this method of interpretation; it is therefore important to examine these concerns before concluding that the human rights approach provides an appropriate basis for the analysis to follow.

Concerns about the legitimacy of the human rights approach

The key objection that could be posited against the comparative treaty interpretation approach is that it is not appropriate to hold states accountable, as a matter of international law, by reference to obligations set out in treaties to which they are not parties. In other words, when interpreting the Refugee Convention, a decision-maker should not make reference to other international treaties that the state of origin might not have ratified. Indeed, it might be argued that art. 34 of the VCLT, which provides that a treaty does not create obligations or rights for a third state without its consent, explicitly prohibits this. The response, of course, is that the fact that a refugee decision-maker refers to a second treaty, such as a human rights treaty, in the course of interpreting the Refugee Convention, does not mean that the home state is being held accountable under the second treaty.[192] The issue is not whether a party will be *bound* by this secondary treaty, but merely whether the *standards* set out therein provide appropriate *guidance* for the interpretation of the first treaty.[193] This is made clear in the use of comparative treaty interpretation in other international law contexts.[194] For example, in the decision of the WTO Appellate Body in the *Shrimp case*, additional treaties and resolutions were used to amplify the obligations to which the parties had bound themselves, not to create new obligations by importing requirements from other treaties into the trade context.[195] If this is acceptable in a context such as international trade, it is *a fortiori* in the refugee context, in which there is no question of the liability of the state of origin.

In practice, courts and tribunals interpreting the Refugee Convention often do not consider the question whether the state of origin has ratified the relevant treaty to which reference is being made in the determination of whether serious harm amounts to persecution. In a number of cases, courts and tribunals have made extensive reference to a particular

---

[192] This is sometimes misunderstood. For example, Nathwani seems to assume that it is only legitimate to take those other treaties into account that the home state has ratified, which seems to assume that the refugee decision-maker is indirectly holding the home state accountable under its other obligations: see Niraj Nathwani, *Rethinking Refugee Law* (The Hague: Martinus Nijhoff Publishers, 2003), pp. 76–7. However, this fundamentally misunderstands the justification for the human rights analogy in refugee law and thus criticisms based on this point are unfounded.

[193] It is unlikely that decision-makers applying one treaty have the jurisdiction or authority to enforce the provisions of a secondary treaty as against a party to the first treaty. It is interesting to note that on occasion the European Convention has alluded to the other obligations of states in the course of adjudicating complaints pursuant to the European Convention, but has not suggested that the ECHR has jurisdiction to enforce these other treaties: Aalt Willem Heringa, 'The Consensus Principle – the Role of "Common Law" in the ECHR Case Law' (1996) 3 *Maastricht Journal of European and Comparative Law* 108 refers to the decision of the ECHR in *Costello-Roberts v. United Kingdom* (1993) 247-C Eur Court HR (ser A), in which the Court 'reminded the respondent state of its (other) international obligations: the United Kingdom was subtly reminded of the fact that it had ratified the UN Convention on the Rights of the Child': at 122.

[194] Indeed, this specific argument was considered and rejected in the most recent ILC study on Article 31(3)(c) in which it concluded that, 'although a tribunal may only have jurisdiction in regard to a particular instrument, it must always *interpret* and *apply* that instrument in its relationship to its normative environment – that is to say "other" international law': Koskenniemi, 'Fragmentation of International Law', p. 179.

[195] *United States – Import Prohibition of Certain Shrimp and Shrimp Products*, WTO Doc. WT/DS58/AB/R (1998) paras. 127–34 (Report of the Appellate Body).

treaty, such as the CEDAW, in assessing whether serious harm amounts to persecution, when research reveals that the particular treaty has not been acceded to by the state of origin.[196] Further, in practice, refugee decision-makers sometimes refer to treaties that their own state has not ratified in interpreting the terms of the Refugee Convention.[197]

This gives rise to the question whether, as a matter of policy, it is appropriate for courts to use standards which the state of origin has not even bound itself to accept in order to assess the home state's behaviour. An argument might be made that the notion of surrogate protection, said to be an underlying rationale for the international refugee system,[198] means that the international community should only be required to provide whatever the home state has agreed to provide. However, the obvious problem with such an approach is that it would produce the incongruous position that the less willing a state is to bind itself to international human rights standards, the less chance its citizens

---

[196] For example, in *Refugee Appeal No. 71427/99*, RSAA, 16 August 2000, extensive reference was made to the CEDAW in assessing the claim of a woman from Iran, despite the fact that Iran is not a signatory to that Convention: see at paras. 74–80. In addition, the Canadian Immigration and Review Board's Chairperson's guidelines on civil war specifically refer to this: 'the standards set out in an instrument may assist the Refugee Division in determining permissible conduct even if the instrument is not binding upon the parties to the conflict. By defining permissible conduct, the instruments may assist the Refugee Division in assessing whether or not the treatment constitutes persecution as that term is understood in Canadian case law': Immigration and Refugee Board, Canada, *Civilian Non-Combatants Fearing Persecution in Civil War Situations: Guidelines Issued by the Chairperson Pursuant to Section 65(3) of the Immigration Act* (1996a) <http://www.cisr-irb.gc.ca/en/about/guidelines/civil_e.htm> at 31 May 2006.

[197] For example, the US Guidelines on Children suggest that treaties (including, of course, the Convention on the Rights of the Child) are not required to have been ratified by the USA in order to provide assistance and relevance in the refugee status inquiry: US Children's Guidelines. Similarly, the USA Gender Guidelines make reference to the CEDAW as providing relevant guidance to the adjudication procedure, despite the fact that the USA has signed but not ratified this Convention: see Phyllis Coven, 'INS Adjudicating Asylum Claims for Women', in Deborah E. Anker, 'Women Refugees: Forgotten No Longer?' (1995) 32 *San Diego Law Review* 771 at 792–4. Further, UK Gender Guidelines refer decision-makers to international conventions to which the UK is not a signatory. For example, they refer to the Convention for the Suppression of the Traffic in Persons and of the Exploitation of the Prostitution of Others, GA Res. 317 (IV), UN GAOR, 264th mtg, UN Doc. 317 (IV) (1949), which the UK has neither signed nor ratified.

[198] See *Canada (Attorney-General) v. Ward* [1993] 2 SCR 689 at 709 (La Forest J) ('*Ward*'); *Applicant A* (1996) 190 CLR 225 at 248 (Dawson J); *R v. Home Secretary, ex parte Sivakumaran* [1988] AC 958, [1988] 1 All ER 193, [1988] 2 WLR 92, [1988] Imm AR 147; *Horvath* [2000] 3 All ER 577 at 581 Lord Hope; 589 (Lord Lloyd); 594 (Lord Clyde).

have of obtaining refugee status. In other words, the home state could indirectly control the recognition of refugee status in respect of its citizens. Moreover, it would mean different standards would apply to applicants depending on their country of origin (and possibly also country of asylum), an untenable position under the Refugee Convention. The Refugee Convention does not provide for any distinction in treatment according to nationality; on the contrary, art. 1A(2) is non-derogable and, following the adoption of the 1967 Protocol, must be applied regardless of the geographical origin of the applicant. In any event, such an approach is not logical when one considers that, as emphasized above, reference to other international conventions is not made in order to hold states accountable to those standards, but to provide an objective barometer of unacceptable treatment. For these reasons, as long as a human rights treaty has attained widespread membership such that it can be said to 'express the common intentions or understanding' of all parties to the Refugee Convention as to the rights to which every individual is entitled, it is not relevant whether it has in fact been ratified by a particular home state (or state of asylum) or whether reservations have been entered, for the purposes of deciding whether the standards set out therein may serve as an aid in the interpretation of the Refugee Convention.

A number of other objections have been voiced relating more specifically to the nature of the Refugee Convention. It is accurate to characterize those objections as concerned with both over- and under-inclusivity. On the one hand, Steinbock criticizes the human rights approach to interpretation on the basis that 'a large body of rights violations are equated with persecution', and the 'practical impact of this approach would be enormous'.[199] Similar invocations of the 'floodgates' concern underlie the reservation expressed by Lady Justice Hale of the English Court of Appeal, who observed that the human rights approach 'has the potential to expand the types of maltreatment involved way beyond what might usually be thought of as persecution'.[200] There are a number of problems with this argument. The first is that it seems to assume that there is a 'usual' or common-sense meaning of persecution, which the Court should be reluctant to distort. However, as the above analysis reveals, reliance on ordinary dictionary meanings has been

---

[199] Daniel J. Steinbock, 'Interpreting the Refugee Definition' (1998) 45 *UCLA Law Review* 733 at 782.
[200] *Horvath* [2000] Imm AR 205 at para. 10.

heavily criticized as producing outcomes inconsistent with the object and purpose of the Refugee Convention. Second, Steinbock's critique is based on the mistaken notion that the human rights approach purports to 'serve as a working definition of the kinds of deprivation that, by themselves, constitute persecution without any showing of a prohibited reason for the human rights infringement'.[201] This appears to overlook the fact that the human rights approach does not necessarily mean that every breach of a human rights provision automatically equates to fulfillment of the criteria for refugee status. On the contrary, in terms of the being persecuted inquiry, in the ultimate analysis discretion still resides with the decision-maker, as human rights treaties are designed to provide guidance, not to constitute an inflexible grid which dictates the outcome in every case. Indeed, art. 31(3)(c) provides that the interpreter should *take into account* other rules of international law – not apply them rigidly to the treaty under review. In addition, an applicant must still satisfy the other aspects of the definition, most notably the requirement that the fear of being persecuted be *for reasons of* race, religion, nationality, membership of a particular social group or political opinion.[202] Third, while there is no doubt that there is the potential (a potential which has indeed been realized in cases that have recognized domestic violence victims as refugees for example) to expand the application of the definition on this analysis, any objection to such an outcome must be made on grounds of principle and not merely on the basis of some inchoate 'floodgates' concern. This is because, as the senior courts in the common law world have emphasized repeatedly, the floodgates argument is not a valid legal argument.[203]

Conversely, some commentators have expressed concern that importing human rights standards into the refugee status assessment results in an overly restrictive approach to the Convention. Nathwani suggests that referring to international human rights principles requires a decision-maker to make a positive finding that the state of origin is responsible for that violation as a matter of international law before finding that

---

[201] Steinbock, 'Interpreting the Refugee Definition', p. 782.
[202] This is made clear by the UK Court of Appeal in *Amare v. Secretary of State for the Home Department* [2005] All ER (D) 300 at para. 27.
[203] See, for example, *Applicant A* (1996) 190 CLR 225 at 241 (Gummow J); *Chan v. Canada (Minister for Immigration and Education)*, at para. 57, *R v. Secretary of State for the Home Department, ex parte Jeyakumaran* [1994] Imm AR at 48. See also the authorities cited in Symes, *Caselaw on the Refugee Convention*, p. 10.

persecution has been established.[204] Thus he concludes that, on the human rights theory, '[a]n act that is not attributable to a State cannot constitute a human rights violation and, thus, does not lead to refugee status'.[205] However, this represents a misunderstanding of the role of human rights standards in refugee adjudication. A refugee decision-maker has neither the jurisdiction nor ability to make a positive finding of state responsibility vis-à-vis the state of origin. Rather, as the New Zealand RSAA has made clear, 'determination of refugee status is no more than an assessment whether, in the event of the refugee claimant returning to the country of origin, there is a real chance of that person "being persecuted" for a Convention reason'.[206] In the course of determining whether the risk of harm feared by the applicant amounts to a violation of human dignity such as to constitute persecution, a decision-maker may refer to international human rights standards in order to ascertain the kinds of harm considered unlawful by the international community. Further, in undertaking that assessment it will often be helpful to refer to the interpretation of international human rights standards by the relevant treaty bodies in order to understand the scope of a particular right. However, it must always be remembered that the 'function of refugee law is palliative'; 'it does not hold states responsible for human rights abuses'.[207]

---

[204] Nathwani also makes another argument against the human rights approach that should be noted for completeness but will not be considered in detail because it is easily dismissed. Nathwani argues that introducing the question whether human rights have been violated risks causing tension between states because it necessarily implies censure of another state. However, it is difficult to understand how this is any different from one state finding that another state is persecuting its citizens either directly, or indirectly (by failing to protect against persecution by non-state agents). In other words, his argument is really directed towards the use of the term 'persecution' (or more accurately 'being persecuted') in the Refugee Convention: see Nathwani, *Rethinking Refugee Law*, p. 21.

[205] *Ibid.*, p. 59. See also Daniel Wilsher, 'Non-State Actors and the Definition of a Refugee in the United Kingdom: Protection, Accountability or Culpability' (2003) 15 *International Journal of Refugee Law* 68 at 98.

[206] *Refugee Appeal No. 74665/03*, RSAA, 22 July 2003, at para. 75.

[207] *Refugee Appeal No. 74665/03*, RSAA, 22 July 2003, at para. 75. As the RSAA explains, a 'refugee decision-maker does not usurp the jurisdiction of the Human Rights Committee ... Nor is it the role of the refugee decision-maker to express "views" as if refugee adjudication were an individual complaint under the First Optional Protocol'. The RSAA has reiterated this point in the context of the ICESCR in *Refugee Appeal No. 75221*, RSAA, 23 September 2005, at para 110: 'the refugee status determination jurisdiction is not a de facto ICESCR individual complaints procedure'.

Another concern related to under-inclusiveness is that the 'persecution as human rights violations' analysis should be used with caution on the basis that, '[i]t is possible that all forms of persecution have not yet been identified or codified in international human rights law'.[208] However, this appears to overlook the fact that it is precisely the human rights approach that has led to the evolution of refugee law to accommodate contemporary refugee flows.[209] Indeed, the analysis in the following chapters suggests that it is *failure* to refer to authoritative human rights standards with respect to socio-economic rights violations which has led to an overly restrictive understanding of 'being persecuted'.[210] As that analysis reveals, the deficiency is not with international human rights standards, but in refugee decision-makers' failure to recognize, interpret and apply them correctly.

Moreover, this concern overlooks the fact that the key international human rights treaties are not static; but are subject to constant supervision and interpretation by the relevant supervisory bodies which are specifically charged with monitoring the implementation of those covenants, thus providing an important source of guidance to refugee decision-makers.[211] The primary interpretive

---

[208] Alice Edwards, 'Age and Gender Dimensions in International Refugee Law' in Feller, Türk and Nicholson, *Refugee Protection in International Law*, p. 50. According to Türk and Nicholson, 'attempts to define it ... could limit a phenomenon that has unfortunately shown itself all too adaptable in the history of humankind': 'Refugee protection in international law: an overall perspective', p. 39.

[209] The NZ RSAA has specifically dealt with this argument in *Refugee Appeal No. 74665/03*, RSAA, 7 July 2004, at para. 70. Furthermore, in none of the papers in which such concerns are raised are the authors able to point to a single case in which a claim has been dismissed on this basis. It appears to be a purely hypothetical concern.

[210] A classic example is the right to education discussed in *Faddoul*, 37 F 3d 185 (5th Cir. 1994); *Li*, 92 F 3d 985 (9th Cir. 1996); *Petkov and Tritchkova*, 114 F 3d 1192 (7th Cir. 1997); and *De Souza*, 999 F 2d 1156 (7th Cir. 1993). See above at note 39.

[211] In the case of most of the major UN international human rights instruments, the relevant supervisory body is established by the covenant itself: see, for example, art. 28(1) of the ICCPR, which establishes the Human Rights Committee, and arts. 40–5 which set out the functions of the Committee. In the case of the ICESCR, the Economic and Social Council is vested with the relevant supervisory functions; however, the ECSR Committee was established by *Review of the composition, organization and administrative arrangements of the Sessional Working Group of Governmental Experts on the Implementation of the International Covenant on Economic, Social and Cultural Rights*, ESC Res. 17, UN ESCOR, 22nd mtg, UN Doc. E/RES/1985/17 (1985): see Wouter Vandenhole, *The Procedures before the UN Human Rights Treaty Bodies: Divergence or Convergence?* (Antwerp: Intersentia, 2004), p. 47.

guidance provided by the UN treaty bodies is in the form of general comments/recommendations which usually address the nature and scope of a particular covenant article, but insight into the meaning and operation of the covenants is also provided in concluding observations issued in the course of assessing reports of individual state parties.[212] In addition, four of the treaty bodies may, in certain circumstances, hear and assess individual communications alleging a violation of rights, and thus produce 'judgments' with respect to these communications.[213] It is generally accepted that these general comments, concluding observations and 'views' with respect to individual communications are of highly persuasive value, carrying 'considerable legal weight'.[214] Indeed, it could be argued that since the views (expressed in various forms) of the treaty bodies represent the conclusions of 'the only expert body entrusted with and capable of making such pronouncements', 'for States parties to ignore or not act on such views would be to show bad faith in implementing their Covenant-based obligations'.[215] In other words, the requirement both to implement and interpret a treaty in good faith requires great deference to the views of

---

[212] For a detailed description of the reporting procedures of the various bodies, see Michael O'Flaherty, *Human Rights and the UN: Practice before the Treaty Bodies*, second edition (The Hague: Kluwer Law International, 2002).

[213] See Optional Protocol to the International Covenant on Civil and Political Rights, GA Res. 2200A (XXI), UN GAOR, UN Doc. A/6316 (1966); Optional Protocol to the Convention on the Elimination of all Forms of Discrimination against Women, GA Res. A/RES/54/4, UN GAOR, 54th sess., Agenda Item 109, UN Doc. A/RES/54/4 (1999); CERD art. 14; CAT, art. 22. See generally, Vandenhole, *The Procedures before the UN Human Rights Treaty Bodies*, p. 243.

[214] *Refugee Appeal No. 74665/03*, RSAA, 7 July 2004, at paras. 73–4. See also *Refugee Appeal Nos. 72558/01 and 72559/01*, RSAA, 19 November 2002, at para. 116 and *Refugee Appeal No. 75221*, RSAA, 23 September 2005, at para. 85. See also Scott Davidson, 'Intention and Effect: The Legal Status of the Final Views of the Human Rights Committee', in Huscroft and Rishworth, *Litigating Rights*, p. 308; Elizabeth Evatt, 'The Impact of International Human Rights on Domestic Law', in Huscroft and Rishworth, *Litigating Rights*, pp. 300–1; Paul Rishworth, 'The Rule of International Law', in Huscroft and Rishworth, *Litigating Rights*, pp. 274–8.

[215] Office of the United Nations High Commissioner for Human Rights, *Fact Sheet No. 16 (Rev. 1): The Committee on Economic Social and Cultural Rights* (1991) <http://www.ohchr.org/english/about/publications/docs/fs16.htm> at 31 May 2006, noted in Sepulveda, *The Nature of the Obligations under the International Covenant on Economic, Social and Cultural Rights*, p. 110. The Economic Committee, for example, is composed of 18 members with 'recognized competence in the field of human rights', who are nominated by State parties to the ICESCR and elected by ECOSOC: Vandenhole, *The Procedures Before the UN Human Rights Treaty Bodies*, pp. 47–9.

the treaty bodies as to the correct interpretation of the human rights covenants.[216]

Turning to the Economic Committee, whose interpretative guidance is particularly relevant to the analysis in the following chapters, it is important to note that it has become increasingly effective in providing normative content to the broad framework of rights set out in the ICESCR. In terms of Concluding Observations issued with respect to the review of individual state parties' reports, observers have noted that the Committee has 'sometimes achieved a level of detail and analysis more commonly associated with judicial bodies',[217] and that the 'strong language used by the committee has provided clearer guidance as to the normative content of the Covenant'.[218] Further, General Comments constitute an 'important mechanism for developing the jurisprudence of a Committee in a way that is not possible in individual comments on State reports'.[219] The Economic Committee's General Comments draw on

---

[216] Article 26 of the VCLT provides: '[e]very treaty in force is binding upon the parties to it and must be performed by them in good faith'. Article 31 provides: 'A treaty shall be interpreted in good faith.' In practice, the Economic Committee's legitimacy is supported by the 'significant level of acceptance of the Covenant's interpretation among States': Sepulveda, *The Nature of the Obligations under the International Covenant on Economic, Social and Cultural Rights*, p. 110. She states that this is reflected both in state practice before the Committee and by a 'plethora of resolutions and decisions adopted by States in international fora': p. 110. She also notes that no state has ever objected to one of the General Comments, and that, in responding to the Committee's Concluding Observations, states parties tend to deny the facts on which the Committee relied rather than 'to deny the scope of the obligations as set out by the Committee', which 'tends to reinforce the validity of the Committee's interpretation': pp. 40, 42. Craven also notes that no states have objected to the Economic Committee's view that it has the jurisdiction to issue General Comments: Matthew C. R. Craven, *The International Covenant on Economic, Social and Cultural Rights: A Perspective on its Development* (Oxford: Oxford University Press, 1995), pp. 89–90. Further, Craven argues that 'the endorsement by ECOSOC and the General Assembly (in which significant numbers of State parties participate) of the Committee's annual report gives considerable weight to the Committee's interpretation': p. 92.

[217] Scott Leckie, 'The Committee on Economic, Social and Cultural Rights: Catalyst for Change in a System Needing Reform', in Alston and Crawford, *The Future of UN Human Rights Treaty Monitoring*, p. 134. Craven also notes that since 1993, the Committee has been issuing Concluding Observations that follow the same structure as those of other treaty bodies, and that these 'represent an important improvement both in terms of the level of detail provided and in the quality of assessment': *The International Covenant on Economic, Social and Cultural Rights*, p. 88.

[218] Sepulveda, *The Nature of the Obligations under the International Covenant on Economic, Social and Cultural Rights*, pp. 37–40.

[219] Craven, *The International Covenant on Economic, Social and Cultural Rights*, p. 90.

'the experience gained ... through the examination of States' reports',[220] and are the 'most suitable of the Committee's tools to clarify the normative content of the Covenant because they are general in nature and provide an abstract picture of the scope of the obligations'.[221] While the early General Comments were directed at more general obligations, the Committee has more recently issued General Comments on a range of individual rights, setting out the normative content, and the nature of state obligations and violations with respect to those rights.[222] Finally, it is important to note that consideration is currently being given to the adoption of a Protocol to the ICESCR which would establish a complaints procedure, thus allowing for the possibility of individual 'judgments' concerning violations of socio-economic rights in the future.[223]

In light of this, it is particularly important that refugee decision-makers defer to the interpretation of international human rights standards by the relevant expert treaty bodies.[224] The importance of this, particularly in the context of socio-economic rights, is highlighted in Chapter 3 wherein the dangers of 'fragmentation' in international law are underlined, following an examination of decisions in which refugee decision-makers have misunderstood fundamental elements of socio-economic rights in international law. As that analysis reveals, reference to the authoritative interpretation of socio-economic rights by the Economic Committee holds the potential to improve the accuracy of refugee decision-making in this area and to allow international refugee law to evolve in line with principled developments in international human rights law.

---

[220] Sepulveda, *The Nature of the Obligations under the International Covenant on Economic, Social and Cultural Rights*, p. 40.

[221] *Ibid.*, p. 41. Craven also explains that '[n]ot only does [the formulation of general comments] provide a means by which jurisprudence may be generated at a faster rate ... but it is also a means by which members of the Committee may come to an agreement by consensus as to an interpretation of a specific provision without facing the difficult issue of addressing individual States': p. 90.

[222] See, for example, Committee on Economic, Social and Cultural Rights, *General Comment No. 13: The Right to Education (Art. 13)*, UN Doc. E/C.12/1999/10 (1999); Committee on Economic, Social and Cultural Rights, *General Comment No. 14: The Right to the Highest Attainable Standard of Health*, UN Doc. E/C.12/2000/4 (2000); Committee on Economic, Social and Cultural Rights, *General Comment No. 15: The Right to Water*, UN Doc. E/C.12/2002/11 (2003); Committee on Economic, Social and Cultural Rights, *General Comment No. 18: The Right to Work*, UN Doc. E/C.12/GC/18 (2005b).

[223] See references in Chapter 4, note 39.

[224] This was explicitly recognized recently by the New Zealand RSAA, in *Refugee Appeal No. 75221*, 23 September 2005, in which it noted that the views of the Economic Committee 'are highly persuasive', and 'ought not to be lightly disregarded': at para. 85.

Concerns about the workability of the human rights approach

The second type of objection relates to the possible unworkability of the human rights framework. It might be posited that, despite its deficiencies, the predominant US approach, for example, is preferable to one which relies on an external framework, since domestic law judges are not experts in human rights law and to require them to engage in an analysis of international human rights provisions would merely serve to complicate their task. In addition, it might be argued that introducing a new body of law into the decision-making process may result in inadequate or incorrect reasoning, if judges are not sufficiently versed in relevant international provisions.[225]

There is of course a possibility that judges will misunderstand provisions in international human rights law and thus incorrectly apply relevant principles in the refugee context.[226] However, this risk is greatly reduced when one considers that, as explained above, all of the widely ratified UN treaties are monitored by a committee of experts, which either have jurisdiction to hear complaints from individuals and/ or, at the very least, to monitor reports by state parties and draw concluding observations in respect of state compliance and provide interpretative guidance through instruments such as general comments/ recommendations, all of which are easily accessible to refugee decision-makers. Indeed, the reports produced by these bodies have long been relied upon by decision-makers in order to obtain factual knowledge

---

[225] Erika Feller has raised this as an issue that might cause difficulty and therefore make domestic judges reluctant to embrace the human rights approach. However, she concludes that 'human rights law and refugee law should each be interpreted in a way that strengthens and enriches the broad protection framework rather than undermines it through aberrant exceptions. On refugee issues, a "purposive" approach to interpreting international law will ensure that the focus is kept on the victim and the palliative purpose of protection. It will also promote the dynamic rather than static character of international law and the State's commitment to it': Erika Feller, 'Address to the Conference of the International Association of Refugee Law Judges', at 382–3.

[226] It must be acknowledged that there are cases in which a lower level court or tribunal has misapplied an international convention in a deleterious way for the applicant concerned. However, such cases are generally swiftly rectified on appeal as they tend to involve fairly blatant misapplications, and are thus not a function of the complexity of international human rights law but merely faulty reasoning by the lower court. See, for example, *Liu v. Minister for Immigration and Multicultural Affairs* [2001] FCA 257 (Unreported, Cooper J, 16 March 2001) and *X (JK) (Re)*, No. M92-01550(T) [1992] CRDD No. 348, 20 November 1992, overturned on appeal to the Federal Court of Canada: [1993] ACF No. 1465 (Unreported, Noel J, 9 June 1993).

about the country conditions in the applicant's state of origin,[227] and decision-makers are increasingly displaying a similar willingness and capacity to seek guidance from these committees in relation to legal issues as well.[228] In any event one could argue that reliance on an objective framework is less prone to error as it provides greater scope for judicial review of erroneous decisions than decisions based only on a decision-maker's subjective assessment of what is 'reasonable' or sufficiently 'offensive' to constitute persecution.

Conclusion

This chapter has explored the emerging tendency to refer to human rights standards in refugee adjudication and has explored a number of theories that explain and justify the human rights approach to the interpretation of the Refugee Convention. It has been established that the practice accords with traditional approaches to treaty interpretation, the most important being the requirement to read the text in context and in light of the object and purpose of the Refugee Convention. In addition, it constitutes further evidence of a growing trend in international law to read treaties in a dynamic manner and in light of other obligations of the parties in order to promote coherence in the international legal system. It has thus been shown that the human rights-based approach is legitimate and well established. This is vital in light of the increasing focus in international human rights law on the importance of economic and social rights, a development on which the following chapters rely in advocating a more creative application of the Refugee Convention to claims based on poverty and economic deprivation.

---

[227] See, for example, *Reference V01/12621*, RRT, 19 May 2002 (referring to Romania's reports to the CEDAW Committee); *Reference N01/38920*, RRT, 11 July 2002 (referring to India's reports to the CEDAW Committee).

[228] See, for example, the authorities set out by the NZ RSAA in *Refugee Appeal Nos. 72558/01 and 72559/01*, RSAA, 19 November 2002, at para. 115.

3 Persecution and socio-economic deprivation in refugee law

[T]here are many more subtle ways of persecuting people than beating them up. Many refugees would probably rather suffer an occasional beating than face a life of repression, poverty and disadvantage because of their ethnic or religious background.
Submissions of counsel, Canadian RPD decision, 2000.[1]

With respect to education, it seems clear that if a person will be excluded from institutions of learning in his home country for political reasons, this will affect his whole life much more profoundly than a relatively short term of imprisonment.
Atle Grahl-Madsen.[2]

Introduction

The question whether a person has a well-founded fear of being persecuted is central to the refugee status determination procedure and is thus an issue on which there is a great deal of jurisprudence and scholarly comment. As explained in Chapter 2, since there is no definition of 'persecution' contained in the Refugee Convention, its meaning must be divined by a process of judicial interpretation.[3] The need for some objective guidance has underpinned the development of the human rights approach to interpreting the Refugee Convention, which is now dominant in the common law world, and increasingly accepted in many

---

[1] *SWE (Re)*, Nos. T99-04041, T99-04042, T99-04043, T99-04044, T99-06333, T99-06363, T99-04047, T99-04048, T99-06334 [2000] CRDD No. 45, 1 March 2000, at para. 6.
[2] Grahl-Madsen, *The Status of Refugees in International Law*, p. 215.
[3] As the UNHCR explained in 1979, '[t]here is no universally accepted definition of "persecution" and various attempts to formulate such a definition have met with little success': UNHCR Handbook, at para. 51.

civil law jurisdictions as well. This chapter explores the extent to which this approach does and can accommodate claims based on the deprivation of economic and social rights.

The notion that persecution may take an economic form is not a modern construct or radical notion; rather there is evidence that from the earliest days of its operation some types of socio-economic claims were considered to fall within the purview of the Refugee Convention definition.[4] However, the current status of such claims, particularly those involving issues other than economic proscription,[5] is far from clear, no doubt largely due to the fact that claims based on economic and social deprivation present the most difficult challenge to some key conceptual assumptions regarding the nature of persecution, and most directly and acutely challenge the distinction between economic migrants and refugees.[6] At present there exists neither jurisprudential consensus nor extensive analysis in the case law that provides guidance on adjudicating such claims; nor is there any significant exploration of the relevant issues available in the refugee law literature.[7]

---

[4] See Hathaway, *The Law of Refugee Status*, p. 103, note 33, citing the drafting history; Grahl-Madsen, *The Status of Refugees in International Law*, p. 215, citing early (mainly German) cases which held that forms of economic persecution were encompassed within the Refugee Convention definition.

[5] Refugee status on the basis of economic proscription is reasonably well accepted: see, for example, the discussion set out in Hathaway, *The Law of Refugee Status*; and below notes 23–64.

[6] The extent to which courts are willing to dismiss claims having an economic element or aspect, on the rationale that the applicant is an economic migrant, is evident in many cases, as will be further discussed in Chapter 5. For one example, see *Agbuya*, 1999 US App. LEXIS 21091 (9th Cir. 2 September 1999), where the US Court of Appeals for the Ninth Circuit upheld the claim of a Filipino woman who feared persecution from a guerrilla group due to the unpopular actions she took as an employee in a private company. The majority took the view that she feared persecution on account of her political opinion. In a strongly worded dissent, Hall J argued that the persecution was 'economically-motivated' and accused the majority of 'conflat[ing] an economic motivation with a political one': at 25.

[7] Hathaway appears to be one of the only refugee law scholars who has analysed these issues in any detail: see *The Law of Refugee Status*, although Anker discusses economic claims in the context of US asylum law: Anker, *Law of Asylum in the United States*, pp. 233–43. By contrast, many other significant jurisprudential developments have been closely analysed in the literature, most notably those related to forms of gender persecution. There is a vast literature on gender issues as pertaining to the persecution question. See, for example, Deborah Anker, 'Boundaries in the Field of Human Rights'; Lisa Gilad, 'The Problem of Gender-Related Persecution: A Challenge of International Protection', in Doreen Indra (ed.), *Engendering Forced Migration: Theory and Practice* (New York: Berghahn Books, 1999); Pamela Goldberg, 'Anyplace but Home: Asylum in the United States for Women Fleeing

Moreover, the jurisprudence is in a state of evolution, as new and novel claims are beginning to challenge decision-makers to explore many of the key conceptual and practical questions engaged in adjudicating claims involving economic and social rights. It is thus an apt time to examine the current status of such claims and evaluate existing approaches in light of international human rights principles.

Some of the key questions raised by these claims and which must be addressed include: what kinds of human rights violations may be implicated in an understanding of serious harm?[8] Should notions of persecution be confined to prohibitions on torture, unlawful imprisonment and other traditional civil and political rights protection, or should they extend to encompass claims involving economic (including property) and social rights? Is there an appropriate hierarchy of rights and how is this implicated in refugee analysis? If economic and social claims are encompassed, how should decision-makers undertake the task of assessing whether violations of such rights have occurred in the particular circumstances of individual claims? Does persecution necessarily imply an infliction of harm or may it involve a *failure to act*? And finally, how do we apply the accepted notion that the particular vulnerabilities of an individual applicant are relevant to assessing the risk of being persecuted, where those vulnerabilities are of an economic or social nature? Are there insuperable barriers to applying the traditional principle in respect of such claims?[9]

This chapter begins the task of exploring these questions by reviewing briefly the current state of the refugee jurisprudence in relation to socio-economic claims, before turning to consider the conceptual foundation

---

Intimate Violence' (1993) 26 *Cornell International Law Journal* 565; Pamela Goldberg, 'Where in the World Is There Safety for Me: Women Fleeing Gender-Based Persecution', in Julie Peters and Andrea Wolper (eds.), *Women's Rights, Human Rights: International Feminist Perspectives* (New York: Routledge, 1995); Jacqueline Greatbatch, 'The Gender Difference: Feminist Critiques of Refugee Discourse' (1989) 1 *International Journal of Refugee Law* 518; Audrey Macklin, 'Refugee Women and the Imperative of Categories' (1995) 17 *Human Rights Quarterly* 213. In addition, there are at least two books dedicated to gender and the Refugee Convention: see Spijkerboer, *Gender and Refugee Studies* and Crawley, *Refugees and Gender*. However, developments relating to new forms of economic claims have generally been overlooked. There are very few articles and textbooks that deal with this topic.

[8] Persecution is often understood as requiring a showing of 'serious harm': see Hathaway, *The Law of Refugee Status*, p. 103.

[9] For an exposition of the traditional principle that the subjective circumstances of the applicant are relevant, see Mark Symes and Peter Jorro, *Asylum Law and Practice* (London: LexisNexis UK, 2003), p. 102.

upon which refugee decision-makers have based their reasoning in such cases. The chapter then proceeds to identify a number of fundamental problems with the way decision-makers have approached these claims to date. These problems reflect certain assumptions and misconceptions regarding the nature and value of socio-economic rights and the nature of states' obligations in international human rights law pertaining to these rights. In light of this analysis, Chapter 4 then reviews these problems in the context of international human rights principles and proposes a reformulation of the existing approach in refugee law, in line with contemporary developments in international law concerning the meaning and significance of socio-economic rights.

Socio-economic rights and persecution: an overview

Claims involving threats to economic rights were envisaged as falling within the refugee definition from the earliest operation of the Refugee Convention, although traditionally these were confined to cases of 'economic proscription', that is, an almost complete denial of the ability to earn a living.[10] For example, Grahl-Madsen explained in 1966 that '[i]t is an established practice that economic proscription so severe as to deprive a person of all means of earning a livelihood' constitutes persecution and that '[s]uch proscription is deemed to exist in the case of systematic denial

---

[10] Grahl-Madsen considered that the economic aspect of 'persecution' was well accepted even prior to the adoption of the term in the 1951 Convention. He explains that, in the practice of the International Refugee Organization (which preceded the 1951 Convention), 'the actual form of persecution was considered immaterial' and that it included 'deprivation of work': *The Status of Refugees in International Law*, p. 194. In addition, he was of the view that the term generally encompasses economic harm: 'It is generally agreed in Convention and non-Convention countries alike that if a man's life, limb or physical freedom is threatened, *or if he will be denied every possibility for earning a livelihood*, he has a valid claim to refugeehood': p. 86 (emphasis added). Indeed, this was the view of even those who posited the most restrictive understanding of 'persecution'. Grahl-Madsen explains that Zink interpreted 'persecution' so as to mean only deprivation of life or physical freedom, although in the former category he included 'enforced, protracted unemployment in the absence of other means of livelihood': p. 193. Similarly, Hathaway argues that '[e]ven the most conservative theorists agree that the sustained or systemic denial of the right to earn one's living is a form of persecution, which can coerce or abuse as effectively as imprisonment or torture': *The Law of Refugee Status*, p. 121. Hathaway cites from the drafting history and, in particular, from an exchange between the representative of the American Federation of Labor and the delegate of France, which revealed that persecution of a 'social or economic' nature would be included within the Refugee Convention definition: p. 103, note 33.

of employment'.[11] This provided solid foundation for an understanding of the notion of 'persecution' as encompassing a more complete range of harms; however, despite this early authority, the jurisprudence remained fairly undeveloped until relatively recently, particularly in respect of aspects of economic and social rights other than the right to work. Indeed, in 1991 Hathaway noted, after making the case for economic proscription claims, that there was only 'vague authority' for the proposition that forms of socio-economic harm not related to the right to work, such as the right to education and health care, could constitute persecution.[12]

Over the past two decades, the range of claims considered by courts and tribunals has expanded considerably, as different factual circumstances have challenged decision-makers to interpret the Refugee Convention so as to accommodate the reality of modern-day refugee movements. Importantly, the jurisprudence has now developed to a point where it is capable of encompassing a far wider range of claims relating both to work and other aspects of economic and social rights. This does not mean that all types of economic and social claims have been accepted, or that there is uniformity in approach as amongst jurisdictions. On the contrary, there are many significant unresolved issues in respect of these claims, which will be explored below. Nonetheless, there is a growing body of case law that is attempting to grapple with the multifaceted issues inherent in cases involving deprivation of economic and social rights and it is instructive briefly to survey these developments before turning to the key conceptual challenges in adjudicating such cases.

Recognition of economic claims reflects three important interpretative developments, relating to the nature and gravity of persecution, which must be clarified and underlined at the outset. First, one possible argument against acceptance of any type of economic claim could have been that 'persecution' encompasses only harm that amounts to an infringement of life or freedom, which necessarily excludes violations of

---

[11] Grahl-Madsen, *The Status of Refugees in International Law*, p. 208.
[12] Hathaway explained that at that stage, there existed only 'vague authority for the proposition that the discriminatory denial of educational or health facilities is a form of persecution', and that while there was one Canadian decision that could support such a finding, other decisions were 'less encouraging'. After reviewing some decisions that held that discrimination in access to schooling and medical care did not amount to persecution, he concluded, 'these precedents take an overly narrow view of the meaning of persecution, and warrant reconsideration in the light of the human rights paradigm set out above: *The Law of Refugee Status*, pp. 123–4.

economic and social rights. However, even if persecution were so narrowly understood, the argument that economic claims are automatically precluded would ignore the potential harm visited upon a person by economic deprivation, as has been acknowledged by courts. For example, in an early decision, the US Court of Appeals for the Third Circuit explained:

> The denial of an opportunity to earn a livelihood in a country such as the one involved here [former communist Yugoslavia] is the equivalent of a sentence to death by means of slow starvation and none the less final because it is gradual. The result of both is the same.[13]

Similarly, the UK IAT acknowledged in a more recent decision:

> The harm need not result from violence or loss of liberty. An inability to earn a living or to find anywhere to live can result in destitution and at least potential damage to health and even life. If discrimination against which the state cannot or will not provide protection produces such a result, the Convention can be engaged.[14]

In other words, decision-makers have recognized that there is no necessary correlation between the nature of harm (economic and social versus civil and political) and the gravity of the impact upon an individual.

Second, it is now well established in any event that the definition of 'persecution' is not confined only to those actions which infringe life or freedom. Although in earlier cases some governments put forward the argument that the language in art. 33 of the Refugee Convention (*non-refoulement* where 'life or freedom' would be threatened)[15] constrains the type of harm encompassed within 'persecution' in art. 1A(2), this has generally been rejected by courts. For example, in *Adan, Subaskaran and Aitseguer*, Simon-Brown LJ held that 'Article 1 must govern the scope of Article 33 rather than the other way around'.[16] Courts have been equally adamant that the phrase 'being persecuted' is capable of encompassing

---

[13] *Dunat v. Hurney*, 297 F 2d 744 (3rd Cir. 1961), as cited in Grahl-Madsen, *The Status of Refugees in International Law*, p. 208. This case was defining the phrase 'physical persecution' – as was then the test in the USA.

[14] *Secretary of State for the Home Department v. Sijakovic* (Unreported, IAT, Appeal No. HX-58113-2000, 1 May 2001), at para. 16 ('*Sijakovic*').

[15] Article 33(1) of the Refugee Convention provides that '[n]o Contracting State shall expel or return ['refouler'] a refugee in any manner whatsoever to the frontiers of territories where his life or freedom would be threatened on account of his race, religion, nationality, membership of a particular social group or political opinion'.

[16] [1999] 4 All ER 774; [1999] 3 WLR 1274, [1999] Imm AR 521. See also *Gashi and Nikshiqi* [1997] INLR 96. See also *Woldesmaet* (Unreported, IAT, Case No. 12892, 9 January 1995),

forms of harm other than direct physical mistreatment.[17] This has underpinned an expansion of claims both in the civil and political,[18] and economic and social rights arena.[19]

The third relevant development is that courts are now uniform in considering the full range of harm feared by an applicant for refugee status, thus making assessments of whether a person is at risk of 'being persecuted' on the basis of an accumulation of all harm feared, even if some elements of harm would not individually be considered sufficiently serious to amount to persecution.[20] This is often explained by the

---

cited in Mark Symes, *Caselaw on the Refugee Convention: The United Kingdom's Interpretation in the Light of the International Authorities* (London: Refugee Legal Centre, 2000), p. 116; and Grahovac (Unreported, IAT, Case no. 11761, 9 January 1995): Symes, *Caselaw on the Refugee Convention*, p. 116. This is also well established in the US cases: see, for example, Sizov v. Ashcroft, 70 Fed. Appx. 374, 2003 US App. LEXIS 13524 (7th Cir. 2003) ('Sizov'), at 377. For NZ authority, see *Refugee Appeal No. 2039/93*, RSAA, 12 February 1996, at para. 36. For Australian authority, see Chan v. Minister for Immigration and Ethnic Affairs (1989) 169 CLR 379 at 429-31 ('Chan'). For Canadian authority, see Oyarzo v. Canada (Minister of Employment and Immigration) [1982] 2 FC 779.

[17] In the UK decision of R v. Secretary of State for the Home Department; ex parte Sasitharan [1998] Imm AR 487, Sedley J stated: '[Counsel] submits that implicit in Staughton LJ's formulation [in a previous decision] is a limitation of persecution to physical abuse. In this I have no hesitation in saying [counsel] is wrong': cited in Symes, *Caselaw on the Refugee Convention*, p. 64. For authority that persecution can consist of purely psychological harm, see SCK (Re), No. MA1-00356 [2001] CRDD No. 401, 15 November 2001 (psychological harm as a result of losing custody of children recognized as persecution); and Fisher v. Immigration and Naturalization Service, 37 F 3d 1371 (9th Cir. 1994), where the US Court of Appeals for the Ninth Circuit held that 'the concept of persecution is broad enough to include governmental measures that compel an individual to engage in conduct that is not physically painful or harmful but is abhorrent to that individual's deepest beliefs': at 1379-81. See also SCAT v. Minister for Immigration and Multicultural and Indigenous Affairs (2003) 76 ALD 625 at 635.

[18] For example, in respect of freedom of religion, the harm involved often impacts upon freedom of conscience or freedom to practice: see, for example, Fatin v. Immigration and Naturalization Service, 12 F 3d 1233 (3rd Cir. 1993). In the context of FGM, the US Court of Appeals for the Sixth Circuit has recognized that 'being forced to witness the pain and suffering of her daughter' which would follow from the infliction of FGM was sufficient to found a successful claim on the part of the mother: see Abay and Amare v. Ashcroft, 368 F 3d 634 (6th Cir. 2004), at 642.

[19] See discussion below, especially at notes 65-90.

[20] As the UK IAT has explained: 'It is an axiom of refugee law that hardships and discriminations must be looked at cumulatively. Whilst we do not see any one of the abovementioned factors as itself giving rise to persecution, we are satisfied that taken together they would amount to persecution': Maksimovic v. Secretary of State for the Home Department [2004] EWHC 1026. This was recognized at an early stage in the UNHCR Handbook, where it is explained that persecution can be established on 'cumulative grounds': at para. 53.

principle that 'discrimination' (a word designed to connote less serious forms of harm) can amount to persecution 'if of sufficient severity and of a sustained or systemic nature'.[21] As the New Zealand RSAA has explained:

> It is recognised that various threats to human rights, in their cumulative effect, can deny human dignity in key ways and should properly be recognised as persecution for the purposes of the Convention. The need to recognise the cumulative effect of threats to human rights is particularly important in the context of refugee claims based on discrimination.[22]

Against this background, it is instructive to turn to a brief overview of the kinds of economic claims that have been considered and accepted by refugee decision-makers in recent years. Beginning with the more traditional types of claim – namely those related to employment – it is now almost indisputable that cases involving a complete denial of the right to work are considered sufficiently serious to warrant characterization as 'persecution'. This is perhaps not surprising given early acceptance of this principle and (most importantly) the impact that the denial of all means to earn a living has on a person's ability to subsist. Thus, courts have recognized claims relating to the inability to obtain employment or to earn a livelihood,[23] particularly where the

---

[21] *Refugee Appeal No. 71404/99*, RSAA, 29 October 1999, at 30–3. See also *Refugee Appeal No. 71404/99*, RSAA, 29 October 1999, at para. 67 and *DG* (Unreported, High Court of New Zealand, Chisholm J, 5 June 2001), at para. 21.

[22] *Refugee Appeal No. 71427/99*, RSAA, 16 August 2000, at para. 53(a).

[23] *Freiberg v. Canada (Secretary of State)* 1994 ACWSJ LEXIS 70958; 1994 ACWSJ 404678; 48 ACWS (3d) 1430, 27 May 1994. In the UK, the Court of Appeal has held that where a person is unable to secure employment for a protected ground, 'a serious issue' arises as to whether that amounts to persecution: *He v. Secretary of State for the Home Department* [2002] EWCA 1150, [2002] Imm AR 590 at paras. 26, 38. For further UK authority, see *Secretary of State for the Home Department v. Chiver* [1997] INLR 212 at 217; *Secretary of State for the Home Department v. Baglan* (Unreported, IAT, Appeal No. HX-71045-94, 23 October 1995), at 7; Symes, *Caselaw on the Refugee Convention*, p. 116. Courts in Australia have recognized that '[d]iscrimination in employment may constitute persecution in the relevant sense if for a Convention reason. However, whether it does so depends on all the circumstances': *Prahastono v. Minister for Immigration and Multicultural Affairs* (1997) 77 FCR 260 at 267 ('*Prahastono*'). See also *Chan* (1989) 169 CLR 379 at 388 (Mason CJ) and *NACR of 2002 v. Minister for Immigration & Multicultural & Indigenous Affairs* [2002] FCAFC 318 at para. 46. In New Zealand, this has been accepted in numerous cases of the RSAA and also endorsed by the High Court: see *H v. Chief Executive of the Department of Labour* (Unreported, High Court of New Zealand, Case No. 183/00, 20 March 2001) at para. 19 (Gendall J).

interference is from the government in the context of a state-controlled economy.[24]

Some courts have made reference to the UNHCR Handbook in support of this interpretation, which notes that discrimination amounts to persecution 'if measures of discrimination lead to consequences of a substantially prejudicial nature' such as 'serious restrictions on [a person's] right to earn his livelihood'.[25] In addition, some courts have referred to the relevant provisions in the UDHR and the ICESCR in support of the principle that infringements on the right to work are relevant to the persecution inquiry.[26] Article 23 of the UDHR provides that '[e]veryone has the right to work, to free choice of employment, to just and favourable conditions of work and to protection against unemployment' and art. 6(1) of the ICESCR provides that '[t]he States Parties to the present Covenant recognise the right to work which includes the right of everyone to the opportunity to gain his living by work which he freely chooses or accepts, and will take appropriate steps to safeguard this right'.

While many cases relating to denial of the right to work involve state-controlled economies in which the applicant is effectively 'blacklisted', there are numerous examples of successful claims in other situations as well, for example, where continual discrimination by either state or non-state actors precludes a person from obtaining or sustaining work. For example, in *Desir v. Ilchert*,[27] the US Court of Appeals for the Ninth Circuit held that a claim for economic persecution was made out because '[i]n addition to this physical abuse, Desir's ability to earn a livelihood was also severely impaired by his refusal to give money to the Macoutes

---

[24] See, for example, *Castillo-Ponce v. Immigration and Naturalization Service*, 1995 US App. LEXIS 27058 (9th Cir. 1995) ('*Castillo-Ponce*'); and *Zhen Hua Li v. Attorney General of the United States; Immigration and Naturalization Service*, 400 F. 3d 157 (3rd Cir. 2005), in which a claim was upheld because the applicant was 'blacklisted from government employment' in China, which also resulted in loss of benefits such as 'health coverage, food and medicine rations, and educational benefits': at 169. For Canadian authority, see: *Xie v. Canada* [1994] FCJ No. 286, at para. 11; *Shao Mei He v. Minister of Employment and Immigration* [1994] FCJ No. 1243; and *Li v. Canada (Minister of Citizenship and Immigration)* [1994] FCJ No. 1745.

[25] See, for example, *Castillo-Ponce*, 1995 US App. LEXIS 27058 (9th Cir. 1995), at 7. I note that the UNHCR has reiterated this in more recent documents: see, for example, *Guidelines on International Protection: Religion-Based Refugee Claims under Article 1A(2) of the 1951 Convention and/or the 1967 Protocol relating to the status of Refugees*, HCR/GIP/04/06 (2004) at para. 17.

[26] See for example, *Refugee Appeal No. 70863/98*, RSAA, 13 August 1998, at 7.

[27] 840 F 2d 723 (9th Cir. 1988).

because the threats on his life precluded both fishing and the selling of curios'.[28] In a more recent decision, the same court overturned the decision of the IJ which had rejected the claim of an Israeli Arab who had faced discrimination in employment his whole life (having been prevented from working as an accountant and a lifeguard, occupations for which he was trained, on the basis of his ethnicity), culminating in constant harassment from the Israeli Marines in the course of working for his family as a fisherman.[29] The applicant established that the Marines 'targeted Baballah's livelihood by purposely destroying his fishing nets... by frightening away his crew, and by singling him out to receive unwarranted citations that were costly to resolve... Ultimately Baballah's fishing boat was destroyed by the Israeli Marines when they ignored Baballah's directions for towing it'.[30]

The more controversial question is the extent to which less severe infringements on the ability to work will be considered sufficiently serious as to constitute persecution. Courts do not always require the complete denial of all forms of work or all possibility of earning a living in order to found a successful claim, although they take different approaches to the extent of exclusion from employment that is required to amount to persecution. At one end of the spectrum,[31] decision-makers are uniform in holding that 'mild' discrimination in the workplace, whereby an individual is demoted[32] or foreclosed from such

---

[28] *Desir*, 840 F 2d 723 (9th Cir. 1988) 727.
[29] *Baballah v. John Ashcroft*, 367 F 3d 1067 (9th Cir. 2003) (*'Baballah'*).
[30] *Baballah*, 367 F 3d 1067 (9th Cir. 2003), at 13.
[31] This term is taken from the decision of Tamberlin J of the Federal Court of Australia in *Ye Hong v. Minister for Immigration and Multicultural Affairs* [1998] 1356 FCA (Unreported, Tamberlin J, 2 October 1998): 'At one end of the spectrum there may be a situation where a person is denied any right to work or is given work of a demeaning nature or of a type which ignores any academic or special experience or qualification to work in a highly skilled area for which the person has been specially trained. At the other extreme, is a situation where the discrimination is merely in the nature of unpleasantness or a conflict of personalities': at para. 37 (*'Ye Hong'*).
[32] Courts have held that the fact that an applicant suffers a demotion at work for a Refugee Convention reason does not of itself amount to 'being persecuted'. See, for example, *PFH (Re)*, Nos. T96-00266, T96-00267, T96-00269 [1997] CRDD No. 327, 3 February 1997, at para. 14; *Kornetskyi v. Gonzales*, 129 Fed. Appx. 254; 2005 US App. LEXIS 7457 (6th Cir. 2005); *Baka v. Immigration and Naturalization Service*, 963 F 2d 1376 (10th Cir. 1992) (which found that lack of promotions and the assignment of less advantageous jobs were not sufficient to constitute persecution); *Ly Ying Sayaxing v. Immigration and Naturalization Service*, 179 F 3d 515 (7th Cir. 1999) (which found that demotion was not sufficient to constitute a claim).

opportunities as promotions or better or more interesting work,[33] does not fall within the notion of 'being persecuted'. In one US decision for example, the Romanian applicant specifically invoked the relevant (US) domestic legislation concerning employment discrimination in support of his application for asylum, which was founded on the differential treatment he had suffered at work due to his religion.[34] However, the court rejected his claim on the basis that '[h]is analogy fails to establish his past persecution; this court has determined that such discriminatory practices do not amount to persecution'.[35]

Violations of the right to work that are more serious than 'mere' discrimination in the workplace but which do not amount to a complete denial of employment are less straightforward. In some cases, decision-makers have recognized claims where a person was repeatedly denied employment in his or her field,[36] while in other cases more widespread exclusion has been required.[37] A particularly interesting issue concerns the right to work in government positions, as courts tend to disagree regarding the extent to which this fact alone constitutes persecution. Such a prohibition potentially violates both the right to work provisions

---

[33] See, for example, *Ni v. Immigration and Naturalization Service*, 54 Fed. Appx. 212, 2002 US App. LEXIS 27189 (6th Cir. 2002), which observed that '[n]or did the school system's decision to reduce Ni's salary and deny him an allegedly deserved promotion impose the hardships necessary to constitute "persecution" ': at 10. See also *El-Hewie v. Immigration and Naturalization Service*, 1994 US App. LEXIS 34660 (9th Cir. 1994).

[34] *Sofinet v. Immigration and Naturalization Service*, 196 F 3d 742 (7th Cir. 1999), at 747 ('*Sofinet*').

[35] *Sofinet*, 196 F 3d 742 (7th Cir. 1999).

[36] See, for example, *Baballah v. Immigration and Naturalization Service*, 335 F 3d 981 (9th Cir. 2003), at 922. In Denmark, 'the Board granted refugee status to an Armenian woman fired from her job and subjected to other forms of threats and harassment because of her political opposition to the authorities': Pia Lynggaard Justesen, 'Denmark' in Carlier, Vanheule, Peña Galiano and Hullman (eds.), *Who is a Refugee?*, p. 325. In addition, '[t]he deprivation of an attorney's license may also make the fear of future persecution well-founded': pp. 325–6.

[37] See, for example, *Urukov v. Immigration and Naturalization Service*, 55 F 3d 222 (7th Cir. 1995), at 228; and *Moro v. The Secretary of State for the Home Department* (Unreported, IAT, Appeal No. HX-72022-98, 11 September 2000), at para. 8 ('*Moro*'), upheld on appeal: see *Moro v. Secretary of State for the Home Department* [2001] EWCA Civ 1680. In *Refugee Appeal No. 70863/98*, RSAA, 13 August 1998, the NZ RSAA held that an Iranian woman who was forced by the Komiteh to cease working as a hairdresser was not a victim of persecution. Interestingly, the Authority made some obiter comments that suggest that it might have taken a different view if the applicant was well established in a profession, stating that '[t]here has not therefore been a substantial investment in terms of years of training and accumulated experience which may make any proscription on following one's normal profession particularly onerous': at 9.

in the ICESCR and art. 25 of the ICCPR, which provides that: 'Every citizen shall have the right and the opportunity, without any of the distinctions mentioned in article 2 and without unreasonable restrictions' (inter alia) '[t]o have access, on general terms of equality, to public service in his country'.[38]

Where the state controls the economy such that it is the only effective employer, decision-makers have had little difficulty in equating such harm with persecution. For example, the Australian RRT has held that where a person is denied employment in the public sector and in practice it is virtually impossible to find employment in the private sector, 'then this amounts to denial of the right to earn a living and constitutes persecution'.[39] However, the position is not so clear in respect of applicants who may have options for employment in the private sector. In a decision by Mansfield J of the Federal Court of Australia, an Indian woman who was precluded from working for the government as a school teacher based on her Christian faith was held to have established a risk of being persecuted on the basis that

> the Tribunal erred in concluding that the ability to obtain work in private enterprise reflects the State upholding the 'right to work', where the State either imposes or tolerates a system which precludes certain of its citizens from working in government employment for reasons of religion or political beliefs. Far from treating its citizens equally, the State then is sanctioning discrimination against some of them for Convention reasons. It is difficult to envisage circumstances where such discrimination may, in a practical sense, be insignificant. That is the more so when there is a significant economic disadvantage consequent upon that restriction, *although actual economic disadvantage in an immediate personal sense is not per se the critical matter.* It is unnecessary to resort specifically to relatively recent historical examples to make the point. To characterise the circumstances as not sufficiently serious to constitute persecution in my view fails to acknowledge the fundamental significance of the State positively excluding certain of its citizens for Convention reasons from employment by the State and its organs.[40]

---

[38] Which, according to Hathaway, is a 'level two' right: see below notes 122–5.
[39] *Reference V94/02820*, RRT, 6 October 1995, at 6, citing *Li Shi Ping and Anor v. Minister for Immigration, Local Government and Ethnic Affairs* (1995) 35 ALD 557.
[40] *Thalary v. Minister for Immigration and Ethnic Affairs* (1997) 50 ALD 349 at 352 (emphasis added) ('*Thalary*'). See also *Seo v. Minister for Immigration and Multicultural Affairs* [2001] FCA 1258 (Unreported, Spender J, 7 September 2001), at para. 24: 'I would respectfully query whether a right to work in a mixed economy, which is coupled with an inability to work in government employment, would not involve a discrimination amounting to persecution'; *SGKB v. Minister for Immigration and Multicultural Affairs & Indigenous Affairs* (2004) 76 ALD 381, where the Full Federal Court of Australia held that the RRT should

By contrast, other decision-makers, such as the New Zealand RSAA, have held that 'the Authority does not accept that the deprivation of state employment, in circumstances where the asylum seeker was able to secure employment in the private sector and absent any other discrimination ... would amount to persecution'.[41] Since the focus of the US jurisprudence, discussed further below, is on substantial economic disadvantage, it is perhaps not surprising that where the applicant may obtain a position in the private sector, the claim for refugee status is generally not made out.[42] The only exception is where this aspect of the claim may be accumulated with a range of other aspects of serious harm.[43] Interestingly, the issue has rarely been decided in any court by reference to art. 25 of the ICCPR.[44]

Some commentators have suggested that economic proscription should not be restricted only to cases of total exclusion from employment, but rather should extend to include the situation where a person 'is denied all work which is "suitable" or commensurate with his training and qualifications'.[45] Hathaway relies on a 'holistic view of the substance of the right to work, including both the right to access employment and the right to "just and favourable conditions of work", established by Articles 6 and 7 respectively of the [Economic] Covenant',[46] in support of

---

have considered (*inter alia*), 'whether or not the risk of losing the opportunity of government employment was itself sufficient to constitute persecution': at 387. For the contra view, see *WAEW of 2002 v. Minister for Immigration and Multicultural and Indigenous Affairs* [2002] FCAFC 260 (Marshall, Weinberg and Jacobson JJ, 22 August 2002), at para. 19; *Prahastono* (1997) 77 FCR 260 at 267.

[41] *Refugee Appeal No. 71605/99*, RSAA, 16 December 1999, at 7. See also *Refugee No. 70597/97*, RSAA, 1 September 1997, at 12; *Refugee No. 70667/97*, RSAA, 18 September 1997, at 10.

[42] *Minwalla v. Immigration and Naturalization Service*, 706 F 2d 831 (8th Cir. 1983), at 834: 'Minwalla has also failed to establish a substantial economic disadvantage, because he has not alleged that he will be deprived of the opportunity for private sector employment as an engineer'; *Largaespada-Galo v. Immigration and Naturalization Service*, 1996 US App. LEXIS 13267 (9th Cir. 1996).

[43] See *Ram v. Immigration and Naturalization Service*, 2000 US App. LEXIS 6811 (9th Cir. 2000).

[44] It seems that the only decision in which this provision is mentioned is *Moro* [2001] EWCA Civ. 1680, in which the applicant submitted 'that the effective dismissal of Mr Moro from his senior post office job because he refused to attend chaka-mchaka amounted to a denial of his second category right [previously described as including "the ability to partake in government, access public employment without discrimination and vote in periodic and genuine elections"] and thus constituted persecution': at para. 24. The case was ultimately rejected, but not on the basis that denial of government employment could not amount to persecution but on the particular facts of this case: at para. 25.

[45] Grahl-Madsen, *The Status of Refugees in International Law*, p. 208.

[46] Hathaway, *The Law of Refugee Status*, p. 123.

the conclusion that persecution can be established where a person is prevented from securing employment other than that which is 'grossly out of keeping with her qualifications and experience'.[47] There is some support for this in the case law: some of the cases that have been recognized include a claim by a Romanian radiologist whose position was terminated due to political activities and who was unable to obtain another position, except that of a farm labourer,[48] and a claim by a teacher who was relegated to work as 'a farm hand and garment worker'.[49] In another decision, the Federal Court of Australia found that the RRT had fallen into error in failing to consider the effect of exclusion from government employment (based on religion) on the applicant's career, 'taking into account both job satisfaction and remuneration'.[50] However, in other cases courts have been reluctant to recognize that 'hard work not commensurate with one's training' amounts to persecution.[51] For example, US courts have denied claims in which

---

[47] Hathaway, *The Law of Refugee Status*, p. 123.
[48] *Borca v. Immigration and Naturalization Service*, 77 F 3d 210 (7th Cir. 1996), at 212 ('*Borca*'). See also *Cabello v. Canada (Minister of Citizenship and Immigration)* [1995] FCJ No. 630. For Australian authority, see *Ji Kil Soon v. Minister for Immigration, Local Government and Ethnic Affairs and the RRT* (1994) 37 ALD 609 and *Ye Hong* [1998] 1356 FCA (Unreported, Tamberlin J, 2 October 1998) at para. 39. See also *Grecu* (Unreported, IAT, Appeal No. HX/64793/96, 8 January 1998), in which the UK IAT said: 'Furthermore, when that expulsion from university results in a failure to obtain employment commensurate with a person's abilities and education the question of the deprivation of the right to work is a matter which should be examined within the context of persecution for a Convention ground': at 5.
[49] *Shao Mei He v. Minister of Employment and Immigration* [1994] FCJ No. 1243 at para. 15.
[50] *Ahmadi v. Minister for Immigration and Multicultural Affairs* [2001] FCA 1070 (Unreported, Wilcox J, 8 August 2001), at para. 48. The Court noted that the applicant had 'completed 16 years education, emerging with qualifications in a specialized field' and that 'opportunities in his field are substantially, if not wholly, confined to the public sector': at para. 46. As a consequence, 'his training and qualifications would be substantially wasted and he would be denied a career in his chosen field'. Accordingly, 'a real question arose before the Tribunal as to whether the harm suffered by the applicant amounted to 'persecution' within the meaning of the Convention': at para. 46.
[51] *Sofinet*, 196 F 3d 742 (7th Cir. 1999), at 747, citing *Krastev v. Immigration and Naturalization Service*, 101 F 3d 1213 (7th Cir. 1996), at 1217. In *Barreto-Clara v. US Attorney General; Immigration and Naturalization Service*, 275 F 3d 1334 (11th Cir. 2001), at 1340, the court held: 'At most, the evidence reflects that when Barreto fell out of favor with the Communist Party, he suffered employment discrimination, lost his job as a taxi driver and was forced to take menial work. This type of employment discrimination which stops short of depriving an individual of a means of earning a living does not constitute persecution'. The position in the US cases remains unclear, however, as in *Ruiz v. Immigration and Naturalization Service*, 1996 US App. LEXIS 14687 (9th Cir. 1996), the court dismissed the claim on the basis that the applicant has not shown that 'she was unable to obtain any *reasonably comparable employment*': at 2 (emphasis added).

a teacher was forced to take a labouring job due to his political views[52] and where a kindergarten teacher was fired because of her religious beliefs and forced to take a job at a furnace factory.[53] The cases that have been successful in the USA tend to involve relegation to menial work as well as a number of other aspects of serious harm.[54] Being forced to work in dangerous conditions is clearly included, although here the focus is not so much on socio-economic issues as physical integrity.[55]

To a certain extent, differential outcomes in the employment cases reflect a more deep-seated disagreement regarding the nature of the harm inherent in discrimination in the sphere of economic and social rights. Should we be concerned only with pure economic impact or is there something more fundamental about work (and other socio-economic rights), relating to dignity, identity and self-worth? This issue can arise directly where it is clear that persistent discrimination prevents access to employment, but alternative means of survival (through for example government benefits) are available to the applicant.[56] In a decision of the Canadian Federal Court for example, a refugee claim was dismissed on the basis that although the applicant was unable to secure employment on a Convention ground, this 'failed to reach the threshold of persecution by reason of the economic support that her

---

[52] *Auriga v. Immigration and Naturalization Service*, 1993 US App. LEXIS 6775 (9th Cir. 1993), at 7.
[53] *Nagoulko*, 333 F 3d 1012 (9th Cir. 2003). See also *Ljuljdjurovic v. Gonzales*, 132 Fed. Appx. 607; 2005 US App. LEXIS 9644 (6th Cir. 2005), at 612.
[54] Anker cites some examples of these cases. She argues that the Kovac standard 'includes being compelled to take menial employment incompatible with a person's qualifications and experience': Anker, *Law of Asylum in the United States*, p. 238. However, often the cases on point do not involve this issue alone; rather, there are other significant aspects to the case.
[55] See Anker, *Law of Asylum in the United States*, p. 238, note 329. Pia Lynggaard Justesen explains that in Denmark, '[a]nother example of persecution by cumulation was the on-going harassment of a Ukranian Jew who was forced to work in Chernobyl after the nuclear disaster, who received telephone threats, who had to take his child out of kindergarten because the teachers beat him and who was finally dismissed from his job': Lynggaard Justesen, 'Denmark' in Carlier, Vanheule, Peña Galiano and Hullman (eds.), *Who is a Refugee?*, p. 319. See also Hathaway, *The Law of Refugee Status*, p. 123; See also *Prahastono* (1997) 77 FCR 260 at 267.
[56] See, for example, *R (on the Application of Secretary of State for the Home Department) v. Immigration Appeal Tribunal* (Queen's Bench Division (Administrative Court), CO/593/1999, 21 November 2000), at para. 26: 'But nowhere is there a consideration of the degree of seriousness of the discrimination in relation to employment, bearing in mind the high level of unemployment generally *and the availability of social security for Roma*' (emphasis added).

husband was able to provide'.[57] This also arises in the context of the 'menial work as persecution' issue. These cases are complex since, on the one hand, they potentially raise issues of class bias if professional asylum seekers are privileged over those who are unskilled; but on the other hand, they raise genuine questions as to the violation of dignity involved in such treatment. This may be what Mansfield J was alluding to when he stated that 'actual economic disadvantage in an immediate personal sense is not per se the critical matter'.[58] This issue has occasionally been explicitly considered in the jurisprudence. In one decision of the RSAA, the Authority reflected that 'work, besides being the normal means of ensuring an adequate standard of living, has a personal and social dimension which is closely related to the realization of self worth and dignity'.[59] However, the Authority ultimately decided the case on the basis of the economic impact of the loss of employment on the applicant. By contrast, in a recent decision of the Refugee Appeal Board of South Africa, the Board upheld the refugee claim of a citizen of Zimbabwe who established that 'he would not easily, if at all, secure gainful employment as a charted accountant' in Zimbabwe due to his political affiliations.[60] In finding that this treatment amounted to a risk of 'being persecuted', the Board referred to a decision of the South African Supreme Court of Appeal in which it had recognized that

[t]he freedom to engage in productive work – even where that is not required in order to survive – is indeed an important component of human dignity, for mankind is pre-eminently a social species with an instinct for meaningful association. Self-esteem and the sense of self worth – the fulfilment of what it is to be human – is most often bound up with being accepted as socially useful.[61]

---

[57] *Barkai v. Canada (Minister of Employment and Immigration)*, 1994 A.C.W.S.J. LEXIS 74622 (27 September 1994) at para. 44.
[58] *Thalary* (1997) 50 ALD 349 at 352 at 448.
[59] *Refugee Appeal No. 70863/98*, RSAA, 13 August 1998, at 9.
[60] Refugee Appeal Board of South Africa, Appeal number 53/2005, 30 November 2004, at para. 33.
[61] *Minister of Home Affairs and Ors v. Watchenuka and Anor*, 2004 (2) BCLR 120 (SCA), at 127. Similarly, in a Belgian decision, the Refugee Appeals Board found that the dismissal of a Romanian hotel manager, who had been falsely accused of smuggling foreign money when he refused to collaborate in spying on foreign travellers, was persecutory, on the basis that, 'the claimant's fear with regard to this inquiry as well as the possible consequences thereof, namely the lack of professional [prospects] in his sector upon his return, can constitute, in this case, an invasion of his integrity and personal dignity': *CPR* (1 ch), 14 September 1993, F217, as cited in Dirk Vanheule, 'Belgium', in Carlier, Vanheule, Peña Galiano and Hullman (eds.), *Who is a Refugee?*, pp. 92–3.

This approach is consistent with the Economic Committee's view that the right to work embodied in art. 6 of the ICECSR 'is essential for realizing other human rights and forms an inseparable and inherent part of human dignity'.[62] If persecution is understood to be concerned fundamentally with serious violations of human dignity,[63] then this is an issue which requires exploration in the case law dealing with socio-economic persecution. However, this has not been adequately addressed in the case law to date.[64]

Turning to cases involving aspects of economic and social rights other than work, one important development in recent years is that courts have begun to recognize claims based on the denial of the right to education, most importantly in the case of children. In some cases the denial of a child's ability to receive education has itself been considered sufficient to found a refugee claim, on the basis that the right to education is a fundamental human right. For example, in *Ali v. Canada (Minister of Citizenship and Immigration)*, the Federal Court of Canada considered that the decision of the Tribunal below, which held that the child applicant could avoid persecution by declining to attend school, was incorrect on the basis that '[e]ducation is a basic human right and I direct the Board to find that she [the applicant] should be found to be Convention refugee'.[65] In a more recent decision, the Canadian RPD made reference to art. 28 of the CRC – which provides that 'States Parties recognise the right of the child to education'[66] – in support of the conclusion that the 'two minor claimants have been persecuted based on their suspension from school'.[67] In many cases deprivation of education is considered in conjunction with a number of other violations of socio-economic rights,[68] although

---

[62] Committee on Economic, Social and Cultural Rights, *General Comment No. 18: The Right to Work*, UN Doc. E/C.12/GC/18 (2005b), at para. 1.
[63] *Refugee Appeal No. 71427/99*, RSAA, 16 August 2000, at para. 53(a).
[64] For a relatively rare reference to the humiliation/dignity aspect of discrimination in US case-law, see *Begzatowski*, 278 F 3d 665 (7th Cir. 2002).
[65] [1997] 1 FCD 26; 1996 FCD LEXIS 592, at para. 13 ('*Ali*').
[66] Article 28 of the CRC relevantly provides: 'States Parties recognise the right of the child to education, and with a view to achieving this right progressively and on the basis of equal opportunity, they shall, in particular: (a) Make primary education compulsory and available free to all'.
[67] *ODO (Re)*, Nos. VA1-03231, VA1-03232, VA1-03233 [2003] RPDD No. 66, 12 March 2003, at paras. 5–10.
[68] Including denial of the right to health care: see *Freiburg v. Canada (Secretary of State)* (1994) 78 FTR 283; *Mirzabeglui v. Canada (Minister of Employment and Immigration)* [1991] FCJ No. 50;

even then emphasis is placed on the central importance of the right to education.[69]

Another issue that is beginning to attract attention from advocates and decision-makers is the right to health, and specifically equal access to medical treatment. While the jurisprudence is nascent, a number of successful claims have been made based primarily on severe discrimination in access to medical treatment. For example, in *TNL (Re)*, the Canadian RPD upheld the claim of an HIV-positive man from Poland who feared severe discrimination on the basis of his HIV status. It noted that he was at risk of the 'following forms of discrimination ... in the area of health care alone: refusal to admit HIV patients to hospitals for fear that they pose a health risk to the staff; refusal of doctors to operate on patients who tested HIV-Positive; and frequent testing of hospital patients for HIV without their consent and sometimes without their knowledge'.[70] In another decision involving the claim of a Russian child with cerebral palsy who faced severe discrimination in respect of both access to medical care and education, the US Court of Appeals for the Ninth Circuit noted, in upholding the claim, that where denial of medical care or education 'seriously jeopardizes the health or welfare of the affected individuals, a finding of persecution is warranted'.[71]

While decision-makers have allowed claims based on a single type of socio-economic deprivation, the most common method by which claims based on the deprivation of economic and social rights have been successful is by reference to the principle that a fear of being persecuted may be established by an accumulation of a number of less serious violations, which may be sufficiently serious in combination as to

---

Madelat v. Canada (Minister of Employment and Immigration) [1991] FCJ No. 49; Ali [1997] 1 FCD 26; 1996 FCD LEXIS 592. Discrimination in educational facilities has been considered relevant in Denmark on a cumulative basis: Pia Lynggaard Justesen explains that '[s]ystematic and ongoing harassment by exclusion from a particular education as well as other complaints such as telephone threats and assaults may also constitute persecution': 'Denmark' in Carlier, Vanheule, Peña Galiano and Hullman (eds.), *Who is a Refugee?*, p. 319.

[69] See Chen Shi Hai (2000) 201 CLR 293; *Cheung et al. v. Canada (Minister of Employment and Immigration)* [1993] 2 FC 314; 153 NR 145; 19 Imm. LR (2d) 81 (FCA), at 325 ('*Cheung*').

[70] No. T95-07647 [1997] CRDD No. 251, 23 October 1997. See also *SBAS v. Minister for Immigration and Multicultural Affairs* [2003] FCA 528 (Unreported, Cooper J, 30 May 2003), at paras. 74–9 ('*SBAS*').

[71] *Tchoukhrova v. Gonzales*, 404 F 3d 1181 (9th Cir. 2005), at 1194.

constitute persecution.[72] As explained by the IAT in *Gudja*, persecution can be established by

a concatenation of individual denials of rights; for example to the right to work, to education, to health or to welfare benefits to such an extent that it erodes the very quality of life in the result that such a combination is an interference with a basic human right to live a decent life.[73]

However, this presents a challenge in identifying the kinds of economic and social rights violations that are deemed sufficiently serious to constitute persecution, since it is difficult to assess the degree of seriousness with which each separate issue is regarded.[74] It is often impossible to ascertain from the decision-maker's reasoning whether certain violations would, on their own, have amounted to a finding of persecution or whether they must necessarily have been consolidated with a range of other types of harm. This is magnified by the fact that courts have sometimes stated that it is the task of the first-level decision-maker (usually at the executive level) rather than the court to 'police the line between discrimination and persecution'.[75] It should be noted that this appears to be a particular problem in the context of economic-related claims, as will be discussed further below.

Among the types of claims that have been successful by engaging the 'accumulation analysis' are the following: withdrawal of ration card and confiscation of property in combination with threats of violence;[76] withdrawal of state benefits, in combination with inability to obtain employment or accommodation due to ethnic origin;[77] denial of state benefits such as housing, food and clothing benefits and subsidies in

---

[72] For example, in a number of cases, courts and tribunals have acknowledged that infringements on the right to work may constitute a factor in assessing persecution: see *Refugee Appeal No. 732/92*, RSAA, 5 August 1994; *Refugee Appeal 71605/99*, RSAA, 16 December 1999; *Minister for Immigration, Local Government and Ethnic Affairs v. Che Guang Xiang* (Federal Court of Australia, Jenkinson, Spender and Lee JJ, 12 August 1994); and *Chen Ru Mei v. Minister of Immigration and Ethnic Affairs* (1995) 130 ALR 405.
[73] *Gudja* (Unreported, IAT, CC/59626/97, 5 August 1999), at 2. See also *VTAO v. Minister for Immigration and Multicultural and Indigenous Affairs* (2005) 81 ALD 332 at 352.
[74] See, for example, the UK IAT: 'Whilst we do not see any one of the abovementioned factors as itself giving rise to persecution, we are satisfied that taken together they would amount to persecution': *Maksimovic v. Secretary of State for the Home Department* [2004] EWHC 1026 at para. 29.
[75] *Sizov*, 70 Fed. Appx. 374, 2003 US App. LEXIS 13524 (7th Cir. 2003), at 7.
[76] *Gonzalez v. Immigration and Naturalization Service*, 82 F 3d 903 (9th Cir. 1996) ('*Gonzalez*').
[77] See for example *Secretary of State of the Home Department v. Padhu* (Unreported, IAT, Appeal No. HX 74530-94, 14 July 1995) at 2.

a state-controlled economy;[78] severe discrimination in 'most civil, social and economic rights' such that the applicant would suffer 'a life of destitution';[79] and discrimination in a range of areas such as employment, housing, child-care and education for children, sometimes combined with infliction of humiliating and degrading treatment from society.[80] In one decision concerning a child born outside the one-child policy in China, the Canadian Federal Court of Appeal held that

if Karen Lee were sent back to China, she would, in her own right, experience such concerted and severe discrimination, including deprivation of medical care, education and employment opportunities and even food, so as to amount to persecution.[81]

---

[78] L (LL) Re, No. A93-81751 [1994] CRDD No. 368, 16 August 1994.

[79] In *Secretary of State for the Home Department* v. *Kondratiev* [2002] UK IAT 08283 ('*Kondratiev*'), the IAT upheld the claim of a stateless woman who, if returned to Russia, could not obtain registration as a 'forced migrant' and thus could not obtain internal Russian passports, since, '[w]ithout such passports there would be no recourse to housing, work or benefits of any kind'. The Adjudicator held that the evidence showed that 'if returned to Russia the respondent would suffer from a 'life of destitution' and that would amount to persecution on the grounds of nationality': at para. 7. See also *Peco* (Unreported, IAT, Appeal No. HX-74935-94, 12 November 1996), where the UK IAT allowed an appeal against the decision to reject a claim by a citizen of Bosnia on the basis that there was evidence that the applicant would experience 'discrimination in fields of housing, employment and welfare, with the latter having particular significance due to the difficulties of obtaining employment': at 6.

[80] See *Refugee Appeal No. 2217/94*, RSAA, 12 September 1996, at 13–14; and *Refugee Appeal No. 74395*, RSAA, 21 January 2004. In *SBAS* [2003] FCA 528 (Unreported, Cooper J, 30 May 2003), the Federal Court of Australia found that the RRT was in error in failing to consider whether a range of socio-economic violations constituted persecutory treatment: at para. 58. See also the Danish cases discussed by Pia Lynggaard Justesen in 'Denmark' in Carlier, Vanheule, Peña Galiano and Hullman (eds.), *Who is a Refugee?*, notes 42, 61. In Greece, '[d]iscrimination on economic and social matters can also be an element of the threat directed against the claimant': Paroul Naskou-Perraki, 'Greece' in Carlier, Vanheaule, Peña Galiano and Hullman (eds.), *Who is a Refugee?*, p. 453. For UK authority, see *Secretary of State for the Home Department* v. *Vujatovic* [2002] UKIAT 02474, 9 July 2002, at paras. 37, 44. For Canadian authority, see *V (OZ) Re*, No. M93-04717 [1993] CRDD No. 164, 10 June 1993; and *JLD (Re)*, No. T95-00305 [1996] CRD No. 291, 9 April 1996. In the USA, see *Levitskaya* v. *Immigration and Naturalization Service*, 43 Fed. Appx. 38; 2002 US App. LEXIS 15799 (9th Cir. 2002), where the 9th Circuit upheld a claim based on the applicant's evidence that 'she and her family were forced to live in overcrowded, substandard housing and were even required to relinquish housing to other residents...that her sister was denied educational opportunities...that she was prohibited as a child from attending church services with her parents, and...that civil police disrupted church services and incarcerated church leaders': at 42.

[81] *Cheung* [1993] 2 FC 314; 153 NR 145; 19 Imm LR (2d) 81 (FCA), at 325. See also *Chen Shi Hai* (2000) 201 CLR 293, where the High Court of Australia found that, in a similar context, '[o]rdinarily, denial of access to food, shelter, medical treatment and, in the case of children, denial of an opportunity to obtain an education involve such a significant

These decisions are sometimes reached by reference to a range of human rights provisions, including those contained in the ICESCR, such as art. 6 (the right to work), art. 11 (the right to an adequate standard of living including adequate food, clothing and housing), art. 12 (the right to health) and art. 13 (right to education).[82]

As is the case in respect of claims involving the denial of employment, 'cumulative' applications have been most easily accepted where the violation of socio-economic rights is either inflicted by the state or clearly sponsored by the state. For example, in a decision of the US Court of Appeals for the Sixth Circuit, the Court held that the BIA had erred in rejecting the refugee claim of a stateless Palestinian family resident in Kuwait, who, after the liberation of Kuwait, suffered a series of human rights violations based on the perception that they had been supporters of Iraq.[83] The evidence was clear in establishing that the Kuwaitis engaged in 'a general campaign to prohibit Palestinians from working, attending school, buying food, obtaining water or obtaining drivers' licenses'.[84] The Oudas were 'not only harassed because they were Palestinians who were perceived enemies of Kuwait, they were unable to earn a livelihood or travel safely in public, forced to sell their belongings to buy food, and expelled from Kuwait with only a percentage of Mr Ouda's pension'.[85] In such circumstances the Court concluded that 'no reasonable factfinder could fail to find that the Oudas were persecuted'.[86]

---

departure from the standards of the civilized world as to constitute persecution': at para. 29 (Gleeson CJ, Gaudron, Gummow, and Hayne JJ).

[82] See, for example, *Refugee Appeal No. 2217/94*, RSAA, 12 September 1996, at 15–16. See also *TNL (Re)*, No. T95-07647 [1997] CRDD No. 251, 23 October 1997.

[83] *Ouda*, 324 F 3d 445 (6th Cir. 2003) ('*Ouda*').

[84] *Ouda*, 324 F 3d 445 (6th Cir. 2003), at 23.

[85] *Ouda*, 324 F 3d 445 (6th Cir. 2003), at 23.

[86] *Ouda*, 324 F 3d 445 (6th Cir. 2003), at 23. See also *El Himri v. Ashcroft*, 378 F 3d 932 (9th Cir. 2004), in which the Ninth Circuit upheld the refugee claim from a stateless Palestinian family from Kuwait on the basis that while they were 'fortunate enough to avoid violent persecution upon their return to Kuwait, they would not be able to avoid the state-sponsored economic discrimination that has been enacted against Palestinians living in Kuwait since the end of the Gulf War': at 937–8. This economic discrimination was evidenced by the fact that after the Gulf War, Palestinians 'were denied the right to work, go to school, or even obtain drinking water': at 937. In addition, 'the government remains reluctant to issue work permits to the Palestinians still living in Kuwait': at 937. The Court also noted that it has been 'particularly sensitive to state-sponsored economic discrimination as distinguished from isolated acts by individuals': at 937. See also *Refugee Appeal No. 74880*, RSAA, 29 September 2005, in which the NZ RSAA upheld a claim by a stateless man, born in Kuwait, who claimed that due to his being a bedoon, he could not 'access social services which are available to Kuwaiti nationals, including education, health care and benefits': at para. 84.

By contrast, applicants appear to have greater difficulty in establishing claims when the exclusion stems from discrimination on the part of non-state actors. This is sometimes compounded by the fact that the issue of whether harm is sufficiently serious becomes intertwined with issues surrounding sufficiency of protection, especially where the state is unable rather than unwilling to provide protection against persecution.[87] Nonetheless, there are numerous examples of successful claims based on violations of economic and social rights by non-state actors.

Tribunals and courts have been willing to acknowledge that a lifetime of discrimination suffered by an ethnic group at the hands of non-state actors can give rise to a well-founded fear of persecution. For example, in a decision of the New Zealand RSAA, the Authority held that the systemic discrimination suffered by a Roma family in the Czech Republic, in a range of areas such as employment, the provision of health care and housing, education of their children, provision of public goods and services, coupled with a number of individual instances of race-motivated violence, was sufficient to constitute persecution.[88] The Authority considered the 'profound effect of the appellants' long experience of involuntary abasement' in reaching its conclusion,[89] thereby alluding

---

[87] In brief, the key issue in this respect is that in some cases the courts require only a 'due diligence' effort on the part of the state, rather than an ability to remove the well founded fear altogether. Thus, courts will sometimes deny claims even where a fear exists on the basis that the home government is 'doing its best' to stop the discrimination/persecution. The cases involving severe discrimination and violence against Roma are good examples of this phenomenon: see for example *Horvath* [2000] 3 All ER 577; [2000] 3 WLR 379. In the specific context of socio-economic claims, see *Refugee Appeal No. 75221*, RSAA, 23 September 2005, in which the NZ RSAA found that while 'Dalits remained discriminated against in every aspect of their lives', the refugee claim was rejected on the basis that 'the Indian state has taken steps to address the de jure and de facto discrimination against Dalits and is taking steps to progressively realize their rights under the ICESCR': at paras. 119, 121. This is arguably asking the wrong question, as the ultimate question is whether the state's ability to protect is sufficient to remove the well-founded fear of being persecuted: see *Refugee Appeal No. 71427/99*, RSAA, 16 August 2000. For further discussion of this issue, see Penelope Mathew, James C. Hathaway and Michelle Foster, 'The Role of State Protection in Refugee Analysis' (2003) 15 *International Journal of Refugee Law* 444.

[88] *Refugee Appeal No. 71193/98*, RSAA, 9 September 1999. The decision outlines the applicant's case regarding a range of discrimination experienced in the past. The claim for future persecution is summarized as follows: 'The appellant said that if he returned to the Czech Republic, he would not have anywhere to live and would be unemployed. The appellant was especially concerned that his children would not have a good life in the Czech Republic. According to the appellant, there was nowhere in the Czech Republic where Roma could live safely': at 12.

[89] *Refugee Appeal No. 71193/98*, RSAA, 9 September 1999, at 12.

to the dignity aspect of socio-economic deprivation. In another case the Authority granted the claim of a Czech Romani on the basis that if he returned home 'he can expect to experience severe discrimination in seeking employment, in the level of and access to education by his children, and in obtaining housing. He can also expect further threats to his life and liberty particularly from the various skinhead groups'.[90]

Finally, the fact that courts have held that 'purely financial grievances'[91] or 'mere economic detriment'[92] will not generally found a successful refugee claim tends to suggest that applications involving confiscation of property would not be considered sufficiently serious to warrant a finding of persecution,[93] although claims based on deprivation of property rights have enjoyed some success. For example, in the US cases, '[c]onfiscation of property has been cited as one type of action that can cross the line from harassment to persecution'[94] and in a French decision, a former official in the presidential security service, 'whose possessions had been confiscated and bank account blocked after a coup d'état', was recognized as a refugee.[95] However, even in the USA, in most cases confiscation of property has been considered to 'contribute to

---

[90] Refugee Appeal No. 71336/99, RSAA, 4 May 2000.
[91] Hathaway, The Law of Refugee Status, p. 119.
[92] This is a phrase used in some US cases, although it can found a claim for persecution if it rises to the level of 'substantial economic disadvantage'– see below note 143. See Ambati v. Reno; Immigration and Naturalization Service, 233 F 3d 1054 (7th Cir. 2000). However, this must be carefully applied to the facts of individual cases, as it may be that in some instances, denial of such 'benefits', or imposition of 'mere' financial penalties, may in fact result in violations of fundamental rights. For example, while some courts have dismissed claims from parents who will be penalized financially for violating the one child policy in China on the basis, for example, that the applicant merely 'faces the objective possibility of incurring fees associated with the cost of housing and educating his son' (Chen v. Immigration and Naturalization Service, 195 F 3d 198 (4th Cir. 1999), at 204), it is important to note that courts have also recognized that such a financial grievance can in fact result in the deprivation of the rights to education and health for the children if the parents are unable to pay the relevant fine and the children are thus precluded from receiving fundamental entitlements to education and health care: see Chen Shi Hai (2000) 201 CLR 293.
[93] For authority in support of the notion that property loss is not sufficient to constitute persecution: see Ramirez v. Canada (Solicitor General) [1994] FCJ No. 1888; Chen v. Canada (Minister of Citizenship and Immigration) [1995] FCJ No. 189, at 4.
[94] Ouda, 324 F 3d 445 (6th Cir. 2003), citing Begzatowski, 278 F 3d 665 (7th Cir. 2002), at 669.
[95] Klaudia Schank and Carlos Peña Galiano, 'France' in Carlier, Vanheule, Peña Galiano and Hullman (eds.), Who is a Refugee?, p. 397.

a finding of persecution',[96] and thus must usually be combined with other elements of serious harm in order to constitute a successful claim.[97] Where the confiscation of property has more serious consequences for the individual, for example, by resulting in loss of housing or livelihood, decision-makers are more likely to view the action as sufficiently serious as to constitute persecution.[98] For example, in *Singh v. Immigration and Naturalization Service*,[99] the US Court of Appeals for the Ninth Circuit overturned the original rejection of the petitioner's claim which was based on the confiscation of his farming land by the Fijian government, holding, '[w]here the petitioner is a farmer, the taking of his land constitutes a substantial economic disadvantage that can be the basis of persecution'.[100]

This brief overview reveals that refugee decision-makers have become increasingly willing to consider a range of socio-economic rights violations as capable of constituting persecution. In addition to the more 'traditional' claims based on economic proscription, recent claims founded on severe discrimination in education, health care and a range of socio-economic rights related broadly to an adequate standard of living have been held to fall within the parameters of the Refugee Convention. This is significant as it makes it clear that the pervasive rhetoric of 'economic migrants' and 'economic refugees' has not precluded successful refugee claims based on threats to economic and social rights.

However, notwithstanding these positive developments, many significant problems remain in the adjudication of refugee claims based on

---

[96] *Ubau-Marenco v. Immigration and Naturalization Service*, 67 F 3d 750 (9th Cir. 1995) (emphasis in original) ('*Ubau-Marenco*'), citing *Samimi v. Immigration and Naturalization Service*, 714 F 2d 992 (9th Cir. 1983), at 995 ('*Samimi*'). In *Ubau-Marenco*, the Sandinistas confiscated the family transportation business without compensation. However, the claim was rejected since 'after this seizure Dr. Ubau-Marenco's family continued to own and profitably operate a farm selling rice to the government': at 754.

[97] For cases where deprivation of property was combined with other factors to find persecution, see *Gonzalez*, 82 F 3d 903 (9th Cir. 1996). See also cases cited by Anker, *Law of Asylum in the United States*, pp. 240–1, note 335.

[98] See, for example, *Chand v. Immigration and Naturalization Service*, 222 F 3d 1066 (9th Cir. 2000), at 1071 ('*Chand*'). In *Samimi*, 714 F 2d 992 (9th Cir. 1983), the court held that the 'seizure of petitioner's father's land and livelihood because of his family's ties to the former Shah could contribute to a finding of persecution' (as cited in *Ubau-Marenco* at 754). See also *Baballah*, 335 F 3d 981 (9th Cir. 2003), which found persecution on the basis of destruction of a fishing business. See also *Reference N01/40702*, RRT, 30 June 2003.

[99] 1999 US App LEXIS 22989 (9th Cir. 1999).

[100] *Singh*, 1999 US App LEXIS 22989 (9th Cir. 1999) at para 14.

infringements of economic and social rights. While some fundamental questions are no longer seriously in dispute, such as the question whether claims based on violations of economic and social rights can ever constitute successful refugee cases,[101] a more subtle set of problems emerges from an analysis of the jurisprudence over the past decade, relating to the *status, importance* and *method of evaluation* of economic and social rights. In other words, decision-makers are becoming increasingly comfortable with the notion of economic and social rights as rights,[102] often by reference to the ICESCR, but remain uncertain in many respects as to how to engage such rights in refugee adjudication. In particular, there is confusion concerning the substance of the rights in light of their formulation as being subject to progressive implementation,[103] their value in terms of a hierarchical approach, and the way in which the rights are measured. It is perhaps this lack of clarity in understanding the nature and method of implementing economic and social rights that explains courts' continuing reticence in practice to grant refugee status on the basis of violations of economic and social rights alone, all the while proclaiming that in principle such claims can give rise to successful applications for refugee status.[104] Before turning to an analysis of the specific problems in the case law, it is important first to understand the two key conceptual approaches espoused in the literature, because many of the difficulties and problems manifested in the case law pertain to confusion or misunderstanding of these different models.

Conceptual approaches to socio-economic rights and persecution

Chapter 2 established the dominance of the human rights approach to determining persecution, but did not consider the precise role of

---

[101] Martin's view that socio-economic rights cannot underpin a convention claim has not been sustained by the subsequent case law: see David Martin, 'Review of The Law of Refugee Status' (1993) 87 *American Journal of International Law* 348 at 351.
[102] It is important to note that the USA is an exception to this because the courts generally do not discuss the issues in terms of rights.
[103] Article 2(1) of the ICESCR provides that parties to the Covenant undertake to 'take steps individually and through international assistance and co-operation, especially economic and technical, to the maximum of its available resources, with a view to achieving progressively the full realization of the rights recognized in the present Covenant by all appropriate means, including particularly the adoption of legislative measures'. See further discussion in Chapter 4.
[104] Anker also recognizes this trend: see *Law of Asylum in the United States*, pp. 237–8.

socio-economic rights in a human rights model. There are two dominant models in the literature, and these will be considered briefly in turn.

Carlier's 'Three Scales': normative hierarchical approach

In recognition of the challenges facing both practitioners and decision-makers in establishing and ascertaining the elements of the refugee definition, Jean-Yves Carlier has developed a theory designed to assist the resolution of the 'central question': 'is there a risk of persecution in the case of return to the country of origin?'[105] In his model, the central question can be divided into three sub-questions: 'At what point does risk exist? At what point does persecution exist? [And] At what point is the risk of persecution sufficiently established?'[106] In Carlier's model, these three questions can be assessed in a 'Theory of the Three Scales or Levels' in which the decision-maker is required to address each element separately and provide cogent reasons in respect of his or her conclusions on each point. This model is motivated in part by the recognition that without a framework to guide decision-making in this field, refugee law is left 'to a great extent, to the unclear and subjective appreciation of administrative officials',[107] and thus 'reinforcement of legal reasoning' is necessary to uphold the protective objective of the Refugee Convention,[108] sentiments that are consistent with the discussion in Chapter 2.

While all three sub-questions must be addressed in assessing a refugee claim according to the Carlier model, it is sufficient for present purposes to focus on the question '[a]t what point does persecution exist?' in order to understand the nature of the human rights model adopted by Carlier. He takes the view that the answer to this question turns on 'the degree of breach of basic human rights amounting to persecution'.[109] Based on his study of appellate level decisions, primarily from civil law jurisdictions,[110] he concludes that the 'only essential criteri[on] applied in case law, either expressly or implicitly, to determine whether an excessive violation of basic human rights has occurred, is disproportionality'.[111]

---

[105] Jean Yves Carlier, 'General Report' in Carlier, Vanheule, Peña Galiano and Hullman (eds.), *Who is a Refugee?*, p. 685.
[106] Ibid.   [107] Ibid., p. 686.   [108] Ibid.   [109] Ibid., p. 687.
[110] Ibid., although he also includes the USA, Canada and the UK in his analysis.
[111] Ibid., p. 702.

In general, he states, the disproportionate nature of the relevant act will be 'a function of the quantitative and qualitative severity of the treatment, on the one hand, and of the basic human right that the treatment violates, on the other'.[112] In other words:

> The more fundamental the right in question is (right to life, physical integrity, freedom ...), the less quantitatively and qualitatively severe the treatment need be. The lower the priority attributed to the violated freedom (economic, social or cultural rights), the more quantitatively and qualitatively severe the treatment must be.[113]

In this model it is clear that there is a priority in the ordering of human rights norms, with civil and political rights being accorded a higher value or weight than economic, social and cultural rights. However, there is little further explanation provided as to the precise content of the respective categories or as to the relationship between the various rights contained within them.[114]

This model has rarely been explicitly referred to in the case law, although, as will be explained below, courts at times implicitly adopt this model while purporting to adopt the Hathaway hierarchical model.

Hathaway's model: hierarchy of obligation

Hathaway's original conception, on which the case law development of the human rights model has been primarily based, was that the 'International Bill of Rights', comprising the UDHR, the ICCPR and the ICESCR, constitutes a persuasive and compelling guide to the interpretation of 'being persecuted', given the 'extraordinary consensus' and acceptance of its standards.[115] In order to provide more specific guidance to decision-makers, Hathaway elaborated on this scheme by explaining that in assessing whether a particular act constitutes persecution, it is necessary to keep in mind that the international covenants impose different levels of obligation on state parties; thus, assessment of whether a right has been breached varies according to the nature of the right.

---

[112] *Ibid.*   [113] *Ibid.*, p. 703.
[114] As the IARLJ notes, 'Carlier's framework implicitly relies on a ranking or hierarchical ordering of human rights without articulating in any detail what that ordering might be'. See Inter-Conference Working Parties: Human Rights Nexus Working Party, *Human Rights Conference Report*, p. 14 (on file with author).
[115] Hathaway, *The Law of Refugee Status*, pp. 106–7.

Hathaway's key definition of persecution is that it is the 'sustained or systemic failure of state protection in relation to one of the core entitlements'.[116] He then proposes a four-level model to explain in what circumstances violation of such core entitlements will amount to persecution. In brief, his scheme proposes that 'four distinct types of *obligation* exist'.[117] First in the hierarchy are the rights contained in the UDHR that were codified into 'immediately binding form' in the ICCPR,[118] and from which no derogation is permitted whatsoever, even in times of compelling national emergency. These include freedom from arbitrary deprivation of life, protection against torture or cruel, inhuman or degrading punishment or treatment, freedom from slavery, the prohibition on criminal prosecution for *ex post facto* offences, the right to recognition as a person in law, freedom of thought, conscience and religion, and protection from imprisonment on the ground of failure to uphold a contractual obligation.[119] He concludes that the 'serious possibility of a violation of a first category right *will always* constitute a risk of persecution'.[120] Thus, he explains, 'the threat of execution, assault, torture, slavery, or enforced conformity of belief exemplifies failure by the state to protect *core* values'.[121]

The second category is composed of those rights set out in the UDHR and codified in binding form in the ICCPR, but from which states may derogate during a public emergency.[122] These include freedom from arbitrary arrest or detention, the right to equal protection for all, including children and minorities; the right in criminal proceedings to a fair and public hearing and to be presumed innocent unless guilt is proved; the protection of personal and family privacy and integrity; the

---

[116] Hathaway, *The Law of Refugee Status*.
[117] Hathaway, *The Law of Refugee Status*, p. 109 (emphasis added).
[118] *Ibid.*
[119] Article 11 of the ICCPR provides that '[n]o one shall be imprisoned merely on the ground of inability to fulfill a contractual obligation'. Hathaway does not explicitly include this in his list, but it would presumably apply since it is a non-derogable right: see Hathaway, *The Law of Refugee Status*, pp. 109–10.
[120] Hathaway, *The Law of Refugee Status*, p. 112 (emphasis added).
[121] *Ibid.*
[122] Article 4(1) of the ICCPR provides that '[i]n time of public emergency which threatens the life of the nation and the existence of which is officially proclaimed, the States Parties to the present Covenant may take measures derogating from their obligations under the present Covenant to the extent strictly required by the exigencies of the situation, provided that such measures are not inconsistent with their other obligations under international law and do not involve discrimination solely on the ground of race, colour, sex, language, religion or social origin'.

right to internal movement and choice of residence; the freedom to leave and return to one's country; liberty of opinion, expression, assembly and association; the right to form and join trade unions; and the ability to partake in government, access public employment without discrimination, and vote in periodic and genuine elections.[123] Hathaway's view is that *failure to ensure any of these rights* will 'generally constitute a violation of a state's basic duty of protection, *unless* it is demonstrated that the government's derogation was strictly required by the exigencies of a real emergency situation, was not inconsistent with other aspects of international law, and was not applied in a discriminatory way'.[124] He is clear that the only exception to the view that a breach of level two will constitute persecution is short-term non-discriminatory emergency derogation.[125] Presumably, other derogable provisions of the ICCPR, including the right to self-determination (art. 1), the right to be treated with humanity and dignity when deprived of liberty (art. 10) and the right of minorities to enjoy their own culture, religion and language (art. 27) also fall within this category.

The third category comprises the rights contained in the UDHR which were codified in the ICESCR. Hathaway explains that in contrast to the ICCPR, the ICESCR does not impose 'absolute and immediately binding standards of attainment, but rather requires states to take steps to the maximum of their available resources to progressively realize rights in a non-discriminatory way'.[126] The relevant rights include the right to work, including just and favourable conditions of employment, remuneration and rest; entitlement to food, clothing, housing, medical care, social security and basic education; protection of the family, particularly children and mothers; and the freedom to engage and benefit from cultural, scientific, literary and artistic expression.[127] Hathaway's view is that a state is in breach of its basic obligations in this respect where it either 'ignores these interests notwithstanding the fiscal ability to respond, or where it excludes a minority of the population from their enjoyment'.[128] In addition, he recognizes that the deprivation of certain socio-economic rights, such as the ability to earn a living, or the

---

[123] Hathaway, *The Law of Refugee Status*, pp. 110–11.
[124] Hathaway, *The Law of Refugee Status*, p. 110 (emphasis added).
[125] Hathaway, *The Law of Refugee Status*, p. 113.
[126] Hathaway, *The Law of Refugee Status*, p. 110.
[127] Hathaway, *The Law of Refugee Status*, p. 111.
[128] *Ibid.*

entitlement to food, shelter or health care 'will at an extreme level be tantamount to the deprivation of life or cruel, inhuman or degrading treatment, and hence unquestionably constitute persecution'.[129]

The fourth and final category comprises two rights contained in the UDHR which were not codified into either the ICCPR or ICESCR. The right to own, and be free from arbitrary deprivation of property, and the right to be protected against unemployment are rights that, according to Hathaway, 'will not ordinarily suffice in and of themselves as the foundation for a claim of failure of state protection' because they are not subject to a binding legal obligation.[130]

Hathaway's four-level model, and in particular the notion that economic and social rights (so-called 'third level rights') may be engaged in refugee determination, has been most prominently accepted and adopted in the UK, Canada and New Zealand. In the UK, the notion that 'third level rights' may form the basis of a refugee claim is very well established in the jurisprudence of the IAT,[131] and is also accepted by the executive government, as evidenced in the guidelines produced to assist decision-makers in determining claims involving gender issues.[132] This principle is also accepted by the Court of Appeal, although has not been fully explored at that level.[133] In Canada the four-level hierarchy,

---

[129] Hathaway, *The Law of Refugee Status*, p. 111.
[130] *Ibid.*
[131] The most important case is *Gashi and Nikshiqi* [1997] INLR 96. This has been applied in many subsequent cases: See, for example, *Kondratiev* [2002] UKIAT 08283, at paras. 7, 19–20; *Karickova v. Secretary of State for the Home Department* [2002] UKIAT 05813, at para. 4; *Kovac* (Unreported, Appeal No. CC3034497, 28 April 2000); *Peco* (Unreported, IAT, Appeal No. HX-74935-94, 12 November 1996); *Macura, Ljiljana, Maletic v. Secretary of State for the Home Department* (Unreported, IAT, Appeal No. HX-61441-00, 11 September 2001), and *HS* [2005] UKIAT 00120, at para. 19, where the IAT noted that 'Professor Hathaway's categorization of human rights' has been approved by the UK IAT and Court of Appeal.
[132] See UK Gender Guidelines, s. 2.
[133] In *Horvath*, a case concerning a claim for refugee status by a Roma family from Slovakia on the basis, inter alia, of a range of deprivations of economic and social rights including education and employment, the UK Secretary of State argued before the Court of Appeal that 'third category' rights could never amount to persecution. The Court of Appeal thought it unnecessary to decide this point (*Horvath v. Secretary of State for the Home Department* [2000] INLR 205 at para. 31 (Stuart-Smith LJ) ('*Horvath*')), although Lord Ward expressed a 'preliminary view' that 'breach of third category rights cannot be said as a matter of law to amount to persecution just as it cannot be said as a matter of law that breach of these rights could never amount to persecution': at para. 10. Although this case was appealed to the House of Lords ([2000] 3 All ER 577; [2000] 3 WLR 379), the economic aspects of the claim were not relevant to the appeal, and the House of Lords did not therefore consider this aspect of the claim at all. In a more recent decision,

including the notion that 'level three rights' are relevant to a claim of persecution, is well entrenched,[134] as a perusal of the case law over the past decade, particularly that of the Federal Court of Canada and the RPD, reveals.[135] Similarly, in New Zealand, the RSAA has long accepted the four-level hierarchy advocated by Hathaway,[136] thus accepting that 'third level rights' may be relevant to the assessment of refugee status.[137] As it has explained:

It is [Hathaway's] approach based on the Universal Declaration of Human Rights 1948, the International Covenant on Civil and Political Rights 1966 and the International Covenant on Economic, Social and Cultural Rights 1966 and the

the Court of Appeal allowed an appeal by a Palestinian man who had claimed refugee status on the basis of deprivations of economic and social rights to which he would be subjected if returned to a refugee camp in Lebanon, on the basis that the IAT had erred in failing properly to consider his claim that 'discrimination and ill treatment suffered by Palestinian refugees in UNRWA camps were such as to amount to persecution on the basis of Professor Hathaway's third category': *Krayem v. Secretary of State for the Home Department* [2003] EWCA Civ. 649, at para. 22 ('*Krayem*'). This clearly implies that breach of 'third level rights' may underpin a finding of persecution in appropriate circumstances. Further, in a number of cases, the UK Court of Appeal has adopted the hierarchical model, thus implying acceptance of the relevance of third-level rights as well: See *R v. Secretary of State for the Home Department, ex parte Ravichandran* [1996] Imm AR 97 at 107; *Demirkaya* [1999] Imm AR 498, at 6; *R (on the application of Okere) v. Immigration Appeal Tribunal* (Queen's Bench Division, Administrative Court, Scott Baker J, CO/5067/1999, 9 November 2000), at paras. 17–18 ('*Okere*'); *R v. Secretary of State for the Home Department, ex parte Blanusa* (Court of Appeal, Civil Division, Henry, Ward and Schiemann LJJ, 18 May 1999), at 2.
[134] This is perhaps most explicit in an Immigration and Review Board ('IRB') document designed to guide decision-makers at the tribunal level: IRB, *Discrimination as a Basis for a Well-Founded Fear of Persecution* (IRB Legal Services, 1991), pp. 8–9 (on file with author).
[135] Many specific decisions will be referred to throughout the chapter, but see for example, *ZWB (Re)*, Nos. T98-03011, T98-03012, T98-03013, T98-03014, T98-03015, T98-03016, T98-03017, T98-07280, T98-09201, T98-09202, T98-09203 [1999] CRDD No. 211, 27 September 1999; *GRF (Re)*, Nos. AA0-01454, AA0-01462 and AA0-01463 [2001] CRDD No. 88, 12 July 2001; *BOG (Re)*, No. VA0-03441 [2001] CRDD No. 121, 16 July 2001, at para. 36, citing from IRB, *Discrimination as a Basis for Well-Founded Fear of Persecution*, which is in turn based on Hathaway's arguments: 'This framework analysis also includes different levels of "type of right or freedom threatened". In this claimant's circumstances the claimant's level of discrimination were primarily under the "third level", which includes the right to work, right to adequate standard of living, right to education.'
[136] See, for example, *Refugee Appeal No. 71427/99*, RSAA, 16 August 2000; *Refugee Appeal No. 71606/99*, RSAA, 31 March 2000, *Refugee Appeal No. 2039/93*, RSAA, 12 February 1996, and *Refugee Appeal No. 74665/03*, RSAA, 7 July 2004.
[137] In the most detailed consideration of the relevance of claims based on socio-economic discrimination to date, the Authority concluded that 'breaches of the ICESCR are in law capable of founding a claim for refugee status': *Refugee Appeal No. 75221/05*, RSAA, 23 September 2005, at para. 111.

associated hierarchy of rights which has largely informed the New Zealand law of refugee status.[138]

The Authority has more recently warned against a rigid application of such a model and has begun to emphasize the importance of a more holistic approach to any categorization of rights,[139] although in some cases has continued to engage the language of 'levels' and 'generations' of rights.[140]

Australian courts have not explicitly adopted the Hathaway model, or one that automatically equates a breach of a human rights provision with persecution, but decision-makers have displayed a willingness to consider a wide range of human rights abuses as relevant to the question whether a person is at risk of 'being persecuted', including socio-economic harm.[141] However, while the four-level human rights framework has not been engaged directly at the appellate level, it is often invoked at the tribunal level where a large proportion of cases

---

[138] *Refugee Appeal No. 2039/93*, RSAA, 12 February 1996, at para. 56, after setting out a list of 10 cases in which the Authority has adopted the view. See also *Refugee Appeal No. 74665/03*, RSAA, 7 July 2004.

[139] *Refugee Appeals Nos. 72558/01 and 72559/01*, RSAA, 19 November 2002, at para. 114. See also *Refugee Appeal No. 71427/99*, RSAA, 16 August 2000, at para. 51; *Refugee Appeal No. 74665/03*, RSAA, 7 July 2004. For the most progressive and detailed discussion of the ICESCR in the context of refugee claims, see *Refugee Appeal No. 75221*, RSAA, 23 September 2005, at paras. 80–1. The Authority notes in that case that '[o]verly rigid categorizations of rights in terms of hierarchies are therefore to be avoided': at para. 81.

[140] In a recent decision, the Authority noted that 'the right to education is a second generation, third level human right in the sense that it is not an absolute human right linked to civil and political status. It does not impose, as stated above, an absolute and immediately binding standard, the breach of which may be a strong indicator of persecutory behaviour – see Hathaway': *Refugee Appeal No. 74754, 74755*, RSAA, 7 January 2004, at para. 42.

[141] For example, in *Chan* (1989) 169 CLR 379, McHugh J noted that 'persecution on account of race, religion and political opinion has historically taken many forms of social, political and economic discrimination. Hence, the denial of access to employment, to the professions and to education or the imposition of restrictions on the freedoms traditionally guaranteed in a democratic society such as freedom of speech, assembly, worship or movement may constitute persecution if imposed for a Convention reason': at 429–31. These sentiments were reiterated in the subsequent decision in *Applicant A* (1997) 190 CLR 225 at 241. In a more recent decision, *S395/2002* (2003) 216 CLR 473, McHugh and Kirby JJ noted that that persecution includes 'discrimination in social life and employment' (at para. 40), while Gummow and Hayne JJ approved an earlier definition of the High Court that 'measures in disregard of human dignity may, in appropriate cases, constitute persecution' (at para. 66). For the most explicit adoption of this reasoning by the High Court, see *Chen Shi Hai* (2000) 201 CLR 293.

is decided.[142] Since the US courts do not, in the main, rely on a human rights approach, the Hathaway framework is not directly engaged, although they have clearly accepted that economic harm may be relevant to the question of persecution, as displayed above.[143]

---

[142] See, for example, *Reference N95/08624*, RRT, 27 March 1997; *Reference N93/02256*, RRT, 20 May 1994; and *Reference N96/11195*, RRT, 10 September 1996.

[143] Although courts emphasize that the concept of persecution 'does not include every sort of treatment our society regards as offensive': *Nagoulko*, 333 F 3d 1012 (9th Cir. 2003), at 1015, citing *Korablina*, 158 F 3d 1038 (9th Cir. 1998), it is clear that the term encompasses economic harm if the applicant is able to establish 'deliberate imposition of substantial economic disadvantage': at 1044. This appears to be accepted in all circuits. In some circuits, courts have imposed the additional requirement that economic harm 'must be deliberately imposed as a form of punishment': *Vura v. Immigration and Naturalization Service*, 1998 US App. LEXIS 10755 (7th Cir. 1998), at 3. In *Lukban v. Immigration and Naturalization Service*, 1998 US App. LEXIS 10854 (7th Cir. 1998), at 2, the Court held that 'the economic harm must be imposed "as a form of punishment"', citing *Borca*, 77 F 3d 210 (7th Cir. 1996). The Fifth Circuit has elaborated on this test by explaining that 'severe economic disadvantage' may involve the 'deprivation of liberty, food, housing, employment or other essentials of life': *Abdel-Masieh v. Immigration and Naturalization Service*, 73 F 3d 579 (5th Cir. 1996), at 583, citing *Matter of Laipenieks*, BIA, 1983 BIA LEXIS 16, 18 I & N Dec. 433, 456-7, 8 September 1983; *Hekmat Wadih Mikhael v. Immigration and Naturalization Service*, 115 F 3d 299 (5th Cir. 1997), at 303. While economic detriment has always been considered capable of establishing a well-founded fear of being persecuted, 'persecution' was initially interpreted to require 'probable denial of all means of livelihood'. This history is well set out in the case that has come to represent the classic (or at least foundational) US case on economic persecution, *Kovac v. Immigration and Naturalization Service*, 407 F 2d 102 (9th Cir. 1969). However, following removal of the adjective 'physical' as a qualification to 'persecution' by Congress in 1965, it is clear that 'probability of deliberate imposition of substantial economic disadvantage' is sufficient to satisfy the refugee definition. Indeed, an expansion of economic claims appears to have been one of the key aims of the legislative amendment: at 105-6. See also Anker, *Law of Asylum in the United States*, p. 237. Anker also explains that the *Kovac* standard was endorsed by Congress in the context of the 1980 Refugee Act 'when it approved an interpretation of persecution including "severe economic disadvantage or the deprivation of liberty, food, housing, employment or other essentials of life"': p. 237 and accompanying notes. Finally, it is also clear that the Department of Homeland Security (formerly INS) recognizes the relevance of socio-economic harm to the persecution inquiry, as it states, in its *Basic Law Manual*, that relevant factors in the persecution assessment 'could include ... deprivation of virtually all means of earning a livelihood; relegation to substandard dwellings; exclusion from institutions of higher learning': see *Basic Law Manual*, p. 25. See also US Department of Justice, Office of General Counsel, 'Legal Opinion: Palestinian Asylum Applicants' (27 October 1995) (on file with author). See also US Immigration and Citizenship Service, *Asylum Officer Basic Training Course: Lesson Plan on Asylum Eligibility*, 5 December 2002, pp. 22-3, as cited in Regine Germanin, *AILA's Asylum Primer: A Practical Guide to US Asylum Law and Procedure*, second edition (Washington, DC: American Immigration Lawyers Association, 2005), p. 28.

Although adoption of the Hathaway model in the UK, Canada and New Zealand (and, to a lesser extent, in Australia) has paved the way for acceptance of claims based on violations of economic and social rights, and is therefore of undoubted importance, a close analysis of the way in which the model has been implemented reveals a significant problem. That is, while purporting to adopt the Hathaway model, many courts and tribunals have in fact implemented a hierarchical model that closely resembles the Carlier idea of hierarchical categorization in terms of the normative value of different types of human rights. In other words, courts and tribunals that rely on a hierarchical model tend to equate the level of hierarchy with the extent to which the relevant right is 'fundamental' or a core entitlement, which in turn determines the extent to which a type of harm can constitute persecution.

In fact, the explication of state obligations under the International Bill of Rights in terms of a hierarchical model in the Hathaway scheme was intended to convey the point that measuring implementation of a right, and consequently the question whether a relevant right has been breached, is less straightforward in the context of economic and social rights; not that such rights are regarded as normatively less important than non-derogable civil and political rights.[144] To this extent there is a clear distinction between the Carlier and Hathaway models: in Hathaway's model, the hierarchy designation refers to the *nature of state obligation*, whereas in Carlier's, there is an implicit assumption that there is some difference *in normative priority* as between different categories.[145] However, rather than these distinctions being made clear in the case law, there is a pervasive conflation of the two conceptually distinct issues.

This confusion is well exemplified by the manner in which the hierarchical approach outlined in Hathaway's model is paraphrased by

---

[144] Perhaps misunderstanding is exacerbated by statements in Hathaway's text where he acknowledges that 'the relative ease of establishing a risk of persecution on the basis of a threat to life or freedom privileges these aspects of human dignity in relation to social, economic, and cultural rights' but that this 'accurately reflects the current hierarchical state of the international law of human rights': Hathaway, *The Law of Refugee Status*, p. 115. In an earlier passage, he asks the question: 'What rights are appropriately considered to be basic and inalienable?' and then immediately following states: 'Within the International Bill of Rights, four distinct types of obligation exist': p. 108. This does tend to suggest that the hierarchy subsequently outlined bears some relation to the question of which rights are 'basic and inalienable'.

[145] The IARLJ background paper also interprets Carlier's model in this way: see Inter-Conference Working Parties: Human Rights Nexus Working Party, *Human Rights Conference Report*, p. 25.

CONCEPTUAL APPROACHES TO SOCIO-ECONOMIC RIGHTS AND PERSECUTION 121

courts and commentators.[146] For example, in the seminal decision of the UK IAT in *Gashi and Nikshiqi*, the UNHCR intervener argued that 'some human rights have *greater pre-eminence* than others and it may be necessary to identify them through a *hierarchy of relative importance*'.[147] This analysis was accepted by the IAT, as it noted the 'four distinct types of obligation *in a hierarchy of relative importance*',[148] and has been repeated in numerous subsequent UK decisions,[149] including in decisions by the Court of Appeal.[150] This approach is also prevalent in Canadian decisions, particularly those of the RPD.[151] Examples abound of the recitation of

[146] For example, in a background paper prepared by a working party of the IARLJ, the Hathaway approach is paraphrased as follows: '[t]here are those who argue that some human rights are more fundamental than others and that, indeed, they have been enshrined as such in the very language of the international human rights instruments': Inter-Conference Working Parties: Human Rights Nexus Working Party, *Human Rights Conference Report*, pp. 2–3. In another paper of the same working party, Hathaway's hierarchical approach is summarized as having the effect that, '[t]he more inviolate a right is considered in those treaties, the less a breach of that right is tolerated. Socio-economic rights, for example, could be violated repeatedly before the breach would reach the requisite threshold of severity. *In this model some rights are clearly more important than others*': IARLJ, *The Application of Human Rights Standards to the 1951 Refugee Convention – the Definition of Persecution* (paper prepared by the Human Rights Nexus Working Party, 24 April 2001), p. 13 (emphasis added) (on file with author).

[147] *Gashi and Nikshiqi* [1997] INLR 96 at 105 (emphasis added). This was most recently approved by the Court of Appeal in *Krayem* [2003] EWCA Civ. 649, at paras. 9–12, 22.

[148] *Gashi and Nikshiqi* [1997] INLR 96 at 100 (emphasis added).

[149] See, for example, *Okere* (Queen's Bench Division, Administrative Court, Scott Baker J, CO/5067/1999, 9 November 2000), where Scott Baker J was reminded of Hathaway's text 'and the four-fold criteria directed towards establishing the gravity and character of human rights abuses necessary to admit of a finding of persecution': at para. 17. See *Doymus* (Unreported, IAT, Appeal No. HX/80112/99, 19 July 2000), at para. 23; and *Puzova v. Secretary of State for the Home Department* [2001] UKAIT 00001 ('*Puzova*').

[150] In *Horvath*, for instance, Ward LJ explained that '[i]n an attempt to *classify the gravity of the breaches* of the human rights, Hathaway proposed the helpful division into four categories': *Horvath* [2000] INLR 205 at para. 48 (emphasis added). It should be noted that Ward LJ went on to say that '[t]he classification is useful but not definitive and should be applied with care': at para. 48. However, the important point for present purposes is his interpretation of the meaning of the Hathaway framework.

[151] This is made most explicit in the Canadian IRB document *Discrimination as a Basis for a Well-Founded Fear of Persecution*, which instructs decision-makers first to 'identify the type of right or freedom threatened' according to the Hathaway typology set out therein': p. 8. The decision-makers should then 'determine whether the discriminatory measures: a. are serious measures against first level rights, *in which case they readily constitute persecution*; or b. where they restrict rights other than the first level rights, are nevertheless systemic and seriously affect the integrity and human dignity of the claimant, in which case they would also amount to persecution': at 9 (emphasis added). This clearly indicates that the IRB interprets the hierarchy as relating to a *normative* hierarchy or hierarchy of *seriousness* of violation.

statements such as the following: 'With denial of access to elementary education, normally considered a third level human right *as compared to the more serious harms of categories one and two*, this family was therefore not seriously deprived in terms of education.'[152] A similar approach is evident in decisions of the Australian RRT and in some New Zealand decisions. For example, in some early decisions in the latter jurisdiction, the RSAA described the rights contained in the ICESCR as 'secondary in importance' to those in the ICCPR,[153] and, more specifically, explained in relation to education that this 'right is therefore a "social" or second generation right and is placed third in the four-tier hierarchy of rights',[154] which places it 'low in the hierarchy of rights'.[155] Further, in relation to the 'right to work' the Authority has said that it is 'a violation of a relatively low-level right',[156] and that 'it is only a third level right ... and is not a basic or core human right'.[157] The language of 'levels' and sometimes 'generations' of rights is highly prevalent in this case law, and it is patent that decision-makers engage such terminology to distinguish between different levels of seriousness of rights; in other words to assess the extent to which a violation of a right constitutes the violation of a core entitlement and thus persecution.[158]

This is not a matter of mere semantics or a minor difference in emphasis; rather it has important ramifications for the assessment of individual claims, because the notion that economic and social rights are inherently inferior to civil and political rights, and thus that breach of such rights is less significant, leads to a corresponding under-valuation of

[152] *WRH (Re)*, Nos. T97-05485, T97-05486, T97-05487, T97-05488, T97-05489 [1999] CRDD No. 112, 31 March 1999 (emphasis added). See also *ZWB (Re)*, Nos. T98-03011, T98-03012, T98-03013, T98-03014, T98-03015, T98-03016, T98-03017, T98-07280, T98-09201, T98-09202, T98-09203 [1999] CRDD No. 211, 27 September 1999.
[153] See *Refugee Appeal No. 1/92*, RSAA, 30 April 1992, at 49.
[154] *Refugee Appeal No. 732/92*, RSAA, 5 August 1994, at 7.
[155] *Refugee Appeal No. 732/92*, RSAA, 5 August 1994, at 9.
[156] *Refugee Appeal No. 732/92*, RSAA, 5 August 1994, at 7.
[157] *Refugee Appeal No. 71163/98*, RSAA, 31 March 1999, at 10. The most recent authority calls this hierarchical approach into question: see *Refugee Appeals Nos. 72558/01 and 72559/01*, RSAA, 19 November 2002, at para. 114; *Refugee Appeal No. 74665/03*, RSAA, 7 July 2004; *Refugee Appeal No. 75221*, RSAA, 23 September 2005.
[158] Economic and social rights are variously labelled 'third level', 'third category', 'category 3' and even 'tertiary rights' in the case law: see, for example, *Macura, Ljiljana, Maletic v. Secretary of State for the Home Department* (Unreported, IAT, Appeal No. HX-61441-00, 11 September 2001), at para. 27. For examples of tribunals using the hierarchical model to distinguish between levels of importance of rights, see *Refugee Appeal No. 71163/98*, RSAA, 31 March 1999; *Refugee Appeal No. 1039/93*, RSAA, 13 February 1995, at 20; *Refugee Appeal No. 2039/93*, 12 February 1996, at para. 80.

refugee claims based on such deprivations. An analysis of cases decided at all levels of the decision-making hierarchy in five common law jurisdictions reveals that there are a number of problems with the way in which refugee claims based in whole or in part upon violations of economic and social rights are currently adjudicated. While some difficulties appear directly related to a mistaken adoption of a normatively hierarchical model of 'being persecuted', others relate more generally to an undervaluation of such rights or a lack of understanding of the nature of economic and social rights in international law. Some of the problems reflect misunderstandings that are capable of rectification by reference to authoritative interpretation of the relevant principles in international human rights law. However, others reflect more intractable problems that suggest that some reconsideration of the existing dominant approach, that is, the hierarchical model, is necessary. These issues will be considered in turn.

Problems and difficulties in the current approach

Problems related to a normative hierarchical approach

Imposition of an erroneously high test

One of the most common and pervasive problems in the current adjudication of refugee claims based on socio-economic deprivation is the tendency to apply a very high test to refugee claims involving economic and social rights; one that is significantly higher than that generally required in refugee adjudication. This has the consequence that only very extreme cases are in practice accepted as sufficient to ground a successful application for refugee status. The rationale appears to be that since the value of the right is lower (as compared to those engaged in more traditional claims involving civil and political rights), the level of violation must be significantly higher in order to reach the requisite level of persecution – a clear (though implicit) application of the Carlier model.[159]

---

[159] The notion that the degree of severity required will turn on the level of right is most explicit in a decision of the IAT in which the President held that since, in that case, the relevant denial was of a right to practise religion, then as a 'higher human right (or first category right) the threshold from discrimination to persecution is lower than in the case of a breach of a lower category of human rights': *Tahir and Saeed*, Case No. 19236, 4 December 1998, as cited in Symes and Jorro, *Asylum Law and Practice*, p. 90. Conversely, in *Barkoci*, Case No. 17610, 10 May 1999, the IAT held that '[t]he lower the category the higher must be the threshold': see Symes and Jorro, *Asylum Law and Practice*, p. 107.

While this inferior treatment of socio-economic rights is often justified by reference to the notion that socio-economic rights are merely 'third level' – and thus apparently inferior to civil and political rights – it is also prevalent in those jurisdictions that do not explicitly adopt the Hathaway (or any other) human rights model, therefore indicating that there is a widespread tendency to undervalue socio-economic rights in refugee adjudication.

Turning first to those jurisdictions that have explicitly adopted the Hathaway model, it is evident that decision-makers frequently interpret the model as encompassing third level violations as persecution only when the harm can be said to be 'extreme' and/or life-threatening. For example, in *Horvath*, the UK IAT purported to adopt 'the view of Professor Hathaway that *in an extreme case* [a breach of level 3 rights] might [constitute persecution].'[160] In some decisions of the UK IAT, the test has been formulated in a similarly stringent manner, for example: '[e]conomic hardship must be extreme and the discrimination must effectively destroy a person's economic existence before surrogate protection can be required'.[161] Similarly, the New Zealand RSAA has stated that 'serious restrictions on his right to earn his livelihood' will amount to persecution 'only to the extent that, at the extreme level, the restrictions are "tantamount to the deprivation of life or cruel, inhuman or degrading treatment"'.[162]

---

[160] *Horvath* [2000] INLR 205 at para. 31 (emphasis added).
[161] *El Deaibes v. Secretary of State for the Home Department* [2002] UKIAT 02582, at para. 13 ('*El Deaibes*'). This is important because the IAT referred to both para. 54 of the UNHCR Handbook, which mentions discrimination which causes 'substantial prejudice', and paras. 62–4, which mention 'economic measures that destroy economic existence', noting that '[t]hese citations indicate an apparent slight difference of emphasis': at para. 11. Without explaining the rationale, the IAT clearly preferred the higher test. It is relevant to note that the UNHCR itself has reiterated the 'substantial prejudice' test in subsequent documents: see UNHCR, *Guidelines on Roma*, cited in Stevens, 'Roma Asylum Applicants in the United Kingdom' and *Guidelines on International Protection: Religion-Based Refugee Claims under Article 1A(2) of the 1951 Convention and/or the 1967 Protocol relating to the status of Refugees*, HCR/GIP/04/06 (2004) at para. 17.
[162] *Refugee Appeal No. 71605/99*, RSAA, 16 December 1999, at 7. See also *Refugee Appeal No. 732/92*, RSAA, 5 August 1994, at 10, where the Authority said: 'To this might be added the observation that at a less extreme level, substantial impairment of ability to earn a living coupled with other discriminatory factors could, depending on the circumstances, constitute persecution'.

The requirement that economic deprivation be classified as 'extreme' or be 'tantamount to the deprivation of life or cruel, inhuman or degrading treatment' is repeated in many other cases,[163] and is arguably a misinterpretation of Hathaway's original framework, in which persecution is capable of being established once a violation of a third-level right is clear. Importantly, Hathaway states that in some cases the severity of a breach of economic and social rights may be so high as to amount to 'the deprivation of life or cruel, inhuman or degrading treatment',[164] but this is not necessarily required in order for violations of third level rights to amount to persecution.[165] However, courts and tribunals appear to have focused on the 'deprivation of life' analogy and extrapolated a general rule from that statement.[166]

The strict nature of the test that results from the attribution of an inferior status to economic and social rights, thus requiring a higher threshold of harm, is well illustrated in cases decided by the Canadian RPD involving ethnic Turks in Bulgaria. In *RMK (Re)*, the applicant claimed that he and his family feared economic persecution by the Bulgarian government because of his membership of a particular social group – ethnic Turkish tobacco growers. The documentary evidence

---

[163] See the debate as to this point in the Canadian jurisprudence, first raised in the decision of the Federal Court in *Bougai v. Canada (Minister of Citizenship and Immigration)* [1995] 3 FC D 32; 1995 FCTD LEXIS 211, and most recently noted in *HQT (Re)*, Nos. T96-03054 and T96-03055 [1997] CRDD No. 149, 8 July 1997. See also *Refugee Appeal No. 71605/99*, RSAA, 16 December 1999.

[164] Hathaway, *The Law of Refugee Status*, p. 111.

[165] Rather, as stated above, Hathaway's view is that 'an absence of state protection can be said to exist only where a government fails to ensure the non-discriminatory allocation of available resources to meet the most basic of socio-economic needs': *The Law of Refugee Status*, p. 117.

[166] For example, in *Refugee Appeal No. 7105/99*, RSAA, 16 December 1999, the RSAA stated that '[t]he statement of the [UNHCR Handbook] that "serious restrictions on his right to earn his livelihood" amounts to persecution is accepted *only to the extent that*, at the extreme level, the restrictions are "tantamount to the deprivation of life or cruel, inhuman or degrading treatment"': at 7 (emphasis added). Importantly, however, this is not what the UNHCR Handbook says. Rather, the Authority has added a restriction based on a mistaken interpretation of what Hathaway actually says. See also *Reference N95/08624*, RRT, 27 March 1997, where the RRT set out the 'third category in Hathaway's hierarchy of rights' and stated, '[a]s Hathaway noted, extreme deprivation of some of these rights, such as the right to earn a living or to food, may be cruel and degrading treatment that would be persecutory. However, restriction on these rights which does not reach that extreme level of deprivation *will not be sufficiently serious harm* to [be] persecution': at 7–8 (emphasis added).

established that 'Bulgarian employers in mass numbers refuse to hire minorities, even for those jobs that require no skills and qualifications'[167] and the claimant gave evidence that as a result of this situation, the only work available was tobacco cultivation, which was 'pure slave work for the ethnic Turks and Roma, and from which the state made very large profits'.[168] The claimant gave evidence (which was accepted as credible by the Tribunal) that because his village was populated only by ethnic Turks, the government withdrew all health, transportation and telephone services from the village after the fall of the communist government in 1991, once the tobacco growers began 'demanding their rights'.[169] Leaders of the Movement for Rights and Freedoms accused the government of 'enforcing a policy of hidden economic assimilation for the Turkish minority in order to force them to emigrate to Turkey'.[170] The evidence established that the Bulgarian government continually suspended payment for the tobacco crop, and when payment was made, reduced the price to 15 per cent of the sale price, thus leaving the tobacco farmers in poverty. The Movement for Rights and Freedoms alleged that this was a deliberate policy to 'push the ethnic Turks ... to the poverty limit'.[171]

The Tribunal accepted that 'the measures which ... the Bulgarian government took with respect to ethnic Turks and tobacco farmers (not all of whom were ethnic Turks), may have been discriminatory' and resulted in 'serious problems for tobacco farmers in sustaining themselves and their families, and that a number of tobacco farmers and their families experienced hunger'.[172] However, the Tribunal rejected the claim on the basis that the treatment was not sufficiently serious as to amount to persecution because the measures 'have not resulted in the loss of ethnic Turks' or ethnic Turk tobacco farmers' ability to earn a living *at an extreme level* or which was systematic',[173] since the claimant had 'managed to eke out a meager living, despite these actions, and continued to cultivate, harvest and sell their crop to [the government

---

[167] *RMK (Re)*, No. TA1-06365 [2002] CRDD No. 300, 16 May 2002, at para. 18.
[168] *RMK (Re)*, No. TA1-06365 [2002] CRDD No. 300, 16 May 2002, at para. 4.
[169] *RMK (Re)*, No. TA1-06365 [2002] CRDD No. 300, 16 May 2002, at para. 21.
[170] *Ibid.*
[171] *RMK (Re)*, No. TA1-06365 [2002] CRDD No. 300, 16 May 2002, at para. 25.
[172] *RMK (Re)*, No. TA1-06365 [2002] CRDD No. 300, 16 May 2002, at para. 35.
[173] *RMK (Re)*, No. TA1-06365 [2002] CRDD No. 300, 16 May 2002, at para. 35 (emphasis added).

owned enterprise], being left with little choice to do otherwise'.[174] In reaching this conclusion, the Tribunal adopted the reasoning of a previous Tribunal decision involving similar facts in which in concluding that the claimants had not established persecution, the Tribunal had noted 'the approach of Hathaway to the problem wherein economic rights occupy the third tier of rights and only in very specific circumstances [are] a basis for persecution'.[175]

This is a very problematic decision. The Tribunal accepted that ethnic Turks due to discrimination had no other choice but to work in conditions that were grossly unfair and indeed barely allowed the applicants to survive: conditions that undoubtedly represented a severe infringement on their human dignity.[176] It nonetheless rejected the claim for refugee status. It is difficult to understand how a policy of economic oppression that causes hunger and threatens a person's ability to survive does not qualify as a measure that constitutes persecution.

This serves to highlight the fact that their description as 'level three' in a four-level hierarchy of obligation has led some decision-makers to treat socio-economic rights as inferior to civil and political rights, such that a much higher level of violation is required of socio-economic rights violations in order to be considered persecution pursuant to the Refugee Convention.

This is not a peculiarity of those jurisdictions which explicitly adopt a human rights framework; decision-makers in other jurisdictions also have a tendency to impose a higher test in respect of socio-economic claims, thus suggesting a widespread under-valuation of socio-economic rights. For example, US courts are also prone to imposing a higher standard of what constitutes persecution on economic related claims compared with other types of claims, often in clear contravention of

---

[174] *RMK (Re)*, No. TA1-06365 [2002] CRDD No. 300, 16 May 2002, at para. 36.
[175] *RMK (Re)*, No. TA1-06365 [2002] CRDD No. 300, 16 May 2002, at para. 37.
[176] 'Persecution' is often paraphrased as action which 'den[ies] human dignity in any way': *Refugee Appeal No. 2039/93*, RSAA, 12 February 1996, at para. 40, citing Hathaway. For a more recent NZ decision, see *Refugee Appeal No. 71427/99*, RSAA, 16 August 2000, at para. 51. See also *Ward* [1993] 2 SCR 689 at 733; *Minister for Immigration and Multicultural Affairs v. Ibrahim* (2000) 204 CLR 1 at 21 (McHugh J). In addition, it has been said to engage those rights 'that are essential to the maintenance of the integrity and inherent human dignity of the individual': Goodwin-Gill, *The Refugee in International Law*, p. 39.

established authority.[177] Although it is very well established in US jurisprudence that persecution exists where there is a 'probability of deliberate imposition of substantial economic disadvantage',[178] and that 'economic persecution' is 'an important part of asylum claims',[179] decision-makers continue to impose a much higher test in practice. While it can be argued that in some cases invocation of an erroneously high standard has not affected the outcome of the application since the harm feared is unlikely to have been considered sufficiently serious under any test of 'being persecuted',[180] there is no question that application of the higher test has had a concrete impact on applicants' claims in many cases.[181] For example, in *Largaespada-Castellanos*,[182] the applicant claimed

---

[177] See, for example, *Bereza v. Immigration and Naturalization Service*, 115 F 3d 468 (7th Cir. 1997), at 474, where the Seventh Circuit discusses the incorrect test in relation to economic harm applied by the BIA and *Borca*, 77 F 3d 210 (7th Cir. 1996). In some very recent cases the courts have set out a very high test for economic claims: see, for example, *Nagoulko*, 333 F 3d 1012 (9th Cir. 2003), at 1015, *Lukwago v. Ashcroft*, 329 F 3d 157 (3rd Cir. 2003) and *Ouda*, 324 F 3d 445 (6th Cir. 2003). These cases appear inconsistent with established authority that only 'substantial economic disadvantage' is required. Indeed, the issue of the appropriate test has recently caused strong disagreement amongst judges (with some strong dissents) and also amongst circuits, with a number of recent judgments emphasizing that the correct test does not require that the severe economic harm amount to a violation of 'life or freedom': see *Gormley v. Ashcroft*, 364 F 3d 1172 (9th Cir. 2004) ('*Gormley*'); and *Jaars v. Gonzales*, 148 Fed. Appx. 310; 2005 US App. LEXIS 15069 (6th Cir. 2005). For disagreement amongst judges on the appropriate standard, see *Damko v. Immigration and Naturalization Service*, 430 F 3d 626 (2nd Cir. 2005), especially at 637 (Circuit Judge Pooler).

[178] See discussion above at note 143.

[179] *Chand*, 222 F 3d 1066 (9th Cir. 2000), at 1073. See also *Gormley*, 364 F 3d 1172 (9th Cir. 2004), at 1178.

[180] Anker also notes that some of the case law 'continues to rely on the old "denial of opportunity to make a living" and "threats of bodily harm" standard, without acknowledging the now longstanding change in statutory language and reiterated legislative intent': *Law of Asylum in the United States*, p. 237. However, she argues that '[t]his misstatement of the current rule ... is largely a failure to articulate the conceptual shift; results in most cases are consistent with the newer standard of "substantial" or "severe" economic detriment, rather than the older Board emphasis on denial of all opportunity to earn a living': p. 237.

[181] For example, see *Gheorghe v. Immigration and Naturalization Service*, 1998 US App. LEXIS 14989 (9th Cir. 1998), in which the Ninth Circuit dismissed the applicant's claim that he had been fired from his job and had difficulty in finding another one on the basis that '[t]o rise to the level of persecution, however, economic deprivations must be "so severe that they constitute a threat to an individual's life or freedom"': at 2, quoting *Matter of Acosta*. The Court held that the applicant's allegations 'simply do not meet this standard'.

[182] *Largaespada-Castellanos v. Immigration and Naturalization Service*, 1995 US App. LEXIS 22919 (9th Cir. 1995) ('*Largaespada-Castellanos*').

that, based on his family's political activities in Nicaragua, the family's ration card had been confiscated, as had the business licence for the family bakery (which was eventually closed down), and the applicant had been forced to leave school and subsequently forced to leave his job as well. In upholding the BIA's rejection of the claim, the Ninth Circuit stated that the evidence 'at most, shows that he suffered some economic and educational discrimination ... This is not a situation in which the economic deprivation was so severe that [the applicant] *was deprived of the necessities of life*'.[183]

A similar approach is evident in some European decisions on point. For example, in Austria, claims based on dismissal from employment on political and religious grounds have been refused unless the applicant is able to show that he or she has lost his or her 'basis for living',[184] and in Germany, work-related difficulties 'may only be taken into consideration where they endanger the asylum-seeker's basic subsistence (*Existenzmnimum*)'.[185]

Perhaps most explicitly, the amended *Migration Act 1958* (Cth) in Australia now provides that 'serious harm' in the context of interpreting 'persecution' relevantly includes, 'significant economic hardship that threatens the person's capacity to subsist; denial of access to basic services, where the denial threatens the person's capacity to subsist; and

---

[183] *Largaespada-Castellanos*, 1995 US App. LEXIS 22919 (9th Cir. 1995) (emphasis added). In this case, the Court also relied on changed circumstances; however, this merely buttresses the previous finding regarding persecution: at 7. See also *Martinez v. Immigration and Naturalization Service*, 1995 US App. LEXIS 27361 (9th Cir. 1995), where the Court again applied the test whether 'the economic deprivation was so severe that Martinez was deprived of the necessities of life': at 3. In another decision, the Ninth Circuit accepted that confiscation of a food ration card which forced the applicant's family to buy food on the black market at five times the regular price combined with denial of a work permit due to political activities constituted 'significant economic deprivation': *Obando-Rocha v. Immigration and Naturalization Service*, 1996 US App. LEXIS 8222 (9th Cir. 1996), at 3. However, the Court rejected the refugee claim because the applicant had not established 'a showing of a severe impairment of the *applicant's ability to earn a living*': at 3 (emphasis added), citing from *Saballo-Cortez v. Immigration and Naturalization Service*, 761 F 2d 1259, 1264 (9th Cir. 1984). It is highly likely that if the accepted test in the US jurisprudence had been applied – namely, substantial economic disadvantage – these applicants' claims are likely to have been successful.

[184] Klaus Hullmann, 'Austria', in Carlier, Vanheule, Peña Galiano and Hullman (eds.), *Who is a Refugee?*, p. 43.

[185] *V. G. Ansbach*, 18 March 1992, 19th Division, AN 19 K 91.39868, cited in Klaus Hullman, 'Germany', in Carlier, Vanheule, Peña Galiano and Hullman (eds.), *Who is a Refugee?*, p. 268.

denial of capacity to earn a livelihood of any kind, where the denial threatens the person's capacity to subsist'.[186] The legislation is clear that the list of factors of which these are part does not limit what is considered serious harm;[187] but the framing of the test in this way in the legislation is likely to have a significant impact on the way in which such claims are treated by the courts (or at the very least by the administrative branch).[188]

One of the major limitations of an approach that requires socio-economic harm to amount to a threat to subsistence is that it has a tendency to exclude types of harm that violate dignity and potentially have significant long-term consequences for the individual concerned, but may not produce an *immediate* economic outcome or harm — most notably denial of education.[189] This has been particularly evident in the

---

[186] Migration Act 1958 (Cth), Section 91R.
[187] This has been explicitly acknowledged by the Federal Court of Australia: see *VTAO v. Minister for Immigration and Multicultural and Indigenous Affairs* [2004] FCA 927 (Unreported, Merkel J, 19 July 2004), at para. 57 and by the Full Federal Court in *NBFP v. Minister for Immigration and Multicultural and Indigenous Affairs* [2005] FCAFC 95 (Kiefel, Weinberg and Edmonds JJ, 31 May 2005), at para. 57.
[188] Indeed, this is arguably already evident in decisions of the RRT that post-date the legislative amendments. See, for example, *Reference N02/43084*, RRT, 5 September 2002, at para. 34; *SCAT v. Minister for Immigration and Multicultural and Indigenous Affairs* [2002] FCA 962 (Unreported, Von Doussa J, 6 August 2002); *SBBA v. Minister for Immigration and Multicultural and Indigenous Affairs* [2002] FCA 1401 (Unreported, Mansfield J, 15 November 2002); *NASB v. Minister for Immigration & Multicultural and Indigenous Affairs* [2003] FCA 1046 (Beaumont, Lindgren and Tamberlin JJ, 2 October 2003), at para. 22 and *SZBQJ v. Minister for Immigration and Multicultural and Indigenous Affairs* [2005] FCA 143 (Unreported, Tamberlin J, 28 February 2005).
[189] However, the problematic cases are not restricted to those involving education. For example, in *Alvarez-Montiel v. Immigration and Naturalization Service*, 1996 US App. LEXIS 4802 (9th Cir. 1996), the court took a rather strange approach to the applicant's claim that, due to his political activities, he had been unable to find work for three years following the Sandinista revolution in Nicaragua, in concluding that 'the record does not contain any evidence to support a finding that Alvarez-Montiel and his family were subjected to "substantial economic disadvantage" when he was unable to find work... or when his wife was terminated from her teaching position': at 3. The focus on measuring economic harm is evident in the way the test is formulated in the USA (substantial economic damage/disadvantage), as well as the way in which it is applied. For example, in *Vega-Garcia v. Immigration and Naturalization Service*, 1996 US App. LEXIS 10881 (9th Cir. 1996), the Court set out the applicant's claim as follows: 'the Sandinistas persecuted [the applicant] by cutting his food rations, expelling him from a Sandinista-run public school, intimidating him through prison tours while he was in the military, and threatening him because of his political beliefs': at 21. The Court dismissed the claim on the basis that, '[b]ecause Vega was able to buy food on the black market and attend private school, the expulsion and reduction in food rations seem to *have minor economic effects at most*': at 1 (emphasis added).

US jurisprudence. In some cases, rejection of claims based in part upon exclusion from educational institutions appears to stem from a narrow view of persecution, which requires some physical type of harm, contrary to existing authority.[190] However, in the main, dismissal of such claims has been premised on the argument that denial of education does not fall within the notion of 'economic disadvantage'. For example, in *Gonzalez-Alvarado*,[191] the Nicaraguan applicant claimed that, as a result of his family's activities, the Sandinistas had rationed his food, denied him his high school diploma which prevented him from attending college and refused to issue him with the documents necessary to work.[192] The Court rejected his claim on the basis, inter alia, that '[t]he denial of Petitioner's diploma also does not reach the level of substantial economic disadvantage so as to be eligible for asylum, particularly as Petitioner has not alleged that he was denied the opportunity to earn a livelihood'.[193]

The requirement that economic-related harm constitute a threat to life in order to amount to 'persecution' is inconsistent with very well-established authority that holds that persecution is not restricted

---

[190] For example, in *Wang v. US Department of Justice*, 2003 US App. LEXIS 11198 (2nd Cir. 2003), the Court of Appeals for the Second Circuit set out the applicant's testimony that, as a result of his participation in student demonstrations, he had been 'stripped of his class presidency, barred from taking college entrance exams, and hindered in his post-graduation job search by the negative reference letter he received from his high school'. The IJ had concluded that '[a]lthough the incidents which Wang recounts may be regrettable and were no doubt demoralizing, Wang was never physically harmed, arrested, or threatened with further investigation': at 365. The Court of Appeals concluded that '[u]nder these circumstances, the IJ's conclusion that Wang had not successfully demonstrated past persecution is supported by substantial evidence and must be upheld'.

[191] *Gonzalez-Alvarado v. Immigration and Naturalization Service*, 1996 US App. LEXIS 16488 (9th Cir. 1996) ('*Gonzalez-Alvarado*').

[192] *Gonzalez-Alvarado*, 1996 US App. LEXIS 16488 (9th Cir. 1996), at 2.

[193] *Gonzalez-Alvarado v. Immigration and Naturalization Service*, 1996 US App. LEXIS 16488 (9th Cir. 1996). See also *Blanco-Herrera v. Immigration and Naturalization Service*, 1996 US App. LEXIS 15280 (9th Cir. 1996), where the court noted, after setting out the 'substantial economic disadvantage' test, that 'Blanco's exclusion from college, even if it was the result of his failure to participate with the CDS, does not constitute past persecution': at 3. See also *Rivera v. Immigration and Naturalization Service*, 100 F 3d 964 (7th Cir. 1997), where the court held that educational discrimination must result in 'such a severe impairment of the ability to earn a livelihood that it rises to the level of persecution': cited in Anker, *Law of Asylum in the United States*, p. 245, note 355.

only to those cases where life or freedom is at risk.[194] The question therefore arises: why is it that courts appear unwilling to apply the tests or approaches established in other types of refugee cases to applications involving the deprivation of economic and social rights? This tends to suggest that there is something inherent in economic claims which gives decision-makers pause, perhaps indicating their lack of comfort with the connection between economic claims and the rhetoric of economic migration. Most fundamentally, the approach appears to be based on a view that socio-economic violations are necessarily less important or significant, thus requiring a higher level of breach in order to amount to persecution. This suggests that the predominant view of socio-economic rights in international refugee law may require reconsideration in light of recent developments in international human rights law, as will be explored in Chapter 4.

The automatic requirement of accumulation

The second problem with the attribution of a normatively inferior status to socio-economic rights in refugee adjudication, closely related to that above, is that there appears to be an assumption in many cases that once the nature of the relevant harm is identified as 'third level', it can amount to persecution only where there is an accumulation of a number of breaches of such rights or where violations of 'third level' rights are combined with more 'traditional' (i.e. civil and political) forms of persecution. While decision-makers have recognized that harm such as 'loss of employment and restrictions on one's right to earn his livelihood ... need not be coupled with any threat to life or liberty' in order to constitute persecution,[195] this is routinely ignored in claims involving socio-economic deprivation.

The recognition that persecution may take the form of 'cumulative harassment' or 'cumulative discrimination' has been an important development in recent years and is a legitimate tool in cases in which an applicant alleges a well-founded fear of a range of *less serious violations*

---

[194] There are many examples of such cases. See, for example, *Refugee Appeal No. 1039/93*, RSAA, 13 February 1995, in which the Authority upheld a claim based on a violation of freedom of religion (ICCPR, art. 18) and the right to privacy (ICCPR, art. 17) and marriage and family (ICCPR, art. 23). See also authorities cited above at notes 16–22.

[195] *Woldesmaet v. Secretary of State for the Home Department* (Unreported, IAT, Case No. 12892, 9 January 1995).

of fundamental rights. However, it appears that courts have a tendency to assume that every breach of a level-three right is automatically 'mere discrimination', and thus requires fortification by a list of other rights violations, particularly involving 'higher level rights', in order to constitute persecution.[196]

This is made clear in a decision of the Canadian RPD, involving the claim of a stateless Palestinian who feared return to Lebanon on the basis that he would be unable to find work in Lebanon (as a result of the restrictions on Palestinians obtaining work, which the Tribunal found 'would effectively prevent him from meaningful employment opportunities'),[197] that he would be denied medical services, education and rations, and, given that the refugee camp in which he had formerly lived had been destroyed, would have difficulty finding somewhere to live. None of these issues could be classified as minor breaches of the relevant international human rights; rather, they arguably go to the core of each of the rights to housing, an adequate standard of living and right to health. Notwithstanding this, the RPD classed them as 'third level' and thus required an accumulation of such instances of 'discrimination' in order to classify the applicant's predicament as one involving 'persecution'. Ultimately, the fear of such treatment was buttressed with a risk of a breach of 'level 2 rights' (arbitrary arrest and detention), which assured the success of this claim.[198] However, it is arguable that any of the socio-economic factors, even standing alone, should have been sufficient to justify a finding of persecution, or at least that the socio-economic factors did not require consolidation by physical violence in order to amount to persecution. This is supported by a submission by Amnesty International to the Committee on Racial Discrimination which argues that '[t]he main problems faced by Palestinian refugees [in Lebanon] are of a social and economic nature' and that '[d]iscrimination levied against Palestinians in relation to the rights to own and inherit property and the right to work,

---

[196] As Anker surmises from a consideration of the US cases, '[a]djudicators seem wary of the concept of discrimination itself, as if it inherently describes types of harm that are not serious': *Law of Asylum in the United States*, p. 215. In a recent major treatise on refugee law, Symes and Jorro state that '[t]o the refugee lawyer, though, "discrimination" in the sense now discussed is that which manifests itself in breaches of *lower order rights*, primarily those recognised by the ICESCR': Symes and Jorro, *Asylum Law and Practice*, p. 106 (emphasis added).

[197] *GRF (Re)*, Nos. AA0-01454, AA0-01462 and AA0-01463 [2001] CRDD No. 88, 12 July 2001, at para. 22.

[198] *GRF (Re)*, Nos. AA0-01454, AA0-01462 and AA0-01463 [2001] CRDD No. 88, 12 July 2001, at para. 25.

creates conditions where Palestinian refugees cannot enjoy an adequate standard of living'.[199]

This requirement that socio-economic violations be combined with breaches of civil and political rights in order to constitute persecution is also evident in cases in other jurisdictions,[200] including in the USA where, although purporting to accept that substantial economic deprivation can itself found a successful refugee claim, courts often decline to grant applications unless the economic related aspect of the claims can be buttressed by fear of violence or other more 'traditional' (civil and political) types of harm.[201]

An analysis of tribunal and court decisions reveals that this approach is often engaged in respect of claims that could potentially have extremely wide ramifications, for example in those by Roma applicants from the Czech Republic and Slovakia,[202] thus suggesting that an implicit

---

[199] Amnesty International, *Lebanon: Economic and Social Rights of Palestinians Refugees, Submission to the Committee on the Elimination of Racial Discrimination* (2004) <http://web.amnesty.org/library/prit/ENGMDE180172003> at 31 May 2006. In particular, Amnesty notes that the rights to education, access to medical care and housing are severely affected by Lebanon's policies vis-à-vis Palestinian refugees.

[200] An analysis of Dutch cases by Spijkerboer tends to confirm this concern, as he notes that there is 'a strong tendency to find violations of [economic and social] rights insufficient except in combination with other, "normal" forms of persecution': Spijkerboer, *Gender and Refugee Studies*, p. 109. He provides the following example: 'a Yugoslav Roma woman, who was in bad health, had no housing, no work, had been denied medical treatment in the past and would possibly be denied treatment again in the future was not considered a refugee. The facts were seen as insufficiently serious to amount to persecution': p. 133, note 10.

[201] For example, see *Nagoulko*, 333 F 3d 1012 (9th Cir. 2003): 'In the precise circumstances of this case, it is significant that Nagoulko never suffered any significant physical violence': at 1015–16. See also *Korablina*, 158 F 3d 1038 (9th Cir. 1998), at 1038–9.

[202] This is a particularly prominent issue in the UK jurisprudence. See, for example, the decision of the IAT in *Puzova* [2001] UKAIT 00001, which is the key IAT decision on Roma in the Czech Republic (identified as such by the IAT). To a certain extent, the same analysis applies in respect of the UK cases dealing with Croatian Serbs – the leading case is *The Secretary of State for the Home Department v. SK (Appellant SK)* [2002] UKIAT 05613 (starred appeal – 'Key Case'). See also *Majkic v. Secretary of State for the Home Department* (Unreported, IAT, Appeal No. CC/12867/01, 10 December 2001); *Macura, Ljiljana, Maletic v. Secretary of State for the Home Department* (Unreported, IAT, Appeal No. HX-61441-00, 11 September 2001); *The Secretary of State for the Home Department v. Rakas* [2002] UKIAT 06426. It is, however, also present in other jurisdictions. For example, in the recent decision in *Refugee Appeal No. 73607*, RSAA, 26 February 2004, the Authority noted, in upholding the claim for refugee status by a Czech Roma, that '[t]he appellant has a profile over and above the average Roma, and can be seen to be somebody who skinhead or other neo-Nazi gangs, and local Czech population, may take particular exception to': at para. 56 (distinguishing this case from the general socio-economic deprivation of the Roma).

(indeed, sometimes explicit) 'floodgates' argument underpins the need to distinguish a particular applicant from the plight of all members of an economically and socially oppressed minority.[203] Moreover, the assumption seems to be that widespread deprivation and degradation resulting in life-long disadvantage on account of, for example, race, can be tolerated, whereas once that is accompanied by the threat of violence, the Refugee Convention must legitimately be engaged, again suggesting that a lower value is placed on the status of economic and social rights.[204]

While this is a generally applicable problem, as Spijkerboer notes, it can be particularly relevant in refugee claims by women, who often allege violation of what he phrases 'soft rights';[205] indeed, it has been argued that 'women encounter the severest human rights problems in

---

[203] A good example of this phenomenon is provided in *El Deaibes* [2002] UKIAT 02582, which concerned a claim by a Palestinian suffering a range of socio-economic deprivations in a refugee camp in Lebanon. In rejecting the claim, the IAT stated: 'Mr Jackson [counsel for the applicant] acknowledges that, if he is right, the majority of the Palestinians at present in refugee camps in Lebanon will not be returnable if they manage to reach the United Kingdom': at para. 9.

[204] In *Horvath*, for example, the UK Court of Appeal upheld the IAT's rejection of the applicant's claims based on 'third category rights' — notwithstanding the evidence presented in that case of widespread severe discrimination against Roma in Slovakia in a range of socio-economic rights (see, for example, paras. 27–33). However, the 'violence from the skinheads' was easily found to constitute persecution: at para. 27. See also *R (on the application of Secretary of State for the Home Department)* v. *Immigration Appeal Tribunal* (Unreported, Queen's Bench Division, CO/593/1999, 21 November 2000).

[205] Spijkerboer, *Gender and Refugee Studies*, p. 109. See also Crawley, *Refugees and Gender*, p. 42. Crawley expresses concern about the hierarchical model since 'discriminatory violations of rights such as the right to work and the right to basic education... conceivably might be more likely to affect women': Heaven Crawley, 'Women and Refugee Status', in Indra (ed.), *Engendering Forced Migration: Theory and Practice*, p. 312. See also Hilary Charlesworth and Christine Chinkin, 'The Gender of Jus Cogens' (1993) 15 *Human Rights Quarterly* 63. As Eva Brems points out, worldwide, women's economic and social status is lower than that of men: see Eva Brems, 'Social and Economic Rights of Women', in Peter Van der Auweraert (ed.), *Social, Economic and Cultural Rights: An Appraisal of Current European and International Developments* (Antwerpen: Maklu, 2002), p. 23. She says, that '[a]ccording to UNIFEM data, there is feminization of poverty in 12 out of 15 developing countries for which data is available': p. 23. She notes that many scholars and women's rights activists have argued for greater importance to be placed on socio-economic rights, given their relevance and impact on the lives of women: see p. 25, note 390.

the area of economic, social and cultural life'.[206] So much was acknowledged by the RSAA where, after reiterating the principle that 'discrimination per se is not enough to establish a case for refugee status',[207] it emphasized that 'decision-makers should consciously strive both to recognize and give proper weight to the impact of discriminatory measures on women'.[208]

Problems related to the hierarchical obligation model

So far we have considered problems that manifest in refugee cases as a result of socio-economic rights being accorded a lower normative status as compared with civil and political rights. As explained above, in some jurisdictions this appears to be a mistaken interpretation of the Hathaway human rights model, in that some decision-makers have misunderstood the hierarchy of *obligation* model as referring to *normative* hierarchy. However, an analysis of the case law reveals that the notion of hierarchy of obligation has itself produced problems in refugee adjudication, in that courts have a mistaken tendency to interpret the 'lower level of enforceability' described in the Hathaway model as negating any content to economic and social rights. It is essential that these problems are identified in order that they may be rectified in future refugee adjudication.

---

[206] Katarina Frostell and Martin Scheinin, 'Women' in Asbjorn Eide, Catarina Krause, Allan Rosas and Martin Scheinin (eds.), *Economic, Social and Cultural Rights: A Textbook*, second edition (Dordrecht: M. Nijhoff Publishers, 2001), p. 331. See also Robert McCorquodale, 'Secrets and Lies: Economic Globalisation and Women's Human Rights' (1998) 19 *Australian Year Book of International Law* 73. The *Montreal Principles on Women's Economic, Social and Cultural Rights* (2002) <http://www.fidh.org/femmes/rapport/2003/ca0110a.pdf>, developed by a leading group of international legal scholars, notes that '[e]conomic, social and cultural rights have a particular significance for women because as a group, women are disproportionately affected by poverty, and by social and cultural marginalization. Women's poverty is a central manifestation, and a direct result of women's lesser social, economic and political power. In turn, women's poverty reinforces their subordination, and constrains their enjoyment of every other right': at 2.

[207] *Refugee Appeal No. 71427/99*, RSAA, 16 August 2000, at para. 54.

[208] *Refugee Appeal No. 71427/99*, RSAA, 16 August 2000, at para. 55. According to Haines, 'discrimination can affect individuals to different degrees and it is necessary to recognise and to give proper weight to the impact of discriminatory measures on women. Various acts of discrimination, in their cumulative effect, can deny human dignity in key ways and should properly be recognized as persecution for the purposes of the Refugee Convention': Rodger P. G. Haines, 'Gender-Related Persecution', in Feller, Türk and Nicholson (eds.), *Refugee Protection in International Law*, p. 331.

Progressive implementation as negating content of socio-economic rights

An analysis of common law decisions reveals that some decision-makers have adopted an erroneous interpretation of economic and social rights provisions, which tends to assume that there is little content to such rights, given their programmatic and progressive nature. There are two aspects to this problematic interpretation.

First, some courts appear to take the approach that international covenants containing economic and social rights do not impose any *immediate duties* on state parties. For example, in a number of decisions of the Australian RRT, the Tribunal has stated that the ICESCR 'does not create obligations that States are required to fulfill immediately and therefore persons whose sole reason for migration is to achieve a better economic standard of living are generally excluded from refugee protection under the Convention'.[209] There is a logical gap in this statement, as it seems to imply that since the ICESCR does not create immediate standards of attainment, refugee claimants may not base their applications on a breach of economic and social rights. Similarly, the New Zealand RSAA has said that '[t]he obligations imposed by the [ICESCR] are not absolute and immediately binding, but rather "programmatic"'.[210] In Hathaway's original formulation it is explained that the ICESCR does not impose 'absolute and immediately binding standards of *attainment*'.[211] While it is true that the ICESCR generally does not provide for immediate *outcomes* in respect of these rights, it certainly imposes immediate *obligations* in a number of important respects. As the Economic Committee has explained, 'while the Covenant provides for progressive realization and acknowledges the constraints due to the limits of available resources, it also imposes various obligations which are of immediate

---

[209] See *Reference N93/02256*, RRT, 20 May 1994, at 3. See also *Reference N96/11195*, RRT, 10 September 1996.
[210] *Refugee Appeal No. 732/92*, RSAA, 5 August 1994, at 9. In a later decision, the Authority noted that 'the right to education is a second generation, third level human right in the sense that it is not an absolute human right linked to civil and political status. It does not impose, as stated above, an absolute and immediately binding standard, the breach of which may be a strong indicator of persecutory behaviour – see Hathaway', *Refugee Appeals Nos. 74754, 74755*, RSAA, 7 January 2004, at para. 42. However, it should be noted that the most recent decision to consider socio-economic claims takes a much more sophisticated approach to the obligations contained in the ICESCR: see *Refugee Appeal No. 75221*, RSAA, 23 September 2005.
[211] Hathaway, *The Law of Refugee Status*, p. 110 (emphasis added).

effect'.[212] This distinction may appear subtle, but it has significant ramifications for applicants in refugee claims because the 'programmatic' nature of these rights is not relevant to cases where a person's economic and social rights are actively withdrawn,[213] or where there is discrimination (on a protected ground) in the provision of such rights.[214] However, this important point seems to have been obscured by the hierarchy of obligation approach.

A second, although closely related, aspect of this erroneous interpretation is that some decision-makers have a tendency to dismiss active violations of economic and social rights as possible cases of persecution based on the reasoning that economic and social rights are always subject to resource constraints and the 'discretion' of individual countries.[215] Thus, violations are not considered capable of constituting persecution. This approach is summarized in the following analysis of the Australian RRT, in relation to a claim by a disabled Korean man who alleged discrimination in employment due to his medical condition:

The right to employment is recognised in Article 23 of the Universal Declaration on Human Rights, Article 6 of the International Covenant on Economic, Social and Cultural Rights and Article 7 of the Declaration on the Rights of Disabled Persons. Similarly the right to an adequate standard of living including the right to social security in the event of disability is recognised in Article 23 of the Universal Declaration on Human Rights, Articles 9 and 11 of the International Covenant on Economic, Social and Cultural Rights and Article 7 of the declaration on the Rights of Disabled Persons. However ... referring to the preamble of the Universal Declaration on Human Rights, and Article 2 of the International Covenant on Economic, Social and Cultural Rights, and the preamble to the Declaration on the Rights of Disabled Persons ... *these rights are relative and are to be progressively implemented and are dependent on the finances*

---

[212] Committee on Economic, Social and Cultural Rights ('CESCR'), *General Comment 3: The Nature of States Parties Obligations (Art. 2, para. 1 of the Covenant)*, UN Doc. E/1991/23 (1990).

[213] The Economic Committee has explained: 'any deliberately retrogressive measures in that regard would require the most careful consideration and would need to be fully justified by reference to the totality of the rights provided for in the Covenant and in the context of the full use of the maximum available resources': CESCR, *General Comment 3: The Nature of States Parties Obligations (Art. 2, para. 1 of the Covenant)*, UN Doc. E/1991/23 (1990), at para. 9.

[214] See CESCR, *General Comment 3: The Nature of States Parties Obligations (Art. 2, para. 1 of the Covenant)*, UN Doc. E/1991/23 (1990), where the Committee explains that one of the obligations of immediate effect is the 'undertaking to guarantee' that relevant rights 'will be exercised without discrimination': at para. 1.

[215] *Reference N96/11195*, RRT, 10 September 1996, at 6.

and resources of the country concerned. As such the Tribunal finds that a breach of such rights, particularly in these circumstances, does not constitute persecution.[216]

This line of reasoning is highly questionable because it appears to assume that even where there has been a violation of a relevant socio-economic right, a lack of resources in the country of origin may nonetheless justify the violation. The problem with such reasoning is that while the financial resources of the country of origin may be relevant to determining whether a violation of a socio-economic right has occurred (which is the feature that can make violations of socio-economic rights more difficult to assess as compared to violations of civil and political rights), these issues are not relevant once it is clear that a violation has been established (which, in the above case was achieved on the basis of discrimination).

An example of a concrete way in which this erroneous interpretation affects refugee claims is provided in the decision of the UK Court of Appeal in *Kagema*,[217] in which the applicant claimed refugee status on the basis of repeated forcible evictions, as a result of ethnic persecution supported by the government, which left he and his family destitute. The evidence established that his house in the Rift Valley was burnt down and he was driven off the land by an ethnic group supported by the government; he was then taken to a camp (populated predominantly by his ethnic group) which was later raided by the police who destroyed the camp and looted and burned the belongings of the inhabitants, and was then forcibly relocated (after being questioned by police) to Central Province – the area regarded as the traditional home of his ethnic group. Families were separated and the displaced were not provided with food or shelter. The applicant and his family then moved to Kirigiti Stadium, from where they were evicted, and ultimately found shelter at a camp run by the Catholic Church, at which they arrived destitute.[218]

In rejecting his claim for asylum, the Special Adjudicator held: '[t]he government have actually provided places for the appellant and his family to live, they have not prevented the church from providing the basic necessities. *It is not realistic to suppose that in a country such as*

---

[216] *Reference N96/11195*, RRT, 10 September 1996, at 4–5 (emphasis added).
[217] *Kagema v. Secretary of State for the Home Department* [1997] Imm AR 137 at 138–9 ('*Kagema*').
[218] *Kagema* [1997] Imm AR 137 at 138–9.

Kenya all citizens will at all times have employment and a solid house in which to live'.[219] The analysis of the Special Adjudicator renders the notion of economic and social rights meaningless, as it appears to suggest that violations, even in the form of active withdrawals of rights, are justified on the basis of the resource constraints on the home state, and thus essentially that there is no content to the notion of economic and social rights as rights.[220] On this reasoning, any active withdrawal, regardless of the level of seriousness, would not amount to a socio-economic rights violation and hence to persecution.

This approach is patently at odds with the authoritative view of the Economic Committee that 'forced evictions' (defined as the 'permanent or temporary removal against their will of individuals, families and/or communities from the homes and/or land which they occupy, without the provision of, and access to, appropriate forms of legal or other protection',[221] which clearly applies in this case), are a 'gross violation of human rights'[222] and are prima facie incompatible with the requirements of the Covenant'.[223] The Economic Committee has explained that, 'in view of the nature of the practice of forced evictions, the reference in article 2.1 to progressive achievement based on the availability of resources will rarely be relevant'.[224] In particular, the 'State must itself refrain from forced evictions and ensure that the law is enforced against its agents or third parties who carry out forced evictions'.[225]

---

[219] *Kagema* [1997] Imm AR 137 at 139 (emphasis added).
[220] Interestingly, on appeal, Lord Justice Ward noted that he 'may well have found that thrice being forcefully displaced from home and camp by agents of the Government could not be anything but persecution'. Ultimately, the Court focused on the risk of future persecution, dismissing the appeal on the basis of changed circumstances: *Kagema* [1997] Imm AR 137 at 139 at 140.
[221] CESCR, *General Comment 7: The Right to Adequate Housing (Art. 11.1): Forced Evictions*, UN Doc. E/1998/22 (1997), annex IV.
[222] In *General Comment 7: The Right to Adequate Housing (Art. 11.1): Forced Evictions*, UN Doc. E/1998/22 (1997), annex IV, the Committee referred to this view by the UN Human Rights Commission in its resolution 1993/77: at para. 2.
[223] CESCR, *General Comment 4: The Right to Adequate Housing (Art. 11(1) of the Covenant)*, UN Doc. E/1992/23 (1991), at para. 18.
[224] CESCR, *General Comment 7: The Right to Adequate Housing (Art. 11.1): Forced Evictions*, UN Doc. E/1998/22, annex IV, at para. 8.
[225] CESCR, *General Comment 7: The Right to Adequate Housing (Art. 11.1): Forced Evictions*, UN Doc. E/1998/22, annex IV, at para. 8.

Another example of this tendency to excuse violations of socio-economic rights by reference to resource constraints is provided in a decision involving the claim of a Russian child with cerebral palsy who, because of his disability, 'was denied rights afforded to all other citizens', including access to medical care and to an elementary education. The US Immigration Judge rejected the refugee claim on the basis that, inter alia, 'Russia does not have the resources to provide medical attention to individuals at the same standards as in developed nations'.[226] In overturning this decision, the US Court of Appeals for the Ninth Circuit found this reasoning to be erroneous because 'claims of economic difficulties cannot be used to justify the deprivation of services essential to human survival and development, if the deprivation is based on the recipient's membership in a statutorily protected group'.[227] The Court's analysis in that case is consistent with the Economic Committee's view that pursuant to the right to health protected by art. 12 of the ICESCR, states parties have a core obligation 'to ensure the right of access to health facilities, goods and services on a non-discriminatory basis, especially for vulnerable or marginalized groups'[228] and that a 'State party cannot, under any circumstances whatsoever, justify its non-compliance with th[is] core obligation'.[229] In other words, resource constraints can never constitute a permissible reason to derogate from the core obligation of non-discrimination in respect of either the right to health or education.[230]

The cases identified in this section, in which the socio-economic aspects to refugee claims have been dismissed based on the mistaken view that the ICESCR does not impose immediate duties or that all violations are explained by a lack of resources, indicate that there is a significant level of confusion and misunderstanding in refugee jurisprudence regarding the nature of socio-economic rights in international law.

---

[226] *Tchoukhrova v. Gonzales*, 404 F 3d 1181 (9th Cir. 2005), at 1194 ('*Tchoukhrova*').
[227] *Tchoukhrova*, 404 F 3d 1181 (9th Cir. 2005), at 1194.
[228] CESCR, *General Comment 14: The Right to the Highest Attainable Standard of Health (Art. 12 of the International Covenant on Economic, Social and Cultural Rights)*, UN Doc. E/C. 12/2000/4 (2000), at para. 43(a).
[229] CESCR, *General Comment 14: The Right to the Highest Attainable Standard of Health (Art. 12 of the International Covenant on Economic, Social and Cultural Rights)*, UN Doc. E/C. 12/2000/4 (2000), at para. 47.
[230] CESCR, *General Comment 13: The Right to Education (Article 13 of the Covenant)*, UN Doc. E/C. 12/1999/10 (1999).

Misunderstanding the nature of discrimination in socio-economic rights

Another key problem in understanding the nature of states' obligations in respect of socio-economic rights relates to the relevance and importance of the concept of discrimination, an issue alluded to above. The essential issue is that refugee decision-makers have a tendency to ignore discrimination in access to socio-economic rights, such as education and health care, unless the particular right is absolutely guaranteed in international law, thus undermining the substance of the non-discrimination provision in the ICESCR and other relevant international treaties.

Article 2(2) of the ICESCR imposes an obligation on States Parties 'to guarantee that the rights enunciated in the present Covenant will be exercised without discrimination of any kind as to race, colour, sex, language, religion, political or other opinion, national or social origin, property, birth or other status'[231] – rights of *immediate obligation*. The Economic Committee takes the view that the prohibition against discrimination enshrined in art. 2(2), in the context of education, for example, 'is subject to neither progressive realization nor the availability of resources; it applies fully and immediately to all aspects of education and encompasses all internationally prohibited grounds of discrimination'.[232] In other words, although a person does not have an absolute right to free secondary or tertiary education or to the full range of health facilities, if the government is able generally to provide secondary or tertiary education or health care to citizens but excludes a section of the population on prohibited grounds, this clearly constitutes a violation of the ICESCR,[233] as well as (potentially) the prohibition of

---

[231] ICESCR art. 2(2). Importantly, the non-discrimination provision in the ICESCR has been pointed to by scholars as holding the greatest potential in the future development of economic and social rights. According to Tomuschat, art. 2(2) 'provides a vast potential for dynamic development of the CESCR': see Christian Tomuschat, *Human Rights: Beyond Idealism and Realism* (Oxford: Oxford University Press, 2003), p. 44.

[232] CESCR, *General Comment 13: The Right to Education (Article 13 of the Covenant)*, UN Doc. E/C. 12/1999/10 (1999).

[233] Both arts. 2(2) and 3 of the ICESCR – which specifically ensure the 'equal right of men and women to the enjoyment of all economic, social and cultural rights set forth in the present Covenant' – are relevant in this regard. There are also other provisions in the context of specific rights. For example, art. 13(2) of the ICESCR provides that higher (tertiary) education 'shall be made *equally accessible to all*, on the basis of capacity, by every appropriate means, and in particular by the progressive introduction of free education' (emphasis added).

discrimination contained in the ICCPR,[234] CEDAW,[235] the CERD[236] and the CRC.[237]

Notwithstanding this, refugee decision-makers in some cases appear to have conflated the separate questions of the absolute nature of the right on the one hand with the prohibition on discrimination on the other, such that discrimination is often held relevant only where the person otherwise has an absolute entitlement to the content of the right. A good example of this problem is provided in the context of discrimination in secondary and tertiary education. In a number of instances, courts have been presented with claims based, at least in part, on a discriminatory denial of higher education, on Refugee Convention grounds such as race or gender. The analysis of whether a relevant right has been breached (the precursor to the persecution question) has, in a number of instances, reflected a fundamental misunderstanding of the nature of economic and social rights. Unlike some US decisions in which courts have summarily dismissed the notion that education engages the concept of rights,[238] other courts have been willing to consider that the right to education is something that is protected in international law (usually by reference to the UDHR and the ICESCR); however, they tend to interpret it in a very narrow way. For example, in one decision of the Australian RRT, the Tribunal noted:

> the Applicant's husband was expelled from his tertiary institution because of his political activities. *However the right to education expressed in the International Covenant on Economic, Social and Cultural Rights and the Convention on the Rights of the Child only extends to primary education.* In the present case the Applicant's

---

[234] The ICCPR provides a general, autonomous, non-discrimination provision in art. 26, which has been held by the Human Rights Committee to apply to discrimination in the provision of economic and social rights on a protected ground. In three cases involving allegations of discrimination in Dutch legislation concerning unemployment benefits, the Committee explained: 'Although Article 26 requires that legislation should prohibit discrimination, it does not of itself contain any obligation with respect to the matters that may be provided for by legislation. Thus it does not, for example, require any State to enact legislation to provide for social security. However, when such legislation is adopted in the exercise of a State's sovereign power, then such legislation must comply with Article 26 of the Covenant': *Zwaan-de Vries v. The Netherlands*, Communication No. 182/1984, as cited in Martin Scheinin, 'Economic and Social Rights as Legal Rights', in Asbjørn Eide, Catarina Krause and Allan Rosas, *Economic, Social and Cultural Rights, A Textbook* (The Hague: Kluwer Law International, 2001), p. 33.

[235] CEDAW, art. 2.   [236] CERD, art. 2.   [237] CRC, art. 2.

[238] See, for example, *Faddoul*, 37 F 3d 185 (5th Cir. 1994), at 188; *Li*, 92 F 3d 985 (9th Cir. 1996), at 987; and *Petkov and Tritchkova*, 114 F 3d 1192 (7th Cir. 1997).

husband had access to secondary education and I do not consider that the fact that he was denied the opportunity to continue his university studies amounts to 'persecution' involving 'serious harm'.[239]

In this decision, it is clear that the Tribunal based its conclusion that the discriminatory denial of education did not amount to 'serious harm' on the premise that he did not enjoy a right to tertiary education in international law. A similar analysis had been adopted in an earlier decision of the RRT in which the Tribunal had rejected that part of the claim based on discriminatory denial of tertiary education on the basis that 'the right to education set out in the [ICESCR] requires universal access only to primary education, with further opportunities conditioned by circumstances'.[240] Similar sentiments can be found in some New Zealand cases in relation to secondary and tertiary education,[241] and, in a recent decision of the Canadian RPD, the Tribunal

---

[239] *Reference N01/39925*, RRT, 18 April 2002, at 12 (emphasis added). See also *Reference N01/39111*, RRT, 15 March 2002, at 6; *Reference N97/13974*, RRT, 10 July 1997, at 8; *Yousefi v. Minister for Immigration and Multicultural Affairs* [2000] FCA 1352 (Unreported, Carr J, 22 September 2000), in which His Honour affirmed the decision of the RRT below, which had held 'the Applicant was refused entry to university because he failed the religious character test. However the right to education expressed in the International Covenant on Economic, Social and Cultural Rights and the Convention on the Rights of the Child only extends to primary education': at 6. In that case, the RRT also concluded that it did not consider the denial of the opportunity to go to university constituted 'such a significant detriment or disadvantage as to amount to "persecution" for the purposes of the Convention', but this conclusion was undoubtedly influenced by the prior incorrect conclusion.

[240] *Reference N97/13974*, RRT, 10 July 1997, at 8. The RRT also misinterpreted the UNHCR Handbook on this issue. Paragraph 54 of the Handbook states that denial of access to normally available educational facilities is an example of 'consequences of a substantially prejudicial nature' that could constitute persecution. However, the RRT in this case paraphrased this as: 'Although denial of access to education may constitute persecution if imposed for a Convention reason ... restricted access to higher education is not of itself normally regarded as amounting to persecution. This will occur only where substantial prejudice arises from the denial of access to normally available educational facilities (UNHCR Handbook ... para. 54)': at 7.

[241] For example, in *Refugee Appeal No. 732/92*, RSAA, 5 August 1994, the RSAA stated that '[t]he appellant is unable to point to an unqualified right to secondary education': at 9. The Authority dismissed the claim mainly on the basis that the applicant did not provide evidence that she was subject to a blanket exclusion from secondary and higher education, thus suggesting that the result may have been different had the applicant shown that the exclusion was 'accompanied by aggravating features, such as her blanket exclusion from all educational institutions'. See also *Refugee Appeal No. 70651/97*, RSAA, 27 November 1997: 'Frankly, even if there

similarly rejected the applicant's claim relating to denial of tertiary education on the basis that, while the denial was discriminatory, 'third level rights' include only access to basic education, which, in any event, only require the state to 'take steps to the maximum of their available resources to progressively realize [these rights] in a non-discriminatory way'.[242]

Although the issue of discrimination in health care has not been as extensively considered in the case law, there is evidence that decision-makers may take a similar approach to this issue. For example, in *Puzova*, the UK IAT explained that:

> With regard to category 3 rights, it should be noted that their scope is also limited by the terms of their incorporation in the relevant International Covenants. Thus, for example, the right to education requires universal access only to primary education and the right to health only obliges the state to work to reduce infant mortality, improve hygiene, control diseases and establish basic medical services... All these passages indicate the high threshold which must be crossed to show that serious harm exists in discriminatory denial of category 3 rights *both* by reason of their restriction to very basic levels to be met, and by reason of the degree of harm necessary to raise the treatment complained of from even severe discrimination to persecution.[243]

As this passage highlights, to a certain extent the erroneous approach in some cases reflects a misunderstanding of Hathaway's text, in which he sets out the minimal nature of the absolute entitlement to rights such as education and health care (from which the IAT in *Puzova* quoted), but also clearly includes discriminatory denial of socio-economic rights as a separate category of violation, in accordance with the ICESCR.[244] However, this important distinction appears to have been overlooked and

---

were a complete prohibition on the appellant undertaking tertiary studies, we are not satisfied that we would find such discrimination to be persecutory in the case of this appellant, given the reasonable level of education already attained by her': at 12 (emphasis added).

[242] *AWC (Re)*, No. AA1-01391 [2003] RPDD No. 71, 27 May 2003, at 7–8.
[243] *Puzova* [2001] UKAIT 00001 at 3 (emphasis added), quoting from Hathaway, *The Law of Refugee Status*, p. 117.
[244] Hathaway notes that there are two distinct duties: 'First, a government must marshal national and international resources and give priority to the expenditure of those resources in achieving the full realization of human rights. Second, and more commonly related to refugee claims, states must implement socio-economic rights on a non-discriminatory basis': Hathaway, *The Law of Refugee Status*, pp. 116–17. This indicates that the obligations are separate and distinct.

collapsed into one requirement.[245] Indeed, even those decision-makers who have rejected the argument that discrimination in secondary or tertiary education is irrelevant in refugee law because of the limited right in international law, have often failed to focus on the independent scope of the non-discrimination right in the ICESCR, relying instead on more general notions such that discrimination in education is 'worthy of serious consideration as persecution'.[246]

This is not to say that discriminatory denial of access to secondary or tertiary education or health care necessarily amounts to persecution in every case; however, proper analysis of this question is hampered by an erroneous understanding of economic and social rights in international law, because the approach taken in many of the above cases results in the socio-economic aspect of the claim being discounted altogether, rather than at least being considered as part of the refugee claim.

The final discrimination point which has been raised in respect of refugee claims based on socio-economic discrimination relates to the exception in art. 2(3) of the ICESCR, which provides that '[d]eveloping countries, with due regard to human rights and their national economy, may determine to what extent they would guarantee the economic rights recognized in the present Covenant to non-nationals'. In *Refugee Appeal No. 73952*,[247] the New Zealand RSAA suggested that this provision may preclude a successful refugee claim by a person who fears discrimination in respect of a range of socio-economic rights due to his or her status as a

---

[245] *Puzova* [2001] UKIAT 00001 at 3. See also *Filiusina v. Secretary of State for the Home Department* (Unreported, IAT, Appeal No. HX/65188/2000, CC/13395/2000, 3 December 2001), in which the UK IAT said: 'there was one other point which had been raised in the grounds of appeal, relating to the potential discrimination against the daughter in relation to her ability to attend university. It was Ms Cronin's submission that this required to be considered as a Convention Issue. We pointed out to her, however, that in dealing with the question of whether breach of third level rights, under Professor Hathaway's classification in the Law of Refugee Status, could be regarded as being of sufficient seriousness to cross the threshold from discrimination to persecution, Professor Hathaway specifically made the point that the nature of the third level right to education was internationally recognized as being limited to primary education. Ms Cronin accepted that on that basis she could not advance her arguments further in relation to any question of persecution under the Refugee Convention on this basis': at para. 8.

[246] *Grecu* (Unreported, IAT, Appeal No. HX/64793/96, 8 January 1998), at 5. See also *Koffi v. Secretary of State for the Home Department* (Unreported, IAT, Appeal No. 18227, HX/60314/96, 17 September 1999) at 5.

[247] RSAA, 26 May 2005.

non-national in the country of origin.[248] However, it is important to note that the general prohibition on discrimination in art. 2(2) of the ICESCR protects non-nationals.[249] Further, it is clear that art. 2(3) was intended 'as a measure of affirmative action in favour of historically underprivileged nationals'[250] and is therefore of very limited scope.[251] Accordingly, it is unlikely ever to be relevant in the refugee context.

Inherent problems with a categorical approach

A problem with any approach that is based on categorical distinctions is that it can lead to a rigid analysis, which fails to take into account the reality of the particular circumstances of the individual applicant and the interconnectedness of levels of rights. A good example of this problem relates to claims involving deprivation of property. It will be recalled that according to the hierarchical model of state obligation, the right to own and be free from arbitrary deprivation of property is categorized as falling within the 'fourth category', and will not, standing alone, normally constitute persecution.[252] While this may be highly appropriate in relation to claims of, for example, small business owners who are at risk of damage to or deprivation of their business property (in the context that such action will not deprive them of the ability to earn a living), it may be highly inappropriate in the context of an applicant who has been or will be deprived of property in the form of a house or other property essential to the realization of certain rights such as the right to an adequate standard of living or the right to housing. This can be particularly relevant for women, who continue to suffer

---

[248] The RSAA ultimately declined to resolve this issue since the evidence in that case did not suggest that the child applicants had a well founded fear of the relevant violations in that case: see *Refugee Appeal No. 73952*, RSAA, 26 May 2005, at paras. 72–3.
[249] Article 2(2) refers to discrimination based on 'national or social origin'.
[250] Bertrand G. Ramcharan, *Judicial Protection of Economic, Social and Cultural Rights: Cases and Materials* (Leiden: Martinus Nijhoff Publishers, 2005), p. 23.
[251] See Sepulveda, *The Nature of the Obligations under the International Covenant on Economic, Social and Cultural Rights*, pp. 414–15. After outlining the drafting history, which supports its limited scope, she notes that in any case, 'no developing State has sought to invoke it': p. 415.
[252] This has generally been accepted by those jurisdictions that adopt the hierarchical model. For example, in NZ the RSAA has noted that 'the right to own private property...[is] a fourth level right and breach of the right will not ordinarily provide the foundation for a claim of failure of state protection': *Refugee Appeal No. 72558/01*, RSAA, 19 November 2002, at para. 143.

from discriminatory laws relating to inheritance and property ownership in many countries, which can result in severe economic deprivation.

An example of the tendency to rely overly on the hierarchical categories is provided in the decision in *Ramirez v. Canada*,[253] in which the Federal Court of Canada considered an application for judicial review by a 64-year-old citizen of Nicaragua whose home had been confiscated by the Sandinista government as a result of her daughter's political activities. She argued that she feared being returned to Nicaragua because she was economically dependent on her daughter in Canada, and that, as a result of the confiscation, would have nowhere to live in Nicaragua. Furthermore, she had no relatives or family on whom she could rely to take care of her there.[254] The Tribunal below had accepted this evidence, but dismissed the claim on the basis that, relying on Hathaway's framework, 'protection from property confiscation is a fourth level right and although recognised in the Universal Declaration of Human Rights is... not codified in either of the binding covenants on human rights, and may be thus outside the scope of a state's basic duty of protection'.[255] The applicant criticized this assessment on the basis that the Tribunal had erroneously categorized the harm as engaging only a fourth-level right, whereas it 'is a third level right as set out in the International Covenant on Economic, Social and Cultural Rights', since 'the confiscation of the family home did, for all intents and purposes, deprive a woman who was almost sixty years of age, of the essential right to shelter'.[256] However, the Court dismissed the application for judicial review, agreeing with the Tribunal as to the inferior importance of fourth-level rights.[257] There are similar examples in the case law in other jurisdictions.[258]

---

[253] [1994] FCJ No. 1888 ('*Ramirez*').
[254] *Ramirez* [1994] FCJ No. 1888, at para. 4.
[255] *Ramirez* [1994] FCJ No. 1888, at para. 12. See also *Sithamparapillai v. Minister for Immigration & Multicultural Affairs* [2000] FCA 897 (Unreported, Goldberg J, 5 July 2000), at para. 19, where the Federal Court of Australia accepted the Hathaway view of property as a fourth level right.
[256] *Ramirez* [1994] FCJ No. 1888, at para. 5.
[257] *Ramirez* [1994] FCJ No. 1888, at para. 12.
[258] See, for example, *Reference N97/13974*, RRT, 10 July 1997. This was a claim by Indo-Fijians who alleged a range of deprivations based on their ethnicity. They claimed, inter alia, that they had lost their house due to a discriminatory land preference system for ethnic Fijians. The RRT responded that '[o]wnership of land is not a fundamental human right. Hathaway refers to 'the rule that core principles of human rights do not include a right to private property' and that 'a claim grounded solely on the actual or anticipated

In another decision involving a claim based on the consequences that followed from a Christian Iranian man's objection to a discriminatory section of the Iranian Civil Code dealing with inheritance laws, the Canadian RPD held that

> it is clear that disputes over inheritance rights have nothing to do with persecution. Inheritance rights are property rights. It is his father's property that the claimant seeks, and that his uncle seeks to prevent him from obtaining. Property rights are not generally-recognised fundamental human rights; after all, even in Canada, property rights are not protected in our Charter of Rights and Freedoms. Article 881 of the Iranian civil code may very well be discriminatory towards non-Muslim beneficiaries of deceased persons. *However, since it affects only property rights, we cannot find it to be persecutory*. It is also, perhaps, significant to note that the law does not confiscate property in favour of the state; it merely ensures its distribution to Muslim heirs. This is unquestionably discriminatory but it is not an example of persecution.[259]

On the facts of that particular case, the consequences of the discrimination may not have been sufficiently serious for the applicant and thus the claim may well have been properly rejected. However, the analysis is worrying as it suggests that one looks only to the so-called *value* of the rights invoked, rather than the *consequences of their breach* for the individual,[260] in assessing whether harm amounts to persecution. It is not difficult to point to examples where 'mere property rights' or 'disputes over inheritance rights' have a great deal to do with persecution. As mentioned above, this is a particularly important issue for women who suffer widespread discrimination resulting from 'gender biased laws, policies and traditions which prevent women from renting, leasing, owning and inheriting land, housing and property independently or at all and which render women's access to and control over land, housing and property dependent on their link to a man'.[261] It is

---

confiscation of property or damage to goods, without any attendant risk to personal security or basic livelihood, is not of sufficient gravity to warrant the granting of refugee status . . . Nor is there any fundamental human right to continued enjoyment of leased property. If it is claimed that the lease was terminated improperly or prematurely, then the remedy lies in the courts in Fiji': at 9.

[259] *PKH (Re)*, No. T96-01209 [1996] CRDD No. 216, 17 December 1996, at paras. 19–20 (emphasis added).

[260] This is arguably inconsistent with Hathaway's explanation that 'a claim grounded solely on the actual or anticipated confiscation of property or damage to goods, *without any attendant risk to personal security or basic livelihood*, is not of sufficient gravity to warrant the granting of refugee status': *The Law of Refugee Status*, p. 120.

[261] Brems, 'Social and Economic Rights of Women', p. 38.

recognized that restrictions on property and ownership rights can 'therefore have devastating consequences for the well-being of women, their children and families'.[262] A concrete example of this phenomenon is provided in a report by Human Rights Watch which highlights the plight of women in Kenya whose rights to property (including land and livestock) are removed following the death of their husbands, according to customary law, relegating many of the women and their children to a position of absolute poverty.[263]

These cases suggest that there is a tendency for decision-makers to apply the hierarchical model in a fixed and simplistic manner, and that such an overly categorical approach can distract attention from the interconnectedness of human rights, for example, the relationship between property and an adequate standard of living, in certain circumstances. In addition, these examples highlight the limitations of a categorical approach which does not take into account the cross-cutting nature of provisions such as art. 3 of the ICESCR;[264] and art. 26 of the ICCPR, which the Human Rights Committee ('HRC') has explained requires that '[w]omen should also have equal inheritance rights to those of men when the dissolution of marriage is caused by the death of one of the spouses'.[265] Nor does it make explicit allowance for consideration of provisions such as art. 15 of the CEDAW which prohibits all forms of discrimination against women in economic life, with explicit reference to the right to administer property, and art. 14 which provides for equal rights of both spouses 'in respect of the

---

[262] Frostell and Scheinin, 'Women', in Eide, Krause, Rosas and Scheinin (eds.), *Economic, Social and Cultural Rights*.
[263] Human Rights Watch, *Double Standards: Women's Property Rights Violations in Kenya* (2003a) <http://www.hrw.org/reports/2003/kenya0303/kenya0303.pdf> at 31 May 2006, especially at Chapter IV: 'Women's Property Rights Violations and their Consequences'.
[264] In CESCR, *General Comment No. 16: The Equal Right of Men and Women to the Enjoyment of all Economic, Social and Cultural Rights*, E/C.12/2005/4 (2005a), the Economic Committee notes that 'Article 3 is a cross-cutting obligation and applies to all the rights contained in articles 6 to 15 of the Covenant' (para. 22). In particular, the Committee notes that implementing art. 3 in conjunction with art. 10 (1) requires states to 'ensure that women have equal rights to marital property and inheritance upon their husband's death' (para. 27) and that implementing art. 3 in relation to art. 11(1) 'requires that women have a right to own, use or otherwise control housing, land and property on an equal basis with men' (para. 28).
[265] Human Rights Committee, *General Comment No. 28: Equality of Rights between Men and Women (Article 3)*, UN Doc. CCPR/C/21/Rev.1/Add.10 (2000), at paras. 19, 26.

ownership, acquisition, management, administration, enjoyment and disposition of property'.[266]

One may argue that this simply supports greater attentiveness on the part of decision-makers to the relationship between the categories in the hierarchical model. However, there is no question that categories signal distinction, and for decision-makers not schooled in international human rights law, there is genuine potential for confusion and misapplication, as these cases clearly suggest.

Inherent difficulties with socio-economic claims

One of the greatest limitations of the socio-economic category is that refugee claims based on socio-economic deprivation simply have not been taken up by advocates or courts in significant numbers; thus analysis is, in the main, relatively limited and unsophisticated. Bhabha focuses on the role of refugee advocates in this respect, arguing that they have a 'heavy onus' and responsibility to 'draw on theoretical innovations in conceptions of rights' in order to expand protection to encompass new types of claims.[267] While this is undoubtedly true, much of the problem is that there is little discussion or analysis in the academic literature or case law which seeks to clarify and develop relevant principles on which advocates can draw in presenting individual claims.

The courts that have accepted the notion that violations of 'third level rights' can amount to persecution in certain circumstances have tended to repeat the principles but have rarely had occasion to analyse and extrapolate their meaning in the context of concrete cases. For example, in the UK, the IAT has accepted the hierarchical rights formulation and often repeated the principle that persecution includes 'failure to

---

[266] The CEDAW Committee has noted: 'The right to own, manage, enjoy and dispose of property is central to a woman's right to enjoy financial independence, and in many countries will be critical to her ability to earn a livelihood and to provide adequate housing and nutrition for herself and for her family... Any law or custom that grants men a right to a greater share of property at the end of a marriage or de facto relationship, or on the death of a relative, is discriminatory and will have a serious impact on a woman's practical ability to divorce her husband, to support herself or her family and to live in dignity as an independent person': CEDAW Committee, *General Recommendation No. 21*, UN Doc. HRI/GEN/1/Rev.4 (2000), cited in Brems, 'Social and Economic Rights of Women', p. 40.

[267] Bhabha, 'Boundaries in the field of Human Rights: Internationalist Gatekeepers?', at 180–1.

implement a right within the third category which is either discriminatory or not grounded in the absolute lack of resources',[268] but has rarely explained how a decision-maker should assess a particular factual situation in light of these principles. This may well explain the tendency of courts and tribunals to decide cases on other bases where possible, noting that the economic and social rights aspect of a particular claim need not be considered.[269] It may also explain the tendency for refugee advocates to focus on the civil and political aspects of claims, neglecting equally important economic aspects.[270]

In some cases the reluctance to entertain the socio-economic aspect of claims appears to stem from a concern regarding the method of measurement or approach to evaluation of such claims. For example, in *Mare v. Canada*,[271] the Federal Court of Canada opined that:

> Counsel then refers me to International Conventions in which it is suggested that states adhering to such agreements have an obligation to undertake steps to the maximum of their available resources to achieve a certain standard of medical care ... To look to refugee boards to determine independently what standard should be applied throughout the world or in each country of origin is not their function, as well it is beyond their expertise. How can they be expected to determine the adequacy of medical care being offered?[272]

It is true that there are considerable challenges in respect of such claims, but it is also true that much work has been carried out by both scholars and international treaty bodies in providing normative content and substance to socio-economic rights in international law in recent years, and that there are considerable resources available to refugee decision-makers to assist in interpreting socio-economic obligations in international law. Most importantly, just as refugee decision-makers rely on reports of the UN HRC in respect of state fulfillment of civil and political

---

[268] *Doymus* (Unreported, IAT, Appeal No. HX/80112/99, 19 July 2000), at para. 12. See also the decision of UK Court of Appeal in *Ravichandran v. Secretary of State for the Home Department* [1996] Imm AR 97 at 107.

[269] One of the best examples is *Horvath*, in which, as explained above, the UK Court of Appeal thought it unnecessary to consider the question of whether 'third level rights' could amount to persecution as the case was resolved on other grounds: *Horvath* [2000] Imm AR 205 at para. 31 (Stuart-Smith LJ). On appeal to the House of Lords, Lord Hope of Craighead noted that this issue was not the subject of appeal; thus it was also not necessary to consider it at this level: see *Horvath* [2000] 1 AC 489 at 492.

[270] See for example Bhabha, 'Boundaries in the field of Human Rights: Internationalist Gatekeepers?'.

[271] *Mare v. Canada (Minister of Citizenship and Immigration)* [2001] FCJ No. 712 ('*Mare*').

[272] *Mare* [2001] FCJ No. 712, at para. 11.

PROBLEMS AND DIFFICULTIES IN THE CURRENT APPROACH 153

rights obligations,[273] there are similar tools available in the context of socio-economic rights, since a number of treaty bodies – most prominently the Economic Committee – are charged with supervising the implementation of the social and economic rights guaranteed by international law. As explained in Chapter 2, the Economic Committee produces concluding observations in respect of individual state party reports (thus providing country-specific information relating to socio-economic violations),[274] as well as General Comments which more generally elucidate the meaning of individual articles in the ICESCR.[275] Moreover, since the CEDAW contains extensive socio-economic guarantees, the CEDAW Committee undertakes review and analysis of state party compliance with socio-economic rights in its assessment of individual country reports,[276] and provides insight into the content and operation of socio-economic rights in its General Comments.[277] The Committee has the potential to develop this further in the context of individual communications pursuant to the Optional Protocol which entered into force in 2000.[278] Finally, non-government

---

[273] See, for example, *Reference N01/38920*, RRT, 11 July 2002, where the RRT cited Human Rights Committee, *Concluding Observations of the UN Human Rights Committee In Respect of India*, UN Doc. CCPR/C/79/Add.81 (1997), p. 4, on the issue of state protection; and *Reference V01/12621*, RRT, 19 May 2002, where the RRT cited from CEDAW Committee, *Consideration of Reports Submitted by States Parties under Article 18 of the Convention on the Elimination of All Forms of Discrimination Against Women: Combined Fourth and Fifth Reports of States Parties (Romania)*, UN Doc. CEDAW/C/ROM/4–5 (1999a), p. 6.
[274] See generally: <http://www.unhchr.ch/tbs/doc.nsf>.
[275] These are available at <http://www.unhchr.ch/tbs/doc.nsf>, and will be drawn on in detail below in Chapter 4.
[276] See generally <http://www.unhchr.ch/tbs/doc.nsf>.
[277] See, for example, the following *General Comments* by the CEDAW Committee: *General Recommendation 13: Equal Remuneration for Work of Equal Value*, UN Doc. A/44/38 (1999a); *General Recommendation 15: Avoidance of Discrimination against Women in National Strategies for the Prevention and Control of Acquired Immunodeficiency Syndrome (AIDS)*, UN Doc. A/45/38 (1990b); *General Recommendation 16: Unpaid Workers in Rural and Urban Family Enterprises*, UN Doc. A/46/38 (1993a); *General Recommendation 17: Measurement and Quantification of the Unremunerated Domestic Activities of Women and Their Recognition in the Gross National Product*, UN Doc. A/46/38 (1993b); *General Recommendation 18: Disabled Women*, UN Doc. A/46/38 (1993c); *General Recommendation 24: Women and Health* UN Doc. A/54/38 (1999b).
[278] *Optional Protocol to the Convention on the Elimination of Discrimination against Women*, GA Res. 54/4, UN GAOR, 54th sess. UN Doc. A/RES/54/4 (1999). The Optional Protocol provides that 'Communications may be submitted by or on behalf of individuals or groups of individuals, under the jurisdiction of a State Party, claiming to be victims of a violation of any of the rights set forth in the Convention by that State Party. Where a communication is submitted on behalf of individuals or groups of individuals, this shall be with their consent unless the author can justify acting on their behalf without such consent': art. 2.

organizations, on which refugee decision-makers and advocates have traditionally relied to obtain country-specific information on civil and political rights violations, have begun explicitly to expand their focus to incorporate violations of socio-economic rights, focusing particularly on 'arbitrary or discriminatory governmental conduct that causes or substantially contributes to an ESC [economic, social and cultural] rights violation'[279] – precisely the kind of violation most pertinent to a refugee claim.

The problem is therefore not that resources are unavailable, but rather that refugee decision-makers and scholars have not drawn on these developments to refine and improve refugee decision-making in this field. In light of this, the next chapter turns to consider developments in international human rights law in order to provide a more principled basis for future determination of socio-economic claims in refugee law.

Conclusion

In this chapter, the key definitional element of the Convention – 'being persecuted' – was analysed from the perspective of the contemporary treatment of claims based on economic deprivation. This chapter reviewed the significant developments that have been made in recent years in terms of refugee decision-makers' increased willingness to consider claims involving a denial of socio-economic rights; thereby revealing that the economic migrant/refugee distinction has not proved an insurmountable hurdle to refugee claims based on socio-economic deprivation. In addition to more traditional claims related to the right to work, courts and tribunals have allowed claims based on a wide range of violations of socio-economic rights, including the right to education and health care. However, although decision-makers have embraced the idea that economic and social rights in international law are potentially relevant to refugee claims, they have had greater difficulty in translating this recognition of principle into positive outcomes for refugee applicants. While this is partly explained by the inherent difficulty in assessing socio-economic claims in some respects, it is also due to fundamental misunderstandings regarding the nature of socio-economic rights in

---

[279] Roth 'Defending Economic, Social and Cultural Rights', at 69. Roth is the Executive Director of Human Rights Watch and made this comment in the context of discussing the most effective role for a non-governmental organization in drawing attention to socio-economic rights violations.

international law. The analysis has revealed that there are several fundamental problems with decision-makers' approaches to the assessment of these rights, most importantly in adopting a hierarchical approach which accords an inferior status to such rights. The next chapter therefore turns to consider the way in which this approach can be reformulated so as to accord with contemporary developments in international human rights law.

4   Rethinking the conceptual approach to socio-economic claims

Introduction

The analysis undertaken in Chapter 3 suggests that refugee decision-makers are currently grappling with fundamental issues regarding the status and importance of economic and social rights in international law, including the way in which such rights are implemented, and how best to measure whether a violation has occurred. In light of the difficulties highlighted in Chapter 3, it is vital that we now turn to a consideration of a more theoretical issue, namely the status of economic and social rights in international law, in order to assess the extent to which refugee decision-makers are adopting an interpretation of socio-economic rights that is consistent with developments in the field of international human rights law. The salient questions include: Is the view that economic and social rights are inherently inferior acceptable according to current understandings of the hierarchy of human rights? If there is a hierarchy of rights, is the concept of enforceability of obligation a useful or legitimate method of organizing the hierarchical model? And finally, is it meaningful to separate different kinds of rights into different categories, or are all rights interdependent and indivisible? After considering these issues in Part One of the chapter, Part Two then turns to consider the way in which the current approach to socio-economic claims should be reformulated in refugee law, in order to ensure consistency with international human rights law.

PART ONE: THE CURRENT APPROACH TO PERSECUTION IN LIGHT OF INTERNATIONAL HUMAN RIGHTS LAW

The question whether there is a hierarchy of norms, standards or obligations in international law is of considerable contemporary relevance in light of a range of recent developments, including the proliferation of treaties and standards and questions about the relationship between different regimes, as well as the growing number of international tribunals capable of adjudicating and interpreting international law.[1] Indeed, the importance and urgency of the issue is evidenced by the fact that the ILC has identified the topic of 'Hierarchy in International Law' as one sub-topic within its new area of reference, 'Fragmentation of International Law: Difficulties Arising From the Diversification and Expansion of International Law'.[2] The scope of the topic of hierarchy in international law is extremely wide,[3] and a thorough examination is beyond the scope of this book.[4] Rather, it is important for present purposes to focus on the specific question whether there is a hierarchy of *norms* in international human rights law, and hence whether recognition of refugee status ought reasonably to reflect such a hierarchy. This issue is perhaps most pronounced in the refugee context, given that the question is not merely whether a human rights violation has occurred (the key question in most other areas of international human rights law), but additionally whether the violation is sufficiently serious as to constitute *persecution*. This may explain the quest for principles, guidelines and models to guide decision-making in this respect in the refugee context.

The legitimacy of a normative hierarchy in human rights

The first question is whether there is a clear superiority, on a normative or philosophical basis, of civil and political rights over economic and

---

[1] See ILC, *Report of the Study Group on Fragmentation of International Law: Difficulties Arising From the Diversification and Expansion of International Law*, UN Doc. A/CN.4/L.644 (2003), at para. 11.
[2] The ILC decided to include this topic in its long-term program of work at its 52nd session in 2000: see *Official Records of the General Assembly*, UN Doc. A/55/10 (2000), chapter IX.A.1, at para. 729. For the latest report of the Study Group, see International Law Commission, *Fragmentation of International Law: Difficulties Arising from the Diversification and Expansion of International Law*, Report of the Study Group of the International Law Commission by Martti Koskenniemi (A/CN.4/L.682, 4 April 2006) at 175 ('Koskenniemi, Fragmentation of International Law').
[3] This is because it potentially encompasses such questions as hierarchy among institutions and hierarchy in international law as a method of resolving conflicts between different obligations. The ILC study examined *jus cogens*, obligations *erga omnes*, and art. 103 of the UN Charter as conflict rules: see Koskenniemi, *Fragmentation in International Law*.
[4] For example, there are entire books dedicated to the issue of hierarchy in international human rights law: see, for example, Ian D. Seiderman, *Hierarchy in International Law: The Human Rights Dimension* (Antwerpen: Intersentia, 2001).

social rights, such that violations of the former category are inherently more serious than violations of the latter. This issue can be resolved relatively easily, as the notion that economic and social rights are inherently inferior or lower in importance than civil and political rights is out of step with contemporary thought in international law. While historically some scholars have posited that a number of apparently clear and obvious distinctions between the different categories of rights supports the notion that 'first generation' liberal civil and political rights are superior to 'second generation' aspirational economic and social rights, these distinctions have been shown to be simplistic and indeed unsustainable in a number of significant respects.

It is unnecessary to outline and consider the various arguments in detail, as a rich and extensive literature has developed over the past few decades examining the various facets of this debate with the result that many issues are no longer seriously in dispute. In particular, reference will not be made to philosophical arguments based on notions of natural law or morality that seek to establish that economic and social rights are not truly rights.[5] An extensive review is beyond the scope of this book and, in any event, is no longer material given that the existence of the ICESCR arguably makes such arguments moot.[6] Moreover, as the above case

---

[5] Proponents of these views include Maurice Cranston, *What Are Human Rights?* (London: Bodley Head, 1973) and Bossuyt discussed in Kitty Arambulo, *Strengthening the Supervision of the International Covenant on Economic, Social and Cultural Rights* (Antwerpen: Intersentia, 1999), p. 71. For the most significant and thorough rebuttal of these views, see G. J. H. van Hoof, 'The Legal Nature of Economic, Social and Cultural Rights: A Rebuttal of Some Traditional Views', in Philip Alston and Katarina Tomasevski (eds.), *The Right to Food* (Utrecht: Stichting Studie-en Informatiecentrum Mensenrechten, 1984), pp. 103–4. See also Taduesz Jasudowicz, 'The Legal Character of Social Rights from the Perspective of International Law as a Whole', in Krzysztof Drzewicki et al. (eds.), *Social Rights as Human Rights: A European Challenge* (Åbo: Institute for Human Rights, Åbo Akademi University, 1994), pp. 23–33 and Koen Raes, 'The Philosophical Basis of Social, Economic and Cultural Rights' in Van der Auweraert (ed.), *Social, Economic and Cultural Rights*, pp. 43–4.

[6] As Rajagopal notes, during the drafting of the ICESCR, 'no delegation deprecated the importance of economic, social and cultural rights at the drafting stage ... and in fact many Western countries such as the UK, France and Canada declared that both sets of rights were equally important': Balakrishnan Rajagopal, *International Law From Below* (Cambridge: Cambridge University Press, 2003), p. 192, citing Farroukh Jhabvala, 'On Human Rights and the Socio-Economic Context', in Frederick E. Snyder and Surakiart Sathirathai (eds.), *Third World Attitudes Toward International Law* (Dordrecht: Martinus Nijhoff, 1987). It is important to note that not only are socio-economic rights codified at the international level, but they are now incorporated in human rights law at the regional level as well. Eide and Rosas explain that they are contained in the

analysis reveals, refugee decision-makers have, in the main, accepted the validity of economic and social rights as rights in international law. Nonetheless, it is important briefly to advert to the key distinctions traditionally relied upon to support a normative hierarchy, and note their resolution in the literature and in the authoritative views of the relevant treaty bodies.

While there are various permutations and nuances in the literature, it is accurate to characterize the salient arguments traditionally relied upon in order to support the hierarchy theory as encapsulated in the following key distinctions: civil and political rights are true liberal rights since they impose only negative duties on the state (that is, duties to abstain from action infringing rights), as opposed to socio-economic rights which impose only positive duties;[7] civil and political rights do not require expenditure of resources (since they impose only duties to refrain from action), while economic and social rights require the expenditure of vast resources in order to be fulfilled, thus underlining the aspirational nature of the latter; and while civil and political rights are justiciable, economic and social rights are not. These propositions are distinct but closely related, and have all been said to support the view that economic and social rights are not as legitimate as more traditional civil and political rights.[8] However, as mentioned above, these distinctions have been challenged extensively in the literature and in the practice of the treaty bodies, with the result that they have been undermined in fundamental ways.

First, it is now trite to note that almost all rights contain both positive and negative components, or duties to abstain and to act, regardless

---

European Social Charter, in the Additional Protocol to the American Convention on Human Rights in the Area of Economic, Social and Cultural Rights, and in the African Charter on Human and Peoples' Rights: Asbjørn Eide and Allan Rosas, 'Economic, Social and Cultural Rights: A Universal Challenge', in Eide, Krause and Rosas (eds.), *Economic, Social and Cultural Rights*, p. 4.

[7] Bossuyt is one of the key proponents of this view: see van Hoof, 'The Legal Nature of Economic, Social and Cultural Rights', p. 103. Koen Raes explains that the differences were argued on the basis of Isaiah Berlin's well-known distinction between positive and negative freedom: Raes, 'The Philosophical Basis of Social, Economic and Cultural Rights', p. 43.

[8] See van Hoof, 'The Legal Nature of Economic, Social and Cultural Rights', pp. 102–3. For an excellent overview of the common misconceptions, see Philip Alston and Gerard Quinn, 'The Nature and Scope of States Parties' Obligations under the International Covenant on Economic, Social and Cultural Rights' (1987) 9 *Human Rights Quarterly* 156 at 159–60.

of their nature.[9] Reference to the provisions of the ICCPR and ICESCR alone is sufficient to highlight this fact, as the specific obligations in each treaty impose both negative and positive duties on state parties. An analysis of the terms of the ICCPR, in conjunction with the HRC's General Comments, reveals that positive duties are potentially engaged in respect of all rights;[10] and specific examples are set out in General Comments pertaining to a range of rights including the right to life,[11] prohibition on torture and cruel treatment or punishment,[12] the right to a fair and public hearing,[13] the right to respect of privacy,[14] the right to vote[15] and rights relevant to non-discrimination[16] and equality between men and women.[17] A particularly clear example is provided

---

[9] This is widely discussed in the literature. For specific consideration of this issue, see, for example, van Hoof, 'The Legal Nature of Economic, Social and Cultural Rights', p. 103; Veli-Pekka Viljanen, 'Abstention or Involvement? The Nature of State Obligations under Different Categories of Rights', in Drzewicki et al. (eds.), *Social Rights as Human Rights*, p. 43; Paul Hunt, *Reclaiming Social Rights: International and Comparative Perspectives* (Aldershot: Dartmouth, 1996), p. 60; Arambulo, *Strengthening the Supervision of the International Covenant on Economic, Social and Cultural Rights*, pp. 71–4; Sepulveda, *The Nature of the Obligations under the International Covenant on Economic, Social and Cultural Rights*, pp. 123–36; Manfred Nowak, *Introduction to the International Human Rights Regime* (Leiden: Martinus Nijhoff Publishers, 2003), pp. 25–30. For recent recognition of this in the refugee jurisprudence, see *Refugee Appeal No. 75221*, RSAA, 23 September 2005, at para. 73.

[10] This is perhaps made most explicit in the HRC's *General Comment No. 31*: 'The legal obligation under article 2, paragraph 1, is both negative and positive in nature': *The Nature of the General Legal Obligation Imposed on States Parties to the Covenant*, UN Doc. CCPR/C/21/Rev.1/Add.13 (2004), at para. 6. See also HRC, *General Comment No. 3: Implementation at the National Level (Art. 2)*, UN Doc. HRI\GEN\1\Rev.1 at 4 (1981).

[11] HRC, *General Comment No. 06: The Right to Life (Art. 6)*, UN Doc. HRI\GEN\1\Rev.1 at 6 (1982), para. 5.

[12] ICCPR, art. 7; HRC, *General Comment No. 20: Replaces General Comment 7 concerning Prohibition of Torture and Cruel Treatment or Punishment (Art. 7)*, UN Doc. HRI\GEN\1\Rev.1 at 30 (1992).

[13] ICCPR, art. 14; HRC, *General Comment No. 13: Equality Before the Courts and the Right to a Fair and Public Hearing by an Independent Court Established by Law (Art. 14)*, UN Doc. HRI\GEN\1\Rev.1 at 14 (1984).

[14] ICCPR, art. 17; HRC, *General Comment No. 16: The Right to Respect of Privacy, Family, Home and Correspondence, and Protection of Honour and Reputation (Art. 17)*, UN Doc. HRI\GEN\1\Rev.1 at 21 (1994d).

[15] ICCPR, art. 25; HRC, *General Comment No. 25: The Right to Participate in Public Affairs, Voting Rights and the Right of Equal Access to Public Service (Art. 25)* UN Doc. CCPR/C/21/Rev.1/Add.7 (1996).

[16] ICCPR art. 2(1); HRC, *General Comment No. 18: Non-discrimination*, UN Doc. HRI\GEN\1\Rev.1 at 26 (1989b).

[17] ICCPR, art. 3; HRC, *General Comment No. 28: Equality of Rights between Men and Women (Art. 3)*, UN Doc. CCPR/C/21/Rev.1/Add.10 (2000). This is perhaps one of the most explicit in this respect, see for example, para. 3.

in art. 24, which states that every child shall have, without discrimination, 'the right to such measures of protection as are required by his status as a minor, on the part of his family, society and the State'.[18] The HRC has explained that this requires that 'every possible economic and social measure should be taken to reduce infant mortality and to eradicate malnutrition among children and to prevent them from being subjected to acts of violence and cruel and inhuman treatment or from being exploited by means of forced labour or prostitution, or by their use in the illicit trafficking of narcotic drugs, or by any other means'.[19]

Conversely, it is clear that the ICESCR imposes 'negative' as well as 'positive' obligations on state parties. This is evident from the terms of the treaty, in which some rights, such as the prohibition on discrimination[20] and the right of everyone to join trade unions,[21] closely resemble those contained in the ICCPR.[22] Further, the Economic Committee has made clear that state parties are under an obligation to 'refrain from interfering directly or indirectly'[23] with the enjoyment of a range of rights including the right to housing,[24] the right to food,[25] the right to education,[26] the right to health,[27] the right to water[28] and the right to work.[29] This brief survey is sufficient to indicate that an attempt to classify rights based only on the positive/negative distinction is an 'artificial, simplistic and arid exercise'.[30]

Second, it is now well recognized that the argument that economic and social rights are more akin to aspirations than rights — given that

---

[18] ICCPR, art. 24(1).
[19] HRC, *General Comment No. 17: Rights of the Child (Art. 24)*, UN Doc. HRI\GEN\1\Rev.1 at 23 (1989a), at para. 3.
[20] ICESCR, art. 2(2).   [21] ICESCR, art. 8.
[22] van Hoof, 'The Legal Nature of Economic, Social and Cultural Rights', p. 103.
[23] Committee on Economic, Social and Cultural Rights ('CESCR'), *General Comment No. 15: The Right to Water*, UN Doc. E/C.12/2002/11 (2002), at para. 21.
[24] See generally CESCR, *General Comment No. 7: The Right to Adequate Housing (Art 11.1): Forced Evictions: 20/05/97*, UN Doc. E/1998/22, annex IV (1997).
[25] CESCR, *General Comment No. 12: The Right to Adequate Food (Art. 11)*, UN Doc. E/C.12/1999/5 (1995), at para. 15.
[26] CESCR, *General Comment 13: The Right to Education (Article 13 of the Covenant)*, UN Doc. E/C.12/1999/10 (1999), at para. 47.
[27] CESCR, *General Comment No. 14: The Right to the Highest Attainable Standard of Health*, UN Doc. E/C.12/2000/4 (2000), at paras. 48–9, discussing acts of *commission* and acts of *omission* (emphasis added).
[28] CESCR, *General Comment 15, The Right to Water*, 20/01/2003, E/C.12/2002/11, at para. 21.
[29] CESCR, *General Comment No. 18: The Right to Work*, UN Doc. E/C.12/GC/18 (2006), at para. 23.
[30] Henry Shue, 'The Interdependence of Duties' in Alston and Tomasevski (eds.), *The Right to Food*, p. 84.

they require, unlike civil and political rights, significant government expenditure – is a 'gross oversimplification'.[31] On the one hand, it is beyond dispute that the fulfillment of many civil and political rights, such as the right to a fair trial and to free and fair elections, require enormous government expenditure.[32] Conversely, it is recognized that economic and social rights can often 'best be safeguarded through non-interference by the state'.[33]

Third, in respect of the issue that has arguably dominated the debate – justiciability[34] – the various strands to this argument have been systemically challenged in the literature. The notion that, unlike civil and political rights, economic and social rights are not justiciable because they require policy choices to be made which are not amenable to judicial determination,[35] has been shown to represent an overly simplistic distinction. In particular, the argument that economic and social rights are vague and ill-defined, as compared with the more precise civil and political rights, has been questioned on the basis that many rights considered civil and political are framed in extremely vague and open terms, and thus require judicial interpretation and, in some cases, policy considerations to inform their interpretation.[36] Moreover, the argument that economic and social rights are not justiciable, because it is difficult

---

[31] Asbjørn Eide, 'Economic, Social and Cultural Rights as Human Rights', in Eide, Krause and Rosas (eds.), *Economic, Social and Cultural Rights*, p. 24.

[32] Many scholars point this out: see, for example, van Hoof, 'The Legal Nature of Economic, Social and Cultural Rights', p. 103; Etienne Mureinik, 'Beyond a Charter of Luxuries: Economic Rights in the Constitution' (1992) 8 *South African Journal on Human Rights* 464 at 466. See also Hunt, *Reclaiming Social Rights*, p. 57. He provides a vivid picture of this fact in his table of annual expenditure of the New Zealand government on civil and political rights: pp. 57–61, and in his extractions from the HRC's General Comments which set out the obligations of states which clearly cost considerable funds: pp. 62–4.

[33] van Hoof, 'The Legal Nature of Economic, Social and Cultural Rights', p. 25.

[34] Henry J. Steiner and Philip Alston, *International Human Rights in Context: Law, Politics, Morals: Text and Materials* (Oxford: Clarendon Press, 1996), p. 298, as cited by Hunt, *Reclaiming Social Rights*, p. 24.

[35] It is argued that judges are neither equipped nor sufficiently accountable to make these types of policy decisions. This view is put forward in E. W. Vierdag, 'The Legal Nature of the Rights Granted by the International Covenant on Economic, Social and Cultural Rights' (1978) 9 *Netherlands Yearbook of International Law* 69.

[36] Robinson argues that civil and political rights are no more conceptually precise or inherently defined than social and economic rights. Rather, 'many civil rights, such as right to trial by jury, were determined by historic experience. The real difficulty with social and economic rights then is inexperience in determining the content of those rights': Kim Robinson, 'False Hope or a Realizable Right? The Implementation of the Right to Shelter Under the African National Congress' Proposed Bill of Rights for South Africa' (1993) 28 *Harvard Civil Rights-Civil Liberties Law Review* 505 at 521. See also Hunt, *Reclaiming Social Rights*, p. 56.

to give normative content to and identify violations of rights framed in terms of progressive realization, has been undermined on the basis that the distinction between rights of immediate application (justiciable civil and political rights) and rights of progressive realization (non-justiciable economic and social rights) is overly broad (as will be further discussed below). In addition, even acknowledging that economic and social rights are framed in less concrete terms, the last decade has witnessed considerable advances in giving meaningful content to these rights in the form of identifying obligations[37] (including a core minimum)[38] and providing a concrete basis for determining violations,[39] thereby undermining the potency of the justiciability critique.[40]

[37] In this regard, there are at least three important developments which have occurred since the late 1980s. First, the Limburg Principles emerged from a meeting organized by the International Commission of Jurists in 1986 and attempted to identify the nature and scope of states' obligations, the role of the implementing mechanism, and set out potential guidelines for the monitoring activities of the CESCR: see 'Limburg Principles on the Implementation of the International Covenant on Economic, Social and Cultural Rights' (1987) 9 *Human Rights Quarterly* 122. The second was the product of a meeting of 30 experts, also convened by the International Commission of Jurists, designed to elaborate upon the Limburg Principles: see 'The Maastricht Guidelines on Violations of Economic, Social and Cultural Rights' (1998) 20 *Human Rights Quarterly* 691. The third is the *Montreal Principles on Women's Economic, Social and Cultural Rights*, which were adopted at a meeting of experts held 7–10 December 2002 in Montreal, Canada. The Principles are designed 'to guide the interpretation and implementation of the guarantees of non-discrimination and equal exercise and enjoyment of economic, social and cultural rights, found, *inter alia*, in Articles 3 and 2(2) of the International Covenant on Economic Social and Cultural Rights, so that women can enjoy these rights fully and equally': p. 1.

[38] The Economic Committee has identified a 'minimum core obligation' to ensure the satisfaction of, at the very least, minimum essential levels of each right: discussed further below. For discussion of the issue of core obligations, see Craig Scott and Philip Alston, 'Adjudicating Constitutional Priorities in a Transnational Context: A Comment on Soobramoney's Legacy and Grootboom's Promise' (2000) 16 *South African Journal of Human Rights* 206 at 250.

[39] One significant development in this regard is that the option of adopting a protocol to the ICESCR which will provide an individual complaints procedure similar to that provided under the First Optional Protocol to the ICCPR, is currently under serious consideration. Concerns about justiciability were dismissed as part of the process of adopting a draft protocol: see generally Erika de Wet, 'Recent Developments Concerning the Draft Optional Protocol to the International Covenant on Economic, Social and Cultural Rights' (1997) 13(4) *South African Journal on Human Rights* 514. For documents produced by the open-ended working group to consider options regarding elaboration of an optional protocol to the ISESCR, see <http://www.ohchr.org/english/issues/escr/group3.htm> at 31 May 2006. On the justiciability of socio-economic rights generally, see Arambulo, *Strengthening the Supervision of the International Covenant on Economic, Social and Cultural Rights*.

[40] The justiciability argument has been considered in depth in the South African context, given that the new Constitution contains enforceable economic and social rights.

The dismissal in principle of the notion that strict and stark distinctions operate to distinguish international human rights into two separate categories, and most importantly, to accord a superior status to one category of rights over the other, is consistent with the traditional position of the UN that, despite compartmentalization into different covenants, both categories of human rights are equally important and no hierarchy exists between different groups of rights. Although some of the distinctions outlined above were relied upon, at least in part, as justification for the separation of the rights contained in the UDHR (which does not distinguish between categories of rights) into two separate binding covenants,[41] the most important explanation for the separation is widely accepted to be ideological considerations related to the Cold War.[42] Craven explains that, due mainly to ideological concerns, the decision was taken to draft two separate instruments, but this was on the understanding that 'the enjoyment of civil and political freedoms and economic, social and cultural rights are interconnected

---

See for example, Mureinik, 'Beyond a Charter of Luxuries', at 466. In the *First Certification Judgment*, the Constitutional Court of South Africa acknowledged that the socio-economic rights in the Constitution would have budgetary and other implications but considered them justiciable and thus upheld their constitutionality: see Nicholas Haysom, 'Constitutionalism, Majoritarian Democracy and Socio-Economic Rights' (1992) 8 *South African Journal on Human Rights* 451 at 451. I also note that regional bodies such as the Inter-American Commission on Human Rights initially expressed reservations about commenting on socio-economic rights violations, but has now acknowledged that those presumed problems are not, in fact, an impediment to adjudication: see Maurice Craven, 'The Protection of Economic, Social and Cultural Rights under the Inter-American System of Human Rights', in David J. Harris and Stephen Livingstone (eds.), *The Inter-American System of Human Rights* (Oxford: Clarendon Press, 1998), p. 315. See also the cases from domestic jurisdictions such as Japan and India contained in Ramcharan, *Judicial Protection of Economic, Social and Cultural Rights*, pp. 211–30. For discussion of the justiciability question in relation to a specific right in international law – education – see *The Right to Education: Report Submitted By the Special Raporteur on the Right to Education*, UN Doc. E/CN.4/2005/50 (2005), at paras. 54–7.

[41] See generally *Draft International Covenants on Human Rights: Annotation – Report of the Secretary-General to the Tenth Session of the General Assembly*, UN Doc. A/2929 (1955).

[42] As Steiner and Alston explain, the debate over the relationship between the two sets of rights 'had become a casualty of the Cold War': *International Human Rights in Context*, p. 109. See also Fons Coomans, *Economic, Social and Cultural Rights* (Utrecht: Advisory Committee on Human Rights and Foreign Policy of the Netherlands, 1995), pp. 4–5. For further explanation of the historical background see Kitty Arambulo, 'Drafting an Optional Protocol to the International Covenant on Economic, Social and Cultural Rights: Can an Ideal Become Reality?' (1996) 2 *University of California Davis Journal of International Law and Policy* 111.

and interdependent'.[43] Accordingly, the Preambles to both the ICCPR and ICESCR recognize that 'the ideal of free human beings enjoying civil and political freedom and freedom from fear and want can only be achieved if conditions are created whereby everyone *may enjoy his civil and political rights, as well as his economic, social and cultural rights*'.[44]

This interdependence and equal importance of the two categories of rights has been consistently reinforced in the UN system since the introduction of the two covenants,[45] at least in principle if not always in practice.[46] From a positivist perspective, this is supported by the fact that as of April 2006, the treaties enjoy almost identical support: 153 parties

---

[43] General Assembly resolution 543 (VI), 5 February 1952, as cited in M. Craven, 'The International Covenant on Economic, Social and Cultural Rights', in Raija Hanski and Markku Suksi (eds.), *An Introduction to the International Protection of Human Rights − A Textbook* (Åbo: Institute for Human Rights, Åbo Akademi University, 1999), p. 102. See also Craig Scott, 'The Interdependence and Permeability of Human Rights Norms: Towards a Partial Fusion of the International Covenants on Human Rights' (1989) 27(4) *Osgoode Hall Law Journal* 769 at 791; see further at 798−811.

[44] ICCPR, Preamble (emphasis added). The Preamble to the ICESCR states: 'Recognizing that, in accordance with the Universal Declaration of Human Rights, the ideal of free human beings enjoying freedom from fear and want can only be achieved if conditions are created whereby everyone may enjoy his economic, social and cultural rights, as well as civil and political rights.'

[45] For example, Coomans explains that resolutions adopted in the UN since the mid-1980s 'no longer accord explicit priority to one category of right over the other', providing as an example the *Declaration on the Right to Development*: Coomans, *Economic, Social and Cultural Rights*, p. 5. He also outlines in detail the renewed interest in economic, social and cultural rights that has taken place at the UN level since 1985: pp. 6−9. On this issue, see also Sepulveda, who outlines in considerable detail developments at the international and regional level: *The Nature of the Obligations under the International Covenant on Economic, Social and Cultural Rights*, pp. 45−70. Eide and Rosas similarly note that at the time of entry into force of the two covenants, the General Assembly passed a resolution emphasizing that the different sets of human rights were interrelated and indivisible and that this 'has been repeated ever since in United Nations fora': Eide and Rosas, 'Economic, Social and Cultural Rights', pp. 3−4.

[46] It is arguable that economic and social rights have traditionally been neglected in terms of the attention given to their breach. See for example the oft-cited statement by the CESCR to the 1993 World Conference on Human Rights: 'the shocking reality ... is that States and the international community as a whole continue to tolerate all too often breaches of economic, social and cultural rights which, if they occurred in relation to civil and political rights, would provoke expressions of horror and outrage and would lead to concerted calls for immediate remedial action. In effect, despite the rhetoric, violations of civil and political rights continue to be treated as though they were far more serious, and more patently intolerable, than massive and direct denials of economic, social and cultural rights': See UN Doc, E/1993/22, Annex III, para. 5, as cited in Steiner and Alston, *International Human Rights in Context*, p. 215. See also, Eide and Rosas, 'Economic, Social and Cultural Rights', p. 3; Diane Otto, 'Defending Women's

have ratified the ICESCR while 156 have ratified the ICCPR.[47] Perhaps most significant is that any argument based on hierarchy is no longer sustainable in light of the statement of principle reflected in the *Vienna Declaration and Programme of Action*, which was approved at the World Conference on Human Rights in 1993, attended by 171 States. It relevantly states that:

> 5. All human rights are universal, indivisible and interdependent and interrelated. The international community must treat human rights globally in a fair and equal manner, on the same footing, and with the same emphasis. While the significance of national and regional particularities and various historical, cultural and religious backgrounds must be borne in mind, it is the duty of States, regardless of their political, economic and cultural systems, to promote and protect all human rights and fundamental freedoms.[48]

In light of this, and of the reduced significance of ideological issues following the end of the Cold War, it is now accurate to describe the predominant approach as a unified one, based on the concept of 'human dignity as inherent in the realization of all human rights'.[49]

Economic and Social Rights: Some Thoughts on Indivisibility and a New Standard of Equality', in Isfahan Merali and Valerie Oostervedl (eds.), *Giving Meaning to Economic, Social and Cultural Rights* (Philadelphia: University of Pennsylvania Press, 2001) pp. 53–4.

[47] See OHCHR, *Status of Ratifications of the Principal International Human Rights Treaties* (2006) <http://www.ohchr.org/english/countries/ratification/index.htm> at 31 May 2006.

[48] World Conference on Human Rights, *Vienna Declaration and Programme of Action*, UN Doc. A/CONF.157/23 (1993). This has been reaffirmed in countless declarations and resolutions of the UN since that time. See, for example, Commission on Human Rights, *Question of the Realization in all Countries of the Economic, Social and Cultural Rights Contained in the Universal Declaration of Human Rights and in the International Covenant on Economic, Social and Cultural Rights, and Study of Special Problems which the Developing Countries Face in their Efforts to Achieve these Human Rights*, UN Doc. E/CN.4/RES/2000/9 (2000a), at paras. 3(c) and (d).

[49] See Danilo Turk, *The New International Economic Order and the Promotion of Human Rights: Realization of Economic, Social and Cultural Rights (Preliminary Report)*, UN Doc. E/CN.4/Sub.2/1989/19 (1989): 'It is the opinion of the Special Rapporteur that the era of the hierarchization of human rights is more or less over and that a unified approach is to be sought in the interpretation of the relationship between the two major sets of human rights. The conceptual basis is already there – it has always been there – and it is embodied in the core concept of human dignity': at para. 26. This view was reiterated and elaborated upon in the Rapporteur's Final Report: Danilo Turk, *The Realization of Economic, Social and Cultural Rights*, UN Doc. E/CN.4/Sub.2/1992/16 (1992), at paras. 26–7. Many commentators argue that debate has been apparently resolved in favour of the principles of 'indivisibility and interdependence': see UN Centre for Human Rights, *Right to Adequate Food as a Human Right* (Geneva: UN Centre for Human Rights, 1989), p. 50; Coomans, *Economic, Social and Cultural Rights*, p. 5. Eva Brems notes that '[i]n theory, there appears

It is thus imperative that refugee decision-makers update their approach to this issue and discard any understanding based on a prior assumption of normative hierarchy between categories of human rights. This is important in order to ensure that refugee jurisprudence does not remain mired in Cold War ideas about the relative importance of rights.[50] Therefore, an approach posited on the notion that economic and social rights are, as a category, 'secondary in importance', 'low in the hierarchy of rights' or do not constitute 'basic or core human right[s]',[51] must be immediately discontinued as being inconsistent with wider principles in international human rights law.[52] This is vital in light of the analysis above which revealed that this mistaken view has a tendency to produce, and indeed has produced, negative consequences for the assessment of refugee claims based on economic and social rights, including the widespread imposition of an erroneously high test in respect of such claims, and the frequent requirement that socio-economic aspects necessarily be buttressed by an accumulation of factors or by a more traditional type of claim, such as a fear of physical violence. Indeed, this dissonance between the treatment of socio-economic rights in international law and international refugee law supports the view of the ILC that the production of conflicting jurisprudence by different interpreters of international law is a negative aspect of the phenomenon of

to be a world-wide consensus that social and economic rights have the same importance as civil and political rights': 'Social and Economic Rights of Women', p. 25. See also 'Introduction', in Merali and Oostervedl (eds.), *Giving Meaning to Economic, Social and Cultural Rights*, p. 1.

[50] Symes and Jorro, while adopting the hierarchical framework, have noted that if the Convention is considered a 'living instrument', the human rights framework 'cannot be allowed to become mired in the first generation of human rights instruments to which reference is most often made': Symes and Jorro, *Asylum Law and Practice*, p. 72.

[51] See Chapter 3, notes 153–7.

[52] This has also been emphasized by refugee scholars. For example, Haines says that 'it cannot be assumed that because these rights are third category that they are of any less significance in the refugee inquiry than first and second category rights': Haines, 'Gender-Related Persecution', in Feller, Türk and Nicholson (eds.), *Refugee Protection in International Law*, p. 329. See also *The Realities of Refugee Determination on the Eve of a New Millennium: The Role of the Judiciary* (Haarlem, The Netherlands: International Association of Refugee Law Judges, 1999), p. 15. In addition, this has also been emphasized by NGOs. For example, the European Council on Refugees and Exiles ('ECRE') believes that 'it is not the nature of the right at stake which matters but the gravity of the harm to the person concerned': *Position Paper on the Interpretation of Article 1 of the Refugee Convention* (2000b) para. 46 <http://www.ecre.org/positions/csrinter.shtml> at 31 May 2006.

fragmentation of the international legal system, and therefore should be avoided.[53] A contemporary approach to these issues would result in a more informed understanding of the importance of socio-economic rights and a greater appreciation of the extent to which their deprivation can constitute persecution.

The merits of a categorical approach based on state obligation

Having rejected an approach premised on a normatively hierarchical relationship between civil and political rights on the one hand, and economic and social rights on the other, it nevertheless remains necessary to consider the validity of another kind of hierarchy – the model of hierarchy of obligation or legal hierarchy posited by Hathaway in his original framework. Consideration of this issue as a separate matter from the above arguments is somewhat artificial given that differences in enforceability have sometimes been relied upon to support an argument about the lack of justiciability of economic and social rights and their inferior place in a normative hierarchy. Nevertheless, given that hierarchy of enforceability is the dominant model relied upon in the refugee context, it is necessary to consider its validity as a matter of international law.

The Hathaway model was set out at length above, and was helpfully summarized in a more recent exposition of the original framework:

> The specific concern – sometimes short-handed as a problem of hierarchy – is that some rights in the International Bill of Rights (such as the prohibition of torture) are absolutely binding and never subject to legitimate exception of any kind for any reason; others (such as freedom of speech and association) are immediately binding, but subject to non-discriminatory suspension in time of genuine and officially declared national emergencies; and other rights, including most socio-economic rights, are enforceable only at the level of a duty of progressive, non-discriminatory implementation, to the maximum of a state's capabilities.[54]

This appears to distinguish rights based on, first, the extent to which the rights are immediately binding or enforceable and second, the extent

---

[53] See ILC, *Fragmentation of International Law: Difficulties Arising From the Diversification and Expansion of International Law*, UN Doc. A/CN.4/537 (2000), p. 49. See also Koskenniemi, 'Fragmentation of International Law' at p. 9.
[54] Hathaway, 'The Relationship between Human Rights and Refugee Law', p. 99.

to which a state may derogate from those rights. The model can be depicted in the following manner:

A. *Immediately binding (levels 1 and 2)*
  1. Absolutely binding – Non-derogable Civil and Political (level 1)
  2. Derogable civil and political (level 2)
B. *Not immediately binding (level 3)*
    'the ICESCR does not impose absolute and immediately binding standards of attainment';[55] it 'does not create obligations that states are required to fulfil immediately upon accession';[56]
    'Enforceable only at the level of a duty of progressive, non-discriminatory implementation, to the maximum of a state's capabilities'[57] (level 3) – thus seems to imply inherent flexibility.

According to Hathaway, a breach of a 'level one' right is always tantamount to persecution, as is a breach of a 'level two' right unless the violation is based on a legitimate derogation in accordance with the terms of the ICCPR.[58] A breach of a 'third level right' may amount to persecution where there is a failure to implement such a right 'which is either discriminatory or not grounded in the absolute lack of resources'.[59] This approach has the benefit of producing certainty and clarity, and reduces the likelihood of decision-makers reaching divergent conclusions in respect of similarly situated individuals. However, reliance on this scheme in the refugee context has produced a degree of confusion regarding the nature of economic and social rights as it has been erroneously assumed that their categorization as 'third level' means that their violation is less significant than violations of levels one and two. Further, their description in contradistinction to the immediately binding and enforceable level one and two rights has been interpreted by some decision-makers as meaning that states are under no duties of an immediate nature in respect of socio-economic rights and that the requirement of progressive realization undermines any solid content to these rights.

The key difficulty with the model is not that international human rights law does not provide for different levels of obligation or enforceability,[60] nor that differences in enforceability do not exist between some

---

[55] Hathaway, *The Law of Refugee Status*, p. 110.
[56] *Ibid.*, p. 116.   [57] *Ibid.*   [58] *Ibid.*, p. 112.   [59] *Ibid.*
[60] On the contrary it is clear that *jus cogens* norms, whatever the content of this category, always prevail in the case of inconsistency with other norms, including treaty provisions, partly because they are non-derogable. Article 53 of the VCLT describes a 'peremptory

socio-economic rights and civil and political rights (since there is no question that some aspects of the fulfillment of socio-economic rights are indeed less immediate than civil and political rights).[61] Rather, the difficulty lies in the fact that the categories are not as simple and stark as might be implied by reference to this scheme. This is so for two key reasons.

First, the notion that the distinction between duties of an immediate nature and those of a progressive nature explains the distinction between civil and political rights and economic and social rights is not consistent with contemporary understandings of international human rights law. Second, reliance on the notion of derogability tends to produce confusion, because it is not a meaningful method of distinguishing between the various categories of rights.

Immediate versus progressive realization

The question of the correct interpretation of the concept of 'progressive realization' embodied in art. 2 of the ICESCR, the key provision establishing state parties' obligations under the Covenant, has been said to be 'the single most complex and misunderstood dimension of economic and social rights'.[62] Thus it is not surprising that refugee decision-makers have sometimes fallen into error in conceiving this duty as lacking concrete components. However, much work has been undertaken by the treaty bodies in the past decade which has served to highlight that in many respects the obligations relevant to socio-economic rights are no different from those involved in civil and political rights.

The notion that duties of progressive implementation (or 'obligations of result'[63] – economic and social rights) are properly juxtaposed against

> norm of general international law', for the purposes of that Convention, as follows: 'a peremptory norm of general international law is a norm accepted and recognized by the international community of States as a whole from which no derogation is permitted and which can be modified only by a subsequent norm of general international law having the character'.
>
> [61] The Economic Committee has acknowledged the differences between the ICCPR and ICESCR: 'In this sense the obligation [in the ICESCR] differs significantly from that contained in article 2 of the [ICCPR] which embodies an immediate obligation to respect and ensure all of the relevant rights': CESCR, *General Comment No. 03*, at para. 9.
>
> [62] Scott and Alston, 'Adjudicating Constitutional Priorities in a Transnational Context', pp. 262-3.
>
> [63] Craven explains that art. 2(1) of the ICESCR has often been interpreted as imposing such an obligation (in contrast to obligations of conduct imposed by the ICCPR): see Craven, *The International Covenant on Economic, Social and Cultural Rights*, p. 109.

duties of an immediate nature (or 'obligations of conduct' – civil and political rights) is the predominant source of confusion, but is clearly mistaken for two key reasons. First, some articles contained in the ICESCR are, on their own terms, immediately binding. In particular, the Economic Committee has made it clear that it considers art. 3 (equality between men and women),[64] art. 7(a)(i) (equal pay),[65] art. 8 (right to form trade unions and to strike),[66] art. 10(3) (protection of children from exploitation),[67] art. 13(2)(a) (free primary education),[68] art. 13(3) (freedom of parents to choose type of education for children)[69] and art. 15(3) (freedom of scientific research and creative activity) to be capable of immediate implementation.[70]

Second, *all* rights in the ICESCR imply two key duties of an *immediate nature*. One of these is the guarantee that relevant rights will be exercised without discrimination (art. 2(2)) on specified grounds.[71] As the Economic Committee has explained, the principle of non-discrimination is 'immediately applicable and is neither subject to progressive implementation nor dependent on available resources'.[72] The other is to *take steps* to realize the rights contained in the ICESCR. The Economic Committee has emphasized that such steps 'should be deliberate, concrete and targeted as clearly as possible towards meeting the obligations recognized in the Covenant'.[73] The ICESCR sets out the specific steps required in

---

[64] CESCR *General Comment No. 03*, para. 5 and CESCR *General Comment No. 09, The domestic application of the Covenant*, U.N. doc. E/C.12/1998/24 (1998) at para. 10.
[65] *Ibid.*
[66] ICESCR, arts. 8(1)(a), (d). As Craven notes, 'article 8 is to be implemented in an immediate manner, and therefore does not contain the flexibility found in other articles': Craven, *The International Covenant on Economic, Social and Cultural Rights*, p. 284.
[67] CESCR, *General Comment No. 03*, para. 5 and CESCR, *General Comment No. 09*, at para. 10.
[68] *Ibid.*   [69] *Ibid.*   [70] *Ibid.*
[71] CESCR, *General Comment No. 3*, at para. 1; CESCR, *General Comment No. 9*, at para. 10. The CESCR has also made this clear in General Comments dealing with specific obligations: see, for example, CESCR, *General Comment No. 18: The Right to Work*, UN Doc. E/C.12/GC/18 (2006), at paras. 19, 33. Craven explains that '[t]he fact of its [article 2(2)'s] physical separation from article 2(1) and the inclusion of the word "guarantee" draw one to the conclusion that States are under an obligation to eliminate discrimination immediately': *The International Covenant on Economic, Social and Cultural Rights*, p. 181. He states that this was the interpretation adopted during the drafting of the covenant and by expert analyses such as the Limburg Principles, as well as the practice of the committee: p. 181.
[72] CESCR, *General Comment No. 18*, at para. 33.
[73] See CESCR, *General Comment No. 3*, at para. 2; Steiner and Alston, *International Human Rights in Context*, p. 265. For discussion of this concept in the refugee context, see *Refugee Appeal No. 75221*, RSAA, 23 September 2005, at paras. 85–8.

respect of certain of the rights. For example, art. 12(2) requires, *inter alia*, that state parties take steps necessary for the 'prevention, treatment and control of epidemic, endemic, occupational and other diseases'.[74]

The obligation to take steps to achieve progressively the rights in the Covenant in turn can be seen to require two additional types of immediately applicable duties. One reflects a negative duty, mentioned above, to refrain from interfering directly or indirectly with the enjoyment of a right. In the case of the right to food, for example, this requires States parties not to take any measures that result in preventing access to adequate food.[75] A violation of the right to food can thus occur where a state repeals or suspends legislation necessary for the continued enjoyment of the right to food, denies access to food to particular individuals or groups, or prevents access to humanitarian food in internal conflicts or other emergency situations.[76] These are by nature duties of immediate obligation.[77] The second type of immediate obligation inherent in the obligation to realize rights progressively pertains to the development of the notion that States parties have a 'core obligation to ensure the satisfaction of, at the very least, minimum essential levels of each of the rights enunciated in the Covenant'.[78] The Economic Committee has made it clear that with respect to such core obligations, 'a State party cannot, under any circumstances whatsoever, justify its non-compliance',[79] thus clearly implying that such core obligations are of immediate binding effect.[80]

---

[74] ICESCR, art. 12(2). Craven points to this provision as an example of an obligation of conduct in the ICESCR: Craven, *The International Covenant on Economic, Social and Cultural Rights*, p. 108.

[75] CESCR, *General Comment No. 12*, at para. 15.   [76] *Ibid.*, at para. 19.

[77] Although the Committee does not always specify explicitly that each of these duties is of an immediate nature, the clear implication is that at least these 'negative' rights are of immediate application: see Sepulveda, *The Nature of the Obligations under the International Covenant on Economic, Social and Cultural Rights*, p. 184 (who takes this view and argues for greater clarity by the Committee in this area). Moreover, in *General Comment No. 3*, the Committee explains that 'any deliberately retrogressive measures in that regard would require the most careful consideration and would need to be fully justified by reference to the totality of the rights provided for in the Covenant and in the context of the full use of the maximum available resources': at para. 9.

[78] This was originally set out in CESCR, *General Comment No. 3*, at para. 9, but has been elaborated upon in relation to specific obligations in later General Comments which deal with specific rights.

[79] See, for example, CESCR, *General Comment No. 14*, at para. 47.

[80] The Committee makes this clear in some of its General Comments: see for example *General Comment No. 15*: 'In the Committee's view, at least a number of core obligations in

THE MERITS OF A CATEGORICAL APPROACH BASED ON STATE OBLIGATION   173

This brief overview serves to highlight the fact that obligations in the ICCPR and ICESCR cannot be strictly and exclusively categorized into those obligations of immediate effect and those of progressive realization respectively. As Scott and Alston have reiterated, '[t]o read the principle of progressive realization as incompatible with immediate duties to ensure key protections would be, in effect, to conceptualize duties to ensure positive rights as never capable of being violated, as constantly receding into the future'.[81]

Indeed, rather than continuing to insist on categorical distinctions between economic and social rights, and civil and political rights, based on a dichotomous understanding of the nature of obligations imposed on state parties, the modern trend has been to understand that all rights, regardless of their 'category', generate similar kinds of obligations and duties. This innovation, shorthanded as a 'typology' of rights, was initially developed in the literature,[82] but has now been explicitly adopted by the Economic Committee[83] and implicitly by the HRC[84] as a useful method of identifying the different types of obligations that each human rights covenant imposes on state parties. The idea is that all human rights (regardless of their category) can be analysed using a 'very simple tripartite typology of interdependent duties of avoidance,

---

relation to the right to water can be identified, *which are of immediate effect*': CESCR, *General Comment No. 15*, at para. 37 (emphasis added).

[81] Scott and Alston, 'Adjudicating Constitutional Priorities in a Transnational Context', p. 227.

[82] Shue is recognized to be the first person to have introduced this idea: see Henry Shue, *Basic Rights: Subsistence, Affluence, and US Foreign Policy* (Princeton: Princeton University Press, 1980). It is beyond the scope of this book to analyse the subtle differences in the models, as the literature discussing the various models is considerable. See for example the critique by Shue of modifications of his model suggested by others: Shue, 'The Interdependence of Duties' in Alston and Tomasevski (eds.), *The Right to Food*, pp. 84–6. For a thorough consideration of the different typologies, see Sepulveda, *The Nature of the Obligations under the International Covenant on Economic, Social and Cultural Rights*, pp. 157–247.

[83] The Economic Committee frequently describes state obligations in respect of particular rights in terms of the typology of obligations: see, for example, CESCR, *General Comment No. 12*, at paras. 14–20; CESCR, *General Comment No. 14*, at paras. 30–7; CESCR, *General Comment No. 15*, at paras. 17–29; and CESCR, *General Comment No. 18*, at para. 22.

[84] The HRC is less explicit in adopting the typology; however, it often points to differences between the different types of obligations, particularly as between 'respect' (non-interference) and 'protect' or 'ensure' (more positive measures): see, for example, HRC, *General Comment No. 31: The Nature of the General Legal Obligation Imposed on States Parties to the Covenant*, UN Doc. CCPR/C/21/Rev.1/Add.13 (2004), at paras. 4–6.

protection and aid'.[85] That is, all human rights 'impose three types or levels of obligations on States Parties: the obligation to respect, to protect and to fulfil'.[86] These can briefly be described as follows: the obligation to respect requires non-interference with a right;[87] the duty to protect 'forces the State to take steps – through legislation or otherwise – which prevent or prohibit others (third persons) from violating recognized rights or freedoms';[88] while the obligation to fulfil or ensure requires states 'to adopt appropriate legislative, administrative, budgetary, judicial, promotional and other measures towards the full realization of the right'.[89]

It is vital to underline that these different types of duties are not constructed in a hierarchical fashion; rather they are 'multi-layered',[90] and 'each layer of obligation is equally relevant to the rights in question'.[91] This is so despite the fact that different levels may apply on a more or less immediate basis.

This conception was originally designed as a valuable tool to highlight the lack of legitimacy in dichotomies between rights constructed on the basis of simplistic distinctions such as positive versus negative obligations and immediate duties versus those of progressive realization. It was not designed, and is not introduced here, as a model to guide decision-makers in assessing whether rights have been violated in individual refugee cases, as it operates on a very general level.[92] Rather, assessment of human rights violations in the refugee context must continue to refer to the normative content of each individual and specific right

---

[85] Henry Shue, 'The Interdependence of Duties', p. 83.
[86] Eide, 'Economic, Social and Cultural Rights as Human Rights', p. 23.
[87] van Hoof, 'The Legal Nature of Economic, Social and Cultural Rights', p. 106.
[88] Ibid.   [89] CESCR, *General Comment No. 14*, at para. 33.
[90] See Hunt, *Reclaiming Social Rights*, p. 31.
[91] *Decision Regarding Communication No. 155/96*, African Commission on Human and Peoples' Rights, ACHPR/COMM/A044/1, 27 May 2002, at para. 44. In addition, van Hoof discusses 'layers' of obligation: 'The Legal Nature of Economic, Social and Cultural Rights', p. 107.
[92] For example, Shue explains that '[a]t best such general categories help to organize the debate over precisely which duty falls to which agent. The bottom-line of the intellectual exercise, however, must be the specific designation of what should be done by whom at a level of detail that will permit assessments of compliance by responsible agents themselves and, where appropriate, by others charged with supervision over their compliance. Typologies are of largely heuristic, mnemonic, pedagogical, and rhetorical value, and like many other ladders they can be left behind once we have reached the next level, which in this case consists of very specific duties': Shue, 'The Interdependence of Duties', p. 84.

as defined and interpreted in international law. However, undertaking such assessments in light of an understanding of these typologies would sensitize refugee decision-makers to the manifold ways in which 'third level' rights may well be engaged in refugee law, often in ways that are very similar to claims involving more traditional types of harm.[93] This is because it is only with respect to the third type of obligation, namely 'to fulfil', that the assessment of what is required by 'progressive realization' becomes more complicated. It thus assists in highlighting the fact that in many respects, consideration of economic claims does not involve the great conceptual leap that might be otherwise implied. This is not to say that there do not remain difficult and challenging cases (for example, those based on failure to fulfil) but that the gap is not as great as seems to have been assumed by many decision-makers to date.

Derogability

The second distinctive factor in the hierarchical model is the notion of derogability, which is posited as a method of distinguishing between different levels of obligation, apparently according to the theory that the more absolute a right, the higher the obligation on a state, and thus the more likely it is that a violation will amount to persecution. This is implied in the explanation that '[s]ome rights are defined to grant states operational flexibility in their definition and implementation, while others are not'.[94] The first three levels are thus portrayed as a hierarchy ranging from an absolute right (non-derogable), to those with only one exception (derogability), to those that permit flexibility and discretion in operation (progressive realization). However, there are a number of limitations on the usefulness of derogability alone to assist in this process.

First, derogability is not necessarily the only relevant factor in ascertaining whether a right is absolute, or the extent of 'operational flexibility' inherent in that right. A close examination of the nature of the individual rights in all categories reveals considerable potential overlap between them, breaking down the validity of distinct categories.

---

[93] As recently recognized by the RSAA, 'not all refugee claims [based on the deprivation of socio-economic rights] will raise complex ICESCR issues': *Refugee Appeal No. 74665/03*, 7 July 2004, at para. 89.

[94] Hathaway, 'The Realities of Refugee Determination', p. 88.

Many of the rights contained in both levels one and two in fact admit of exceptions and limitations in addition to the availability of derogability in an emergency situation. Even one of the non-derogable rights in level one – freedom of religion – provides for limitations,[95] highlighting that even non-derogable rights are not necessarily absolute.[96] In respect of level two rights, many articles permit limitations 'necessary in a democratic society in the interests of national security or public safety, public order, the protection of public health or morals or the protection of the rights and freedoms of others'.[97] Ascertaining whether a state has properly relied on one of these limitations involves an element of proportionality[98] and can often involve a delicate balancing exercise, such that '[t]he dividing line between an ICCPR right and its limitations is by no means clear, especially at the "edges" of a right'.[99]

Moreover, although it is certainly true that the obligations in the ICESCR are subject to progressive realization, and thus allow for considerations such as resource constraints to justify failure to comply, all rights in the ICESCR are non-derogable. Rosas and Sandvik-Nylund argue that since the ICESCR does not contain a derogability clause relating to public emergencies, it is, 'in principle, fully applicable in times of armed conflict and other public emergencies'.[100] This has been

---

[95] Article 18(3) of the ICCPR states: 'Freedom to manifest one's religion or beliefs may be subject only to such limitations as are prescribed by law and are necessary to protect public safety, order, health, or morals or the fundamental rights and freedoms of others.'

[96] Indeed, the HRC has been explicit on this point. In *General Comment No. 29*, it explained: 'Conceptually, the qualification of a Covenant provision as a non-derogable one does not mean that no limitations or restrictions would ever be justified. The reference in article 4, paragraph 2, to article 18, a provision that includes a specific clause on restrictions in its paragraph 3, demonstrates that the permissibility of restrictions is independent of the issue of derogability': HRC, *General Comment No. 29: States of Emergency (Art. 4)*, UN Doc. CCPR/C/21/Rev.1/Add.11 (2001), at para. 7.

[97] See ICCPR, art. 21. See also arts. 12, 13, 19 and 22. Also, the in-built limitation clauses are actually easier for the state party to satisfy because procedurally they do not require special measures to be taken in order to be relied upon – unlike derogation, which is very precise and is available only in very limited circumstances.

[98] Joseph, Schultz and Castan, *The International Covenant on Civil and Political Rights*, p. 20.

[99] *Ibid.*, p. 21.

[100] Allan Rosas and Monika Sandvik-Nylund, 'Armed Conflicts' in Eide, Krause and Rosas (eds.), *Economic, Social and Cultural Rights*, p. 407. The ICESCR does contain a general limitation clause in art. 4, giving states the right to subject ICESCR rights to such limitations as are 'determined by law' and are compatible with the nature of these rights and are resorted to 'solely for the purpose of promoting the general welfare in a democratic society'. However, it is clear that art. 4 is interpreted in a 'very restrictive

explained on the basis that derogation of ICESCR rights would not be appropriate or justified even in a public emergency.[101] Craven has noted that since no derogation is permitted from the ICESCR, an inconsistency may arise in that a state may derogate from its obligation to ensure the right to join and form trade unions contained in the ICCPR, but 'may not do so under the terms of the ICESCR'.[102] In addition, as explained above, the Economic Committee has begun to define core obligations in respect of individual rights which are immediately binding, and from which no derogation is permitted. For example, in relation to the right to health, the Economic Committee has set out the core minimum obligations of State parties pursuant to art. 12 of the ICESCR, emphasizing that 'a State party cannot, under any circumstances whatsoever, justify its non-compliance with the core obligations set out in paragraph 43 above, *which are non-derogable*'.[103] Further, in relation to art. 3, whereby states undertake to ensure the equal rights of women and men to ICESCR rights, the Committee has explained that this sets 'a non-derogable standard for compliance with the obligations of States parties as set out in articles 6 through 15 of ICESCR'.[104] This reveals that in many instances, the level

manner' (see Sepulveda, *The Nature of the Obligations under the International Covenant on Economic, Social and Cultural Rights*, p. 279), since the intention of the drafters was that it was 'meant to be protective rather than limitative' (Ramcharan, *Judicial Protection of Economic, Social and Cultural Rights*, p. 23). The Economic Committee itself has stressed that 'the Covenant's limitations clause, article 4, is primarily intended to be protective of the rights of individuals rather than permissive of the imposition of limitations by the State': CESCR, *General Comment No. 13*, at para. 42. Further, there are some Covenant rights that cannot be subject to restrictions: see Sepulveda, *The Nature of the Obligations under the International Covenant on Economic, Social and Cultural Rights*, p. 279. See also Rosas and Sandvik-Nylund who note that the 'provision does not give any extensive limitation rights and can, in any case, not imply departure from a minimum standard of livelihood and health, even in times of armed conflict': 'Armed Conflicts', p. 413. Indeed, the Economic Committee has made it clear that core obligations cannot be limited: see, for example, CESCR, *General Comment No. 14*, at paras. 43 and 47; see Sepulveda, *The Nature of the Obligations under the International Covenant on Economic, Social and Cultural Rights*, p. 281. For a restrictive approach to art. 4, see *Legal Consequences of the Construction of a Wall in the Occupied Palestinian Territory*, Advisory Opinion (I.C.J. July 9, 2004), 43 I.L.M. 1009 (2004) at para. 136.

[101] Sepulveda, *The Nature of the Obligations under the International Covenant on Economic, Social and Cultural Rights*, pp. 277–92.
[102] Craven, *The International Covenant on Economic, Social and Cultural Rights*, p. 27. See also Sepulveda, *The Nature of the Obligations under the International Covenant on Economic, Social and Cultural Rights*, pp. 293–303.
[103] CESCR, *General Comment No. 14*, at para. 47 (emphasis added).
[104] CESCR, *General Comment No. 16: The Equal Right of Men and Women to the Enjoyment of All Economic, Social and Cultural Rights*, UN Doc. E/C.12/2005/4 (2005a), at para. 17.

of obligation or enforceability of 'level 3' rights will be higher or stricter than in the case of level two rights.[105]

The HRC has noted that even though art. 26 and the other ICCPR provisions related to non-discrimination (arts. 2, 3, 14(1), 23(4), 24(1) and 25) have not been listed among the non-derogable provisions, 'there are elements or dimensions of the right to non-discrimination that cannot be derogated from in any circumstances'.[106] The fact that non-discrimination in the ICCPR applies to areas engaging socio-economic rights thus further erodes the strict categories based on derogability.[107]

Further, other important, widely ratified instruments such as the CEDAW, the CERD and the CRC, on which courts have been increasingly willing to rely in evaluating whether an applicant is at risk of being persecuted, not only contain both civil and political and economic and social rights within the one document (at least in the case of CEDAW and the CRC), but fail to provide for derogability.[108] It is thus not clear where the rights contained within these covenants would fall within a hierarchical scheme of state obligation.

In light of this analysis we can conclude that derogability is not a useful method by which to construct a clear distinction between the categories of civil and political rights on the one hand, and economic and social rights on the other.

Having resolved this issue, the question remains, however, whether all rights in international law are equal, or whether there is some distinction or hierarchy of importance between rights? Although Hathaway did not invoke derogability as a means of distinguishing the normative value of rights, it is likely that some courts have mistakenly assumed this to be

---

[105] A similar criticism was voiced in Martin, 'Review of The Law of Refugee Status', at 352.
[106] HRC, *General Comment No. 29*, at para. 8.
[107] See for example HRC, *General Comment No. 28*, at paras. 10, 28 and 31.
[108] The HRC has clearly taken this approach to the interpretation of the fact that there is no derogability clause in the CRC. In *General Comment No. 29*, the HRC notes that art. 4(1) of the ICCPR requires that no measure derogating from the provisions of the Covenant may be inconsistent with the State party's other obligations under international law, particularly the rules of international humanitarian law: at paras. 9–10. In providing examples of how this provision may interact with other obligations in international law, it provides the following example: 'Reference is made to the Convention on the Rights of the Child which has been ratified by almost all States parties to the Covenant and does not include a derogation clause. As article 38 of the Convention clearly indicates, the Convention is applicable in emergency situations': see note 5. For an explicit discussion of this point in the refugee context, see *Refugee Appeal No. 71427/99*, RSAA, 16 August 2000, at para. 51.

the case because of the association between derogability and normative hierarchy, given that non-derogability is sometimes identified as the hallmark of fundamental rights. Thus relying on derogability in any hierarchical framework raises the likelihood that it will be interpreted in a way that assigns normative significance to the different categories. On one level, this may accord with common sense. After all, if we were to construct a hierarchy, perhaps a logical place to start would be with norms from which states can never derogate.[109] However, such a task is fraught with complexity. As the HRC has explained in relation to non-derogable provisions in the ICCPR:

> While there is no hierarchy of importance of rights under the Covenant, the operation of certain rights may not be suspended, even in times of national emergency. But not all rights of profound importance, such as articles 9 and 27 of the Covenant, have in fact been made non-derogable. One reason for certain rights being made non-derogable is because their suspension is irrelevant to the legitimate control of the state of national emergency (for example, no imprisonment for debt, in article 11). Another reason is that derogation may indeed be impossible (as, for example, freedom of conscience). At the same time, some provisions are non-derogable exactly because without them there would be no rule of law.[110]

Similar observations have led some scholars to conclude that 'tracing superiority with the help of non-derogable rights dwells on the assumption that those rights are non-derogable because they are superior – a classic circular argument'.[111]

---

[109] See for example, Teraya Koji, 'Emerging Hierarchy in International Human Rights and Beyond: From the Perspective of Non-Derogable Rights' (2001) 12 *European Journal of International Law* 917.

[110] HRC, *General Comment No. 24: Issues Relating to Reservations Made upon Ratification or Accession to the Covenant or the Optional Protocols thereto, or in Relation to Declarations under Article 41 of the Covenant*, UN Doc. CCPR/C/21/Rev.1/Add.6 (1994e), at para. 10. See also *General Comment No. 29*, at para. 11: 'However it is apparent that some other provisions of the Covenant were included in the list of non-derogable provisions because it can never become necessary to derogate from these rights during a state of emergency (e.g. articles 11 and 18).'

[111] Susanne Zühlke and Jens-Christian Pastille, 'Extradition and the European Convention – Soering Revisited' (1999) 59 *Zeitschrift für ausländdisches öffentliches Recht und Völkerrecht* 749, cited in Gregor Noll, *Negotiating Asylum: The EU Acquis, Extraterritorial Protection and the Common Market of Deflection* (The Hague: Martinus Nijhoff Publishers, 2000), p. 462. Noll states, in relation to the European Convention, that 'the Convention text is no more than a structure of technical solutions to the problem of formulating rights with sufficient precision. There is no indication whatever that the chosen technical solutions are signs of superiority': p. 462.

An attempt to construct a hierarchy of international legal norms has proved difficult and controversial. As Brownlie points out, attempts to classify rules, or rights and duties, by use of terms such as 'fundamental' or 'inalienable' (in respect of rights), 'have not had much success'.[112] One exception to this is the notion that peremptory norms, or *jus cogens* norms, are the primary, core or most fundamental or important rights and thus represent a normative hierarchy in international law. There is some logic to this idea as it must be that the international community views these rights as more fundamental than others since there must be some normative justification for according them superior enforceability.[113] However, there is a question as to how helpful this insight is in the context of refugee law, as it does not advance the analysis very far. Although the precise parameters of the category *jus cogens* are unclear, it is accurate to note that only a very limited number of rights can properly and uncontroversially be described as *jus cogens* norms,[114] and it is well established in refugee law that persecution may be constituted by a far wider range of harm than is represented by the *jus cogens* category.[115] Therefore, reference to *jus cogens* merely tells us that

---

[112] Ian Brownlie, *Principles of Public International Law*, sixth edition (Oxford: Oxford University Press, 2003), p. 488. Theodore Meron also points out, in a seminal piece of scholarship on the hierarchy issue, that examination of the Charter and the key international human rights instruments reveals that 'the terms "human rights", "freedoms", "fundamental human rights", "fundamental freedoms", "rights and freedoms" and, most commonly, "human rights and fundamental freedoms" appear, in general, to be used interchangeably': Theodor Meron, 'On a Hierarchy of International Human Rights' (1986) 80 *American Journal of International Law* 1 at 4. He concludes that this suggests that 'there is no substantive or definable legal difference between these terms': at 4.

[113] The VCLT provides that a treaty is void if it conflicts with a peremptory norm of general international law: art. 53. It should be noted, however, that while *jus cogens* norms are non-derogable, not all non-derogable rights are *jus cogens* norms. As the HRC has explained: 'The enumeration of non-derogable provisions in article 4 is related to, but no identical with, the question whether certain human rights obligations bear the nature of peremptory norms of international law': HRC, *General Comment No. 29*, at para. 11.

[114] These are, most relevantly, prohibitions on genocide, torture, crimes against humanity, slavery, and systematic racial discrimination: Koskenniemi, 'Fragmentation of International Law' at pp. 158-9. See also Brownlie, *Principles of Public International Law*, p. 489.

[115] See generally Chapter 3, particularly notes 15-19. Indeed, reliance on *jus cogens* norms in the refugee context is dangerous given that it may result in refugee decision-makers confining analysis to those claims alone: see Daniel Steinbock, 'Interpreting the Refugee Definition' (1998) 45 *UCLA Law Review* 733 at 784.

violations of some rights will always constitute persecution, but does not assist in resolving less clear-cut cases.[116] Thus, one returns to the task of assessing the level of seriousness in each particular case.

The interdependence of human rights

The above two sections have questioned the notion that there is a clear and simple hierarchical relationship between the categories of civil and political rights on the one hand and economic and social rights on the other, based either on a theory of normative hierarchy or on one of hierarchical obligation. This is important in illuminating the deficiencies in the current approach to human rights analysis in refugee law. However, there is a deeper problem with reliance on a categorical framework, implicit in each of the above critiques: the notion that rights can be neatly compartmentalized into two broad and neatly distinguishable categories is highly questionable in light of contemporary understandings of the interdependence of all human rights.

The emphasis in the Vienna Declaration on the indivisibility, interdependence and interrelatedness of all human rights has long been reflected and confirmed in the academic literature and, more recently, by the various treaty bodies in their Concluding Observations and General Comments. The 'permeability' of human rights was initially developed on a theoretical or philosophical level,[117] but more recently has been implemented in practice by human rights courts and tribunals as they have interpreted 'traditional' protections in the form of civil and political rights in a manner that encompasses violations traditionally considered to be of an economic and social nature.[118] These

---

[116] It is interesting to note that the HRC describes the right to life as 'the supreme right from which no derogation is permitted even in time of public emergency which threatens the life of the nation': HRC, *General Comment No. 06*. However, it does not elaborate on this hierarchy issue in respect of other rights, thus underlining the point that the hierarchy approach does not assist with anything other than the most fundamental rights.

[117] The seminal piece on this topic is Scott, 'The Interdependence and Permeability of Human Rights Norms': see particularly at 771. See also Craig Scott, 'Reaching Beyond (Without Abandoning) the Category of Economic, Social and Cultural Rights' (1999b) 21 *Human Rights Quarterly* 634.

[118] There are various aspects to the wider debate about interdependence and indivisibility. For example, Diane Otto refers to three types of indivisibility: see Otto, 'Defending Women's Economic and Social Rights', p. 54. See also Scott, 'The Interdependence and Permeability of Human Rights Norms'.

developments have highlighted that the categories of rights are interconnected and fluid, since obligations in the separate categories may overlap, and even those rights traditionally considered 'civil and political' may include socio-economic aspects; thus, a particular act may involve a violation of both civil and political and economic and social rights obligations. In other words, it is not always possible to categorize an action as engaging strictly *either* a civil and political right or an economic and social right. This is important in the refugee context because it highlights the limitations of a hierarchical model that assumes that each act or violation can be neatly categorized and apportioned a degree of significance to the persecution inquiry accordingly. As Sachs J of the South African Constitutional Court has opined, 'a single situation can give rise to multiple, overlapping and mutually reinforcing violations of ... rights'.[119]

There are two key methods by which the concrete interdependence of human rights has been established. First, even in terms of the text of the treaties, the strict distinction is undermined on the basis that, as a number of commentators have pointed out, there is some overlap between the Covenants.[120] For example, both the ICCPR and the ICESCR contain provisions of a socio-economic nature (or even of a 'communitarian' nature in some cases)[121] including at least some aspects of the right to self-determination,[122] equal protection,[123] prohibition on arbitrary interference with the home,[124] freedom of association,[125] rights of minorities (including in relation to cultural and language rights),[126] education of

---

[119] *National Coalition for Gay and Lesbian Equality and Anor v. Minister of Justice and Others* (1998) (12) BCLR 1517 (CC), 1998 SACLR LEXIS 26, 9 October 1998, at para. 114. In that case, His Honour was clearly talking about constitutional rights, but the principle is more generally relevant.

[120] Similar observations have been made in respect of regional human rights treaties. For example, Eide and Rosas point out that the right to education is included in Protocol No. 1 to the European Convention and there has been discussion of a new protocol on the cultural rights of minorities: see Eide and Rosas, 'Economic, Social and Cultural Rights', p. 5.

[121] For example, those commonly referred to as 'third generation rights', such as the right to self-determination: contained in ICCPR, art. 1 and ICESCR, art. 1.

[122] ICCPR, art. 1; ICESCR, art. 1.

[123] ICCPR, arts. 2 and 3; ICESCR art. 2(2) and art. 3. As Tomuschat argues, non-discrimination cannot be described in terms of the generations of rights: 'Equality does not fit into the classification scheme which distinguishes between first generation and second generation rights': Tomuschat, *Human Rights*, p. 41.

[124] ICCPR, art. 17; ICESCR, p. 11.   [125] ICCPR, art. 22; ICESCR, art. 8.

[126] ICCPR, art. 27; ICESCR, art. 15(1)(a).

children,[127] family[128] and the right to work.[129] Thus, it is possible that a single incident or act, such as a forcible eviction by the government, could constitute both a violation of art. 17 of the ICCPR and art. 11 of the ICESCR.[130] In other words, one act could simultaneously constitute a violation of two levels of rights, as illustrated in Chapter 3 in relation to the right to housing (level three) and property (level four).[131]

Further, it has been noted that most international human rights instruments that post-date the International Bill of Rights, such as the CERD and the CEDAW, are not structured in terms of their distinction between civil and political rights on the one hand, and economic, social and cultural rights on the other. Rather, they make provision with respect to both types of rights in one instrument.[132] For example, Eide points out that the Convention on the Rights of the Child, which has now been

---

[127] In the ICESCR, the right to education is encapsulated in art. 13, while in the ICCPR, there is protection with respect to religious education: see ICCPR, art. 18(4).

[128] See ICESCR, art. 10 and ICCPR, arts. 23 and 24.

[129] The ICESCR contains the most inclusive provisions in respect of the right to work: see art. 7. However the ICCPR also addresses the right to work in the context of government service: see art. 25(c).

[130] See CESCR, *General Comment No. 4*; CESCR, *General Comment No. 7*. In *General Comment No. 7*, the Committee states: 'The State itself must refrain from forced evictions and ensure that the law is enforced against its agents or third parties who carry out forced evictions... Moreover, this is reinforced by article 17, paragraph 1, of the International Covenant on Civil and Political Rights, which complements the right not to be forcefully evicted without adequate protection. That provision recognizes, *inter alia*, the right to be protected against arbitrary or unlawful interference with one's home. It is to be noted that the State's obligation to ensure respect for that right is not qualified by considerations relating to its available resources': at para. 9.

[131] Another example is provided in a recent Amnesty report documenting the impact of movement restrictions on Palestinians in the occupied territories, where it is explained that these restrictions have resulted in violations of other important rights as well, including the right to work: see Amnesty International, *Israel and the Occupied Territories, Surviving Under Siege: The Impact of Movement Restrictions on the Right to Work* (2003c) <http://web.amnesty.org/library/print/ENGMDE150012003> at 31 May 2006. Indeed, this was explicitly recognized by the ICJ in *Legal Consequences of the Construction of a Wall in the Occupied Palestinian Territory*, Advisory Opinion (I.C.J. July 9, 2004), 43 I.L.M. 1009 (2004), where the Court found that the construction of the wall impeded the liberty of movement of the inhabitants in violation of art. 12 (1) of the ICCPR, as well as 'the right to work, to health, to education and to an adequate standard of living' guaranteed in the ICESCR: at para. 134.

[132] Eide and Rosas, 'Economic, Social and Cultural Rights', p. 4. See also the *International Convention on the Protection of the Rights of All Migrant Workers and Members of Their Families* (adopted by General Assembly resolution 45/158 of 8 December 1990). However, as at 8 May 2006, the Convention has only 34 parties: <http://www.ohchr.org/english/countries/ratification/13.htm> at 31 May 2006.

ratified by 192 states,[133] protects traditional civil rights[134] alongside the right to health (art. 24), to social security (art. 25), to an adequate standard of living (art. 27), to education (art. 28) and to protection from economic exploitation (art. 32).[135] So much has been emphasized by the Committee on the Rights of the Child in a General Comment:

> There is no simple or authoritative division, of human rights in general or of Convention rights, into the two categories ... Enjoyment of economic, social and cultural rights is inextricably intertwined with enjoyment of civil and political rights ... the Committee believes that economic, social and cultural rights, as well as civil and political rights, should be regarded as justiciable.[136]

This is significant because it is not clear where the rights contained in these instruments would be situated in a model of persecution based on categories which assumes a distinction between civil and political rights on one hand and economic, social and cultural rights on the other.

Second, it is widely acknowledged that many traditional civil and political rights have been interpreted in a manner that incorporates obligations of a socio-economic nature, further underlining the interdependence of the two 'categories' of rights. At the international level, the HRC has made clear in both General Comments and jurisprudence that a number of provisions in the ICCPR incorporate socio-economic aspects.

---

[133] As at 19 April 2006: see OHCHR, *Status of Ratifications of the Principal International Human Rights Treaties* (2006) <http://www.ohchr.org/english/countries/ratification/index.htm> at 31 May 2006.

[134] Although importantly, as Pieterse points out, even the civil and political rights have a social dimension. For example, art. 6 of the CRC provides: 'State Parties recognize that every child has the inherent right to life. 2. State Parties shall ensure to the maximum extent possible the survival and development of the child': at 374. She quotes from Julia Sloth-Nielsen, 'Ratification of the United Nations Convention on the Rights of the Child: Some Implications for South African Law' (1995) 11 *South African Journal on Human Rights* 401 at 410, where the author states that the intent of art. 6 'was to incorporate into the Convention a phrase "the right to survival"': Marius Pieterse, 'A Different Shade of Red: Socio-Economic Dimensions of the Right to Life in South Africa' (1999) 15 *South African Journal on Human Rights* 372 at 375, note 17.

[135] Eide, 'Economic, Social and Cultural Rights as Human Rights', p. 11. See also Scott and Alston, 'Adjudicating Constitutional Priorities in a Transnational Context', p. 227: 'The CRC ... entrenches the human rights of children from both categories of so-called "civil and political" and "economic, social and cultural rights" in a way that does not segregate them, nor, indeed, even indicate whether a given right falls into one category or the other – or into both, in the manner of the evolving knitting together of the ICCPR and the ICESCR.'

[136] Committee on the Rights of the Child, *General Comment No. 5: General Measures of Implementation for the Convention on the Rights of the Child*, UN Doc. CRC/GC/2003/5 (2003), at para. 6.

In its General Comments, for example,[137] the HRC has clarified that the right to life is not to be 'narrowly interpreted' and in this regard 'considers that it would be desirable for States parties to take all possible measures to reduce infant mortality and to increase life expectancy, especially in adopting measures to eliminate malnutrition and epidemics',[138] and that, when reporting on compliance with obligations in respect of art. 6, states should provide, *inter alia*, 'data on birth rates and on pregnancy- and childbirth-related deaths of women, 'gender-disaggregated data ... on infant mortality rates' and 'information on the particular impact on women of poverty and deprivation that may pose a threat to their lives'.[139] Similarly, the HRC has reiterated that in respect of art. 24 of the ICCPR, concerning the obligation to protect children, 'States parties should report on measures taken to ensure that girls are treated equally to boys in education, in feeding and in health care'.[140]

In terms of jurisprudence developed in response to individual complaints and in concluding observations on States parties reports, the HRC has further consolidated the 'permeability' of rights in finding, for example, that a failure to take adequate steps to address the situation of homelessness may compromise the right to life of those persons,[141] that art. 7 (prohibition on cruel, inhuman and degrading treatment) can apply where a person is subjected to conditions in detention that violate basic minimum standards including (*inter alia*) 'provision of food of nutritional value adequate for health and strength',[142] and that art. 26 (right to non-discrimination) is capable of applying to social security legislation (including unemployment benefits)[143] and to cuts in social

---

[137] Hunt extracts the relevant principles from nine of the HRC's General Comments: Hunt, *Reclaiming Social Rights*, pp. 61–4.
[138] See HRC, *General Comment No. 6*, at para. 5.
[139] HRC, *General Comment No. 28*, at para. 10.   [140] *Ibid.*, at para. 28.
[141] This was the case in respect of Canada: see Scott and Alston, 'Adjudicating Constitutional Priorities in a Transnational Context', p. 226, note 51. See also Craig Scott, 'Canada's International Human Rights Obligations and Disadvantaged Members of Society: Finally into the Spotlight?' (1999a) 10(4) *Constitutional Forum* 97 at 102, where he summarizes both the HRC and CESCR's views on Canada's compliance with its human rights obligations: 'Canada's failure to take adequate measures to prevent and respond to homelessness represents a failure to ensure rights to housing, health and life itself. Positive measures must be taken to tackle this combined rights violation.'
[142] Communication No. 458/1991, UN Doc. CCPR/C/51/D/458/1991 (1994), at para. 9.3.
[143] The cases on this issue are frequently cited in this debate: *SWM Broeks v. the Netherlands*, Communication No. 172/1984, UN Doc. CCPR/C/29/D/172/1984 (1987); *LG Danning v. the Netherlands*, Communication No. 180/1984, UN Doc. CCPR/C/29/D180/1984 (1987);

assistance rates that do 'not have a neutral effect across all poor persons but necessarily operate[ ] to exacerbate disproportionately the poverty of disadvantaged social groups such as women and children'.[144]

These jurisprudential developments have also taken place at the regional level,[145] most notably in decisions of the ECHR.[146] Perhaps the most oft-cited example is the early decision of *Airey*, in which the ECHR held that art. 6 (right of access to courts) of the European Convention for the Protection of Human Rights and Fundamental Freedoms ('European Convention')[147] required the State party (Ireland) to provide legal aid to a person seeking legal separation from a spouse if he/she is unable to afford his or her own lawyer, thereby observing that 'there is no water-tight

---

and *FH Zwaan-de Vries* v. *the Netherlands*, Communication No. 182/1984, UN Doc. CCPR/C/29/D/182/1984 (1987), cited in Scott, 'The Interdependence and Permeability of Human Rights Norms', pp. 852–3. In the three cases, the HRC applied art. 26 of the ICCPR to legislation dealing with social security. See also Scheinin, 'Economic and Social Rights as Legal Rights', pp. 32–4, where he also discusses the case of *Gueye et al.* v. *France*, Communication No. 196/1985, *Official Records of the Human Rights Committee 1988/89*, vol. II, pp. 409–10, in which the HRC 'found a violation of Article 26 whereby French legislation afforded lower pensions to returned Senegalese soldiers of the French army than to French citizens in an otherwise equal position'.

[144] Scott and Alston, 'Adjudicating Constitutional Priorities in a Transnational Context', p. 226, note 51; see also Scott, 'Canada's International Human Rights Obligations and Disadvantaged Members of Society', p. 102.

[145] There are also some very interesting domestic examples, although it is well beyond the scope of this book to engage in any discussion of these developments. India is perhaps the jurisdiction most often referred to because it has interpreted the civil and political rights protections in its Constitution, such as the right to life, so as to incorporate socio-economic rights such as health: see for example, Nihal Jayawickrama, *The Judicial Application of Human Rights Law* (Cambridge: Cambridge University Press, 1998), pp. 258–60. This is distinct from the important development in South Africa, where the interdependence argument is not necessary given that specific provisions on socio-economic rights are found in the text of the Constitution itself: see generally Haysom, 'Constitutionalism, Majoritarian Democracy and Socio-Economic Rights'.

[146] Although there have also been developments in the Inter-American Court: see generally Craven, 'The Protection of Economic, Social and Cultural Rights under the Inter-American System of Human Rights'. See also Craig Scott and Patrick Macklem, 'Constitutional Ropes of Sand or Justiciable Guarantees? Social Rights in a New South African Constitution' (1992) 141 *University of Pennsylvania Law Review* 1 at 110. With respect to the Inter-African system, there is less need to rely on 'permeability' arguments since the text of the relevant instrument itself contains socio-economic rights. This has led some commentators to note that it is more advanced with respect to these issues: see generally, Sisule Fredrick Musungu, 'International Trade and Human Rights in Africa: A Comment on Conceptual Linkages' in Frederick M. Abbott, Christine Breining-Kaufmann and Thomas Cottier (eds.), *International Trade and Human Rights: Foundations and Conceptual Issues* (Ann Arbor: University of Michigan Press, 2006), pp. 321–8.

[147] Rome, 4 November 1950, in force 3 September 1953, 312 UNTS 221.

division separating that sphere [economic and social rights] from the field covered by the Convention'.[148] The Court has continued to display a willingness to interpret the mostly 'civil and political' rights in the European Convention in a more expansive manner. For example, it has recognized that forced evictions can violate the right to privacy (art. 8),[149] that serious environmental damage and accompanying health problems can amount to a violation of art. 8 (protection of private and family life)[150] and that both the non-discrimination principle in art. 14 and procedural safeguards in art. 6 can apply in the field of social insurance, including welfare assistance.[151] In one of the most significant jurisprudential developments to date, the Court held in *D v. the United Kingdom*[152] that the UK would be in violation of art. 3 (prohibition on inhuman or degrading treatment) if it returned a man with AIDS to St Kitts (his home country), where his removal would entail 'the abrupt withdrawal' of the 'sophisticated treatment and medication' which he was receiving in the UK, and

---

[148] *Case of Airey v. Ireland* (1979) Eur. Court HR, Application No. 6289/73, 9 October 1979, cited in Viljanen, 'Abstention or Involvement?', p. 55.

[149] See *Akdivar v. Turkey* (1996) Eur. Court HR, Case No. 99/1995/605/693, 30 August 1996, cited in Shedrack C. Agbakwa, 'Reclaiming Humanity: Economic, Social and Cultural Rights as the Cornerstone of African Human Rights' (2000) 5 *Yale Human Rights and Development Law Journal* 177 at 209. See also *Selçuk and Asker v. Turkey* (1998) Eur. Court HR, Case No. 12/1997/796/998–9, 24 April 1998; *Dulas v. Turkey* (2001) Eur. Court HR, Case No. 25801/94, 3 January 2001; and *Bilgin v. Turkey* (2000) Eur. Court HR, Case No. 23819/94, 16 November 2000, cited in Agbakwa, 'Reclaiming Humanity', at 209.

[150] See *Lopez Ostra v. Spain* (1994) Eur. Court HR, Case No. 41/1993/436/515, 9 December 1994, as cited in Scheinin, 'Economic and Social Rights as Legal Rights', pp. 41–2. See also Walter Kaelin, 'Trade and the European Convention on Human Rights' in Abbott, Breining-Kaufmann and Cottier (eds.), *International Trade and Human Rights*, pp. 297–8.

[151] *Schuler-Zgraggen v. Switzerland* (1993) Eur. Court HR, Case No. 17/1992/362/436, 24 June 1993, cited in Agbakwa, 'Reclaiming Humanity', at 209. Agbakwa also cites *Feldbrugge v. The Netherlands* (1986) Eur. Court HR, Case No. 8562/79, 29 May 1986 and *Deumeland v. Germany* (1986), Eur. Court HR, Case No. 9384/81, 29 May 1986, in which the court extended the non-discrimination right to health insurance allowances: at 209. Scheinin also discusses *Salesi v. Italy* (1993) Eur. Court HR, Case No. 11/1992/356/430, 26 February 1993, in which art. 6 was held to apply to a monthly disability allowance and *Gaygusuz v. Austria* (1996) Eur. Court HR, Case No. 39/1995/545/631, 16 September 1996, where 'a violation of Article 14 taken in conjunction with the property rights clause in Article 1 of Protocol No. 1 was established due to denial of social assistance to a Turkish migrant worker on the basis of a distinction based on nationality': at 34. See also *Cyprus v. Turkey* (2001) Eur. Court HR, Case No. 25781/94, 10 May 2001, in which Röhl explains the Court found that the Turkish authorities had violated art. 3 of the European Convention in 'restricting the access of Greek Cypriots living in Northern Cyprus to adequate health care': Katharina Röhl, *Fleeing Violence and Poverty*.

[152] (1997), Eur. Court HR, Case No. 146/1996/767/964, 21 April 1997.

subjection to conditions of adversity which would 'further reduce his life expectancy and subject him to acute mental and physical suffering' in St Kitts.[153] In particular, any medical treatment which he 'might hope to receive [in St Kitts] could not contend with the infections which he may possibly contract on account of his lack of shelter and sanitation problems which beset the population of St Kitts'.[154]

The combined significance of an interpretation of a number of articles in the European Convention which permits their application both to socio-economic issues and to removal proceedings, has underpinned the growing reliance by refugee applicants in European Convention signatory countries on European Convention-related claims as an alternative to refugee status.[155] This is particularly so where a claim involves harm in the form of a denial of socio-economic rights, and has led to developing jurisprudence on the extent to which art. 3 (inhuman and degrading treatment) prohibits the removal of a person in the context that he or she will face seriously disadvantaged economic conditions on return. For example, the UK IAT has confirmed that '[i]t is uncontroversial that if as a result of a removal decision a person would be exposed to a real risk of existence below the level of bare minimum subsistence that would cross the threshold of Art. 3 harm'.[156] Accordingly, claimants have successfully argued that art. 3 prohibits their removal in various situations, including where the applicant would be returned to 'a camp where conditions are described as "sub-human" and [he or she would] face medical conditions described as some of the worst in the world';[157] where an applicant was 'an amputee who had serious mental problems who would not receive either financial or medical support in the Gambia and

---

[153] *D* (1997), Eur. Court HR, Case No. 146/1996/767/964, 21 April 1997, at paras. 51–2.
[154] *D* (1997), Eur. Court HR, Case No. 146/1996/767/964, 21 April 1997, at para. 52. It should be noted that in subsequent decisions, the European Court of Human Rights has emphasized the exceptional nature of the circumstances in *D* v. *UK*, thus limiting its application to other applications by persons with HIV: see Röhl, *Fleeing Violence and Poverty*. For a strict approach to *D* v. *UK* in UK law, see *N* v. *Secretary of State for the Home Department* [2005] 4 All ER 1017.
[155] This remedy varies depending on domestic arrangements. In the UK for example, this avenue has fairly recently been opened by the passage of the Human Rights Act 1998. The IAT now has jurisdiction to hear cases under the Convention/Act and thus many applicants submit alternative claims (i.e. a claim for refugee status and in the alternative, claim for protection under the Human Rights Act provisions). For further discussion, see Chapter 7.
[156] *Mandali* v. *Secretary of State for the Home Department* (Unreported, IAT, Appeal No. HX16991-02, 27 March 2003), at para. 10.
[157] *Paul Owen* v. *Secretary of State for the Home Department* [2002] UKIAT 03285, at para. 27.

would only have recourse to begging for his support';[158] and where a 16-year-old boy would be subject to destitution and the absence of any protection in Kosovo.[159] It is striking that it is the same decision-makers who, while acknowledging and implementing in a very practical way the idea of the permeability of rights in the European Convention removal context, continue to insist on categories in the context of refugee law.[160]

This brief analysis of the interdependence of human rights illuminates further the problems in relying on categories as a method of assessing which rights are capable of constituting 'persecution' in the refugee context, and supports the view that rather than compartmentalizing and hierarchically ordering the harms involved in an individual case, '[h]uman rights are better approached and defended in an integrated rather than a disparate fashion'.[161] These concerns are not merely theoretical; the categorical approach in the refugee jurisprudence has, as explained in Chapter 3, been prone to misunderstanding, as categories tend to mask the overlap and similarities between rights. In light of the above analysis it must be concluded that the construction of 'overly broad categories',[162] such as the contrast between civil and political rights and economic and social rights, has 'limited conceptual integrity'[163] and serves to 'obscure more than [it] illuminate[s]'.[164]

---

[158] *R v. Secretary of State for the Home Department, ex parte Kebbeh* (Queen's Bench Division, Crown Office List, Case No. CO/1269/98, 30 April 1999), at 8.

[159] *Korca v. Secretary of State for the Home Department* (Unreported, IAT, Appeal No. HX-360001-2001, 29 May 2002), at para. 9. The IAT also found that art. 8 (right to family life) would be breached given the 'appellant's age, the absence of any home or family in Kosovo and the establishment of some degree of home here [the UK]': at para. 9.

[160] The IAT is one of the jurisdictions in which the four-level categorical approach is most entrenched: see the discussion in Chapter 3.

[161] *National Coalition for Gay and Lesbian Equality and Anor v. Minister of Justice and others* (1998) (12) BCLR 1517, at para. 112 (Sacks J).

[162] James Nickel, 'How Human Rights Generate Duties to Protect and Provide' (1993) 15 *Human Rights Quarterly* 77 at 80.

[163] Scott and Alston, 'Adjudicating Constitutional Priorities in a Transnational Context', p. 240. See generally Scott, 'Reaching Beyond (Without Abandoning) the Category of Economic, Social and Cultural Rights'.

[164] Nickel, 'How Human Rights Generate Duties to Protect and Provide', p. 80. See also Scott Leckie, 'Another Step Towards Indivisibility: Identifying the Key Features of Violations of Economic, Social and Cultural Rights' (1998) 20 *Human Rights Quarterly* 81, in which he argues that the permeability approach provides 'a very convincing case that the continued categorization of rights is a flawed approach to understanding or interpreting human rights law and related violations thereof': at 104.

Conclusion on hierarchies and models in refugee law

The key insight of the above analysis is that the current hierarchical approach threatens to hamper future evolution of the degree to which socio-economic harm can constitute persecution in refugee law. As an IARLJ Working Party has noted, it 'leaves little room for growth as international perspectives on the relative importance of these [economic, social and cultural] rights shifts'.[165] The argument of this book is that the importance and normative development of these rights has shifted, and refugee law must reflect this change in order to ensure its contemporary relevance and, more importantly, to ensure an evolutionary approach to an interpretation of the Refugee Convention as required by the VCLT.

The question remains whether it is possible to provide any guidance as to the way in which refugee decision-makers should apply the human rights approach to determining persecution. Are there risks in abandoning the current predominant approach and is there an acceptable alternative? One argument against abandoning the hierarchy approach is that it departs from a certain, consistent standard, and leaves decision-makers too much subjectivity or discretion. This is premised on the argument that, at present, while the hierarchical model may have some limitations or problems (primarily in relation to the application of level three rights), it at least ensures that level one and two rights are always considered tantamount to persecution, since, according to the hierarchical model, violations of these rights will almost always amount to 'the sustained or systemic denial of core human rights'.[166] The problem with this argument is that it is not necessarily supported by the case law, since it is well established that not every breach of a human right (even level one and two rights) will automatically constitute persecution; the ultimate question of whether particular harm amounts to persecution is subject to assessment on a case-by-case basis.[167] For example, in *Q* v. *RSAA*, the applicant argued before the High Court of New Zealand that

---

[165] IARLJ, Inter-Conference Working Parties: Human Rights Nexus Working Party, *Human Rights Conference Report*, p. 14 (on file with author). See also Symes and Jorro, *Asylum Law and Practice*, p. 72; *Refugee Appeal No. 71427/99*, RSAA, 16 August 2000. Goodwin-Gill has also noted that the 'list of fundamental protected interests [whose breach will be considered persecution] . . . can be expanded in the future . . . as the value of certain economic and social rights is increasingly accepted': *The Refugee in International Law*, p. 79.

[166] Hathaway, *Law of Refugee Status*, p. 108.

[167] The case law is relatively clear that 'not every threat of harm to a person or interference with his or her rights . . . constitutes being persecuted': *Chan* (1989) 169 CLR 379

the Vietnamese government restricts its citizens' privacy rights and freedom of speech, and that this should be recognized as persecution in accordance with Hathaway's view that 'failure to ensure such rights as that of freedom of thought was tantamount to persecution'.[168] The Court rejected this argument on the basis that 'it must surely go too far to suggest that every such breach [of a human right] is per se a persecution'.[169] In another decision, the RSAA concluded that the applicants' claims failed because, although they were able to establish breaches of arts. 17 and 23 of the ICCPR (level two in Hathaway's model), such breaches were not 'significant'.[170] Thus, even with respect to level one and two breaches, courts do not necessarily accept a strict correlation of persecution with human rights violations and are thus open to making different findings in respect of similar rights depending on the circumstances of a case. This is because not every violation of a human right is equally serious, nor has the same level of impact upon the individual concerned.

Although, as revealed in the analysis in Chapter 3, refugee decision-makers have predominantly adopted a hierarchical approach to 'being persecuted', which prioritizes some forms of harm over others, there is

at 429–30. Thus, as one Justice of the High Court of Australia has opined, '[f]raming an exhaustive definition of persecution for the purpose of the Convention is probably impossible': *Minister for Immigration and Multicultural Affairs* v. *Haji Ibrahim* (2000) 204 CLR 1 at 21 (McHugh J). See also *MMM* v. *Minister for Immigration and Multicultural Affairs* (1998) 170 ALR 411 at 414. For Canadian authority, see *Ling, Che Kueung* v. *Minister of Employment and Immigration* (FCTD, Case No. 92-A-6555, Muldoon J, 20 May 1993), at 2; and *Sulaiman, Hussaine Hassan* v. *MCI* (FCTD, Case No. IMM-525-94, Mackay J, 22 March 1996). For UK authority: see *Amare* v. *Secretary of State for the Home Department* [2005] All ER (D) 300, at paras. 27–31. This is also supported by the view of the IARLJ working party which concluded, after briefly surveying the approach in Canada, New Zealand, Australia, UK, the USA and some European countries, that '[n]one of the jurisdictions surveyed above, whether countries that make explicit references to human rights instruments or implicit, take[s] the position that any violation of a right articulated in an international human rights instrument automatically leads to a finding of persecution. There is still the requirement that the violation be serious': IARLJ, *Human Rights Conference Report*, p. 12.

[168] Q v. *Refugee Status Appeals Authority* [2001] NZAR 472, at para. 3. See also *H* v. *Chief Executive of the Department of Labour* (Unreported, High Court of New Zealand, Case No. 183/00, 20 March 2001), at para. 6 ('*H*').
[169] *H* (Unreported, High Court of New Zealand, Case No. 183/00, 20 March 2001), at para. 5.
[170] *Refugee Appeal Nos. 72558/01 and 72559/01*, RSAA, 19 November 2002, at para. 141. See also *Refugee Appeal No. 71404/99*, RSAA, 29 October 1999, at para. 65; *Refugee Appeal No. 2039/93*, RSAA, 12 February 1996, at para. 42; *Refugee Appeal 71163/98*, RSAA, 31 March 1999, at 9; and *Refugee Appeal No. 71427/99*, RSAA, 16 August 2000, at para. 54.

also evidence of an evolution in thought by some courts, from outright adoption of the hierarchical model,[171] to acceptance with limited caveats,[172] to a position that is much less rigid. As an example of the latter phenomenon, the RSAA has stated in a recent case that 'overly rigid categorizations of rights in terms of hierarchies are ... to be avoided'.[173] It has suggested that

> the question whether the anticipated harm rises to the level of 'being persecuted' depends not on a rigid or mechanical application of the categories of rights, but on an assessment of a complex set of factors which include not only the nature of the right threatened, but also the nature of the threat or restriction and the seriousness of the harm threatened. It must also be remembered that all human rights and fundamental freedoms are universal, indivisible, interdependent and interrelated.[174]

This is reminiscent of the approach advocated by Goodwin-Gill, who states that whether a human rights violation will amount to persecution will 'again turn on an assessment of a complex of factors, including (1) the nature of the freedom threatened, (2) the *nature and severity of the restriction*, and (3) the likelihood of the restriction eventuating in the

---

[171] The most important case is *Refugee Appeal No. 2039/93*, RSAA, 12 February 1996, in which the RSAA attempted to link derogability with hierarchy.

[172] See for example *Refugee Appeal No. 71427/99*, RSAA, 16 August 2000. In the UK, the Court of Appeal has found the four-level division 'helpful', but warned that the classification is 'not definitive' and 'should be applied with care': *Horvath* [2000] Imm AR 205 at para. 55 (Ward LJ). See also *Kovac* (Unreported, Appeal No. CC3034497, 28 April 2000), at 15.

[173] *Refugee Appeal No 75221*, RSAA, 23 September 2005, at para. 81. Moreover, guidelines produced by the Australian Department of Immigration and Multicultural Affairs advise decision-makers that 'as there is no agreed or settled position on a hierarchy of human rights obligations, it is open for delegates to use the International Bill of Human Rights to formulate their own': DIMA, *Refugee Law Guidelines* (2001), ch. 4–3, cited in DIMIA, Refugee and Humanitarian Division, 'Gender-Related Persecution (Article 1A(2)) – An Australian Perspective' (paper prepared as a contribution to the UNHCR's expert roundtable series, 2001), at 9–10, note 29 (on file with author). This less rigid position can be seen in recent RRT cases. For example in *Reference N03/46534*, RRT, 17 July 2003, the RRT listed the range of rights violations relevant to the conclusion that the applicant faced persecution, without regard to their category or place in any hierarchy: see at 21. See also the UK IAT's decision in *Kovac* (Unreported, Appeal No. CC3034497, 28 April 2000), at 15. See also *R v. Secretary of State for the Home Department, ex parte Blanusa*: 'it appears that what amounts to persecution is a flexible concept and depends on the gravity of the invasion of an individual's human rights, gravity being established by reference to the nature of the invasion and the length of time of invasion': (Unreported, UK Court of Appeal (Civil Division), Henry, Ward and Schiemann LJ, 18 May 1999) at 2 ('*Blanusa*').

[174] *Refugee Appeals Nos. 72558/01 and 72559/01*, RSAA, 19 November 2002, at para. 114

individual case'.[175] It is unclear what precisely is meant by the *nature of the freedom/right threatened* (for example, it is unclear whether this is similar to the Carlier model in which rights are ranked in terms of normative significance), but it is apparent that a much less structured approach is envisioned in which the decision-maker ultimately considers the seriousness of the violation in light of all relevant circumstances. The least structured approach (in that there is not even a reference to the nature of the right in this conception) has been put forward by an IARLJ Working Party as follows:

> A framework which accepts that all widely ratified human rights conventions should be used in assessing the kinds of breaches that might be persecutory; and then further requires an assessment of the seriousness of the breach in terms of its impact on the dignity of the person, would provide consistency and fairness. The resort to all human rights instruments provides flexibility and sensitivity, while the requirement of seriousness in the breach lessens the fear of overly liberalizing the interpretation of the Convention.[176]

In this model, the key method of distinguishing those human rights violations which are properly considered 'persecution' from those which are not is the test of *seriousness*. This appears to suggest that refugee decision-makers rely on international human rights law in order to decide which harms are to be considered potentially relevant to persecution, but the ultimate evaluation of the persecution question must remain an individual one within the discretion of the particular decision-maker. In other words, there is a two-step test:

1. Is there a human rights violation?
2. Is the violation sufficiently *serious* to warrant a finding of persecution?[177]

---

[175] Goodwin-Gill, *The Refugee in International Law*, p. 68 (emphasis added).
[176] *The Realities of Refugee Determination on the Eve of a New Millennium: The Role of the Judiciary* (Haarlem, The Netherlands: International Association of Refugee Law Judges, 1999), p. 15. Symes and Jorro also note this advantage: 'By this sensible linkage between formal breach of a human right and its conversion into persecution by means of the gravity of its invasion, the principal criticism of the Hathaway approach, that it might extend the forms of harm capable of constituting persecution too far, is overcome': Symes and Jorro, *Asylum Law and Practice*, p. 88.
[177] This is supported by the view of the IARLJ Working Party that '[w]hat decision-makers do when they try to make findings on persecution is, whether they acknowledge it or not, measure the activity on two levels. The first level asks the question, "is the harm the claimant fears the kind of harm the international community identifies as a violation of an important right?" and the second level then asks, "if the right violated is one that ought to be protected, is the violation sufficiently serious to warrant international protection?"' IARLJ, *Human Rights Conference Report*, p. 15.

This approach has the advantage of eschewing any rigid (or even more fluid) hierarchical model, but there may be a danger that such an approach represents an abandonment of the 'quest for standards'.[178] On the one hand, it is simply not possible to provide a grid or rigid guideline that will predict whether, in every case, a given set of conditions will amount to persecution. Such an exercise is neither possible nor fruitful. On the other hand, it is well recognized that it is necessary to protect against 'the unclear and subjective appreciation of administrative officials',[179] and thus ensure the 'reinforcement of legal reasoning',[180] in order to uphold the protective objectives of the Refugee Convention. The IARLJ Working Party position may represent a compromise in that reliance on human rights principles ensures some degree of consistency, since decision-makers are considering the same kinds of harms as relevant. Importantly, it prevents summary dismissal of claims based on subjective notions of what is or is not important. But is it possible to provide any further guidance to decision-makers in respect of the second step of the test, other than that they must engage in an assessment of 'seriousness'? Can we devise a workable guideline or framework that provides more assistance than simply stating that human rights should be referenced, but does not rely on categorical distinctions between rights based on their classification as civil and political on the one hand or socio-economic on the other?

Close consideration of the approach of courts in the refugee field reveals that what they are attempting to do when they undertake an assessment of persecution is to analyse the degree of violation, or of *how much* of a given human right/s is violated. For example, in *Chan*, LaForest J of the Canadian Supreme Court expressed the test as follows: '[t]he essential question is whether the persecution alleged by the claimant threatens his or her basic human rights *in a fundamental way*'.[181] Similarly, the New Zealand High Court has explained that in order to amount to persecution, '[t]here must be a denial *in a key way* of a human right',[182] and

---

[178] *Applicant A* (1997) 190 CLR 225 at 245 (Gummow J).
[179] Jean Yves Carlier, 'General Report', p. 686.
[180] Ibid.   [181] *Chan* (1995) 3 SCR 593 at 634–5 (emphasis added).
[182] 'Refugee law is concerned with actions that deny human dignity in any key way which requires an assessment of degree': *H* (Unreported, High Court of New Zealand, Case No. AP 183/00, 20 March 2001), citing *Q* v. *RSAA* (Unreported, High Court of New Zealand, Case No. CP57/2000, 24 October 2000). See also the INS Basic Law Manual (copy on file with author), which defines persecution as 'serious violations of basic human rights'.

CONCLUSION ON HIERARCHIES AND MODELS IN REFUGEE LAW 195

the New Zealand RSAA has more recently characterized the relevant focus in determining persecution as being 'on the minimum core entitlement conferred by the relevant right'.[183] The UK Court of Appeal has referred to the *'gravity of the invasion'*[184] and the new EU Directive defines 'being persecuted' as the *'severe violation* of basic human rights'.[185]

Although they do not always use the precise words, the approach of these decision-makers could be characterized as an attempt to ascertain whether the *core* of a relevant right has been violated. There is implicit recognition that if the violation in question is not *fundamental, key or grave*, or, in other words, does not impinge on the core of the right, then it will not, at least alone, be considered sufficiently serious as to amount to persecution.

The notion that human rights contain core and more peripheral elements is reflected both in the theory and practice of international human rights law.[186] The concept has been developed in the context of ascertaining what limitations on a right are permissible, or, in other words, 'how far can a right be regulated and limited before it becomes vacuous or even illusory?'[187] Orucu argues that the scope of every right 'must be analysed in terms of an outer edge, a circumjacence and a core', such that '[t]he essential elements of the norm which are unrelinquishable and unchangeable for the guaranteed core must be determined'.[188] In practice, scholars and the treaty bodies have not approached the interpretation of individual human rights protections in such a mechanical manner, since this three-part description is arguably intended to operate at a metaphorical level only; however, the concepts of core and

---

[183] *Refugee Appeal 74665/03*, RSAA, 7 July 2004, at para. 90.
[184] *Blanusa* (Unreported, UK Court of Appeal (Civil Division), Henry, Ward and Schiemann LJ, 18 May 1999), at 2.
[185] See EU Directive on a Common Asylum Policy, art. 9 (1)(a).
[186] It should be noted that H L A Hart initially introduced the notion of the 'core' and 'penumbra' of a legal rule, albeit in a different context. In his seminal article entitled 'Positivism and the Separation of Law and Morals' (1958) 71(4) *Harvard Law Review* 593, Hart explained that '[t]here must be a core of settled meaning, but there will be, as well, a penumbra of debatable cases in which words are neither obviously applicable nor obviously ruled out': at 607.
[187] Esin Orucu, 'The Core of Rights and Freedoms: The Limit of Limits', in Tom Campbell et al. (eds.), *Human Rights: From Rhetoric to Reality* (New York: Blackwell, 1986), p. 46. As the HRC explained in *General Comment No. 10: Freedom of Expression*, '[i]t is the interplay between the principle of freedom of expression and such limitations and restrictions which determines the actual scope of the individual's right': HRC, *General Comment No. 10: Freedom of Expression (Art. 19)*, UN Doc. HRI\GEN\1\Rev.1 at 11 (1994c), at para. 3.
[188] Orucu, 'The Core of Rights and Freedoms', p. 55.

periphery have proved useful in the interpretation of treaty terms and in some domestic jurisdictions in the context of interpreting constitutional rights.[189] In particular, the notion that it is necessary to identify an 'unrelinquishable nucleus'[190] of a right in order to determine its *raison d'être* has proved highly influential in the context of the obligations contained in the ICESCR, where this tool has been engaged as the most effective method of developing the normative content of the rights therein.[191] The concept was first introduced in 1990 in *General Comment No. 3* dealing generally with state obligations under the Covenant, in which the Economic Committee explained that if the ICESCR were to be read in such a way as not to establish a minimum core obligation, 'it would be largely deprived of its *raison d'être*'.[192] The rationale is that the core or essence of a right is identified by 'some essential element[s] without which it loses its substantive significance as a

---

[189] In the domestic context, the notion of core elements of a right can be useful in determining the kinds of restrictions that may be permissible by the state. See for example, in Canada: R v. *Sharpe*, 2001 SCCDJ 42; 2001 SCCDJ LEXIS 2, at paras. 23, 181–5 (McLachlin CJ, for the Court); *RJR-MacDonald Inc.* v. *Canada (Attorney General)*, 1995 Can. Sup. Ct. LEXIS 69, at paras. 71–5; and *United States of America* v. *Cotrobi* [1989] 1 SCR 1469 at 1491. I also note that s. 33 of the Constitution of South Africa provides that '[t]he rights entrenched in this Chapter may be limited by law of general application, provided that such limitation . . . (b) *shall not negate the essential content of the right in question*': see *S* v. *Makwanyane and Anor* (1995) (6) BCLR 665 (CC), at para. 98 (emphasis added) ('*Makwanyane*'). However, it is important to note that the South African Constitutional Court has not taken up the core-periphery idea in any meaningful way in the context of socio-economic rights thus far: see generally, David Bilchitz, 'Towards a Reasonable Approach to the Minimum Core: Laying the Foundations for Future Socio-Economic Rights Jurisprudence' (2003) 19 *South African Journal on Human Rights* 1.

[190] Orucu, 'The Core of Rights and Freedoms', p. 52.

[191] It should be noted that this approach is acknowledged to carry some risks, for example, 'that identifying core elements of a right and corresponding minimum obligations might lead to neglect of peripheral elements of the same right and to an undermining of the universal character of that right': Fons Coomans, 'In Search of the Core Content of the Right to Education', in Audrey R. Chapman and Sage Russell (eds.), *Core Obligations: Building a Framework for Economic, Social and Cultural Rights* (Antwerp; New York: Transnational Publishing, 2002), p. 245. Further, Chapman and Russell note that there is a concern 'that the identification of minimum core content will reveal to State parties how little they have to do in order to be in compliance with their obligations, and that States will do that minimum and nothing more'. However, as they note, 'if States actually *did* fulfil their minimum obligations, that would in many cases represent progress': Audrey R. Chapman and Sage Russell, 'Introduction' in Chapman and Russell, *Core Obligations*, p. 9.

[192] CESCR, *General Comment No. 3*, at para. 10. Alston appears to have been one of the first scholars to have suggested the application of the core content concept in this context: Philip Alston, 'Out of the Abyss: The Challenges Confronting the New UN Committee on Economic, Social and Cultural Rights' (1987) 9 *Human Rights Quarterly* 332 at 352–3.

human right'.[193] Building upon this development, the Economic Committee has begun to undertake the task of identifying the core content of a number of specific rights, including the right to education,[194] health,[195] food,[196] water[197] and work,[198] and has identified those core elements in relation to which 'a State party cannot, under any circumstances whatsoever, justify its non-compliance'.[199]

The notion of a core or essential element has not been engaged as directly by the HRC, although in a number of General Comments concerning those rights which may be limited in certain circumstances, the HRC has emphasized that states should be guided by the principle that 'the restrictions must not impair the essence of the right', 'vitiate'[200] or 'put in jeopardy'[201] the right itself; thus, the 'relation between right and restriction, between norm and exception, must not be reversed',[202] suggesting an indirect reliance on the notion of the core of a right.

How might the idea that human rights protections comprise a core element be engaged in the context of refugee law? The notion of core and periphery helps to explain why a risk of a violation of certain types of rights will *always* amount to persecution, for example right to life and prohibition on torture, while other violations will amount to persecution in only certain circumstances. This is because, in respect of such rights,

---

[193] Fons Coomans, *Economic, Social and Cultural Rights*, p. 18.
[194] CESCR, *General Comment No. 13*, at para. 57.
[195] CESCR, *General Comment No. 14*, at paras. 43–5.
[196] CESCR, *General Comment No. 12*, at paras. 6–8.
[197] CESCR, *General Comment No. 15*, at para. 37.
[198] CESCR, *General Comment No. 18*, at para. 31.
[199] See for example, CESCR, *General Comment No. 14*, at para. 47. For discussion of these issues in the refugee context, see *Refugee Appeal No. 75221*, RSAA, 23 September 2005, at para. 98. It should be noted that there is some imprecision in the terminology. As Chapman and Russell note, the minimum core idea 'is variously referred to as minimum core content, core content, essential elements, core entitlements, core obligations, minimum State obligations, and other variations on these themes', and that these terms are not synonymous: Chapman and Russell, 'Introduction', pp. 8–9. They explain that the approach favoured by the Economic Committee is the minimum core obligation formulation, which attempts to explain to a state party, 'what things [it] must do immediately to realize the right': p. 9.
[200] HRC, *General Comment No. 22: The Right to Freedom of Thought, Conscience and Religion (Art. 18)*, UN Doc. CCPR/C/21/Rev.1/Add. 4 (1993), at para. 8: 'Limitations imposed must be established by law and must not be applied in a manner that would vitiate the rights guaranteed in article 18.'
[201] HRC, *General Comment No. 10*, at para. 4.
[202] HRC, *General Comment No. 27: Freedom of Movement (Art. 12)*, UN Doc. CCPR/C/21 Rev. 1/Add.9 (1999), at para. 13.

the core is entirely or almost entirely co-extensive with the right itself. By contrast, other rights, such as privacy, religion, free speech and fair trial, may have an essential core and then a wider 'grey zone' or periphery, in which a violation of the right may occur but such breach may not be sufficiently central to the right as to constitute persecution. For example, it is unlikely that a breach of the right to life could be considered anything other than a core violation, whereas it is possible to envisage violations of the right to freedom of religion that would not be considered to reach the very core of the right.

This approach suggests a more principled method of explaining the common-sense notion developed in the refugee case law that not all violations of human rights are equally serious, and thus provides a useful tool for conceptualizing what it is that refugee judges are attempting to do when they undertake the persecution assessment. Indeed, analysis of the case law reveals that this is what decision-makers are effectively doing when they uphold claims (described in Chapter 3) based on, for example, a violation of the core of the right to work (that is, complete, or effectively complete, denial of the right to work generally or in relation to a specific occupation), while rejecting claims based solely on more peripheral violations such as minor discrimination in the workplace. It would explain why a denial of access to food to particular individuals or groups,[203] or the prevention of access to humanitarian food in internal conflicts or other emergency situations,[204] would amount to persecution, while discriminatory denial 'of such perquisites as discounts on food' would not alone establish persecution, especially where the denial of a ration card does not prevent the applicant from buying food.[205] Similarly, forced evictions, such as were described in *Kagema* in Chapter 3,

---

[203] The Full Federal Court of Australia has recognized, for example, that '[o]ne can envisage circumstances in which the taking of harvests of those perceived as "enemies", rather than those perceived as "allies", might found a conclusion of persecution for a Convention reason': *Hagi-Mohamed v. Minister for Immigration and Multicultural Affairs* [2001] FCA 1156 (Wilcox, Weinberg and Hely JJ), at para. 31. A concrete example is provided in the current situation in North Korea, in which it has been suggested that the government has in fact 'created a famine': Marcus, 'Famine Crimes in International Law', at 258. In particular, it has been suggested that the 'government is knowingly manipulating the famine to target certain populations that threaten its political survival': at 260.

[204] CESCR, *General Comment No. 12*, at para. 19. See also von Sternberg, *The Grounds of Refugee Protection in the Context of International Human Rights and Humanitarian Law*, pp. 298–311.

[205] For example, in a number of US decisions involving Nicaraguan applicants, courts have found that denial 'of such perquisites as discounts on food and a special work permit' does not establish persecution: see *Molinares v. Immigration and Naturalization Service*, 1995

clearly touch the core of the right to housing and thus constitute persecution, whereas less serious violations, such as the provision of inferior accommodation, may not alone suffice to warrant a refugee claim.[206] Hathaway has also (at least implicitly) acknowledged the logic of this approach, noting that, 'incapable of establishing persecution, are circumstances in which the rights at risk are related to core entitlements, but the threat does not go to the heart of the right as elaborated in international law', distinguishing this situation from those claims 'which evince a *serious* risk to core human rights' and 'hence justify a finding of fear of persecution'.[207]

It is important to note, however, that the identification of a core *does not* render non-core violations irrelevant to the persecution inquiry; on the contrary, a series of non-core violations can be considered in combination to amount to persecution, in accordance with well-established authority. An emphasis on the core aspects of human rights ensures that certain types of harm will always amount to persecution alone, without the necessity to accumulate such violations with other kinds of human rights violations. In this regard, this approach holds the most significant potential for providing a more principled framework for an assessment of claims in the field of economic and social rights, in respect of which, as previously mentioned, the Economic Committee has begun to elaborate the core content of many of the fundamental rights in the ICESCR.

Another advantage of this approach is that it obviates the concerns of those who question the appropriateness of referencing human rights

---

US App. LEXIS 36930 (9th Cir. 1995), citing *Saballo-Cortez*, 761 F 2d 1259 (9th Cir. 1984), especially where the denial of ration card or work permit does not prevent the applicant from buying food or working: at 1264. In *Raudez-Hurtada* v. *Immigration and Naturalization Service*, 1994 US App. LEXIS 28409 (9th Cir. 1994), the Ninth Circuit found that although the applicant established that her food ration card was reduced, eventually to nothing, and that she was denied a Sandinista party letter she needed to get a job, the denial did not prevent her 'from getting food or a job. She established at most that she would have to pay more for food and would be excluded from some jobs': at 1. See also *Benevides* v. *Immigration and Naturalization Service*, 1996 US App. LEXIS 8623 (9th Cir. 1996) and *Escobar-Chavez* v. *Immigration and Naturalization Service*, 1996 US App. LEXIS 17795 (9th Cir. 1996). However, the dissent of Judge Pregerson should be noted in *Saballo-Cortez*: 'it is unreasonable to require Saballo-Cortez to show that the Sandinista's refusal to issue a food ration card or work permit would result in his total inability to find food or work': at 1270.

[206] I say 'may not', because it may be that relegation to inadequate housing facilities constitutes persecution (see INS Basic Law Manual) but inferior accommodation, such as described by Hathaway, *The Law of Refugee Status*, will not.

[207] Hathaway, *The Law of Refugee Status*, p. 120.

(particularly economic and social rights) in the persecution inquiry on the basis that this approach is overly expansive, in that it provides a principled method of distinguishing between fundamental or key breaches and less serious violations.

Perhaps most important, this approach provides a broad framework or 'markers' to guide decision-makers, but does not purport to provide a definitive model, as it allows for evolution as the composition of the core of different rights develops.[208] In particular, there has been dramatic development in the past decade in terms of defining the core content of many of the rights contained in the ICESCR, most importantly by the Economic Committee,[209] but also in the scholarship, which can and should be engaged by refugee decision-makers in order to ensure the contemporary relevance of the Refugee Convention.

One potential problem with the core/periphery approach is that it may introduce a layer of complexity, in that refugee decision-makers are required to undertake the difficult task of ascertaining the core and periphery of a range of rights.[210] However, it is important to note that this approach does not require the construction of a categorical list of those violations falling within the core, or the delineation of a 'bright line' between those cases that will always amount to persecution and those which will not. As explained above, the persecution inquiry cannot be reduced to a simple reference to a categorical list. Rather, this operates as a method of providing analytical structure to what decision-makers are already effectively doing in respect of more traditional claims. While the assessment of claims and interpretation of the Refugee Convention

---

[208] Leckie, for example, notes that: 'Definitions of the core and supplemental contents of civil and political rights are being expanded continually. The search for similar clarity with respect to economic, social and cultural rights will continue to advance rapidly, and should by no means be viewed as an obstacle to addressing violations of these rights': Leckie, 'Another Step Towards Indivisibility: Identifying the Key Features of Violations of Economic, Social and Cultural Rights', at 102.

[209] See also Craven, who explains that the minimum core approach is also taken by the Inter-American Court of Human Rights: 'The Protection of Economic, Social and Cultural Rights under the Inter-American System of Human Rights', p. 343.

[210] The difficulty of this task has been noted by the Constitutional Court of South Africa in the context of s. 33 of the Constitution of South Africa, which prevents negation of the essential content of a right: see *Makwanyane* (1995) (6) BCLR 665 (CC), at para. 132. Notwithstanding these reservations, the Court has engaged the core-periphery idea in subsequent decisions: see, for example, *Van der Walt* v. *Metcash Trading Limited* (2002) (5) BCLR 454 (CC), at para. 37 and *Phillips and Anor* v. *Director of Public Prosecutions (Witwatersrand Local Division) and Others* (2003) (4) BCLR 357 (CC), at para. 58.

will continue to take place on an incremental basis, reference to core obligations provides much-needed guidance in the most cutting-edge and developing area – socio-economic rights. With this in mind, the second part of this chapter turns to a consideration of how this approach may operate to assist refugee decision-makers to evaluate claims based on deprivations of socio-economic rights in the future.

PART TWO: REVISITING VIOLATIONS OF SOCIO-ECONOMIC RIGHTS AND PERSECUTION

The core obligations approach: general considerations

This part of the chapter begins the task of demonstrating how the core/periphery idea can be implemented in practice by reference to some particular case studies. It is, of course, not possible to consider every potential way in which socio-economic claims may be relevant to the 'being persecuted' inquiry. Rather, the aim is to consider two of the most important emerging issues in the case law in recent years – education and health care – in order to provide some guidance for future consideration of a broader range of socio-economic claims. Before turning to these specific topics, there are a number of more general points that must be addressed.

First, it is important to emphasize that conceptually there are different ways by which refugee claims based on socio-economic deprivation may be established. Just as in the case of more traditional claims, a person may be at risk where the action emanates either from a government source, or from a non-government entity when the government is complicit, condones or is indifferent to the action, or is merely unable to control the non-government entity.[211] While it is necessary to establish, in the case of persecution by non-state agents, that the state is unable or unwilling to provide protection in order to establish a successful claim, it must be remembered that the ultimate question is always whether the applicant has a well-founded fear of being persecuted for a Convention reason. For this reason, it is only where the availability of state protection removes a person's well-founded fear of being persecuted that a refugee claim will fail on the

---

[211] See generally Mathew, Hathaway and Foster, 'The Role of State Protection in Refugee Analysis'.

'state protection' ground.[212] In other words, it is not sufficient that the state is endeavouring to fulfil its obligations pursuant to international human rights law; it must provide sufficient protection to remove the well-founded fear.[213]

Second, it has been recognized that persecution may be characterized by a government's *failure to act*. In the Australian High Court's decision in *Khawar*, the Court explained that failure on the part of the state to provide protection against persecution by non-state agents can *itself* constitute persecution.[214] In this context, Gleeson CJ explained that 'whether failure to act amounts to conduct often depends upon whether there is a duty to act'.[215] His Honour chose examples from private domestic law to illustrate this concept,[216] but it is more appropriate (and arguably more relevant) to refer to international human rights law to ascertain whether a state has a duty to act in a certain respect. Since international human rights law recognizes that states have a duty to act to respect and to fulfil human rights obligations, a violation can occur by virtue of an act of commission as well as of omission.[217] This is, of course, not to say that every time a state cannot provide socio-economic rights to its

---

[212] As the NZ RSAA has explained, '[i]f the net result of a state's "reasonable willingness" to operate a system for the protection of the citizen is that it is incapable of preventing a real chance of persecution of a particular individual, refugee status cannot be denied that individual': *Refugee Appeal No. 71427/99*, RSAA, 16 August 2000.

[213] This is important because decision-makers sometimes take the erroneous approach that requires only that the state is attempting to comply with its international obligations. For an example of this phenomenon in the context of a refugee claim based on socio-economic deprivation, see *Refugee Appeal No. 75221*, RSAA, 23 September 2005, where the NZ RSAA held that notwithstanding the evidence that Dalits in India 'remained discriminated against in every aspect of their lives', the refugee claim was not made out because 'the Indian State has taken steps to address the *de jure* and *de facto* discrimination against Dalits and is taking steps to progressively realize their rights under the ICESCR': at paras. 121, 199.

[214] *Khawar* (2002) 210 CLR 1. Since there are five different judgments, it is difficult to encapsulate the majority opinion. However McHugh and Gummow JJ were clearly of this view (at 29), while Gleeson CJ appeared also to accept this reasoning, where he stated that the Convention 'refers to persecution, which is conduct of a certain character. I do not see why persecution may not be a term aptly used to describe the combined effect of conduct of two or more agents; or why conduct may not, in certain circumstances, include inaction': at 12. Kirby J adopted the House of Lords' decision in *Shah*. See also *S152/2003* (2004) 205 ALR 487.

[215] *Khawar* (2002) 210 CLR 1 at 12 (Gleeson CJ).

[216] *Ibid*.

[217] The Economic Committee explicitly uses the language of omission and commission: see for example CESCR, *General Comment No. 15*, at paras. 42–3.

citizens, a person is entitled to refugee status. Rather, failure to provide will only amount to persecution where the state is clearly in breach of a legal duty as defined in international human rights law. Although assessing when this is so in the context of socio-economic rights has traditionally been a difficult task, the most significant aspect of the Economic Committee's work over the past decade is that it has elaborated on the specific aspects of state duties pursuant to the ICESCR and, in particular, has made it clear which 'positive' aspects of those obligations are essentially independent of the issue of resources.

This is highly significant in the context of refugee law because it means that, even in respect of cases where the state has failed to provide a basic right (as opposed to having actively withdrawn it), a refugee decision-maker may be able to ascertain a core violation of the ICESCR, without needing to assess in any detail the question whether the state has 'done enough', thus alleviating the most pressing concerns of decision-makers in this regard.[218]

Refugee decision-makers have begun to display a willingness to view critically state attempts to fulfil basic or core obligations. For example, in *JDJ (Re)*, the Canadian RPD held, in relation to Zaire:

> In *Cheung* the child's deprivations would result from an express government policy working against her particular social group, namely, second children. No such government policy is directed against impoverished children [in Zaire]. At the same time, the potential deprivations the claimant would face are the indirect result of government policies. The teachers, or for that matter, other civil servants are not being paid. No funds are provided for medical services or other service to assist the poor, particularly youth. The government has established a one-party state which suppresses political opposition and maintains an occupation army in the street, much of it made up of Rwandans. Such policies have directly contributed to continuing political and economic instability which is the cause of many of the social and economic problems in Kinshasa. It may reasonably be assumed that the government is well aware of the problems of homeless youth in the capital and that it chooses not to implement policies which would address the problem. It must be emphasised that the dilemma of homeless youth is not solely a result of Zaire's unfortunate history. Despite its pronouncements about future democratic possibilities, the Kabila government has embarked on a program of strict political repression and narrow tribal preferences which exacerbate the problems of the poor, including homeless youth.[219]

---

[218] See for example *Mare* [2001] FCJ No. 712.
[219] *JDJ (Re)*, No. A95-00633 [1998] CRDD No. 12, 28 January 1998, at para. 12.

Significantly, the Tribunal concluded that, comparing the case to *Cheung* (which concerned the deprivation of socio-economic rights in respect of children born outside the one-child policy in China), 'one would suffer harm because of the government's express policy, the second would suffer similar harm because of the *government's calculated indifference and deliberate failure to act*'.[220]

While not referring to the work of the Economic Committee in this regard, this decision represents an accurate approach to these issues. Rather than simply dismissing this case as being too difficult or beyond the scope of the expertise of the refugee decision-maker, the RPD recognized that the home state was under obligations in international law to take steps to fulfil core rights and that it had failed to take any steps whatsoever to fulfil these duties. Thus, it effectively held that a deliberate failure to act or to *take any steps whatsoever* to fulfil a duty, in the circumstances that a state has a positive duty in international law so to act, may constitute persecution where the failure has a disproportionate impact on a particularly vulnerable group such as children.[221] This willingness to scrutinize apparent resource-related explanations for a government's inability to provide protection (albeit in a different context) is also evident in a decision of the US Court of Appeals for the Ninth Circuit in which the Court queried the explanation that financial considerations may have accounted for the Russian government's inability to protect against ethnic persecution on the basis that 'any lack of funding might be labeled as a governmental choice (contrast the current military campaign in Chechnya)'.[222]

This is an approach that remains to be developed further, but the fact that decision-makers have begun to recognize that it is both feasible and

---

[220] *JDJ (Re)*, No. A95-00633 [1998] CRDD No. 12, 28 January 1998, at para. 13 (emphasis added).
[221] For authority that a 'neutral' act (such as a piece of legislation) may nonetheless result in a successful refugee claim, see *Chen Shi Hai* (2000) 201 CLR 293, in which the High Court of Australia noted that 'To say that, ordinarily, a law of general application is not discriminatory is not to deny that general laws, which are apparently non discriminatory, may impact differently on different people and, thus, operate discriminatorily': at 301 (Gleeson CJ, Gaudron, Gummow and Hayne JJ).
[222] *Maya Avetova-Elisseva v. Immigration and Naturalization Service*, 213 F 2d 1192 (9th Cir. 2000), at 1198. It is true that this involves more traditional claims based on a well-founded fear of violence, but the Court's analysis is nonetheless relevant as it displayed a willingness to scrutinize the home state's use of resources to provide sufficient protection. See also *Refugee Appeal No. 75221*, RSAA, 23 September 2005, at paras. 99–102, where the NZ RSAA discusses states' core obligations under the ICESCR in the refugee context.

appropriate to examine the fulfillment of international legal obligations by the home state, even where this involves scrutiny of a state's use of limited resources, is highly significant, and suggests the possibility of a more nuanced and sophisticated approach to socio-economic rights in refugee decision-making as the socio-economic jurisprudence evolves.

It is interesting to note that the cases that have displayed a willingness to address state obligations in a more detailed manner have concerned the most vulnerable groups. This is consistent with the views of the Economic Committee that 'even in times of severe resource constraints . . . the vulnerable members of society can and indeed must be protected by the adoption of low-cost targeted programmes'.[223] Thus, the instinct in refugee law that states do have greater responsibility for vulnerable groups is in fact reflected in the authoritative views of the Economic Committee.

This leads to a third important point, namely that the notion of what constitutes the core of a right may well be different according to the particular vulnerabilities of the applicant. In other words, decision-makers must take into account the individual circumstances pertaining to the applicant in assessing whether harm is sufficiently serious as to amount to persecution.[224] For example, in *Velluppillai*, the Federal Court of Canada held:

In both versions of its reasons, the CRDD notes: 'Short detentions for the purpose of preventing disruption or dealing with terrorism do not constitute persecution'. While this statement may be generally true, the CRDD fails to take into account the special circumstances of the applicant herein, in particular, his age and, given that age, the impact of the applicant's prior experiences, as forecasted in the foregoing quotation from the psychological report.[225]

---

[223] See CESCR, *General Comment No. 3*, at para. 12; CESCR, *General Comment No. 14*, at para. 49; CESCR, *General Comment No. 5: Persons with Disabilities*, UN Doc. E/C.12/1994/13 (1994).
[224] This is recognized in art. 4(3) of the new EU Directive on a Common Asylum Policy, which provides that '[t]he assessment of an application for international protection is to be carried out on an individual basis and includes taking into account: '(c) the individual position and personal circumstances of the applicant, including factors such as background, gender and age, so as to assess whether, on the basis of the applicant's personal circumstances, the acts to which the applicant has been or could be exposed would amount to persecution or serious harm'.
[225] *Velluppillai v. Minister for Citizenship and Immigration* (Case No. IMM-2043–99, 9 March 2000), as cited in Symes and Jorro, *Asylum Law and Practice*, pp. 79–80.

There is no reason in principle why the same approach should not be taken in cases involving a deprivation of socio-economic rights. Indeed, such an approach is increasingly being adopted in respect of such claims, as will be seen below in the context of the provision of health care, although the range of claims extends beyond this context. For example, in *KBA (Re)*, the Canadian RPD allowed a claim by an ethnic Russian citizen of Kyrgyzstan because of her 'special profile', namely that she and her children could be described as a 'family including two minor children led by a single parent female with serious mental health problems, in a country with serious social and economic problems with a documented negative effect on women and children'.[226] The evidence established that the 'high level of unemployment among Kyrgyz women; absence of programs targeted to more vulnerable, out of work women compounded the problem of the increase in trafficking and prostitution'.[227] While the RPD concluded that not all ethnically Russian citizens of Kyrgyzstan were at risk of persecution, the applicant's special vulnerability (namely, mental health problems) compounded and magnified the discrimination she would otherwise face, so as to elevate the claim to one warranting refugee status.[228] Similarly, in a decision of the UK IAT, the Tribunal allowed the claim of a Somali woman who, if returned, would have had no family support which would have exacerbated the problems of her minority group, the Eyle clan, which continues 'to live in conditions of great poverty and suffer numerous forms of discrimination and exclusion. They are considered to be inferior without full rights, hence their low social, economic and political status'.[229]

The importance of a particularized approach is underlined in the context of claims involving children. One of the most important contributions of the infusion of human rights principles into the refugee definition is the insight that 'serious harm', like other aspects of the refugee definition, has traditionally been understood in a manner that tends to reflect a male-centred paradigm. Reliance on other widely

---

[226] *KBA (Re)*, Nos. T98-03163, T98-03164, T98-03165 [2001] CRDD No. 56, 7 May 2001, at para. 2.
[227] *KBA (Re)*, Nos. T98-03163, T98-03164, T98-03165 [2001] CRDD No. 56, 7 May 2001, at para. 31.
[228] *KBA (Re)*, Nos. T98-03163, T98-03164, T98-03165 [2001] CRDD No. 56, 7 May 2001, at paras. 33–8.
[229] *G (Somalia)* [2003] UKIAT 00011, at paras. 5–9. This decision is not an example of the clearest reasoning, but it seems a fair reading to say that the economic problems (as well as risk of rape, etc.) were exacerbated because of her status as a woman.

ratified conventions, such as the CEDAW, has been central to the ability of refugee decision-makers to apply the Refugee Convention to the specific forms of harms faced by women. Similarly, it has more recently emerged that there is a need to 'fashion a jurisprudence that is responsive to the specificity of child persecution'.[230] While still at a nascent stage, there is growing recognition by refugee decision-makers that the notion of 'serious harm' must be understood in a way that is able to reflect the nature of harm faced by children.[231] The challenges posed by applications for refugee status by children are twofold: first, levels of harm that may not, in the case of adults, be sufficiently serious to constitute 'persecution' can in fact amount to persecution in the case of children; second, the notion of what we understand to fall within the realm of persecution may need to be expanded to take into account the reality of children's lives. The most important reference point in such claims is the CRC – one of the most widely ratified human rights conventions. Indeed, the CRC specifically addresses the needs of refugee children in art. 22:

State parties shall take appropriate measures to ensure that a child who is seeking refugee status or who is considered a refugee in accordance with applicable international or domestic law and procedures shall, whether unaccompanied or accompanied by his or her parents or by any other person, receive appropriate

---

[230] Bhabha, 'Boundaries in the Field of Human Rights: Internationalist Gatekeepers?', at 175.

[231] In the UK, the IAT has noted that '[e]ven though the determination of what is a "serious possibility" or "reasonable likelihood" of persecution is to be judged objectively, that objective judgment must specifically address the risk created by the facts as found and the background upon this minor. In our view the same matrix of facts for an adult claimant do not necessarily lead to the same conclusions as they would for a minor': *Jakitay v. Secretary of State for the Home Department* (Unreported, IAT, Appeal No. 12658, 15 November 1995), at 5 ('*Jakitay*'). See also *Latheef v. Secretary of State for the Home Department* (Unreported, IAT, 7 March 2002). Although the UK IAT also noted in *Jakitay* that 'there is very little authority to guide an adjudicator when a minor claims an asylum in his own right', this is an increasingly important issue that is attracting attention in both the scholarship and case law. For example, both the USA and Canada have developed guidelines relevant to claims by children: see US Children's Guidelines, pp. 2–4; Immigration and Review Board (Canada), *Child Refugee Claimants – Procedural and Evidentiary Issues: Guidelines Issued by the Chairperson Pursuant to Section 65(3) of the Immigration Act* (1996b) <http://www.irb-cisr.gc.ca/en/references/policy/guidelines/child_e.htm> at 31 May 2006 (although the latter deals mainly with procedural questions rather than substantive issues). In addition, refugee children are beginning to attract increasing attention at the international level: see for example UNHCR, *Refugee Children – Global Consultations on International Protection*, UN Doc. EC/GC/02/9 (2002b). For a particularly thoughtful discussion of these issues, see *Mansour v. Ashcroft*, 390 F 3d 667 (9th Cir. 2004), at 679–83 (Circuit Judge Pregerson in dissent).

protection and humanitarian assistance in the enjoyment of applicable rights set forth in the present Convention and in other international human rights or humanitarian instruments to which the said states are parties.[232]

With respect to the first issue – when a violation will be considered a breach of the core of a right in the context of children – a number of decision-makers (and executive guidelines in the USA)[233] have emphasized that the level of discrimination necessary to elevate a claim to one of persecution will often be considerably lower in the case of a child than in respect of an adult.[234] In addition, harm that is also faced by adults

---

[232] The RPD has specifically relied on this provision to underline the importance of assessing the refugee claims of children in their own right, rather than subsuming the claim within that of the parents or other family members: see for example *U (NX) (Re)*, Nos. T93-12579 and T93-12586 [1995] CRDD No. 74, 25 July 1995 at 18. Indeed, the Federal Court of Canada has held that the RPD commits a reviewable error when it fails 'to assess the children's risk of persecution' when the evidence suggests that they have 'claims of their own': *Akhter v. Canada (Minister of Citizenship and Immigration)* [2000] FCJ No. 1125, at para. 13. See generally CRC, *General Comment No. 6: Treatment of Unaccompanied and Separated Children outside their country of origin*, CRC/GC/2005/6 (2005). See also Jacqueline Bhabha and Wendy Young, 'Not Adults in Miniature: Unaccompanied Child Asylum Seekers and the US Guidelines' (1999) 11(1) *International Journal of Refugee Law* 84 at 87 and Ninette Kelley, 'Canadian Refugee-Determination Procedures and the Minor Claimant', in *The Realities of Refugee Determination on the Eve of a New Millennium: The Role of the Judiciary* (Haarlem, The Netherlands: International Association of Refugee Law Judges, 1999), pp. 142–55. In addition, other treaties, such as the ICCPR, also acknowledge the special position of children, and the HRC has noted that 'some provisions of the Covenant expressly indicate to States measures to be adopted with a view to affording minors greater protection than adults': HRC, *General Comment No. 17: Rights of the Child (Art. 24)*, UN Doc. HRI\GEN\1\Rev.5 (1989a), at para. 2.

[233] See US Children's Guidelines: 'The harm a child fears or has suffered... may be relatively less than that of an adult and still qualify as persecution.' The Guidelines also note that children 'may be particularly vulnerable to sexual assault, forced labour, forced prostitution, infanticide, and other forms of human rights violations such as the deprivation of food and medical treatment': p. 4.

[234] See for example, *KRQ (Re)*, Nos. T95-01828, T95-01829 [1996] CRDD No. 232, 1 October 1996 (discrimination suffered by a Black child in Russia amounted to persecution in the case of the child.) See also *Y (QH) Re*, No. V93-02093 [1994] CRDD No. 203, 4 May 1994, and *WMI (Re)*, Nos. T96-02166 and T96-02168 [1997] CRDD No. 113, 14 May 1997. See also *Refugee Appeal No. 71336/99*, RSAA, 4 May 2000, in which the Authority noted that the breaches of human rights suffered by the applicants ('specifically his right to freedom of movement, his right to work, his right to privacy and security of home and person') produced a climate of fear and insecurity that 'directly affected' his children. 'Specifically, they were denied the opportunity to learn their own language for fear of identifying them as Roma and were required to spend the first years of their lives attending separate schools, effectively pretending that they had no relationship to each other': at 14.

may have a more dramatic or serious impact on children.[235] For example, harm such as violence in the home has a significant impact on children, because they often have no alternative means of support. Thus, refugee claims have been recognized by decision-makers in both the USA and Canada where there is a risk that a child will be forced to live on the streets as a result of his or her need to escape violence in the home.[236] For example, in *MZJ (Re)*,[237] the 16-year-old applicant submitted that, as a consequence of violence in the home, he would end up on the streets in Mexico. The RPD accepted the claim, finding that 'the state in Mexico is incapable of helping the many children left abandoned in the streets ... I find him to be a child who could very easily be victimized by drug dealers, pimps and other predators on the street and that the State is unwilling — or by the sheer numbers of street children in need — unable, to protect the claimant'.[238]

Where a child will effectively have no protection or care because of the death or other absence of a parent, decision-makers have recognized that the resulting harm can constitute persecution in itself,[239] and/or can exacerbate the discrimination that the child applicant would face based on another factor such as race. For example, in *U (NX) Re*, the RPD emphasized that the child claimant's application must 'be assessed keeping in mind her vulnerability which results partly from her dependence on adults' and that '[g]iven her tender years she is unable to provide

---

[235] In *Chen Shi Hai* (2000) 201 CLR 293, for example, the High Court of Australia held that '[o]rdinarily, denial of access to food, shelter, medical treatment and, in the case of children, denial of an opportunity to obtain an education involve such a significant departure from the standards of the civilized world as to constitute persecution': at para. 29 (Gleeson CJ, Gaudron, Gummow, and Hayne JJ).

[236] For example, an Immigration Judge has recognized the claim by twins from Honduras whose experience of violence left them vulnerable to living on the street; their fear was a 'well-founded fear of future abuse because they would end up as street children': see James Pinkerton, 'Judge Grants Orphan-Twins Asylum After Hearing about Abuse by Family', in *Houston Chronicle* (Houston: 8 February 2000), cited in Bhabha, 'Boundaries in the field of Human Rights: Internationalist Gatekeepers?'. See also Bhabha and Young, 'Not Adults in Miniature', at 105, note 105. See also Jacqueline Bhabha, 'Minors or Aliens? Inconsistent State Intervention and Separate Child Asylum-Seekers' (2001) *European Journal of Migration and Law* 283 at 308, note 115.

[237] *MZJ (Re)*, No. V97-03500 [1999] CRDD No. 118, 31 May 1999.

[238] *MZJ (Re)*, No. V97-03500 [1999] CRDD No. 118, 31 May 1999, at para. 14.

[239] In *QDS (Re)*, Nos. A99-00215, A99-00256, A99-00258 [1999] CRDD No. 235, 30 September 1999, the RPD held that '[h]er young age — I think she is not yet three — alone is sufficient to establish that she would have more than a mere possibility of persecution in Djibouti should she be forced to return there, there being no close family members who would be able to take care of her': at para. 20.

for her own needs or to protect herself from harm'.[240] In that case, the RPD held that the discrimination she would face as an unprotected Tamil child would rise to persecution because of her vulnerability caused by age.[241] Similarly, in *KBA*, the RPD found that 'there is no appropriate care for the children in Kyrgyzstan other than the care that the adult claimant would provide' and that, given the mother's problems and inability to care for the children, 'the life of these children could well be affected by the conditions for children described in Kyrgyzstan . . . such as . . . problems in the economy, of female unemployment, of a lack of basic resources for shelter, food and clothing, of problems in the educational system, of trafficking in girls and women, of child abuse and growing numbers of street children'.[242] Similar concerns have been relied upon in the context of children with HIV, whose parents have died, or are likely to die of AIDS, thus rendering them particularly vulnerable to discrimination on the basis of their medical status.[243] In this regard, decision-makers should take into account the socio-economic background of the country of origin, and in particular the existence of infrastructure such as child protection services, in assessing the claims of orphaned or abandoned children, as a lack of governmental services can exacerbate the level of harm faced by children, as implicitly recognized in *MZJ (Re)*.[244]

With respect to the second key way in which the interpretation of 'being persecuted' may need to be reshaped to take into account the

---

[240] *U (NX) (Re)*, Nos. T93-12579 and T93-12586 [1995] CRDD No. 74, 25 July 1995.
[241] *U (NX) (Re)*, Nos. T93-12579 and T93-12586 [1995] CRDD No. 74, 25 July 1995, at 19. See also *QQX (Re)*, No. T95-00479 [1996] CRDD No. 52, 5 July 1996, where the RPD held, in relation to a six-year old Somali female of the Majerteen clan, that '[b]y virtue of her age and in particular, her status as an orphan without close relatives on whom to rely for support and protection, and membership in the Majerteen clan, the panel is of the opinion that were the claimant to return to Somalia she would be significantly marginalized, and such marginalization would amount to persecution': at para. 13. See also *RRF (Re)*, No. T99-00210 [1999] CRDD No. 220, 21 September 1999.
[242] *KBA (Re)*, Nos. T98-03163, T98-03164, T98-03165 [2001] CRDD No. 56, 7 May 2001, at para. 24.
[243] See *Reference V95/03256*, RRT, 9 October 1995.
[244] When engaging in the 'being persecuted' inquiry in relation to children, it is also important to note that related issues, such as whether they have an 'internal protection alternative' will also need to take into account the particular vulnerabilities of children, such that while an IPA may be found to be available for an adult, this may not be the case in respect of a child, particularly where the child would be alone in the proposed IPA. For a discussion of the internal protection issue generally, see Hathaway and Foster, 'Internal Protection/Relocation/Flight Alternative as an Aspect of Refugee Status

needs of child applicants, Bhabha and Young note that there are many types of harm that are inflicted only on children, including 'infanticide, conscription as a child soldier,[245] child abuse, incest, female genital mutilation (in countries where this practice is confined to young girls), bonded or hazardous child labour, child sale, child marriage, and religious sexual servitude'.[246] In addition, a Canadian decision provides relevant insight into the unique harm that can be visited upon children. In the context of a case concerning a boy who was bullied at school because of race and ethnicity, the RPD framed the relevant issues as follows:

> Was his school experience persecutory? From the lordly perch of an adult, one could say it was not. The reason for such a view is, of course, that the Convention refugee definition and its evolving law is mostly about adults. 'Persecution' – the single most important concept in refugee law takes adult situations into account. For example, a series of detentions in prison is deemed to be persecution. This is because the adult cherishes freedom. The regime of rights that adults have developed is in response to adult needs, the unjust denial of which is tantamount to persecution. I believe, however, that the term 'persecution', needs to be made relevant to the world of the child as well.[247]

This suggests that 'psychological' harm may be particularly relevant to claims by children. For example, some tribunals have found that the harm inflicted on a child as a result of witnessing domestic violence can amount to persecution,[248] sometimes by reference to provisions such as

---

Determination', in Feller, Türk and Nicholson (eds.), *Refugee Protection in International Law*, pp. 353–413. A detailed discussion is beyond the scope of this book. However, for authority for the particular approach to IPA in the case of children, see *KNA (Re)*, No. T97-05827 [1998] CRDD No. 148, 16 July 1998, at para. 8; and *STI (Re)*, No. T98-00366 [1999] CRDD No. 11, 18 January 1999, at para. 7.

[245] In a series of cases, the RPD has held that young Tamils were particularly at risk for forced recruitment in Sri Lanka. See *ESO (Re)*, No. U96-04191 [1997] CRDD No. 27, 21 January 1997; *O (QB) (Re)*, No. U93-04790 [1993] CRDD No. 283, 8 December 1993; *DUR (Re)*, No. U96-03325 [1996] CRDD No. 243, 16 December 1996; *MCK (Re)*, No. U97-00412 [1997] CRDD No. 156, 2 July 1997; *OXJ (Re)*, No. U96-03098 [1997] CRDD No. 224, 15 July 1997; *QJV (Re)*, No. U97-01267 [1997] CRDD No. 249, 8 October 1997; *PKM (Re)*, No. V98-00452 [1998] CRDD No. 179, 11 September 1998; *VBJ (Re)*, No. T98-09801 [1999] CRDD No. 62, 30 April 1999; *UKT (Re)*, No. T99-10465 [2000] CRDD No. 129, 12 July 2000.

[246] Bhabha and Young, 'Not Adults in Miniature', at 101–2.

[247] *BNY (Re)*, Nos. TA1-03656, TA1-03657, TA1-03658 [2002] RPDD No. 223, 19 December 2002, at paras. 7–9.

[248] *FYM (Re)*, Nos. V97-00708, V97-00709, V97-00710, V97-00711 [1998] CRDD No. 153, 11 August 1998, at para. 37. See also *FOO (Re)*, Nos. MA1-11675, MA1-11676, MA1-11677 [2003] RPDD No. 83, 16 June 2003, at para. 24, where the RPD held that the children

art. 19 of the CRC, which obliges state parties to take all appropriate measures to 'protect the child from all forms of physical and mental violence, injury or abuse, neglect or negligent treatment, maltreatment or exploitation including sexual abuse, while in the care of parent(s), legal guardian(s) or any other person who has the care of the child'.[249] Further, in *QJQ (Re)*, the RPD held that the possibility that custody would be awarded to their paternal grandfather following their father's death (based on discriminatory laws against women in Iran) constituted persecution of the children since 'the children have a fundamental human right to be with the surviving parent, their mother'.[250] In addition, the loss of or separation from a parent can itself constitute persecution, even though this would be unlikely to amount to persecution in the case of an adult.[251]

The final general point in relation to the core violations approach to persecution is that despite the focus on core violations, a non-core (or peripheral) violation may nonetheless be considered, in combination with other violations, to amount to persecution depending on the facts of the case. This general proposition is, as explained in Chapter 3, well

'suffered psychological abuse in witnessing the mistreatment inflicted by their father on their mother' and that, '[s]ince young children, who are much more emotionally fragile than adults, are involved, the opinion of the panel is that the treatment imposed on their mother and the fact that young children are powerless in such circumstances, that is, the entire situation could have a persecutory effect on them': at para. 26.

[249] *B (TD) (Re)*, Nos. T91-01497, T91-01498 [1994] CRDD No. 391, 9 August 1994, at 6. The RPD also referred to CRC art. 24 concerning the right of the child to the 'enjoyment of the highest attainable standards of health': at 6.

[250] *QJQ (Re)*, Nos. V97-01419, V97-01420, V97-01421, V98-02335, V98-02345, V98-02346 [1999] CRDD No. 189, 9 August 1999, at para. 53. The RPD added that 'the harm they would suffer as a result, through the loss of their mother's care and countless life decisions made on their behalf, is so serious and repetitious that it amounts to persecution': at para. 53. See also *QDS (Re)*, Nos. A99-00215, A99-00256, A99-00258 [1999] CRDD No. 235, 30 September 1999, at para. 20.

[251] See Simon Russell, 'Unaccompanied Refugee Children in the United Kingdom' (1999) 11(1) *International Journal of Refugee Law* 126 at 141–2. See also Bhabha and Young, 'Not Adults in Miniature', at 105; *Kahssai v. Immigration and Naturalization Service*, 16 F 3d 323 (9th Cir. 1994): 'when a young girl loses her father, mother and brother – sees her family effectively destroyed – she plainly suffers severe emotional and developmental injury'. For further support in the case law, see *QDS (Re)*, Nos. A99-00215, A99-00256, A99-00258 [1999] CRDD No. 235, 30 September 1999, at para. 20: 'I do believe it would be persecutory in itself to separate such a young child [in that case 3 years old] from her mother, where that separation would be the result of the State's persecutory intent towards the mother. I have in mind the Convention on the Rights of the Child, in particular, at Articles 9 and 16. As well, I take note of provisions in this connection, in particular, in Article 24 of the International Covenant on Civil and Political Rights'.

established in the case law and is central to the success of claims based on socio-economic deprivation. The difficulty is in attempting to discern principles or guidelines as to when such a claim will amount to persecution. In other words, when can we say that a claim based on less serious violations of core human rights (or 'discrimination' as frequently used in the case law) has 'crossed the persecution threshold'?[252]

Some courts have attempted to provide 'definitions' or state principles to explain what distinguishes a claim that is sufficiently serious from one that is not. For example, the Federal Court of Canada has posed the test as being whether the 'discriminatory acts . . . [are] sufficiently serious and occur over such a long period of time that it can be said that the claimants' physical or moral integrity is threatened'.[253] On the other hand, in the USA, it has been said that '[t]he difference between persecution and discrimination is one of degree, which makes a hard and fast line difficult to draw'.[254] As these quotes reveal, it is not possible to provide a strict guideline that will enable one to predict whether, in any given case or in light of any particular set of circumstances, a claim based on non-core violations of fundamental human rights will amount to persecution.

However, the traditional approach of decision-makers to socioeconomic claims, based as it is on an assumption about the automatic inferiority of socio-economic rights, has arguably produced the result that claims based on a violation of these rights have tended to be treated as less serious than other types of claims. Thus, in undertaking the task of weighing the gravity of the harm in a particular case, decision-makers must abandon notions of a hierarchy as between starkly defined categories, and recognize that violations of a range of socio-economic rights are capable of constituting persecution.

This is evident in more recent jurisprudence that has begun to recognize successful refugee claims based on the denial of a number of socio-economic rights (without the need to combine those violations with breaches of civil and political rights),[255] or which has emphasized the

---

[252] *Secretary of State for the Home Department* v. *Gudja* (Unreported, IAT, Case No. CC/59626/97, 5 August 1999) at 2 ('*Gudja*').
[253] *NK* v. *Canada*, Federal Court Trial Division, 9 June 1995, cited in Lorne Waldman, *The Definition of Convention Refugee* (Markham: Butterworths, 2001), at 8.80.
[254] *Bucur* v. *Immigration and Naturalization Service*, 109 F 3d 399 (7th Cir. 1997) ('*Bucur*').
[255] See for example the decision of the RPD in *KCS (Re)*, No. MA1-03477 [2002] CRDD No. 5, 16 January 2002, which upheld a claim based on socio-economic rights violations suffered by

socio-economic aspects of a claim involving a range of rights violations. An example of the latter phenomenon is provided in *OQU (Re)*, in which the Canadian RPD noted that the Cuban applicant was at risk of a range of civil and political as well as socio-economic rights violations, but placed particular significance on the fact that some of the violations 'deal with basic subsistence needs' in finding that the harm amounted to persecution.[256]

In upholding these 'accumulation' claims, decision-makers have begun to characterize the ultimate test in a way that closely resembles art. 11 of the ICESCR, namely the 'right of everyone to an adequate standard of living'. For example, the UK IAT has expressed the principle as follows:

> Agglomeration can occur if the evidence supports it by a concatenation of individual denials of rights, for example to the right to work, to education, to health or to welfare benefits to such an extent that it erodes the very quality of life in the result that such a combination is an *interference with a basic human right to live a decent life*.[257]

This is reflected in other decisions which have recognized claims based on a violation of a range of rights that amounts to a denial of 'basic living standards';[258] or would result in 'a life of destitution',[259] suggesting that the Convention regime is open to evolution in this regard.

Having considered these general principles, it is now instructive to turn to a more detailed consideration of the two issues that have proved most relevant to refugee claims based on socio-economic deprivation thus far in the emerging case law – education and health care.

Right to education and persecution

The relevance of the right to education to the persecution question was considered briefly in Chapter 3, where it was noted that courts have frequently had difficulty appreciating the independent operation of the non-discrimination clause in this context. This section attempts to rectify

---

a Palestinian living in a refugee camp in Lebanon. Unlike *GRF (Re)*, Nos. AA0-01454, AA0-01462 and AA0-01463 [2001] CRDD No. 88, 12 July 2001, the CRDD did not require accumulation with other forms of harm such as violence in order to accept the claim.

[256] No. T98-09064 [1999] CRDD No. 157, 19 July 1999, at para. 75.
[257] *Gudja* (Unreported, IAT, Case No. CC/59626/97, 5 August 1999).
[258] *Glowacka v. Secretary of State for the Home Department* (Unreported, IAT, Appeal No. 18928, 9 July 1999).
[259] *Kondratiev* [2002] UKIAT 08283.

some of the misunderstandings in the jurisprudence and suggest the ways in which a claim based on education may be relevant to the Refugee Convention.

There are two key provisions relevant to the right to education in international law: art. 13 of the ICESCR and art. 28 of the CRC. Both provisions state that '[p]rimary education shall be compulsory and available free to all'.[260] In addition, secondary education 'shall be made generally available and accessible to all by every appropriate means, and in particular by the progressive introduction of free education',[261] and higher education 'shall be made accessible to all, on the basis of capacity, by every appropriate means, and in particular by the progressive introduction of free education'.[262]

The fundamental nature of the right to education has been emphasized by the Economic Committee, which has repeated that it is 'of vital importance'[263] and is inextricably related to dignity and the 'development of the human personality'.[264] The Economic Committee has aptly described 'a well-educated, enlightened and active mind' as 'one of the joys and rewards of human existence'.[265] Denial of the right to education is recognized to be 'of particular significance in terms of its consequences, as the loss of a lifetime of opportunities and personal fulfillment that may ensue from [not] having one's right to education respected are considerable'.[266]

---

[260] ICESCR, art. 13(2)(a). Also note that art. 28(1)(a) of the CRC is in very similar terms.
[261] ICESCR, art. 13(2)(b). See also CRC, art. 28.
[262] ICESCR, art. 13(2)(c). See also CRC, art. 28.
[263] CESCR, *General Comment No. 11*, at para. 2.
[264] Ibid.   [265] CESCR, *General Comment No. 13*, at paras. 1, 4.
[266] Symes and Jorro, *Asylum Law and Practice*, p. 109. A good example of the importance of sensitivity to this issue is provided in the UK Court of Appeal's decision in *Horvath* in which the Court upheld the IAT's finding that the 'problems associated with unemployment amongst the Roma in Slovakia are due primarily to poor education and lack of professional qualifications making it difficult for them to compete successfully in the labour market', thus distinguishing this from Convention persecution: see *Horvath* [2000] Imm AR 205 at para. 31 (Stuart-Smith LJ). Neither the Tribunal nor the Court apparently made the connection between this finding and the fact that one of the bases of the applicant's claim was that his children would suffer discrimination in educational opportunities. The applicant submitted: 'The whites in the village were mostly hostile to us. There was a nursery class that my son could have attended but the teacher made it very clear to me that there were others who didn't wish me to come bothering her about my son going here': at para. 4. His son was then only 5. Such evidence was also presented in an RRT decision in which the RRT noted that workplace discrimination against minorities continued to be a problem in Bulgaria, especially

Turning initially to the right to primary education, its central importance to children has been emphasized by both the Economic Committee and Committee on the Rights of the Child. In particular, the former has explained:

> the work of the Committee has shown that the lack of educational opportunities for children often reinforces their subjection to various other human rights violations. For instance these children, who may live in abject poverty and not lead healthy lives, are particularly vulnerable to forced labour and other forms of exploitation. Moreover, there is a direct correlation between, for example, primary school enrolment levels for girls and major reductions in child marriages.[267]

The Economic Committee has emphasized that the obligation 'to provide primary education for all' is an immediate duty of all States parties[268] and constitutes part of the 'minimum core obligation' of the right to education.[269]

In light of this, there is no question that denial of the right to primary education in and of itself amounts to persecution.[270] As the RRT has stated, '[d]iscriminatory denial of access to primary education is such a denial of a fundamental human right that it amounts to persecution'.[271] In this regard, it is vital that decision-makers consider both explicit forms of denial (for example, exclusion because of birth status, political opinion of parents, race or gender),[272] as well as effective forms of denial. This is

---

for Roma, and that '[e]mployers justify such discrimination on the basis that most Roma have only elementary training and little education': *Reference V98/09164*, RRT, 12 January 2001, at 7. However, this is undoubtedly related to the fact that the evidence also suggested that 'only one-half of all students at these schools [special Roma schools] attend class regularly and only about 10 percent successfully graduate' (this decision was ultimately resolved on other grounds). This underlines the grave and continuing harm visited upon an applicant by the denial of (or effective preclusion from) education, given the lifelong impact of its denial.

[267] CESCR, *General Comment No. 11*; CESCR, *General Comment No. 13*, at para. 1.
[268] CESCR, *General Comment No. 13*, at para. 57.
[269] *Ibid.*, at para. 57.
[270] See for example, *ODO (Re)*, Nos. VA1-03231, VA1-03232, VA1-03233 [2003] RPDD No. 66, 12 March 2003. See also *Freiberg v. Canada (Secretary of State)* 78 FTR 283 (1994); *Mirzabeglui v. Canada (Minister of Employment and Education)*, 1991 ACWAJ LEXIS 20946, 28 January 1991; and *Castillo-Ponce*, 1995 US App. LEXIS 27058.
[271] *Reference V95/03256*, RRT, 9 October 1995, at para. 47.
[272] HRW has found that '[o]n nearly every continent ... children suffer discrimination in gaining access to education, based on their race, ethnicity, religion, or other status': HRW, *Failing Our Children: Barriers to the Right to Education* (2005a) p. 24 <http://hrw.org/reports/2005/education0905/education0905.pdf> at 31 May 2006.

particularly relevant in the case of girls who, in addition to being excluded de jure from access to educational institutions in some countries, are more often in practice not provided the same opportunities as boys due to endemic societal discrimination.[273] Indeed, the Economic Committee has emphasized that states must protect the accessibility of education 'by ensuring that third parties, including parents and employers, do not stop girls from going to school'.[274] In addition to parents with limited resources often preferring to educate their sons, other circumstances, such as illness, can disproportionately affect the opportunities for girls to remain in education. For example, the Committee on the Rights of the Child has noted that in many communities where HIV has spread widely, 'children from affected families, in particular girls, are facing serious difficulties staying in school'.[275] This is supported by a HRW study of the impact of HIV/AIDS in Kenya which notes that '[g]irls are more readily pulled out of school when someone in the household is ill with Aids', providing the example that in one heavily AIDS-affected province, girls make up only 6 per cent of those who are promoted to grade five after four years of primary school.[276]

In addition, discrimination on racial and ethnic grounds can often make attendance at school unbearable for children, resulting in

---

[273] For example, Brems notes that '[a] particularly serious issue is the gap in education, because education is essential for both women and men to improve their living conditions and their level of enjoyment of social and economic rights. In Sub-Saharan Africa, only 5 out of 34 countries listed in UNIFEM data have eliminated the relative disadvantage of girls in terms of secondary education enrolment (ranging from 31 girls per 100 boys in Guinea to 94 girls per 100 boys in Cape Verde)': 'Social and Economic Rights of Women', p. 23. See also ZAJ (Re), Nos. T96-04022, T96-04023, T96-04024, T96-04025, T96-04026 and T96-04027 [1997] CRDD No. 205, 15 September 1997, concerning discrimination against girls in education and other socio-economic rights.

[274] CESCR, General Comment No. 13, at para. 50. See also at para. 55: 'State parties are obliged to remove gender and other stereotyping which impedes the educational access of girls, women and other disadvantaged groups'. In para. 58, the Committee states that a violation occurs on 'the failure to take measures which address de facto educational discrimination'. See also CESCR, General Comment No. 16, which provides that 'States parties should ensure ... that families desist from giving preferential treatment to boys when sending their children to school': at para. 30.

[275] CRC, General Comment No. 3: HIV/Aids and the Rights of the Children, UN Doc. CRC/GC/2003/3, 17 March 2003, at para. 18.

[276] HRW, In the Shadow of Death: HIV/AIDS and Children's Rights in Kenya (2001) <http://www.hrw.org/reports/2001/kenya/kenya0701.PDF> at 31 May 2006. See also HRW, Letting Them Fail: Government Neglect and the Right to Education for Children Affected by AIDS (2005b) <http://hrw.org/reports/2005/africa1005/africa1005.pdf> at 31 May 2006.

de facto exclusion from basic educational facilities.[277] The willingness to consider de facto exclusion as relevant to the persecution inquiry is displayed in the decision of *SBO (Re)*, in which the Canadian RPD recognized that the minor claimants of Chinese origin were 'harassed and bullied' in Peru to the extent that they no longer wished to attend school and, since they were unable to find another school where they would receive better treatment, had suffered serious harm which 'involved denial of human dignity in a key way', since education 'is essential to the development and well-being of a child'.[278] Indeed, in a number of decisions in both Australia and Canada, decision-makers have been willing to consider harassment and bullying of school children as itself amounting to persecution.[279] For example, the RRT has recognized that Sabean Mandaean children in Iran 'suffer discrimination in schools from other pupils and teachers and constant attempts to convert them to Islam by a variety of means'.[280] In particular, when a Mandaean child and a Muslim child develop a friendship 'it is not uncommon for the Muslim child to be instructed by his or her parents to inform the Mandaean child that the Mandaean is not to touch the Muslim, nor to share food, nor to be in any sort of contact, as this would render the Muslim child 'unclean'".[281]

---

[277] HRW has also focused on this type of exclusion from education: the Executive Director explains that HRW has been able to show 'that governments' failure to address violence against certain students (girls in South Africa, gays and lesbians in the United States) or bonded child labor (in India and Egypt) discriminatorily deprives these disfavored children of their right to education': Röth, 'Defending Economic, Social and Cultural Rights: Practical Issues Faced by an International Human Rights Organization', at 70. Research by HRW specifically in the area of education has also revealed that children with HIV/AIDS in India and Russia are often pressured to withdraw from educational facilities due to severe discrimination and from pressure being brought to bear by the parents of other children: see HRW, *Failing Our Children*. In relation to Russia, see HRW, *Positively Abandoned: Stigma and Discrimination against HIV-Positive Mothers and their Children in Russia* (2005c) pp. 35–8 <http://hrw.org/reports/2005/russia0605/russia0605.pdf> at 31 May 2006. Further, severe discrimination against Dalit children in India 'encourages Dalit children to drop out of school' and the fear of sexual violence and abduction in Baghdad had resulted in only 50 per cent of girls attending schools in recent years: HRW, *Failing Our Children*, pp. 29, 38.
[278] SBO (Re), Nos. VA1-02828, VA1-02826, VA1-02827, VA1-02829 [2003] RPDD No. 17, 27 February 2003, at para. 36.
[279] BNY (Re), Nos TA1-03656, TA1-03657, TA1-03658 [2002] RPDD No. 223, 19 December 2002, at paras. 7–9.
[280] *Reference N03/46534*, RRT, 17 July 2003, at 10.
[281] Ibid.

The RRT has held that this 'has a serious psychological impact on the Mandaean child, amounting substantially to persecution'.[282]

In considering these cases, it is important to recall that the assessment is a forward-looking appraisal of the well-founded risk of being persecuted, which may be established even if the probability of being persecuted is low. This was implicitly recognized in *YSC (Re)*, in which the Canadian RPD allowed the claim of a Roma child from Hungary on the basis that:

> Now that she has been labeled as a gypsy at school, [her] opportunities have greatly diminished. As noted above, she will be considered mentally inferior by some of her teachers and may be shunted to a remedial class. She has a 50% chance of completing her primary education. If she does finish primary school, the chances of her obtaining a secondary education [are] practically non-existent since less than 2% of gypsy teenagers go on to high school and the drop-out rate is higher than the national average. The documents suggest that there is not a strong tradition amongst gypsies to get an education (although xxxxxxxx parents are not of this mindset.) These attitudes in part may be the result of the deep-seated prejudices about the abilities of gypsy children and a corresponding lack of programmes for gypsy children or even training for teachers to enable them to respond to the needs of gypsy students. Many parents simply do not see the point of encouraging their children to persevere in the face of such daunting odds.[283]

On this basis, the Tribunal concluded that 'there is a reasonable chance that the minor claimant would face persecution should she return to Hungary'.[284]

This decision is also important in highlighting that it is not open to refugee decision-makers to dismiss such claims based on 'cultural differences about the importance of education', or on the basis that certain groups of children simply do not want to go to school. Rather, the stipulation in the Covenant that primary education shall be *compulsory* 'serves to highlight the fact that neither parents, nor guardians, nor the State are entitled to treat as optional the decision as to whether the child should have access to primary education.'[285]

---

[282] *Reference N03/46534*, RRT, 17 July 2003, at 10. See also *Reference N03/47996*, RRT, 10 February 2004, at 15; *SBAS* [2003] FCA 528 (Unreported, Cooper J, 30 May 2003), at para. 63.
[283] *YSC (Re)*, Nos T97-00096, T97-00097, T97-00098 [1998] CRDD No. 26, 22 January 1998, at para. 25.
[284] *YSC (Re)*, Nos T97-00096, T97-00097, T97-00098 [1998] CRDD No. 26, 22 January 1998, at para. 26. See also *SBO (Re)*, Nos. VA1-02828, VA1-02826, VA1-02827, VA1-02829 [2003] RPDD No. 17, 27 February 2003.
[285] CESCR, *General Comment No. 11*, at para. 6.

Article 14 of the ICESCR requires that those states which have not been able to secure compulsory primary education, free of charge, undertake within two years 'to work and adopt a detailed plan of action for the progressive implementation, within a reasonable number of years, to be fixed in the plan, of the principle of compulsory education free of charge for all'. This serves to emphasize that the obligation to *take steps* is a concrete one, and a state that makes no effort to comply with arts. 13 and 14 of the ICESCR, is in violation of a core obligation. In particular, the obligation to 'ensure the right of access to public educational institutions and programmes on a non-discriminatory basis' is a core obligation;[286] thus, failure to take measures which address de facto educational discrimination is a violation of art. 13 which may give rise to a refugee claim.[287] Accordingly, the RPD was correct to point to the lack of programmes designed to combat societal prejudice as further evidence of the risk that the applicant child would be denied basic education in the above case.[288]

The Economic Committee has also made clear that where there are separate educational systems or institutions for different groups they must offer equivalent 'access to education, providing a teaching staff with qualifications of the same standard as well as school premises and equipment of the same quality, and afford the opportunity to take the same or equivalent courses of study'.[289] This is a particular issue in respect of ethnic groups such as Roma communities in various countries in which special schools are often established, notwithstanding that this is often a result of altruistic motives.[290]

---

[286] CESCR, *General Comment No. 13*, at para. 57.
[287] *Ibid.*, at para. 59.
[288] Another example is in the evidence presented to the RRT, which noted in respect of Romani children in Bulgaria that '[l]ack of effective government infrastructure and programs and economic and social factors thus combine to deprive increasing numbers of Romani youths of an education and a better future': *Reference V98/09164*, RRT, 12 January 2001, at 8.
[289] Article 2 of the *UNESCO Convention Against Discrimination in Education*, referenced by the Economic Committee in General Comment 13, at para. 34. As Nowak has noted, if governments 'wish to prevent certain groups from equally participating in the political, social, economic or cultural life in their countries, one of the most efficient methods is to deny them equal access to education or to maintain segregated educational facilities with different educational standards': Manfred Nowak, 'The Right to Education' in Eide, Krause and Rosas (eds.), *Economic, Social and Cultural Rights*, p. 259.
[290] The Committee on the Elimination of Racial Discrimination has issued a General Recommendation on the treatment of Roma, noting, in respect of the field of education, that States should adopt a number of measures, including:

Since 'there is a strong presumption of impermissibility of any retrogressive measures taken in relation to the right to education',[291] where a state removes educational opportunities from a particular region or section of the population, persecution may be established. In particular, the Economic Committee makes clear that a state must respect the availability of education by not closing private schools.[292] This may be particularly relevant in the context of the obligation in art. 18(4) of the ICCPR which requires states to have respect for the liberty of parents 'to ensure the religious and moral education of their children in conformity with their own convictions'.[293] While states are not required publicly to fund religious schools, denial of the ability to provide such education to children may give rise to a claim of persecution.[294]

Turning to denial of access to secondary and tertiary education, the jurisprudence displays far less clarity or consensus concerning the seriousness with which such denials are regarded. As noted above,

---

17. To support the inclusion in the school system of all children of Roma origin and to act to reduce drop-out rates, in particular among Roma girls, and, for these purposes, to cooperate actively with Roma parents, associations and local communities.
18. To prevent and avoid as much as possible the segregation of Roma students, while keeping open the possibility for bilingual or mother-tongue tuition; to this end, to endeavour to raise the quality of education in all schools and the level of achievement in schools by the minority community, to recruit school personnel from among members of Roma communities and to promote intercultural education.
22. To ensure that their programmes, projects and campaigns in the field of education take into account the disadvantaged situation of Roma girls and women': Committee on the Elimination of Racial Discrimination, *General Recommendation No. 27: Discrimination Against Roma*, UN Doc. A/55/18 (2000).

[291] CESCR, *General Comment No. 13*, at para. 45.   [292] *Ibid.*, at para. 50.
[293] It should be noted that the Economic Committee also includes the obligation 'to ensure free choice of education without interference from the State or third parties' in its minimum core (at para. 57), although this is subject to conformity with 'minimum educational standards', thus permitting the state to regulate this in some way. See also *SBO (Re)*, Nos. VA1-02828, VA1-02826, VA1-02827, VA1-02829 [2003] RPDD No. 17, 27 February 2003, where the RPD also relied on the right to cultural identity in the context of education.
[294] See *Bucur*, 109 F 3d 399 (7th Cir. 1997), where the court noted that if children were forced to go to public school because religious schools were intentionally closed by the government, this could amount to persecution: at 404. See also *SBAS* [2003] FCA 528 (Unreported, Cooper J, 30 May 2003), where His Honour quashed the decision of the RRT on the basis that, *inter alia*, it did not address 'the claims that the [Mandaean] children were denied the right to be taught their religion at school, were denigrated for their beliefs and put under pressure to convert to Islam in order to get access to a university education and employment in government service': at para. 59.

the Economic Committee regards the obligation to 'ensure the right of access to public educational institutions and programmes on a non-discriminatory basis' as a minimum core obligation,[295] which applies 'to all aspects of education'.[296] Coomans explains that '[t]he essence of the right to education means that no one shall be denied an education', thus 'individuals have a right of access to the existing public educational institutions on a non-discriminatory basis'.[297] As explained in Chapter 3, in those cases in which courts have dismissed claims based on a discriminatory denial of tertiary education, the reasoning in the main has relied on the incorrect conclusion that the ICESCR does not prohibit discrimination at the secondary or tertiary level. But does it necessarily follow that, having understood that this conclusion is incorrect, and that non-discrimination is a core obligation, courts will (or should) automatically hold that such discrimination is sufficiently serious as to warrant a finding of persecution?

In assessing such claims, the fundamental importance of education must be borne in mind. In particular it must be emphasized that, as 'an empowerment right, education is the primary vehicle by which economically and socially marginalized adults and children can lift themselves out of poverty and obtain the means to participate fully in their communities',[298] playing a particularly vital role in empowering women.[299] Thus, denial of access to higher education, particularly on a systemic scale in relation to particular groups, can result in marginalization and a lack of basic opportunities. This has been recognized by some decision-makers. For example, in an RRT decision concerning the treatment of Baha'i in Iran, the Tribunal noted:

> Public and private universities continue to deny admittance to Baha'i students, a particularly demoralizing blow to a community that traditionally has placed a high value on education. Denial of access to higher education appears *aimed at the eventual impoverishment of the Baha'i community*.[300]

In another decision, the evidence suggested that the Burmese government's denial of, *inter alia*, access to tertiary education for Rohingya Muslims, was aimed at 'emptying Arakan of its Rohingya population,

---

[295] CESCR, *General Comment No. 13*, at para. 57.   [296] *Ibid.*, at para. 31.
[297] Fons Coomans, 'In Search of the Core Content of the Right to Education', p. 225.
[298] CESCR, *General Comment No. 13*, at para. 1.   [299] *Ibid.*
[300] *Reference V01/13122*, RRT, 19 August 2003, at 10 (emphasis added).

though in an insidious and incremental way so as not to attract the attention of the international community'.[301]

There is no question that denial of higher education is at least a factor in assessing a refugee claim,[302] but there is growing authority for the proposition that denial of higher education can, in and of itself, constitute serious harm such as to found a claim of persecution. This is recognized by the UNHCR,[303] and in the executive guidelines in some countries.[304] There is also growing judicial authority for this view.[305] For example,

---

[301] *Reference N01/38085*, RRT, 18 February 2002, at 6, under 'Claims and Evidence'. The claim was ultimately successful, although on a range of socio-economic and civil and political rights violations.

[302] For example, in Denmark, 'prevention from obtaining future employment or education because of political activities may, in a general assessment, be an indication for future persecution': Justesen, 'Denmark', p. 326. Similarly, in the Netherlands it is clear that '[t]he exclusion from a certain education, even though the applicant fulfilled all prerequisites to be admitted, can also be considered to form persecution, if the applicant has other complaints to add to his or her claim': Dirk Vanheule, 'The Netherlands', in Carlier, Vanheule, Peña Galiano and Hullman (eds.), *Who is a Refugee?*, 505–6 (and cases cited therein). In a recent decision of the RRT, the Tribunal took into account a range of rights violations in finding that the Sabean Mandaean applicants were at risk of being persecuted, including discriminatory withholding of tertiary education: see *Reference N03/46534*, RRT, 17 July 2003, at 21.

[303] Interestingly, the 1979 UNHCR Handbook, on which many refugee decision-makers rely, notes that 'consequences of a substantially prejudicial nature' that may amount to persecution include discriminatory denial of 'access to normally available educational facilities': UNHCR Handbook, para. 54. In addition, more recent UNHCR documents reiterate this view: see for example: UNHCR, *Guidelines on International Protection, Gender-Related Persecution within the context of Article 1A(2) of the 1951 Convention and/or its 1967 Protocol relating to the status of refugees*, HCR/GIP/02/02, 7 May 2002 at para. 14; *Guidelines on International Protection: Religion-Based Refugee Claims under Article 1A(2) of the 1951 Convention and/or the 1967 Protocol relating to the status of Refugees*, HCR/GIP/04/06 (2004) at para. 17.

[304] In the USA, the INS Basic Manual sets out a number of elements 'that may be significant in determining if human rights have been violated or whether discrimination has been overwhelming', including 'exclusion from institutions of higher learning', as well as 'deprivation of virtually all means of earning a livelihood' and 'relegation to substandard dwellings': INS Basic Law Manual, p. 25. In the UK, the Home Office Guidelines also include denial of education as a relevant indicator of persecution. In *Popik*, the UK IAT cites the Home Office Guidelines as: 'Discrimination. In certain circumstances ill-treatment, which we might call discrimination can amount to persecution. This might be so if incidents of discrimination were frequent or could be expected to occur over a long period of time or if the consequences of the discrimination were substantially prejudicial for the person concerned, inhibiting his freedom to exercise basic human rights, e.g. to earn his livelihood, to practice his religion, or to have access to education facilities normally available in his country': *Popik* (Unreported, IAT, Case No. HX/70116/98, 20 May 1999), at 7.

[305] It is interesting to note that some of this authority is emerging in the recent US jurisprudence, notwithstanding the high test imposed in respect of economic deprivation claims in US law (discussed in Chapter 3). See for example, *Zhang v. Gonzales*,

in *Bucur v. Immigration and Naturalization Service*, the US Court of Appeals for the Seventh Circuit noted, in obiter, '[i]f Romania denied its Ukrainian citizens the right to higher education enjoyed by ethnic Romanians, this would be, we imagine, a form of persecution',[306] and the UK IAT has held that 'deprivation of education from primary through to further education can, in appropriate circumstances, amount to persecution'.[307] The issue has perhaps been most closely considered by the IAT in *Grecu*:

> In our view the deprivation of a person's right to university education, once he has been accepted for university and once he has embarked upon his degree course, by reason of his expression of political opinion, is worthy of serious consideration as persecution for a Convention reason. Furthermore, when that expulsion from university results in a failure to obtain employment commensurate with a person's abilities and education the question of the deprivation of the right to work is a matter which should be examined within the context of persecution for a Convention ground.[308]

Such views suggest that courts are increasingly willing to recognize the fundamental nature of the right to education, including at the secondary and tertiary level.

As recognized by the IAT, the question whether a violation of the right to education amounts to persecution depends on 'appropriate

---

408 F 3d 1239 (9th Cir. 2005), at 1247: 'Denial of access to educational opportunities available to others on account of a protected ground can constitute persecution'; *Chen v. Ashcroft*, 113 Fed. Appx. 135; 2004 US App. LEXIS 22942 (6th Cir. 2004), at 9: 'A government's treatment of individuals due to their membership in a group against whom the government's policies are directed, such as the exclusion of Jewish students from German universities under the Nurnberg Laws, constitutes persecution'; *Korniejew v. Ashcroft*, 371 F 3d 377 (7th Cir. 2004), at 383: 'we have suggested that an official policy denying an ethnic or religious minority the right to a higher education could be a form of persecution'; and *Chen v. Gonzales*, 2006 US App. LEXIS 2741 (2nd Cir. 2006) at 3. For Australian authority suggesting that discrimination in access to higher education may amount to persecution, see *Hapuarachchige v. Minister for Immigration and Ethnic Affairs* (1997) 46 ALD 496; *Harirchi v. Minister for Immigration and Multicultural Affairs* [2001] FCA 1576 (Sackville, Kiefel and Hely JJ, 7 November 2001) ('*Harirchi*') and *Chan Yee Kin v. Minister for Immigration and Multicultural Affairs* (1989) 169 CLR 379 at 431 (McHugh J).

[306] *Bucur*, 109 F 3d 399 (7th Cir. 1997).
[307] *Koffi v. Secretary of State for the Home Department* (Unreported, IAT, Case No. HX/60314/96, 17 September 1999), at 5 ('*Koffi*').
[308] *Grecu* (IAT, Appeal No. 16049, HX/64793/96 (8/1/1998)). See also *Oyarzo v. Canada (Minister of Employment and Immigration)* [1982] 2 FC 779: 'The fact that because of his political opinion and involvement he was not permitted to continue his education is, in itself, evidence of a continuing disability resulting from his political opinion and that he can expect to suffer further discrimination and disability in his country because of his opinion': at 785.

circumstances', thus it is difficult to make broad and sweeping conclusions concerning such claims. However, it is possible to identify some relevant factors that may assist in determining when denial of higher education will constitute persecution. First, it is relevant to consider the level of higher education, for example, denial of secondary education is likely to be considered more serious than denial of tertiary education, and, at the tertiary level, there are also distinctions between different levels of education (for example, college level versus doctoral studies). Another relevant question would be whether attendance at school or university is completely prohibited or merely made more difficult, for example, by the denial of scholarships, or imposition of discriminatory fees.[309] Of course, it must be remembered that in many cases, denial of access to scholarship funds or other necessary resources may amount to an effective preclusion from higher education. Another question would be whether, in respect of claims based on denial of access to public universities, private education is still available (and accessible) to the applicant.[310] In summary, if discrimination in the provision of education is present, but does not result in a de jure or de facto denial of education, the violation will properly be considered at the periphery of the right to education, and will not necessarily be sufficiently serious alone to amount to persecution.[311] It should still be considered as part of the

---

[309] See *Refugee Appeal No. 70846/98*, RSAA, 28 May 1998, at 4: 'That there may have been some discrimination in favour of Fijians in the granting of government scholarships does not amount to persecution'. See also *Reference N03/46492*, RRT, 24 July 2003 (finding that affirmative action for Malays in Malaysia not persecution of Chinese: 'The programs do not prevent the Chinese from finding employment in, and dominating the private sector or from gaining public university entrance, albeit in limited numbers'). See also *Gunaseelan v. Minister for Immigration and Multicultural Affairs* (1997) 49 ALD 594 at 6 (responding to claim of persecution in terms of education discrimination): 'As to that the Tribunal found that he was never denied the opportunity for education although he may have had to pay for his tertiary course.'

[310] See for example, *Reference N03/46893*, RRT, 5 December 2003, finding that persecution was not made out when the applicant could still attend a private school, notwithstanding inability to attend a public school.

[311] For example, in *Harirchi* [2001] FCA 1576 (Sackville, Kiefel and Hely JJ, 7 November 2001), the Federal Court held that the RRT had properly rejected the applicant's claim (finding that the discrimination in education did not amount to persecution), where the applicant's claim was primarily based on the alleged receipt of lower grades and other similar educational disadvantage because of his political opinion. Importantly, the Court noted that the RRT had accepted that 'denial of access to education could amount to persecution and could bring an applicant within the scope of the Convention'.

refugee claim, but will need to be weighed in the balance with the other forms of harm to which the applicant is at risk. However, if the discrimination amounts to preclusion of access to higher education, it is very likely sufficient to amount to a finding of persecution.

Right to health and persecution

The right to health has been described as a 'fundamental human right indispensable for the exercise of other human rights'.[312] As with other rights in the ICESCR, the right to health implies duties both of an immediate and progressive nature, although even the latter requires State parties to *take steps* progressively to realize the right.

Although an applicant may not establish a refugee claim merely on the basis that medical treatment he or she could or is receiving in the asylum state is superior to that available in the country of origin,[313] there are a number of important methods by which a refugee claim may be established based on the denial of the right to health.

States have a core obligation to 'ensure the right of access to health facilities, goods and services on a non-discriminatory basis, especially for vulnerable or marginalized groups'[314] and this obligation has been the foundation on which most successful refugee claims in this area have been based. Refugee claims have been recognized, at least in part, on the basis of denial of health care on religious grounds (for example, the RRT took into account the fact that Sabean Mandaeans in Iran 'are not adequately treated in hospitals ... and because of their alleged "uncleanness" it is difficult for them to obtain medical attention' in finding that the applicants were at risk of being persecuted)[315] and on the grounds of disability (for example, the RPD took into account the fact that persons with motor or physical disabilities in Burkina Faso cannot obtain medical care and 'medical personnel may refuse to care for them since

---

[312] CESCR, *General Comment No. 14*, at para. 1.
[313] This is because nexus would not be established in such a case: see generally Chapter 5. For a specific example of this point, see *GCH (Re)*, Nos. T99-00524, T99-00525 [2000] CRDD No. 12, 12 January 2000, in which the RPD rejected a claim from a disabled woman from Lebanon on the basis that Lebanon could not 'be expected to provide medical service to its citizens which is as sophisticated and specialized as the Canadian health care service': at para. 8.
[314] CESCR, *General Comment No. 14*, at para. 43.
[315] *Reference N03/46534*, RRT, 17 July 2003, at 21.

they cannot touch them' in finding that the applicant was at risk of being persecuted).[316] However, the successful claims to date have primarily concerned persons with HIV;[317] such applications have been recognized in the USA,[318] Canada[319] and Australia.[320] The RRT has stated that 'access to medical care and treatment is a fundamental human right and that actions amounting to an effective denial may constitute persecution'[321] and that, in certain circumstances, 'systematic denial of medical services to those with HIV/Aids ... amounts to a de facto death sentence'.[322] The fact that the country of origin is poor and undeveloped, and thus has only basic health services, does not preclude a claim where 'people infected with HIV may be denied even the low level of care available to others on account of their membership of a particular social group'.[323]

It should be emphasized that denial of medical treatment, particularly in the context that a person suffers from a life threatening illness, is itself sufficient to found a claim for persecution.[324] Although often considered

---

[316] *OGW (Re)*, No. MA1-08719 [2002] CRDD No. 53, 16 April 2002, at para. 13.

[317] Much research has been undertaken by human rights groups in recent years regarding discrimination faced by persons with HIV/AIDS in many countries: see for example, HRW, *Rhetoric and Risk: Human Rights Abuses Impeding Ukraine's Fight against HIV/AIDS* (2006) <http://hrw.org/reports/2006/ukraine0306/ukraine0306web.pdf> at 31 May 2006, particularly at 44–6 concerning denial of health care. See also HRW, *Hated to Death: Homophobia, Violence and Jamaica's HIV/AIDS Epidemic* (2004a) <http://hrw.org/reports/2004/jamaica1104/jamaica1104.pdf>, particularly at 36–41, concerning discrimination in the health care system against persons with HIV, including denial of medical treatment altogether.

[318] See 'Ostracism, Lack of Medical Care Support HIV-Positive Alien's Asylum Quest, IJ Rules' 78(3) *Interpreter Releases* 233. See also 'US-Asylum Granted to Person Living with HIV' (1996) 3(1) *Canadian HIV/Aids Policy and Law Newsletter*, in which it is explained that the IJ decision concerned a man from Togo and the Ivory Coast where, as a result of HIV, 'hospitals and families shun HIV-positive persons'.

[319] *TNL (Re)*, No. T95-07647 [1997] CRDD No. 251, 23 October 1997.

[320] *Reference N95/08165*, RRT, 6 June 1997; *Kuthyar v. Minister for Immigration and Multicultural Affairs* [2000] FCA 110 (Unreported, Einfeld J, 11 February 2000).

[321] *Reference N95/08165*, RRT, 6 June 1997, at 9. See also *TNL (Re)*, No. T95-07647 [1997] CRDD No. 251, 23 October 1997, where the fact that access to medical treatment was considered a 'low level human right' did not preclude persecution finding: see at para. 11.

[322] *Reference N03/45504*, RRT, 1 July 2003, at 5.

[323] *Reference N94/04178*, RRT, 10 June 1994, at 10.

[324] Of course, it would have to be clear that the denial was systematic. That is, a one-off instance of discrimination would not suffice. In other words, the internal protection alternative question would be relevant here: see generally Hathaway and Foster, 'Internal Protection/Relocation/Flight Alternative as an Aspect of Refugee Status Determination', pp. 353–413. The UNHCR has stated that denial of access to 'normally

as one of many factors that, in combination, amount to persecution, such denial is a core violation of the right to health and is therefore capable of constituting a refugee claim in its own right. As the RRT has held, '[d]enial of access to medical facilities *of itself is such a denial of fundamental human rights* that it amounts to persecution'.[325]

It is clear that the socio-economic background of the country of origin is relevant to these claims, in that societal discrimination and, in particular, ostracism from friends and family, have far more devastating and serious consequences in terms of health care for an applicant from a country which does not have adequate health care facilities due to a lack of resources. So much was recognized by the RRT in a decision concerning an HIV-positive man from an undisclosed country in Africa in which 'people who are HIV positive are stigmatized and isolated'.[326] The RRT found that 'families must play an integral part in caring for people in the position of the Applicant',[327] since 'the family ... has been the major structure responsible for caring for individual health and well-being, and effective government social welfare systems to supplement family support are virtually non-existent'.[328] Thus, where a condition such as HIV-positive status results in 'social stigma and ostracism'[329] from family and social networks on which the person primarily relies for care, the consequences, such as being forced to live on the street because there is

---

available health services' can constitute persecution: UNHCR Handbook, para. 54. In addition, more recent UNHCR documents reiterate this view: see for example: UNHCR, *Guidelines on International Protection, Gender-Related Persecution within the context of Article 1A(2) of the 1951 Convention and/or its 1967 Protocol relating to the status of refugees*, HCR/GIP/02/02, 7 May 2002 at para. 14; *Guidelines on International Protection: Religion-Based Refugee Claims under Article 1A(2) of the 1951 Convention and/or the 1967 Protocol relating to the status of Refugees*, HCR/GIP/04/06 (2004) at para. 17 and UNHCR, *Guidelines on International Protection: The application of Article 1A(2) of the 1951 Convention and/or Protocol relating to the status of refugees to the victims of trafficking and persons at risk of being trafficked*, HCR/GIP/06/07 (7 April 2006) at para. 15.

[325] *Reference V95/03256*, RRT, 9 October 1995, at para. 44 (emphasis added).
[326] *Reference V94/02084*, RRT, 23 February 1996, at 2.
[327] *Reference V94/02084*, RRT, 23 February 1996, at 7.
[328] *Reference V94/02084*, RRT, 23 February 1996, at 7. The claim was ultimately upheld on the basis that, *inter alia*, although the government did not directly discriminate against those with HIV, 'discrimination likely to be endured by the Applicant in the general community would be systematic and persistent and of such a degree as to amount to serious harm. It is apparent that the State is powerless to intervene and protect the Applicant at this level and that it does not have the facilities to remove him from such a discriminatory environment': at 10.
[329] *Reference V94/02084*, RRT, 23 February 1996, at 7.

no social safety net, will amount to persecution.[330] The degree to which the non-existence of government infrastructure can transform discrimination into persecution has been recognized in the context of disabled persons, who suffer severe discrimination in many countries. For example, in *OGW (Re)*, the Canadian RPD allowed a claim by a disabled man from Burkina Faso, holding that:

> The repeated and persistent injury and annoyance suffered by the disabled persons of Burkina Faso ... greatly undermine the fundamental rights of disabled persons, in particular their right to work to support themselves, thus potentially jeopardizing their survival in a country where medical care is not free of charge and where there is no system of state protection for those persons and they rely solely on the aid of their family or charities to survive.[331]

Similarly, decision-makers are displaying an increasing willingness to consider the relevance of the applicant's poverty to his/her ability to overcome discrimination and stigmatization. For example, a recent decision of a US Immigration Judge upheld a claim of a 'low income individual with HIV' from Mali on the basis that 'country conditions indicated that only individuals with wealth and large sums of money can access treatment and avoid stigmatization'.[332] In another decision, the RRT took into account evidence that in the (undisclosed) country in question, HIV/AIDS sufferers who are poor and without family support or money 'will not receive adequate treatment in a government hospital.

---

[330] HRW points to other forms of social ostracism which can lead to denial of health care. For example, their research shows that in Jamaica, 'people known or perceived to be living with HIV are denied access to public and private transportation, relegating many to lives isolated from important sources of social support and undermining their capacity to obtain even basic medical care': HRW, *Hated to Death*, p. 50. See also HRW, *Future Forsaken: Abuses against HIV/AIDS-Affected Children in India* (2004) <http://hrw.org/reports/2004/india0704/> at 31 May 2006.

[331] *OGW (Re)*, No. MA1-08719 [2002] CRDD No. 53, 16 April 2002, at para. 16. See also *IPJ (Re)*, No. A99-01121 [2000] CRDD No. 141, 11 September 2000, in which the Canadian RPD held that a young mentally handicapped woman from Lebanon was a refugee in light of the fact that documentary evidence suggested that 'what support exists for people in the claimant's situation is heavily dependant on the active involvement of family members' (at para. 6) and that, due to discrimination by her family, she was not able to receive such support. The evidence suggested that 'the government of Lebanon has made sincere efforts towards improving the situation of the mentally handicapped in that country, but those efforts are fundamentally compromised by a lack of financial resources, in particular a result of the country still recovering from decades of warfare and as well, still effectively under occupation by Syrian forces': at para. 5.

[332] This was a decision of the Newark Asylum Office, 2003. The decision of the INS is unavailable because the US Asylum Office does not provide reasons for decisions. However, the basis of the argument before the INS office was obtained through

Access will be denied due to lack of drugs, money, dedicated service providers and discrimination against PWAs [people with Aids]'.[333] Thus, the 'applicant faces a real chance of persecution'.[334]

While lack of available medical treatment for a condition is not per se sufficient to found a refugee claim, as explained above, it may be that there are issues of discriminatory allocation of resources, which may indeed be relevant to such a claim.[335] As the Economic Committee has held:

> Inappropriate health resource allocation can lead to discrimination that may not be overt. For example, investments should not disproportionately favour expensive curative health services which are often accessible only to a small, privileged fraction of the population, rather than primary and preventive health care benefiting a far larger part of the population.[336]

This has been argued in at least one refugee application. In the RRT case *Reference N97/19558*, the applicant submitted that 'the problems with the supply of drugs are part of a differential treatment of Aids sufferers not simply an issue of resources within the health system. According to him, a reported lack of treatment for people with tuberculosis mentioned in the primary decision was an isolated problem whereas he believes that lack of treatment for Aids sufferers is a political matter'.[337] The Tribunal rejected the claim, but it is conceivable that such a claim could be

---

correspondence with the lawyer, Thu Tran, and the HIAS and Council Migration Service of Philadelphia (on file with author). The asylum applicant's lawyer explained that she relied on 'a report on the INS IRC site that said AIDS victims often died alone in hospitals and were ostracized by their communities.'

[333] *Reference V95/03256*, RRT, 9 October 1995, at para. 32.

[334] *Reference V95/03256*, RRT, 9 October 1995, at para. 35. I note that the RRT also found that 'there is a real chance that the applicant will not have access to medical services, even those basic ones which are available to xxxx suffering from other illnesses; she may be excluded from employment and housing. She may suffer social isolation, being stigmatised and ostracised by many of those around her': at para. 34. However it appeared to base its conclusion on the fact that '[d]enial of access to medical services, to a person with the applicant's health status, amounts to persecution': at para. 35.

[335] Walker also takes this view. She argues that '[i]f it could be demonstrated that a country's facilities for treating HIV/Aids were inadequate or "basic" because of a discriminatory failure to devote resources to HIV/Aids treatment, then the inadequacy of the treatment ought to amount to persecution'. See Kristen L. Walker, 'Sexuality and Refugee Status in Australia' (2000) 12(2) *International Journal of Refugee Law* 175.

[336] CESCR, *General Comment No. 14*, at para. 19. See also *Minister of Health v. Treatment Action Campaign* (2002) (5) SA 721 (CC) in which the Constitutional Court of South Africa held that 'the government must provide the antiretroviral drug, nevirapine, to pregnant mothers and their children where this is medically indicated and the capacity exists to do so'. See Bilchitz, 'Towards a Reasonable Approach to the Minimum Core', at 1.

[337] *Reference N97/19558*, RRT, 22 April 1999, at 8.

established in the future, especially given that there is significant discrimination in many countries against those with diseases such as HIV. References in some decisions to the fact that a particular state of origin does not treat seriously the AIDS epidemic[338] suggest that decision-makers may well be open to such arguments where the consequences are that those with HIV/AIDS do not receive access to available treatment. The willingness of a refugee decision-maker to scrutinize the action of the government in the country of origin in terms of the adequacy of efforts in relation to HIV treatment is well illustrated in a decision of the RRT in which it held, in relation to an undisclosed country, that:

> The spread of HIV/AIDS has reached alarming proportions in the country [unnamed] and government attempts to check it appear belated and cursory; although medical and nursing staff are well-trained and competent, their efforts are clearly being hampered by poor sanitary conditions, outmoded hospital equipment and a backward health infrastructure; there exists a critical shortage of drugs to prevent or treat opportunistic infections afflicting patients in the later stages of the illness; NGOs have been hindered in their activities by logistical and attitudinal problems on the part of national authorities; the national government is dominated by a highly authoritarian regime widely condemned for its serious human rights abuses which has created an anti-humanitarian culture which cannot be conducive for creating the compassionate and caring environment fundamental for effective control of a problem of this nature. In these circumstances, it may be concluded that, at a minimum, the Applicant faces a real chance of being denied access to medical treatment and palliative care of his condition which accords with universally-accepted minimal standards.[339]

Thus, decision-makers should not automatically assume that a lack of available medical facilities is necessarily due to a lack of resources; reference should be made to the state's obligations to take steps on a non-discriminatory basis to implement the right to health in international law and to the fact that violations of the right to health will occur when a state deliberately withholds or misrepresents information vital to health protection or treatment,[340] fails 'to provide education and access to information concerning the main health problems in the community, including methods of preventing and controlling them', or 'suspends legislation or adopts laws or policies that interfere with the enjoyment of

---

[338] See 'IJ Grants Asylum to HIV Positive Man, General Counsel Issues HIV Instructions' (1996) 73(26) *Interpreter Releases* 901.
[339] *Reference V5/03396*, RRT, 29 November 1995, at 7.
[340] CESCR, *General Comment No. 14*, at para. 50.

the components of the right to health'.[341] This could well be relevant given policies in some African countries of failing to provide information about diseases such as HIV, particularly where this is a result of discriminatory attitudes and/or has a disproportionate impact on certain groups.[342]

In addition to direct denial of medical treatment, the existence of a medical condition, such as HIV-positive status, can lead to other persecutory consequences. For example, in some countries, while medical treatment is not precluded altogether, it is administered in such a way as to constitute inhuman and degrading treatment. This was recognized by the Canadian RPD in *OPK (Re)*[343] in the context of a claim from a Singaporean man with HIV, where the evidence established that people with HIV/AIDS were 'housed in a special hospital [and] ... the spatial separation has earned the Centre the reputation of an isolation ward – a medical jail where no bail is permitted ... Inmates are sentenced to confinement in bed away from the rest of society and fellow inmates'.[344] The RPD held that this amounted to inhuman treatment in accordance with art. 7 of the ICCPR and refugee status was thus appropriately recognized.[345]

Another example of the discriminatory consequences that can befall persons suffering from a particular medical condition, such as HIV/AIDS, is provided by the position of children suffering with HIV/AIDS in Kenya, where HRW reports that 'as a class, AIDS-affected children are likely to be targeted for dispossession of their property', which 'contributes to the impoverishment of children and increases the likelihood that they will be unable to enjoy the highest attainable standard of health and the right to education guaranteed them in the Convention on the Rights of the Child'.[346]

An important way in which the right to health may be engaged in refugee decisions is in respect of the obligation of states not to apply

[341] *Ibid.*
[342] For example, HRW has noted that '[t]he response of African governments to the AIDS epidemic has generally been grossly inadequate' and that a range of human rights violations and issues account for the high prevalence and widespread accompanying problems in many African countries: see HRC, *In the Shadow of Death*. It is possible therefore that the response of governments to the HIV/AIDS epidemic could found a refugee claim in appropriate circumstances.
[343] *OPK (Re)*, No. U95-04575 [1996] CRDD No 88, 24 May 1996, at para. 47.
[344] *OPK (Re)*, No. U95-04575 [1996] CRDD No 88, 24 May 1996.
[345] *OPK (Re)*, No. U95-04575 [1996] CRDD No 88, 24 May 1996, at para. 48.
[346] HRW, *In the Shadow of Death*.

'coercive medical treatments, unless on an exceptional basis for the treatment of mental illness or the prevention and control of communicable diseases'.[347] Successful claims have hence been recognized in the USA and Australia, involving cases such as electro-shock treatment of lesbians in Russia,[348] enforced health treatment on the basis of religion in Russia,[349] and subjection to a series of 'degrading and dangerous mystical treatments' in respect of an autistic boy from Pakistan who was perceived to have the 'curse of Allah'.[350]

Finally, it is vital for refugee decision-makers to be open to the way in which action by state and non-state actors can violate the right to health of particular communities, beyond the direct denial of medical treatment. For example, severe pollution and environmental degradation caused by state or non-state actors (which the state fails to control) may seriously affect the right to health of individuals and may give rise to a refugee claim where the harm can be linked to a Convention ground.[351] An example of this point is provided in the decision of the African Commission on Human and Peoples' Rights in *SERAC and CESR v. Nigeria*, which held that the Nigerian government had violated a range of rights related to the right of health, including, *inter alia*, the right to food, of the Ogoni people by facilitating and condoning the actions of an oil consortium which exploited oil reserves in Ogoniland 'with no regard for the health or environment of the local communities, disposing toxic wastes into the environment and local waterways'.[352] The Commission found that the 'destruction of farmlands, rivers, crops and animals' created 'malnutrition and starvation among certain Ogoni communities', and constituted a violation of the right to food in a number of significant respects.[353] In addition, the Nigerian government was found

---

[347] CESCR, *General Comment No. 14*, at para. 34. See also *Report of the Special Rapporteur on the Right of Everyone to the Enjoyment of the Highest Attainable Standard of Physical and Mental Health*, UN Doc. E/CN.4/2005/51 (2005), at para. 34.
[348] *Pitcherskaia v. Immigration and Naturalization Service*, 118 F 3d 641 (9th Cir. 1997).
[349] *Reference N02/43487*, RRT, 29 September 2003.
[350] Julie Deardroff, 'Mom Wins Asylum for Autistic Son with Autism', *Chicago Tribune*, 21 February 2001. See also 'INS Grants Asylum to Autistic Child Persecuted due to Disability' (2001) 78(13) *Interpreter Releases* 604. This was a decision of the INS Chicago's Asylum Office and therefore reasons are not available.
[351] See for example the ECHR jurisprudence on environmental damage, discussed above at note 150.
[352] *Decision Regarding Communication No. 155/96*, ACHPR/COMM/A044/1, 15th Annual Activity Report of ACHPR, 7 May 2002, annex V, at para. 44.
[353] *Ibid.*

to have committed 'massive violations' of the right to shelter in that, for the purposes of the oil production project, it 'destroyed Ogoni houses and villages and then, through its security forces, obstructed, harassed, beaten and, in some cases, shot and killed innocent citizens who have attempted to return to rebuild their ruined homes'.[354] While this was not a refugee claim, it nonetheless indicates the potential for such action to be considered a core violation of fundamental human rights and thus, potentially, persecution.

This example also highlights the important point that while this chapter has focused on two of the most important socio-economic rights which have emerged in the refugee jurisprudence in recent years – the right to education and to health care – it is vital that advocates and decision-makers remain open and sensitive to possibilities for future evolution. For example, the Federal Court of Canada, the Federal Court of Australia, and the New Zealand RSAA have alluded to the potential for refugee claims to be based on denial of the right to food in noting respectively that 'denial of famine relief in anti-government areas' may constitute persecution;[355] that the 'taking of harvests of those perceived as "enemies", rather than those perceived as allies, might found a conclusion of persecution for a Convention reason';[356] and that 'the right to life ... in conjunction with the right to adequate food ... should permit a finding of "being persecuted" where an individual faces a real risk of starvation'.[357] Future claims based on the right to food could be supported by reports of international organizations which have begun to establish factual links between famine and/or food deprivation and human rights violations. For example, human rights organizations have recently produced reports on the politicization of food in Zimbabwe,[358] the human rights causes of famine in Sudan[359] and violations of the right

---

[354] *Ibid.*, at para. 62.
[355] *Chan v. Canada (Minister of Employment and Immigration)* [1993] 3 FC 675, 20 Imm. LR (2d) 181 at para. 69.
[356] *Hagi-Mohamed* [2001] FCA 1156 (Wilcox, Weinberg and Hely JJ).
[357] *Refugee Appeal 74665/03*, RSAA, 7 July 2004, at para. 89.
[358] HRW, *Not Eligible: The Politicization of Food in Zimbabwe* (2003c) <http://www.hrw.org/reports/2003/zimbabwe1003/zimbabwe1003.pdf> at 31 May 2006. See also, HRW, *The Politics of Food Assistance in Zimbabwe* (2004b) <http://www.hrw.org/backgrounder/africa/zimbabwe/2004/zimbabwe0804.pdf> at 31 May 2006, especially p. 4 where HRW documents the various groups who have been excluded from purchasing food and from receiving food aid for political reasons.
[359] HRW, *Famine in Sudan, 1998: The Human Rights Causes* (1999) <http://www.hrw.org/reports/1999/sudan/SUDAWEB2.htm> at 31 May 2006.

to food in North Korea,[360] all of which challenge the common perception that hunger and famine are apolitical issues.

Conclusion

The analysis in this chapter followed from that undertaken in Chapter 3, which revealed that although refugee decision-makers have embraced the idea that economic and social rights in international law are potentially relevant to refugee claims, they have had greater difficulty in properly understanding the nature and importance of socio-economic rights in international law. The chapter thus began by evaluating the extent to which the hierarchical approach currently entrenched in refugee status assessment is consistent with broader developments in international law. It was revealed that the hierarchical approach, whether based on a model of normative hierarchy or of hierarchy of obligation, is not consistent with contemporary understandings of the interdependence of all human rights. However, the analysis undertaken in Part Two of this chapter makes it clear that by revisiting the hierarchy question, and in particular by adopting an approach to socio-economic violations consistent with international human rights law, refugee decision-making in this area can continue to evolve in a creative yet principled and legally sustainable manner so as to embrace persons fleeing the full range of human rights violations.

---

[360] Amnesty International, *Starved of Rights: Human Rights and the Food Crisis in the Democratic People's Republic of Korea* (2004b) <http://web.amnesty.org/library/pdf/ASA240032004ENGLISH/$File/ASA2400304.pdf> at 31 May 2006. In particular, Amnesty notes that the impact of food shortages in North Korea is uneven, partly because '[m]any North Koreans are victimized because of their class and social status': pp. 13–14.

5 Economic deprivation as the reason for being persecuted

> *A desire to achieve a better life or for economic improvement cannot of itself justify asylum. Nevertheless, the line between the need to escape persecution which results in penury and economic migration is often difficult to draw.*
> United Kingdom's Immigration Appeal Tribunal, 2001.[1]
>
> *The question is not, of course, whether they are economic migrants but whether they fall within the Convention.*
> United Kingdom's Immigration Appeal Tribunal, 1998.[2]

Introduction

This chapter turns to consider the second of those aspects of the refugee definition that present the most formidable obstacles to successful applications based on violations of economic and social rights, namely the question of when persecution can properly be characterized as being 'for reasons of' a Refugee Convention ground – race, nationality, religion, political opinion or membership of a particular social group.

In addition to invoking existing controversies inherent in this aspect of the definition, including the degree of causal connection required to satisfy the nexus ('for reasons of') clause,[3] as well as the appropriate interpretation of the malleable and wide notion of 'membership of a

---

[1] *Sijakovic* (Unreported, IAT, Appeal No. HX-58113-2000, 1 May 2001), at para. 16.
[2] *Bukusa v. Secretary of State for the Home Department*, 24 June 1998, cited in Symes and Jorro, *Asylum Law and Practice*, p. 109.
[3] See Foster, 'Causation in Context', p. 265; James C. Hathaway and Michelle Foster, 'The Causal Connection ("Nexus") to a Convention Ground' (2003b) 15 *International Journal of Refugee Law* 461.

236

particular social group',[4] claims involving economic and social rights also challenge decision-makers to examine the wider societal context of poverty and inequality in analysing the underlying or complex explanation for a person's predicament, rather than merely focusing on the immediate explanatory factor for the person's fear of harm.

This chapter addresses the multifaceted issues raised in the jurisprudence pertaining to nexus, as related to claims based on violations of socio-economic rights. As analysis of the case law across five common law jurisdictions reveals, decision-makers continue to display a tendency to dismiss claims involving economic and social rights deprivation on the basis that the person's fear of harm is explained by a non-Convention-related reason, such as the search for a 'better life' or for 'economic reasons'; on the basis that the Convention ground is not a sufficiently relevant factor; or on the basis that the perpetrator of the persecution has an 'economic' (and therefore non-Convention) motive for persecuting the applicant. The economic migrant–refugee distinction thus arises in a number of different but important ways in relation to the nexus clause.

When is persecution for a Convention reason? The particular challenge of socio-economic claims

The requirement that a person's fear of being persecuted be 'for reasons of' a Refugee Convention ground has emerged in recent times as one of the most difficult and least understood aspects of the refugee definition. It is well settled that the 'for reasons of' clause requires some kind of causal connection to be established between the applicant's well-founded fear of being persecuted and one of the Refugee Convention grounds – race, religion, nationality, membership of a particular social group and political opinion. In other words, refugee protection is delimited to those persons at risk of being persecuted for a relevant Convention ground and is therefore not available to all those who fear serious human rights violations. However, the nature of the causal link and, in particular, the question of the relevance of intention to the analysis, is less well settled and is subject to evolving developments in the jurisprudence.

---

[4] See Hathaway and Foster, 'Membership of a Particular Social Group'. This issue is considered in depth in Chapter 6.

These challenges are magnified in the context of claims involving economic deprivation or where economic deprivation provides the context or conditions for other types of persecution, as the close connection between such claims and the 'economic migrant' issue has given rise to much confusion in the case law. This chapter identifies and analyses the salient problems, and assesses how such problems can be resolved by reference to existing and developing principles pertaining to the nexus clause.

The desire for a 'better life': economic migrants versus political refugees

Before turning to technical and complex questions related to the nature of the causal link, an initial question that must be addressed is whether there is an inherent incompatibility between a claim based on socio-economic deprivation and the need to link persecution to civil and political status. This question arises because one of the most prevalent problems in the case law is a tendency on the part of decision-makers to focus on the perceived motivations of the applicant in leaving his/her country of origin and/or for seeking protection, and to assign economic factors to those motivations, which then automatically results in a dismissal of the refugee claim. In particular, decision-makers have a predilection to invoke concepts such as 'economic' or 'voluntary' migrant as a method of dismissing claims. The focus in such an inquiry is on identifying the 'true' motivation of the applicant for seeking protection and, when the motivation can be explained on the basis that the applicant is searching for 'a better life' or seeks 'economic improvement', then the refugee claim is denied. The question is whether such labels are relevant or helpful to an assessment of whether a person is a Convention refugee.

This issue is often invoked in assessing the credibility of the applicant, which is often closely connected with the assessment of whether the applicant in fact has a well-founded fear of being persecuted.[5] The economic position of the applicant tends to play a pivotal role in

---

[5] For example, in *Nelson* v. *Immigration and Naturalization Service*, 232 F 3d 258 (1st Cir. 2000), the Court dismissed the applicant's claim based on persecution for reasons of her political activity on the basis that she had introduced testimony that 'she moved to the United States "to have a quiet life ... and bring up her children" '. Thus, '[o]bjectively, any fear that Nelson genuinely had was not "well-founded" ': at 10.

many claims, particularly where the applicant is from a poor country. In such a case, it sometimes appears as though the applicant needs to overcome an assumption that he or she has migrated solely in order to improve his or her economic position.[6] The corollary is that decision-makers often appear more comfortable with an applicant from a poor country when he or she can establish some independent wealth. For example, in *Florante de Leon v. Immigration and Naturalization Service*,[7] the US Court of Appeals for the Ninth Circuit explained in finding the Filipino applicants credible, that:

> It is hard to see why Mr and Mrs De Leon would leave their lives as wealthy celebrities, even if the change of regimes would reduce their wealth, for the lives they now lead in America, were it not for the fear they claim. It's been a long way down, from folk singing star to night security guard at a hospital. His Philippine fame is of little economic value here, as it might be in the Philippines if he continued singing, or even just opened a bar or restaurant.[8]

In another decision, the same Court thought it significant that '[d]espite being put out of business, [the applicant] testified that she did not leave Nicaragua for economic reasons, stating, 'we have money".[9] This is a problematic trend as it raises an additional barrier to applicants from poor countries and results in discrimination against refugee applicants on the basis of their country of origin.

Conversely, the question of economic wealth can also prove detrimental to a refugee applicant, as it tends to undermine a claim based on the deprivation of economic and social rights. In a number of decisions, courts and tribunals have questioned the credibility of a claimant who professes to face economic persecution on the basis that if he or she managed to raise the funds to travel to a developed asylum state, then the refugee claim is unlikely to be true. For example, in *FOS (Re)*, the RPD explained, in concluding that the applicants' claim must be dismissed, that '[i]n the first place, although they claim they did and would face hunger, they managed to raise the necessary funds to bring four people to North America, not an insignificant sum'.[10]

---

[6] See for example *Todorovici v. Immigration Appeal Tribunal* (Queen's Bench Division, Administrative Court, Jackson J, CO/4263/2000, 23 March 2001), at paras. 22–3.
[7] 1995 US App. LEXIS 3690 ('*Florante de Leon*').
[8] *Florante de Leon*, 1995 US App. LEXIS 3690, at 4–5.
[9] See *Gonzalez*, 82 F 3d 903 (9th Cir. 1996), at 906.
[10] Nos. TA0-01421, TA0-01422, TA0-01423, TA0-01424 [2001] CRDD No. 262, 16 May 2001, at para. 15.

Similarly, in *Moro v. Secretary of State for the Home Department*, the UK's IAT noted:

> Although this appellant has been forced out of his job for political reasons, he was not prevented from earning a living, and after two years doing so was able to pay a considerable sum of money, he says, for his journey here. We do not regard that part of his history as amounting to Convention persecution.[11]

The assumption that the mere fact of having garnered the necessary resources to seek protection in another country precludes a credible claim based on socio-economic deprivation is highly questionable for two reasons. First, whether or not an applicant has money is irrelevant to many types of claim based on the deprivation of economic and social rights, since a person may suffer a range of socio-economic harm, such as denial of access to educational and health care facilities or access to certain types of employment, at a level sufficient to constitute persecution, regardless of the amount of money to which the person has access. In other words, not all claims based on the denial of fundamental socio-economic rights require that the applicant be destitute. Second, even in those cases where one may well expect a claimant not to have money (for example, where the claim is based on the complete denial of an ability to make a living), the fact that he or she does manage to fund passage to a developed country does not automatically impugn credibility, since it is extremely common for refugee claimants to call on the resources of a wide range of friends and family (and even to enter into significant debt, including debt bondage) in order to secure the ability to flee from a persecutory situation. This serves to underline the problem with preconceived assumptions about the profile of a 'true' or 'genuine' refugee, as claims risk being summarily dismissed without regard to the true position of the individual applicant.

---

[11] Unreported, IAT, Appeal No. HX-72022-98, 11 September 2000, at para. 8. A good example of this is provided in *Zhang v. Gonzales* 408 F 3d 1239 (9th Cir. 2005) in which the IJ had dismissed the applicant's claim on the basis, *inter alia*, that '[i]f funds were available to pay for her to be smuggled out of China' then 'surely' funds were available to counteract the persecutory consequences of her parents' violation of the one-child policy: see at 1248. The Ninth Circuit overturned this decision on the basis that there was no evidence to support this finding. See also *Zalega v. Immigration and Naturalization Service*, 916 F 2d 1257 (7th Cir. 1990) in which the Court found that 'Zalega was able to start a business and support himself consistent with his prior standard of living. He presumably had enough money to buy land and a round-trip airline ticket to the United States': at 1260.

Another salient way in which the 'economic migrant' issue arises is by the application of a simple dichotomy: either the applicant is a genuine refugee *or* he/she is seeking a better economic future. However, the problem with this label is that where the persecution is based on the deprivation of economic and social rights, such claims inevitably and necessarily involve the search for better economic (and life) opportunities; thus, the invocation of the economic migrant label automatically precludes such claims.[12] For example, in *Peco*,[13] the UK Special Adjudicator concluded that the facts of the case pointed to 'a deliberate decision by both families to do something to improve the prospects of their young people rather than a departure of necessity to escape persecution',[14] and thus the application for refugee status was dismissed. However, the IAT overturned this decision on the basis that the applicant did face persecution: 'based on evidence first as to discrimination in fields of housing, employment and welfare, with the latter having particular significance due to the difficulties in obtaining employment and secondly the uncertainty as to return to Bosnia'.[15] Similarly, in another UK decision, the Special Adjudicator decided that the appellant left his country 'for reasons of personal convenience, for example the lack of educational and employment opportunities',[16] and was thus not a refugee. However, on appeal the IAT held that the adjudicator had focused on the wrong question, noting, '[t]hat he left because of the lack of opportunities and facilities is undoubtedly correct; the question is whether that was for personal convenience or because the situation was

[12] See, for example, *Mohamad v. Secretary of State for the Home Department* (Unreported, IAT, Appeal No. HX/74489/94, 21 October 1996), where the applicant claimed that he had been dismissed from his employment in Sudan and was unlikely to gain other employment for political reasons. The Secretary of State dismissed the claim on the basis that 'your reasons for remaining in the United Kingdom were economically motivated and that this further detracted from your credibility': at 3. Similarly, the adjudicator held that 'the appellant has now become an economic migrant': at 5. The IAT declined to interfere with the adjudicator's factual findings. For a blatant example of a decision-maker taking the view that the label 'economic migrant' excludes claims based on socio-economic deprivation, see *Refugee Appeal No. 70618/97*, RSAA, 30 June 1989, where the Tribunal stated that 'asylum-seekers who are properly characterized as economic migrants will normally be excluded from the protection of the Refugee Convention': at 8. But, of course, this begs the question as to who is properly characterized as an 'economic migrant'.
[13] Unreported, IAT, Appeal No. HX-74935-94, 12 November 1996.
[14] *Peco* (Unreported, IAT, Appeal No. HX-74935-94, 12 November 1996), at 5.
[15] *Peco* (Unreported, IAT, Appeal No. HX-74935-94, 12 November 1996), at 6.
[16] *El Deaibes* (Unreported, IAT, Appeal No. CC-06299-2001, 12 July 2002), at para. 12 ('*El Deaibes*').

so intolerable that he could not reasonably be expected to remain',[17] and that '[e]conomic hardship and persecution are distinct, although it is possible, if the hardship is sufficiently severe, for the two to merge with each other'.[18]

These cases highlight the fact that in claims involving economic and social rights, framing the pivotal inquiry as being whether the applicant was seeking to 'improve prospects' or opportunities is unhelpful and indeed dangerous, as it obscures the salient legal question of whether the person fears being persecuted for a Refugee Convention reason. Indeed, the artificiality of the dichotomy is highlighted by the fact that all persons seeking refuge in a state other than their own are, to a certain extent, seeking a 'better life' for themselves and their family, although this insight is rarely applied in respect of more traditional claims. However, decision-makers are increasingly displaying sensitivity to the fact that the two concepts are not mutually exclusive. For example, in a decision of the New Zealand RSAA holding that a Roma family from the Czech Republic had made out a successful refugee claim based on life-long economic deprivation, the Authority noted:

> The appellant and his wife decided to leave the Czech Republic because they wanted a better life, especially for their children, who they wanted to live in an environment of safety and not of fear.[19]

The obfuscatory nature of an analysis focused primarily on whether the applicant is seeking 'better opportunities' has been explicitly acknowledged by courts and tribunals, which are becoming increasingly vocal in criticizing such an approach. In the UK, the Queen's Bench Division has held, in *R (on the application of Vuckovic)* v. *Special Adjudicator and anor*,[20] that the Special Adjudicator erred in law in holding that the applicant was 'to be treated as an economic migrant and to be refused asylum',[21] given that the claim was based at least in part on discrimination against Croatian Serbs in employment.[22] Indeed, the IAT has held that 'a positive finding that the Appellant and his wife were economic migrants'

---

[17] *El Deaibes* (Unreported, IAT, Appeal No. CC-06299-2001, 12 July 2002).
[18] *El Deaibes* (Unreported, IAT, Appeal No. CC-06299-2001, 12 July 2002), at para. 11.
[19] See *Refugee Appeal No. 71193/98*, RSAA, 9 September 1999, at 12.
[20] Queen's Bench Division (Administrative Court), CO/3021/2000, 18 December 2000 (Newman J) ('*Vuckovic*').
[21] *Vuckovic*, Queen's Bench Division (Administrative Court), CO/3021/2000, 18 December 2000 at para. 15 (Newman J).
[22] *Vuckovic*, Queen's Bench Division (Administrative Court), CO/3021/2000, 18 December 2000 at para. 16 (Newman J).

represents 'an unfortunate error in approach to asylum appeals'.[23] It has explained:

> It may well be that in reaching the conclusion that the story given is not worthy of belief, the Adjudicator comes to the conclusion that an Appellant is motivated by reasons such as looking for a better life. That does not, however, mean that there is any issue which requires positive findings that an Appellant is an economic migrant any more than that he is a bogus refugee – neither of these expressions have any place in determinations in these Tribunals and, with great respect, in our view, *they should be avoided*. The question is not, of course, whether they are economic migrants but whether they fall within the Convention.[24]

A similar conclusion should be drawn in respect of the increasing tendency on the part of decision-makers to consider whether an applicant is a 'voluntary migrant', presumably in contrast to genuine refugees who are necessarily 'forced migrants'. This has proven to be especially pertinent to claims by women and children who fear being trafficked for the purposes of prostitution or other forms of forced labour, either based on the fact that they have already been trafficked to the country of asylum and/or that they are particularly at risk of falling victim to traffickers on return to their home country (or at risk of harm from those to whom they are indebted as a result of having been trafficked in the past). Where the applicant was 'duped' into the trafficking process, decision-makers appear to be somewhat amenable to upholding refugee claims.[25] However, where the applicant was not initially kidnapped but rather either lured into a trafficking ring based on false promises of high-paying employment in a foreign country or, in some cases, became involved with traffickers knowing that the work to be undertaken in the foreign country would involve some kind of prostitution activities (but often not realizing that this would involve being held in slavery-like conditions), decision-makers have a tendency to approach the assessment of claims from the perspective that the applicant is a person in poor economic circumstances merely searching for a better life, rather than seeking to escape harm due to the applicant's civil or political status. One of the most common methods of dismissing such claims is by

---

[23] *Bukasa v. Secretary of State for the Home Department* (Unreported, IAT, Appeal No. HX/60692/96, 24 June 1997), at 4, cited in Symes and Jorro, *Asylum Law and Practice*, p. 109.
[24] *Ibid.* (emphasis added).
[25] However, there is generally much inconsistency in respect of these claims: see further below at notes 131–40.

reference to the concept of 'voluntariness'.[26] For example, in one claim before the RPD involving an 18-year-old girl from China who alleged that she had been forcibly smuggled to Canada by her parents and would be at risk of being re-trafficked on return, the applicant submitted that her potential mistreatment could be causally liked to her powerlessness in Chinese society, which was, in turn, a direct consequence of her youth, rural status and particularly gender.[27] She presented evidence that

> young women in rural Fuzhou and Wenzhou face numerous other gender-based disadvantages. Among other things, they are increasingly likely to be denied a basic education, and they often face the prospect of being forced by their families to enter into an arranged marriage . . . In particular, many young persons (especially girls) are not registered with the state authorities at birth, either as state-imposed punishment for their parents' breach of the one-child policy, or because of their parents' efforts to avoid detection or punishment for this breach . . . Unregistered status brings with it a number of legal, social and economic disadvantages.[28]

Ultimately in this case the Tribunal reduced the question to whether there was 'volition in a particular claimant [in] that she adverted to a risk of harm of her own will' and thus 'is a voluntary economic migrant taking risks to secure a better living for herself and perhaps her family'.[29]

The problem with this analysis is that whether or not there was some volition on the part of an applicant in the initial decision to depart his or her home country (and note that the question of volition is very

---

[26] This is particularly prevalent in a series of RPD decisions concerning women from Thailand: see *PYM (Re)*, No. U98-01933 [1999] CRDD No. 163, 3 June 1999, at para. 24; *HDO (Re)*, T98-17677 [1999] CRDD No. 116, 26 May 1999, at para. 24; and *NWX (Re)*, T99-01434 [1999] CRDD No. 183, 25 August 1999.

[27] *TZU*, No. TAO-03660 [2000] CRDD No. 249, 20 October 2000, at 14.

[28] *TZU*, No. TAO-03660 [2000] CRDD No. 249, 20 October 2000, at 15. See also a series of Canadian cases regarding Chinese minors smuggled into the USA by their parents – who paid 'snakeheads' – in which the claims were refused on the notion that they were voluntary, economic migrants: *ICR (Re)*, Nos. V99-03509, V99-03511, V99-03532, V99-03536, V99-03540, V99-03544, V99-03547, V99-03548 [2000] CRDD No. 199, 14 February 2000; *TEK (Re)*, No. V99-03528 [2000] CRDD No. 21, 27 January 2000; *SNJ*, No. V99-03818 [2000] CRDD No. 119, 8 June 2000; *YDJ (Re)*, Nos. V99-02955, V99-02956, V99-02953, V99-02914, V99-02933, V99-02912, V99-02951, V99-02913, V99-02960, V99-02927, V99-02931, V99-02919, V99-02928, V99-02949, V99-02923, V99-02961 [2000] CRDD No. 401, 9 May 2000; *AFW (Re)*, No. V99-03532 [2001] CRDD No. 215, 12 October 2001; *END (Re)*, No. VA1-01344 [2002] CRDD No. 22, 3 January 2002. See also *Zheng v. Canada (Minister of Citizenship and Immigration)* [2002] FCJ No. 580. By contrast, in *THK (Re)*, VA0-02635 [2001] CRDD No. 30, 22 March 2001, the RPD found that the minor was not a voluntary migrant in the extreme facts of that case (the child had suffered violence and abuse at the hands of his father).

[29] *TZU*, No. TAO-03660 [2000] CRDD No. 249, 20 October 2000, at 30.

problematic in the context of children[30] and even of women who may face few alternative prospects in their home country),[31] the question nonetheless remains whether he or she is at risk of future persecution for a Refugee Convention ground.[32] If the applicant does face such a risk,

---

[30] So much was acknowledged by Gibson J in *Li v. Canada (Minister of Citizenship and Immigration)* [2000] FCJ No. 2037 (*'Li'*), in respect of a claim involving children from the Fuijian Province in China who were smuggled into Canada at the behest of their parents in order to work. Gibson J accepted 'without reservation' the argument of counsel for the applicants, which included the submission that 'the applicants could not "consent" to being "trafficked", whether or not they were of "tender years" ': at paras. 23, 26. This has also been recognized in some RPD decisions: see *PEF (Re)*, No. VA0-00091 [2000] CRDD No. 110, 29 May 2000, in which the RPD recognized that the claimant had not wanted to leave China, but that his family forced him to do so: at paras. 5, 18–20. See also *ZOI (Re)*, Nos. V99-02926, V99-02950, V99-02926, V99-02950 [2000] CRDD No. 91, 9 May 2000, at paras. 17, 24–5. However, the case law is very mixed, with many RPD decisions rejecting these claims based on the finding that the claimant was a 'voluntary migrant'.

[31] See the report prepared by the United Nations Children's Fund ('UNICEF'), United Nations Office of the High Commissioner for Refugees ('UNOHCR') and the Organization for Security and Cooperation in Europe ('OSCE')/Office for Democratic Institutions and Human Rights, entitled *Trafficking in Human Beings in Southeastern Europe* (2002) <http://www.unicef.org/ceecis/Trafficking.Report.2005.pdf> at 31 May 2006, where it is noted that, 'The root causes of migration and vulnerability to trafficking include not only the weak economic situation of women but also discrimination against them in their countries of origin. Discrimination against women in the labour market, growing unemployment among women, lower wages, lack of skills and training – essentially, the feminisation of poverty – all these factors contribute to the growing number of young women willing to take their chances by searching for opportunities and a better life in the West': at 6. These findings concerning the root causes of trafficking are well documented in the burgeoning literature, both in terms of country-specific research, and in terms of international legal remedies, that has emerged on the trafficking issue in recent years. As has been noted by Human Rights Watch, the focus in the international community has shifted from viewing trafficking as 'solely a criminal justice issue' to one requiring the remedy of the 'underlying human rights abuses that created the conditions for trafficking', including 'poverty, discrimination – particularly against women, children and minorities – violence, and general insecurity often related to armed conflict': Widney Brown, 'A Human Rights Approach to the Rehabilitation and Reintegration into Society of Trafficked Victims' (Speech delivered at the 21st Century Slavery – The Human Rights Dimension to Trafficking in Human Beings Conference, Rome, 15–16 May 2002).

[32] This was acknowledged in the RPD decision in *GVP (Re)*, No. T98-06186 [1999] CRDD No. 298, 2 November 1999, involving a Thai sex worker who feared persecution by criminal gangs to whom she owed a debt bondage if she returned to Thailand. The majority held that '[t]he fact that the claimant made an individual choice to become a sex trade worker and remain in the sex trade for some time cannot be reason to find that the ground of membership in a particular social group does not apply in this case': at para. 27. The dissenting judge found that 'the claimant came to Canada, not because she was fleeing Thailand, but because she felt that her earnings in Thailand would be insufficient for her needs. Therefore, I find that her reason for leaving Thailand was for economic reasons, and as such has no nexus to a Convention ground': at para. 33.

issues such as volition and economic opportunism simply have no relevance to the inquiry as a matter of law.[33] An example of the correct approach is provided in the decision of the Australian RRT in *Reference N02/42226*, in which the Tribunal recognized that the applicant left Uzbekistan to 'improve her economic situation in the context of a declining economy and consequent limited employment opportunities in Uzbekistan, especially for women',[34] but nonetheless considered whether her subsequent experience of being trafficked and the risk of harm that followed from that experience constituted persecution for a Refugee Convention reason.

The High Court of Australia has acknowledged that there are dangers in 'creating and applying a scheme for classifying claims to [refugee] protection' in that such classification carries the risk 'that the individual and distinctive features of a [refugee] claim are put aside in favour of other, more general features which define the chosen class'.[35] While these comments were made in the context of an artificial dichotomy constructed in the Australian jurisprudence concerning claims by homosexual men and women, the Court's critique remains valid for other types of refugee claims, and particularly to those where claims are classified using such crude tools as the labels 'economic migrants' and 'voluntary refugees'. The Refugee Convention sets out well-defined and closely circumscribed grounds for exclusion[36] and it is clear that none of them includes the fact that a person is a 'voluntary migrant',

---

[33] The UNHCR has recognized that '[t]he forcible or deceptive recruitment of women or minors for the purposes of forced prostitution or sexual exploitation is a form of gender-related violence or abuse that can even lead to death... In individual cases, being trafficked for the purposes of forced prostitution or sexual exploitation could therefore be the basis for a refugee claim where the State has been unable or unwilling to provide protection against such harm or threats of harm': UNHCR, *Guidelines on International Protection: Gender-Related Persecution within the Context of Article 1A(2) of the 1951 Convention and/or its 1967 Protocol relating to the Status of Refugees*, UN Doc. HCR/GIP/02/02 (2002a), at para. 18. The UNHCR speaks of 'deceptive recruitment', thus going beyond the cases where women are abducted to include those where the woman was, for example, deceived as to the true nature of the work involved. Clearly the UNHCR does not accord any relevance to the initial motivation of the applicant. See also UNHCR, *Guidelines on International Protection: The application of Article 1A (2) of the 1951 Convention and/or Protocol relating to the status of refugees to the victims of trafficking and persons at risk of being trafficked*, HCR/GIP/06/07 (7 April 2006).

[34] *Reference N02/42226*, RRT, 30 June 2003, at 11.

[35] *Appellant S395/2002 v. Minister for Immigration and Multicultural Affairs; Appellant S* (2003) 216 CLR 473 at 499 (Gummow and Hayne JJ in the majority); at 495–6 (McHugh and Kirby JJ, also in the majority).

[36] See Article 1(F).

'economic migrant' or seeks a 'better life'. Nor is it open to state parties to introduce additional grounds for exclusion. Thus decision-makers should assess such claims within the parameters of existing principle and doctrine. It is true that many of the cases in which such issues are invoked raise difficult and challenging questions for decision-makers, some of which will be explored further below. However, it is imperative that these emerging claims be dealt with in the same way as other types of claims that have challenged our vision of Refugee Convention refugees, such as gender-based claims and claims from homosexual men and women, that is, 'fairly and squarely in terms of the refugee definition',[37] rather than by reference to irrelevant and confusing additional labels.

The causal connection to a refugee convention ground

Having established that there is no inherent incompatibility between refugee claims based on socio-economic deprivation and the need to establish nexus to a Convention ground, it is necessary to turn to the precise issues involved in establishing nexus and identify the particular challenges that arise in the context of socio-economic claims. This section deals with various aspects of the causal connection, that is, with issues related to the degree of connection required between the Convention ground and predicament of the applicant. The following section considers the important question of intention.

Sole versus mixed motives: particular difficulties in economic claims

It is well settled in the case law that it is not necessary for an applicant to establish that his or her risk of harm is *solely* attributable to a Convention-related ground, since decision-makers have recognized that to impose such a test 'would render the Convention protection largely ineffectual'.[38] The corollary is that a refugee claim may be established when there are 'mixed motives' for the applicant's fear of harm or decision to seek protection. As the Canadian Federal Court has explained,

---

[37] *Re RS, Refugee Appeal No. 135/92*, RSAA, 19 June 1993, at 8. This comment was made in the context of the internal protection question, and the Authority was particularly commenting on the trend in other jurisdictions to formulate the question as being one of internal flight. However, the same sentiment applies in the present context.

[38] *Minister for Immigration and Multicultural Affairs v. Abdi* (1999) 162 ALR 105 at 112 ('*Abdi*'). For further authority on this point, see discussion and cases cited in Foster, 'Causation in Context', pp. 269–70.

'people frequently act out of mixed motives, and it is enough for the existence of political motivation that one of the motives was political'.[39] However, the application of this principle has proved problematic in two important ways in the context of claims based on or involving a socio-economic element.

First, the correct application of this principle means that even in cases where the applicant has truly chosen to seek refugee status in the asylum state for economic reasons (unrelated to the fear of being persecuted), this does not preclude a claim if the person nonetheless has a well-founded fear of being persecuted in his or her home state for a Convention reason. As Hathaway states, the 'fact of this auxiliary [economic] motivation is quite irrelevant to the issue of refugee status' where the person has a genuine fear of persecution on Convention grounds.[40]

However, decision-makers continue to display a tendency to focus on non-Convention (economic) factors as a method of dismissing claims, ignoring the simultaneous presence of Refugee Convention-related harm.[41] While such mistakes are often corrected on appeal, the tendency is nonetheless worrying, given that so few cases reach the appellate level. As explained by the US Court of Appeals for the Ninth Circuit, it is 'quite reasonable' for an individual fleeing persecution 'to seek a new homeland that is insulated from the instability [of his home country] and that offers more promising economic opportunities'.[42] This affirmed the Court's conclusion in an earlier decision that it is not 'inconsistent with a claim of fear of persecution that a refugee, after he flees his homeland, goes to the country where he believes his opportunities will be best'.[43]

The second issue in this respect is that while decision-makers often acknowledge in principle that the nexus clause does not impose a 'sole cause' test, and thus a successful claim may be established where there are 'mixed motives' or mixed factors which explain the fear of being persecuted, in practice decision-makers have a tendency to reduce a

---

[39] *Zhu v. Canada*, 1994 ACWSJ LEXIS 68679; 1994 ACWSJ 402290; 46 ACWS (3d) 715 ('*Zhu*').
[40] Hathaway, *The Law of Refugee Status*, pp. 118–19.
[41] See, for example, the decision of the IJ in *Arout Melkonian v. Ashcroft*, 320 F 3d 1061 (9th Cir. 2003), at 1071, which dismissed the applicant's claim because his reasons for leaving Abkhazia were in part to 'improve himself and his family economically', thus disqualifying him from a grant of asylum: at 1072.
[42] *Arout Melkonian v. Ashcroft*, 320 F 3d 1061 (9th Cir. 2003), at 1071.
[43] *Arout Melkonian v. Ashcroft*, 320 F 3d 1061 (9th Cir. 2003), citing *Garcia-Ramos v. Immigration and Naturalization Service*, 775 F 2d 1370 (1985), at 1374–5.

complex predicament, or a persecutor's motives, to a simple 'economic' explanation, thus dismissing the claim due to failure to establish the requisite nexus. This often operates as an *effective* sole cause test, in that decision-makers appear to assume that, as soon as the relevant factor or motive can be described as economic, the claim falls outside the Refugee Convention. In such cases, since only one factor or motive is identified by the decision-maker, the 'mixed motive' doctrine is not even enlivened. While this is an issue that also arises in more 'traditional' types of refugee claims, it appears that it is particularly acute in cases involving economic elements, perhaps indicating decision-makers' discomfort with cases that resemble those of 'economic migrants'.

A number of courts have emphasized that when decision-makers treat 'the presence of a nonpolitical [often economic] motive as evidence of the absence of a political motive', this constitutes an error of law.[44] The deficiency in the either/or reasoning, often employed by tribunals such as the US BIA, is well highlighted in the decision of the US Court of Appeals for the Second Circuit in *Osorio* v. *Immigration and Naturalization Service*, a case involving a Guatemalan union leader who feared persecution by the government as a result of his union activities.[45] The BIA rejected the claim on the basis that the 'fundamental nature' of the dispute between Osorio and the government was 'economic' and therefore his well-founded fear of being persecuted could not be said to be 'for reasons of' political opinion or membership of a particular social group.[46] In overturning the BIA decision, the Court noted that to 'jump from the characterisation of a dispute as economic to the conclusion that Osorio is ineligible for asylum, the BIA must have assumed that if a dispute is properly characterised as economic, it cannot be characterised as political'.[47] The Court held that this was an error because the nexus clause 'does not mean persecution *solely* on account of the victim's

---

[44] For example, in *Sarrazola* (2001) 107 FCR 184, the Full Court of the Federal Court of Australia stated: 'To elevate having the means to pay to be the *only* reason motivating the respondent's persecutor is, bearing in mind "the broad policy of the Convention"... illogical and wrong... The RRT cannot immunise itself from review by correctly stating the tests to be applied in order to determine whether the causal nexus requirements of Art 1(2A) are satisfied. It must also correctly apply the tests': at 199 (emphasis in original). See also *Villasenor* v. *Immigration and Naturalization Service*, 2000 US App. LEXIS 781 (9th Cir. 2000), at 2; *Tarubac* v. *Immigration and Naturalization Service*, 182 F 3d 1114 (9th Cir. 1999), at 1119; and *Borja* v. *Immigration and Naturalization Service*, 175 F 3d 732 (9th Cir. 1999) ('*Borja*').
[45] 18 F 3d 1017 (2nd Cir. 1994) ('*Osorio*').   [46] *Osorio*, 18 F 3d 1017 (2nd Cir. 1994), at 1028.
[47] *Osorio*, 18 F 3d 1017 (2nd Cir. 1994), at 1028.

political opinion' and that in light of the evidence that Osorio and his union posed a political threat to the Guatemalan government's authority, '[a]ny attempt to unravel economic from political motives is untenable'.[48] The BIA's decision thus revealed 'a complete lack of understanding of the political dynamics in Guatemala'.[49] This underlines the need for decision-makers to be attuned to the wider context of an individual claim.[50]

Notwithstanding this acknowledgement, however, courts continue to apply this binary reasoning – either a dispute is economic or it is political – in assessing cases involving economic issues.[51] This tends to occur in a number of different types of case – where the subject matter of the dispute involves an economic element, and where the sanction involves an economic element.

An excellent example of this phenomenon is provided in the decision by the US Court of Appeals for the Fifth Circuit in *Ontunez-Tursios v. Ashcroft*,[52] a case involving the claim by a Honduran man who feared for his life as a result of his activities as a key member of a cooperative of peasant farmers aiming to gain ownership of land via an agrarian reform plan, opposed by a group of landlords.[53] The refugee claim was dismissed by both the IJ and the BIA on the basis that 'his conflict with the landlords was not shown to arise other than solely from a private fight over land'.[54] Ontunez appealed to the Fifth Circuit, submitting that the BIA 'looked at his evidence only as proof of economic conflict without considering that it also demonstrates a political struggle', and that the BIA had therefore erred in requiring him to demonstrate that his persecution was 'primarily on account of a protected ground rather than merely that his persecution had some nexus to a protected ground'.[55] The majority of the

---

[48] *Osorio*, 18 F 3d 1017 (2nd Cir. 1994), at 1029.   [49] Ibid.
[50] For another positive example of the Ninth Circuit taking a broad approach to the political context of an 'economic dispute', see *Agbuya v. Immigration and Naturalization Service*, 1999 US App. LEXIS 21091 (9th Cir. 1999) ('*Agbuya*').
[51] For some early examples, see Hathaway, *The Law of Refugee Status*, p. 115. See also Foster, 'Causation in Context', pp. 270–4, and Spijkerboer, *Gender and Refugee Studies*, pp. 74–6, where he notes a similar phenomenon in Dutch cases which led him to conclude that 'the opposition between "economic" and "political" refugees is so strong and so total in the context of refugee law that anything related to the economic is assumed to be non-political': p. 76
[52] 303 F 3d 341 (5th Cir. 2002) ('*Ontunez-Tursios*').
[53] For a description of background, see *Ontunez-Tursios*, 303 F 3d 341 (5th Cir. 2002), at 345–9.
[54] *Ontunez-Tursios*, 303 F 3d 341 (5th Cir. 2002), at 350.
[55] *Ontunez-Tursios*, 303 F 3d 341 (5th Cir. 2002), at 352.

Fifth Circuit dismissed his appeal, holding that the BIA was correct to conclude that the evidence 'showed no motive of the persecutors other than a private, economic one and failed to establish persecution to any extent on account of or motivated by Ontunez's political opinion or membership of a particular social group'. Importantly, it held that the BIA 'did not disregard mixed motive; Ontunez *failed to meet his burden of proof of a mixed motive*'.[56] Thus the majority found that there was only *one* explanation for the applicant's predicament – economic – thus precluding a nexus finding.

In a strongly worded dissent, which highlights the deficiency in the majority's reasoning, Circuit Judge Wiener held that 'shoe-horning his reasonable fears of persecution into the single "economic" cubbyhole and failing to recognise the fallacy of attempting to ascribe that (or any) single persecution motive to the Facusse Group based on its perception of Ontunez's belief, turns a blind eye to the realities of the situation', since the situation pertaining in that case was 'the stuff that mixed motivation is made of'.[57] Wiener J explained:

> Recorded history is replete with examples of class struggles over land between the land-less and the landed. Some clashes have been armed and violent; others have been political and non-violent. In most instances, the land-less protagonist comprised the poor, the dispossessed, the disenfranchised; the landed protagonist comprised the wealthy, the socially prominent, the politically potent. In combination, these traits have produced multi-faceted motivations, defying analytical efforts to isolate any single factor as the sole producing 'cause' of the conflict. Indeed, in these class struggles cum land or ownership struggles, the intertwining of the political, economic, social, and property-holding motivations inevitably proves inextricable, rendering fruitless any analytical effort to isolate one causal factor. As such, attempts to parse these elements invariably prove speculative at best, presenting classic examples of the venerable riddle, 'which came first, the chicken or the egg?'[58]

In addition to being engaged when the *subject matter of the dispute* involves an economic element, this phenomenon also arises in a unique way in a subset of economic-related cases, namely, those where the *method of harm* has an economic element, for example, in cases of extortion. In *Mohan v. Immigration and Naturalization Service*,[59] for instance, the

---

[56] *Ontunez-Tursios*, 303 F 3d 341 (5th Cir. 2002), at 352 (emphasis added).
[57] *Ontunez-Tursios*, 303 F 3d 341 (5th Cir. 2002), at 355.
[58] *Ontunez-Tursios*, 303 F 3d 341 (5th Cir. 2002), at 356.
[59] Mohan v. *Immigration and Naturalization Service*, 1997 US App. LEXIS 6721 (9th Cir. 1997) ('Mohan').

Ninth Circuit upheld the BIA's rejection of a claim by an Indian man who had been harassed by a terrorist group of Sikh militants, on the basis that there was no 'compelling evidence that the purpose of the extortion was anything more than an attempt to obtain money'.[60] Rather, 'the Sikh militants utilize their terrorist attacks to forward their movement [and] carry out indiscriminate attacks on civilians'. In a dissenting opinion which reflects a more complex understanding of the situation, Circuit Judge Reinhardt criticized the majority of the Ninth Circuit's characterization of the situation, as it ignored evidence that the Sikh militants targeted the applicant 'because he was a Hindu residing in a predominantly Sikh, and historically violent, region of India'. Reinhardt J concluded that, like the BIA, the majority had reasoned

> in effect, that because the form of persecution experienced by Mohan was partly economic (and partly physical beating), the reason for the persecution was entirely economic. Even if the form of the persecution were entirely economic, the form that the persecution takes does not determine the answer to the controlling question: what was the reason for the persecution?[61]

As is the case when the subject matter of the dispute involves an economic element, it is vital that decision-makers remain attuned to the wider political context of what might at first appear to be a case of apolitical harm with an economic aspect, such as extortion.[62] This was acknowledged by the Ninth Circuit in *Desir*,[63] a case concerning a Haitian man who, in exchange for the right to fish in certain waters (his livelihood), was expected to pay bribes to the Haitian security forces known as the Ton Ton Macoutes. The BIA had rejected the claim on the basis that the Macoutes 'wish to extort money from him for personal reasons' and that Desir had not shown that his refusal to pay the bribes 'was an expression of political opinion rather than the product of other motivations such as inability to pay'.[64] In overturning this decision, the Ninth Circuit noted that the Haitian government, under the dictator Duvalier, 'operated as a "kleptocracy", or government by thievery, from

---

[60] *Mohan*, 1997 US App. LEXIS 6721 (9th Cir. 1997), at 3.
[61] *Mohan*, 1997 US App. LEXIS 6721 (9th Cir. 1997), at 7.
[62] It should be noted that the argument here is not that every case of extortion necessarily gives rise to a Convention claim. Rather, it should not be assumed that it automatically precludes a claim: see, for example, *Re Minister for Immigration and Multicultural Affairs, ex parte PT* (2001) 178 ALR 497 at 504 (Kirby J): 'I would not approach my conclusion . . . on the footing that there is a general rule relating to extortion that takes such cases outside the Convention definition of "refugees" '.
[63] 840 F 2d 723 (9th Cir. 1988).   [64] *Desir*, 840 F 2d 723 (9th Cir. 1988), at 725.

the highest to the lowest level'.⁶⁵ Thus, Desir's refusal to 'accede to extortion in a political system founded on extortion resulted in his classification and treatment as subversive'.⁶⁶

Similarly, in Singh v. Immigration and Naturalization Service,⁶⁷ the Ninth Circuit noted that '[w]hile the immediate purpose behind the cancellation of the lease on the land Singh occupied may have been to build a hotel, the cancellation occurred in the context of generally legally sanctioned race-based discrimination in land tenure' which was 'enough to establish that the harm was on account of race'.⁶⁸

These cases make it clear that the fact that economic issues are relevant to a refugee claim (either because there is a coexisting economic motivation for harm or because the nature of the harm is economic) should not and does not preclude a refugee claim.⁶⁹ The Federal Court of Australia, for example, has criticized the approach of some decision-makers to determine the nexus issue by the application of a simple dichotomy: 'was the perpetrator's interest in the [applicant] personal or was it Convention related?'⁷⁰ Rather, the court has insisted that decision-makers undertake a more sophisticated evaluation, allowing 'for the possibility that the extortive activity has [a] dual character'.⁷¹ It is therefore vital for decision-makers to consider the context of a claim in a global manner and not seek to identify the one non-Convention factor that can explain the situation, without regard to the possible existence of other Refugee Convention factors. In other words, it is not sufficient to acknowledge that there is no sole cause test; decision-makers must implement this principle in practice.

---

[65] Desir, 840 F 2d 723 (9th Cir. 1988), at 727.
[66] Desir, 840 F 2d 723 (9th Cir. 1988), at 727. The Court also quoted from a decision of the Southern District of Florida Court (affirmed by the Fifth Circuit), in which it had concluded: 'Because the Macoutes are an organization created for political purposes, they bring politics to the villages of Haiti. To challenge the extortion by which the Macoutes exist is to challenge the underpinnings of the political system. Accordingly, to resist extortion is to become an enemy of the government': Haitian Refugee Center v. Civiletti, 503 F Supp 442 at 498–500, cited in Desir, 840 F 2d 723 (9th Cir. 1988), at 727.
[67] 1999 US App. LEXIS 22989 (9th Cir. 1999).
[68] 1999 US App. LEXIS 22989 (9th Cir. 1999), at 4.
[69] This is also recognized in 'Political Legitimacy in the Law of Political Asylum' (1985) 99 Harvard Law Review 450, in which the author emphasizes the need for courts to consider 'structural persecution': at 468–9.
[70] Rajaratnam v. Minister for Immigration and Multicultural Affairs [2000] FCA 1111 (Moore, Finn and Dowsett JJ, 10 August 2000) ('Rajaratnam').
[71] Rajaratnam [2000] FCA 1111 (Moore, Finn and Dowsett JJ, 10 August 2000). The Court noted that 'the reason why the extorting party has that interest may or may not have foundation in a Convention reason': at 13.

Quantum of connection and economic claims

Another important issue in relation to the standard of causation pertains to the situation where, unlike in the above examples, the decision-maker identifies various possible explanations for a person's well-founded fear of persecution (some of which are Refugee Convention related and some of which are not), and it is necessary to ascertain the degree to which the Refugee Convention ground accounts for the well-founded fear of being persecuted. While it is well settled that the Refugee Convention reason need not be the *only* factor in the person's well-founded fear, this does not answer the question of what degree of connection is necessary. In other words, where the decision-maker identifies a number of possible reasons for the person's fear, must the Convention ground/s be shown to be the dominant or essential cause/factor, the 'but for' cause or merely one contributing cause? This question has proved to be an issue of considerable significance in recent years, attracting both judicial and legislative attention.[72]

This issue has particular relevance to refugee claims set against a background of economic difficulty, as there is a tendency on the part of decision-makers to accord great significance to the economic explanations for a person's predicament, with reduced significance to the Convention-related factors. The issue has arisen particularly acutely in cases where the perpetrators of harm are likely influenced, at least partly, by economic factors or by non-Convention factors such as greed, revenge and profit-making (such as in the case of extortion and trafficking), as well as Convention factors such as race, gender and political opinion. In such cases, decision-makers have often had difficulty in apportioning the relevant weight of the Convention-related factors, as opposed to the non-Convention factors, as an explanation for the person's well-founded fear of being persecuted. It has also arisen in cases involving economic deprivation where it can be difficult to separate the effects of the persecutory behaviour from the impact of a generally depressed or poor economy.

The way in which different approaches to the level of causation question operate in the context of a particular case is well illustrated in the decision of the Ninth Circuit in *Gafoor* v. *Immigration and*

---

[72] The issue of causation has generally proved to be a difficult question in many areas of the common law. For a classic work on this topic, see H. L. A. Hart and A. M. Honore, *Causation in the Law* (Oxford: Clarendon Press, 1959).

Naturalization Service,[73] a case involving the claim of an Indo-Fijian police officer who feared harm from his ethnic Fijian colleagues after he had arrested a prominent ethnic Fijian for rape. The BIA rejected the refugee claim on the basis that the attacks 'were motivated solely by revenge for the arrest of the army officer'.[74] In a decision that displayed sensitivity to the particular context of refugee law, the majority of the Ninth Circuit overturned the BIA's decision, applying the principle that the applicant need only establish that the harm 'was motivated, at least in part, by an actual or implied protected ground'.[75] The majority specifically rejected an argument that the applicant was required to establish that a Convention ground (in that case race) standing alone, would have led to the persecution, or that the persecution would not have occurred in the absence of a Convention ground.[76] By contrast, the dissenting judge was highly critical of the majority's approach, concluding that 'for the majority, a motivating factor need not have any causal significance at all'.[77] The dissenting judge took the view that the applicant's claim should be rejected since he had failed to establish that 'he would have been treated any differently were he an ethnic Fijian', thus applying an effective 'but for' test.

In light of the complexity in determining refugee claims, which often involves assessment of complicated and intricate factual circumstances and contexts undertaken against a range of particular challenges, including evidentiary limitations, the requirement of a stringent causation standard, such as that advocated by the dissenting judge in Gafoor, would prove unworkable. Many courts have acknowledged the difficulty and often artificiality in attempting to 'surgically differentiate'[78] the various contributing factors to a person's particular situation, since Convention and non-Convention factors are often 'inextricably linked';[79] thus an attempt to separate and apportion causal significance to different contributing factors is impossible in many cases. In light of this, most common law courts have concluded that a simple 'one part' or one

---

[73] Gafoor v. Immigration and Naturalization Service (2000) 231 F 3d 645 (9th Cir. 2000) ('Gafoor').
[74] See Hathaway and Foster, 'Causal Connection', at 470, where this case is discussed in more detail.
[75] Ibid.   [76] Ibid.   [77] Ibid.
[78] See In Re T-M-B-, BIA, 1997 BIA LEXIS 7; 21 I & N Dec. 775, 778, 20 February 1997 (Rosenberg in dissent). The majority BIA decision was ultimately overturned in Borja, 175 F 3d 732 (9th Cir. 1999).
[79] Sarrazola (2001) 107 FCR 184 at 199.

factor test is the most practical in light of the object and purposes of the Refugee Convention.[80]

This is supported by reference to relevant standards in other areas of the law. The more strict 'but for' standard of causation is notoriously inadequate in the tort context (from which it derives) in its application to cases involving multiple possible causes, and has been modified accordingly to accommodate such cases.[81] Moreover, its speculative and hypothetical nature is said at times to 'demand the impossible' since it 'challenges the imagination of the trier to probe into a purely fanciful and unknowable state of affairs'.[82] Interestingly, such a high test has been rejected in other areas of domestic law, such as anti-discrimination law,[83] an area in which the policy objectives and factual context more closely resemble those of refugee law. In light of the evidentiary difficulties and remedial objectives of anti-discrimination law, courts and legislators have preferred the adoption of a 'one factor test'.[84] As one Canadian tribunal explained, 'the declared purpose of the [Human Rights] Act can be better accomplished by the much less involved method of determining merely whether a prohibited reason formed part of the reasons for the decision'.[85]

Importantly, the similarity between anti-discrimination law and refugee law has been noted by a number of common law courts, which have relied on flexible and liberal causation tests in the discrimination context as additional support for the adoption of a liberal standard in the refugee context. In *Gafoor*[86] and *Chokov v. Minister for Immigration and Multicultural Affairs*,[87] the US Court of Appeals for the Ninth Circuit and the Federal Court of Australia referred to the 'one factor' test prescribed in US federal anti-discrimination law[88] and Australian

---

[80] See generally Foster, 'Causation in Context', pp. 283–6. For a discussion of the object and purpose of the Refugee Convention, see Chapter 2. The NZ RSAA has specifically held that 'we accept that as a matter of principle the only proper conclusion to be drawn from the language, object and purpose of the Refugee Convention is that the Convention ground need not be shown to be the sole, or even the dominant, cause of the risk of being persecuted. It need only be a contributing factor to the risk of being persecuted': *Refugee Appeal No. 72635/01*, RSAA, 6 September 2002, at para. 177.

[81] See Foster, 'Causation in Context', pp. 274, 306–10.

[82] Wex S. Malone, 'Ruminations on Cause-in-Fact' (1956) 9 *Stanford Law Review* 60 at 67, cited in Hathaway and Foster, 'Causal Connection', at 471.

[83] It has also been rejected in equity cases: see Foster, 'Causation in Context', pp. 310–17.

[84] See the detailed discussion at *ibid.*, at 324–6.

[85] *Holloway* [1983] 4 CHRR D/1454, at para. 12485.

[86] *Gafoor* (2000) 231 F 3d 645 (9th Cir. 2000) at 671.

[87] [1999] FCA 823 (Unreported, Einfeld J, 25 June 1999) ('*Chokov*').

[88] *Civil Rights Act of 1991*, amending Title VII (employment discrimination): see Foster, 'Causation in Context', p. 333.

anti-discrimination law,[89] respectively, concluding that such a test was equally (and perhaps even more) appropriate in the refugee context.[90] As Lord Rodger of Earlsferry explained in R *(on the application of Sivakumar)* v. *Secretary of State for the Home Department*, '[s]o long as the decision-maker is satisfied that one of the reasons why the persecutor ill-treated the applicant was a Convention reason and the applicant's reasonable fear relates to persecution for that reason, that will be sufficient... [A]s in the fields of sex and race discrimination, there is little to be gained from dwelling unduly on the precise adjective to use to describe the reason'.[91]

While views similar to that of the dissenting judge in *Gafoor*, that the 'for reasons of' clause requires a 'but for' standard of causation, are present in the case law and have been recently adopted in Australian legislation,[92] the overwhelming trend in the common law jurisprudence is to eschew strict tests such as dominant, predominant, essential or 'but for' cause in favour of a more liberal 'in part' or 'a factor' test.[93] Courts

---

[89] For example, s. 18 of the *Racial Discrimination Act 1975* (Cth) provides that 'where an act is done for two or more reasons, and one of the reasons is the race, colour, descent, or national or ethnic origin of a person (regardless of whether it is the dominant reason or a substantial reason for doing the act) then the act is considered to have been done for that "protected" reason': see *Chokov* [1999] FCA 823 (Unreported, Einfeld J, 25 June 1999); Foster, 'Causation in Context', pp. 325–6, note 279, for a discussion of other Australian legislation embodying a similar test.

[90] Indeed in *Gafoor* (2000) 231 F 3d 645 (9th Cir. 2000), the Court stated that the dissent 'offers no reason for imposing a higher burden on asylum applicants than on employees in Title VII cases': at 653. The Court continued: 'the equities cut the other way. An employee at least has the opportunity to gather evidence of the employer's motive and to put the employer on the stand to explain the reasons behind the employment action. The evidentiary obstacles for asylum applicants, by contrast, are enormous. "Persecutors", we have stated, "are hardly likely to provide their victims with affidavits attesting to their acts of persecution". Nor are they likely to submit declarations explaining exactly what motivated them to act. And individuals fleeing persecution do not usually have the time or ability to gather evidence of their persecutor's motives': at 654.

[91] [2003] UKHL 14, [2003] 2 All ER 1097, at para. 41.

[92] As a result of a perception that this 'one factor' standard is too lenient, the Australian Parliament amended the *Migration Act 1958* (Cth) to provide that art. 1A(2) of the Convention does not apply in relation to persecution for one or more reasons 'unless that reason is the essential and significant reason, or those reasons are the essential and significant reasons, for the persecution': *Migration Legislation Amendment Act (No. 6) 2001* (Cth). Similarly, the US Department of Justice has proposed an amendment to the Immigration and Naturalization Service regulations governing the determination of asylum eligibility that would provide that in cases 'involving a persecutor with mixed motivations' the applicant 'must establish that the applicant's protected characteristic is central to the persecutor's motivation to act against the applicant': see *Asylum and Withholding Definitions*, 65 Federal Register 236 (to be codified at 8 CFR '208).

[93] See generally Foster, 'Causation in Context', pp. 283–6, 334–9.

and tribunals in the USA,[94] Canada,[95] Australia,[96] New Zealand[97] and the UK[98] have formulated the test in slightly different ways but are quite consistent in holding that 'it is sufficient if one of the reasons for which persecution is feared is a [Convention] ground'[99] or that the relevant act of harm be motivated 'in part' by a Convention ground.[100] The application of the 'a factor/motive/cause' test is not accompanied by any requirement that the decision-maker attribute any particular degree of significance to the Convention factor (such as the 'but for', dominant, essential, substantial or main cause); it requires only that the Convention ground be 'a motive',[101] 'one of the motives'[102] or

[94] See *Gafoor* (2000) 231 F 3d 645 (9th Cir. 2000); *Navas v. Immigration and Naturalization Service*, 217 F 3d 646 (9th Cir. 2000); *In re S-P-*, BIA, 1996 BIA LEXIS 25; 21 I & N Dec. 486, 18 June 1996; *In Re T-M-B-*, BIA, 1997 BIA LEXIS 7; 21 I & N Dec. 775, 778, 20 February 1997.
[95] *Zhu*, 1994 ACWSJ LEXIS 68679; 1994 ACWSJ 402290; 46 ACWS (3d) 715; *Shahiraj v. Minister of Citizenship and Immigration*, 2001 Fed Ct Trial LEXIS 443; 2001 FCT 453 ('*Shahiraj*').
[96] *Sarrazola* (2001) 107 FCR 184; *Abdi* (1999) 162 ALR 105 at 112.
[97] *Refugee Appeal No. 72635/01*, RSAA, 6 September 2002.
[98] See *R (on the application of Sivakumar) v. Secretary of State for the Home Department* [2003] 2 All ER 1097, in which Lord Rodger of Earlsferry adopted the minimalist evidentiary test posited by the Court of Appeal in *Suarez v. Secretary of State for the Home Department* [2002] 1 WLR 2663, namely that 'so long as an applicant can establish that one of the motives of his persecutors is a Convention ground and that the applicant's reasonable fear relates to persecution on that ground, that will be sufficient': at para. 41.
[99] *Sarrazola* (2001) 107 FCR 184 at 186 (Heerey J). See also *Garcia-Martinez v. Ashcroft* 371 F. 3d 1066 (9th Cir. 2004) at 1076: 'the protected ground need only constitute a motive for the persecution'.
[100] This is generally the test adopted in the US cases. In applying the 'in part' test set out in *Gafoor* (2000) 231 F 3d 645 (9th Cir. 2000), the Ninth Circuit has allowed refugee claims even where the Convention ground is clearly not the essential, significant or most important factor in the person's well-founded fear: see for example *Lim v. Immigration and Naturalization Service*, 224 F 3d 929 (9th Cir. 2000), *Briones v. Immigration and Naturalization Service*, 175 F 3d 727 (9th Cir. 1999) and *Ali v. Ashcroft* 394 F. 3d 780 (9th Cir. 2005). The Trial Division of the Federal Court of Canada has also framed the test as: 'the law is clear that mixed motivation is sufficient if the motivation *in part* is linked to a Convention ground': *Cabarcas v. Minister of Citizenship and Immigration*, 2002 FCT 297, 19 March 2002 at para. 6 (emphasis added). In *Shahiraj*, 2001 Fed Ct Trial LEXIS 443; 2001 FCT 453, the Federal Court of Canada framed the test as being that the Convention ground is relevant 'at least partially': at para. 20.
[101] *Navas v. Immigration and Naturalization Service*, 217 F 3d 646 (9th Cir. 2000), at 656.
[102] *Zhu v. Canada (Minister for Citizenship and Immigration)* [1994] FCJ No. 80. See also *Popova v. Immigration and Naturalization Service*, 273 F 3d 1251 (9th Cir. 2001), at 1258. See also *Applicant in V488 of 2000 v. Minister for Immigration and Multicultural Affairs* [2001] FCA 1815 (Unreported, Ryan J, 19 December 2001), at para. 36: 'the need for a Convention reason will be satisfied if only one of those motives is referable to, for example, the victim's race or membership of a social group'. In the UK, see *Suarez v. Secretary of State for the Home Department* [2002] 1 WLR 2663: 'However, so long as an applicant can establish that one of the motives of his persecutor is a Convention ground...that will be sufficient': at para. 29 (Potter J).

'a motivating factor'[103] in explaining the reason for the applicant's well-founded fear of being persecuted. Indeed, two tribunals have specifically approved the Michigan Guidelines test, which posits that the Convention ground need only be a 'contributing factor' in the well-founded fear of being persecuted,[104] a test also recently advocated by the UNHCR.[105] The case law generally does not appear to require any 'minimum level' of causation (other than the Convention ground be 'a factor'); however, the two tribunals that have approved the Michigan Guidelines 'contributing factor' test have also adopted the proviso that 'if the Convention ground is remote to the point of irrelevance, causation has not been established'.[106]

While these developments in principle are vital to the operation of the Refugee Convention, decision-makers continue to display difficulty (and perhaps reticence) in applying the liberal causation standard to cases involving economic elements. One prevalent issue relates to claims based on economic discrimination and disadvantage against a particular racial or ethnic group in the context of a generally poor country, in which the population generally has few opportunities for economic advancement.

---

[103] *Hagi-Mohamed v. Minister for Immigration and Multicultural Affairs* [2001] FCA 1156 (Wilcox, Weinberg and Hely JJ, 23 August 2001), at para. 8.

[104] See James C. Hathaway, 'The Causal Nexus in International Refugee Law' (2002) 23 *Michigan Journal of International Law* 207 ('Michigan Guidelines'). The two tribunals are the NZ RSAA and the UK IAT. For the New Zealand authority, see *Refugee Appeal No. 72635/01*, RSAA, 6 September 2002 at para. 177. See also *Refugee Appeal No. 73361/02*, RSAA, 19 June 2003, confirming that the NZ position is that, in line with the Michigan Guidelines, 'provided the Convention ground is a contributing factor to the persecution, it need not be the sole or dominant one': at para. 51. The UK IAT has also considered the causation issue in refugee law in *Ameen v. Secretary of State for the Home Department* [2002] UKIAT 07246 ('*Ameen*') at paras. 39–43, approving the Michigan Guidelines.

[105] See UNHCR *Guidelines on International Protection: Gender-Related Persecution within the Context of Article 1A(2) of the 1951 Convention and/or its 1967 Protocol relating to the Status of Refugees*, UN Doc. HCR/GIP/02/02 (2002), at para. 20: 'The Convention ground must be a relevant contributing factor, though it need not be shown to be the sole, or dominant, cause' and UNHCR, *Guidelines on International Protection: The application of Article 1A(2) of the 1951 Convention and/or Protocol relating to the status of refugees to the victims of trafficking and persons at risk of being trafficked*, HCR/GIP/06/07 (7 April 2006) at para. 29: 'It is sufficient that the Convention ground be a relevant factor contributing to the persecution'.

[106] *Refugee Appeal No. 72635/01*, RSAA, 6 September 2002, at para. 173. The UK IAT is not as clear, although appears to approve of authority that states that there must be some minimum level, especially approving the NZ adoption of the Michigan Guidelines approach, in which, 'if the Convention ground is remote to the point of irrelevance refugee status should not be recognized': *Ameen* [2002] UKIAT 07246, 17 March 2003, at para. 51.

As Hathaway explains, the fact that general opportunities are limited 'is not pertinent to the issue of whether the claimant has been disadvantaged beyond the norm' as a result of persecutory acts.[107] However, decision-makers continue to be distracted by such issues.[108]

The issue is well illustrated in a series of decisions of the New Zealand RSAA relating to the situation of the Bihari in Bangladesh, in which claims based mainly on socio-economic deprivation have been denied on the basis that, while facing discrimination in a range of socio-economic areas based on ethnicity, the harm visited upon the Bihari must be assessed in light of the general economic difficulties of one of the world's poorest countries. The RSAA has accepted the documentary evidence which establishes that the 'historical legacy' of the subcontinent's separation in 1947 and the ensuing treatment of the Bihari who remained

---

[107] Hathaway, *The Law of Refugee Status*, p. 123.
[108] The courts seem willing to dismiss cases based on socio-economic deprivation on the basis that other people suffer the same type of harm for non-Convention reasons. For example, in an Austrian decision, the refugee claim by a couple from Albania who had lost their jobs for political reasons was rejected because in 'Albania you find people having lost their work for economic reasons but who still survive there': *VwGH*, Case No. 93/01/0982, 93/01/0997, 16 March 1994, as cited in by Klaus Hullman, 'Austria', in Carlier, Vanheule, Hullman and Peña Galiano (eds.), *Who is a Refugee?*, p. 44. See also *The Queen on the Application of Secretary of State for the Home Department* v. *The IAT, re Oto Koncek* (Unreported, High Court of Justice, CO-593-99, 21 November 2000), at para. 26: 'But nowhere is there a consideration of the degree of seriousness of the discrimination in relation to employment, *bearing in mind the high level of unemployment generally* and the availability of social security for Roma' (emphasis added). See also *Refugee Appeal No. 71605/99*, RSAA, 16 December 1999, in which the RSAA applied the same type of reasoning to an applicant from Vietnam; *Vura* v. *Immigration and Naturalization Service*, 1998 US App. LEXIS 1075510755 (7th Cir. 1998) ('*Vura*'), regarding economic persecution in the context of Hungary and *SZBQ J* v. *Minister for Immigration* [2005] FCA 143 (28 February 2005) in which the Federal Court of Australia upheld the rejection of an asylum claim by a 'black child' from China finding that notwithstanding the socio-economic consequences of the one-child policy for the child, the detriments to the child arose 'from the poverty of the parents' who were unable to ameliorate the economic impact of government policy (at para. 23). This also sometimes applies in extortion cases: see, for example, the decision in *Reference N02/43928*, RRT, 1 July 2003. The problem is that this analysis is never adopted in the context of civil and political claims. For example, the fact that many people go to jail for non-Convention reasons does not preclude a valid refugee claim on the basis of risk of imprisonment. See, for example, the decision of the Federal Court of Australia in *WAKZ* v. *Minister for Immigration* [2005] FCA 1965 (2 August 2005) in which French J noted, 'It is ludicrous to suggest that where a woman is imprisoned on account of her political views and is repeatedly raped, the rape should not be considered as an element of her persecution on account of those views merely because everybody gets raped in prison': at para. 41.

in East Pakistan (now Bangladesh) has left the Bihari 'in the position of a poverty stricken and discriminated against minority',[109] thus finding that 'the evidence clearly shows that they are marginalized in Bangladesh as a people, and can find it difficult to secure work and an adequate standard of living'.[110] However, it has consistently denied claims based on the argument that, whilst their ethnic origins are 'a factor' in the poor circumstances of applicants, the conditions faced by the Bihari are 'not predominantly because of his Bihari origins but the result of Bangladesh's economic situation'.[111] Underlying these decisions is a clear floodgates concern,[112] as well as scepticism concerning claims based on socio-economic deprivation given the connection with the economic migrant label.[113]

Such an approach appears to impose a higher nexus test on an applicant from a poor country. For example, in *Refugee Appeal No. 70618/97*,[114] the RSAA accepted that the Bihari applicant was denied entry into primary school based on his ethnic origins, refused employment from time to time for reasons including his insufficient education, lack of experience, lack of citizenship (related to his ethnicity) and simply because he was Bihari, and, when he was given employment, was paid less for the same work due to his ethnic origins. However, given the 'gross economic problems' of Bangladesh, the RSAA concluded that the appellant's difficulties were 'not predominantly because of his Bihari origins' but were 'overwhelmingly a function of Bangladesh's economic situation'.[115] This runs the risk of imposing a higher test on applicants from poor countries as opposed to more prosperous countries[116] and, in particular, appears to impose a 'but for' test, in that

---

[109] *Refugee Appeal No. 71018/98*, RSAA, 30 October 1998, at 4.
[110] *Refugee Appeal No. 71018/98*, RSAA, 30 October 1998, at 11.
[111] *Refugee Appeal No. 72024/2000*, RSAA, 13 July 2000, at para. 28. See also *Refugee Appeal No. 70618/97*, RSAA, 30 June 1998.
[112] This is made very clear in *Refugee Appeal No. 71018/98*, RSAA, 30 October 1998: 'If the Authority were to accept counsel's argument, then all Bihari would, ipso facto, be characterised as refugees. Counsel conceded such a conclusion. We cannot agree': at 11.
[113] This is very clearly displayed in *Refugee Appeal No. 70618/97*, RSAA, 30 June 1998.
[114] *Refugee Appeal No. 70618/97*, RSAA, 30 June 1998, at 17.
[115] *Refugee Appeal No. 70618/97*, RSAA, 30 June 1998, at 17.
[116] This was acknowledged by Hathaway, where he discussed some early Canadian decisions involving different facts but a similar issue, noting that '[s]uch analysis misses the central issue of whether or not persecution occurred, and results in discrimination against claimants from economically depressed countries': *The Law of Refugee Status*, p. 123.

applicants from poor countries are required to establish that they would not be in an impoverished economic situation 'but for' the relevant Convention factor. In other words, if the Convention ground only contributes to their dire position, then nexus is held not to have been established. This is inconsistent with a liberal 'in part' or contributing cause test accepted in respect of other types of Refugee Convention claims. It is difficult in principle to understand why a different test should be imposed in the case of claims based on socio-economic deprivation.

This approach can be contrasted with cases in which courts have recognized that, even in the context of a country that faces generalized violence and/or hardship, an applicant's Convention status can *elevate* the risk of persecution or *magnify* the harm feared by the applicant. For example, in one decision of the RRT, membership of a particular Somali clan left the applicant particularly vulnerable in a time of unrest;[117] in a UK IAT decision, the Somali applicant's underclass status made him particularly vulnerable in the situation of general violence;[118] and in a number of RPD decisions, the applicant's young age was found to make the applicant especially susceptible to harm in the context of generalized unrest.[119] In a particularly interesting analysis of the claim by a Salvadoran woman who had been (and feared being) abducted and brutally raped by the Farabundo Marti National Liberation Front (FLMN) in retaliation for the political activities of her family,

---

[117] *Reference N97/17592*, RRT, 5 August 1997.
[118] See *Mohamud Osman Amin*, in which the UK IAT found that even against a background of civil unrest, the applicant from the Jaaji clan of Somalia was particularly at risk because of his underclass status. He thus was able to 'link the vulnerability of him and his family in Mogadishu to the fact that it was the lack of unstructured protection within Somali society which led to them being vulnerable': *Mohamud Osman Amin v. Secretary of State for the Home Department* [2002] UKIAT 04084, at 7. See also the decision of the NZ RSAA in *Refugee Appeal No. 75233* (1 February 2005) at paras. 24–6.
[119] See *RRF (Re)*, No. T99-00210 [1999] CRDD No. 220, 21 September 1999, in which the RPD noted that 'you [the applicant] have no de facto protection in Somalia and that, as a minor, you are at particular risk in that country': at para. 13. See also *MGG (Re)* [2000] CRDD No. 191, 5 September 2000: 'The panel is aware of the political situation in the DRC and finds that the claimant, a young girl without male protection in a war zone, has established a subjective and objective basis for a well-founded fear of persecution in her country of habitual residence': at para. 17. The RPD has also applied this in the socio-economic context. For example, in *IPJ (Re)*, No. A99-01121, [2000] CRDD No. 141, the RPD found that the applicant's mental disability and gender made her particularly vulnerable to persecution in the context of generalized poor economic conditions and occupation by foreign forces.

the RPD held that the applicant was persecuted 'in part because she is a woman and therefore more vulnerable than her father'.[120] In all of these cases, the general situation of unrest and difficulty faced by all or a large percentage of members of the relevant society, and thus the fact that the applicant's connection to a Convention ground only *contributed* to the reason for the harm, did not detract from the claim. This is the preferable approach and is consistent with principle.

The meaning of the nexus clause: is intention required?

One of the most vexed and fraught issues which has pervaded refugee jurisprudence in recent times, and which is particularly pertinent to the present topic, is the question whether the causal nexus clause requires an element of intention. Although it is well accepted that causation and intention are analytically distinct concepts in other areas of law,[121] in the refugee context they are frequently conflated such that the nexus clause will not be satisfied unless the applicant can establish that the perpetrator *intended* to inflict persecution for a Convention reason. The key dispute relates to the role or function of the nexus clause, that is whether its purpose is to link the Convention grounds to the persecutor's intention, to the intention of the state which fails to protect the applicant, or to the applicant's well-founded fear of being persecuted.[122] The salient issue is encapsulated in the question as to whether the nexus clause requires a decision-maker to ask 'why does the persecutor wish to harm (or withhold protection from) the applicant?' Or rather, 'why is the applicant at risk of being harmed?' Interestingly, despite the significance of this issue, courts rarely explicitly acknowledge the different possible approaches or consciously choose one interpretation over another, although this has begun to change in the most recent cases. Given the lack of conceptual clarity that often pervades this important issue, and its central relevance to the present topic, this section will briefly identify the three key approaches, and evaluate their relative merits, in the context of discussing the ramifications of the nexus clause for claims involving socio-economic deprivation.

[120] *S (ZD) (Re)*, No. T94-02002 [1995] CRDD No. 75, 20 June 1995, at 4. See also note 108 above.
[121] For example, in 'no fault' tort law: see Hathaway and Foster, 'Causal Connection', at 461.
[122] Hathaway and Foster, 'Causal Connection', at 461.

Intention of the persecutor

The first approach that has been adopted in the case law is to require the applicant to establish that the persecutor intended to harm the applicant for a Convention reason; in other words, that the persecutor was or is motivated by a Convention-related attribute of the applicant (such as race) rather than by a non-Convention factor. This approach is particularly prevalent in the US cases, following the decision of the US Supreme Court in *Elias Zacarias* in which the Court held that the nexus clause 'makes motive critical'.[123] Such an interpretation requires the applicant to provide direct or circumstantial evidence of the persecutor's motive in order to establish nexus and hence a successful claim.[124] The intention requirement is made most explicit in the US jurisprudence relating to economic deprivation, in which courts formulate the test as being 'the *intentional* imposition of substantial economic disadvantage'.[125] The intention requirement is not confined to US jurisprudence; it has been adopted in decisions in Australia,[126] Canada and the UK. While in more recent cases courts have made it clear that the persecutor's intention need not be malevolent — and indeed the persecutor may even believe that he or she is 'doing the victim a favour'[127] — there is no doubt that, despite rejecting the need for malignity or enmity on the part of

---

[123] *Elias Zacarias* (1992) 502 US 478.
[124] Hathaway and Foster, 'Causal Connection', at 463. See also Shayna S. Cook, 'Repairing the Legacy of INS v. Elias-Zacarias' (2002) 23 *Michigan Journal of International Law* 223.
[125] This test appears to be accepted in all circuits. See, for example, *Abdel-Masieh v. Immigration and Naturalization Service* 73 F 3d 579 (5th Cir. 1996), at 583, citing *Matter of Laipenieks*, BIA, 1983 BIA LEXIS 16; 18 I & N Dec. 433, 8 September 1983; *Hekmat Wadih Mikhael v. Immigration and Naturalization Service*, 115 F 3d 299 (5th Cir. 1997), at 303. It is also sometimes framed as the 'deliberate' imposition of substantial economic disadvantage: see *Nagoulko*, 333 F 3d 1012 (9th Cir. 2003), at 1015, citing *Korablina v. Immigration and Naturalization Service*, 158 F 3d 1038 at 1044. In some circuits, courts have imposed the additional requirement that the economic harm 'must be deliberately imposed "as a form of punishment"': *Vura*, 1998 US App. LEXIS 10755 (7th Cir. 1998), at 3; *Lukban v. Immigration and Naturalization Service*, 1998 US App. LEXIS 10854 (7th Cir. 1998), at 2: 'Additionally, the economic harm must be imposed "as a form of punishment"', citing *Borca*, 77 F 3d 210 (7th Cir. 1996), at 215. See discussion in Chapter 3, note 143.
[126] See especially *Ram v. Minister for Immigration* (1995) 57 FCR 565 at 570 ('*Ram*').
[127] *Minister for Immigration and Multicultural Affairs v. Khawar* (2002) 210 CLR 1 at 36 (Kirby J) ('*Khawar*'). See also *Chen Shi Hai v. Minister for Immigration and Multicultural Affairs* (2000) 201 CLR 293 ('*Chen Shi Hai*') and *Pitcherskaia*, 118 F 3d 641 (9th Cir. 1997).

the persecutors, the focus nonetheless remains on the intention of the persecutor.[128]

This approach has proven particularly problematic in relation to claims by women, since women are often persecuted by non-state agents (such as their husbands or men in general) whose motivations are presumed to be personal and non-political (for example, in the case of rape the motivation is often said to be lust or sexual deviancy; in the case of domestic violence, the woman is merely unlucky to have a violent or nasty husband)[129] and thus outside the Convention regime.[130]

A good example of the particular prominence of this approach in the context of claims involving socio-economic issues is provided by refugee claims by women and children who have been, or who fear being, trafficked for sexual or labour purposes, often against the background that they constitute a particularly vulnerable group in their home country as a result of a combination of discrimination, poverty and disadvantage. The adoption of an 'intention of the persecutor' standard

---

[128] See Hathaway and Foster, 'Causal Connection', at 463–4. This is made clear in the US cases that have implemented the *Elias-Zacarias* approach. For example, the US Court of Appeals for the Tenth Circuit denied asylum to a woman who was repeatedly raped by the Chechen mafia for over two years because 'her attackers never explained anything to her': *Basova v. Immigration and Naturalization Service*, 185 F 3d 873 (10th Cir. 1999). See also *Tecun-Florian v. Immigration and Naturalization Service*, 207 F 3d 1107 (9th Cir. 2000), at 1110. See also Cook, 'Repairing the Legacy of INS v. Elias-Zacarias'.

[129] See, for example, the decision of the BIA in *In re R-A-*, BIA, 2001 BIA LEXIS 1; 22 I & N Dec. 906, 11 June 1999, in which the BIA rejected the claim of a Guatemalan woman who had fled a violent husband, primarily on the basis of a lack of nexus to a Convention ground. The majority stated: 'He harmed her, when he was drunk and when he was sober, for not getting an abortion, for his belief that she was seeing other men, for not having her family get money for him, for not being able to find something in the house, for leaving a cantina before him, for leaving him, for reasons related to his mistreatment in the army, and "for no reason at all". Of all these apparent reasons for abuse, none was on account of a protected ground, and the arbitrary nature of the attacks further suggests it was not the respondent's claimed social group characteristics that he sought to overcome': at para. 36. This decision was vacated by (then) Attorney-General Reno; however, its resolution remains uncertain following the change of government in 2000: see <http://cgrs.uchastings.edu//campaigns/alvarado.php> for a summary of developments in this case.

[130] See also Spijkerboer, *Gender and Refugee Studies*, who observed a similar trend in his analysis of Dutch cases. As he noted, in relation to claims by women, 'acts of persecution are often assumed to be inspired by motives on the side of persecutors which are, in the eyes of decision makers, irrelevant in the context of refugee law. Most notably, acts of persecution are often deemed to be random or private violence in a speculative way': p. 100.

in these cases diverts attention from the wider societal context of discrimination and socio-economic disadvantage which frequently underlies the predicament of individual applicants, thus reducing persecutory motivation to personal and private matters.[131]

This point is well exemplified in a decision of the RRT, which concerned the asylum application of a young woman from Colombia who had travelled to Australia under the mistaken assumption that she would have the opportunity to travel and work there. In fact, she became unwittingly involved in a trafficking operation. She feared retaliation from the traffickers if returned to Colombia. In refusing her claim the RRT concluded:

The Applicant's own personal circumstances in Colombia (including her expressed desire to travel overseas), together with the fact that she is a young woman, presented the opportunity for certain criminals to identify her as a suitable victim but does not of itself necessarily provide the motivation for the harm she suffered or feared. The Tribunal is satisfied that the motivation in first luring the Applicant into prostitution and then demanding regular payments from her was opportunistic self-interested criminality to make money ... and there was no motivation to persecute or harm her because she was a member of a cognizable particular social group of young Colombian women or vulnerable young Colombian women. Further, the Tribunal is satisfied that the harm the Applicant fears on return to Colombia arises out of her particular circumstances and is essentially a harm directed at her as an individual and not for any Convention reason.[132]

This analysis is replicated in many cases involving trafficking decided by tribunals in Australia,[133] Canada[134] and the

---

[131] For example, the RRT dismissed the claim of an Albanian applicant who feared being trafficked on the basis that it was not clear that the applicant was at risk for a Convention reason since it was equally likely women were targeted because 'as individuals ... [they] are suitable victims': *Reference V01/13868*, RRT, 6 September 2002, at 21.

[132] *Reference N98/24000*, RRT, 13 January 2000, at 11.

[133] *Reference V01/13868*, RRT, 6 September 2002. See also *Reference V00/11003*, RRT, 29 September 2003: 'Even if I were prepared to accept that the applicant is a member of a particular social group, I do not accept that she was threatened and raped for reasons of her membership of a particular social group. I find that the threats and violence perpetrated against her [in the context of trying to force her into prostitution] were criminal acts that were aimed at her as an individual': at 5.

[134] In *Zhu v. Canada* [2001] FCJ No. 1251, the Federal Court of Canada upheld the RPD decision that '[t]here was no evidence before the tribunal that the snakeheads or the applicant's parents smuggled or trafficked the applicants because of their status as minors from

USA,[135] in which decision-makers have focused on the criminal, economic and profit-making motives of the persecutors, thus deducing that women are at risk of being persecuted solely because of the criminal motives of their potential persecutors rather than because they are women, poor, or otherwise a member of a particular social group. In another decision of the RRT, involving a claim of a Thai woman who had been traded by her family in order to repay a debt and forced into prostitution, the Tribunal concluded that 'the applicant was essentially the victim of criminal activity' and that 'she was subjected to a form of "private persecution" unrelated to a Convention reason'.[136] In one US decision the IJ acknowledged that '[i]t is sad that there are men who kidnap women and sell them to others for purposes of prostitution. It is a horrible crime, and very demeaning to women, however, this is not a ground for the grant of asylum'.[137] This approach overlooks the reality that, as recognized by the UNHCR, '[s]cenarios in which trafficking can flourish frequently

---

Fujian province, or because of any other Convention ground. There was clear evidence that the snakeheads smuggled or trafficked the applicants for profit. There was evidence that the parents ... were equally motivated by financial reasons': at para. 39. In many of the cases in which applications have been rejected, decision-makers have compared trafficking cases to others involving general criminal activity, noting, for example, that 'victims of crime cannot generally establish a link between their fear of persecution and one of the five grounds in the definition': *NWX (Re)*, No. T99-01434 [1999] CRDD No. 183, 25 August 1999. See also *DJP (Re)*, No. T98-06446 [1999] CRDD No. 155, 3 August 1999 and *AFW (Re)*, No. V99-03532 [2001] CRDD No. 215, 12 October 2001 at para. 49.

[135] See for example *Matter of O-*, Portland, 7 February 2000, discussed in Karen Musalo and Stephen Knight, 'Gender-Based Asylum: An Analysis of Recent Trends' (2000) 77(42) *Interpreter Releases* 1533. See also *In the Matter of L*, IJ Anna Ho, Anchorage, Alaska, 24 July 1998 (on file with author). See also the decision of Immigration Judge Sandy Hom in *In the Matter of Ann*, in which the applicant trafficking victim's refugee claim was dismissed based on the finding that she 'was merely a victim of "personal" and "criminal" actions': *Brief of Amicus Curiae in Support of Respondent Ann's Appeal from the Judgment of the Immigration Judge*, Center for Gender & Refugee Studies, March 29, 2005 (on file with author). This analysis is adopted by Immigration Judges in other contexts as well. See for example, *Gao v. Gonzales* 440 F 3d 62 (2nd Cir. 2006) in which the Second Circuit overturned an IJ decision which had found that the applicant's risk of forced marriage was the result of a 'dispute between two families' (at 64). The Second Circuit instead found that the risk was on account of membership in the group: 'women who have been sold into marriage' (at 69).

[136] *Reference N02/43293*, RRT, 24 October 2002, at 6.

[137] *In the Matter of L*, IJ Anna Ho, Anchorage, Alaska, 24 July 1998 at 30 (on file with author).

coincide with situations where potential victims may be vulnerable to trafficking precisely as a result of [Convention] characteristics'.[138]

Part of the problem in such reasoning is related to the causal connection issue discussed above. That is, applying the 'mixed motive' doctrine, the fact that the motivation of the traffickers may be related to a personal desire to make a profit does not preclude the possibility that the applicant is also at risk because of her status as a woman.[139] So much was recognized by the Canadian RPD in a case involving the application for refugee status of a Thai woman who feared persecution due to her past status as a sex trade worker. The majority reasoning stated:

it is enough if the prospective harm is in some respect related to an innate characteristic of the claimant. The fact that the claimant is a woman is a major cause of her predicament; not the only cause, but a major one nonetheless.[140]

However, the key difficulty is clearly the intent requirement and confusion concerning the role of the nexus clause as this presents the most onerous barrier to such claims.

Intention of the persecutor or of the home state

The second method of understanding the nexus clause is closely related to the first. It continues to require an element of intention, although represents an important extension, in that it looks both to the state of mind of the individual persecutor(s), as well as to the intention of the state in failing to protect the applicant. This approach has been developed in the context of, and has been particularly important in, claims by women, which, as explained above, often fail when reference to the intention of the persecutor is the only method by which nexus can be established. This second, 'bifurcated' approach, recognizes that persecution has two elements – the infliction of serious harm, and failure of the state to provide protection – and it is sufficient for one of those elements to connect to a Convention ground for a successful claim to be

---

[138] UNHCR, *Guidelines on International Protection: The application of Article 1A(2) of the 1951 Convention and/or Protocol relating to the status of refugees to the victims of trafficking and persons at risk of being trafficked*, HCR/GIP/06/07 (7 April 2006) at para. 31.

[139] See UNHCR, *Guidelines on International Protection: The application of Article 1A(2) of the 1951 Convention and/or Protocol relating to the status of refugees to the victims of trafficking and persons at risk of being trafficked*, HCR/GIP/06/07 (7 April 2006) at para. 31: 'This overriding economic motive [for trafficking] does not, however, exclude the possibility of Convention-related grounds in the targeting and selection of victims.'

[140] *GVP (Re)*, No. T98-06186 [1999] CRDD No. 298, 2 November 1999, at 5.

established. Accordingly, courts have upheld claims by women who fear domestic violence in countries such as Pakistan[141] and Iran[142] where the evidence is that 'the state would not assist them because they were women',[143] or where women are 'fundamentally disenfranchised and marginalized by the state'.[144]

In the context of the trafficking of women and children for sex, for example, this approach was relied upon by the UK IAT in allowing a claim from an Albanian woman where evidence suggested that the state is complicit in the trafficking of women, and that there is police corruption and failure to prosecute corrupt police, in the context of a country that is traditionally very male-dominated and patriarchal.[145]

While this has proven to be an important development, and has been hailed as such by many scholars and advocates,[146] it contains similar limitations to the first approach to the extent that intent is still required. This is made clear in the reasoning of those courts that have adopted the bifurcated analysis.[147] For example, in the important Australian High Court decision on point, *Khawar*, Gleeson CJ explained that '[i]t would not be sufficient for Ms Khawar to show maladministration, incompetence, or ineptitude, by the local police. That would not convert personally

---

[141] See, for example, *R v. Immigration Appeal Tribunal, ex parte Shah* [1999] 2 AC 629; *Khawar* (2002) 210 CLR 1.
[142] See *Refugee Appeal No. 71427/99*, RSAA, 16 August 2000.
[143] *R v. Immigration Appeal Tribunal, ex parte Shah* [1999] 2 AC 629 at 644.
[144] See *Refugee Appeal No. 71427/99*, RSAA, 16 August 2000, at para. 108.
[145] *Judgment of K* [2003] UKIAT 00023, 7 July 2003.
[146] See, for example, Karen Musalo, 'Revisiting Social Group and Nexus in Gender Asylum Claims: A Unifying Rationale for Evolving Jurisprudence' (2003) 52 *DePaul Law Review* 777, argues that, in the context of gender claims, 'if the role of the State as well as the individual persecutor is considered, nexus can easily be established': at 805.
She criticizes the USA for not having yet adopted this approach: at 807. See also Stephen Knight, 'Reflections on Khawar: Recognizing the Refugee from Family Violence' (2003) 14 *Hastings Women's Law Journal* 27.
[147] This is made clear in Lord Hoffman's judgment in the ground-breaking *Shah* case. As his Lordship stated, '[a]ssume that during a time of civil unrest, women are particularly vulnerable to attack by marauding men, because the attacks are sexually motivated or because they are thought weaker and less able to defend themselves. The government is unable to protect them, not because of any discrimination but simply because its writ does not run in that part of the country. It is unable to protect men either. It may be true to say women would not fear attack but for the fact that they were women. But I do not think that they would be regarded as subject to persecution within the meaning of the Convention. *The necessary element of discrimination is lacking*': *R v. Immigration Appeal Tribunal, ex parte Shah* [1999] 2 AC 629 at 641 (emphasis added).

motivated domestic violence into persecution on one of the grounds'.[148] Therefore it is evident that where women (or other groups) are the only victims or vastly disproportionately represented as victims in relation to a particular harm, and the state is merely unable rather than truly unwilling to provide protection, the claim will fail unless it is possible to point to a Convention explanation for the motivation of the perpetrator (that is, to a specific intent to hurt women *qua* women).[149] Thus, for example, in the trafficking context, claims routinely fail where, by contrast to the Albanian decision mentioned above, the applicant is unable to establish that the state is unwilling, as opposed to merely unable, to protect her from the risk of being trafficked or otherwise harmed by traffickers.[150]

Each of these approaches requires an intentional identification of the victim, as well as a particular motivation for that identification. In other words, it is not enough that women are being identified or 'singled out' as the particular victims (in the case of trafficking for example); there must be a Convention ground motivation for the selection of women as victims.

The predicament approach

The third possible method of interpreting the nexus clause eschews a focus on the intention either of the persecutor or the state, and focuses instead on why the person is in the predicament of fearing persecution. A good example of this approach (as opposed to the intent-based method)

---

[148] *Khawar* (2002) 210 CLR 1 at 12.
[149] This is borne out by analysis of decisions of the RRT that post-date *Khawar*. While some involving similar facts to *Khawar* have been successful, others have not. For example, in *Reference V01/12813*, RRT, 1 December 2003, the claim from a Polish woman who feared domestic violence was denied on the basis that 'the Applicant's spouse did not attack her for reason of her membership of such a group [women]. Rather, he was a violent drunkard who attacked her for purely personal reasons, unrelated to the Convention': at 5. Further, none of the evidence led the Tribunal 'to conclude that the Polish State authorities withhold or deny protection to victims of domestic violence for Convention reasons. The information does not demonstrate "state tolerance or condonation of domestic violence, and systematic discriminatory implementation of the law"': *ibid.* citing *Khawar* (2002) 210 CLR 1 at 12.
[150] This is especially a problem in the UK jurisprudence, which appears to impose only a 'due diligence' standard on the home state: see, for example, *Gjoni v. Secretary of State for the Home Department* [2002] UKIAT 06307, and *R (on the application of C) v. Immigration Appeal Tribunal* [2003] EQHC 883 (Admin), 9 April 2003 and *VD (Trafficking) Albania CG* [2004] UKIAT 00115 (26 May 2004). For a general discussion of the problem of the test applied in respect of adequacy of state protection, see Mathew, Hathaway and Foster, 'The Role of State Protection in Refugee Analysis'.

is provided in the decision of Branson J of the Federal Court of Australia in *Okere*,[151] which involved a claim by a Nigerian man who feared death from a satanic sect because he had refused to agree to become the head of the sect. Although the sect had not chosen him for his religious beliefs (but rather through local custom by a fortune teller), he was unable to comply with their demands because of his Catholic beliefs. Thus, while his religious beliefs played no part in the decision of the cult members to seek his participation, they were the key reason why the applicant refused their demands. The RRT rejected the claim on the basis that the harm would not be directed against the applicant for a Convention reason. However the Federal Court overturned this decision on the basis that the applicant's fear was motivated 'indirectly' by reason of his religion and that his religious beliefs constituted the 'true reason' for his fear of being persecuted. Branson J explained:

> I reject the contention ... that Art. 1A(2) of the Refugees Convention is to be construed as excluding from the protection afforded by the Refugees Convention persons who have a well-founded fear of persecution which is motivated not directly by reason, for example, of their religion, but only 'indirectly' by reason of their religion. According to this contention, for example, persons who have a well-founded fear of persecution for reason of their refusal to work on the Sabbath could not be found to have a well-founded fear of persecution for reason of their religion; the persecution feared by them would be related to their refusal to work and not to their religion.[152]

While not formulated precisely in such terms, the Court's reasoning is based on a predicament approach which focuses on the reason for the applicant's fear, rather than the reason for the persecutor's decision to harm the applicant. The example provided is reminiscent of an indirect discrimination (or disparate impact) claim in which the relevant question is whether an apparently neutral law or policy has a disproportionately discriminatory impact on a protected group.

The predicament approach has also been applied in other contexts,[153] including in trafficking cases where some decision-makers have focused

---

[151] *Okere v. Minister for Immigration and Multicultural Affairs* (1998) 157 ALR 678 ('*Okere*').

[152] *Okere* (1998) 157 ALR 678 at 681, cited in Hathaway and Foster, 'Causal Connection', p. 466. The significance of this decision is seen by comparison to the UK decision in *Omoruyi v. Secretary of State for the Home Department* [2001] Imm AR 175 ('*Omoruyi*'), which involved almost identical facts, but which resulted in the opposite conclusion.

[153] One of the issues that has consistently raised this dilemma is that of military conscription, where the applicant cannot serve due to, for example, religious convictions, but the law of general application in the home country does not permit

not on why the persecutor wishes to harm the applicant, but on why the applicant is in the predicament of being particularly susceptible to the risk of being trafficked. For example, in one decision of the RPD, the tribunal found that the applicant 'has a link as a member of a particular social group – namely, minors. The child's vulnerability [to being trafficked] arises as a result of his status as a minor'.[154]

In considering how best to resolve this interpretative challenge as a matter of international law, those courts that have recently begun explicitly to consider these issues have properly done so by considering the requirements of the VCLT, which direct the interpreter's attention to the ordinary meaning of the text, in light of its context, object and purpose (as discussed in depth in Chapter 2). It should be emphasized that the crucial question is not whether intention is ever relevant; rather in many cases intention will provide the requisite nexus. The issue is whether it is *necessarily* required; in other words, whether it is the *only* method of satisfying the nexus clause.

While, as mentioned above, courts that have adopted the intention approach rarely provide an overt rationale for this choice, it would appear that the approach is primarily premised on the idea that the 'plain' or 'ordinary' meaning of the word 'persecution' denotes an element of intention on the part of the persecutor; so much is confirmed by reference to English dictionary definitions. This was articulated in an early (and oft cited) decision of the Federal Court of Australia in *Ram*:

> Persecution involves the infliction of harm, but it implies something more: an element of an attitude on the part of those who persecute which leads to the infliction of harm, or an element of motivation (however twisted) for the infliction of harm. People are persecuted for something perceived about them or attributed to them by their persecutors.[155]

---

exceptions for conscientious or religious objectors. In the USA these claims have failed for lack of intent on the part of the government. For the most recent decision, see *Tesfu v. Ashcroft*, 322 F 3d 477 (7th Cir. 2003). In the UK, the House of Lords has recently rejected such claims on the basis that there is no right in international law to conscientious objection, thus obviating the need to consider the nexus question in this context: see *Sepet* [2003] 3 All ER 304. In NZ a successful claim has been made out: see *Refugee Appeal No. 73378*, RSAA, 11 December 2003, at para. 63. In some jurisdictions such claims have been successful at the lower level: see *Maksimovic v. Secretary of State for the Home Department* (Unreported, IAT, Case No. 01TH00432, 16 May 2001). See also EU Directive on a Common Asylum Policy, art. 9(2)(e).

[154] *GAF (Re)*, No. V99-02929 [2000] CRDD No. 48, 21 February 2000, at para. 21.
[155] *Ram* (1995) 57 FCR 565 at 571.

However, as set out in Chapter 2, there is a danger in relying on dictionary definitions alone, as such reliance tends to import elements into the persecution test that have no proper place in refugee determination. For example, early cases that heavily relied on dictionary definitions imposed the requirement that the applicant establish enmity or malignity on the part of the persecutor; the corollary being that if such enmity was not present, nexus was not satisfied. However, in *Chen Shi Hai*, the High Court of Australia rejected this approach (as have other common law courts),[156] with Kirby J warning against reliance on 'earlier more extreme meanings of persecution', which placed greater emphasis on discriminatory intent.[157] In a subsequent decision Kirby J further opined that reliance on dictionary definitions can 'incorrectly direct the mind of the decision-maker to the intention of the persecutor instead of to the effect on the persecuted'.[158] As His Honour noted, '[i]t is the latter that is important if the "fear" (twice referred to in the Refugee Convention definition) is to be understood and the complex motivations and causes of the flight and the claim of the applicant to protection are to be analysed correctly'.[159]

In addition to indicating that it is the 'fear' of the applicant that is arguably the focus of the refugee definition, attention to the text of the definition reveals that while frequently described as the short-hand 'persecution', in fact the definition speaks of a refugee's well-founded fear of 'being persecuted'. The fact that the test is framed in the passive voice is significant, as it again underlines the focus on the predicament of the applicant, rather than on an assessment of the situation from the perspective of the persecutor.[160] So much was acknowledged by Heerey J in the decision of the Full Federal Court of Australia in *Minister for Immigration and Multicultural and Indigenous Affairs v. Kord*, in which His Honour noted that '[t]he Refugees Convention's definition of "refugee" speaks of a person's "fear of being persecuted". The use of the passive voice conveys a compound notion, concerned both with the conduct of the persecutor and the effect that conduct has on the person being persecuted'.[161] The significance of the use of the passive voice has also

---

[156] See for example, *Pitcherskaia*, 118 F 3d 641 (9th Cir. 1997).
[157] *Chen Shi Hai* (2000) 201 CLR 293 at 312 (Kirby J).
[158] *Khawar* (2002) 210 CLR 1 at 36.   [159] *Khawar* (2002) 210 CLR 1 at 36.
[160] As other scholars have noted, the Convention test does not explicitly mention the intention of the persecutor: see Goodwin-Gill, *The Refugee in International Law*, pp. 50–1; Michigan Guidelines, at 215.
[161] [2002] FCA 334 (Heerey, Marshall and Dowsett JJ, 28 March 2002), at para. 2.

been noted by Madgwick J of the Federal Court of Australia, who in departing from the traditional approach of Australian courts which have historically elevated the notion that persecutory motivation will suffice in satisfying the nexus clause to a *requirement* that intention be established,[162] observed:

> In using the passive voice of the verb 'to persecute', it seems to me that the Convention sets up a test, conformable with dictionary definitions of 'persecute', of being seriously oppressed. That idea is also consistent with the causational expression 'for reasons of' (which introduces the Convention-proscribed attributes of the person concerned) being linked to the oppressed condition of that person. Thus, it appears textually to suffice, among other things, if it can reasonably and realistically be said that the putative refugee fears being persecuted because, in fact, he or she holds a political opinion, whether or not the persecutor knows of this.[163]

The RSAA has similarly concluded that the language of the Refugee Convention 'draws attention to the fact of exposure to harm, rather than to the act of inflicting harm. The focus is on the reasons for the claimant's predicament rather than on the mindset of the persecutor'.[164]

This textual analysis is further buttressed by reference to the context, object and purpose of the Refugee Convention, as required by the VCLT.[165] The object of the Refugee Convention is, as explained in Chapter 2, to ensure the protection of victims of persecution and is not, on any possible reading, concerned to punish the perpetrators of such persecution.[166] In this regard, the aims and purposes of international refugee law are fundamentally different from those underpinning international criminal responsibility for example.[167] This has been implicitly recognized by

---

[162] *NACM of 2002* v. *Minister for Immigration and Multicultural and Indigenous Affairs* [2003] FCA 1554 (Unreported, Madgwick J, 22 December 2003), at para. 50 ('*NACM of 2002*').
[163] *NACM of 2002* [2003] FCA 1554 (Unreported, Madgwick J, 22 December 2003), at para. 51.
[164] See *Refugee Appeal No. 72635/01*, RSAA, 6 September 2002, at para. 168: 'The employment of the passive voice ("being persecuted") establishes that the causal connection required is between a Convention ground and the *predicament* of the refugee claimant. The Convention defines refugee status not on the basis of a risk "of persecution" but rather "of *being* persecuted" ' (emphasis in original). For the most recent authority, see *Refugee Appeal No. 74665/03*, RSAA, 7 July 2004.
[165] See generally the discussion in Chapter 2.
[166] See Foster, 'Causation in Context', p. 294. See also *Refugee Appeal No. 72635/01*, RSAA, 6 September 2002: 'In our view the primary object of the Refugee Convention is to provide the surrogate protection of the international community for those genuinely in need of protection. The focus is on assisting the (potential) victim, not on assigning guilt to the persecutor': at para. 171.
[167] As mentioned in Chapter 2, notes 118–19.

those courts that have criticized the intention approach on the basis of its impractical implementation. As noted by Muldoon J of the Federal Court of Canada, 'who knows what is the intention of the persecutor? Who knows what is the particular knowledge of the persecutor?'[168] After all, the 'alleged persecutors are obviously not present at the hearing . . . and cannot testify as to their own subjective state of mind'.[169] It is thus difficult to understand the relevance of an inquiry into the state of mind of the persecutors to the question whether an applicant is a person in need of protection.

In addition, given the humanitarian object of the treaty as a whole, it is well established that the text should be read in a liberal rather than restrictive manner. In other words, a possible meaning that unduly constrains the protective scope of the Refugee Convention is to be subordinated to a permissible reading that upholds its object and purpose. Courts are increasingly willing to acknowledge that an interpretation of the Refugee Convention which focuses on the intent of the persecutor would impose an extremely onerous if not impossible burden on applicants,[170] and would 'confine the scope of Convention protection in a straightjacket so tight as to mock the words in the [Convention's] recital . . . "the widest possible exercise of these fundamental rights and freedoms"'.[171] In perhaps the strongest critique of the intent approach to date, Madgwick J of the Australian Federal Court has asserted that

it would make a mockery of the international human rights guarantees if a person in fear of oppression because he or she has acted or threatened to act on a political conviction could be denied refugee status merely because an official oppressor is motivated by an intention to prevent, or to seek revenge for, the act impelled by the victim's political conviction, but is too distracted or for other reasons fails to appreciate also that the person fearing oppression had been

---

[168] *Nejad, Hossein Hamedi* v. *Minister of Citizenship and Immigration*, 1997 ACWSJ LEXIS 159001; 1997 ACWSJ 419632; 73 ACWS (3d) 1017, at para. 4.
[169] *Shahiraj*, 2001 Fed Ct Trial LEXIS 443; 2001 FCT 453. See also Cook, 'Repairing the Legacy of INS v. Elias-Zacarias', in which she discusses the problems that have ensued in the lower US courts of appeals from the *Elias-Zacarias* decision: at 232–41.
[170] *Refugee Appeal No. 72635/01*, RSAA, 6 September 2002, at para. 171: 'the Convention cannot be interpreted so as to impose on the claimant the often impossible task of establishing intent. A low evidentiary threshold is more in keeping with the humanitarian purpose of the Convention'. See also UNHCR, *Written Submission on Behalf of the UN High Commissioner for Refugees in the UK Court of Appeal in Sepet* [2001] EWCA Civ 681, extracted in Musalo, Moore and Boswell, *Refugee Law and Policy*, pp. 313–17.
[171] *Sepet* [2001] EWCA Civ. 681 at para. 92.

motivated by such conviction, or where the victim's motivation simply does not concern the oppressor. The putative refugee is nevertheless in his or her predicament because of political belief.[172]

As His Honour noted, given that the Refugee Convention is concerned not only with political opinion (the relevant ground in that case) but also with race, religion, nationality and membership of a particular social group, an 'unwarrantedly narrow view of "being persecuted" is likely to disadvantage people in relation even to the expression of their natures or innate characteristics', if claims are dismissed because the intention of the persecutor cannot be established to be related to a Convention ground.[173] Such a 'narrow, literalist approach' appears 'disconsonant with the concerns properly to be imputed, as a matter of interpretation, to the framers of the Convention'.[174]

The only argument under the rubric of object and purpose that could reasonably militate in favour of an intent approach is the well-established concept that anti-discrimination principles underpin the object and purpose of the Refugee Convention. In *Omoruyi*, for example, the UK Court of Appeal rejected a claim based on almost identical facts to those in *Okere* above, on the basis that discrimination 'is essential to the concept of persecution under the Convention' and that 'some element of conscious discrimination against the victim based on a Convention reason' is a necessary element of a Refugee Convention claim,[175] which was found to be lacking in that case.

However, reliance on anti-discrimination principles does not warrant the imposition of an intent test. On the contrary, as Madgwick J acknowledged in *NACM*, discrimination law 'treats as uncontroversial the proposition that discrimination may be legally established where either the intent or effect of conduct is discriminatory'.[176] This is established in both international and domestic human rights law.[177] First, it is important to note that courts and legislatures in many domestic jurisdictions

---

[172] *NACM of 2002* [2003] FCA 1554 (Unreported, Madgwick J, 22 December 2003), at para. 57.
[173] *NACM of 2002* [2003] FCA 1554 (Unreported, Madgwick J, 22 December 2003), at para. 58.
[174] *NACM of 2002* [2003] FCA 1554 (Unreported, Madgwick J, 22 December 2003), at para. 58.
[175] *Omoruyi* [2001] Imm AR 175 at 181.
[176] *NACM of 2002* [2003] FCA 1554 (Unreported, Madgwick J, 22 December 2003), at para. 59. See also *Sepet* [2003] 3 All ER 304, where Lord Hoffman observed that 'at any rate for the purposes of article 14 [of the *European Convention*] a law of general application may have a discriminatory effect if it contains no exceptions for people who have a right to be treated differently': at para. 30.
[177] For authority in relation to international treaties dealing with anti-discrimination, see Hathaway and Foster, 'Causal Connection', p. 469.

have eschewed a subjective test of intention, even with respect to cases of direct discrimination or disparate treatment, in favour of an objective assessment of whether the treatment suffered by the applicant can be explained by reference to a discriminatory policy or act, regardless of the intention of the defendant.[178] It has been said that although there is 'some force' in the argument that expressions such as 'on the ground of' look to an intent or motive on the part of the alleged discriminator that is related to the protected status of the other person, to require the plaintiff to establish an intent to discriminate 'would significantly impede or hinder the attainment of the objects of' anti-discrimination legislation and would 'subvert the achievement of the purposes' of the relevant legislation.[179] An objective test is said to avoid 'complicated questions relating to concepts such as intention, motive reason or purpose, and the danger of confusion arising from the misuse of those elusive terms'.[180] Second, in respect of disparate impact or indirect discrimination, it is clear that a neutral policy which disproportionately impacts upon a protected group can constitute unlawful discrimination.[181] Applying these principles to the Refugee Convention, it would be necessary only to establish that an applicant was at risk of being persecuted because of a distinction or difference in treatment based on a Convention ground, or that the applicant's Convention ground status puts him or her at a disproportionately high risk of the relevant harm feared.

In UK decisions post-*Omoruyi*, while continuing to emphasize the importance of non-discrimination principles to an interpretation of the Refugee Convention, the Court of Appeal and House of Lords have resiled, at least partially, from the strict approach taken in *Omoruyi*, albeit in *obiter* comments only.[182] In *Sepet*, Laws LJ of the

---

[178] See Foster, 'Causation in Context', p. 320, for detailed references in the domestic context.
[179] Foster, 'Causation in Context', p. 321, citing Australian High Court decisions in *Waters v. Public Transport Corporation* (1992) 173 CLR 349 at 359; *IW v. The City of Perth and Others* (1997) 191 CLR 1.
[180] *James v. Eastleigh Borough Council* [1990] 2 AC 751, 765.
[181] *James v. Eastleigh Borough Council* [1990] 2 AC 751, 765.
[182] Both the Court of Appeal and House of Lords have confined *Omoruyi* to the particular facts of the case: see *Sepet* [2001] EWCA Civ. 681 at para. 91 (Laws J); *Sepet* [2003] 3 All ER 304, where Lord Hoffman described the case as 'bizarre': at para. 54. It is also interesting to note that there is *dicta* in previous UK Court of Appeal decisions to the effect that intent is not required: see *R v. Immigration Appeal Tribunal, ex parte De Melo and Anor* (Unreported, IAT, Appeal No. CO/1866/96, 19 July 1996), at 5 (Laws J) and *Montoya v. Secretary of State for the Home Department* [2002] EWCA Civ. 620, where the Court (Schiemann, May and Parker LJJ) at para. 31.

Court of Appeal (with whom Parker LJ agreed) rejected outright the submission that motive is always required, concluding that this view 'confuses what is meant . . . by the words, "for reasons of" with *one* of the modes of proving that the words apply',[183] and rejected 'out of hand the view that the autonomous, international meaning of the Refugee Convention involves the proposition that the whole sense of "for reasons of" has a single reference, namely the motive of the putative persecutor'.[184] In upholding the Court of Appeal's decision in *Sepet*, the House of Lords was less adamant in rejecting the intent approach, adopting instead an approach that has been said to come 'half-way' to the predicament approach.[185] As Lord Bingham explained:

> However difficult the application of the [causation] test to the facts of particular cases, I do not think that the test to be applied should itself be problematical. The decision-maker will begin by considering the reason in the mind of the persecutor for inflicting the persecutory treatment . . . But the decision maker does not stop there. He asks if that is the real reason, or whether there is some other effective reason. The victims' belief that the treatment is inflicted because of their political opinion is beside the point unless the decision-maker concludes that the holding of such opinion was the, or a, real reason for the persecutor's treatment.[186]

Similarly tentative steps away from the strict intent/motivation approach can be detected in Australia (where support can be found for an approach

---

[183] *Sepet* [2001] EWCA Civ. 681 at para. 92 (Laws J) (emphasis added).
[184] *Sepet* [2001] EWCA Civ. 681 at para. 92. Laws J further explained that 'the question is always whether the applicant faces discrimination on a Convention ground. There will be, are, cases where that is made out by reference to the persecutor's motives. There will be, are, others where his motive matters not'. In the House of Lords decision in *Sepet*, Lord Bingham characterized the Court of Appeal decision as having 'unanimously rejected [the intention] argument': at para. 21.
[185] *NACM of 2002*, at para. 67 (Madgwick J).
[186] *Sepet* [2003] 3 All ER 304 at para. 23 (Lord Bingham of Cornhill, with whom Lord Rodger of Earlsferry specifically agreed on this point: at para. 59). His Lordship also observed that '[d]ecision-makers are not concerned...to explore the motives or purposes of those who have committed or may commit acts of persecution, nor the belief of the victim as to those motives or purposes. Having made the best assessment possible of all the facts and circumstances, they must label or categorise the reason for the persecution': at para. 23. Lord Hoffman stated that although unnecessary to decide in this case, His Lordship's 'present inclination is to agree with Laws LJ that it would be inconsistent to say that a general conscription law which did not make an exception for conscientious objectors was an infringement of their fundamental human rights but that punishing conscientious objectors under such a law was not persecution for reasons of their opinions': at para. 54.

akin to indirect discrimination or disparate impact)[187] and Canada,[188] and in some civil law jurisdictions such as Germany.[189] The UNHCR strongly supports the predicament approach,[190] recent developments in

[187] The High Court of Australia has indicated the need for a more objective approach: see *Chen Shi Hai* (2000) 201 CLR 293 at 301 where the Court (Gleeson CJ, Gaudron, Gummow and Hayne JJ) noted that 'general laws, which are apparently non-discriminatory, may impact differently on different people and, thus, operate discriminatorily'. The House of Lords characterized this decision as a more objective approach in *Sepet* [2003] 3 All ER 304 at para. 21 (Lord Bingham of Cornhill). Further, in *Minister for Immigration and Multicultural Affairs* v. *Haji Ibrahim* (2000) 204 CLR 1, McHugh J held that although 'the motivation of this relatively small group of Marehans might arguably throw some light on what Marehans generally might do to the applicant', His Honour did 'not think that a finding as to the motivation for this incident was so necessary that, by failing to find that motivation, the Tribunal erred in law': at 21. For further Federal Court authority, see *Wang* v. *Minister for Immigration and Multicultural Affairs* (2000) 105 FCR 548 at 562 (Merkel J); and *Applicant VEAZ of 2002* v. *Minister for Immigration and Multicultural Affairs* [2003] FCA 1033 (Unreported, Gray J, 2 October 2003) at para. 26.
[188] See *Cheung* v. *Canada (Minister of Employment and Immigration)* [1993] 102 DLR (4th) 214 at para. 9: '[The Refugee Board] also wrongly required that a "persecutory intent" be present, whereas a persecutory effect suffices'. See also *Hassan Mare* v. *Canada (Minister of Citizenship and Immigration)*, 2001 ACWSJ LEXIS 14683; 2001 ACWSJ 612342; 105 ACWS (3d) 502, at para. 10; *Shahiraj*, 2001 Fed Ct Trial LEXIS 443; 2001 FCT 453, and *Flores* v. *Canada (Minister of Citizenship and Immigration)*, 2002 ACWSJ LEXIS 5953; 2002 ACWSJ 8570; 116 ACWS (3d) 420, at paras. 12–13. See also *IVV (Re)*, No. TA2-00027 [2003] CRDD No. 64, 26 May 2003, where the Tribunal allowed a claim involving almost identical facts to *Okere* and *Omoruyi*, thereby adopting an approach which analyses the situation from an objective point of view.
[189] See the UNHCR's submission in *Sepet*: '[The no intent required] position is further supported by the clear position taken by the German Constitutional Court. In a 1987 decision concerning Ahmadis in Pakistan, the Court firmly rejected the concept of motivation of persecution until then applied by the Federal Administrative Court. The Court stated that persecution for reasons of political opinion could not be denied simply because Pakistan was motivated, when enacting certain criminal laws, to guarantee public order. What was decisive was whether the acts in question, based on laws of general application or not, amounted to persecution in an objective sense. That decision was again confirmed in a 1989 decision of the German Constitutional Court concerning the application of a Turkish national of Kurdish origin. The Court there held that the subjective motives of the persecutor were irrelevant for the determination of the right to asylum or refugee status': at para. 40, as cited in Musalo, Moore and Boswell, *Refugee Law and Policy*, p. 317, citing cases of Bundesverfassungsgericht (Federal Constitutional Court), 2 BvR 478, 962/86, 1 July 1987, BverfGE 76, 143 at 166 and 2 BvR 958/85, 20 December 1989.
[190] The UNHCR says that persecution comprising serious harm may, among other things, arise where a law of general application has a differential impact on a person or group of persons on account of one of the Convention grounds, or where the enforcement of the law risks or does violate human rights: see UNHCR, 'The International Protection of Refugees: Interpreting Article 1 of the 1951 Convention Relating to the Status of Refugees' (2001) 20(3) *Refugee Survey Quarterly* 77 at 83. See also *Brief Amicus Curiae of the Office of the United Nations High Commissioner for Refugees in Support of Respondents in*

the EU appear to admit of this approach,[191] and academic commentary is also increasingly adopting the view that intention is not necessary.[192] However, the predominant approach in the common law jurisprudence as a whole undoubtedly remains one of requiring intent.[193] Notwithstanding this, in addition to growing (although still nascent) explicit recognition of the logic of a predicament approach, and some explicit justification of this approach as a matter of treaty interpretation, there is an emerging body of case law that is implementing the predicament approach *in practice* by focusing on the predicament of the applicant rather than on the motivation of the persecutor, even if this important interpretative move is not always overtly acknowledged. This development has been particularly relevant and important in the context of trafficking and other economic-related claims involving

Elias-Zacarias, No. 90-1342, 8, n. 11. In addition, the UNHCR intervened in *Sepet* at the Court of Appeal level, arguing that in considering 'the drafting history, there is no indication at all that the drafters intended the motive or intent of the persecutor to be a (or the) controlling factor in either the definition of "refugee" or in the determination of refugee status': at paras. 34–5, quoted in Musalo, Moore and Boswell, *Refugee Law and Policy*, p. 317.

[191] See EU Directive on a Common Asylum Policy, art. 9, 'Acts of persecution'. Article 9(2) sets out the kinds of acts that can constitute '[a]cts of persecution' as long as they are 'qualified as such in accordance with paragraph 1'. These include '(c) prosecution or punishment, *which is disproportionate or discriminatory*, (d) denial of judicial redress resulting in a *disproportionate or discriminatory punishment*, (e) prosecution or punishment for refusal to perform military service in a conflict, where performing military service would include crimes or acts falling under the exclusion clauses, as set out in Article 12(2)' (emphasis added). Both the reference to acts having a disproportionate impact and to the conscientious objector principle suggests a move away from intent. In particular the 'refusal to perform military service' scenario is well recognized to raise acutely the intention question, which was in fact the very question in *Sepet*. Lord Bingham of Cornhill made reference to the EU Directive in *Sepet* [2003] 3 All ER 304 at para. 16, but at that stage it was in draft form only.

[192] Goodwin-Gill, *The Refugee in International Law*, pp. 50–1, Symes and Jorro, *Asylum Law and Practice*, p. 109; Michigan Guidelines, at 215, and Hugo Storey, 'The Advanced Refugee Law Workshop Experience: An IARLJ Perspective' (2003) 15 *International Journal of Refugee Law* 422 at 427–8. For an earlier critique of the *Elias-Zacarias* intent approach, see Karen Musalo, 'Irreconcilable Differences? Divorcing Refugee Protections from Human Rights Norms' (1994) 15 *Michigan Journal of International Law* 1179.

[193] At present, it is only accurate to say that NZ has fully embraced the predicament approach. In Australia, for example, despite the support for the predicament approach outlined above, the predominant authority still appears to require intent. As Madgwick J acknowledged in *NACM of 2002*, at least a Full Court of the Federal Court would need to consider this in order for the predicament approach to be more widely and authoritatively accepted: [2003] FCA 1554 (Unreported, Madgwick J, 22 December 2003), at para. 66.

applicants who are particularly vulnerable, such as children, the disabled and the seriously ill, in which their predicament puts them at heightened risk of a range of harm.

There are two key ways by which claims have been successful based on this effective predicament analysis. First, in a number of decisions, courts and tribunals have focused on the question of which groups in society are primarily the victims of the particular type of harm faced by the applicant. Where, for example, all or almost all of the victims are women, a number of decision-makers have been willing to characterize the reason for the applicant's fear of being persecuted as membership of a particular social group – women. In such decisions, the adjudicator has not engaged in an inquiry or consideration as to what the individual motives or thoughts of the persecutor (or future persecutor) may have been, or even as to whether the state had the requisite intent; the fact that one group is significantly over-represented amongst victims is deemed sufficient to establish nexus.

This approach has sometimes been engaged by women and children whose refugee claims are based on their fear of being trafficked or otherwise harmed by traffickers in the future. While, as explained above, some decision-makers have compared trafficking claims to those involving victims of crime generally, other decision-makers have recognized that while in the latter class of case the applicant cannot establish that he or she is more at risk than any other member of society, or at most that he or she will be targeted for a non-Convention factor such as wealth, in trafficking cases women (and/or children) are often the *only* group at risk. As recognized by one IJ in the USA, '[a] house of prostitution by force is something that only a woman can be victimized by, not a man'.[194] This analysis has been adopted in the UK at the Special Adjudicator level, where, for example, it has been accepted that an orphaned child from Vietnam who had been trafficked to the UK was at risk of being

---

[194] Ms M, Immigration Judge, 3 December 1996; upheld on appeal to the BIA, 30 March 2001 (both decisions on file with author). One might also add that children (including boys) are also potential victims and thus refugee claims may also potentially be open to child victims of trafficking on this analysis. In an Austrian High Administrative Court decision involving a Nigerian citizen who was sold into forced prostitution, the Court annulled the earlier decision on the basis that it had 'wrongly reasoned that "the risk she claimed was clearly not attributable to the reasons set forth in the [1951] Geneva Convention"': see Alice Edwards, 'Age and Gender Dimensions in International Refugee Law', in Feller, Türk and Nicholson (eds.), *Refugee Protection in International Law*, p. 61.

persecuted in the future for reasons of membership in the social group – 'females in Vietnam'.[195]

Another example is provided in the context of domestic or sexual violence against women, where some decision-makers have not found it necessary to engage in a bifurcated analysis (that is, an inquiry into whether intent can be linked either to the agent of harm or the state), finding simply that 'the claimant fears persecution on account of her membership in the particular social group "women", since spousal abuse is fundamentally a form of violence against women'[196] (in one case) and 'that the form of harm feared by the claimant is one that is experienced predominantly by women because of their exposure or vulnerability for physical violence and denial of fundamental rights' (in another).[197]

While many courts continue to rely on the intention analysis (either of the persecutor or the state), others are beginning to consider the wider context of societal discrimination against a particular group, such as women, to provide the factual background to the conclusion that women are the primary victims in respect of certain harms as a consequence of general societal discrimination, which is deemed sufficient to establish nexus to a Convention ground.[198] This is particularly important since the predominance of women (for example) as victims of particular types of grave human rights violations is often not an 'accident' or a 'coincidence'; it is often the function of widespread underlying

---

[195] *Tam Thi Dao* v. *Secretary of State for the Home Department* (Unreported, IAT, Appeal No. HX/28801/2003, 1 September 2003), as reported in Catriona Jarvis, 'Can Trafficked Persons Be Refugees?' in Immigration Appellate Authority, *Legal and Research Unit Update*, 29 February 2004, p. 8 (on file with author).

[196] *C(UY) (Re)*, Nos. T94-00416, T94-00418 and T94-00419 [1994] CRDD No. 389, 25 August 1994, at 4.

[197] *G (BB) (Re)*, Nos. T93-09636, T93-09638 and T93-09639 [1994] CRDD No. 307, 26 January 1994, at 4. See also *L (HX) (Re)*, Nos. T93-05935, T93-05936 [1993] CRDD No. 259, 31 December 1996, in which the Tribunal allowed the claim of a woman who feared losing custody of her child for reasons of her gender. See also the decision of the RRT in *Reference V02/14674*, RRT, 13 February 2004, finding that women from Papua Niugini are a particular social group and that the applicant in that case 'was gang raped and persecuted for the essential and significant reason of her membership of this particular social group'. In the USA, see *Mohammed* v. *Gonzales* 400 F. 3d 785 (9th Cir. 2005) in the context of female genital mutilation.

[198] For example, in a decision of the RRT involving a claim by a mother and daughter from Afghanistan, the Tribunal noted that 'women, particularly single women and widows . . . are at risk of persecution in Afghanistan today': *Reference N02/44244*, RRT, 1 October 2003, at 24. It was satisfied that 'the persecution experienced by women in Afghanistan occurs for the reason of their gender'. See also *Reference N03/45573*, RRT, 24 February 2003, where the RRT invoked a similar analysis in respect of Burmese women trafficked into Thailand.

societal discrimination.[199] A predicament approach thus allows for a more realistic assessment of the wider context of a person's fear of being persecuted, admitting of the possibility that, where the predicament is the result of widespread discrimination against a group on a ground protected by the Refugee Convention, refugee status will be established. In this way, the analysis closely resembles that undertaken in cases of direct discrimination or disparate treatment in anti-discrimination law, in which the question is whether the individual has been treated differently on the basis of a protected criterion (gender) and not (in most jurisdictions)[200] on whether the discriminator intended to discriminate on the basis of the protected ground.

The second key way in which the predicament approach has begun to be implemented in practice is displayed in cases in which decision-makers focus on the factors that led to or contributed to the person's vulnerability to the relevant harm feared, concluding that if those factors can be related to a Convention ground (most commonly membership of a particular social group) then nexus is established. In such cases, as in those described above, the focus is not on the intention of the persecutor or even of the state (although the state protection issue is relevant); rather the decision-maker simply asks, 'why is the person in this predicament?'

This approach has been adopted most frequently in respect of groups such as children, whose particular vulnerability is often the reason for exposure to the risk of being persecuted. This was the approach adopted in a decision of the US Board of Immigration Appeals concerning the claim by a Honduran woman who had been forced into prostitution as a minor after she was abandoned by her biological family. In overturning the decision of the IJ which had rejected her claim, the BIA held, in an analysis that represents a dramatic departure from the mainstream 'intent of the persecutor' standard in US jurisprudence:

In this case, the respondent has shown that the acts of persecution occurred because of her membership in a group of children who have been abandoned

---

[199] See also Spijkerboer, *Gender and Refugee Studies*, who observes that 'a phenomenon that primarily befalls women is simply not undifferentiated': p. 127.
[200] Of the five common law jurisdictions studied, only the USA continues to require intent to be proved in domestic discrimination cases: see Foster, 'Causation in Context', pp. 320–2.

by their parents and who have not received a surrogate form of protection. Because the respondent was not protected by her parents or surrogate protector, she lived in an extreme state of vulnerability. In such a state, dangerous actors persecuted her because they could do so without any negative repercussions. The respondent, a powerless child with no one looking after her, was an easy target over which they could assert their power ... But for her extreme vulnerability caused by her parents' abandonment and lack of a surrogate protector, the respondent would not have fallen prey to the act of persecution described above.[201]

A similar approach was adopted by the UK Special Adjudicator in a claim by a trafficked Nigerian girl who was an 'orphaned street child without support from her family'. The Adjudicator found that as a female street child 'she was obliged to beg and was vulnerable' and that her fear of future persecution was due, *inter alia*, to her membership of the social group 'orphaned female street children without support from a family' or 'trafficked child'.[202]

Similarly, the Canadian RPD has held that a Chinese child who had been subjected to violence and debt bondage by his father was at risk of future persecution and that this risk was due to his vulnerable status as a minor.[203] In another decision, the RPD held that a child separated from her family in Somalia was at risk of being persecuted since there were no government agencies or blood relatives or extended family members in Somalia who 'would take the responsibility for her care and protection',[204] making her particularly vulnerable to inter-clan and inter-faction violence because of her status as a minor.[205] Similarly, the RPD found that a young stateless girl from the Democratic Republic of Congo, who was at risk of being raped by soldiers and other thugs, was held to satisfy the Refugee Convention definition since she was a 'young girl without male protection in a war zone',[206] her vulnerability thus arising from a combination of her gender and age.

As the above cases suggest, decision-makers have recognized that being poor, particularly in combination with other attributes such as gender or age, can put the applicant in an extremely vulnerable position

---

[201] Unnamed File, Board of Immigration Appeals, 3 June 2003 at 6 (on file with author).
[202] *AS/54991/2003*, December 2003, discussed in Jarvis, 'Can Trafficked Persons Be Refugees?', p. 8.
[203] *GAF (Re)*, No. V99-02929 [2000] CRDD No. 48, 21 February 2000, at para. 21.
[204] *WDK (Re)*, No. T96-04645 [1997] CRDD No. 187, 25 August 1997, at paras. 16–18.
[205] *WDK (Re)*, No. T96-04645 [1997] CRDD No. 187, 25 August 1997, at para. 18.
[206] *MGG (Re)*, No. T99-10153 [2000] CRDD No. 191, 5 September 2000, at paras. 17–18.

THE MEANING OF THE NEXUS CLAUSE: IS INTENTION REQUIRED? 285

and thus constitute the necessary causal link to a Convention ground.[207] For example, in a decision of the Canadian RPD involving the claim of Chinese minors trafficked for labour purposes, the Tribunal noted that

> there is a wealth of other evidence ... before us suggesting that, by virtue of family patriarchy, filial piety, ignorance, and the restricted choices of many rural Fuzhounese families caused by poverty, residence restrictions and other government policies, many young rural Fuzhounese are victimized and exploited by their poor rural families, and that, pursuant to this exploitation, they are at risk of forced migration to work abroad illegally and remit funds to the family, with an attendant risk of a number of serious human rights abuses, and an even greater risk of forced re-migration should the initial attempt at illegal migration fail ... If the claimant fits within [this] poorer, exploitative profile, then he might face a serious possibility of forced remigration should he return to China.[208]

A similar approach is beginning to emerge in relation to sex trafficking cases. For example, the UK Immigration Appellate Authority has recognized the claim of another 16-year-old Nigerian girl trafficked to the UK, identifying her vulnerability as arising due to her status as a 'young girl from Nigeria whose economic circumstances are poor'.[209] Similarly, the Canadian RPD recognized the claim of a young woman from the Ukraine who had been 'duped' into a trafficking ring, since her fear of being persecuted could be linked to her membership of the particular social group – 'impoverished young women from the former Soviet Union recruited for exploitation in the international sex trade'.[210] These cases are consistent with UNHCR Guidelines on Trafficking which recognize that '[m]embers of a certain race or ethnic

---

[207] See, for example, the IJ's decision in *Unnamed*, 18 June 2001 (case on file with author) in which the IJ upheld a claim from a trafficked woman on the basis that her fear was 'on account of' her membership in an 'ethnic group in Thailand, who has been forced into indentured servitude and deprived of the right to citizenship': at 8.
[208] *XUG (Re)*, No. TAO-02066 [2000] CRDD No. 248, 20 October 2000, at 5. See also *Li* [2000] FCJ No. 2037 at para. 22.
[209] See decision of the Immigration Appeal Authority in *Ogbeide v. Secretary of State for the Home Department* (Unreported, IAT, Appeal No. HX/08391/2002, 10 May 2002), cited in Anti-Slavery International, *The Migration-Trafficking Nexus: Combating Trafficking Through the Protection of Migrants' Human Rights* (2003) <http://www.antislavery.org/homepage/resources/the%20migration%20trafficking%20nexus%202003.pdf> at 31 May 2006, p. 19. See also Jarvis, 'Can Trafficked Persons Be Refugees?', at 7.
[210] *YCK (Re)*, No. V95-02904 [1997] CRDD No. 261, 26 November 1997, at para. 4.

group in a given country may be esepecially vulnerable to trafficking', as may be 'children or women generally' or 'subsets of children or women'.[211]

Although these cases are far more inclusive than those which adopt a strict intent-based standard, they raise the danger that a claim is satisfied once the person is shown to be at risk of serious harm *and* to be a member of a particular social group. As recognized by courts, this analysis is not sufficient, as it remains necessary to establish that the harm is *feared for reasons of* membership of the group. However, a closer analysis of these cases suggests that courts appear to be adopting the approach (although not explicitly stated as such) that the nexus clause is satisfied if a person's status makes him or her particularly vulnerable (or, to put it another way, at heightened risk) of potential persecution. In this way, the analysis resembles a disparate impact or indirect discrimination claim, in which the question is whether the member of a protected group faces a disproportionate risk of harm on the basis of his or her status, regardless of the intent of the person carrying out the discriminatory harm. Thus, to be an orphaned child, for example, puts the child at a significantly heightened risk of harm and, as recognized in many of the decisions, makes the applicant an attractive victim for potential persecutors, given the child's vulnerability and weakness. The logic of this analysis was recognized by the Full Federal Court of Australia in *Rajaratnam*, albeit in a different context, where the Court noted that: '[t]he extorted party ... may have become the subject of extortion because of the known susceptibility of a vulnerable social group to which he or she belongs, that social group being identified by a Convention reason',[212] concluding that in such a case a claim could be established.

Evidentiary issues: singling out versus group-based harm

The final issue which must be addressed in respect of the nexus clause relates not so much to the *test* to be satisfied (for example, issues of sole/mixed causes or questions of intention), but the *method* by which

---

[211] UNHCR, *Guidelines on International Protection: The application of Article 1A(2) of the 1951 Convention and/or Protocol relating to the status of refugees to the victims of trafficking and persons at risk of being trafficked*, HCR/GIP/06/07 (7 April 2006) at para. 32.

[212] *Rajaratnam* [2000] FCA 1111 (Unreported, Moore, Finn and Dowsett JJ, 10 August 2000).

applicants must establish that the nexus clause has been satisfied. The key issue is that there remains a tendency to dismiss applications on the basis that the harm which the applicant fears is also feared by an entire group; thus, since the applicant is not 'singled out' for harm, he or she is not being persecuted for a Convention ground. This is potentially exacerbated in the context of economic claims, given that economic and social rights are often denied to an entire class of people rather than only to particular individuals in society. It is vital that courts approach this issue in conformity with existing principle and do not allow the group-based nature of economic and social rights violations to defeat an 'individual' refugee claim.

This trend is particularly prevalent in US decisions in which refugee claims are dismissed on the basis that the applicant fears only 'generalised economic disadvantage'.[213] It is certainly true that if nothing more is in fact proven, then nexus is not established. However, the problem in many of the cases that have invoked such principles in dismissing applications is that such conclusions are often drawn even where the evidence suggests that the generalized economic disadvantage is in fact suffered particularly (or even only) by persons of the applicant's racial or ethnic origin. For example, in *Patel*, the Court dismissed the claim on the basis that '[t]here is no indication that Patel faces a danger of persecution that is appreciably different from that faced by the hundreds of thousands of other Indo-Fijians still in Fiji'.[214]

By engaging in such reasoning, the court appears to be imposing a requirement that the applicant show that he or she was 'singled out' or targeted in a way different from the majority of persons comprising the race, ethnicity or particular social group to which the applicant belongs. Such an analysis is inconsistent with the relevant

---

[213] See, for example, *Patel* (1999) US App. Lexis 30517 (9th Cir. 1999). This has particularly been engaged in a series of cases concerning applications from Nicaraguans, where, in assessing whether the denial of a food ration card (and other socio-economic deprivations) amounted to persecution, the Ninth Circuit has stated, *inter alia*, that 'something more than generalized economic disadvantage' was required: see for example, *Ruiz v. Immigration and Naturalization Service* (1996) US App. LEXIS 14687 (9th Cir. 1996), at 6; *Vega-Gonzalez v. Immigration and Naturalization Service* (1996) US App. LEXIS 8489 (9th Cir. 1996), at 5; and *Molinares v. Immigration and Naturalization Service* (1995) US App. LEXIS 36930 (9th Cir. 1995), at 3.

[214] *Patel* (1999) US App. Lexis 30517 (9th Cir. 1999), at 6.

INS regulations[215] and with well-established authority that has rejected the 'singled out' requirement.[216] As has been explained by the US Court of Appeals for the Ninth Circuit, 'the more members of the group that are targeted, less important is individual showing'.[217] The crucial distinction is perhaps best explained in *Subramaniam v. Immigration and Naturalization Service*:[218]

> Generalised conditions of dislocation, such as might be caused by famine, earthquake or war, do not entitle a person to refugee status. At the same time, when there is ongoing violence specifically directed against many or all members of a particular race, religion, nationality or social or political group sufficient to cause a reasonable person under the circumstances to have a fear of persecution, a member of that group might meet the statutory definition of refugee.[219]

However, it should be noted that even in conditions of famine and civil war, an applicant may establish an individual claim to asylum if he or she can establish that the group to which he or she belongs is subject to harm for reason of that group membership.[220]

---

[215] The US regulations provide (at 8 CFR §1208.13):
'(iii) In evaluating whether the applicant has sustained the burden of proving that he or she has a well-founded fear of persecution, the asylum officer or immigration judge shall not require the applicant to provide evidence that there is a reasonable possibility he or she would be singled out individually for persecution if:
   (A) The applicant establishes that there is a pattern or practice in his or her country of nationality or, if stateless, in his or her country of last habitual residence, of persecution of a group of persons similarly situated to the applicant on account of race, religion, nationality, membership in a particular social group, or political opinion; and
   (B) The applicant establishes his or her own inclusion in, and identification with, such group of persons such that his or her fear of persecution upon return is reasonable.'

[216] For example, in *Chen v. Immigration and Naturalization Service*, 195 F 3d 198 (4th Cir. 1999), the Court held that '[t]he "well founded fear" standard ... does not require an asylum petitioner to show that he will be individually targeted, or "singled out", for persecution': at 203.

[217] See *Chand v. Immigration and Naturalization Service*, 222 F 3d 1066 (9th Cir. 2000), at 1074. See also *Baballah*, 335 F 3d 981 (9th Cir. 2003): at 991.

[218] 724 F Supp. 799 (9th Cir. 1989) ('*Subramaniam*').

[219] *Subramaniam*, 724 F Supp 799 (9th Cir. 1989), at 801.

[220] This has proven to be particularly contentious in the context of civil war cases: see Storey and Wallace, 'War and Peace in Refugee Law Jurisprudence'. In Canada, the 'comparative approach', developed in the context of civil war cases, has also been applied in other contexts. For example, the Canadian Gender Guidelines state: 'A gender-related claim cannot be rejected simply because the claimant comes from a country where women face generalized oppression and violence and the claimant's fear of persecution is not identifiable to her on the basis of an individualized set of facts. This so-called "particularized evidence rule" was rejected by the Federal Court of Appeal in *Salibian v. MEI*, and other decisions.'

Indeed, where evidence suggests that the applicant's ethnic, racial or gender group (for example) suffers disproportionately in respect of core human rights, decision-makers have relied on such evidence to buttress a claim that the fear of being persecuted is attributable to the applicant's connection to a Convention ground. For example, in *Refugee Appeal No. 71336/99*, in finding that the Roma applicant had established a well-founded fear of violation of core rights such as (*inter alia*) the right to work, education and housing, and that such persecution was for reasons of his race, the New Zealand RSAA relied on evidence which established, in the Czech Republic,

> continued discrimination against Roma in the area of housing, employment and access to education. [The documentary evidence] relevantly notes that 'although the unemployment rate in the Czech Republic is approximately 7%, the unemployment rate among Roma is quite high, with estimates reaching 70% and in some areas, 90%'. With many migrants now taking over the market in the area of labouring and unskilled work 'many Roma therefore rely on state benefits and live at or below the poverty line'.[221]

Thus, in this case evidence that this was the 'generalized' situation of Roma people served to fortify the applicant's claim to racial persecution, rather than to undermine it.

Conclusion

This chapter has identified the key issues and challenges raised by socio-economic claims in terms of establishing nexus between the risk of being persecuted and the Refugee Convention grounds. This is vital because the nexus clause is often assumed to be a key reason for excluding socio-economic claims from the rubric of the Convention regime. The analysis undertaken in this chapter has established that while there is no question that socio-economic claims raise important conceptual challenges and difficulties for decision-makers, and that the limits of the Convention definition will necessarily exclude many applicants fleeing socio-economic deprivation (most obviously where the applicant cannot differentiate his or her situation from that of the

---

[221] *Refugee Appeal No. 71336/99*, RSAA, 4 May 2000, at 13. Similarly, in *Refugee Appeal No. 2217/94*, RSAA, 12 September 1996, the RSAA referred to evidence that established that 'women account for 90% of worker layoffs', and other evidence of 'widespread employment discrimination' against women, particularly single women with children (the situation of the applicant) in support of its finding that the applicant had a well-founded fear based on gender and race (because of the race of her son): at 9–10.

general population in the home state), application of existing principle produces the result that a wide range of socio-economic claims may indeed fall within the Refugee Convention definition. As highlighted in this chapter, the economic migrant–refugee distinction has often been invoked, whether explicitly or implicitly, in a way that has tended to distract decision-makers from the key issues relevant to a refugee claim based on socio-economic deprivation. By contrast, it has been established that when decision-makers focus instead on analysing socio-economic claims in accordance with existing principle, including correct application of the 'mixed motives' doctrine and the related notion that the Convention ground need only constitute part of the reasons for the person's well-founded fear, as well as acknowledgement that 'singling out' is not required to be established, many of the traditional obstacles to socio-economic claims are found to be surmountable. These principles are alone sufficient to ensure a more inclusive and nuanced approach to socio-economic claims. An additional development, namely the move away from an approach which requires proof of intent to harm (either on the part of the persecutor or the state) towards one that focuses on the reason for the person's predicament, holds considerable promise in extending the Convention regime even further so as to encompass those claims in which the reasons for an applicant's socio-economic deprivation can be linked to a Convention ground, notwithstanding an inability to establish individual intent. Following on from this analysis, the next chapter now turns to consider the correct interpretation of the final aspect of the definition, namely the Convention grounds.

6 Economic disadvantage and the Refugee Convention grounds

Introduction

Chapter 5 focused on the various ways in which the 'for reasons of' clause, which requires the applicant to link his/her relevant 'well-founded fear of being persecuted' to a Convention ground, raises difficulties for refugee claims based on socio-economic deprivation. It focused on the nature of that causal link, and the particular challenges involved in establishing the causal link in the context of economic claims. This chapter now turns to consider the second aspect of the requirement to establish a link to a Convention ground: the correct interpretation of those grounds as relevant to economic-related claims.

As explained in the previous chapter, it is necessary for an applicant to establish that his or her fear of being persecuted is for reasons of his or her race, nationality, religion, political opinion or membership of a particular social group. All of these grounds are potentially relevant to claims based on economic deprivation, as has been made clear throughout this book. Numerous examples have been provided of cases where economic persecution is inflicted on the basis of race (for example, the Roma cases), religion (for example, the Sabean cases) and political opinion (for example, the cases involving land disputes which are properly understood as involving a political element). Claims based on socio-economic deprivation may also be made on the basis of nationality,[1] and a number of recent cases in different jurisdictions

---

[1] Nationality is defined very widely, and goes beyond mere citizenship. See for example, EU Directive on a Common Asylum Policy, art. 10(1)(c): 'the concept of nationality shall not be confined to citizenship or lack thereof but shall in particular include membership of a group determined by its cultural, ethnic, or linguistic identity, common geographical or political origins or its relationship with the population of another State'.

have concerned claims by non-nationals who face serious socio-economic deprivation by virtue of their non-citizenship status.[2]

Notwithstanding the potential relevance of all Convention grounds, the focus of this chapter is primarily on the interpretation and application of the 'membership of a particular social group' ('MPSG') ground, as it has proven to be the most promising in terms of encompassing a range of new types of claim and is the ground upon which many emerging economic-related claims are being made by groups such as women, children, disabled persons and the poor. For this reason it is important that its interpretation be undertaken in a principled and objective manner, in order to ensure that the expansion to new types of claims is sustainable in terms of existing principles of treaty interpretation. Accordingly, this chapter begins with a brief overview of the key conceptual approaches existing in the case law today, assessing the merits of the two most prominent approaches. This is vital because the subsequent analysis, which turns to consider the application of these principles to those social groups most relevant to the current topic, namely economic class and occupation, disabled persons, and women and children, must be informed by an established analytical approach to the social group category.

Interpreting the social group ground: conceptual approaches

The question of the proper interpretation of the MPSG ground has proven to be a highly controversial topic in recent years,[3] having been considered

---

[2] These types of claims primarily concern persons who are non-citizens either in their place of birth/country of origin or who are stateless, where the state in which they reside declines to afford them citizenship or equivalent status. This fact alone raises issues pertinent to the present topic, since such a position often results in significant socio-economic deprivation. See: in the US: *Ahmed v. Ashcroft*, 341 F 3d 214 (3rd Cir. 2003); in the UK: *Kondratiev* [2002] UKIAT 08283; *Kovac v. Secretary of State for the Home Department* (Unreported, IAT, Appeal No. CC3034497, 28 April 2000) and *Peco* (Unreported, IAT, Appeal No. HX-74935-94, 12 November 1996); and in NZ: *Refugee Appeal No. 74880*, RSAA, 29 September 2005.

[3] It is widely recognized to be the least straightforward and most difficult Convention ground. As Justice North of the Federal Court of Australia has noted: 'The Convention grounds are limited in number. Most of them are clear cut, and easily ruled applicable or not. The "particular social group" ground is, in that respect, in a class of its own. It is more difficult to assess': *Minister for Immigration and Multicultural Affairs v. Applicant S* (2002) 124 FCR 256 at 271.

extensively by courts and commentators,[4] and examined closely by an expert roundtable under the auspices of the UNHCR's Global Consultations in 2001.[5] As the Global Consultations discussion concluded, following detailed consideration of existing jurisprudence, the category is 'the Convention ground with the least clarity'.[6] Given its potentially wide application, decision-makers have struggled to strike a balance between an overly expansive view and an unduly narrow approach to its interpretation.

Notwithstanding the struggle to develop consistent and coherent principles of interpretation, there is consensus on some basic principles of interpretation. First, it is clear that there must be some limit to the term MPSG and that it is not intended to act as a 'catch-all' provision to accommodate all cases that do not fall within the other four grounds. It is well recognized that to interpret this ground as all-encompassing would make the nexus clause superfluous.[7]

Second, it is clear that the group must exist independently of the persecution − to hold otherwise would mean, in the words of McHugh J of the High Court of Australia, that 'persons who had a well-founded fear of persecution were members of a particular social group because they feared persecution':[8] a result based on circular reasoning. Notwithstanding this principle, a number of courts have noted that the actions of persecutors may 'serve to identify or even cause the creation of a particular social group in society'.[9]

---

[4] There are many academic articles that consider the social group ground, often in the context of a particular type of claim, for example by women: see below note 145. For an overview of the approaches to MPSG generally in the case law, see Thomas Alexander Aleinikoff, 'Protected Characteristics and Social Perceptions: An Analysis of the Meaning of "Membership of a Particular Social Group"', in Feller, Türk and Nicholson (eds.), *Refugee Protection in International Law*, pp. 263–11, and Hathaway and Foster, 'Membership of a Particular Social Group'.

[5] See 'Summary Conclusions: Membership of a Particular Social Group, Expert Roundtable, San Remo, September 2001', in Feller, Türk and Nicholson (eds.), *Refugee Protection in International Law*, pp. 312–13 ('UNHCR Summary Conclusions').

[6] Ibid., p. 312. See also UNHCR, *Guidelines on International Protection: 'Membership of a particular social group' within the context of Article 1A(2) of the 1951 Convention and/or its 1967 Protocol relating to the Status of Refugees*, HCR/GIP/02/02, 7 May 2001 at para. 1 ('UNHCR Guidelines on Social Group').

[7] See Hathaway and Foster 'Membership of a Particular Social Group', at 479–80.

[8] *Applicant A* (1996) 190 CLR 225, adopted by Lord Steyn in *Shah* [1999] 2 AC 629 at 645; by Lord Hoffman (at 652–3) and by Lord Hope (at 658).

[9] See *Refugee Appeal No. 71427/99*, RSAA, 16 August 2000, at para. 101, citing *Ward* [1993] 2 SCR 689, *Applicant A* (1996) 190 CLR 225 and *Shah* [1999] 2 AC 629 in support.

Third, it is now clear that there is no requirement that the applicant establish that he or she is 'joined together in a group with some degree of cohesiveness, co-operation or interdependence'[10] or that there exists a 'voluntary associational relationship'[11] between members of the 'particular social group' ('PSG'). Nor is there a requirement that the PSG constitutes any particular size. Indeed, as Gleeson CJ of the High Court of Australia has noted, '[t]here are instances where the victims of persecution in a country have been a majority. It is power, not number, that creates the conditions in which persecution may occur'.[12] In the same judgment, McHugh and Gummow JJ noted that the members of a PSG may be 'very numerous' and that 'the inclusion of race, religion and nationality in the Refugee Convention definition shows that that of itself can be no objection to the definition of such a class'.[13]

[10] See *Shah* [1998] 4 All ER 30 at 48 (Staughton LJ), who in fact held that this was a requirement; however, this decision of the Court of Appeal was overturned on appeal to the House of Lords: see *Shah* [1999] 2 AC 629 at 640–3 (Lord Steyn); at 651 (Lord Hoffmann) and at 657 (Lord Hope). See also *Khawar* (2002) 210 CLR 1, in which the High Court of Australia rejected a cohesiveness requirement in relation to MPSG: at 13 (Gleeson CJ); at 26–28 (Gummow and McHugh JJ) and at 43 (Kirby J). The UNHCR Summary Conclusions also found that '[t]here is no requirement that a group be cohesive in order to be recognised as a particular social group within the meaning of the Convention; that is, there need be no showing that all members of a group know each other or associate together': at para. 4.

[11] This was originally required by the US Court of Appeals for the Ninth Circuit in *Sanchez-Trujillo v. Immigration and Naturalization Service*, 801 F 2d 1571 (9th Cir. 1986) ('*Sanchez-Trujillo*'). However, it has been rejected in most other common law courts: see for example *Shah* [1999] 2 AC 629; *Applicant A* (1996) 190 CLR 225 at 241; *Re ZWD, Refugee Appeal No. 3/91*, RSAA, 20 October 1992. Indeed, even the Ninth Circuit has moved away from it in recent cases: see *Hernandez-Montiel v. Immigration and Naturalization Service*, 225 F 3d 1084 (9th Cir. 2000) ('*Hernandez-Montiel*'). In that case, the 9th Circuit held that a particular social group 'is one united by a voluntary association, including a former association, *or* by an innate characteristic that is so fundamental to the identities or consciences of its members that members either cannot or should not be required to change it': at 1093 (emphasis in original). See also *Thomas v. Gonzales*, 409 F 3d 1177 at 1187 (9th Cir. 2005) where the Court explictly adopted the *Acosta* standard.

[12] *Khawar* (2002) 210 CLR 1 at 13. The Canadian Gender Guidelines also note that '[t]he fact that the particular social group consists of large numbers of the female population in the country concerned is irrelevant – race, religion, nationality, and political opinion are also characteristics that are shared by large numbers of people'.

[13] *Khawar* (2002) 210 CLR 1 at 28. See also Kirby J: 'The Minister conceded in argument that the number of persons potentially involved in a "particular social group" would not of itself put an applicant otherwise within that group outside the Convention definition. This must be correct. After all, there were six million Jews who were incontestably persecuted in countries under Nazi rule. The mere fact that they were many would not have cast doubt on their individual claims to protection had only there

Finally, as is the case in relation to other Convention grounds, an applicant need not demonstrate that all members of a PSG are at risk of being persecuted in order to establish the existence of the PSG.[14]

While a number of different approaches to the interpretation of the MPSG ground proliferated in the early jurisprudence, it is accurate to say that there are currently two dominant approaches in the common law: the *ejusdem generis*, or 'protected characteristics' approach, and the social perception or sociological approach.[15] Some civil law jurisdictions have also adopted one of the two approaches,[16] although the majority of civil law jurisdictions have not developed this ground at all.[17]

The first, the *ejusdem generis* or protected characteristics approach, was initially articulated in the decision of the US Board of Immigration Appeals in *Matter of Acosta*,[18] and is now the predominant approach in the common law, having been adopted in Canada, New Zealand and

---

been an international treaty such as the Refugees Convention in force in the 1930s and 1940s': at 43.

[14] UNHCR, *Guidelines on Social Group*, at para. 17. See also Hathaway and Foster, 'Membership of a Particular Social Group', at 478.

[15] Hathaway and Foster, 'Membership of a Particular Social Group', at 480; UNHCR Summary Conclusions. Although there is still some inconsistency between the Circuit Courts of Appeal in the USA, the case law has recently converged so that the *Acosta* test (*ejusdem generis* or protected characteristics) is now the predominant approach. In *Castellano-Chacon*, 341 F 3d 533 (6th Cir. 2003), the Sixth Circuit noted that the First, Third and Seventh Circuits have 'explicitly adopted the BIA's approach' in *Acosta*, which the Sixth Circuit decided to follow in that case: at 560. See also *Thomas v. Gonzales*, 409 F 3d 1177 (9th Cir. 2005).

[16] For example, in Belgium the Refugee Appeals Board explicitly adopts the 'protected characteristics approach': see Dirk Vanheule, 'Belgium', in Carlier, Vanheule, Peña Galiano and Hullman (eds.), *Who is a Refugee?*, pp. 100–2; while the German Administrative Court implicitly adopts this approach: Klaus Hullman, 'Germany', in Carlier, Vanheule, Peña Galiano and Hullman (eds.), *Who is a Refugee?*, pp. 283–4.

[17] As noted in the UNHCR Summary Conclusions, '[i]n civil law jurisdictions, this ground is less developed, with more focus placed on the interpretation of persecution and on the other four grounds': p. 312. For example, in Austria, the Administrative Court has 'always been very hesitant to make use' of the MPSG ground: Klaus Hullman, 'Austria' in Carlier, Vanheule, Peña Galiano and Hullman (eds.), *Who is a Refugee?*, pp. 49–50. In Denmark the Refugee Appeals Board 'interprets the concept very strictly and appears to be most likely to grant F-status [non-refugee status] in cases concerning social groups': Pia Lynggaard Justesen, 'Denmark', in Carlier, Vanheule, Peña Galiano and Hullman (eds.), *Who is a Refugee?*, pp. 330–1. In Spain '[n]o relevant decision based on membership of a particular social group could be found': Carlos Galiano, 'Spain', in Carlier, Vanheule, Peña Galiano and Hullman (eds.), *Who is a Refugee?*, p. 368.

[18] *Matter of Acosta*, BIA, 1985 BIA LEXIS 2, 19 I & N Dec. 211, 1 March 1985.

the UK.[19] This formulation invokes the well-established doctrine of *ejusdem generis*, which holds that general words used in an enumeration with specific words should be construed in a manner consistent with the specific words.[20] In applying this doctrine to the Refugee Convention, the BIA explained that '[e]ach of [the other grounds of being persecuted] describes persecution aimed at an immutable characteristic: a characteristic that either is beyond the power of an individual to change or is so fundamental to individual identity or conscience that it ought not be required to be changed'.[21] Applying this analysis to the MPSG ground, the BIA concluded that, properly construed, the MPSG ground, includes 'persecution that is directed toward an individual who is a member of a group of persons all of whom share a common, immutable characteristic. The shared characteristic might be an innate one such as sex, color or kinship ties, or in some circumstances it might be a shared past experience such as former military leadership or land ownership ... Whatever the common characteristic that defines the group, it must be one that the members of the group either cannot change, or should not be required to change because it is fundamental to their individual identities or conscience'.[22] As adopted in a number of other jurisdictions, it is now understood as comprising the following categories:

- Groups defined by an immutable characteristic.
- Groups whose members are voluntarily associated with a particular *status* for reasons 'so fundamental to their human dignity that they should not be forced to forsake that association'[23] or that 'the association or group exists by virtue of a common attempt made by its members to exercise a fundamental human right'.[24]
- Groups associated by a former voluntary status, unalterable due to its historical permanence.

---

[19] For Canadian authority, see *Ward* [1993] 2 SCR 689. For UK authority see *Shah* [1999] 2 AC 629 at 651 (Lord Hoffmann) and at 658 (Lord Hope), although Lord Hope of Craighead also discussed the MPSG ground in a more general manner consistent with the sociological approach (set out by the IAT in *Montoya v. Secretary of State for the Home Department* [2002] INLR 399 ('*Montoya*')). For a recent IAT decision clearly adopting the Acosta/Ward formulation, see *HS* [2005] UKAIT 00120 (Unreported, 4 August 2005) at paras. 144–5. The approach has also been adopted in New Zealand: see *Re ZWD, Refugee Appeal No. 3/91*, RSAA, 20 October 1992; *Re GJ, Refugee Appeal No. 1312/93*, RSAA, 30 August 1995 and *Refugee Appeal No. 71427/99*, RSAA, 16 August 2000. For US authority, see above note 15.
[20] Hathaway, *The Law of Refugee Status*, p. 160.   [21] Hathaway, *The Law of Refugee Status*, p. 160.
[22] Hathaway, *The Law of Refugee Status*, p. 160.
[23] *Chan* [1995] 3 SCR 593 at 643–4 (La Forest J dissenting, but not relevantly, and his judgment has been widely subsequently cited).
[24] *Chan* [1995] 3 SCR 593 at 643–4.

The corollary is that excluded from this approach are groups 'defined by a characteristic which is changeable or from which disassociation is possible, so long as neither option requires renunciation of basic human rights'.[25]

The second key approach is the sociological or social perception approach, which differs from the 'protected characteristics' approach because it focuses less on the internal characteristics of the members of the group and more on a 'social perception', 'external' or 'sociological approach' to MPSG. It attempts to elucidate the 'ordinary' meaning of the term MPSG. This approach is predominantly followed by Australian courts,[26] and is best articulated in the leading decision of the High Court in *Applicant A*,[27] a case concerning the question whether opponents of China's one-child policy constituted a PSG for the purposes of the Refugee Convention. The Court took the view that the phrase 'membership in a particular social group' should be given a broad interpretation 'to encompass all those who fall fairly within its language and should be construed in light of the context in which it appears'[28] and considered that 'not only is it impossible to define the phrase exhaustively, it is pointless to do so'.[29] Thus, the Court chose to set out broad principles to

---

[25] Hathaway, *The Law of Refugee Status*, p. 161. This principle is derived from *Ward* [1993] 2 SCR 689 at 737–8, where the Court said: '[s]urely there are some groups, the affiliation in which is not so important to the individual that it would be more appropriate to have the person disassociate him- or herself from it before Canada's responsibility should be engaged'. See also the NZ RSSA: '[w]hat is excluded by this definition are groups defined by a characteristic which is changeable or from which disassociation is possible, so long as neither option requires renunciation of basic human rights': *Refugee Appeal 71427/99*, RSAA, 16 August 2000, at para. 97. See also *Re GJ*, *Refugee Appeal No. 1312/93*, RSAA, 30 August 1995, at 4.

[26] Although it is also supported by some academic commentators (see, for example, Goodwin-Gill, *The Refugee in International Law*, p. 365) and arguably by the UNHCR Handbook: see paras. 77–8. In addition, it appears to find some support in the approach of the US Court of Appeals for the Second Circuit, which requires that the members of the group be 'externally distinguishable': 'Like the traits which distinguish the other four enumerated categories – race, religion, nationality and political opinion – the attributes of a particular social group must be recognisable and discrete': *Gomez v. Immigration and Naturalization Service*, 947 F 2d 660 (3rd Cir. 1991), at 664, cited in *Castellano-Chacon*, 341 F 3d 533 (6th Cir. 2003). This external perception test was considered by the Sixth Circuit in *Castellano-Chacon*, wherein it noted that the UNHCR also seems to advocate that the external perception test 'can be considered as an additional factor in the overall calculus of what makes up a "particular social group"' (at 540, citing the UNHCR's *Guidelines on Social Group*), but ultimately refrained from incorporating this test in its own jurisprudence.

[27] *Applicant A* (1996) 190 CLR 225.   [28] *Applicant A* (1996) 190 CLR 225 at 241 (Dawson J).

[29] *Applicant A* (1996) 190 CLR 225 at 259 (Dawson J).

guide the adjudication of future cases, rather than provide a comprehensive framework of analysis. Dawson J explained:

> A 'group' is a collection of persons ... the word 'social' is of wide import and may be defined to mean 'pertaining, relating, or due to... society as a natural or ordinary condition of human life'. 'Social' may also be defined as 'capable of being associated or united to others' or 'associated, allied, combined'. The adjoining of 'social' to 'group' suggests that the collection of persons must be of a social character, that is to say, the collection must be cognisable as a group in society such that its members share something which unites them and sets them apart from society at large. The word 'particular' in the definition merely indicates that there must be an identifiable social group such that a group can be pointed to as a particular social group. A particular social group, therefore, is a collection of persons who share a certain characteristic or element which unites them and enables them to be set apart from society at large. That is to say, not only must such persons exhibit some common element; the element must unite them, making those who share it a cognisable group within their society.[30]

It is clear that, under this approach, significance is placed upon the external perception of the group, including the perception of the relevant persecutors.[31] While eschewing an approach that defines a PSG solely by reference to a fear of being persecuted, in *Applicant A* McHugh J nonetheless explained that the actions of the persecutors might serve to identify or even cause the creation of a PSG in society. For example, His Honour explained that while left-handed men are not a PSG, 'if they were persecuted because they were left-handed, they would no doubt quickly become recognizable in their society as a [PSG]'.[32] Thus the question is whether the group is perceived by people in the relevant country as a distinct social group 'by reason of some characteristic, attribute, activity, belief, interest or goal that unites them'.[33]

In an attempt to resolve the question of which of these competing approaches should be adopted in interpreting the MPSG ground, it is necessary once again to resort to the principles of treaty interpretation

---

[30] *Applicant A* (1996) 190 CLR 225 at 241 (Dawson J). For a more recent exposition of the social group ground by the High Court of Australia, see *Applicant S v. Minister for Immigration & Multicultural Affairs* (2004) 217 CLR 387.

[31] Carlier is of the opinion that 'it is the persecutor who imputes the social character to a group by persecuting it'. He argues that the classic notion of social class, probably in the mind of the Swedish delegate who proposed the MPSG category, can only be defined by way of opposites, i.e. with respect to another social class. He argues that 'it is the persecutor who identified, qualifies or labels the social group': Carlier, Vanheule, Peña Galiano and Hullman (eds.), *Who is a Refugee?*, pp. 713–14.

[32] *Applicant A* (1996) 190 CLR 225 at 264 (McHugh J).

[33] *Applicant A* (1996) 190 CLR 225 at 264 (McHugh J).

set out in the VCLT. It is arguable that the requirement that treaty terms be given their 'ordinary' meaning, in light of the context and object and purpose of the treaty, dictates that the protected characteristics approach is to be preferred as a matter of international law.[34] Given that the phrase 'membership of a particular social group' does not have an 'ordinary meaning',[35] attention must be focused on the object and purpose of the Refugee Convention. In this regard, the protected characteristics approach has been specifically developed so as to accord with the underlying object and purpose of the Refugee Convention,[36] as it resonates with a human rights approach to refugee determination, which, as developed in Chapter 2, is the preferable method of interpreting the Refugee Convention.[37] It thus provides an objective, principled approach, which is 'sufficiently open-ended to allow for evolution', 'but not so vague as to admit persons without a serious basis for claim to international protection'.[38] By contrast, the social perception test has been criticized on the basis that it is an open-ended and unprincipled approach, with the only truly limiting factors being that (a) purely individuated risk would not be sufficient to constitute a PSG and (b) the group identity could not be solely a function of the persecution feared.[39]

This is also buttressed by policy considerations since, on a practical level, the protected characteristics approach has provided the basis for some important decisions extending the application of the Refugee Convention to groups such as women and homosexual men and women. In addition, it provides a helpful analytical framework for decision-makers, which assists in ensuring consistency in decision-making.

---

[34] For an analysis of the competing approaches, see Hathaway and Foster 'Membership of a Particular Social Group', at 484–9.
[35] In other words, the phrase is not one of common parlance, unlike, for example, race or religion. Nor is it found in other international treaties.
[36] See Lord Hoffmann in *Shah*: 'In choosing to use the general term "particular social group" rather than an enumeration of specific social groups, the framers of the Convention were in my opinion intending to include whatever groups might be regarded as coming within the anti-discriminatory objectives of the Convention': see [1999] 2 AC 629 at 645.
[37] Aleinikoff, 'Protected Characteristics and Social Perceptions', p. 290; *Re GJ, Refugee Appeal No. 1312/93*, RSAA, 30 August 1995, at 28.
[38] Hathaway, *The Law of Refugee Status*, p. 161.
[39] As the NZ RSAA has warned, '[t]he difficulty with the "objective observer" approach is that it enlarges the social group category to an almost meaningless degree. That is, by making societal attitudes determinative of the existence of the social group, virtually any group of persons in a society perceived as a group could be said to be a particular social group. The Refugee Convention, however, was not intended to afford protection to every such persecuted group': *Re GJ, Refugee Appeal No. 1312/93*, RSAA, 30 August 1995, at 28.

The social perception approach by contrast raises practical concerns, as adjudicators may encounter difficulties in assessing the 'social perceptions' of other societies, particularly those that are very different from their own.[40]

The protected characteristics approach is the dominant approach in the common law world,[41] and was endorsed by the relevant Expert Roundtable under the auspices of the UNHCR's Global Consultations Project, where it concluded that a PSG 'is a group of persons who share a common characteristic other than their risk of being persecuted, and which sets them apart. The characteristic will ordinarily be one which is innate, unchangeable or which is otherwise fundamental to human dignity'.[42]

The major criticism[43] of the protected characteristics approach is said to be that it may be overly and unnecessarily narrow and risks excluding a number of claims that ought properly to be included in the Refugee Convention definition.[44] For example, both judges and

[40] Hathaway and Foster 'Membership of a Particular Social Group', at 484.
[41] The approach has been adopted in the UK, Canada, NZ and in the majority of Circuits in the USA: see above note 19. See generally Hathaway and Foster, 'Membership of a Particular Social Group'.
[42] UNHCR Summary Conclusions, at 312. These summary conclusions 'reflect broadly the understandings emerging from the discussion' held at the San Remo Expert Roundtable on this topic, 6–8 September 2001. Paragraph 9 of the Conclusion states that '[c]onsideration could be given to the continued evolution of the membership of a particular social group category in particular by exploring the relevance of a "social perception" test'. This confirms the view that the opinion of this Roundtable was that the protected characteristics approach is the accepted position. However, it should be noted that in the subsequent UNHCR *Guidelines on Social Group*, the UNHCR took the position that 'the two approaches should be reconciled' such that the decision-maker first applies the protected characteristic approach and if this is unsuccessful then 'further analysis should be undertaken to determine whether the group is nonetheless perceived as a cognizable group in that society': paras. 10–13. For a critique of this approach, see Hathaway and Foster, 'Membership of a Particular Social Group', at 489–91.
[43] Goodwin-Gill challenges the appropriateness of the applicability of the rule since this is not a situation 'where general words follow enumerations of particular items, so that the general words should be construed in a manner consistent with the general nature of the enumerated items'. He is of the view that there is no reason to limit the interpretation of MPSG in light of characteristics believed to be necessarily common to the other listed grounds for persecution: see Guy Goodwin-Gill, 'Judicial Reasoning and "Social Group" after *Islam* and *Shah*' (1999) 11 *International Journal of Refugee Law* 537 at 541.
[44] For example, Morritt LJ of the English Court of Appeal has warned that 'to add the requirement of some distinguishing civil or political status [i.e. the *ejusdem generis* approach] would narrow the types of persecuted minority capable of being recognised as entitled to asylum without, in my view, sufficient justification': *Quijano v. Secretary of State for the Home Department* [1997] Imm AR 227 at 233.

commentators have raised the concern that groups such as street children,[45] students, professionals and refugee camp workers[46] may not fall within the categories formulated by the 'protected characteristics' approach. A similar concern has been raised by Aleinikoff, by reference to cases that have dismissed claims based on the social groups of wealth or land-ownership, arguing that while such claims do not fall within the 'protected characteristics' approach, they properly fall within the 'common-sense' notion of MPSG.[47] However, the true difficulty with the approach is not that such claims may not be encompassed, but that decision-makers have sometimes misapplied the approach resulting in an overly narrow application. For example, it is not clear why 'street children' are not considered to possess an 'immutable characteristic' (as will be further considered below). In addition, deserving claims are often dismissed on the basis that they are not encompassed within the protected characteristics approach when they should properly have been considered within another ground, such as political opinion or religion. These observations serve to emphasize the importance of close and careful application of the protected characteristics approach in order to ensure that it is applied in the most expansive but principled way possible.

Finally, it should be noted that some decision-makers who purport to apply the protected characteristics approach sometimes seek nonetheless to define the group by reference to additional considerations,

---

[45] This concern was expressed by Sedley J in *Shah* at the first stage of judicial review: 'It is not in my judgment necessary ... to situate the applicant within one of the Ward categories, though it would no doubt be valuable to be able to do so. These are aids to interpretation, not an exhaustive definition of the phrase "a particular social group" in the Convention. The dangers of a prescriptive approach will be apparent on any consideration of the shifting focus of systemic persecution in what has been a dreadful century for much of the human race. Take the street children of many South American cities, at constant risk of being killed by armed men beyond the control of the state. It might be difficult in the case of any one street child who reached a safe country to allocate him or her to a closely affiliated or cohesive social group except one defined by the fact that it is persecuted; yet it is hard to think that the framers of the 1951 Convention would have expected such a child to fall outside the protection which they were providing': *R v. Immigration Appeal Tribunal and Secretary of State for the Home Department; ex parte Shah* (Queen's Bench Division, CO 4330/95, 12 November 1996).

[46] Goodwin-Gill argues that 'there are social groups other than those that share immutable characteristics, or which combine for reasons fundamental to their human dignity': Goodwin-Gill, 'Judicial Reasoning', at 365.

[47] Aleinikoff, 'Protected Characteristics and Social Perceptions', p. 295.

such as whether there is discrimination against the relevant group in that society, or even whether there is 'a perception by society of the particularity of the social group'.[48] The latter consideration appears to require the applicant to satisfy *both* MPSG tests (and to provide the decision-maker with an additional reason to reject the claim even where the protected characteristics test is satisfied). Storey has sought to justify the approach that 'possession of an immutable characteristic is a necessary but not a sufficient condition for establishing a PSG' by reference to 'common sense, at least to the extent that in a society where women for example face no discrimination, it is hard to see in what way they could be regarded as set apart so as to qualify as a PSG for Refugee Convention purposes'.[49] However, it is not clear how this additional element is justified; it appears to breach the principle that the group must exist independently of the persecution and adds an additional layer of complexity to the

---

[48] A good example of this is provided in the decision of the UK Court of Appeal in *Skenderaj v. Secretary of State for the Home Department* [2002] EWCA Civ 567, [2002] 4 All ER 555 ('*Skenderaj*') where Auld LJ held: 'I suggest that membership of a particular social group exhibits the following uncontroversial and sometimes over-lapping features: (1) some common characteristic, either innate or one of which, by reason of conviction or belief, its members, cannot readily accept change; (2) some shared or internal defining characteristic giving particularity, though not necessarily cohesiveness, to the group, a particularity which, in some circumstances can usefully be expressed as setting it apart from the rest of the society; (3) subject to possible qualification that I discuss below, a characteristic other than a shared fear of persecution; and (4) subject to possible qualification in non-state persecution cases, a perception by society of the particularity of the social group': at para. 17. This is clearly requiring protected characteristics *plus* social perception. See also *Skenderaj* [2002] EWCA Civ 567, [2002] 4 All ER 555 at para. 17. The EU Directive on a Common Asylum Policy appears to adopt this approach. Article 10 (1)(d) provides that 'a group shall be considered to form a particular social group where in particular: members of that group share an innate characteristic, or a common background that cannot be changed, or share a characteristic or belief that is so fundamental to identity or conscience that a person should not be forced to renounce it; *and* that group has a distinct identity in the relevant country, because it is perceived as being different by the surrounding society' (emphasis added).

[49] Storey, 'The Advanced Refugee Law Workshop Experience', at 428–9. Interestingly, Storey criticizes Hathaway and Foster's rejection of the UNHCR's proposed merger approach on the basis that Hathaway and Foster 'do not note that some of the leading cases espousing the *ejusdem generis* approach ... do give some scope, at least on the outer margins, to the social perception dimension'. However, he seems to misunderstand that this is the *opposite* of what the UNHCR suggests – the UNHCR suggests that the *ejusdem generis* is to be the first inquiry, but if an applicant fails consideration is then given to the social perception test: see UNHCR, *Guidelines on Social Group*, at para. 13. However, in the cases Storey cites, the courts used the additional tests to *limit* the *ejusdem generis* approach.

MPSG analysis.[50] As Gleeson CJ of the High Court of Australia has observed (in relation to women but equally applicable to other groups):

> Women in any society are a distinct and recognizable group; and their distinctive attributes and characteristics exist independently of the manner in which they are treated, either by males or by governments. Neither the conduct of those who perpetrate domestic violence, or of those who withhold the protection of the law from victims of domestic violence, identifies women as a group. Women would still constitute a social group if such violence were to disappear entirely. The alleged persecution does not define the group.[51]

The approach adopted in the analysis to follow accordingly comports with the protected characteristics method of interpreting the MPSG ground, which requires close analysis of the relevant international human rights principles and doctrines in order to identify 'fundamental characteristics', but does not require reference to extraneous and additional elements.

---

[50] This trend is prevalent in the jurisprudence of the lower courts and tribunals, even in the face of authority from superior courts in the same jurisdiction. For example in both Australia and the UK, the tribunals are arguably misapplying *Khawar* and *Shah*, respectively. For example, in *Reference N03/45756*, RRT, 28 January 2004, the RRT considered the claim by a Moldovan woman previously kidnapped by traffickers from whom she only narrowly escaped, who feared being trafficked for the purposes of sex if returned to Moldova. Although accepting the applicant's evidence, the RRT rejected the claim on the basis that the applicant's fear of being persecuted was not for a Convention reason. In particular, the RRT rejected the contention that 'women in Moldova' or 'young women in Moldova' constitute a PSG on the basis that 'significant indices', including that 'the law provides for equal rights between women and men', 'the proportion of girls in secondary education is slightly higher than that of boys' and that 'the Law on Political Parties provides that parties and socio-political organisations must promote the principle of equality between women and men in decision-making organs at all levels', indicated that 'women are not distinguished from society at large': at 15. Where relevant at all to a trafficking claim, these considerations may pertain to the question whether the state is failing to protect women (and therefore whether the state is able or willing to protect), but are not relevant to the PSG question. Although the reference to being 'distinguished from society at large' is related to the social perception test adopted by the Australian courts, this approach is not confined to the Australian decisions; rather, examples can be found in other jurisdictions, most notably in the UK. For example, an identical approach was adopted by the IAT in *Secretary of State for the Home Department v. Kircicek* [2002] UKIAT 05491, in which the applicant's fear of being the victim of an honour killing was found not to be for a Convention reason, because, unlike the position of women in Pakistan (found to constitute a PSG in *Shah*), women in Turkey, whilst 'undoubtedly' still the victims of discrimination, 'can no longer be said to be discriminated against by the law and, we find, they are not unprotected by the State. We do not find that societal discrimination against women is either condoned or sanctioned by the State in Turkey': at para. 21. This is clearly confusing a number of different issues and introducing unnecessary complication into the PSG ground.

[51] *Khawar* (2002) 210 CLR 1 at 14.

Particular social groups

Economic class

In this category a range of possible social groups related to economic class will be considered, including caste and the poor as an economic class. The question whether such groups can legitimately fall within the definition of PSG is central to many types of refugee claims based on socio-economic deprivation. Many of these issues have been considered in recent case law and have given rise to conflicting views amongst different courts.

The most straightforward type of case in this category is that based on membership of an economic class that is undoubtedly immutable, such as caste, in respect of which there is no possible method by which the applicant can alter his or her position. Such cases clearly fall within the description of 'groups defined by an innate or unchangeable characteristic'.[52] In *MMS (Re)*, for example, the RPD found that the applicant married couple who had been born into the 'Nai' caste – a 'Dalit' or lower Hindu caste – were persecuted because of 'their membership [of] the caste which is a particular social group' given the 'unchangeable character of their membership in lower or scheduled caste within their country, India'.[53] Similarly, decision-makers in a number of jurisdictions have considered claims from the Midgan caste in Somalia, which documentary evidence suggests is 'a low caste, akin to the Dalits or "untouchables" in India' and that the Midgan are 'often kept as slaves by other clans'.[54] In a decision of the New Zealand RSAA, the Tribunal allowed the claim of a Midgan man on the basis that he was at risk of preclusion from paid employment and indeed risked enslavement on the basis of his caste which, 'unlike the situation of the "untouchables" or Dalits in India ... receive no government protection or positive discrimination measures to assist them to counter entrenched

---

[52] *Ward* [1993] 2 SCR 689 at 738. In addition, in Australia, where the 'protected characteristics' approach has not been adopted, both the RRT and Federal Court have assumed that caste constitutes a PSG: see, for example, *Salem Subramaniam and Ors v. Minister for Immigration and Multicultural Affairs* [1998] 483 FCA (Unreported, Davies J, 4 May 1998), at 4 (*'Salem Subramaniam'*); *Applicants S61 of 2002 v. Refugee Review Tribunal* [2003] FCA 1274 (Unreported, Lindgren J, 11 November 2003), at para. 67; *Reference N01/37224*, RRT, 12 August 2002, at 20.

[53] Nos. M95-02275, M95-02276 [1996] CRDD No. 162, 8 October 1996. See also *Refugee Appeal No. 75221* (23 September 2005) where the NZ RSAA stated, in relation to Dalits in India: 'Caste status can also denote membership of a particular social group; caste being an innate or internal defining characteristic': at para. 11.

[54] *Refugee Appeal No. 71509/99*, RSAA, 20 January 2000, at 2.

traditional discrimination'.[55] Decisions of the UK IAT have also held that persons of the Midgan caste (or 'underclass')[56] constitute a particular social group – for example 'Midgen women'[57] – and can also be characterized as suffering persecution on racial or ethnic grounds to the extent that the Midgen are considered akin to a different race within Somali society.[58]

The second and more difficult type of case relates to claims based on 'economic class' where the immutable nature of the class is not as straightforward or indisputable as in respect of caste. Although this issue could arguably relate both to wealthy and poor economic classes, the latter is most relevant for present purposes and is thus the focus in the following discussion.[59] An analysis of common law decisions

[55] *Refugee Appeal No. 71509/99*, RSAA, 20 January 2000, at 10.
[56] *Ferdowsa Ismail Beldeq* [2002] UKIAT 06753, at 1.
[57] *Ferdowsa Ismail Beldeq* [2002] UKIAT 06753, at 3.
[58] 'Midgen in Somalia are perceived as a race apart and there are substantial racial as well as historical and familial elements which establish whether an individual is or is not Midgen': *Ferdowsa Ismail Beldeq* [2002] UKIAT 06753, at 3. See also *Mohamud Osman Amin* [2002] UKIAT 04084, 30 August 2002, at 7 and *YS and HA Somalia CG* [2005] UKIAT 00088, 22 April 2005. For US authority, see *Deqa Ahmad Haji Ali v. Ashcroft*, 394 F. 3d 780 (9th Cir. 2005).
[59] However, it should be noted that the PSG, wealth or land ownership, has also been contentious. Hathaway states that the members of a privileged social class who resist renunciation of economic privilege are not protected, since it is within their ability voluntarily to renounce their property, an interest which is not protected under core human rights norms: Hathaway, *Law of Refugee Status*, at 166. However, this is not indisputable because it is possible to point to international human rights provisions protecting private property, such as art. 17 of the UDHR, which provides that everyone has the right to own property and that no one shall be arbitrarily deprived of his or her property (for reliance on this provision, see Krista Daley and Ninette Kelley, 'Particular Social Group: A Human Rights Based Approach in Canadian Jurisprudence' (2000) 12(2) *International Journal of Refugee Law* 148 at 169). A number of commentators support the notion of economic class as a PSG: for example, Grahl-Madsen cites as examples of PSGs economic and occupational groupings such as landowners, civil servants, capitalists, businessmen, professional people, farmers and workers: Grahl-Madsen, *The Status of Refugees in International Law*, p. 219. See also Goodwin-Gill, *The Refugee in International Law*, p. 366. In some jurisdictions that adopt the 'protected characteristics approach', it has been held that 'persons of substantial financial standing could not be regarded as a social group within the meaning of the Convention': *Re HS, Refugee Appeal No. 24/91*, RSAA, 9 June 1992, discussed in *Re ZWD, Refugee Appeal No. 3/91*, RSAA, 20 October 1992. However, it could be argued that in some of these cases the claim should properly have been characterized as one involving political opinion: see, for example, *Montoya* [2002] INLR 399, which was upheld by Court of Appeal: *Montoya v. Secretary of State for the Home Department* [2002] EWCA Civ. 620. By contrast, in jurisdictions that adopt a social perception/sociological approach such as Australia, it has been stated that wealth and land ownership may well be capable of constituting a PSG: see, for example, *Ram* (1995) 57 FCR 565 at 570; *Morato v. Minister of Immigration* (1992) 39 FCR 401 at 416 (Lockhart J); *Applicant A* (1996) 190 CLR 225 at 286 (McHugh J).

pertaining to the poor as an economic class reveals that the key disagreement relates to whether 'being poor' is a sufficiently immutable condition as to fall within the 'protected characteristics' approach to social group.

On one hand, a number of Canadian decisions, including from the Federal Court of Appeal, have held in a very straightforward manner that 'the poor' may constitute a PSG.[60] For example, in *UNN (Re)*,[61] the RPD noted that in the applicant's country of origin, Colombia,

[d]iscrimination based on race and socio-economic status is common. The murder rate is extremely high, and attacks of the type experienced by the claimant in Buenaventura occur in many regions of the country. Gangs and groups of the type he described sometimes operate with the tacit approval of the government, and indeed in many cases are alleged to be made up of policemen. Street children, poor young black men, and other 'undesirables' are common targets ... I find that the claimant suffered from discrimination amounting to persecution ... because of his race and socio-economic group.[62]

Other decisions have recognized that 'poor campesinos' from El Salvador[63] and 'impoverished young women from the former Soviet Union recruited for exploitation in the international sex trade'[64] can constitute PSGs. In perhaps the most expansive claim to date, the Federal Court of Canada held that the tribunal erred in failing to consider whether the (minor) applicants' fear of being re-trafficked on return to China was due to their membership in a social group, namely:

children from Fujian province, a province of China that the evidence before the RPD indicated was economically under-developed and a source of out-migration over a long period of years ... The applicants had further characteristics in common, those being that they were all from poor families, they all had little education and they all faced the depressing prospect of little opportunity to rise above the level of poverty in Fujian province.[65]

---

[60] In *Sinora v. Minister of Employment and Immigration* [1993] FCJ No. 725, for example, the Federal Court of Appeal held that the applicant, a citizen of Haiti, was claiming refugee status based on his membership in a particular social group – 'the poor'. Noel J stated that 'it is important to note that this group has been recognized as a social group by the Federal Court of Appeal': at para. 2. In a number of decisions, the RPD has clearly assumed that low socio-economic status can constitute a PSG, but has dismissed claims for other reasons: see, for example, *GIY (Re)*, No. T95-02172, [1996] CRDD No. 64, 25 July 1996, at para. 9.
[61] No. V95-00138, [1997] CRDD No. 12, 16 January 1997.
[62] *UNN (Re)*, No. V95-00138, [1997] CRDD No. 12, 16 January 1997, at paras. 13–14.
[63] *WBT (Re)*, No. V98-00787, [1997] CRDD No. 119, 4 June 1999.
[64] *YCK (Re)*, No. V95-02904, [1997] CRDD No. 261, 26 November 1997, at para. 4.
[65] *Li* [2000] FCJ No. 2037 at para. 22.

Social groups with a low socio-economic element have also been recognized in the UK ('young girls from Nigeria whose economic circumstances are poor')[66] and the USA ('low-income individuals with HIV').[67] In these decisions little if any analysis has been undertaken in respect of the question whether a poor socio-economic status can constitute a PSG, it being treated as rather self-evident and obvious in many of the successful decisions to date.

By contrast, however, some tribunals have rejected the notion that a poor economic class may constitute a PSG, on the basis that it fails the 'protected characteristics' test for want of immutability.[68] For example, in *UKS (Re)*, the RPD rejected the applicant's claim that he feared persecution in El Salvador on the basis of membership in the PSG (*inter alia*) 'young, male, poor, returnees from the USA and Canada to El Salvador' on the basis that:

being a male is innate, and being young is not changeable other than by the natural ageing process. *Being poor, however, is neither innate nor unchangeable.*[69]

Similarly, in a more recent decision regarding an application from a Jamaican woman, the RPD held that the PSG posited by the applicant – 'member of a lower income group' (membership of which was alleged to put her at greater risk from criminals who target such people and often

[66] See *Ogbeide v. Secretary of State for the Home Department* (Unreported, IAT, Appeal No. HX/08391/2002, 10 May 2002) cited in Anti-Slavery International, *The Migration-Trafficking Nexus*, p. 19. See also Jarvis, 'Can Trafficked Persons Be Refugees?', p. 7.
[67] This was a decision of the Newark Asylum Office in 2003 regarding HIV positive persons in Mali. The decision of the INS is unavailable because the US Asylum Office does not provide reasons for decisions. However, the basis of the argument before the INS office was obtained through correspondence with the lawyer, Thu Tran, and the HIAS and Council Migration Service of Philadelphia (on file with author). In a decision of the Supreme Administrative Court of the Czech Republic, *M.I. (Ukraine) v. Ministry of Interior*, 5 Azs 63/2004-60 (19.05.2004), the Court held that the group 'unemployed' can form a particular social group for the purposes of the Convention: summary of decision available on the University of Michigan Law School Refugee Caselaw Website <http://www.refugeecaselaw.org/> at 31 May 2006.
[68] For example, in *Li v. Immigration and Naturalization Service*, 92 F 3d 985 (9th Cir. 1996), the Ninth Circuit rejected the notion that 'low economic status' could constitute a PSG on the basis that members of such a group are not 'a collection of people closely affiliated with each other, who are actuated by some common impulse or interest', nor is there 'a voluntary associational relationship among the purported members, which impart[s] some common characteristic that is fundamental to their identity as a member of that discrete group': at 987. However, that case was based on the old test (adopted only by the Ninth Circuit), and the Ninth Circuit itself has moved away from it in recent cases: see *Hernandez Montiel*, 225 F 3d 1084 (9th Cir. 2000), at 1093 and *Thomas v. Gonzales*, 409 F. 3d 1177 (9th Cir. 2005).
[69] No. T96-02313, [1997] CRDD No. 223, 9 May 1997, at para. 70 (emphasis added).

go unpunished) – 'did not conform to the criteria of particular social group set out in the Ward decision' because '"lower income" is not an innate or unchangeable characteristic, neither is it fundamental to one's human dignity'.[70] Similar sentiments were also expressed in a decision of the New Zealand RSAA, where the Tribunal asserted that '[p]overty *per se* is not immutable, nor is it so fundamental to the identity of the members that they ought not to be required to change it', before adding: '[i]ndeed, it is surely a characteristic which the impecunious would be happy to change'.[71] However, this was immediately followed by the concession that '[t]he Authority does not overlook that there may be other circumstances where poverty might in fact be immutable because a state deliberately operates to prevent the poor from rising above their poverty'.[72]

The difficulty with such decisions is that they reflect a fundamental misunderstanding of the protected characteristic approach. As mentioned above, the justification for dismissing a potential PSG when it is not based on immutable characteristics or those fundamental to the applicant's human rights or identity is, as explained by the Canadian Supreme Court in *Ward*, that '[s]urely there are some groups, the affiliation in which is not so important to the individual that it would be more appropriate to have the person disassociate him- or herself from it before [the country of destination's] responsibility should be engaged'.[73] Thus, the corollary of the reasoning in the above cases is that refugee status was not justified (or even necessary) because the respective applicants could simply 'disassociate' themselves from being poor and thus avoid the persecution altogether. This disassociation or ability to change, however, must logically be a *present* option, not one that is merely possible on an abstract or theoretical level.

Applying this understanding to the above cases that have dismissed the notion of 'the poor' as a PSG, we can readily apprehend that such decisions are not grounded in a realistic assessment of the reasons for and difficulties in alleviating poverty. First, in none of the above cases was any assessment of the situation of the poor in the relevant countries undertaken, such as would sustain the finding that 'being poor' is not immutable. Second, while it is conceivable that in specific individual circumstances an applicant's present position of poverty could be changeable, this is simply not the case for most

---

[70] *ANK (Re)*, No. TA1-19010, [2002] CRDD No. 172, 26 August 2002, at para. 5.
[71] *Refugee Appeal No. 71553/99*, RSAA, 28 January 2000, at 9.
[72] *Refugee Appeal No. 71553/99*, RSAA, 28 January 2000, at 9.   [73] *Ward* [1993] 2 SCR 689 at 738.

of the world's poor. As the World Bank has recognized, 'poverty remains a global problem of huge proportions. Of the world's 6 billion people, 2.8 billion live on less than $2 a day, and 1.2 billion on less than $1 a day. Six infants of every 100 do not see their first birthday and 8 do not survive to their fifth'.[74] The Committee on Economic, Social and Cultural Rights ('Economic Committee') has explained that

[p]overty is not confined to developing countries and societies in transition, it is a global phenomenon experienced in varying degrees by all States. Many developed States have impoverished groups, such as minorities or indigenous people, within their jurisdictions. Also, within many rich countries there are rural and urban areas where people live in appalling conditions – pockets of poverty amid wealth. In all States, women and girls bear a disproportionate burden of poverty, and children growing up in poverty are often permanently disadvantaged.[75]

In these circumstances, the notion that the poor can simply change their status is unrealistic. On the contrary, the Economic Committee takes the view that 'these shocking figures signify massive and systemic breaches of the Universal Declaration of Human Rights and the two International Covenants, as well as of the Convention on the Elimination of All Forms of Discrimination against Women, the Convention on the Rights of the Child and other international human rights instruments'[76] and that 'poverty is a structural problem',[77] especially in developing countries,[78] the alleviation of which requires 'national action and international action and cooperation'.[79]

---

[74] See *Substantive Issues Arising in the Implementation of the International Covenant on Economic, Social and Cultural Rights: Poverty and the International Covenant on Economic, Social and Cultural Rights*, ESC Res E/C. 12/2001/10, UN ESCOR, 25th sess., Agenda Item 5, para. 4, UN Doc. E/C. 12/2001/10 (2001).

[75] Ibid., at para. 5.   [76] Ibid., at para. 4.

[77] Commission on Human Rights, *Report of the Expert Seminar on Human Rights and Extreme Poverty*, 7–10 February 2001, UN Doc. E/CN.4/2001/54/Add.1 (2001), at para. 20.

[78] *Substantive Issues Arising in the Implementation of the International Covenant on Economic, Social and Cultural Rights: Poverty and the International Covenant on Economic, Social and Cultural Rights*, ESC Res E/C. 12/2001/10, UN ESCOR, 25th sess., Agenda Item 5, para. 4, UN Doc. E/C. 12/2001/10 (2001) at para. 21: 'The Committee is deeply aware that there are structural obstacles to the eradication of poverty in developing countries ... some of the structural obstacles confronting developing States' anti-poverty strategies lie beyond their control in the contemporary international order. In the Committee's view it is imperative that measures be urgently taken to remove these global structural obstacles, such as unsustainable foreign debt, the widening gap between rich and poor, and absence of an equitable multilateral trade, investment and financial system, otherwise the national anti-poverty strategies of some States have limited chance of sustainable success'.

[79] United Nations Commission on Human Rights, *Human Rights and Extreme Poverty*, UN Doc. E/CN.4/RES/2000/12 (2000), at para. 1(e). As the Commission notes, 'the lack of political commitment, not financial resources, is the real obstacle to the eradication of poverty': at para. 1(f).

Moreover, as has been noted in both the case law and literature, 'economic conditions underlying ... poverty [may be] attributable to the exercise or the maintenance of political power'.[80] As noted by King J of the US District Court for the Southern District of Florida in *Haitian Refugee Center v. Smith*:

> The purpose of this discussion has been to show the degree to which Haitian economics is a function of the political system. Much of Haiti's poverty is a result of Duvalier's efforts to maintain power. Indeed it could be said that Duvalier has made his country weak so that he could be strong. To broadly classify all of the class of plaintiffs as 'economic refugees', as has been repeatedly done, is therefore somewhat callous. Their economic situation is a political condition.[81]

Thus, while being poor in and of itself will certainly not constitute persecution for a Convention reason,[82] it is clear that the poor can properly be considered a PSG, such that if being poor makes one vulnerable to persecutory types of harm, whether socio-economic or not, then a refugee claim may be established.[83]

The only remaining potential problem with considering the poor as a social group is raised in the New Zealand RSAA decision above, in which the Authority rejected the submission that 'the poor' constitutes a PSG on the basis (in addition to the immutability problem) that it 'is simply not a group capable of definition in this manner because poverty is a

---

[80] 'Political Legitimacy in the Law of Political Asylum', at 459.
[81] 503 F Supp 442 (1980), at 508.
[82] As was properly held in two decisions of the NZ RSAA relating to applicants from Tuvalu – a poor country in which the applicants were treated no differently from anyone else – see *Refugee Appeal No. 72189/2000*, RSAA, 17 August 2000 and *Refugee Appeal Nos. 72179/2000, 72180/2000, 72181/2000*, RSAA, 31 August 2000.
[83] This is supported by the UNHCR, *Guidelines on International Protection: The application of Article 1A(2) of the 1951 Convention and/or 1967 Protocol relating to the Status of Refugees to victims of trafficking and persons at risk of being trafficked*, HCR/GIP/06/07, 7 April 2006 ('UNHCR Trafficking Guidelines'), which recognizes that '[s]cenarios in which trafficking can flourish frequently coincide with situations where potential victims may be vulnerable to trafficking precisely as a result of characteristics contained in the 1951 refugee definition. For instance, States where there has been significant social upheaval and/or economic transition or which have been involved in armed conflict resulting in a breakdown in law and order, are prone to increased poverty, deprivation and dislocation of the civilian population. Opportunities arise for organized crime to exploit the inability, or lack of will, of law enforcement agencies to maintain law and order, in particular the failure to ensure adequate security for specific or vulnerable groups': see pp. 11–12. The difficulty is that this is often misunderstood, and decision-makers are sometimes reluctant to allow claims based on floodgates concerns: see for example *Escobar v. Gonzales*, 417 F. 3d 363 (3rd Cir. 2005) at 367.

relative concept'.[84] That is, '[t]o a wealthy person, a labourer may well be considered poor, but the same labourer would seem wealthy to a beggar. The "poverty line" in New Zealand, for example, would far exceed the income level of the middle classes in many third world countries'.[85] Thus the Authority concluded 'that there are insoluble difficulties in attempting to ... define "the poor" as a social group'.[86] The problem with this analysis is that it appears to assume that one definition of the poor (such as 'all those earning less than $1 per day') must be formulated which would apply to all societies and thus to all PSGs. However, this ignores the fact that whether or not the applicant is 'being persecuted' for reasons of his or her MPSG will always need to be determined in light of the particular factual circumstances of each individual case. In addition, the 'economic relativity' argument ignores contemporary understandings of 'poverty' as going beyond 'insufficient income to buy a minimum basket of goods and services' to more broadly refer to 'the lack of basic capabilities to live in dignity' which is reflected in the definition proposed by the Economic Committee: 'Poverty may be defined as a human condition characterized by sustained or chronic deprivation of the resources, capabilities, choices, security and power necessary for the enjoyment of an adequate standard of living and other civil, cultural, economic, political and social rights.'[87] In light of the country information available from both the Economic Committee and human rights groups, it is highly unlikely that decision-makers will be unable to identify a person as falling within the PSG 'the poor' in a particular society.

Finally, it should be kept in mind that, as has been alluded to above, 'being poor' will often intersect with other Convention grounds, such as gender, to constitute either one PSG or a set of combined Convention explanations for the risk of being persecuted. For example, a recent submission to the UN Commission on Human Rights from a Nepali women's human rights group noted that Nepali Dalit women are 'being trafficked

[84] *Refugee Appeal No. 71553/99*, RSAA, 28 January 2000, at 7.
[85] *Refugee Appeal No. 71553/99*, RSAA, 28 January 2000, at 7.
[86] *Ibid*. In general, the reasoning in this decision is very confused. The Tribunal appears to dismiss the claim based on a lack of nexus, a finding correct on the facts of this case. However, it adds in many other reasons, perhaps indicating its concern about the poor as a social group for future cases.
[87] *Substantive Issues Arising in the Implementation of the International Covenant on Economic, Social and Cultural Rights: Poverty and the International Covenant on Economic, Social and Cultural Rights*, ESC Res E/C. 12/2001/10, UN ESCOR, 25th sess., Agenda Item 5, para. 4, UN Doc. E/C. 12/2001/10 (2001) at para. 8.

and sexually harassed by the people from high caste due to their poverty and lack of societal status and prestige',[88] thus highlighting the potential effect of the intersection of class (in this example, caste) and gender. This combination of poverty with other grounds has also been recognized in a decision of the RRT which upheld the claim of a HIV-positive Colombian man on the basis that the combination of his poverty and HIV status would identify him as a member of the group considered 'desechables (disposables)' and thus make him susceptible to being persecuted by criminal gangs.[89] In reaching this conclusion, the RRT noted that while homosexuals generally may not be 'targeted', 'the treatment of gay men and lesbians may differ according to their economic and social status in Colombia'.[90] The RRT found that the identification of poor gay men as 'disposables' would put them at risk of 'social clean up operations', which also target the 'urban poor ... transvestites, male and female prostitutes, street children, vagrants and petty criminals'.[91]

The third and final type of case to be considered in this category relates to membership in a class-based organization such as a trade union or agricultural cooperative.[92] When a person fears persecution for reasons of membership in such an organization or association, decision-makers have had little difficulty in recognizing the PSG. In light of the importance of relevant international human rights principles, such as freedom of association,[93] such groups can be described as existing 'by virtue of a common attempt made by its members to exercise a fundamental human right'.[94]

For example, in *T (LR) (Re)*, the RPD recognized the claim on both political opinion and PSG grounds from a Guatemalan man suspected of being a union activist since 'persons who are union activists or who are

[88] Binda Kumari Magar, Forum for Women, Law and Development, *Submission to UN Commission on Human Rights, Sub-Commission on the Protection and Promotion of Human Rights, Working Group on Minorities*, 10th Session (Nepal: 1–5 March 2004), p. 2 (on file with author).
[89] *Reference: N98/22948*, RRT, 20 November 2000, at 10–15.
[90] *Reference: N98/22948*, RRT, 20 November 2000, at 12.
[91] *Reference: N98/22948*, RRT, 20 November 2000, at 12.
[92] Hathaway, *The Law of Refugee Status*, p. 169.
[93] Freedom of association is protected in both the ICCPR, art. 22, and the ICESCR, art. 8. It is also one of the four fundamental principles of the ILO which the ILO has held apply to all its members by virtue of their membership and irrespective of whether they have signed the relevant Conventions: see ILO, *Declaration on Fundamental Principles and Rights at Work* (1998) <http://www.ilo.org/dyn/declaris/DECLARATIONWEB.static_jump?var_language=EN&var_pagename=DECLARATIONTEXT> at 31 May 2006.
[94] *Chan* [1995] 3 SCR 593 at 643–4.

suspected of being such, face severe reprisals in Guatemala'.[95] In another decision, the RPD recognized that the members of an agricultural cooperative in Honduras were members of a PSG, since

> [t]he agricultural cooperative in question was the means the claimant and her co-workers had to support their families. In a country where major landholders, with impunity and the use of violence, still oppose agrarian reforms designed to provide poor and disadvantaged peasants with a minimum of dignity and chance for survival, membership in such an agricultural cooperative is a sacred and essential right which no one should be compelled to waive.[96]

Occupation

The question whether occupation can qualify as a PSG is an important one in the present context, given that refugee applicants from many countries suffer both socio-economic and other persecutory consequences as a result of the pursuit of their choice of occupation. It has proven to be one of the most difficult issues in the case law, given that occupation looks less like an 'immutable characteristic' than other well-accepted categories.

In considering whether a fear of being persecuted for reason of a person's employment or occupation is protected under the Refugee Convention, decision-makers have tended to reach different conclusions depending on whether the 'protected characteristics' or the 'social perception' approach is adopted. It has been argued that, according to the protected characteristics approach, groups defined by employment or profession fall within the social group category since freedom to choose one's occupation is a basic right pursuant to art. 6 of the ICESCR and art. 23 of the UDHR.[97] However, this has not generally been adopted in the case law, given that art. 6 of the ICESCR provides for 'the right of everyone to the opportunity to gain his living by work which he freely chooses or accepts', which is not necessarily the same thing as a right to a particular occupation of one's choosing.[98] This issue arose in

---

[95] No. V93-01037, [1994] CRDD No. 406, 29 March 1994, at 6.
[96] *ORL (Re)*, No. MAO-06253, [2001] CRDD No. 2, 18 January 2001, at para. 17.
[97] Hathaway, *The Law of Refugee Status*, p. 168. See also Daley and Kelley, 'Particular Social Group', at 170.
[98] It appears that the phrase in art. 6 – 'work which he freely chooses or accepts' – was designed to prohibit forced labour and that it was agreed that the State could not be expected to provide everyone with work of their own choosing: see Craven, *The International Covenant on Economic, Social and Cultural Rights*, pp. 197–9.

R v. Secretary of State for the Home Department, ex parte Ouanes,[99] in which the UK Court of Appeal considered an appeal by the Secretary of State against the decision of the IAT, which had held that government-employed midwives in Algeria constituted a PSG for the purposes of the Convention. The applicant was required, as part of her midwifery duties, to provide advice to women regarding contraception, and the IAT had concluded that she had a well-founded fear of being persecuted because fundamentalists were opposed to such duties and the authorities were unable to provide protection from the threats of the fundamentalists. On these facts, the IAT had held that her well-founded fear of being persecuted was for reasons of her MPSG. On appeal, Pill LJ (with whom Mummery LJ and Hobhouse LJ agreed) found that the midwives in that case 'do have common interests which are identifiable'; but, in applying the *ejusdem generis* approach advocated by the Secretary of State, concluded that:

The Convention, as its preamble recites, is concerned with fundamental rights and freedoms. I am not unmindful that the 'right to work' appears in article 23 as such a right, but that does not readily convert into a right of asylum for inability to do a specific job. 'Membership of a group of employees' does not appear as a specific ground for relief in article 1A(2). *The characteristic that defines the social group must, in situations such as the present, be one that the members should not be required to change because it is fundamental to 'their individual identities or conscience'* ... A *common employment does not ordinarily have that impact upon individual identities or conscience necessary to constitute its employees a particular social group within the meaning of the Convention.*[100]

Pill LJ went on to say that there might be a possibility that fellow employees may constitute a particular social group if, by reason of the nature of their employment or the addition of other links to those of employment, the 'protected characteristics' principle applies, providing employment as a member of a religious order as an example. However, it is questionable whether the approach leaves any independent operation for the MPSG category, given the close connection of the example provided to another Convention ground, namely religion.

This application of the protected characteristics approach has been followed in some other common law jurisdictions,[101] and is perhaps not

---

[99] [1998] 1 WLR 218 ('*Ouanes*'). [100] *Ouanes* [1998] 1 WLR 218 at 225 (emphasis added).
[101] For example, in New Zealand, see *Re KR, Refugee Appeal No. 61/92*, RSAA, 22 July 1992, in which the RSAA rejected an argument that taxi drivers constituted a social group (at 10); and in *Ward* [1993] 2 SCR 689 at 739, the Canadian Supreme Court approved the outcome in *Matter of Acosta*, BIA, 1985 BIA LEXIS 2, 19 I & N Dec. 211, 1 March 1985. In *Leticia*

surprising given that in *Matter of Acosta* itself (the origin of the *ejusdem generis* approach) the BIA held that a group of taxi drivers did not meet the immutable or protected characteristic requirement because 'the members of the group [the taxi cooperative] could avoid the threats of the guerillas either by changing jobs or by cooperating in work stoppages'.[102] While the BIA considered that it may be unfortunate that 'the [refugee applicant] either would have to change his means of earning a livelihood or cooperate with the guerillas in order to avoid their threats', this outcome was justified since 'the internationally accepted concept of a refugee simply does not guarantee an individual right to work in the job of his choice'.[103]

By contrast to the above, some claims based on occupational groups as PSGs have been accepted in the Australian jurisprudence under the social perception test. For example, in *Nouredine* v. *Minister for Immigration and Multicultural Affairs*,[104] the applicant was an Algerian beauty industry worker, an occupation condemned by Muslim extremists in Algeria. In overturning the decision of the Tribunal below, that beauty industry workers could not constitute a PSG, Burchett J quoted from a previous decision of the Federal Court in which it had been stated that '[t]here will no doubt be cases in which persons who have in common no more than a shared occupation do form a cognisable group in their society. This may well come about ... when persons who follow a particular occupation are persecuted by reason of the occupation that they follow'.[105] Burchett J explained:

In my [previous] judgment ... I referred to the situation in Cambodia under Pol Pot, where 'teachers, lawyers, doctors and others ... were regarded as potentially dangerous to the new order', as a textbook example of persecution for membership of a social group ... In *Zamora*, the Full Court instanced human rights workers in some countries. It is easy to think of further illustrations,

Bartolome Vicente v. *Immigration and Naturalization Service*, 2000 US App. LEXIS 29893, the US Court of Appeals for the Ninth Circuit held that 'health care professionals in the Philippines' are not a PSG because they are not a 'cohesive and homogenous' group: at 4. However this is the only jurisdiction – even in the USA – to impose this requirement and the Court has itself recently abandoned the cohesiveness test, thus casting doubt on the validity of this decision.

[102] *Matter of Acosta*, BIA, 1985 BIA LEXIS 2, 19 I & N Dec. 211, 1 March 1985, at 56.
[103] *Matter of Acosta*, BIA, 1985 BIA LEXIS 2, 19 I & N Dec. 211, 1 March 1985, at 56.
[104] (1999) 91 FCR 138 ('*Nouredine*').
[105] *Nouredine* (1999) 91 FCR 138 at 143, citing a previous decision, *Minister for Immigration and Multicultural Affairs* v. *Zamora* (1998) 84 FCR 458 ('*Zamora*'). However, in *Zamora* the Court held that '[o]rdinarily ... persons who have in common no more than a shared occupation are not recognizable as a particular social group in their society': at 464–5.

such as landlords after the revolutions in China and Vietnam, prostitutes almost anywhere, swineherds in some countries, and ballet dancers or other persons who followed occupations identified with Western culture in China during the Cultural Revolution.[106]

His Honour concluded that the beauty workers in that case were seen by religious extremists as purveyors of immorality and therefore as a group within society that should be eliminated, plainly bringing them within the MPSG ground.[107] On the other hand, other claims, such as those by an Ecuadorian tourist guide[108] and a Malaysian former policeman,[109] have been rejected.

Leaving aside the fact that a number of these cases could properly have been determined within other categories, most relevantly 'political opinion', or on the basis of former status, the question remains whether a person should be required to relinquish his or her occupation in order to avoid persecution. One of the problems in the existing case law is that there is a conflation of two analytically distinct issues, namely the question whether inability to pursue the occupation of one's choosing itself constitutes persecution (not relevant to the present question) and the presently pertinent question whether persecution feared as a result of pursuing an occupation may found a successful refugee claim, a confusion well illustrated in the BIA's assessment that 'the internationally accepted concept of a refugee simply does not guarantee an individual right to work in the job of his choice'.[110] The other key

---

[106] *Nouredine* (1999) 91 FCR 138 at 143–4.   [107] *Nouredine* (1999) 91 FCR 138 at 144.
[108] In *Zamora* (1998) 84 FCR 458, the Federal Court of Australia held that 'one should be cautious in characterising an occupational group as a particular social group. Quite apart from the risk of using persecution or the fear of persecution as a defining feature, in many cases an occupational group will not satisfy the requirement that it be recognised within the society as a group, even though it may fairly be said that the members of an occupational group have common characteristics not shared by their society. Indeed, members of an occupational group will have characteristics in common simply by reason of the fact that they all follow the same occupation, but this does not of itself make those who follow the same occupation members of a particular social group': at 464.
[109] For example, in *Vam v. Minister for Immigration and Multicultural Affairs* [2002] FCAFC 125 (Black CJ, Drummond and Kenny JJ, 10 May 2002), the Full Federal Court of Australia held, in relation to a claim by a man who based his claim on his fear of being persecuted for reason of his status as a former policeman, that '[i]t would seem unlikely in the extreme that possession by each of a number of people of those two characteristics ["former" and "policemen"] could give rise to a perception within Malaysian society that those people were a group set apart, as a social group, from the rest of the community in which they lived': at para. 14.
[110] *Matter of Acosta*, BIA, 1985 BIA LEXIS 2, 19 I & N Dec. 211, 1 March 1985, at 56.

problem is that the inconsistency in outcome arguably reflects a class bias in analysis since decision-makers appear more willing to uphold a claim from a professional person,[111] or one whose occupation is deemed noble,[112] than a relatively unskilled person such as a tourist guide or taxi driver. This risks privileging certain occupations and is also open to criticism on the basis that unskilled or semi-skilled workers may have far more difficulty in finding alternative work than more skilled or professional workers.

Applying the protected characteristics approach, the relevant question in determining the existence of a PSG is whether the expectation that a person may 'disassociate' from his or her occupation would infringe an established principle of international human rights law. The focus in answering this question has to date been on art. 6 of the ICESCR and specifically whether there is a right to the occupation of one's choosing. While this is certainly a relevant provision, perhaps a better focus would be on the fact that the ICESCR's requirement that the Covenant's rights will be exercised 'without discrimination' (art. 2(2)) and that states guarantee to 'take all appropriate steps to safeguard' the right to work (art. 6) means, at a minimum, that a person has a right not to be arbitrarily deprived of work.[113] As one Committee member has said, '[w]ithout a fundamental guarantee against arbitrary dismissal, the right to work would be meaningless'.[114] Requiring an applicant to abandon his or her occupation in order to avoid persecution thus conflicts with the right not to be arbitrarily deprived of work. Accordingly, a PSG based on occupation should properly be recognized

---

[111] Note the examples provided in *Nouredine* (1999) 91 FCR 138.
[112] For example, in *Zamora* (1998) 84 FCR 458, the Federal Court of Australia stated that '[t]here will no doubt be cases in which persons who have in common more than a shared occupation do form a cognisable group in their society... The persecution for following a particular occupation may well create a public perception that those who follow the occupation are a particular social group. Human rights workers in certain nations subject to totalitarian rule come to mind as a possible example': at 464–5. See also the example provided by Pill J in *Ouanes* [1998] 1 WLR 218, regarding members of a religious order.
[113] This is supported by Craven, *The International Covenant on Economic, Social and Cultural Rights*, p. 221. Von Sternberg also takes this view in relation to the occupational PSG cases: see von Sternberg, *The Grounds of Refugee Protection in the Context of International Human Rights and Humanitarian Law*, pp. 202–3, although his analysis is slightly different from the above.
[114] Cited by Craven, *The International Covenant on Economic, Social and Cultural Rights*, p. 221. This has recently been clearly affirmed by the Economic Committee in *General Comment No. 18, The Right to Work*, E/C.12/GC/18 (2006) at paras. 4 and 6.

as falling within the ambit of the Refugee Convention definition, based on the protected characteristics approach to determining the existence of a PSG.

Disabled and ill persons

The question whether a person who suffers from a chronic or serious illness or disability may establish membership in a PSG is an issue particularly relevant to socio-economic-related claims, as such persons in many societies are subject to a range of socio-economic deprivations, such as denial of education, employment and health care; they often suffer social ostracism, which leads to poverty and degrading treatment, and are often subject to violations of a range of other rights including the right to liberty.[115]

While the question of disability/illness as a PSG has not been considered extensively by the higher common law courts, a substantial body of tribunal and other administrative decisions has emerged in recent years, which supports the view that those suffering disability/illness can properly constitute a PSG.

Applying the protected characteristics approach, Canadian decisionmakers have had little difficulty in finding that a person suffering from a disability satisfies the definition of membership in a PSG. For example, in a decision concerning the claim by an unaccompanied 14-year-old from Poland suffering from an undisclosed disability which resulted (*inter alia*) in an inability to speak, the RPD found that he suffered abuse amounting to persecution from his parents and that this was inflicted by virtue of his membership in a PSG – a disabled minor.[116] Applying the principles set out in *Ward*, the RPD held that the 'first category' set out in the Supreme Court's decision

would also embrace those individuals, such as the claimant, who are physically disabled. The claimant was born xxxx (and cannot communicate properly except through sign language) and for all intents and purposes his condition is permanent and unchangeable. He also cannot change the fact that he is inflicted with xxxxxxx xxxxxxxx, which is publicly obvious since he is unable to control the xxx, which afflict him.[117]

---

[115] See generally Arlene Kanter and Kristin Dadey, 'The Right to Asylum for People with Disabilities' (2000) 73 *Temple Law Review* 1117 at 1118.
[116] *LXC (Re)*, No. TAO-05472, CRRD No. 96, 30 May 2001, at paras. 5–6.
[117] *LXC (Re)*, No. TAO-05472, CRRD No. 96, 30 May 2001, at para. 16.

While the protected characteristics approach may potentially encompass a range of disabilities,[118] it has been applied most frequently to HIV-positive persons who face persecution in their home countries by virtue of this status. As the RPD explained in a decision regarding the claim of an HIV-positive man from Poland, following citation of the first *Ward* category:

> While having a medical disability is not necessarily an 'innate' characteristic, once a condition such as being HIV-Positive has developed, [it] is not something within the power of an individual to change. It thus becomes an 'unchangeable characteristic' for the purposes of refugee determination. Moreover, while individuals fearing persecution on the basis of a medical disability are not specifically enumerated under the first category in Ward, the principle of assigning meaning to 'particular social group' by taking into account 'the general underlying themes of the defence of human rights and anti-discrimination' would clearly include individuals such as the claimant who are HIV-Positive. This is consistent with The Charter of Rights and Freedoms which specifically enumerates 'physical disability' in its anti-discrimination provision.[119]

Although the Canadian RPD referred to domestic law to buttress the finding that 'disability' is a protected status in human rights law, reference might more appropriately be made to international human rights law in which 'disability' has been considered to fall within 'other status' for the purposes of the ICCPR[120] and

---

[118] For example, it seems to have been assumed by the RPD in *BOG (Re)*, No. VAO-03441, [2001] CRDD No. 121, 16 July 2001, that the visually impaired could constitute a PSG, although the claim there was unsuccessful because the claimant failed to establish that the discrimination she would face on this basis was sufficiently serious as to amount to persecution. In *I.P.J. (Re)* No. A99-01121, [2000] CRDD No. 141, 11 September 2000, the RPD found that 'mentally handicapped persons' constitute a particular social group: at para. 10; and in *H. (G.Y.) (Re)* Nos. T94-05654 and T94-05655, [1995] CRDD No. 70, 1 February 1995, the RPD found that the applicants were members of the PSG 'disabled persons' based on their 'profound congenital deafness and inability to verbally communicate': at p. 4.

[119] *TNL (Re)*, No. T95-07647, [1997] CRDD No. 251, 23 October 1997, at para. 17. See also *OPK (Re)*, No. U95-04575, [1996] CRDD No. 88, 24 May 1996, at para. 31: 'Guided by Ward which includes sexual orientation in the category of groups defined by an innate or unchangeable characteristic, this claimant is identified as a member of a particular social group, that being Singapore homosexuals who have AIDS'; and *GPE (Re)*, No. U96-02717, [1997] CRDD No. 215, 16 September 1997, at para. 12: 'We therefore find that he would also be persecuted as a member of a particular social group, that is persons diagnosed as HIV positive'.

[120] See Sarah Joseph, Jenny Schultz and Melissa Castan, *The International Covenant on Civil and Political Rights* (Oxford: Oxford University Press, 2000), pp. 518–71, where they note that disability 'seems likely' to be a relevant 'ground' for the purpose of ICCPR's non-discrimination guarantees.

the ICESCR.[121] Indeed, the Economic Committee has issued a General Comment on the topic of 'Persons with Disabilities' in which it states that the non-discrimination clause 'clearly applies to discrimination on the grounds of disability',[122] and notes that '[m]ore recent international human rights instruments' have 'addressed the issues specifically', including, 'the Convention on the Rights of the Child (Article 23); the African Charter on Human and Peoples' Rights (Article 18(4)) and the Additional Protocol to the American Convention on Human Rights in the Area of Economic, Social and Cultural Rights (Article 18)'.[123] Reference might also be made to the UN Declaration on the Rights of Disabled Persons, which provides that:

> Disabled persons shall enjoy all the rights set forth in this Declaration. These rights shall be granted to all disabled persons without any exception whatsoever and without distinction or discrimination on the basis of race, colour, sex, language, religion, political or other opinions, national or social origin, state of wealth, birth or any other situation applying either to the disabled person himself or herself or to his or her family.[124]

International law sources also provide assistance with the potentially problematic issue of definition, since the Economic Committee has noted that while there is no 'internationally accepted definition of the term "disability", significant guidance can be obtained from that adopted in the 1993 Standard Rules':

> The term 'disability' summarizes a great number of different functional limitations occurring in any population . . . People may be disabled by physical, intellectual or sensory impairment, medical conditions or mental illness. Such impairments, conditions or illnesses may be permanent or transitory in nature.[125]

---

[121] Committee on Economic, Social and Cultural Rights ('CESCR'), *General Comment No. 5: Persons with Disabilities*, UN Doc. E/1995/22 (1994), (CESCR, *General Comment No. 5*).

[122] In CESCR, General Comment No. 5 the Committee states that the requirement in art. 2(2) of the ICESCR that the rights 'enunciated . . . will be exercised without discrimination of any kind', based on certain specified grounds "or other status" clearly applies to discrimination on grounds of disability': at para. 5.

[123] CESCR, *General Comment No. 5*, at para. 6. See also the Convention on the Rights of Persons with Disabilities, opened for signature on 30 March 2007 (see: http://www.un.org/disabilities/convention).

[124] GA Res. 3447 (XXX), UN GAOR, 2433rd mtg, UN Doc. 3447 (XXX) (1975), art. 2. The rights contained in the Declaration include all civil, political, economic and social rights. For more recent international activity in the field of disability rights, see Paul Hunt and Judith Mesquita, 'Mental Disabilities and the human right to the highest attainable standard of health' (2006), 28 *Human Rights Quarterly* 332.

[125] CESCR, *General Comment No. 5*, at para. 3. In addition, the UN Declaration on the Rights of Disabled Persons defines disability as 'any person unable to ensure by himself or herself, wholly or partly, the necessities of a normal individual and/or social life, as a result of deficiency, either congenital or not, in his or her physical or mental capabilities'. See also the Convention on the Rights of Persons with Disabilities, Article 1 (not yet in force).

Turning to other common law jurisdictions, despite early disagreement in the Australian case law concerning the question whether a PSG based on disability was sufficiently cognizable under the 'social perception test',[126] it is now very well established in the jurisprudence of the RRT that the fact of having a serious illness, such as HIV, can constitute membership in a PSG,[127] a finding that has been approved by the Federal Court.[128] This conclusion is often reached based on rather circular reasoning (one of the problems with the 'social perception' approach to defining a PSG), in that decision-makers assess whether there is discrimination against people with HIV in the relevant society (amounting to persecution in the successful cases) in order to ascertain the existence of a PSG. For example, in one typical decision the RRT concluded:

---

[126] In *Lo v. Minister for Immigration and Ethnic Affairs* (1995) 61 FCR 221 ('*Lo*'), Tamberlin J of the Federal Court of Australia considered whether 'persons who have the hepatitis B infection or are hepatitis B carriers ("hepatitis B sufferers")' in China were members of a particular social group. In upholding the RRT's decision that no such PSG existed, Tamberlin J said that 'the fortuitous circumstance of a common illness does not make those persons afflicted, members of a particular social group': at 231. See also *Reference N94/04748*, RRT, 10 June 1998. However, despite its apparently clear holding that illness/disability does not constitute a PSG, in subsequent decisions the Court has clearly departed from the reasoning in *Lo*. In the subsequent decision in *Subermani Gounder v. Minister for Immigration and Multicultural Affairs* (1998) 87 FCR 1, Lindgren J of the Federal Court of Australia held, after concluding that the applicant's condition (renal failure) did not make him a member of a PSG, that '[t]his is not to say that persons suffering from a common illness or physical disability can never form such a group (I do not understand Tamberlin J to have held otherwise in Lo v. Minister for Immigration and Ethnic Affairs)': at 8. Further, in *Salem Subramaniam* [1998] 483 FCA (Unreported, Davies J, 4 May 1998), His Honour implicitly accepted that disability may constitute a PSG when he noted that '[t]he Tribunal was content to accept that, on the basis of his disability or caste, or these factors combined, Ganesh could be characterised as being of a particular social group': at 4. Finally, in the most recent decision on point, *Kuthyar v. Minister for Immigration and Multicultural Affairs* [2000] FCA 110 (Unreported, Einfeld J, 11 February 2000) ('*Kuthyar*'), His Honour noted that 'the Tribunal conceded that the applicant may in fact be a member of the particular social group of people with HIV or AIDS, but it was not satisfied that the treatment of the members of the group constituted persecution within the meaning of the Convention on Refugees': at para. 78. Einfeld J overturned the RRT decision because it had not sufficiently considered whether the applicant was able to avail himself of protection from the Indian government which would counteract the 'persecutory discrimination' suffered on account of his status.
[127] There have been many successful applications determined at the RRT level on HIV grounds: see, for example, *Reference N94/04178*, RRT, 10 June 1994, at 7; *Reference V95/03256*, RRT, 9 October 1995, at 7; *Reference V5/03396*, RRT, 29 November 1995, at 15; *Reference V94/02084*, RRT, 23 February 1996, at 10; *Reference N98/21471*, RRT, 21 September 1998, at 8; *Reference N03/45504*, RRT, 1 July 2003.
[128] See *Kuthyar* [2000] FCA 110 (Unreported, Einfeld J, 11 February 2000).

People with HIV and AIDS are treated as a group in xxxx, they are feared, ostracized, stigmatized and persecuted not for anything they have done or may do, as individuals, but because they are considered to be part of a group which poses an unacceptable risk to xxxx society. A person may suffer this way whether or not he or she actually is HIV+, if others suspect or think that he or she fits within that group ... It appears to the Tribunal that the persecution which the applicant may face would indeed be 'for reasons of' her membership in the particular social group defined above.[129]

Thus, although the reasoning would be more persuasively based on the 'protected characteristics' approach, this provides further support for the view that illness and disability may constitute a PSG.

In the USA, where the reasoning underpinning MPSG analysis remains somewhat inconsistent across the circuit courts of appeal, the Eighth Circuit has held that the 'mentally disabled' in Jamaica do not constitute a PSG since they are not 'a collection of people closely affiliated with each other, who are actuated by some common impulse or interest',[130] and are 'too large and diverse a group to qualify' as a PSG.[131] The difficulty with this reasoning is that it is based on principles that have now been clearly rejected by a preponderance of common law jurisdictions and the UNHCR. By contrast, the Ninth Circuit, applying the 'protected characteristics' approach, has found that persons with disabilities 'are precisely the kind of individuals' contemplated by the PSG ground.[132] As the Court noted in *Tchoukhrova*, '[w]hile not all disabilities are "innate" or "inherent" ... they are usually, unfortunately, "immutable"'.[133] Accordingly, the Court held that persons whose disabilities 'are serious and long-lasting or permanent in nature' – in that case disabled children in Russia – are within the PSG category.[134]

Further, a number of successful claims have been made at the Departmental and IJ level based on PSGs such as autism[135] and

---

[129] *Reference V95/03256*, RRT, 9 October 1995, at 7. See also *Reference N94/04178*, RRT, 10 June 1994, at 7. For the most recent decision on point, see *Reference N03/45504*, RRT, 1 July 2003, where the RRT held that 'persons with HIV and homosexuals in Nepal do constitute separate particular social groups. Both groups are quite obviously set apart, and indeed ostracized, from the mainstream of society, they are united because of the fact that they [are] either HIV positive or homosexual, and the rest of Nepalese society regards them as particular groups'.
[130] *Raffington v. Immigration and Naturalization Service*, 340 F 3d 720 (8th Cir. 2003), at 730.
[131] *Raffington v. Immigration and Naturalization Service*, 340 F 3d 720 (8th Cir. 2003), at 730.
[132] *Tchoukhrova v. Gonzales*, 404 F 3d 1181 (9th Cir. 2005), at 1189 ('*Tchoukhrova*').
[133] *Tchoukhrova* at 1189. [134] *Tchoukhrova* at 1189.
[135] See 'INS Grants Asylum to Autistic Child Persecuted Due to Disability' (2001) 78(13) *Interpreter Releases* 604.

HIV-positive status.[136] Indeed, following one positive decision of an Immigration Judge in relation to an HIV-positive man, the (then) INS General Counsel released a memorandum dealing with cases involving HIV infection which states that:

When permitted by statute, the INS and the Executive Office of Immigration Review (EOIR) should grant ... asylum based on the social group category of HIV-positive individuals.[137]

This has now been adopted by the BIA and Court of Appeals for the Third Circuit.[138]

Finally, in addition to disability falling within the MPSG ground, it is important to note that persons associated with a disabled or ill person may establish a claim on the basis of this association, in particular on the basis of membership of the disabled person's family (where the person faces persecution because of this association). This was recognized by the RPD in *YHI (Re)*, in which the Tribunal considered the claim of a Romanian man who alleged that, as an immediate family member of an AIDS-infected person, he was denied the right to earn a living.[139] Although the claim failed on other grounds, the RPD noted that 'the claimant defined the social group to be an immediate family member of an AIDS infected person' and that 'this is an appropriate social group and it has been demonstrated that his membership in it is relevant to the claim'.[140] This is consistent with existing case law which establishes that family can constitute a PSG for the purposes of the Refugee Convention.[141]

---

[136] See 'Ostracism Lack of Medical Care Support HIV-Positive Alien's Asylum Quest, IJ Rules' (2001) 78(3) *Interpreter Releases* 233; 'IJ Grants Asylum to HIV Positive Man, General Counsel Issues HIV Instructions' (1996) 73 *Interpreter Releases* 901. See also the recent decision of the INS office regarding HIV persons from Mali, note 67.
[137] Memorandum from David A. Martin, INS Office of General Counsel (16 February 1996) reported in 73 *Interpreter Releases* 909 (8 July 1996), cited in *Karouni v. Gonzales*, 399 F 3d 1163 (9th Cir. 2005).
[138] In *Okado v. Attorney-General of the United States*, 2005 U.S. App. LEXIS 24989 (3rd Cir. 2005) the BIA had determined that 'Okado fell within a particular social group – HIV-positive individuals' (at *6) and this was not disputed on appeal to the Third Circuit: at *9.
[139] No. T95-07066, [1996] CRDD No. 65, 16 August 1996.
[140] *YHI (Re)*, No. T95-07066, [1996] CRDD No. 65, 16 August 1996, at para. 26. See also *Tchoukhrova* at 1189–90.
[141] In the USA, family has been recognized as a 'prototypical example' of a PSG: see *Sanchez-Trujillo*, 801 F 2d 1571 (9th Cir. 1986), at 1576; *Hernandez-Montiel*, 225 F. 3d 1084 (9th Cir. 2000) and *Thomas v. Gonzales*, 409 F 3d 1177 at 1187 (9th Cir. 2005). It has also been recognized as a PSG in other jurisdictions. In Australia, see: *Applicant A* (1996) 190 CLR 225 at 241 (Dawson J); *Sarrazola* (2001) 107 FCR 184. In New Zealand, see: *Re SSS*,

Women

The question whether women constitute a PSG for the purposes of the Refugee Convention is highly relevant to the present topic, in light of the discrimination faced by women throughout the world in relation to a range of fundamental rights, but most particularly in the context of economic, social and cultural rights.[142] While claims by women are often properly made and accepted on other Convention grounds (and these other grounds should be interpreted in a gender-sensitive manner),[143] the MPSG ground remains that most frequently and successfully relied upon by women at risk of persecution because they are women. In much of the discussion in previous chapters concerned with 'being persecuted' and nexus, it was assumed that 'gender' or women[144] can constitute a relevant Convention ground (gender not otherwise being a ground in the Convention definition), so as to sustain a refugee claim on this basis. It is thus necessary to consider briefly the application of the principles relating to MPSG to this subject.

The question whether women constitute a PSG has perhaps been the most debated and analysed issue within the PSG topic as a whole, having been extensively considered in the literature,[145] and by superior common

---

Refugee Appeal No. 17/92, RSAA, 9 July 1992; *Re NS, Refugee Appeal No. 547/92*, RSAA, 2 June 1994; *Refugee Appeal No. 71145/98*, RSAA, 28 May 1999. There is one very controversial factual scenario related to PSG claims based on family — where members of a family have sought to rely on the MPSG ground in the circumstance that a family member originally attracted persecution for a non-Convention reason such as extortion or retribution for whistle-blowing, and the perpetrators of the persecution now seek to inflict harm on the family members in order either to put pressure on the original victim or to seek payment of the outstanding debt. There exists conflicting authority in many jurisdictions as to this question: see *R v. Immigration Appeal Tribunal, ex parte Bolanus* [1999] Imm AR 350 (Moses J); *Serrano v. Canada (Minister of Citizenship and Immigration)*, 1999 FTR LEXIS 745; 166 FTR 227; *Gonzalez v. Canada (Minister of Citizenship and Immigration)*, 2002 ACWSJ LEXIS 1317; 2002 ACWSJ 1921; 113 ACWS (3d) 126, for authority that these claims are outside the Refugee Convention. For the opposite authority, see *Sarrazola v. Minister for Immigration and Multicultural Affairs* [1999] FCA 101 (Unreported, Hely J, 17 February 1999), at para. 22, now amended by the *Migration Legislation Amendment Act (No. 6) 2001* (Cth) which inserted a new s. 91S into the *Migration Act 1958* (Cth); *R v. Immigration Appeal Tribunal, ex parte De Melo and De Araujo* [1997] Imm AR 43 at 49; and *Jian Chen v. Ashcroft*, 289 F 3d 1113 (9th Cir. 2002).

[142] See Chapter 3, above, notes 205–6.
[143] As also emphasized by Crawley, *Refugees and Gender*, pp. 72–5.
[144] Courts do not generally tend to make a distinction between women and gender; while gender is sometimes used, the most common formulation is 'women'.
[145] There is a vast number of academic articles on the topic of gender-based refugee claims and on the PSG question in particular. Some of the most important include: Anker,

law courts and executive governments (in the form of Gender Guidelines) in recent years.[146] As a consequence of these developments, many of the more contentious issues, such as whether women can ever constitute a PSG, are no longer in dispute. As the UNHCR has stated in its Guidelines on International Protection on Gender-Related Persecution, 'sex can properly be within the ambit of the social group category, with women being a clear example of a social subset defined by innate and immutable characteristics, and who are frequently treated differently than men'.[147]

However, notwithstanding the important progress that has been made in achieving recognition of the fundamental notion that women are capable of constituting a PSG, decision-makers continue to display difficulty (and sometimes reticence) in upholding gender-based claims. Much of the problem relates to the manner in which the PSG is defined.[148] Courts and tribunals have recognized the broad category 'women' or 'gender' to constitute a PSG, as well as more specific subsets of these

'Boundaries in the Field of Human Rights'; Jane Connors, 'Legal Aspects of Women as a Particular Social Group' (1997) 9 *International Journal of Refugee Law* 115; Maryellen Fullerton, 'A Comparative Look at Refugee Status Based on Persecution Due to Membership in a Particular Social Group' (1993) 26 *Cornell International Law Journal* 505; Gilad, 'The Problem of Gender-Related Persecution'; Goldberg, 'Anyplace but Home'; Goldberg, 'Where in the World Is There Safety for Me'; Greatbatch, 'The Gender Difference'; Haines, 'Gender-related Persecution' in Feller, Türk and Nicholson (eds.), *Refugee Protection in International Law*, pp. 319–50; Macklin, 'Refugee Women and the Imperative of Categories'; David L. Neal, 'Women as a Social Group: Recognising Sex-Based Persecution as Grounds for Asylum' (1988) 20 *Columbia Human Rights Law Review* 203; and 'UNHCR Symposium on Gender-Based Persecution, Geneva, 22–23 February 1996' (1997) *International Journal of Refugee Law* 1. In addition, there are two excellent books dedicated to gender and the Refugee Convention: see Spijkerboer, *Gender and Refugee Studies* and Crawley, *Refugees and Gender*, pp. 70–7 for the MPSG issue specifically.
[146] See, for example, in the UK: *Shah* [1999] 2 AC 629; in Australia: *Khawar* (2002) 210 CLR 1; *Applicant S469 of 2002* v. *Minister for Immigration and Multicultural and Indigenous Affairs* [2004] FCA 64 (Unreported, Bennett J, 6 February 2004); in NZ: *Refugee Appeal No. 71427/99*, RSAA, 16 August 2000. See also the UK, US, Canadian and Australian Gender Guidelines; EU Directive on a Common Asylum Policy, art. 12(1)(d) (in the context of setting out the interpretative approach to PSG): 'gender related aspects might be considered, without by themselves alone creating a presumption for the applicability of this Article'.
[147] UNHCR, Guidelines on International Protection, *Gender-Related Persecution within the context of Article 1A(2) of the 1951 Convention and/or its 1967 Protocol relating to the Status of Refugees*, HCR/GIP/02/01, 7 May 2002 at para. 30. See also UNHCR *Guidelines on Social Group*, at paras. 12, 19.
[148] Another very important issue is the question of the availability of state protection, in that there are many worrying examples of decision-makers finding that state protection is available based on the 'sufficiency of protection' argument, when the applicant arguably has a well-founded fear of being persecuted: see generally Mathew, Hathaway and Foster, 'The Role of State Protection in Refugee Analysis'.

categories, which, in many cases, are appropriately defined by a combination of sex or gender and other fundamental characteristics such as age, marital status, education and economic class.[149] Successful claims have been recognized based on PSGs, such as 'married women in Tanzania',[150] 'educated women',[151] 'young Somali women',[152] 'women in Albania without the protection of male relatives'[153] and 'westernized young women',[154] to provide but a few examples.[155]

While this more specific formulation is appropriate in cases in which a number of characteristics or factors forms the basis of the well-founded fear of being persecuted, there is a tendency, found generally in the PSG jurisprudence, but particularly heightened in that relating to gender, to formulate overly complicated and unnecessarily detailed PSGs, rather than simply to find that 'women' or 'gender' constitutes the relevant PSG.[156] Perhaps the most extreme example is provided in a decision of

[149] As the Economic Committee has noted, 'Many women experience distinct forms of discrimination due to the intersection of sex with such factors as race, colour, language, religion, political and other opinion, national or social origin, property, birth, or other status, such as age, ethnicity, disability, marital, refugee or migrant status, resulting in compounded disadvantage': CESCR, *General Comment No. 16 (2005): The equal right of men and women to the enjoyment of all economic, social and cultural rights*, E/C.12/2005/4, 11 August 2005, at para. 5.
[150] *Minister for Immigration and Multicultural Affairs v. Ndege* [1999] FCA 783 (Unreported, Weinberg J, 11 June 1999).
[151] *Ali v. Canada (Minister of Citizenship and Immigration)* (1997) 1 FCD 26.
[152] *Minister for Immigration and Multicultural Affairs v. Cali* [2000] FCA 1026 (Unreported, North J, 3 August 2000). In *Refugee Appeal No. 75233*, 1 February 2005, the NZ RSAA recognized a claim based on the harm feared on return to Somalia for reason of membership in the PSG, 'a woman member of a minority clan': at para. 27.
[153] *Reference V01/13062*, RRT, 16 March 2004, at 19. An additional PSG is a 'female citizen of Somalia without adult male protection': *SCP (Re)*, No. A95-00837, [1996] CRDD No. 244, 3 May 1996, at para. 8.
[154] *CSE (Re)*, No. VA0-00566, [2001] CRDD No. 29, 9 March 2001, at paras. 35–6.
[155] See also the examples provided in the UNHCR *Trafficking Guidelines*, where after noting that women may be considered as a MPSG, it is noted also that 'certain subsets of women may also constitute particular social groups ... Examples of social subsets of women or children could, depending on the context, be single women, widows, divorced women, illiterate women, separated or unaccompanied children, orphans or street children': p. 14.
[156] Research reveals that the Canadian RPD is the most comfortable with the notion that 'women' or 'gender' may constitute a PSG, while the other jurisdictions have a tendency to try to define more circumscribed PSGs. This may be because in *Ward*, the Supreme Court mentioned 'gender' as an example of a 'group defined by innate or unchangeable characteristics', which may explain the lower courts' and tribunals' acceptance of this principle: see for example *B (TD) (Re)*, Nos. T91-01497, T91-01498, [1994] CRDD No. 391, 9 August 1994, at 5. See also *S (ZD) (Re)*, No. T94-02002, [1995] CRDD No. 75, 20 June 1995, at 4–5.

the Canadian Federal Court which held the PSG in that case to be composed of, '[w]omen who have recently immigrated to Israel from the former Soviet Union and who, despite generous support by the host government, fail to integrate, are subsequently lured into prostitution, and are confronted with indifference by the front-line supervisors responsible for their safety'.[157] This tendency is widespread,[158] as evidenced in a decision of the Federal Court of Australia, which rejected the submission that the RRT had committed a jurisdictional error in failing properly to consider the applicant's claim based on MPSG on the basis that the RRT was not required to consider the 'numerous alternative hypothetical social groups' to which the applicant might be said to belong.[159] The interesting point for present purposes is that the Court provided examples of the potentially relevant PSGs as follows:

> 'young women in Thailand',
> 'female prostitutes in Thailand',
> 'young female prostitutes in Thailand',
> 'females who have been sold by their parents into prostitution in Thailand',
> 'female prostitutes in Thailand who have no practicable way of extracting themselves from the life of a prostitute', and
> 'female prostitutes in Thailand who have no practicable way of extracting themselves from the life of a prostitute and who have attempted to do so',

The court concluded that, '[n]o doubt, this list could be extended'.[160]

While not overtly acknowledged, this tendency appears to stem from a concern that if the group is defined too broadly it cannot properly be described as a PSG, with an implicit 'floodgates' argument underpinning such concerns. However, these attempts at more narrow formulations are inconsistent with many of the otherwise settled principles of interpretation related to the PSG ground generally. As has been emphasized

---

[157] *Litvinov* v. *Canada (Secretary of State)* [1994] FCJ No. 1061, at 4.
[158] There are many examples, but the following provide some illustrations of the tendency: 'young women of the Tchamba-Kunsuntu tribe who have not had FGM, as practiced by that tribe, and who oppose the practice': *Matter of Kasinga*, BIA, 1996 BIA LEXIS 15; 21 I & N Dec. 357; 'unmarried Chinese women, who have been subjected to arranged marriages for money according to feudal practices, and who oppose such practices': *In the Matter of Unnamed*, File No. A76-512-001, 18 October 2001, IJ Zerbe, at 6 (on file with author).
[159] *SZAFS* v. *Minister for Immigration and Multicultural and Indigenous Affairs* [2004] FCA 112 (Unreported, Lindgren J, 20 February 2004) ('*SZAFS*').
[160] *SZAFS* [2004] FCA 112 (Unreported, Lindgren J, 20 February 2004) at para. 23.

repeatedly by superior courts, the size of the group does not determine its eligibility for characterization as a PSG and, importantly, formulation of a large group as a PSG does not mean that every member of the PSG is potentially at risk of being persecuted. As Lord Steyn explained in *Shah*, the fact that some women in the relevant group are able to avoid persecution 'is no answer to treating women ... as a relevant social group'.[161]

Moreover, not only do these formulations frequently incorporate the risk of persecution at issue (women who 'are subsequently lured into prostitution'; or 'who have been sold by their parents into prostitution'), which raises the circularity problem, but they also contain factors that are simply not relevant to the definition of a PSG but to other aspects of the refugee definition, such as whether the fear is well-founded and whether the state is willing or able to protect the applicant. The danger with this approach is that a PSG will be rejected based on inappropriate considerations. An instructive example of this problem is provided in the decision of the UK IAT in *Secretary of State for the Home Department* v. *Muchomba*,[162] which concerned the claim by a Kenyan girl who feared female genital mutilation ('FGM'). The Adjudicator had allowed the refugee claim on the basis that the applicant belonged to the PSG, 'young girls living in tribal communities in Kenya where there is an ingrained practice of FGM'.[163] On appeal, the IAT overturned the decision (and thus rejected the refugee claim) on the basis that 'this group of girls does not have an immutable characteristic. The fact that there is an ingrained practice in the tribal communities in Kenya of itself does not give this group an immutable characteristic, because no matter how ingrained the practice, not all the girls in such rural tribal communities will be forced to undergo FGM as many of the girls undergo FGM voluntarily without any means of force or coercion'.[164] This conflation of a number of irrelevant factors with the appropriate PSG inquiry (immutable characteristics) highlights the need for a more straightforward approach which acknowledges that, as explained by Lord Steyn in *Shah*, the notion that women are a PSG is 'neither novel nor heterodox'; rather it is 'simply a logical application of the seminal reasoning in *Acosta* [the protected characteristic approach]'.[165]

[161] *Shah* [1999] 2 AC 629 at 644. [162] [2002] UKIAT 1348 ('*Muchomba*').
[163] *Muchomba* [2002] UKIAT 1348, at para. 3. [164] *Muchomba* [2002] UKIAT 1348, at para. 18.
[165] *Shah* [1999] 2 AC 629 at 644. For an application of this straightforward approach to the women as a PSG issue in UK decision-making, see *NS Afghanistan CG* [2004] UKIAT 00328, 30 December 2004, at paras. 76–9 and in US law, see *Mohammed* v. *Gonzales*, 400 F. 3d 785 (9th Cir. 2005) at 797–8.

Children

The question whether children constitute a PSG for Convention purposes is another pertinent issue given that children's socio-economic needs are generally more poignant than those of adults in light of their dependence on adults and unique developmental needs. Refugee claims by children have traditionally been most frequently considered in the context of the well-founded fear of the family unit as a whole; however, it is increasingly the case that children's claims are being considered in their own right, either because their claims are distinct from and/or independent of those of their accompanying family members (for example in the case of 'black children' from China, whose claims are distinct from their parents who fear sterilization), or because they have arrived unaccompanied and thus their claims must be considered on their own terms. As was discussed in Chapter 4, decision-makers are beginning to recognize that the refugee claims of children require a particularized approach, which takes into account the vulnerability and special needs of children. This manifests most obviously in the need to interpret 'being persecuted' in a way that recognizes that both the type and degree of harm necessary to constitute persecution for children might well be quite different from that relevant to the claims of adults, an issue with particular resonance in the field of socio-economic rights. However, there is a remaining important issue, namely the way in which nexus to a Convention ground is assessed in the context of claims by children and, in particular, whether children (and/or particular sub-sets of children) are capable of constituting a PSG for the purposes of the Convention definition.

Before turning to consider the different methods by which children may be held to constitute a PSG, an initial definitional question may arise as to which persons are included in the category of children or minors. The consensus appears to be that the definition contained in the CRC – 'a child means every human being below the age of eighteen years'[166] – is an appropriate guide.[167] Further, the UK IAT has held, in response to

---

[166] CRC, art. 1. Article 1 goes on to say: 'unless, under the law applicable to the child, majority is attained earlier'.
[167] This is the approach that appears to be taken generally in the case law. In addition, art. 2(1) of the EU Directive on a Common Asylum Policy provides: ' "Unaccompanied minors" means third-country nationals and stateless persons below the age of eighteen, who arrive on the territory of the Member States unaccompanied by an adult responsible for them whether by law or custom.'

a submission that an applicant was 'only marginally a minor' and therefore appropriately treated as an adult, that '[t]o adopt a rigidity however in this respect is in our view to fail to recognize that in many areas of the world even today exact ages and dates of birth are imprecise. It is better to err on the side of generosity'.[168] This is an important principle to bear in mind in assessing such claims. This is not to say that there is no difference between the claim of a 17-year-old and one of an 8-year-old child; each claim must still be assessed on its merits and all aspects of the Refugee Convention definition must be satisfied.[169] Moreover, it is arguable that a child should not be considered outside the relevant PSG simply because he or she is 18 or slightly above, since it is often the fact of being young and vulnerable which identifies the person as a target or otherwise makes the person particularly susceptible to being persecuted. This was explicitly recognized by the RPD in a case concerning a refugee claim by a 19-year-old Chinese boy who had been 'involuntarily trafficked' to Canada by his parents in order to work and remit money to them.[170] The RPD rejected the view that his age nullified his claim to membership in the PSG 'children', since the CRC should be 'generously' interpreted and,[171] in that case, '[t]he claimant's past persecution [abuse by his family] has prevented him from developing the normal defenses that he would as a child ... While he is a chronological adult, he remains ... a psychological child'.[172] In such a case, the applicant should properly be considered either within the PSG children or that of 'young adults'.

Turning to the question whether 'children' can constitute a PSG, the key point of contention is whether such a group is too broad and diverse to constitute a PSG, which in turn depends on the conceptual analysis adopted by the court. As is the case with the PSG 'women',

---

[168] *Jakitay v. Secretary of State for the Home Department* (Unreported, IAT, Appeal No. 12658, 15 November 1995), at 6.
[169] In particular, the age difference will often go to the well-foundedness of the fear and perhaps to other issues such as the extent of an internal protection alternative.
[170] *THK (Re)*, No. VA0-02635, [2001] CRDD No. 30, 22 March 2001.
[171] *THK (Re)*, No. VA0-02635, [2001] CRDD No. 30, 22 March 2001, at para. 41.
[172] *THK (Re)*, No. VA0-02635, [2001] CRDD No. 30, 22 March 2001, at para. 42. See also *MYS (Re)*, Nos. V97-00156, V97-00962, [1998] CRDD No. 149, 23 July 1998, which concerned refugee claims made by two brothers subject to severe abuse by their father, where one brother was under 18 and one was 19. The RPD rejected the view that the older brother's age nullified his claim to membership in the PSG 'children of an abusive father' since '[w]hat is at issue is the nature of the relationship with the abusive parent, rather than merely the age of the applicant': at para. 27.

decision-makers in those jurisdictions that adopt the protected characteristics approach – most notably Canada – have had little difficulty in finding that children may constitute a PSG, such that an applicant's fear may be said to be for reasons of her status as a minor. For example, in *GAF (Re)*,[173] the RPD held that the applicant's 'vulnerability as a minor is an innate and unchangeable characteristic, notwithstanding that the child will grow into an adult'.[174] As the RPD had noted in an earlier decision, the fact that the minor will eventually grow older is irrelevant since 'a panel is determining the facts as presented at the time of the hearing' and '[a]t the time of hearing the minor claimants are minors'.[175] The notion that minors or children may constitute a PSG has also been accepted by the Federal Court of Canada.[176] By contrast, the US Court of Appeals for the Third Circuit has questioned whether children may constitute a PSG, even when applying the 'protected characteristic approach', since

it is undeniable that youth is an important component of a child's identity. Children share many general characteristics, such as innocence, immaturity, and

---

[173] No. V99-02929, [2000] CRDD No. 48, 21 February 2000.
[174] *GAF (Re)*, No. V99-02929, [2000] CRDD No. 48, 21 February 2000, at para. 21. See also *G (BB) (Re)*, Nos. T93-09636, T93-09638 and T93-09639, [1994] CRDD No. 397, 26 January 1994, at 8: 'A child's vulnerability arises due to his or her status as a minor and we find that this is an innate and unchangeable characteristic notwithstanding the child will grow into an adult' and *B (TD) (Re)*, Nos. T91-01497, T91-01498, [1994] CRDD No. 391, 9 August 1994, at 6: 'The panel finds that the minor claimant is a member of a particular social group, namely, minors, based on the "innate and unchangeable characteristic" of being under the age of majority – a fact she cannot change for the foreseeable future'. See also *U (NX) (Re)*, Nos. T93-12579 and T93-12586, [1995] CRDD No. 74, 25 July 1994, at 19: 'I find that the minor claimant is a member of a particular social group, namely, minors, based on the "innate or unchangeable characteristic" of being under the age of majority – a fact she cannot change for the foreseeable future'. In *AFW (Re)*, No. V99-03532, [2001] CRDD No. 215, 12 October 2001, the RPD noted that '[t]here is considerable case law to the effect that "children" can be considered a particular social group': at para. 49. The RPD does not list the decisions relied upon; however, presumably they would include those cited in this note. See also *THK (Re)*, No. VA0-02635, [2001] CRDD No. 30, 22 March 2001.
[175] *G (BB) (Re)*, Nos. T93-09636, T93-09638 and T93-09639, [1994] CRDD No. 397, 26 January 1994, at 8. See also *MZJ (Re)*, No. V97-03500, [1999] CRDD No. 118, 31 May 1999, at para. 12: 'These groups [PSGs] are defined by an innate or unchangeable characteristic, in this case – children. While it is true that children do change, in that they grow up to become adults, it is clear that a 16 year old is still a child . . . He is vulnerable and incapable of accessing state protection on his own.'
[176] In a series of decisions concerning young Chinese boys and girls who had been smuggled to Canada, the Federal Court accepted that minors and children can constitute a PSG, even though some of the claims were rejected for other reasons: see *Canada (Minister of*

impressionability. However, *unlike innate characteristics*, such as sex or color, *age changes over time*, possibly lessening its role in personal identity. Moreover, children as a particular social group represent an extremely large and diverse group, and children, even within a single neighborhood, have a wide degree of varying experiences, interests and traits.[177]

This is arguably an incorrect application of the protected characteristics approach for two reasons. First, as the RPD has pointed out, age is logically considered unchangeable for the purposes of assessing a present risk of persecution for a Convention reason. A minor applicant is clearly unable to disassociate himself from his age in order to avoid the persecutory conduct feared.[178] It may be that the eventual change in age will underpin a cessation application,[179] but the fact that the applicant's age will eventually change cannot justify rejection of the PSG ground. Second, the Third Circuit appears to have superimposed additional requirements onto the protected characteristics test, in that it considered that the size and diversity of the group militated against its correct characterization as a PSG. As explained above, these

---

Citizenship and Immigration) v. Li [2001] FCJ No. 620, at para. 11: 'The Crown did not take issue with the principle that children can constitute a particular social group'; Zhu v. Canada (Minister of Citizenship and Immigration) [2001] FCJ No. 1251, at para. 39: 'There was no evidence before the tribunal that the snakeheads or the applicant's parents smuggled or trafficked the applicants because [of] their status as minors from Fujian province, or because of any other Convention ground'; Xiao v. Canada (Minister of Citizenship and Immigration) [2001] FCJ No. 349, at para. 14: 'When counsel attempted to develop the argument regarding the applicant's particular social group, the presiding member implied that this aspect of the claim was fundamental and did not have to be reiterated. In oral submissions, counsel introduced the leading Supreme Court of Canada decision on membership in a particular social group and referred the tribunal to a number of RPD and Federal Court decisions to support the proposition that persons under the age of 18 constitute a particular social group, i.e. children'; Li [2000] FCJ No. 2037.

[177] *Lukwago v. Ashcroft*, 329 F 3d 157 (3rd Cir. 2003). In this case, the BIA had 'seemed to question whether a group based on age may qualify as a "particular social group" '; and the comments quoted here appear to support this finding: at 171. The Court ultimately went on to find another PSG, namely former child soldiers, although the claim was still not successful for other reasons. For a more recent decision of the Third Circuit applying similar reasoning, see *Escobar v. Gonzales*, 417 F. 3d 363 (3rd Cir. 2005): 'Nor is youth alone a sufficient permanent characteristic, disappearing as it does with age' (at 367).

[178] As the Court said in *Ward*, 'surely there are some groups, the affiliation in which is not so important to the individual that it would be more appropriate to have the person disassociate him- or herself from it before [the country of destination's] responsibility should be engaged': *Ward* [1993] 2 SCR 689 at 738.

[179] See Refugee Convention, art. 1(C) for conditions in which the Convention 'shall cease to apply'.

considerations have been uniformly rejected at the international level, and should therefore be deemed irrelevant to determining the existence of a PSG. As the Federal Court of Australia held in *SGBB* v. *Minister for Immigration and Multicultural and Indigenous Affairs* (following a discussion of the High Court's decision in *Khawar* which held that women may constitute a PSG in certain situations, and that the potential size of the group does not affect its formulation as a PSG),[180] 'there is no obvious reason why unaccompanied youths, or unaccompanied youths with no family connections could not constitute a "particular social group" for the purpose of the Convention'.[181]

The second and more common method by which children have been held to constitute a PSG is not so much by reference to the broad group 'children' or 'minors', but by reliance on a more precisely defined group. This was alluded to above, where it was noted that specific sub-groups within the poor as a class and women, particularly as a result of the intersection of age or gender with poverty, may define a PSG.[182] In addition to the examples provided above, decision-makers have considered that groups such as 'orphaned children',[183] 'abandoned children',[184]

---

[180] [2003] FCA 709 (Unreported, Selway J, 16 July 2003) ('*SGBB*').
[181] *SGBB* [2003] FCA 709 (Unreported, Selway J, 16 July 2003), at para. 23. This is also supported by the UNHCR in its *Trafficking Guidelines*: 'children or certain subsets of [this] group may also constitute [a] particular social group': at para. 38
[182] See also *JDJ (Re)*, No. A95-00633, [1998] CRDD No. 12, 28 January 1998, in which the RPD held that 'impoverished children' in Zaire constituted a PSG for the purposes of the Convention.
[183] Case no. AS/54991/2003, December 2003, discussed in Jarvis, 'Can Trafficked Persons Be Refugees?', p. 8. In *WBT (Re)*, No. V98-00787, [1999] CRDD No. 119, 4 June 1999, the RPD held that 'orphaned children of war' in El Salvador constituted a PSG 'in that being an orphan of war is defined by innate and unchangeable characteristics': at para. 28. See also *QQX (Re)*, No. T95-00479, [1996] CRDD No. 52, 5 July 1996, where the RPD held that '[b]y virtue of her age and in particular, her status as an orphan without close relatives on whom to rely for support and protection, and membership in the Majerteen clan, the panel is of the opinion that were the claimant to return to Somalia she would be significantly marginalized, and such marginalization would amount to persecution': at para. 13.
[184] Unnamed File, Board of Immigration Appeals, 3 June 2003, at 6 (on file with author). The RPD has rejected a claim based on the PSG 'unaccompanied children' since '[b]eing unaccompanied is a situation which can be changed': *WMI (Re)*, Nos. T96-02166 and T96-02168, [1997] CRDD No. 113, 14 May 1997, at para. 9. However, it has recognized claims where the child will be unprotected on return. For example in *MZJ (Re)*, No. V97-03500, [1999] CRDD No. 118, 31 May 1999, the Tribunal held that 'abandoned children in Mexico can be a particular social group who have a well-founded fear of persecution': at para. 14.

'illegitimate children',[185] 'young Tamil males or females',[186] 'female children' or 'girls',[187] 'children of an inter-clan marriage'[188] and even 'children of widowed mothers in Iran'[189] may constitute a PSG for the purposes of the Refugee Convention. In addition, both the High Court of Australia and the Canadian Federal Court of Appeal have held that 'black-market', 'black' or 'second' children' (children born outside the one-child policy in China) can constitute a PSG for the purposes of the Refugee Convention,[190] applying either of the two key analytical approaches to the interpretation of PSG. In *Chen Shi Hai*, the

---

[185] See *EKD (Re)*, Nos. MA1-02054, MA1-02055, MA1-02056, [2001] CRDD No. 174, 21 December 2001; *V (HY) (Re)*, No. V91-00998, [1991] CRDD No. 746, 15 November 1991. See also the decision of Immigration Judge, John M. Bryant, in which an applicant from Congo who suffered domestic violence including rape was granted asylum based on her membership in a social group 'composed of female children who are illegitimate, motherless daughters in the Congo': see Center for Gender and Refugee Studies, *Case Summaries: Case Summary 584* (on file with author).

[186] In a series of cases, the RPD has held that young Tamils were particularly at risk of forced recruitment in Sri Lanka, and that their fear of being persecuted was for reasons of their membership in the PSG, 'young Tamil male' (in most cases) or 'young Tamil female' (in some others – see *ESO (Re)*, No. U96-04191, [1997] CRDD No. 27, 21 January 1997). See, for example, *O (QB) (Re)*, No. U93-04790, [1993] CRDD No. 283, 8 December 1993; *DUR (Re)*, No. U96-03325, [1996] CRDD No. 243, 16 December 1996; *MCK (Re)*, No. U97-00412, [1997] CRDD No. 156, 2 July 1997; *OXJ (Re)*, No. U96-03098, [1997] CRDD No. 224, 15 July 1997; *QJV (Re)*, No. U97-01267, [1997] CRDD No. 249, 8 October 1997; *PKM (Re)*, No. V98-00452, [1998] CRDD No. 179, 11 September 1998; *VBJ (Re)*, No. T98-09801, [1999] CRDD No. 62, 30 April 1999; *UKT (Re)*, No. T99-10465, [2000] CRDD No. 129, 12 July 2000.

[187] The intersection of age and gender is important, as girls are often at risk of being persecuted because of this intersection. For example, many cases based on a fear of female genital mutilation are based on this combination of factors, see *QDS (Re)*, Nos. A99-00215, A99-00256, A99-00258, [1999] CRDD No. 235, 30 September 1999. Also, forced marriage has been recognized as persecution on the basis of gender, a form of serious harm that primarily affects girls: see for example, 'IJ Grants Asylum to Chinese Girl Fleeing Forced Marriage' (2000) 77(45) *Interpreter Releases* 1634. This is especially relevant with respect to many socio-economic rights such as education, see Chapter 3.

[188] *UZG (Re)*, Nos. T96-06291 and T96-06292, [1997] CRDD No. 209, 2 September 1997.

[189] *QJQ (Re)*, Nos. V97-01419, V97-01420, V97-01421, V98-02335, V98-02345, V98-02346, [1999] CRDD No. 189, 9 August 1999, at para. 54. This was in the context that as a result of discrimination against women in Iran, the mother of the children would lose custody of the minor claimants, and since 'the children have a fundamental human right to be with the surviving parent, their mother' they had a well-founded fear of being persecuted if returned: at para. 53. In a more recent decision, the RPD held that three young girls were 'part of a social group of young women who are members of a single-parent family in Mexico': *Unnamed*, MA1-07954, 16 August 2002, at 7.

[190] See *Cheung v. Canada (Minister of Employment and Immigration)* [1993] FCJ No. 309, at para. 19. The Court did not undertake extensive analysis of this issue, apparently assuming that it was self-evident.

High Court of Australia explained that '[s]uch children are... persecuted [by being deprived of a range of socio-economic rights] for what they are (the circumstances of their parentage, birth and status) and not by reason of anything they themselves have done'.[191] Other groups include 'street children', with a number of US Immigration Judges having recognized claims on this basis, particularly where violence in the home has forced the claimants to live 'on the street' and there is evidence that street children are subject to serious harm, including socio-economic deprivation.[192] Although the UK IAT has held that 'street children in Vietnam... do not share a common immutable characteristic' and thus do not constitute a PSG,[193] this is questionable since for most such street children (and certainly in respect of the applicant in that case) they are not able 'by their own actions' to avoid persecution.

In these cases, decision-makers are correct to characterize the applicants' status as constituting a PSG for the purposes of the Refugee Convention, since these predicaments are unchangeable or immutable. In addition, it may be appropriate to identify the group as being more specifically characterized, if it is clear that in a given society it is only children of a particular status, gender or class who are at risk of being persecuted.[194] However, as explained above in the context of women, it is

---

[191] *Chen Shi Hai* (2000) 201 CLR 293 at 301 (Gleeson CJ, Gaudron, Gummow and Hayne JJ).
[192] See 'IJ Grants Asylum to Guatemalan Street Child' (2002) 79 *Interpreter Releases* 440 and *In the Matter of Juan*, BIA, IJ Burkhart, 12 March 1998 (on file with author).
[193] *Tong v. Secretary of State for the Home Department* [2002] UKIAT 08062, at para. 13. This appears to be based on the fact that evidence suggested that there are three categories of street children, including 'children who spend most of their time on the streets but do return home': at para. 12. However, in that case, this option was not available to the applicant since '[h]e has no parents in Vietnam and it would appear that he has no immediate family in that country': at para. 16. In addition, the IAT seemed persuaded by the fact that the treatment received did not amount to persecution: at para. 13. The claim was ultimately upheld on human rights grounds pursuant to art. 8 of the European Convention on Human Rights: at para. 18. For authority that 'street children' could be considered a PSG, see *R v. IAT; ex parte Shah* (Queen's Bench Division, Co 4330/95, 12 November 1996) per Sedley J.
[194] See also the UNHCR *Trafficking Guidelines* which note that appropriate subsets of the PSG children may include 'separated or unaccompanied children, orphans or street children': p. 14. It may be that certain groups of children are particularly at risk of persecution. This was recognized in a concrete context by Human Rights Watch in its report, *Future Forsaken: Abuses against HIV/AIDS Affected Children in India*, July 2994, < http://hrw.org/reports/2004/india0704/ > at 31 May 2006, in which it noted that, 'Children already facing other forms of discrimination, such as sex workers, children of sex workers, street children, children from lower castes and Dalits (so-called untouchables) suffer more': at p. 2.

important that the group not be formulated so narrowly as to effectively define it by reference to the exact harm feared. One example of such a tendency is provided in domestic violence cases, where decision-makers have sometimes defined the relevant PSG as being, for example, 'children in South Korea who are abused by their father',[195] or 'Salvadorian children subject to incest and domestic violence',[196] formulations open to criticism on appeal because they define the group according to the persecution feared (and thus appear to employ the circular reasoning that the applicant has a well-founded fear of being persecuted because he or she is at risk of being persecuted). Such narrow formulations appear to result from a concern that the group must be defined so as to encompass only those who have a well-founded fear. However, as explained above in the context of women, the fact that some members of a group do not have a well-founded fear of being persecuted does not prevent its characterization as a PSG for Convention purposes.

One important developing and related issue is the extent to which claims by children may be made based on membership of the PSG 'family', where a family member is the source of the persecution. While family-related claims are well established in the situation where a child will likely suffer persecution because of his or her association with a political or religious family member, for example,[197] a more recent set of cases has raised the question whether the family can constitute a PSG when a family member is inflicting the relevant harm. This issue has been most extensively considered by the RPD (and some other common law decision-makers) in the context of claims based on domestic violence

---

[195] *ITU (Re)*, Nos. T99-11540, T99-11541, [2001] CRDD No. 95, 31 May 2001, at paras. 1, 16–17.

[196] *QWY (Re)*, No. T98-07956, [1999] CRDD No. 271, 29 November 1999, at paras. 1, 8. See also *TCV (Re)*, Nos. U95-00646, U95-00647 and U95-00648, [1997] CRDD No. 5, 15 January 1997, in which the RPD found that the claimant fell within the PSG 'young children who are victims of incest': at para. 44. This decision was overturned on appeal to the Federal Court but this was on the basis of the state protection issue: see *Canada (Minister of Citizenship and Immigration)* v. *Smith* [1998] FCJ No. 1613; [1999] 1 FC 310. See also *KWB (Re)*, Nos. A99-00789, A99-00790, A99-00791, A99-00792, A99-00793, [2002] CRDD No. 50, 8 April 2002, at para. 23, where the PSG was defined as 'abused women and children in Poland'.

[197] See, for example, *QDS (Re)*, Nos. A99-00215, A99-00256, A99-00258, [1999] CRDD No. 235, 30 September 1999, at para. 18; *L (YO) (Re)*, No. V93-02851, [1995] CRDD No. 50, 3 October 1995 (Sikh boy from India feared persecution based on uncle's activities – a Sikh militant); *L (LL) (Re)*, Nos. A93-81751, A93-81752 and A93-81753 [1994] CRDD No. 368, 16 August 1994; *NCM (Re)*, Nos. U94-04870, U94-04871, U94-04872 and U94-04873 [1996] CRDD No. 147, 19 July 1996; *SLH (Re)*, No. T95-07396 [1997] CRDD No. 121, 27 May 1997. See also Bhabha and Young, 'Not Adults in Miniature', at 111–12.

(which harm often has serious socio-economic consequences for the children if forced to leave home and live on the street). More recently the analysis has been applied to cases where parents have trafficked their children for sex or labour.[198] The reasoning is perhaps best set out by the US Court of Appeals for the Ninth Circuit in *Aguirre-Cervantes*,[199] a case concerning the refugee claim by a young Mexican girl who had been abused by her father. The Court found that the applicant was a member of a PSG – family – because '[f]amily membership is clearly an immutable characteristic, fundamental to one's identity'.[200] The Court held that the applicant's fear of being persecuted was 'on account of' her membership in the PSG family since '[t]he undisputed evidence demonstrated that Mr Aguirre's goal was to dominate and persecute members of his immediate family'.[201] While not relying on such detailed reasoning, a number of RPD decisions have similarly held that a minor applicant's fear of domestic violence is for reasons of membership in the PSG family.[202] As the RPD has held, '[t]he fact that the agents of persecution, the parents, are also members of that same family does not detract from the claimant being a bona fide member of a particular social group'.[203]

It is arguable that such claims are best analysed in terms of the PSG 'children', since it is children's dependence on their family and/or other guardians which gives rise to the vulnerability to persecution within the family unit. Further, in many societies the view that parents have ultimate control over their children contributes to their vulnerability,

---

[198] See, for example, *PEF (Re)*, No. VA0-00091 [2000] CRDD No. 110, 29 May 2000.
[199] *Aguirre-Cervantes v. Immigration and Naturalization Service*, 242 F 3d 1169 (9th Cir. 2001) ('*Aguirre-Cervantes*').
[200] However, it should be noted that the Court also held that 'Mexican society recognises the family as a discrete unit, and members of a family view themselves as such': *Aguirre-Cervantes*, 242 F 3d 1169 (9th Cir. 2001), at 1177. This reflects the Ninth Circuit's particular approach which appears to encompass both tests of PSG, as explained above. The Court also noted that '[i]n the domestic violence context, Mexican society also treats members of a family differently from non-members because it regards violence within a family as a 'domestic matter', rather than a matter for government intervention': at 1177.
[201] *Aguirre-Cervantes*, 242 F 3d 1169 (9th Cir. 2001) at 1178.
[202] See *FYM (Re)*, Nos. V97-00708, V97-00709, V97-00710, V97-00711 [1998] CRDD No. 153, 11 August 1998, at para. 37; *UWB (Re)*, Nos. MA0-10528, MA0-10529 [2001] CRDD No. 212, 15 November 2001, at para. 1; *UCR (Re)*, Nos. M99-07094, M99-07096 and M99-07098 [2001] CRDD No. 94, 31 May 2001, at para. 141; *RGC (Re)*, Nos. MA1-03752, MA1-03753 [2002] CRDD No. 23, 4 January 2002, at paras. 1, 8; *FOO (Re)*, Nos. MA1-11675, MA1-11676, MA1-11677 [2003] CRDD No. 83, 16 June 2003, at para. 27; *MOQ (Re)*, No. VA2-03015, 6 August 2003, at 5.
[203] *PEF (Re)*, No. VA0-00091 [2000] CRDD No. 110, 29 May 2000, at para. 20.

as recognized in some decisions that have considered claims from Chinese minors smuggled to North America to provide income for their family, in which the 'custom of filial piety'[204] has been recognized to place children in a particularly vulnerable position.[205] As the RPD has noted, to a certain extent, claims based on domestic violence by children are 'no different than those of abused women';[206] just as the persecution feared by women in such cases is properly understood as being for reasons of their gender, the persecution feared by children is properly understood as being for reasons of their status as children or minors. Indeed, the RPD explicitly adopted this approach in one decision in which it paraphrased the Canadian Gender Guidelines, in a way appropriate to claims by children:

> What is relevant is evidence that the particular social group suffers or fears to suffer discrimination of harsh and inhuman treatment that is distinguished from the situation of the general population or from other [children]. A subgroup of [children] may be identified by reference to their exposure or vulnerability for physical, cultural or other reasons to violence, including domestic violence, in an environment that denies them protection. These [children] face violence amounting to persecution because of their particular vulnerability as [children] in their societies and because they are so unprotected.[207]

The final point to note is that one important category that is sometimes overlooked in PSG analysis as a whole, but particularly in relation to claims by children and women, is that described in both *Acosta* and *Ward* as 'groups associated by a former voluntary status, unalterable due to its historical permanence'.[208] One example of the potential application of this category is provided in the judgment of the US Court of Appeals for the Third Circuit in *Lukwago*, in which the Court held that 'membership in

---

[204] *PEF (Re)*, No. VA0-00091 [2000] CRDD No. 110, 29 May 2000, at para. 18.
[205] See for example, *PEF (Re)*, No. VA0-00091 [2000] CRDD No. 110, 29 May 2000, in which the RPD recognized that the claimant had not wanted to leave China, but that his family forced him to do so: at paras. 5, 18–20. See also *ZOI (Re)*, Nos. V99-02926, V99-02950, V99-02926, V99-02950 [2000] CRDD No. 91, 9 May 2000, at paras. 17, 24–5.
[206] *MYS (Re)*, Nos. V97-00156, V97-00962 [1998] CRDD No. 149, 23 July 1998, at para. 25. See also *B (TD) (Re)*, Nos. T91-01497, T91-01498 [1994] CRDD No. 391, 9 August 1994, where, in the context of domestic violence on the child, the RPD followed the Supreme Court decision in *Ward* and found that 'the minor claimant is a member of a particular social group, namely, minors, based on the "innate and unchangeable characteristic" of being under the age of majority – a fact she cannot change for the foreseeable future. Her fear of persecution in Bulgaria is by reason of her membership in that particular social group': at 6.
[207] *MYS (Re)*, Nos. V97-00156, V97-00962 [1998] CRDD No. 149, 23 July 1998, at para. 26.
[208] See *Ward* [1993] 2 SCR 689 at 739.

the group of former child soldiers who have escaped LRA activity fits precisely within the BIA's own recognition that a shared past experience may be enough to link members of a "particular social group"'.[209] Another example that is particularly pertinent to the present topic relates to women and children who are at risk of being trafficked for sex or labour, in the situation that they have been trafficked previously by their parents or others, and thus face serious harm on this basis. In addition to such claims being dismissed on irrelevant grounds, such as notions of voluntariness or of their being characterized as 'economic migrants' discussed above in Chapter 5, decision-makers sometimes have difficulty in identifying the relevant PSG, often overlooking the fact that children (as well as women) are often at particular risk of harm because of their status as having been trafficked in the past.[210] As the RRT recognized in one decision, it was the fact that the young Uzbekistani female applicant had been forced into prostitution (a former status) that gave rise to the risk of future harm on the basis that she would be perceived to have 'contravene[d] Uzbek religious and societal codes'[211] and was therefore at risk of being seriously harmed by her family.[212]

Conclusion

This chapter has identified the key issues and challenges raised by socio-economic claims in terms of interpreting the Refugee Convention grounds. While it was observed that all of the Convention grounds are potentially relevant to claims based on the deprivation of socio-economic rights, it was noted that the membership of a particular social group ground has the potential for the most extensive application.

---

[209] *Lukwago*, 329 F 3d 157 (3rd Cir. 2003) at 161, citing *Acosta*. The Court explained that Lukwago's proffered group is not dissimilar from that suggested in Acosta where the BIA stated that the shared characteristic 'might be a shared past experience such as former military leadership'. Ultimately the Court held that the claimant did not fear being persecuted on this ground, thus the asylum claim was rejected.
[210] This is recognized in the UNHCR *Trafficking Guidelines*, p. 14.
[211] *Reference N02/42226*, RRT, 30 June 2003, at 11.
[212] The importance of the applicant's previous involvement in trafficking/prostitution has correctly been identified as the key reason for risk of future harm in other cases as well: see, for example, *YCK (Re)*, No. V95-02904, [1997] CRDD No. 261, 26 November 1997, where the RPD upheld a claim by a Ukrainian woman who was at risk because 'she would be targeted by organized criminals because she did not do what was expected of her and reported their agents in Canada to the police': at para. 3. See also *The Secretary of State for the Home Department* v. *Dzhygun* (Unreported, IAT, Appeal No. 00TH00728, 13 April 2000), in which the UK IAT upheld a claim by a Ukrainian woman in similar circumstances.

Analysis of the 'membership of a particular social group' ground demonstrated that adhering to well-established principle holds significant promise in terms of encompassing a range of groups who are at particular risk of socio-economic deprivation, including the poor, children and the disabled. This chapter thus further supports the hypothesis of this book that the Refugee Convention is capable of transcending the simplistic 'economic migrant' versus 'genuine refugee' distinction so as to encompass a broader range of claims involving socio-economic deprivation.

7 Conclusions

This book has explored the extent to which the key treaty in international law for the protection of refugees — the Refugee Convention — is capable of accommodating claims based on the deprivation of economic and social rights. The impetus arose, in part, from the identification of an emerging class of case that has begun to challenge the distinction between economic migrants and refugees, and a recognition that, while such cases raise important conceptual and interpretive challenges, recent developments in refugee law may have permitted an openness to encompassing this new type of claim.

As explained in Chapter 1, the notion that the distinction between economic and political factors is not as clear and stark as is often portrayed both in the rhetoric of states and even in judicial and executive decision-making, is not a new proposition. On the contrary, a body of migration literature has explored the interconnectedness of economic and political factors in producing migration flows and has highlighted the difficulty in distinguishing between forced and voluntary migrants, given the close connection between migration and a range of human rights violations. However, while these insights have long been acknowledged in the wider literature, they have seldom been applied to the Refugee Convention; rather, it has often been assumed that the Refugee Convention simply does not accommodate claims based on the severe deprivation of socio-economic rights and thus appropriate international responses must lie elsewhere. Even those studies that have considered the potential application of the Refugee Convention to such claims have frequently done so in broad and unspecific terms.

Against this background, this book has undertaken a principled analysis of the precise legal challenges inherent in such claims, by methodically reviewing the key elements necessary to establish a refugee claim and identifying those aspects that prove particularly challenging to the success of claims based on socio-economic deprivation. The guiding rationale is that an interpretation of the Refugee Convention which seeks to ensure its contemporary relevance by allowing for an evolutionary understanding of key concepts such as 'being persecuted', arguably required by the authoritative principles of treaty interpretation set out in Chapter 2, has the potential to accommodate a range of economic-based claims, and that many of the apparent obstacles may be overcome by the application or extrapolation of existing settled principles to these new factual situations.

In Chapter 3, the key definitional element – 'being persecuted' – was analysed from the perspective of the contemporary treatment of claims based on economic deprivation. It was revealed that, in the main, decision-makers have had little difficulty with the general proposition that a violation of economic and social rights may give rise to persecution, thus accepting the anterior proposition that economic and social rights are of considerable importance. This was shown to constitute a logical extension of the now predominant notion that 'being persecuted' is appropriately assessed in light of contemporary norms of international human rights law.

However, while displaying sensitivity to and awareness of the existence of economic, social and cultural rights in international law, the analysis revealed that in several fundamental ways, decision-makers' approaches to the assessment of these rights, most importantly in adopting a hierarchical approach which accords an inferior status to such rights, are considerably out-of-step with the theoretical and practical advancements that have been made in recent decades in according equal status and more precise normative content to economic and social rights in international law. These issues were further explored in Chapter 4, in which it was argued that this lack of correlation between the treatment of economic rights in refugee law vis-à-vis international human rights law is unjustifiable, but is capable of being remedied by a reformulation of the human rights approach to assessing persecution. In particular, a focus on core violations of all types of rights would realign the appropriate focus on the nature of the *violation*, rather than disproportionately on the nature (and so-called status) of the *right* at issue. The chapter sought to provide a conceptual framework for the assessment of the 'being persecuted' question that would permit greater scope for the consideration of violations of economic and social rights.

The central conclusion was that, while decision-makers currently have a tendency to undervalue and otherwise dismiss economic claims based on mistaken notions about their content and value, an approach focused on correct principles of international human rights law holds considerable promise in accommodating a new range of claims based on economic deprivation.

Chapter 5 then turned to consider the second key definitional requirement of the Refugee definition, namely the issue of when persecution can be said to be 'for reasons of' the Convention grounds race, religion, nationality, membership of a particular social group or political opinion. It was established in this chapter that important interpretive developments which have allowed for a liberal causation standard and a move away from a strict intent-based approach, reduce the extent to which nexus presents a barrier to claims based on the deprivation of economic and social rights. Chapter 6 then turned to consider the correct interpretation of the Convention grounds, concluding that the 'membership of a particular social group' ground holds the greatest potential relevance to claims based on economic deprivation. In particular, it was noted that contemporary developments in interpreting this ground, which equate the ground to immutable characteristics or those based on fundamental human rights norms, have enabled groups such as children, persons with disabilities and the poor to establish claims when their status can be linked to the serious harm they fear.

The salient conclusion of the analysis undertaken in this book is that the Refugee Convention is indeed capable of encompassing a range of claims previously thought to be outside the scope of the terms of the treaty. This conclusion is not merely based on theoretical possibility, but is buttressed by the nascent jurisprudence which has shown that decision-makers are both able and willing to transcend simplistic labels, such as 'economic migrant' and 'voluntary migrant', to uphold economic claims based on a creative yet legally sustainable application of existing principle.

This conclusion immediately gives rise to a number of important policy questions that must be addressed. The first set relates to a practical concern that a more expansive interpretation, such as has been advocated in this book, while justifiable in law is inadvisable in policy since it has the potential to break down the refugee–immigration distinction and create an unmanageable situation in light of the limited capacity of refugee-receiving states. Such concern was implicitly voiced by Steinbock when, after considering the proposition that economic and social rights should be considered relevant to the 'being persecuted' inquiry, he concluded:

In sum, a large body of rights violations are equated with persecution. The broad range of human rights identified in this list would make millions of people potential refugees in today's world. Either such an extensive description of persecution would revolutionize refugee law, or choice among potential refugees would need to be made on some other basis than the kind or quality of harm (such as the quantity or probability). With either alternative, the practical impact of this approach would be enormous.[1]

In part this reflects a 'floodgates' concern, often identified throughout this book as either explicitly or implicitly underpinning decision-makers' caution when considering claims based on economic deprivation, although the issue is not confined to such claims. The difficulty with the floodgates argument is that it is clearly not a legal argument, as has been reiterated by many senior common law courts.[2] Indeed, it has been said that the argument that certain decisions may 'open floodgates', 'is no argument at all'.[3] As a Justice of the High Court of Australia has explained:

The mere fact that, potentially, very large numbers of persons might qualify for refugee status in Australia if the appeal to this Court were upheld ... is not, of itself, sufficient to show that decision was wrong.[4]

Thus, to enter into a consideration of the validity of the floodgates concern as a matter of fact and/or policy may be perceived to give cogency to an argument otherwise considered outside the scope of an analysis based on law. On the other hand, there is a risk that adopting such a narrow, albeit legally correct position, is impractical given the relevance of policy issues to the treatment of refugees by executive governments. It may then be necessary to give some consideration to this issue, since to ignore it may risk undermining the cogency of an otherwise valid analysis.

The 'floodgates' argument is often evoked on the supposition that the mere fact that a group of persons may suffer a kind of harm that

---

[1] Steinbock, 'Interpreting the Refugee Definition', at 781.
[2] In *Chan* [1995] 3 SCR 593, La Forest J of the Canadian Supreme Court stated that the 'floodgates' argument is 'not an appropriate legal consideration': at para. 57. See also *R v. Secretary of State for the Home Department, ex parte Jeyakumaran* [1994] Imm AR 45 at 48: 'Whilst I am conscious of the administrative problem of numbers seeking asylum, it cannot be right to adopt artificial and inhuman criteria in an attempt to solve it.'
[3] Decision of the UK IAT in *Stula v. Secretary of State for the Home Department*, cited in Symes, *Caselaw on the Refugee Convention*, p. 10.
[4] *Applicant A* (1997) 190 CLR 225 at 241 (Gummow J).

potentially falls within the definition of being persecuted means they would automatically qualify for refugee status. Accordingly, the consideration of the potential application of the definition to claims based on economic deprivation has a tendency to precipitate exaggerated reactions to the potential implications of such an expansion, based on the assumption that all of the world's poor or indigent could, and probably will, claim refugee status once a more liberal understanding of persecution is accepted by refugee-receiving states.

There are two key problems with such a response. The first is that it assumes a much more expansive conclusion than is justified by the analysis undertaken in this book. Since the current analysis is undertaken within the parameters of the existing refugee definition (rather than, for example, advocating the revision or amendment of the Refugee Convention definition to include new categories of claim or advocating the introduction of 'open borders'), its scope and potential application is inevitably limited by the constraints of the Refugee Convention language. In particular, the harm suffered must be sufficiently serious to warrant the description 'persecution', that is, it must be possible to point to a core violation of socio-economic rights, which involves establishing a failure on the part of the state to ensure non-discriminatory provision of basic rights or to take steps to implement the core obligations in the Covenant. Moreover, it must be possible to link the harm feared to a Refugee Convention ground. This will necessarily continue to exclude a broad range of claims based on economic harm, most obviously where the applicant cannot differentiate his or her situation from that of the general population in the home state. More generally, since the analysis remains firmly based in the terms of the Refugee Convention definition, it does not seek to diminish or obliterate the refugee–migration distinction, but rather to clarify and sharpen the distinction to a certain degree. The book is based on the notion that there is a distinction between those who flee because their fundamental human rights are violated and those who flee for other reasons, and that this distinction should be upheld. The key point of departure is in assessing what kinds of violations are relevant to a refugee claim, with the salient argument being that the fact that some people leave their country for non-persecutory economic reasons should not obscure the fact that many leave for persecutory economic reasons, and that the latter type of claim properly falls within the terms, as well as objects and purposes, of the Refugee Convention.

The second problem with the floodgates argument is that it is usually based on the assumption that all persons who are capable of satisfying the refugee definition will in fact leave their home countries and seek protection in another state (specifically in a developed, northern state), so that to expand the potential scope of the definition will necessarily impose impractical obligations on developed states. The answer is that while it is true that the interpretation promoted in this book offers the scope for a more expansive and liberal interpretation of the Refugee Convention, such that a wider range of claims may well be encompassed, this does not mean that every person who qualifies will ultimately seek protection. On the contrary, it is widely acknowledged that most of the world's refugees remain in their own country, and even those who do leave their country of origin overwhelmingly remain in their own region.[5] Thus, the burden imposed on northern states (that is, those states that usually raise such arguments) is vastly negatively disproportionate to the actual number of refugees and displaced persons in the world. This is borne out by the fact that previous important interpretative developments that have widened the potential scope of the Refugee Convention have not produced the result that all or even a significant proportion of potential refugees falling within that particular definition have in fact left their countries to seek protection. For example, following *Shah*[6] and *Khawar*,[7] neither the UK nor Australia, respectively, has been inundated with women seeking refuge from Pakistan or elsewhere. This is perhaps (paradoxically) even more pertinent to the present topic, since many of those suffering a deprivation of economic and social rights will find it particularly difficult to flee their home countries in search of protection.

However, while the floodgates argument may not prove to be a compelling factor militating against the conclusions set out in this book, the perception of the potential for floodgates may nonetheless prove instrumental in influencing policies of both the executive and the legislature in domestic jurisdictions. In other words, a more progressive approach by the judiciary may precipitate an attempt on the part of other arms of government to constrain the scope of a state's international obligations. For example, a liberal approach to an interpretation of the Refugee Convention by the judiciary may lead (and indeed in some circumstances has led) to the legislature amending domestic legislation

---

[5] The 2002 World Refugee Survey notes that 'Although developed countries contribute most of the funding for programs that assist refugees, the least-developed countries host the overwhelming majority of the world's refugees': US Committee for Refugees, *World Refugee Survey 2002* (Washington DC, 2002), p. 11.
[6] *Shah* [1999] 2 AC 629 at 641.   [7] *Khawar* (2002) 210 CLR 1.

so as to limit the scope of domestic refugee law, even where such amendment brings the domestic jurisdiction into conflict with its international legal obligations.[8] In addition, the perception that once an immigrant is permitted to reach the territory of a state party it will be difficult to remove him or her due to an expansive interpretation of the state's legal obligations may lead (and indeed has led) to the executive in some countries implementing restrictive policies designed to prevent such persons from reaching the territory of the state, for example by physically preventing their arrival. Numerous examples of this phenomenon abound in recent history, with perhaps the most infamous being the actions of the Australian government in 2001 in preventing the refugees on the Tampa from entering Australian territorial waters,[9] and in its subsequent action in declaring parts of Australia to be outside the 'migration zone' and thus, for refugee law purposes, not part of Australian territory.[10] Thus, one might perceive concrete dangers in advocating a more liberal approach to be taken by the judiciary, in that it may simply produce more restrictive policies in other respects.

On the other hand, it might be argued that in the current climate of an increased focus and priority on immigration control throughout the

---

[8] For a good example of the legislature directly responding to the perceived liberal approach of the judiciary to an interpretation of the Convention, see *Migration Legislation Amendment Act (No. 6) 2001* (Cth), which amended the 'causation' test in refugee law (in the *Migration Act 1958* (Cth)) so as to provide for a more narrow test following expansive tests developed by the Federal Court of Australia. See Information and Research Services (Cth), *Migration Legislation Amendment Bill (No. 6) 2001: Bills Digest No. 55* (2001–02), p. 1: 'Over recent years the interpretation of the definition of a refugee by various courts and tribunals has expanded the interpretation of the definition of a refugee so as to require protection to be provided in circumstances that are clearly outside those originally intended.' See also *Migration Legislation Amendment Bill (No. 6) 2001*, Revised Explanatory Memorandum, at para. 3, and The Hon. Philip Ruddock MP, Minister for Immigration and Multicultural Affairs, Second Reading Speech, House of Representatives, 28 August 2001: 'These generous interpretations [by the Federal Court] of our obligations encourage people who are not refugees to test their claims in Australia, adding to perceptions that Australia is a soft touch.'

[9] See generally, Penelope Mathew, 'Current Development: Australian Refugee Protection in the Wake of the Tampa' (2002) 96 *American Journal of International Law* 661. Another example is the US Coast Guard's policy, particularly prominent in the early 1980s, of interdicting Haitian refugees at sea, a practice that was upheld by the US Supreme Court in *Sale v. Haitian Centers Council Inc* (1994) 113 S Ct 2549. See generally: Keith Highet, George Kahale III and Thomas David Jones, 'Decision: Sale v. Haitian Centers Council, Inc, 113 S Ct 2549' (1994) 88 *American Journal of International Law* 114.

[10] This is well described in Goodwin-Gill, 'Refugees and Responsibility in the Twenty-First Century', at 28–9.

developed world, where legislatures and executives are generally prone to restrictive policies, the only remaining feasible site for contestation remains rights-based litigation. Accordingly, advocates are correct to make creative arguments to the judicial branch in order to ensure that those persons traditionally neglected by the Refugee Convention, but arguably within its scope, are provided international protection. This is particularly so in light of the fact that the judiciary will often be more receptive to valid, principled legal arguments, untrammelled by extraneous considerations of 'floodgates' and 'unintended consequences', a proposition which tends to be supported by the analysis undertaken in this book.

In addition to the above criticisms potentially being raised in respect of the conclusions reached in this book, the converse argument, namely that reliance on the Refugee Convention alone does not provide sufficient protection to all those arguably deserving of protection, may also be advanced. The basis for such an argument is outlined in the following explanation of protection gaps by the UNHCR:

> The discrepancies between refugees recognized under the 1951 Convention and the wider group of persons in need of international protection arise in part from the way in which the definition of refugee in the 1951 Convention has been interpreted by some States, in part from the way the 1951 Convention together with the 1967 Protocol has been applied, and in part from the limitations inherent in the refugee instruments themselves.[11]

This underlines the fact that regardless of the extent to which the definition is interpreted in a liberal and expansive manner, consistent with appropriate principles of treaty interpretation, the definition itself contains insurmountable obstacles which prevent application to all those in need. The most obvious limitation is the nexus clause,[12] which ensures that, regardless of the level of serious harm, a claim will fail if it cannot be causally linked to a protected ground. This is often the basis for claims that the Refugee Convention does not apply to generalized suffering, such as produced by civil war, generally poor economic conditions or 'natural' disasters such as famine,

---

[11] UNHCR, 'Note on International Protection', UN Doc A/AC.96/830 (1994), as cited in Oldrich Andrysek, 'Gaps in International Protection and the Potential for Redress through Individual Complaints Procedures' (1997) 9 *International Journal of Refugee Law* 392 at 394.

[12] Others include the exclusion clauses (Refugee Convention, art. 1(F)), which, for example, have been held not to apply to a case under art. 3 of the European Convention on Human Rights: see *Chahal v. United Kingdom* (1996) 23 EHRR 413 at para. 80.

earthquakes or floods. While, as this book has displayed, it is possible (and indeed preferable) to interpret the nexus clause in a liberal manner, so as to allow such claims in specific circumstances, its proper application will nonetheless result in the exclusion of many arguably deserving claims.

One of the most important developments in recent years that has assisted in bridging this lacuna in international protection is an expansive interpretation of international and regional human rights treaties, which has effectively implied a *non-refoulement* provision[13] into such treaties by holding that signatory states are in breach of their human rights obligations if they expel or return an individual to a situation in which he/she will be subjected to treatment prohibited by the relevant treaty, such as art. 3 of the European Convention (torture or degrading treatment) or art. 6 of the ICCPR (right to life).[14] Indeed, recent developments in domestic jurisdictions reveal an increasing convergence between the refugee regime and remedies based on international and regional human rights covenants. The USA was one of the first jurisdictions to provide for a direct remedy based on a non-refugee treaty, the CAT;[15] Canada has now introduced an even more comprehensive scheme

---

[13] It should be noted that art. 3 of the CAT contains an explicit *non-refoulement* provision. By contrast, the other relevant international human rights treaties do not contain an explicit *non-refoulement* provision, but have been interpreted so as to effectively contain such a provision.

[14] For some of the literature on this general issue: see Jane McAdam, *Complementary Protection in International Refugee Law* (OUP, 2007), Andrysek, 'Gaps in International Protection and the Potential for Redress through Individual Complaints Procedures'; Matti Pellonpaa, 'ECHR Case-law on Refugees and Asylum-Seekers and Protection under the 1951 Refugee Convention: Similarities and Differences', in *The Changing Nature of Persecution: IARLJ 4th Conference* (Bern, Switzerland: Institute of Public Law, University of Berne, 2001); Eeva Nykanen, 'Protecting Children? The European Convention on Human Rights and Child Asylum Seekers' (2001) 3 *European Journal of Migration and the Law* 315; Lisbeth Steendijk, 'The Application of Human Rights Standards to Asylum Cases: The Dutch Example' (2001) 3 *European Journal of Migration and the Law* 185; Bertold Huber, 'The Application of Human Rights Standards by German Courts to Asylum-Seekers, Refugees and Migrants' (2001) 3 *European Journal of Migration and the Law* 171; and Nicholas Blake, 'Entitlement to Protection: A Human Rights-Based Approach to Refugee Protection in the United Kingdom', in Frances Nicholson and Patrick Twomey (eds.), *Current Issues of UK Asylum Law and Policy* (Dartmouth: Ashgate, 1998), pp. 252–9. For an overview of the complementary protection regimes in the European Union, the USA and Canada, see Jane McAdam, 'Complementary Protection and Beyond: How States Deal with Human Rights Protection', *UNHCR New Issues in Refugee Research: Working Paper 118* (2005) <http://www.unhcr.org/cgi-bin/texis/vtx/research/opendoc.pdf?tbl=RESEARCH&id=42fb1f045> at 31 May 2006.

[15] See 8 CFR 1208.18 for definitions and procedure to be followed in adjudicating such claims. See also Anker, *Law of Asylum in the United States*, pp. 465–522.

based on both the CAT[16] and the ICCPR;[17] the UK has recently introduced additional remedies for those outside the Refugee Convention based on the European Convention,[18] while the recently enacted EU Directive promises to yield the most comprehensive scheme to date, in which there will be a partial fusion of the refugee and international human rights-based protection schemes.[19] Moreover, it has been argued that a principle of *non-refoulement* has been established in customary international law which prohibits return or expulsion where there are substantial grounds for believing that a person 'would face a real risk of being subjected to torture, cruel, inhuman or degrading treatment or punishment'.[20]

These developments have particular relevance to the present topic since, although the nature of these international legal obligations is often more akin to civil and political rights, the relevant adjudicatory bodies are increasingly recognizing, at least in the European system, that states can, in exceptional circumstances, be in breach of their treaty obligations if they expel a person to a situation in which their economic and social rights will be infringed. As explained in Chapter 4, the ECHR has held (in a decision representing an important conceptual shift) that art. 3 may prohibit the return of a person with HIV/AIDS to a country in which he or she would not receive any treatment or family support;[21] and the UK IAT has extrapolated from this decision the principle that '[i]t is uncontroversial that if as a result of a removal decision a person would be exposed to a

---

[16] See *Immigration and Refugee Protection Act* S.C. 2001, c. 27 (IRPA), s 97 (1)(a), providing that a person in need of protection is a person who would be subject on return 'to a danger, believed on substantial grounds to exist, of torture within the meaning of Article 1 of the Convention Against Torture'.

[17] See *Immigration and Refugee Protection Act*, s 97(1)(b), providing that a person in need of protection is a person who would be subject on return, 'to a risk to their life or to a risk of cruel and unusual treatment or punishment'. A list of limitations is then set out: see s 97(1)(b)(i)–(iv).

[18] In a scheme beginning 1 April 2003, the Immigration and Nationality Directorate has changed the system of granting exceptional leave to provide for Humanitarian Protection and Discretionary Leave to remain in the UK. The Directorate explains that, 'A stand alone human rights claim may also result in a grant of Discretionary Leave if the qualifying criteria are met': see UK Immigration and Nationality Directorate, 'Discretionary Leave' (2006) <http://www.ind.homeoffice.gov.uk/ind/en/home/laws_policy/policy_instructions/apis/discretionary_leave.html> at 31 May 2006.

[19] I say partial, because the EU Directive refers only to specific provisions of the European Convention as a basis for 'subsidiary protection' (see art. 15) and still differentiates between the schemes in terms of rights accorded to those given protection (see Chapter VII – 'Content of International Protection').

[20] Sir Elihu Lauterpacht and Daniel Bethlehem, 'The Scope and Content of the Principle of Non-Refoulement', in Feller, Türk and Nicholson (eds.), *Refugee Protection in International Law*, p. 87.

[21] *D v. United Kingdom* (Unreported, Case No. 146/1996/767/964, 21 April 1997).

real risk of existence below the level of bare minimum subsistence that would cross the threshold of Art 3 harm'.[22] In addition, art. 8 of the European Convention (respect for private and family life) may be invoked where the treatment which the applicant fears does not reach the level of severity of art. 3 treatment. For example, it has been held that treatment might breach art. 8 in its private life aspect 'where there are sufficiently adverse effects on physical and moral integrity',[23] such that reliance may be placed on art. 8 to 'resist an expulsion decision' based on the consequences for [the applicant's] mental health of removal to the receiving country'.[24] Although the circumstances in which such a claim will be successful are very narrow,[25] this nonetheless holds promise for persons outside the scope of the Refugee Convention who are in need of protection.

[22] *Mandali v. Secretary of State for the Home Department* [2002] UKIAT 0741, at para. 10. See also generally *Secretary of State for the Home Department v. Kacaj* (Unreported, IAT, Appeal No. 23044/2000, 19 July 2001), for a discussion of general principles relating to art. 3 and expulsion. Interestingly, the Immigration and Nationality Directorate has also acknowledged that '[t]here may be some extreme cases (although such cases are likely to be rare) where a person would face such poor conditions if returned – e.g. absence of water, food or basic shelter – that removal could be a breach of the UK's Article 3 obligations': see UK Immigration and Nationality Directorate, 'Discretionary Leave'. The Directorate also notes that '[i]t can be a breach of Article 3 to remove someone from the UK if to do so would amount to inhuman or degrading treatment owing to the suffering which would be caused because of that person's medical condition. The threshold for inhuman and degrading treatment in such cases is extremely high and will only be reached in truly exceptional cases involving extreme circumstances'.
[23] *Case of Bensaid v. United Kingdom* (2001) 33 EHRR 10, at para. 46 ('*Bensaid*').
[24] *R (on the application of Razgar) v. Secretary of State for the Home Department* [2004] All ER (D) 169 at 175 ('*Razgar*').
[25] There are three key limitations. First, the House of Lords has made clear in *Razgar* that 'an applicant could never hope to resist an expulsion decision without showing something very much more extreme than relative disadvantage [in respect of medical treatment] as compared with the expelling state': at 176. Second, these issues have been raised overwhelmingly in general deportation cases, rather than in refugee claims. This may be explained on the basis that an asylum-seeker is less likely to have established family ties or to have established ongoing medical treatment in the asylum state prior to the decision to expel. Moreover, comments in the Court's decisions may suggest that these principles are less relevant to refugee claims. For example, in *Berrehab*, the Court considered it significant that 'the instant case did not concern an alien seeking admission to the Netherlands for the first time but a person who had already lawfully lived there for several years': *Berrehab v. The Netherlands* (1988) 11 EHRR 322, at para. 29. Third, the ECHR has said that the home country may weigh migration considerations against the harm caused to the applicant. In *Bensaid*, the Court there rejected the art. 8 argument on the basis that even 'assuming that the dislocation caused to the applicant by removal from the United Kingdom where he has lived for the last eleven years was to be considered by itself as affecting his private life, in the context of the relationships and support framework which he enjoyed there', the interference was justified under art. 8(2) as pursuing the aims of protection and economic well-being of the country and the prevention of disorder and crime.

In the Canadian context, while a claim based only on 'inadequate health or medical care' in the country of origin is expressly excluded from protection under the relevant human rights based provisions,[26] the Federal Court of Canada has held that a lack of health care may nonetheless form the basis of a claim where, due to a mental condition such as schizophrenia or depression, and an absence of family support, an applicant 'would be particularly vulnerable in the unstable conditions prevailing in [his or her country of origin]'.[27]

The potential scope of other provisions of the European Convention and the ICCPR, particularly those with socio-economic dimensions,[28] in the removal context is yet to be defined,[29] although it is important to note

---

[26] See *Immigration and Refugee Protection Act*, s 97(1)(b)(iv).
[27] *Ahmed v. Canada (Minister of Citizenship & Immigration)* (2002) 7 Imm LR (3d) 286, at 5. There is little case law on this issue, given that the legislation only came into force in 2002, but the relevant commentary by Legal Services, Immigration and Refugee Board, *Consolidated Grounds in the Immigration and Refugee Protection Act: Persons in Need of Protection, Risk to Life or Risk of Cruel and Unusual Treatment or Punishment* (15 May 2002) (on file with author), states that 'individuals who are denied treatment may be able to establish a claim under [the relevant legislation] because in their case, their risk arises from the country's unwillingness to provide them with adequate care'. In addition, '[c]are must be taken in analysing a claim where the risk arises, not because of the lack of health care, but because the person has a medical condition that will make him or her more vulnerable to the unstable conditions in his or her country': p. 11.
[28] For example, it is not clear whether the eviction cases, held to be in breach of art. 8 (see Chapter 4, notes 149–50), would apply to a removal case.
[29] The ECHR has considered other provisions in this context. It impliedly accepted that art. 2 can, in certain circumstances, give rise to extra-territorial application in *Mohamed Dougoz v. Greece* (Unreported, Application No. 40907/98, 8 February 2000) ('*Dougoz*'). It has also held art. 6 to be relevant: *Soering Case* (Unreported, Case No. 1/1989/161/217); *Case of Drozd and Janousek v. France and Spain* (Unreported, Case No. 21/1991/273/344, 26 June 1992), at para. 110; *Pellegrini v. Italy* (Unreported, Case No. 30882/96, 20 July 2001). It is established that an expulsion to face the death penalty will be in breach of Protocol 6: *Aylor-Davis v. France* (Unreported, Case No. 22742/93, 20 January 1994). In two very recent House of Lords decisions, the House confronted this precise issue, concluding that other provisions of the European Convention, including the 'qualified rights', such as those contained in arts. 8 and 9, may be engaged in the removal context, although the test will be a high one: 'The reason why flagrant denial or gross violation is to be taken into account is that it is only in such a case – where the right will be completely denied or nullified in the destination country – that it can be said that removal will breach the treaty obligations of the signatory state however those obligations might be interpreted or whatever might be said by or on behalf of the destination state': *R (on the application of Ullah) v. Special Adjudicator; Do v. Secretary of State for the Home Department* [2004] 3 All ER 785, at *12, citing the UK IAT in *Devaseelan v. Secretary of State for the Home Department* [2002] IAT 702. The Human Rights Committee has appeared to take a more inclusive approach to the relevance of provisions of the ICCPR to the expulsion/removal context. In General Comment 15, the HRC has explicitly interpreted Article 7 as including the

that the new EU Directive applies subsidiary protection only to those at risk of execution, torture or inhuman or degrading treatment or punishment, or a 'serious and individual threat to a civilian's life or person by reason of indiscriminate violence in situations of international or internal armed conflict'.[30]

In all of these cases, while the level of proof required to establish a claim is high,[31] it is not necessary to establish that the harm feared is related to a specific ground (for example, race or religion), thus circumventing one of the most formidable barriers to successful complaints under the Refugee Convention. Nonetheless, it must be acknowledged that these remedies are still very much in their infancy in terms of development and, more importantly, have limited application geographically. Moreover, it is widely accepted that the Refugee Convention should remain the key governing regime for the protection of those who cannot or should not be required to return to their country of origin,[32] most importantly because it confers a range of civil and political and socio-economic rights on those recognized as refugees, and thus provides far greater protection than the right of non-return which (albeit essential) is often the only remedy available under the subsidiary schemes. Therefore, while these developments are certainly important (and must be considered in any review of remedies available to those in need of protection), they do not obviate the concern that the Refugee Convention may be overly narrow in scope and accordingly difficult to justify ethically.

---

principle of *non-refoulement*. See also *ARJ* v. *Australia* (Communication No. 692/1996, 11 August 1997) at para. 6.9.

[30] EU Directive, Article 15.

[31] In *Dougoz*, the ECHR explained: 'As regards the substance of the complaint, the Court recalls that, under its case-law, the expulsion of an asylum-seeker may engage a Contracting Party's responsibility under Article 3 of the Convention where substantial grounds have been shown for believing that the person concerned faces a real risk of being subjected to torture or to inhuman or degrading treatment or punishment' (the Vilvarajah and Others v. the United Kingdom judgment of 30 October 1991, Series A no. 215, p. 34, §102).

[32] The Refugee Convention continues, in the words of the UNHCR, to 'serve as the cornerstone of the international refugee protection regime': UNHCR Executive Committee, *Conclusion on the Provision of International Protection Including Through Complementary Forms of Protection* (2005) <http://www.unhcr.org/cgi-bin/texis/vtx/excom/opendoc.htm?tbl=EXCOM&id=43576e292> at 31 May 2006; Inter-Conference Working Parties: Human Rights Nexus Working Party, *Human Rights Conference Report* (IARLJ Annual Conference, Ottawa, 12–17 October 1998) (on file with author), p. 12.

The question whether the Refugee Convention is 'outdated' or otherwise in need of revision is a complex and multifaceted one that is clearly beyond the scope of this book to resolve. However, it should be noted that the fact that it is of limited scope does not necessarily suggest that it is no longer sustainable in terms of wider humanitarian principles or goals. Hathaway, for example, puts forward a convincing argument that if we are to accept that 'the world's asylum capacity is insufficient to accommodate those who would be likely to advance refugee claims based simply on the risk of serious harm', then the nexus criterion provides a principled way to extend protection to those who are 'fundamentally marginalized' in their state of origin.[33] As he explains:

> if persons affected by fundamental forms of socio-political disfranchisement are less likely than others ever to be in a position to seek effective redress from within their state, then their need for external protection is indeed more profound.[34]

The question of how best to allocate necessarily limited resources to all the world's displaced persons is one of undoubted importance but also one of enormous complexity. In addition to difficult ethical, legal and moral arguments, there are also fundamental practical concerns about the political will of western governments to commit necessary resources to provide meaningful solutions to the multifarious problems. While not seeking to minimize or ignore the importance of the wider policy debate, this book has focused not on questions of future remedies or schemes for the protection of refugees, but has sought to examine the extent to which the key remedy currently available in international law – the Refugee Convention – may be interpreted and implemented in a manner that reflects contemporary understandings of the scope of human rights protection, most importantly the equal value of economic, social and cultural rights. As this book has established, while certainly not constituting an ideal scheme for the protection of refugees, the Refugee Convention is capable of evolving so as to accommodate contemporary developments, being 'constant in motive but mutable in form'.[35] An ability

---

[33] James C. Hathaway, 'Is Refugee Status Really Elitist? An Answer to the Ethical Challenge', in Carlier and Vanheule (eds.), *Europe and Refugees: A Challenge?*, pp. 85–6.
[34] *Ibid.*, p. 86.
[35] R v. *Immigration Appeal Tribunal and Another, Ex parte Shah* (The Times, 12 November 1996, CO 4330/95 25 October 1996), adopted in *Chen Shi Hai* (2000) 201 CLR 293 at 317–18 (Kirby J).

to evolve so as to incorporate the protection needs of those who suffer socio-economic deprivation for a Refugee Convention reason has and will make significant progress in upholding the human rights and humanitarian objectives of the Refugee Convention and in achieving its purpose of providing protection to those most in need of international protection.

Bibliography

Articles and books

Agbakwa, Shedrack C., 'Reclaiming Humanity: Economic, Social and Cultural Rights as the Cornerstone of African Human Rights' (2000) 5 *Yale Human Rights and Development Law Journal* 177.

Aleinikoff, Thomas Alexander, 'The Refugee Convention at Forty: Reflections on the IJRL Colloquium' (1991) 3 *International Journal of Refugee Law* 617.

Aleinikoff, Thomas Alexander, David A. Martin and Hiroshi Motomura, *Immigration and Citizenship: Process and Policy* (St Paul, MN: West Group, 1998).

Alston, Philip, 'Conjuring Up New Human Rights: A Proposal for Quality Control' (1984) 78 *American Journal of International Law* 607.

'Out of the Abyss: The Challenges Confronting the New UN Committee on Economic, Social and Cultural Rights' (1987) 9 *Human Rights Quarterly* 332.

Alston, Philip and Gerard Quinn, 'The Nature and Scope of States Parties' Obligations under the International Covenant on Economic, Social and Cultural Rights' (1987) 9 *Human Rights Quarterly* 156.

Andrysek, Oldrich, 'Gaps in International Protection and the Potential for Redress through Individual Complaints Procedures' (1997) 9 *International Journal of Refugee Law* 392.

Anker, Deborah, 'Women Refugees: Forgotten No Longer?' (1995) 32 *San Diego Law Review* 771.

Law of Asylum in the United States (Boston, MA: Refugee Law Center, 1999).

'Refugee Status and Violence Against Women in the "Domestic" Sphere: The Non-State Actor Question' (2001) 15 *Georgetown Immigration Law Journal* 391.

'Boundaries in the Field of Human Rights: Refugee Law, Gender and the Human Rights Paradigm' (2002) 15 *Harvard Human Rights Journal* 133.

Arambulo, Kitty, 'Drafting an Optional Protocol to the International Covenant on Economic, Social and Cultural Rights: Can an Ideal Become Reality?' (1996) 2 *University of California Davis Journal of International Law and Policy* 111.

Strengthening the Supervision of the International Covenant on Economic, Social and Cultural Rights (Antwerp: Intersentia, 1999).

Aust, Anthony, *Modern Treaty Law and Practice* (Cambridge: Cambridge University Press, 2000).

Bhabha, Jacqueline, 'Minors or Aliens? Inconsistent State Intervention and Separate Child Asylum-Seekers' (2001) *European Journal of Migration and Law* 283.

'Boundaries in the Field of Human Rights: Internationalist Gatekeepers?: The Tension Between Asylum Advocacy and Human Rights' (2002) 15 *Harvard Human Rights Journal* 155.

Bhabha, Jacqueline and Wendy Young, 'Not Adults in Miniature: Unaccompanied Child Asylum Seekers and the US Guidelines' (1999) 11(1) *International Journal of Refugee Law* 84.

Bilchitz, David, 'Towards a Reasonable Approach to the Minimum Core: Laying the Foundations for Future Socio-Economic Rights Jurisprudence' (2003) 19 *South African Journal on Human Rights* 1.

Blake, Nicholas, 'Entitlement to Protection: A Human Rights-Based Approach to Refugee Protection in the United Kingdom', in Frances Nicholson and Patrick Twomey (eds.), *Current Issues of UK Asylum Law and Policy* (Dartmouth: Ashgate, 1998).

Boyle, Allan, 'Some Reflections on the Relationship of Treaties and Soft Law', in Vera Gowlland-Debbas (ed.), *Multilateral Treaty Making, The Current Status of Challenges to and Reforms Needed in the International Legislative Process* (The Hague, Boston: M. Nijhoff, 2000).

Brems, Eva, 'Social and Economic Rights of Women', in Peter Van der Auweraert (ed.), *Social, Economic and Cultural Rights: An Appraisal of Current European and International Developments* (Antwerp: Maklu, 2002).

Breyer, David and Edmund Cairns, 'For Better? For Worse? Humanitarian Aid in Conflict' (1997) 7(4) *Development in Practice* 363.

Brownlie, Ian, *Principles of Public International Law*, sixth edition (Oxford: Oxford University Press, 2003).

Buffard, Isabelle and Karl Zemanek, 'The "Object and Purpose" of a Treaty: an Enigma?' (1998) 3 *American Review of International and European Law* 311.

Carlier, Jean-Yves, Dirk Vanheule, Carlos Peña Galiano and Klaus Hullman (eds.), *Who is a Refugee? A Comparative Case Law Study* (The Hague: Kluwer Law International, 1997).

Charlesworth, Hilary and Christine Chinkin, 'The Gender of Jus Cogens' (1993) 15 *Human Rights Quarterly* 63.

Chisanga Puta-Chekwe and Nora Flood, 'From Division to Integration: Economic, Social and Cultural Rights as Basic Human Rights', in Isfahan Merali and Valerie Oostervedl (eds.), *Giving Meaning to Economic, Social and Cultural Rights* (Philadelphia: University of Pennsylvania Press, 2001).

Clark, Tom and Francois Crêpeau, 'Mainstreaming Refugee Rights: the 1951 Refugee Convention and International Human Rights Law' (1999) 17(4) *Netherlands Quarterly of Human Rights* 389.

Connors, Jane, 'Legal Aspects of Women as a Particular Social Group' (1997) 9 *International Journal of Refugee Law* 115.

Cook, Shayna S., 'Repairing the Legacy of INS v. Elias-Zacarias' (2002) 23 *Michigan Journal of International Law* 223.
Coomans, Fons, *Economic, Social and Cultural Rights* (Utrecht: Advisory Committee on Human Rights and Foreign Policy of the Netherlands, 1995).
  'In Search of the Core Content of the Right to Education', in Audrey R. Chapman and Sage Russell (eds.), *Core Obligations: Building a Framework for Economic, Social and Cultural Rights* (Antwerp, New York: Transnational Publishing, 2002).
Cottier, Thomas, 'Trade and Human Rights: a Relationship to Discover' (2002) 5(1) *Journal of International Economic Law* 111.
Cranston, Maurice, *What Are Human Rights?* (London: Bodley Head, 1973).
Craven, Matthew C.R., *The International Covenant on Economic, Social and Cultural Rights: A Perspective on its Development* (Oxford: Oxford University Press, 1995).
  'The Protection of Economic, Social and Cultural Rights under the Inter-American System of Human Rights', in David J. Harris and Stephen Livingstone (eds.), *The Inter-American System of Human Rights* (Oxford: Clarendon Press, 1998).
  'The International Covenant on Economic, Social and Cultural Rights', in Raija Hanski and Markku Suksi (eds.), *An Introduction to the International Protection of Human Rights – A Textbook* (Åbo: Institute for Human Rights, Åbo Akademi University, 1999).
Crawley, Heaven, *Refugees and Gender: Law and Process* (Bristol: Jordan Publishing, 2001).
Daley, Krista and Ninette Kelley, 'Particular Social Group: A Human Rights Based Approach in Canadian Jurisprudence' (2000) 12(2) *International Journal of Refugee Law* 148.
Dauvergne, Catherine, 'Chinese Fleeing Sterilisation: Australia's Response Against a Canadian Backdrop' (1998) 19 *International Journal of Refugee Law* 77.
Dauvergne, Catherine and Jenni Millbank, 'Before the High Court: Applicants S396/2002 and S395/2002, A Gay Refugee Couple from Bangladesh' (2003) 25 *Sydney Law Review* 97.
Davy, Ulrike, 'Refugees from Bosnia and Herzegovina: Are They Genuine?' (1995) 18 *Suffolk Transnational Law Review* 53.
de Wet, Erika, 'Recent Developments Concerning the Draft Optional Protocol to the International Covenant on Economic, Social and Cultural Rights' (1997) 13(4) *South African Journal on Human Rights* 514.
Diller, Janelle M., *In Search of Asylum: Vietnamese Boat People in Hong Kong* (Washington: Indochina Resource Center, 1988).
Drzemczewski, Andrew, 'The Sui Generis Nature of the European Convention on Human Rights' (1980) 29 *International and Comparative Law Quarterly* 60.
Dummett, Michael, *On Immigration and Refugees* (London: Routledge, 2001).
Einfeld, His Honour Justice Marcus, 'Is There a Role for Compassion in Refugee Policy?' (2000) 23(3) *University of New South Wales Law Journal* 303.

El Hassan Bin Talal, HRH Crown Prince, 'Refugee Law: Protection for the Minority' (1993) 6 *Journal of Refugee Studies* 1.
Evatt, Elizabeth 'The Impact of International Human Rights on Domestic Law', in Grant Huscroft and Paul Rishworth (eds.), *Litigating Rights: Perspectives from Domestic and International Law* (Oxford: Hart Publishing, 2002).
Farer, Tom, 'How the International System Copes with Involuntary Migration: Norms, Institutions and State Practice' (1995) 17 *Human Rights Quarterly* 72.
Feller, Erika, 'Address to the Conference of the International Association of Refugee Law Judges' (2000–2001) 15 *Georgetown Immigration Law Journal* 381.
  'The Evolution of the International Refugee Protection Regime' (2001a) 5 *Washington University Journal of Law and Policy* 129.
Findley, Sally E., 'Compelled to Move: the Rise of Forced Migration in Sub-Saharan Africa', in M. A. B. Siddique (ed.), *International Migration into the 21st Century* (Cheltenham: Edward Elgar, 2001).
Foster, Michelle, 'Causation in Context: Interpreting the Nexus Clause in the Refugee Convention' (2002) 23(2) *Michigan Journal of International Law* 265.
French, Duncan, 'Treaty Interpretation and the Incorporation of Extraneous Legal Rules' (2006) 55 *International and Comparative Law Quarterly* 281.
Frostell, Katarina and Martin Scheinin, 'Women', in Asbjorn Eide, Catarina Krause, Allan Rosas and Martin Scheinin (eds.), *Economic, Social and Cultural Rights: A Textbook*, second edition (Dordrecht: M. Nijhoff Publishers, 2001).
Fullerton, Maryellen, 'A Comparative Look at Refugee Status Based on Persecution Due to Membership in a Particular Social Group' (1993) 26 *Cornell International Law Journal* 505.
Germanin, Regine, *AILA's Asylum Primer: A Practical Guide to US Asylum Law and Procedure*, second edition (Washington, DC: American Immigration Lawyers Association, 2005).
Ghosh, Bimal, *Huddled Masses and Uncertain Shores: Insights into Irregular Migration* (The Hague: Martinus Nijhoff Publishers, 1998).
Gilad, Lisa, 'The Problem of Gender-Related Persecution: A Challenge of International Protection', in Doreen Indra (ed.), *Engendering Forced Migration: Theory and Practice* (New York: Berghahn Books, 1999).
Goldberg, Pamela, 'Anyplace but Home: Asylum in the United States for Women Fleeing Intimate Violence' (1993) 26 *Cornell International Law Journal* 565.
  'Where in the World Is There Safety for Me: Women Fleeing Gender-Based Persecution', in Julie Peters and Andrea Wolper (eds.), *Women's Rights, Human Rights: International Feminist Perspectives* (New York: Routledge, 1995).
Goodman, Ryan, 'The Incorporation of International Human Rights Standards into Sexual Orientation Asylum Claims: Cases of Involuntary "Medical" Intervention' (1995) 105(1) *Yale Law Journal* 255.
Goodwin-Gill, Guy, *The Refugee in International Law* (Oxford: Clarendon Press, 1996).

Goodwin-Gill, Guy, 'Judicial Reasoning and "Social Group" after *Islam* and *Shah*' (1999) 11 *International Journal of Refugee Law* 537.

'Refugees and Responsibility in the Twenty-First Century: More Lessons learned from the South Pacific' (2003) 12 *Pacific Rim Law and Policy Journal* 23.

Grahl-Madsen, Atle, *The Status of Refugees in International Law* (Leyden: A. W. Sijthoff, 1966).

Greatbatch, Jacqueline, 'The Gender Difference: Feminist Critiques of Refugee Discourse' (1989) 1 *International Journal of Refugee Law* 518.

Haines, Rodger P. G., James C. Hathaway and Michelle Foster, 'Claims to Refugee Status Based on Voluntary but Protected Actions' (2003) 15(3) *International Journal of Refugee Law* 430.

Harding, Jeremy, *The Uninvited: Refugees at the Rich Man's Gate* (London: Profile Books, 2000).

Harris, David, 'The ICCPR and the UK: An Introduction', in David Harris and Sarah Joseph (eds.), *The International Covenant on Civil and Political Rights and United Kingdom Law* (Oxford: Clarendon Press, 1995).

Hart, H. L. A., 'Positivism and the Separation of Law and Morals' (1958) 71(4) *Harvard Law Review* 593.

Hart, H. L. A. and A. M. Honore, *Causation in the Law* (Oxford: Clarendon Press, 1959).

Harvey, C. J., 'Review Essay: Gender, Refugee Law and the Politics of Interpretation' (2001) 12(4) *International Journal of Refugee Law* 680.

Hathaway, James C., 'A Reconsideration of the Underlying Premise of Refugee Law' (1990) 31 *Harvard International Law Journal* 129.

  The Law of Refugee Status (Toronto: Butterworths, 1991).

  'The Causal Nexus in International Refugee Law' (2002) 23 *Michigan Journal of International Law* 207.

  The Rights of Refugees under International Law (Cambridge: Cambridge University Press, 2005).

Hathaway, James C. and Michelle Foster, 'Internal Protection/Relocation/Flight Alternative as an Aspect of Refugee Status Determination', in Erika Feller, Volker Türk and Frances Nicholson (eds.), *Refugee Protection in International Law: UNHCR's Global Consultations on International Protection* (Cambridge: Cambridge University Press, 2003a).

  'The Causal Connection ("Nexus") to a Convention Ground' (2003b) 15 *International Journal of Refugee Law* 461.

  'Membership of a Particular Social Group' (2003) 15(3) *International Journal of Refugee Law* 477.

Haysom, Nicholas, 'Constitutionalism, Majoritarian Democracy and Socio-Economic Rights' (1992) 8 *South African Journal on Human Rights* 451.

Helfer, Laurence R. and Anne-Marie Slaughter, 'Toward a Theory of Effective Supranational Adjudication' (1997) 107 *Yale Law Journal* 273.

Helton, Arthur C. and Eliana Jones, 'What is Forced Migration?' (1999) 13 *Georgetown Immigration Law Journal* 521.
Heringa, Aalt Willem, 'The Consensus Principle – the Role of "Common law" in the ECHR Case Law' (1996) 3 *Maastricht Journal of European and Comparative Law* 108.
Higgins, Rosalyn, 'The United Nations: Still a Force for Peace' (1989) 52 *The Modern Law Review* 1.
  'Ten Years on the UN Human Rights Committee: Some Thoughts upon Parting' (1996) *European Human Rights Law Review* 572.
Highet, Keith, George Kahale III and Thomas David Jones, 'Decision: Sale v. Haitian Centers Council, Inc, 113 S Ct 2549' (1994) 88 *American Journal of International Law* 114.
Huber, Bertold, 'The Application of Human Rights Standards by German Courts to Asylum-Seekers, Refugees and Migrants' (2001) 3 *European Journal of Migration and the Law* 171.
Hunt, Paul, *Reclaiming Social Rights: International and Comparative Perspectives* (Aldershot: Dartmouth, 1996).
Hunt, Paul, and Judith Mesquita 'Mental Disabilities and the human right to the highest attainable standard of health' (2006) 28 *Human Rights Quarterly* 332.
IARLJ, *The Realities of Refugee Determination on the Eve of a New Millennium: The Role of the Judiciary* (Haarlem, The Netherlands: International Association of Refugee Law Judges, 1999).
Inter-Conference Working Parties: Human Rights Nexus Working Party, *Human Rights Conference Report* (IARLJ Annual Conference, Ottawa, 12–17 October 1998) (on file with author).
Jackson, Ivor, 'The 1951 Convention relating to the Status of Refugees: A Universal Basis for Protection' (1991) 3 *International Journal of Refugee Law* 403.
Jacobs, Francis G. and Robin C. A. White, *The European Convention on Human Rights*, second edition (Oxford: Clarendon Press, 1996).
Jamail, Milton H. and Chandler Stolp, 'Central Americans on the Run: Political Refugees or Economic Migrants?' (1985) 31(3) *Public Affairs Comment* 1.
Jasudowicz, Taduesz, 'The Legal Character of Social Rights from the Perspective of International Law as a Whole', in Krzysztof Drzewicki et al. (eds.), *Social Rights as Human Rights: A European Challenge* (Åbo: Institute for Human Rights, Åbo Akademi University, 1994).
Jayawickrama, Nihal, *The Judicial Application of Human Rights Law* (Cambridge: Cambridge University Press, 1998).
Jennings, Sir Robert and Sir Arthur Watts (eds.), *Oppenheim's International Law*, vol. I, ninth edition (Boston: Addison-Wesley, 1997).
Jhabvala, Farroukh, 'On Human Rights and the Socio-Economic Context', in Frederick E. Snyder and Surakiart Sathirathai (eds.), *Third World Attitudes Toward International Law* (Dordrecht: Martinus Nijhoff, 1987).

Joseph, Sarah Jenny Schultz and Melissa Castan, *The International Covenant on Civil and Political Rights: Cases, Materials, and Commentary* (Oxford: Oxford University Press, 2000).
Kanter, Arlene and Kristin Dadey, 'The Right to Asylum for People with Disabilities' (2000) 73 *Temple Law Review* 1117.
Keely, Charles B., 'Demography and International Migration', in Caroline B. Brettell and James F. Hollifield (eds.), *Migration Theory: Talking across Disciplines* (New York: Routledge, 2000).
Klabbers, Jan, 'Some Problems regarding the Object and Purpose of Treaties' (1997) 8 *The Finnish Yearbook of International Law* 138.
Knight, Stephen, 'Reflections on Khawar: Recognizing the Refugee from Family Violence' (2003) 14 *Hastings Women's Law Journal* 27.
Koji, Teraya, 'Emerging Hierarchy in International Human Rights and Beyond: From the Perspective of Non-Derogable Rights' (2001) 12 *European Journal of International Law* 917.
Kushner, Tony and Katharine Knox, 'The Kurds: A Moment of Humanity in an Era of Restriction?', in Tony Kushner and Katharine Knox, *Refugees in an Age of Genocide: Global, National and Local Perspectives during the Twentieth Century* (London: Frank Cass, 1999).
Lambert, Helene, 'The Conceptualisation of "Persecution" by the House of Lords: *Horvath v. Secretary of State for the Home Department*' (2001) 13 *International Journal of Refugee Law* 19.
Lawson, R. A. and H. G. Schermers (eds.), *Leading Cases of the European Court of Human Rights*, second edition (Nijmegen: Ars Aequi Libri, 1999).
Leckie, Scott, 'Another Step Towards Indivisibility: Identifying the Key Features of Violations of Economic, Social and Cultural Rights' (1998) 20 *Human Rights Quarterly* 81.
Legomsky, Stephen H., *Immigration and Refugee Law and Policy*, third edition (New York: Foundation Press, 2002).
'Limburg Principles on the Implementation of the International Covenant on Economic, Social and Cultural Rights' (1987) 9 *Human Rights Quarterly* 122.
Macklin, Audrey, 'Refugee Women and the Imperative of Categories' (1995) 17 *Human Rights Quarterly* 213.
Malone, Wex S., 'Ruminations on Cause-in-Fact' (1956) 9 *Stanford Law Review* 60.
Marceau, Gabrielle, 'A Call for Coherence in International Law' (1999) 33(5) *Journal of World Trade* 87.
  'WTO Dispute Settlement and Human Rights' (2002) 13 *European Journal of International Law* 753.
Marcus, David, 'Famine Crimes in International Law' (2003) 97 *American Journal of International Law* 245.
Martin, David, 'Review of the Law of Refugee Status' (1993) 87 *American Journal of International Law* 348.

Martin, Susan F., *New Issues in Refugee Research: Global Migration Trends and Asylum* (2001) UNHCR working paper no. 41.
Mathew, Penelope, 'Current Development: Australian Refugee Protection in the Wake of the Tampa' (2002) 96 *American Journal of International Law* 661.
Mathew, Penelope, James C. Hathaway and Michelle Foster, 'The Role of State Protection in Refugee Analysis' (2003) 15 *International Journal of Refugee Law* 444.
McAdam, Jane, 'Complementary Protection and Beyond: How States Deal with Human Rights Protection', *UNHCR New Issues in Refugee Research: Working Paper 118* (2005).
  Complementary Protection in International Refugee Law (Oxford: OUP, 2007).
McCorquodale, Robert, 'Secrets and Lies: Economic Globalisation and Women's Human Rights' (1998) 19 *Australian Year Book of International Law* 73.
McGoldrick, Dominic, *The Human Rights Committee: Its Role in the Development of the International Covenant on Civil and Political Rights* (Oxford: Clarendon Press, 1991).
McLachlan, Campbell, 'The Principle of Systemic Integration and Article 31(3)(c) of the Vienna Convention' (2005) 54 *International and Comparative Law Quarterly* 279.
Menjívar, Cecilia, 'History, Economy and Politics: Macro and Micro Level Factors in Recent Salvadorean Migration to the US' (1993) 6 *Journal of Refugee Studies* 350.
Meron, Theodor, 'On a Hierarchy of International Human Rights' (1986) 80 *American Journal of International Law* 1.
Mureinik, Etienne, 'Beyond a Charter of Luxuries: Economic Rights in the Constitution' (1992) 8 *South African Journal on Human Rights* 464.
Musalo, Karen, 'Irreconcilable Differences? Divorcing Refugee Protections from Human Rights Norms' (1994) 15 *Michigan Journal of International Law* 1179.
  'Revisiting Social Group and Nexus in Gender Asylum Claims: A Unifying Rationale for Evolving Jurisprudence' (2003) 52 *DePaul Law Review* 777.
Musalo, Karen and Stephen Knight, 'Gender-Based Asylum: An Analysis of Recent Trends' (2000) 77(42) *Interpreter Releases* 1533.
  'Steps Forward and Steps Back: Uneven Progress in the Law of Social Group and Gender-Based Claims in the United States' (2001) 13 *International Journal of Refugee Law* 51.
Musalo, Karen, Jennifer Moore and Richard Boswell, *Refugee Law and Policy: Cases and Materials* (Durham, NC: Carolina Academic Press, 1997).
Musungu, Sisule Fredrick, 'International Trade and Human Rights in Africa: A Comment on Conceptual Linkages', in Frederick M. Abbott, Christine Breining-Kaufmann and Thomas Cottier (eds.), *International Trade and Human Rights: Foundations and Conceptual Issues* (Ann Arbor: University of Michigan Press, 2006).
Nathwani, Niraj, *Rethinking Refugee Law* (The Hague: Martinus Nijhoff Publishers, 2003).

Neal, David L., 'Women as a Social Group: Recognising Sex-Based Persecution as Grounds for Asylum' (1988) 20 *Columbia Human Rights Law Review* 203.
Nickel, James, 'How Human Rights Generate Duties to Protect and Provide' (1993) 15 *Human Rights Quarterly* 77.
Nkiwane Muzenda, Tandeka, 'The Role of Social and Economic Factors and Natural Disasters in Forced Population Displacements in Africa' (1995) 7 *International Journal of Refugee Law* 46.
Noll, Gregor, *Negotiating Asylum: The EU Acquis, Extraterritorial Protection and the Common Market of Deflection* (The Hague: Martinus Nijhoff Publishers, 2000).
North, Justice A. M. and Nehal Bhuta, 'The Future of Protection – the Role of the Judge' (2001) 15 *Georgetown Immigration Law Journal* 479.
Nowak, Manfred, *Introduction to the International Human Rights Regime* (Leiden: Martinus Nijhoff Publishers, 2003).
Nykanen, Eeva, 'Protecting Children? The European Convention on Human Rights and Child Asylum Seekers' (2001) 3 *European Journal of Migration and the Law* 315.
O'Flaherty, Michael, *Human Rights and the UN: Practice before the Treaty Bodies*, second edition (The Hague: Kluwer Law International, 2002).
Ogata, Sadako, 'Human Rights, Humanitarian Law and Refugee Protection', in Daniel Warner (ed.), *Human Rights and Humanitarian Law: The Quest for Universality* (The Hague: Martinus Nijhoff, 1997).
Oloka-Onyango, Joe, 'Human Rights, The OAU Convention and the Refugee Crisis in Africa: Forty Years after Geneva' (1991) 3 *International Journal of Refugee Law* 452.
Orucu, Esin, 'The Core of Rights and Freedoms: The Limit of Limits', in Tom Campbell, et al. (eds.), *Human Rights: From Rhetoric to Reality* (New York: Blackwell, 1986).
Otto, Diane, 'Defending Women's Economic and Social Rights: Some Thoughts on Indivisibility and a New Standard of Equality', in Isfahan Merali and Valerie Oostervedl (eds.), *Giving Meaning to Economic, Social and Cultural Rights* (Philadelphia: University of Pennsylvania Press, 2001).
Palmeter, David and Petros Mavroidis, 'The WTO Legal System: Sources of Law' (1998) 93(3) *American Journal of International Law* 398.
Parker, Mary Caroline, ' "Other Treaties": The Inter-American Court of Human Rights Defines its Advisory Jurisdiction' (1982) 33 *American University Law Review* 211.
Pauwelyn, Joost, 'The Role of Public International Law in the WTO: How Far Can We Go?' (2001) 95 *American Journal of International Law* 535.
Pellonpaa, Matti, 'ECHR Case-law on Refugees and Asylum-Seekers and Protection under the 1951 Refugee Convention: Similarities and Differences', in *The Changing Nature of Persecution: IARLJ 4th Conference* (Bern, Switzerland: Institute of Public Law, University of Berne, 2001).
'Political Legitimacy in the Law of Political Asylum' (1985) 99 *Harvard Law Review* 450.

Rajagopal, Balakrishnan, *International Law From Below* (Cambridge: Cambridge University Press, 2003).
Ramcharan, Bertrand G., *Judicial Protection of Economic, Social and Cultural Rights: Cases and Materials* (Leiden: Martinus Nijhoff Publishers, 2005).
Ress, George, 'The Interpretation of the Charter', in Bruno Simma et al. (eds.), *The Charter of the United Nations: A Commentary*, second edition (Oxford: Oxford University Press, 2002).
Richmond, Anthony H., 'Reactive Migration: Sociological Perspectives on Refugee Movements' (1993) 6 *Journal of Refugee Studies* 7.
  Global Apartheid: Refugees, Racism, and the New World Order (Toronto: Oxford University Press, 1994).
Robinson, Kim, 'False Hope or a Realizable Right? The Implementation of the Right to Shelter Under the African National Congress' Proposed Bill of Rights for South Africa' (1993) 28 *Harvard Civil Rights-Civil Liberties Law Review* 505.
Röhl, Katharina, 'Fleeing violence and poverty: non-refoulement obligations under the European Convention of Human Rights' (UNHCR, New Issues in Refugee Research, Working Paper No. 111, January 2005).
Rosenne, Shabtai, *Developments in the Law of Treaties, 1945–1986* (Cambridge: Cambridge University Press, 1989).
Roth, Kenneth, 'Defending Economic, Social and Cultural Rights: Practical Issues Faced by an International Human Rights Organization' (2004) 24 *Human Rights Quarterly* 63.
Russell, Simon, 'Unaccompanied Refugee Children in the United Kingdom' (1999) 11(1) *International Journal of Refugee Law* 126.
Sands, Philippe, 'Treaty, Custom and the Cross-Fertilization of International Law' (1998) 1 *Yale Human Rights and Development Law Journal* 85.
Scheinin, Martin, 'Economic and Social Rights as Legal Rights', in Asbjørn Eide, Catarina Krause and Allan Rosas (eds.), *Economic, Social and Cultural Rights, A Textbook* (The Hague: Kluwer Law International, 2001).
Schmeidl, Susanne, 'Conflict and Forced Migration: A Quantitative Review, 1964–1995', in Aristide R. Zolberg and Peter M. Benda (eds.), *Global Migrants, Global Refugees: Problems and Solutions* (New York: Berghahn Books, 2001).
Scott, Craig, 'The Interdependence and Permeability of Human Rights Norms: Towards a Partial Fusion of the International Covenants on Human Rights' (1989) 27(4) *Osgoode Hall Law Journal* 769.
  'Canada's International Human Rights Obligations and Disadvantaged Members of Society: Finally into the Spotlight?' (1999a) 10(4) *Constitutional Forum* 97.
  'Reaching Beyond (Without Abandoning) the Category of Economic, Social and Cultural Rights' (1999b) 21 *Human Rights Quarterly* 634.
Scott, Craig and Philip Alston, 'Adjudicating Constitutional Priorities in a Transnational Context: A Comment on Soobramoney's Legacy and Grootboom's Promise' (2000) 16 *South African Journal of Human Rights* 206.

Scott, Craig and Patrick Macklem, 'Constitutional Ropes of Sand or Justiciable Guarantees? Social Rights in a New South African Constitution' (1992) 141 *University of Pennsylvania Law Review* 1.
Seiderman, Ian D., *Hierarchy in International Law: The Human Rights Dimension* (Antwerp: Intersentia, 2001).
Sen, Amartya, *Development as Freedom* (New York: Knopf, 1999).
Sepulveda, Magdalena, *The Nature of the Obligations under the International Covenant on Economic, Social and Cultural Rights* (New York: Intersentia, 2003).
Shue, Henry, *Basic Rights: Subsistence, Affluence, and US Foreign Policy* (Princeton: Princeton University Press, 1980).
Simma, Bruno, 'Consent: Strains in the Treaty System', in R. St. J. MacDonald and Douglas M. Johnston (eds.), *The Structure and Process of International Law: Essays in Legal Philosophy, Doctrine and Theory* (The Hague: Martinus Nijhoff Publishers, 1983).
  'International Human Rights and General International Law: A Comparative Analysis' in *Collected Courses of the Academy of European Law*, vol. IV, book II (Oxford: Oxford University Press, 1993).
Sinclair, Sir Ian, *The Vienna Convention on the Law of Treaties*, second edition (Manchester: Manchester University Press, 1984).
Sitaropoulos, Nicholas, *Judicial Interpretation of Refugee Status: In Search of a Principled Methodology Based on a Critical Comparative Analysis, with Special Reference to Contemporary British, French, and German Jurisprudence* (Athens: Sakkoulas, 1999).
Sloth-Nielsen, Julia, 'Ratification of the United Nations Convention on the Rights of the Child: Some Implications for South African Law' (1995) 11 *South African Journal on Human Rights* 401.
Smith, Charles David, 'Women Migrants of Kagera Region, Tanzania: The Need for Empowerment', in Doreen Indra (ed.), *Engendering Forced Migration: Theory and Practice* (New York: Berghahn Books, 1999).
Spijkerboer, Thomas, *Gender and Refugee Studies* (Aldershot: Ashgate, 2000).
Steendijk, Lisbeth, 'The Application of Human Rights Standards to Asylum Cases: The Dutch Example' (2001) 3 *European Journal of Migration and the Law* 185.
Steinbock, Daniel, 'Interpreting the Refugee Definition' (1998) 45 *UCLA Law Review* 733.
Steiner, Henry J. and Philip Alston, *International Human Rights in Context: Law, Politics, Morals: Text and Materials* (Oxford: Clarendon Press, 1996).
  International Human Rights in Context, second edition (Oxford: Oxford University Press, 2000).
Sternberg, Mark R., *The Grounds of Refugee Protection in the Context of International Human Rights and Humanitarian Law: Canadian and United States Case Law Compared* (The Hague: M Nijhoff Publishers, 2002).
Stevens, Dallal, 'Roma Asylum Applicants in the United Kingdom: "Scroungers" or "Scapegoats" ', in Joanne van Selm et al. (eds.), *The Refugee Convention at Fifty: A View from Forced Migrations Studies* (Maryland: Lexington Books, 2003).

Storey, Hugo, 'The Internal Flight Alternative Test: The Jurisprudence Re-Examined' (1998) 10(3) *International Journal of Refugee Law* 499.
'The Advanced Refugee Law Workshop Experience: An IARLJ Perspective' (2003) 15 *International Journal of Refugee Law* 422.
Storey, Hugo and Rebecca Wallace, 'War and Peace in Refugee Law Jurisprudence' (2001) 95 *American Journal of International Law* 349.
Symes, Mark, *Caselaw on the Refugee Convention: The United Kingdom's Interpretation in the Light of the International Authorities* (London: Refugee Legal Centre, 2000).
Symes, Mark and Peter Jorro, *Asylum Law and Practice* (London: LexisNexis UK, 2003).
Sztucki, 'The Conclusions on the International Protection of Refugees Adopted by the Executive Committee of the UNHCR Programme' (1989) 1(3) *International Journal of Refugee Law* 285.
'The Maastricht Guidelines on Violations of Economic, Social, & Cultural Rights' (1998) 20 *Human Rights Quarterly* 691.
Tistounet, Eric, 'The Problem of Overlapping among Different Treaty Bodies', in Philip Alston and James Crawford (eds.), *The Future of UN Human Rights Treaty Monitoring* (Cambridge: Cambridge University Press, 2000).
Tomuschat, Christian, *Human Rights: Beyond Idealism and Realism* (Oxford: Oxford University Press, 2003).
Tuitt, Patricia, *False Images: Law's Construction of the Refugee* (London: Pluto Press, 1996).
UN Centre for Human Rights, *Right to Adequate Food as a Human Right* (Geneva: UN Centre for Human Rights, 1989).
US Committee for Refugees, *World Refugee Survey 2002* (Washington DC, 2002).
van Dijk, Pieter, G. J. H. van Hoof and A. W. Heringa, *Theory and Practice of the European Convention on Human Rights* (The Hague: Kluwer Law International, 1998).
van Hoof, G. J. H., 'The Legal Nature of Economic, Social and Cultural Rights: A Rebuttal of Some Traditional Views', in Philip Alston and Katarina Tomasevski (eds.), *The Right to Food* (Utrecht: Stichting Studie-en Informatiecentrum Mensenrechten, 1984).
Vandenhole, Wouter, *The Procedures before the UN Human Rights Treaty Bodies: Divergence or Convergence?* (Antwerp: Intersentia, 2004).
Vanheule, Dirk, 'A Comparison of the Judicial Interpretations of the Notion of Refugee', in Jean-Yves Carlier and Dirk Vanheule (eds.), *Europe and Refugees: A Challenge?* (The Hague: Kluwer Law International, 1997).
Vierdag, E. W., 'The Legal Nature of the Rights Granted by the International Covenant on Economic, Social and Cultural Rights' (1978) 9 *Netherlands Yearbook of International Law* 69.
Villiers, Janice D., 'Closed Borders, Closed Ports: The Flight of Haitians Seeking Political Asylum in the United States' (1994) 60 *Brooklyn Law Review* 841.

Vincent, R. J., 'Political and Economic Refugees: Problems of Migration, Asylum and Resettlement' (1989) 2 *Journal of Refugee Studies* 504.
Waldman, Lorne, *The Definition of Convention Refugee* (Markham: Butterworths, 2001).
Walker, Kristen L., 'Sexuality and Refugee Status in Australia' (2000) 12(2) *International Journal of Refugee Law* 175.
Watts, Sir Arthur, *The International Law Commission, 1949—1998*, 2 vols. (Oxford: Oxford University Press, 1999).
Weiner, Myron, 'The Clash of Norms: Dilemmas in Refugee Policies' (1998) 11 *Journal of Refugee Studies* 433.
Weston, Burns H., Richard A. Falk and Hilary Charlesworth, *International Law and World Order: A Problem-Oriented Coursebook* (St Paul, MN: West Group, 1997).
Wichert, Tim, 'Human Rights, Refugees and Displaced Persons: the 1997 UN Commission on Human Rights' (1997) 9 *International Journal of Refugee Law* 500.
Wilsher, Daniel, 'Non-State Actors and the Definition of a Refugee in the United Kingdom: Protection, Accountability or Culpability' (2003) 15 *International Journal of Refugee Law* 68.
Yong-Joong Lee, Eric, 'National and International Legal Concerns regarding Recent North Korean Escapees' (2001) 13 *International Journal of Refugee Law* 142.
Zolberg, Aristide R., Astri Suhrke and Sergio Aguayo, *Escape from Violence: Conflict and the Refugee Crisis in the Developing World* (New York: Oxford University Press, 1989).

Conference papers and speeches

Brown, Widney, 'A Human Rights Approach to the Rehabilitation and Reintegration into Society of Trafficked Victims' (speech delivered at the 21st Century Slavery – The Human Rights Dimension to Trafficking in Human Beings Conference, Rome, 15—16 May 2002) (on file with author).
Coker, Jane, Heaven Crawley and Alison Stanley, 'A Gender Perspective on the Human Rights Paradigm' (paper presented at the IARLJ Human Rights Nexus Working Party, London, 12 May 1998), p. 3 (on file with author).
DIMIA, Refugee and Humanitarian Division, 'Gender-Related Persecution (Article 1A(2)) – An Australian Perspective' (paper prepared as a contribution to the UNHCR's expert roundtable series, 2001) (on file with author).
Feller, Erika, 'Challenges to the 1951 Convention in its 50th Anniversary Year' (speech delivered at the Seminar on International Protection within One Single Asylum Procedure, Norrkoping, Sweden, 23—24 April 2001b) (on file with author).
Human Rights Watch, International Catholic Migration Committee and the World Council of Churches, *NGO Background Paper on the Refugee and Migration*

Interface (paper presented to the UNHCR Global Consultations on International Protection, Geneva, 28–29 June 2001a) (on file with author).

IARLJ, *The Application of Human Rights Standards to the 1951 Refugee Convention – the Definition of Persecution* (paper prepared by the Human Rights Nexus Working Party, 24 April 2001) (on file with author).

Penz, Peter, 'Economic Refugees and Political Migrants: An Ethical Analysis of "Forced Migration" ' (paper presented at the 7th International Conference of the International Research and Advisory Panel ('IRAP') of the International Association for the Study of Forced Migration, South Africa, 2001) (on file with author).

Simeon, James C., *Background Paper: The Human Rights Paradigm and the 1951 Refugee Convention* (London: Human Rights Nexus Working Party, 1998) (on file with author).

EU documents

Council of the European Union, *Joint Position of 4 March 1996 Defined by the Council on the Basis of Article K.3 of the Treaty on European Union on the Harmonized Application of the Definition of the Term 'Refugee' in Article 1 of the Geneva Convention of 28 July 1951 relating to the Status of Refugees*, 96/196/JHA, 13 March 1996.

Council of the European Union, *Directive on Minimum Standards for the Qualification and Status of Third Country Nationals and Stateless Persons as Refugees or as Persons who Otherwise Need International Protection and the Content of the Protection Granted*, 29 April 2004, 2004/83/EC.

UN documents

CEDAW Committee, *Consideration of Reports Submitted by States Parties under Article 18 of the Convention on the Elimination of All Forms of Discrimination Against Women: Combined Fourth and Fifth Reports of States Parties (Romania)*, UN Doc. CEDAW/C/ROM/4–5 (1999a).

CEDAW Committee, *General Recommendation 13: Equal Remuneration for Work of Equal Value*, UN Doc. A/44/38 (1990a).

CEDAW Committee, *General Recommendation 15: Avoidance of Discrimination against Women in National Strategies for the Prevention and Control of Acquired Immunodeficiency Syndrome (AIDS)*, UN Doc. A/45/38 (1990b).

CEDAW Committee, *General Recommendation 16: Unpaid Workers in Rural and Urban Family Enterprises*, UN Doc. A/46/38 (1993a).

CEDAW Committee, *General Recommendation 17: Measurement and Quantification of the Unremunerated Domestic Activities of Women and Their Recognition in the Gross National Product*, UN Doc. A/46/38 (1993b).

CEDAW Committee, *General Recommendation 18: Disabled Women*, UN Doc. A/46/38 (1993c).

CEDAW Committee, *General Recommendation 21, Equality in marriage and family relations*, UN Doc. HRI/GEN/1/Rev.4 (2000).

CEDAW Committee, *General Recommendation 24: Women and Health* UN Doc. A/54/38 (1999b).

Commission on Human Rights, *Question of the Realization in All Countries of the Economic, Social and Cultural Rights Contained in the Universal Declaration of Human Rights and in the International Covenant on Economic, Social and Cultural Rights, and Study of Special Problems which the Developing Countries Face in their Efforts to Achieve these Human Rights*, UN Doc. E/CN.4/RES/1998/33 (1998).

Commission on Human Rights, *Question of the Realization in All Countries of the Economic, Social and Cultural Rights Contained in the Universal Declaration of Human Rights and in the International Covenant on Economic, Social and Cultural Rights, and Study of Special Problems which the Developing Countries Face in their Efforts to Achieve these Human Rights*, UN Doc. E/CN.4/RES/2000/9 (2000a).

Commission on Human Rights, *Report of the Expert Seminar on Human Rights and Extreme Poverty, 7–10 February 2001*, UN Doc. E/CN.4/2001/54/Add.1 (2001).

Commission on Human Rights, *Report of the Special Rapporteur on Adequate Housing as a Component of the Right to an Adequate Standard of Living*, UN Doc. E/CN.4/2005/48 (2005a).

Commission on Human Rights, *Report of the Special Rapporteur on the Right of Everyone to the Enjoyment of the Highest Attainable Standard of Physical and Mental Health*, UN Doc. E/CN.4/2005/51 (2005b).

Commission on Human Rights, *Report Submitted by the Special Rapporteur on the Right to Education*, UN Doc. E/CN.4/2005/50 (2004a).

Commission on Human Rights, *The Right of Everyone to the Enjoyment of the Highest Attainable Standard of Physical and Mental Health*, UN Doc. E/CN.4/RES/2002/31 (2002).

Commission on Human Rights, *The Right to Education: Report Submitted by the Special Rapporteur on the Right to Education*, UN Doc. E/CN.4/2005/50 (2004b).

Commission on Human Rights, *The Right to Food*, UN Doc. E/CN.4/RES/2000/10 (2000b).

Commission on Human Rights, *The Right to Food: Note by the Secretary-General*, GA Res. A/60/350, UN GAOR, 60th sess, Agenda Item 73(b), UN Doc. A/60/350 (2005).

Committee on Economic, Social and Cultural Rights, *General Comment 3: The Nature of States Parties Obligations (Art. 2, para. 1 of the Covenant)*, UN Doc. E/1991/23 (1990).

Committee on Economic, Social and Cultural Rights, *General Comment 4: The Right to Adequate Housing (Art. 11(1) of the Covenant)*, UN Doc. E/1992/23 (1991).

Committee on Economic, Social and Cultural Rights ('CESCR'), *General Comment 5: Persons with Disabilities*, UN Doc. E/1995/22 (1994).

Committee on Economic, Social and Cultural Rights, *General Comment 7: The Right to Adequate Housing (Art. 11.1): Forced Evictions*, UN Doc. E/1998/22 (1997).
Committee on Economic, Social and Cultural Rights, *General Comment 13: The Right to Education (Art. 13)*, UN Doc. E/C.12/1999/10 (1999).
Committee on Economic, Social and Cultural Rights, *General Comment 14: The Right to the Highest Attainable Standard of Health*, UN Doc. E/C.12/2000/4 (2000).
Committee on Economic, Social and Cultural Rights, *General Comment 15: The Right to Water*, UN Doc. E/C.12/2002/11 (2003).
Committee on Economic, Social and Cultural Rights, *General Comment 16: The Equal Right of Men and Women to the Enjoyment of All Economic, Social and Cultural Rights*, UN Doc. E/C.12/2005/4 (2005a).
Committee on Economic, Social and Cultural Rights, *General Comment 18: The Right to Work*, UN Doc. E/C.12/GC/18 (2005b).
Committee on the Elimination of Racial Discrimination, *General Recommendation 27: Discrimination Against Roma*, UN Doc. A/55/18 (2000).
Committee on the Rights of the Child, *General Commment No. 3: HIV/Aids and the Rights of the Children*, UN Doc. CRC/GC/2003/3, 17 March 2003.
General Comment 5: General Measures of Implementation for the Convention on the Rights of the Child, UN Doc. CRC/GC/2003/5 (2003).
Comprehensive and Integral International Convention to Promote and Protect the Rights and Identity of Persons with Disabilities, GA Res. 56/168, UN GAOR, 3rd Comm, 56th sess, 88th mtg, Agenda Item 119(b), UN Doc. A/RES/56/168 (2001).
Danilo Turk, *The New International Economic Order and the Promotion of Human Rights: Realization of Economic, Social and Cultural Rights (Preliminary Report)*, UN Doc. E/CN.4/Sub.2/1989/19 (1989).
Danilo Turk, *The Realization of Economic, Social and Cultural Rights*, UN Doc. E/CN.4/Sub. 2/1992/16 (1992).
Draft International Covenants on Human Rights: Annotation – Report of the Secretary-General to the Tenth Session of the General Assembly, UN Doc. A/2929 (1955).
Economic and Social Council, *Review of the Composition, Organization and Administrative Arrangements of the Sessional Working Group of Governmental Experts on the Implementation of the International Covenant on Economic, Social and Cultural Rights*, ESC Res. 17, UN ESCOR, 22nd mtg, UN Doc. E/RES/1985/17 (1985).
Human Rights Committee, *General Comment No. 1: Reporting by States Parties*, UN Doc. E/1989/22 (1989).
Human Rights Committee, *General Comment No. 3: Implementation at the National Level (Art. 2)*, UN Doc. HRI\GEN\1\Rev.1 at 4 (1981).
Human Rights Committee, *General Comment No. 06: The Right to Life (Art. 6)*, UN Doc. HRI\GEN\1\Rev.1 (1982).
Human Rights Committee, *General Comment No. 7: Prohibition of Torture and Cruel Punishment*, UN Doc. HRI\GEN\1\Rev.1 at 7 (1994a).

Human Rights Committee, *General Comment No. 9: Humane Treatment of Persons Deprived of Liberty*, UN Doc. HRI\GEN\1\Rev.1 at 9 (1994b).
Human Rights Committee, *General Comment No. 10: Freedom of Expression (Art. 19)*, UN Doc. HRI\GEN\1\Rev.1 at 11 (1994c).
Human Rights Committee, *General Comment No. 13: Equality Before the Courts and the Right to a Fair and Public Hearing by an Independent Court Established by Law (Art. 14)*, UN Doc. HRI\GEN\1\Rev.1 at 14 (1984).
Human Rights Committee, *General Comment No. 16: The Right to Respect of Privacy, Family, Home and Correspondence, and Protection of Honour and Reputation (Art. 17)*, UN Doc. HRI\GEN\1\Rev.1 at 21 (1994d).
Human Rights Committee, *General Comment No. 17: Rights of the Child (Art. 24)*, UN Doc. HRI\GEN\1\Rev.1 at 23 (1989a).
Human Rights Committee, *General Comment No. 18: Non-discrimination*, UN Doc. HRI\GEN\1\Rev.1 at 26 (1989b).
Human Rights Committee, *General Comment No. 20: Replaces General Comment 7 concerning Prohibition of Torture and Cruel Treatment or Punishment (Art. 7)*, UN Doc. HRI\GEN\1\Rev.1 at 30 (1992).
Human Rights Committee, *General Comment No. 22: The Right to Freedom of Thought, Conscience and Religion (Art. 18)*, UN Doc. CCPR/C/21/Rev.1/Add. 4 (1993).
Human Rights Committee, *General Comment No. 24: Issues Relating to Reservations Made upon Ratification or Accession to the Covenant or the Optional Protocols thereto, or in Relation to Declarations under Article 41 of the Covenant*, UN Doc. CCPR/C/21/Rev.1/Add.6 (1994e).
Human Rights Committee, *General Comment No. 25: The Right to Participate in Public Affairs, Voting Rights and the Right of Equal Access to Public Service (Art. 25)* UN Doc. CCPR/C/21/Rev.1/Add.7 (1996).
Human Rights Committee, *General Comment No. 27: Freedom of Movement (Art. 12)*, UN Doc. CCPR/C/21 Rev. 1/Add.9 (1999).
Human Rights Committee, *General Comment No. 28: Equality of Rights between Men and Women (Art. 3)*, UN Doc. CCPR/C/21/Rev.1/Add.10 (2000).
Human Rights Committee, *General Comment No. 29: States of Emergency (Art. 4)*, UN Doc. CCPR/C/21/Rev.1/Add.11 (2001).
Human Rights Committee, *General Comment No. 31: The Nature of the General Legal Obligation Imposed on States Parties to the Covenant*, UN Doc. CCPR/C/21/Rev.1/Add.13 (2004).
Human Rights Committee, *Concluding Observations of the UN Human Rights Committee In Respect of India*, UN Doc. CCPR/C/79/Add.81 (1997).
ILC, *Fragmentation of International Law: Difficulties Arising From the Diversification and Expansion of International Law*, UN Doc. A/CN.4/537 (2000).
ILC, *Report of the International Law Commission: Fifty-Fifth Session*, UN Doc. A/CN.4/537 (2004).
ILC, *Report of the International Law Commission: Fifty-Seventh Session*, UN Doc. A/60/10 (2005).

ILC, *Report of the Study Group on Fragmentation of International Law: Difficulties Arising From the Diversification and Expansion of International Law*, UN Doc. A/CN.4/L.644 (2003).

ILC, *Fragmentation of International Law: Difficulties Arising from the Diversification and Expansion of International Law*, Report of the Study Group of the International Law Commission by Martti Koskenniemi, UN Doc. A/CN.4/L.682, 4 April 2006.

ILO, *Declaration on Fundamental Principles and Rights at Work* (1998) <http://www.ilo.org/dyn/declaris/DECLARATIONWEB.static_jump?var_language=EN&var_pagename=DECLARATIONTEXT>.

Office of the UN High Commissioner for Refugees, *Introductory Note to the Convention and Protocol Relating to the Status of Refugees* (1996) <http://www.unhcr.org/cgi-bin/texis/vtx/protect/opendoc.pdf?tbl=PROTECTION&id=3b66c2aa10>.

Office of the United Nations High Commissioner for Human Rights, *Fact Sheet No. 16 (Rev. 1): The Committee on Economic Social and Cultural Rights* (1991) <http://www.ohchr.org/english/about/publications/docs/fs16.htm>.

Office of the United Nations High Commissioner for Human Rights, *Status of Ratifications of the Principal International Human Rights Treaties* (2006) <http://www.ohchr.org/english/countries/ratification/index.htm>.

UNHCR, *Agenda for Protection*, third edition (2003) <http://www.unhcr.org/cgi-bin/texis/vtx/protect/opendoc.pdf?tbl=PROTECTION&id=3e637b194>.

UNHCR, *Composite Flows and the Relationship to Refugee Outflows, Including Return of Persons not in Need of International Protection as Well as Facilitation of Return in its Global Dimension*, UN Doc. EC/48/SC/CRP.29 (1998).

UNHCR, *Discussion Paper: Reconciling Migration Control and Refugee Protection in the European Union: A UNHCR Perspective* (Geneva, 2000) (on file with author).

UNHCR Division of International Protection, 'Gender-Related Persecution: An Analysis of Recent Trends' (1997) 9 *International Journal of Refugee Law* 79.

UNHCR Executive Committee, *Note on International Protection* (1990) <http://www.unhcr.org/cgi-bin/texis/vtx/excom/opendoc.htm?tbl=EXCOM&id=3ae68c6114>.

UNHCR Executive Committee, *General Conclusion on International Protection* (1993a) <http://www.unhcr.org/cgi-bin/texis/vtx/excom/opendoc.htm?tbl=EXCOM&id=3ae68c6814>.

UNHCR Executive Committee, *General Conclusion on International Protection* (1993b) <http://www.unhcr.org/cgi-bin/texis/vtx/excom/opendoc.htm?tbl=EXCOM&id=3ae68c6814>.

UNHCR Executive Committee, *Conclusion on International Protection* (1998) <http://www.unhcr.org/cgi-bin/texis/vtx/excom/opendoc.htm?tbl=EXCOM&id=3ae68c6e30>.

UNHCR Executive Committee, *Conclusion on the Provision of International Protection Including Through Complementary Forms of Protection* (2005), para (c) <http://www.unhcr.org/cgi-bin/texis/vtx/excom/opendoc.htm?tbl=EXCOM&id=43576e292>.

374 BIBLIOGRAPHY

UNHCR, *Executive Committee of the High Commissioner's Programme*, UN Doc. A/AC.96/1020/Rev.1 (2005).

UNHCR, Executive Committee of the High Commissioner's Programme, *Conclusion on the Provision on International Protection Including Through Complementary Forms of Protection* (2005) <http://www.unhcr.org/cgi-bin/texis/vtx/excom/opendoc.htm?tbl=EXCOM&id=43576e292>.

UNHCR Executive Committee, *Conclusion on the Civilian and Humanitarian Character of Asylum* (2002) <http://www.unhcr.org/cgi-bin/texis/vtx/excom/opendoc.htm?tbl=EXCOM&id=3dafdd7c4> at 31 May 2006.

UNHCR, 'General Briefing Note: UNHCR, Human Rights and Refugee Protection', REFWORLD, July 1997.

UNHCR, *Global Consultations on International Protection, Refugee Protection and Migration Control: Perspectives From UNHCR and IOM*, UN Doc. EC/GC/01/11 (2001).

UNHCR, *Guidelines on International Protection: Gender-Related Persecution within the Context of Article 1A(2) of the 1951 Convention and/or its 1967 Protocol relating to the Status of Refugees*, UN Doc. HCR/GIP/02/02 (2002a).

UNHCR, *Handbook on Procedures and Criteria for Determining Refugee Status under the 1951 Convention and the 1967 Protocol Relating to the Status of Refugees* (1992), para. 51 <http://www.unhcr.org/cgi-bin/texis/vtx/home/opendoc.pdf?tbl=PUBL&id=3d58e13b4>.

UNHCR, 'Note on International Protection' (2001) 20(3) *Refugee Survey Quarterly* 34.

UNHCR, *Refugee Children – Global Consultations on International Protection*, UN Doc. EC/GC/02/9 (2002b).

UNHCR, *Report on International Protection*, UN Doc. A/AC.96/527 (1996).

UNHCR, 'The International Protection of Refugees: Interpreting Article 1 of the 1951 Convention Relating to the Status of Refugees' (2001) 20(3) *Refugee Survey Quarterly* 77.

World Conference on Human Rights, *Vienna Declaration and Programme of Action*, UN Doc. A/CONF.157/23 (1993).

Websites (current as at 31 May 2006)

Amnesty International, *Change in the Air for AI* (2001) <http://web.amnesty.org/wire/October2001/ICM>.

Amnesty International, *Amnesty International Report 2004 – Building an International Human Rights Agenda: Upholding the Rights of Refugees and Migrants* (2004) <http://web.amnesty.org/report2004/hragenda-8-eng>.

Amnesty International, *Israel and the Occupied Territories Surviving under Siege: The Impact of Movement Restrictions on the Right to Work* (2003a) <http://web.amnesty.org/library/index/ENGMDE150012003>.

Amnesty International, *Lebanon: Economic and Social Rights of Palestinian Refugees* (2003c) <http://web.amnesty.org/library/index/ENGMDE180172003>.

Amnesty International, *Starved of Rights: Human Rights and the Food Crisis in the Democratic People's Republic of Korea (North Korea)* (2004b) <http://web.amnesty.org/library/index/engasa240032004>.
Anti-Slavery International, *The Migration-Trafficking Nexus: Combating Trafficking Through the Protection of Migrants' Human Rights* (2003) <http://www.antislavery.org/homepage/resources/the%20migration%20 trafficking%20nexus%202003.pdf>.
DIMA, *Guidelines on Gender Issues for Decision-Makers* (1996) <http://www.immi.gov.au>.
European Council on Refugees and Exiles, *Position Paper on the Interpretation of Article 1 of the Refugee Convention* (2000) <http://www.ecre.org/positions/csrinter.shtml>.
Human Rights Watch, *Economic, Social and Cultural Rights* <http://hrw.org/esc/>.
Human Rights Watch, *Famine in Sudan, 1998: The Human Rights Causes* (1999) <http://www.hrw.org/reports/1999/sudan/SUDAWEB2.htm>.
Human Rights Watch, *In the Shadow of Death: HIV/AIDS and Children's Rights in Kenya* (2001b) <http://www.hrw.org/reports/2001/kenya/kenya0701.PDF>.
Human Rights Watch, *The Invisible Exodus: North Koreans in the People's Republic of China* (2002) <http://www.hrw.org/reports/2002/northkorea/norkor1102.pdf>.
Human Rights Watch, *Double Standards: Women's Property Rights Violations in Kenya* (2003) <http://hrw.org/reports/2003/kenya0303/>.
Human Rights Watch, *Not Eligible: The Politicization of Food in Zimbabwe* (2003c) <http://www.hrw.org/reports/2003/zimbabwe1003/zimbabwe1003.pdf>.
Human Rights Watch, *Hated to Death: Homophobia, Violence and Jamaica's HIV/AIDS Epidemic* (2004a) <http://hrw.org/reports/2004/jamaica1104/jamaica1104.pdf>.
Human Rights Watch, *The Politics of Food Assistance in Zimbabwe* (2004b) <http://www.hrw.org/backgrounder/africa/zimbabwe/2004/zimbabwe0804.pdf>.
Human Rights Watch, *Failing Our Children: Barriers to the Right to Education* (2005a) <http://hrw.org/reports/2005/education0905/education0905.pdf>.
Human Rights Watch, *Letting Them Fail: Government Neglect and the Right to Education for Children Affected by AIDS* (2005b) <http://hrw.org/reports/2005/africa1005/africa1005.pdf>.
Human Rights Watch, *Positively Abandoned: Stigma and Discrimination against HIV-Positive Mothers and their Children in Russia* (2005c) <http://hrw.org/reports/2005/russia0605/russia0605.pdf>.
Human Rights Watch, *Rhetoric and Risk: Human Rights Abuses Impeding Ukraine's Fight against HIV/AIDS* (2006) <http://hrw.org/reports/2006/ukraine0306/ukraine0306web.pdf>.
Immigration and Refugee Board (Canada), *Civilian Non-Combatants Fearing Persecution in Civil War Situations: Guidelines Issued by the Chairperson Pursuant to*

Section 65(3) of the Immigration Act (1996a) <http://www.cisr-irb.gc.ca/en/about/guidelines/civil_e.htm>.

Immigration and Review Board (Canada), *Child Refugee Claimants – Procedural and Evidentiary Issues: Guidelines Issued by the Chairperson Pursuant to Section 65(3) of the Immigration Act* (1996b) <http://www.irb-cisr.gc.ca/en/references/policy/guidelines/child_e.htm>.

Quinn, Gerard and Theresia Degener, *Human Rights and Disability: The Current Use and Future Potential of United Nations Human Rights Instruments in the Context of Disability* (2002) <http://www.unhchr.ch/html/menu6/2/disability.doc>.

Sané, Pierre, Amnesty International Secretary General, *Globalisation: AI and Socio-Economic Rights* (2001) Amnesty International <http://web.amnesty.org>.

Swedish Migration Board, *Gender-Based Persecution: Guidelines for Investigation and Evaluation of the Needs of Women for Protection* (2001) <www.migrationsverket.se>.

UK Immigration and Nationality Directorate, 'Discretionary Leave' (2006) <http://www.ind.homeoffice.gov.uk/ind/en/home/laws___policy/policy_instructions/apis/discretionary_leave.html>.

UK Immigration Appellate Authority, *Asylum Gender Guidelines* (2000) <http://www.asylumsupport.info/publications/iaa/gender.pdf>.

United Nations Children's Fund, United Nations Office of the High Commissioner for Refugees and the Organization for Security and Cooperation in Europe/Office for Democratic Institutions and Human Rights, *Trafficking in Human Beings in Southeastern Europe* (2002) <http://www.unicef.org/ceecis/Trafficking.Report.2005.pdf>

United Nations International Research and Training Institute for the Advancement of Women, *International Agreements* (2006) <http://www.un-instraw.org/en/index.php?option=content&task=blogcategory&id=178&Itemid=239> at 31 May 2006.

US Department of Justice, Immigration and Naturalization Service, *Guidelines for Children's Asylum Claims* (1998) <http://uscis.gov/graphics/lawsregs/handbook/10a_ChldrnGdlns.pdf>.

Others

Deardroff, Julie, ' Mom Wins Asylum for Autistic Son with Autism ', *Chicago Tribune*, 21 February 2001.

'IJ Grants Asylum to Chinese Girl Fleeing Forced Marriage' (2000) 77(45) *Interpreter Releases* 1634.

'IJ Grants Asylum to Guatemalan Street Child' (2002) 79 *Interpreter Releases* 440.

'IJ Grants Asylum to HIV Positive Man, General Counsel Issues HIV Instructions' (1996) 73 *Interpreter Releases* 901.
Immigration and Review Board, *Discrimination as a Basis for a Well-Founded Fear of Persecution* (IRB Legal Services, 1991).
'INS Grants Asylum to Autistic Child Persecuted due to Disability' (2001) 78(13) *Interpreter Releases* 604.
Jarvis, Catriona, 'Can Trafficked Persons Be Refugees?', in Immigration Appellate Authority, *Legal and Research Unit Update*, 29 February 2004.
Legal Services, Immigration and Refugee Board, *Consolidated Grounds in the Immigration and Refugee Protection Act: Persons in Need of Protection, Risk to Life or Risk of Cruel and Unusual Treatment or Punishment* (15 May 2002).
Magar, Binda Kumari, Forum for Women, Law and Development, *Submission to UN Commission on Human Rights, Sub-Commission on the Protection and Promotion of Human Rights, Working Group on Minorities, 10th Session* (Nepal: 1–5 March 2004).
Musalo, Karen and Stephen Knight, 'Unequal Protection', *Bulletin of the Atomic Scientists*, November/December 2002.
'Ostracism, Lack of Medical Care Support HIV-Positive Alien's Asylum Quest, IJ Rules' 78(3) *Interpreter Releases* 233.
US Department of Justice, Office of General Counsel, 'Legal Opinion: Palestinian Asylum Applicants' (27 October 1995).
'US-Asylum Granted to Person Living with HIV' (1996) 3(1) *Canadian HIV/Aids Policy and Law Newsletter*.

Index

For page references in relation to cases and treaties, please refer to the Table of Cases and Table of Treaties respectively.

absolute rights 175–8
accommodation, denial of; *see* housing *and* evictions
accumulation of harm of persecution 105, 107, 132–6, 214
adequate standard of living 108–9, 213–14; *see also* food; health; housing
administrative tribunals 21
affirmative action 147
African Charter on Human and Peoples' Rights 66, 320
African Commission on Human and Peoples' Rights 233
agents of persecution 98, 107–9, 201–2; *see also* persecution, by non-state agents
agricultural co-operatives 312–13
AIDS 187, 210, 217, 322, 323, 350
Albania 269–70, 326
Aleinikoff, T.A. 301
Algeria 314, 315
Alston, Philip 173
American Convention on Human Rights 67, 320
Amnesty International 19, 133
anti-discrimination principles 276–7, 283, 319
arbitrary detention 87, 113, 114
arranged marriages 244
association, freedom of, *see* freedom of association
associations, voluntary, fear on account of membership in 297
asylum applications 3, 6, 97, 99, 102, 128–31, 139, 266, 267, 288, 323
Australia 22, 45, 48, 118–20, 129, 246, 253, 256–8, 264, 269, 271–4, 278, 286, 297, 315, 321, 333–5, 344, 346–7

Refugee Review Tribunal (RRT) 73, 98, 100, 122, 137–9, 143–4, 202, 216–18, 222, 226–31, 233, 246, 262, 266–7, 271, 312, 321–2, 327, 339
Austria 129
autism 322

Bangladesh 260–1
beauty industry 315–16
'being persecuted' *see* persecution
Bhabha, Jacqueline 151, 211
Bingham Lord 278
blacklisting 95
Bosnia 241
Branson J 271
Brownlie, Ian 180
Bulgaria 125–6
bullying 211, 218
Burchett J 315–16
Burkina Faso 226, 229
Burma 222
'but for' test 255–6, 261

Cambodia 315
Canada 22, 29, 101, 103, 106, 116, 120, 121, 125, 148, 152, 227, 247, 264, 279, 295, 306, 308, 318, 327, 330–1, 334, 349, 352
Refugee Protection Division (RPD) 103–4, 117, 122, 133, 144, 149, 203–4, 206, 209–12, 214, 218–19, 226, 229, 232, 239, 244, 262–3, 272, 284, 285, 304, 306–7, 312–13, 318–19, 323, 330–2, 336–8
Carlier, Jean-Yves 112–13, 120, 123, 193
caste 304, 312
categories of human rights 113–23, 147–51, 168–70

causation 254–63
Chechnya 204
child soldiers 339
children
  abandoned 209, 210, 333
  and the right to education 216–21
  as a particular social group 329–39
  born outside 'one child policy' 4, 104, 106, 334
  definition of 329–30
  exploitation of 216
  harms faced by 243–5, 265, 269, 272, 281, 283, 286, 309, 339
  needs of 329
  persecution of 206–12, 335
  protection of 171, 207–10, 212
  psychological harm done to 211
  rights of 161, 183–4
  trafficking of see trafficking
  with HIV 210, 232
China 2, 4, 106, 204, 244, 284, 285, 297, 306, 316, 329, 330
citizenship status 292
civil and political rights 15, 16, 19, 46, 66, 99, 113, 122, 127, 134, 152–4, 157–9, 165, 170–1, 173, 178, 183–9, 213–14, 353
civil society 19
civil war 11, 288, 348
class-based organizations 312
class, fear on account of 304–13
Coker, Jane 66
Cold War 15, 16, 164, 166–7
Colombia 306, 312
Committee on Economic, Social and Cultural Rights see Economic Committee
Committee on Racial Discrimination 133
Committee on the Rights of the Child 184, 216–17
common law 21, 23, 30, 137, 257, 295, 305
complementary protection 349–53
concluding observations, of treaty bodies 81–5
confiscation of property 109–10
Congo, Democratic Republic of 4, 284
constitutional rights 196
Convention Against Torture (CAT) 349–50
Convention on the Elimination of All Forms of Discrimination Against Women (CEDAW) 64–6, 72, 77, 143, 150, 153, 178, 183, 207, 309
  Preamble to 66
Convention on the Elimination of All Forms of Racial Discrimination (CERD) 64, 143, 178, 183

Convention on the Rights of the Child 64–5, 103, 143, 178, 183, 207–8, 212, 215, 232, 309, 320, 329–30
Convention Relating to the Status of Refugees see Refugee Convention
Coomans, Fons 222
core entitlements and obligations 141, 177, 190, 195–214, 201–13, 216, 226, 228, 289, 345
Council of Europe 67, 68
Craven, M. 164, 177
credibility of applications for refugee status 238–40
criminal justice system 58
Croatia 242
cruel, inhuman or degrading treatment 21, 114, 116, 124–5, 160–1, 185, 350;
  see also inhuman or degrading treatment
Cuba 214
cultural differences 219
cultural relativity 66, 68–9
cumulative harm see accumulation of harm as persecution
customary international law 53–4, 350
Czech Republic 4, 108–9, 134, 242, 289

Dawson J 298
death penalty 353
'deliberate imposition of substantial economic disadvantage' 119, 128
derogation from rights 114–15, 169–70, 175–81
detention, arbitrary see arbitrary detention
developing countries 146, 309
dictionary definitions of terms 47–9, 78, 272–4
Director of International Protection 32
disabled persons 73, 138, 141, 226, 229, 281, 318–23
  definition of 320
discrimination
  against non-nationals 146–7
  as distinct from persecution 213, 229
  educational 222
  indirect 271, 277, 279, 286
  in distribution of resources 230–2
  in the workplace 127
  racial 217, 306
  right to non-discrimination 150–1
  societal 282
  socio-economic 94–8, 142–7
  see also anti-discrimination principles
disease control 172, 233
dismissal from work 129, 317
disparate treatment and disparate impact 271, 277, 279, 283

dissenters, political and religious 8
dissidents 7
domestic violence *see* violence, domestic
Duvalier, Jean-Claude 252, 310

economic class as a social grouping 304–13
Economic Committee 17, 83–4, 103, 137, 140–2, 153, 171–3, 177, 197, 196–200, 203, 205, 215–17, 220–2, 230, 236–8, 241–7, 261, 290, 309, 311, 320
general comments 82–4, 153, 171–8, 196
economic deprivation *see* persecution; and socio-economic rights
economic migrants 2–14, 88, 110, 154, 238–47, 339–41, 343
definition of 5–7, 21, 25
economic persecution *see* persecution; and socio-economic rights
economic/political distinction 1–11, 18–19, 249–51
economic proscription 90–1, 99, 110
economic refugees 2–14, 238–47
economic relativity 311
economic and social rights
see socio-economic rights
Ecuador 316
education
as empowerment 215, 222
deprivation of as persecution 103–4, 214–26
free and compulsory education 215, 219
non-discrimination in 142–5
obligation of the state to provide 214–20
primary education 215–20
private schools 221
right of parents to choose the education of their children 221
right to 103–7, 115, 130–1, 133, 141–6, 154, 171, 182, 184, 185, 197, 214–26, 244
religious education 221
secondary 221–6
segregation in 220
Special Rapporteur on 17
tertiary 142–3, 221–6
ejusdem generis doctrine 295–6, 314–5; *see also* protected characteristics
El Salvador 262, 306–7, 318–36
emergencies, public 176–7, 179
employment *see* work
employment status *see* occupation
enforceability of rights 168–9, 178, 180
environmental degradation 233

equal pay 171
equality/equal protection
see anti-discrimination principles; discrimination; women
ethnic minorities 108, 125–7, 139
European Convention for the Protection of Human Rights and Fundamental Freedoms 67–8, 70, 186–9, 349–52
European Court of Human Rights (ECHR) 59, 69, 186, 350
European Union 280
Directives of 195, 350, 353
evictions 139–40, 187, 198
evidence, for refugee claim 286–9
ExCom resolutions 71–2
ex post facto offences 114
extortion 251–4, 286
Eyle clan 206

failure to act *see* persecution
family members 329, 336–7
famine 10, 234–5, 288, 348
fear of persecution 201–2, 254, 271, 273, 274, 281–3, 286, 288, 290, 298, 313, 314, 316, 337–8; *see also* persecution; well-founded fear of
female genital mutilation (FGM) 48, 65, 211
Fiji 110, 255, 287
financial grievances (as distinct from persecution) 109–10
first level rights 114
'floodgates' argument 79, 135, 261, 327, 344–8
food
deprivation of as persecution 234–5
right to 172, 185, 197–8, 233–4
Special Rapporteur on 18
'for reasons of' *see* nexus
forced evictions *see* evictions
forced labour 161, 216
forced migration 341
Forest J 194
fourth-level rights 147–8
France 110
freedom of association 168, 182, 312
freedom of conscience 179
freedom of movement 183
freedom of religion *see* religious discrimination/freedom
freedom of speech 168, 191, 198
fundamental rights and freedoms 43, 54, 120, 133, 149, 179, 180, 192, 199, 212, 213, 216, 224, 226–8, 230, 234, 275, 282, 312, 314, 324, 343, 345, 354

Gambia 188
Gender Guidelines 325, 338

'generalized economic disadvantage' 287, 289
gender, *see* women
general comments, of treaty bodies 81–4, 153, 181; *see also* Economic Committee, general comments, Human Rights Committee, general comments
generations of human rights, *see* categories of human rights
Germany 11, 129, 279
girls *see also* children; women
girls, discrimination and other harms faced by 217, 244, 284–5, 309, 328
Gleeson CJ 202, 269, 294, 303
Goodwill-Gill, Guy 192
government employees 97–101
government policies 203–4, 343–4, 346–8
Grahl-Madsen, Atle 87, 90
group-based harm/persecution 286–9
Guatemala 28–36, 312–13
Gummow J 294

Haiti 2, 252, 310
Hale LJ 78
handbook, UNHCR *see* United Nations High Commissioner for Refugees
Harding, Jeremy 9, 10
hardship, *see* socio-economic rights
Hathaway, James C. 27, 56, 58–9, 64, 70, 91, 99, 113–25, 127, 136, 137, 145, 148, 168–9, 178, 191, 199, 248, 259, 354
health
    content of right to 226–7
    deprivation of as persecution 104, 226–35
    environment and the right to health 233–4
    equal access to health services 226–7
    resource allocation of services 230–2
    right to 104–5, 116, 133, 141–2, 145–6, 154, 177, 184, 185, 197, 206, 226–35
    Special Rapporteur on 18
Heerey J 273
hierarchy of human rights 112–23, 123–54, 147–8, 150–1, 155–68, 178–82, 186–9, 192, 194, 213, 235, 342
    normative 157–68, 235
    problems with 123–32, 136, 138
hierarchy of obligation 168, 181, 235
Higgins, Rosalyn 70
HIV status 104, 210, 217, 227–32, 307, 312, 319, 321–3, 350
Hobhouse LJ 314
Hoffmann, Lord 57

'holistic' approach to refugee claims 25
homelessness 185, 203
homosexuality 48, 233, 246–7, 299, 312
Honduras 250, 283, 313
Hong Kong 2
housing, right to
    and property rights 147–50
    deprivation as persecution 139–40
    Special Rapporteur on 18
    see also evictions
human dignity 102–3, 127, 130, 166, 193, 215, 300, 308, 311, 313
human rights 13, 15–7, 23–4
    interdependence of 181–9, 235
    international principles of 27, 36–44, 50–1, 58, 79–81, 84, 89, 301, 303, 312; *see also* international law of human rights
    universality and indivisibility of 166, 181, 192
human rights approach to refugee determination 27–36, 87, 190–201, 299, 342
    confirmation by context 49–51
    legitimacy of 75–84
    workability of 85–6
Human Rights Committee (HRC) 68, 70, 150, 152, 160–1, 173, 178, 179, 184–5, 197
    General comments 160–1, 184–5
human rights violations 46, 80–1, 157, 174, 190–3, 282, 341–5
    seriousness of 193–5, 198
Human Rights Watch (HRW) 19, 150, 217, 232
human rights workers 315
Hungary 219

illegitimate children *see* children; 'one child policy'
immediate obligation, duties of 172–4, 177; *see also* obligations (of states)
immigration control 347
inability to protect *see* agents of persecution
India 252, 304
infant mortality 161, 185
inhuman or degrading treatment 187–8, 232; *see also* cruel; inhuman or degrading treatment
innate or immutable characteristics *see* membership of a particular social group
intention 237, 263–70, 272, 274–86, 290
    and the *nexus* criterion 263–70
    of the persecutor or home state 264–70
Inter-American Court of Human Rights 69

INDEX 383

interdependence and indivisibility
  (of human rights) 17, 150–1, 164–6,
  181–9
internal protection alternative 28
International Association of Refugee Law
  Judges (IARLJ) 33, 35, 37, 113, 120–1,
  193–4
International Bill of Rights (IBR) 27, 56, 66,
  113, 120, 168
International Court of Justice (ICJ) 61
International Covenant on Economic,
  Social and Cultural Rights (ICESCR)
  17, 27–8, 64, 83–4, 95, 98, 103, 107,
  111, 113, 115–17, 122, 137, 138,
  141–8, 150, 153, 158–61, 170–3,
  176–7, 182–3, 196, 199–200, 203, 214,
  215, 220, 222, 226, 309, 313, 317,
  320
  Preamble to 165–6
International Covenant on Civil and
  Political Rights (ICCPR) 27, 64, 68, 98,
  99, 113–17, 122, 143, 150, 160–1, 169,
  173, 176–9, 182–5, 191, 221, 232, 309,
  318–9, 350, 352
  Preamble to 165–6
international law 15, 17, 18, 22, 25, 33–5, 40,
  50–3, 60, 75–6, 79, 86, 204
  criminal law 57–8
  fragmentation of 157, 167–8
  of human rights 50–2, 75, 81, 85, 90,
    155–7, 167, 169–70, 183, 193, 195,
    202–3, 235, 271, 276, 317–19,
    342–3
  possible conflict with domestic
    jurisdiction 347
  relevance of 57–8, 61, 67
  see also customary international law
International Law Commission (ILC) 35, 52,
  55, 56, 60, 157, 167
Iran 149, 212, 218, 222, 226, 269, 334
Ireland 14, 186
Israel 96, 327

Jacobs, Francis G. 68
Jamaica 322
Jewish communities 11
judicial conversations 22, 69
judicial review 86
jus cogens norms 53–4, 180
justiciability of rights 162–3, 168, 184

Kenya 139, 150, 217, 328
kidnapping 267
King J 310
Kirby J 45, 273
Klabbers, Jan 42
Kosovo 189

Kuwait 107
Kyrgyzstan 206, 210

Laws LJ 277–8
Lebanon 133
legal aid 186–9
legislation, domestic 346
liberal approach to rights 159, 259, 262, 275,
  345–9
liberty and security of the person, right to
  92, 114–15, 132
life
  right to 114, 160, 181, 197, 198
  social dimensions of 185, 234
life expectancy 185
Limburg principles 163, 171
limitations/restrictions (on rights) 176, 177,
  195–7
livelihood, right to earn see work
Lloyd, Lord 41–2

Maastricht Guidelines on Violations of
  Economic, Social and Cultural Rights
  163
Macoutes 95, 252
Madgwick J 274–6
Malaysia 316
Mali 229
malnutrition 161, 185
Mansfield J 98, 102
margin of appreciation 68–9
McHugh J 293–4, 298
medical treatment 104, 107, 115, 133, 141,
  188, 226–33, 352
  forced/coerced 232–3
membership of a particular social group
  (MPSG) 236, 267, 272, 281–5, 288, 292,
  296, 323, 339, 343
  as a Refugee Convention ground
    292–303
Mexico 209, 337
Michigan Guidelines 259
Midgan caste 304–5
midwives 314
migrant workers 183, 187
minimum state obligations, see core
  obligations
minorities, see ethnic minorities
mixed motives 247–51, 268, 290
Montreal Principles on Women's
  Economic, Social and Cultural Rights
  163
motivation
  of applicants for refugee status 238,
    243, 276
  of persecutors 267, 272, 280–1
  see also mixed motives

Muldoon J 275
Mummery LJ 314

Nathwani, Niraj 79
nationality 291
natural disasters 9, 348
natural law arguments 158
Nepal 311
Netherlands 3
New Zealand 22, 116, 120, 122, 144, 190, 258, 260–1, 295
  Refugee Status Appeals Authority (RSAA) 48, 71, 80, 94, 99, 102, 108–9, 117–18, 124, 136, 137, 146, 195, 234, 242, 274, 289, 304, 308, 310–11
nexus criterion 24, 236–8, 247–51, 261, 262, 270, 272–4, 281–3, 286–7, 289, 293, 324, 329, 343, 348–9, 354
  methods of satisfying and the requirement for intention 263–70
Nicaragua 129, 148, 239
Nigeria 233, 271, 285, 307
non-derogable rights *see* derogation from rights
non-discrimination, *see* discrimination
non-government organizations 4, 19–20, 153, 231
non-state actors, *see* agents of persecution
non-refoulement 21, 25, 45, 92, 349, 350
North Korea 2, 235

obligations (of states)
  positive/negative 159–61
  progressive/immediate 169–72
  requiring expenditure 161–2
  to fulfil 174–5
  to protect 174–5
  to respect 174–5
  vague/precise 162–3
object and purpose of treaty 40–9
obligation to fulfil 174–5
obligation to respect 174
obligations of result and of conduct 171
occupation defining a social group 313–18
Ogoni people 233–4
omissions of state *see* persecution, failure to act
one child policy 4, 106, 204, 297, 334
'one factor' test 256–9, 261
orphans 209–10, 212, 284, 286, 333
Orucu, Esin 195
Optional Protocol to the ICESCR 163

Pakistan 269, 346
Parker LJ 278

particular social groups (PSGs) 294–5, 297–304, 306–8, 310, 312–15, 317–19, 321–39; *see also* membership of a particular social group
permeability of rights 185, 189
persecution
  agents of, *see* agents of persecution
  and socio-economic rights 90–123
  as distinct from discrimination 213, 229
  by non-state agents 107–9, 201–2, 265
  current approach to 156–7, 342
  definition of 27–34, 37, 39, 48, 53, 56–8, 62, 64, 73, 76–81, 86, 97, 114, 124–5, 127, 138, 149, 151, 154, 169, 175, 178, 180–1, 190–2, 204–5, 212–18, 234, 236, 310, 316, 344–5
  economic 88, 90–123
  of women and children 65–6, 206–12, 335
  ordinary meaning of 272–3
  passive-voice terminology for ('being persecuted') 273–4
  risk of 219, 226–7, 230, 284, 286, 311–12, 324, 330, 332, 339
  through *failure* to act 161, 202–5
  well-founded fear of 87, 108, 238, 248, 249, 259, 271, 291, 326, 336;
  see also fear of persecution
Peru 218
Philippines, the 239
Pill LJ 314
Poland 319
Pol Pot 315
police corruption 269
political opinion, persecution on basis of 249–53
political rights *see* civil and political rights
political will 354
poor, *see* poverty
positivism, legal 70
poverty 19, 66, 185–6, 206, 216, 222, 229, 237, 265, 267, 284, 306, 311, 317–19, 333
  defining a social group 305–12
  definition of 311
  'predicament' approach 270–86
privacy, right to 160, 187, 191, 198
professional workers 317
professions, *see* work
programmatic rights 138
progressive realization of rights 170–6
property rights 109, 116, 147–51
  and the right to housing 110, 147–50, 183, 232
  of women 147–51
proportionality 176

prostitution 161, 206, 243, 266–7, 281, 283, 312, 316, 327–8, 339
protected characteristics 295, 299–303, 306–8, 313, 314, 317–19, 322, 331–2
protection *see also* internal protection alternative; agents of persecution
protection, duty of 108, 161, 174, 202–5
public/private distinction 65–6
'pull' and 'push' factors in migration 7

quality of life 105, 214

racial discrimination *see* discrimination
rape 265, 284
'reactive migration' (Richmond) 9
Refugee Convention 1–6, 15–17, 20–2, 236, 237, 245, 341, 348, 353–4
  common understanding of 78
  context for 49, 274
  evolutionary approach to 63, 354
  grounds under 24, 28, 237, 246–63, 268–70, 276, 277, 282–3, 285, 289–92, 324, 339, 343, 348, 353
  implementation of 50–1, 207
  inclusivity of 78, 81
  interpretation of 22–4, 27–32, 36–44, 49, 51, 54–5, 62, 71, 75–7, 86, 91, 190, 200, 275, 277, 299
  object and purpose of 42–9, 58, 79, 86, 256, 274–5, 299, 345
  Preamble to 16, 42–4, 49, 314
  Protocol to (1967) 62, 78, 348
refugee status
  assessments of 79–80, 167
  definition of 15, 21, 23, 25–6, 28, 32–3, 35, 46, 49, 52, 79–80, 206, 236, 273
  rights attaching to 22
regional human rights bodies and standards 51, 67–70, 186
Reinhardt J 252
religious discrimination and religious freedom 93, 98, 100, 129, 176, 198, 226, 233, 271, 291
religious education 221
religious orders 314
reservations, treaties 78
resource constraints 138–41, 140–2, 176, 205, 228
retrogressive measures 138, 172, 221
return to country of origin 112
Richmond, Anthony H. 8–9
Rodger of Earlsferry, Lord 257
Roma communities 4, 108–9, 126, 134, 219–20, 242, 289, 291
Romania 224, 323
Russia 48, 141, 204, 206, 233, 322

Sachs J 182
St Kitts 187–8
schizophrenia 352
Scott, Craig 173
second-level rights 176, 178, 188
Sedley LJ 25
sex, persecution on account of *see* women
sex trade 268, 285, 306
sexual harassment 312
sexual orientation *see* homosexuality
sexual violence 208, 211, 212, 265, 282, 327–8; *see also* rape
shelter *see* housing
Simma, Bruno 62, 71
Simon-Brown LJ 92
Singapore 232
singling out of individuals for refugee status 10–11, 287–8, 290
slavery 114
Slovakia 134
social class 298, 304–7, 306–7
social group *see* membership of a particular social group
social perception approach to MPSG 297, 299–300, 313, 315, 321
social rights *see* socio-economic rights
socio-economic rights 15–26, 28, 46, 52, 84, 86, 90–123, 132–6, 142–7, 157–9, 169–70, 182–90, 199–206, 213–14, 235–42, 247–8, 287, 289–91, 318–19, 324, 335, 339–46, 350, 353–5
  group-based nature of 287
  hierarchical approaches to 113–23, 136, 138
  inherent difficulties over claims to 151–4, 237–8
  progressive implementation of 137–41
soft law 70–5, 135
sole motives 247
Somalia 206, 262, 284, 304–5, 326
South Africa 102
South Korea 328
Spijkerboer, Thomas 135
Steinbock, Daniel 78–9, 343
Steyn, Lord 328
stigmatization 228–9, 322
Storey, Hugo 302
street children 301, 306, 312, 335–7
subjective approach to human rights 38–9
Sudan 234
sufficiency of protection 270, 325; *see also* protection
surrogate protection 77, 284

Tanzania 326
targeting requirement *see* singling out; *see also* intention
taxi drivers 315, 317
terrorism 252
Thailand 267-8, 327
third-level rights 116-17, 122, 124-7, 132-3, 148, 151-2, 169, 175, 187-8, 337
tort 256
torture 114, 160, 168, 197, 349, 350, 353
trade unions 171, 177, 312-13
trafficking 4, 8, 74, 161, 206, 243-4, 246, 254, 265-72, 280-1, 284-6, 306, 311, 330, 337, 339
treaties
　common intentions of parties to 56-7
　evolutionary aspect of 59-63
　interpretation of 40-1, 53, 55, 59-63, 71, 72, 75-6, 86, 196, 298, 342, 348
　inter-temporality issue for 60-1
　object and purpose 40-9
　on human rights 55-6, 64
　preambles of 42-3, 45
treaty bodies 75, 81-5, 152-3, 159, 170, 195
Tuitt, Patricia 6
typology of state obligation 173-5

unable to protect 108; *see also* agents of persecution
unemployment *see* work
union membership, right to 312-13
United Kingdom 23, 29, 116, 120, 187, 258, 264, 281, 296, 307, 346, 350
　Court of Appeal 116, 121, 139, 195, 276-8, 314
　House of Lords 277-8
　Immigration Appeal Tribunal (IAT) 92, 105, 116, 121, 124, 145, 151, 188, 206, 214, 224, 236, 240-3, 262, 269, 305, 314, 328, 329, 335, 350-1
　Queen's Bench Division 242
　Special Adjudicator 241, 242, 284
United Nations 164-5
　Charter 43
　Commission on Human Rights 17, 311
　Declaration on the Rights of the Disabled 320
　General Assembly 72, 73
　High Commissioner for Refugees (UNHCR) 9-10, 22, 32, 37, 44, 49, 51, 58, 71, 72, 75, 121, 223, 259, 267, 279, 285, 293, 300, 322, 325, 348
　　Handbook (1979) 11-13, 32, 71-2, 95
　see also Human Rights Committee; Economic Committee

United States 2, 23, 37, 85, 99-101, 109, 119, 127-8, 130, 134, 141, 208-10, 213, 227, 233, 256-8, 264, 287, 307, 322, 349
　Board of Immigration Appeals (BIA) 249-52, 255, 283-4, 296, 315, 316, 323, 339
　Immigration and Naturalization Service (INS) 287, 323
　Supreme Court 264
Universal Declaration of Human Rights (UDHR) 16, 27-8, 43, 49, 64, 95, 113-17, 138, 143, 148, 164, 309, 313
university education 224-5; *see also* education
unwilling to protect 108; *see also* agents of persecution
Uzbekistan 246, 339

Vienna Convention on the Law of Treaties (VCLT) 35, 40-1, 49, 51, 55, 60-1, 72, 75, 190, 272, 274, 299
　Art 31 41-2
　Art 31 (2) 49
　Art 31 (3)(c) 51-62, 79
Vienna Declaration and Programme of Action (1993) 166, 181
Vietnam 2, 191, 316, 335
violence
　domestic 79, 209, 211, 265, 269, 282, 303, 335-6
　fear of 167
voluntary migration 6-9, 25, 238, 243-7, 246, 341, 343
voting rights 160
vulnerable groups 205-6, 226, 265, 268, 272, 281, 283-6, 310

warlords 10
water, right to 107, 161, 172-3, 197
wealth of applicants for refugee status 239
well founded fear *see* persecution
White, R.C.A. 68
Wiener J 251
women
　as a particular social group 285-6, 303, 324-8
　discrimination against 38, 72
　empowerment of 222
　equality for 66, 171
　harms faced by 185, 207, 243-5, 265-70, 281-2, 309
　persecution of 65-6
　rights of 15, 16, 135, 147-50
　violence against 72

work
  dangerous 101
  denial of as persecution 94–103
  freedom of choice of occupation 313–18
  just and favourable working conditions 99–101
  personal and social dimension of 101–2
  right not to be arbitrarily deprived of 315–18
  right to 90–1, 94–103, 105–7, 115–16, 124, 126, 130–3, 138, 154, 183, 197–8, 313, 314, 323
  suitable/commensurate with qualifications 99–101

World Bank 309
World Conference on Human Rights (1993) 166
World Trade Organization (WTO) 76

Young, Wendy 151, 211
Yugoslavia 92

Zaire 203
Zimbabwe 102, 234
Zolberg, Aristide R. 7–9, 13

CAMBRIDGE STUDIES IN INTERNATIONAL AND COMPARATIVE LAW

Books in the series

The Concept of Non-International Armed Conflict in International Humanitarian Law
Anthony Cullen

The Challenge of Child Labour in International Law
Franziska Humbert

Shipping Interdiction and the Law of the Sea
Douglas Guilfoyle

International Courts and Environmental Protection
Tim Stephens

Legal Principles in WTO Dispute
Andrew D. Mitchell

War Crimes in Internal Armed Conflicts
Eve La Haye

Humanitarian Occupation
Gregory H. Fox

The International Law of Environmental Impact Assessment: Process, Substance and Integration
Neil Craik

The Law and Practice of International Territorial Administration: Versailles, Iraq and Beyond
Carsten Stahn

Cultural Products and the World Trade Organization
Tania Voon

United Nations Sanctions and the Rule of Law
Jeremy Farrall

National Law in WTO Law
Effectiveness and Good Governance in the World Trading System
Sharif Bhuiyan

The Threat of Force in International Law
Nikolas Stürchler

Indigenous Rights and United Nations Standards
Alexandra Xanthaki

International Refugee Law and Socio-Economic Rights
Michelle Foster

The Protection of Cultural Property in Armed Conflict
Roger O'Keefe

Interpretation and Revision of International Boundary Decisions
Kaiyan Homi Kaikobad

Multinationals and Corporate Social Responsibility
Limitations and Opportunities in International Law
Jennifer A. Zerk

Judiciaries within Europe
A Comparative Review
John Bell

Law in Times of Crisis
Emergency Powers in Theory and Practice
Oren Gross and Fionnuala Ní Aoláin

Vessel-Source Marine Pollution
The Law and Politics of International Regulation
Alan Tan

Enforcing Obligations Erga Omnes *in International Law*
Christian J. Tams

Non-Governmental Organisations in International Law
Anna-Karin Lindblom

Democracy, Minorities and International Law
Steven Wheatley

Prosecuting International Crimes
Selectivity and the International Law Regime
Robert Cryer

Compensation for Personal Injury in English, German and Italian Law
A Comparative Outline
Basil Markesinis, Michael Coester, Guido Alpa, Augustus Ullstein

Dispute Settlement in the UN Convention on the Law of the Sea
Natalie Klein

The International Protection of Internally Displaced Persons
Catherine Phuong

Imperialism, Sovereignty and the Making of International Law
Antony Anghie

Necessity, Proportionality and the Use of Force by States
Judith Gardam

International Legal Argument in the Permanent Court of International Justice
The Rise of the International Judiciary
Ole Spiermann

Great Powers and Outlaw States
Unequal Sovereigns in the International Legal Order
Gerry Simpson

Local Remedies in International Law
C. F. Amerasinghe

Reading Humanitarian Intervention
Human Rights and the Use of Force in International Law
Anne Orford

Conflict of Norms in Public International Law
How WTO Law Relates to Other Rules of Law
Joost Pauwelyn

Transboundary Damage in International Law
Hanqin Xue

European Criminal Procedures
Edited by Mireille Delmas-Marty and John Spencer

The Accountability of Armed Opposition Groups in International Law
Liesbeth Zegveld

Sharing Transboundary Resources
International Law and Optimal Resource Use
Eyal Benvenisti

International Human Rights and Humanitarian Law
René Provost

Remedies Against International Organisations
Karel Wellens

Diversity and Self-Determination in International Law
Karen Knop

The Law of Internal Armed Conflict
Lindsay Moir

International Commercial Arbitration and African States
Practice, Participation and Institutional Development
Amazu A. Asouzu

The Enforceability of Promises in European Contract Law
James Gordley

International Law in Antiquity
David J. Bederman

Money Laundering
A New International Law Enforcement Model
Guy Stessens

Good Faith in European Contract Law
Reinhard Zimmermann and Simon Whittaker

On Civil Procedure
J. A. Jolowicz

Trusts
A Comparative Study
Maurizio Lupoi

The Right to Property in Commonwealth Constitutions
Tom Allen

International Organizations Before National Courts
August Reinisch

The Changing International Law of High Seas Fisheries
Francisco Orrego Vicuña

Trade and the Environment
A Comparative Study of EC and US Law
Damien Geradin

Unjust Enrichment
A Study of Private Law and Public Values
Hanoch Dagan

Religious Liberty and International Law in Europe
Malcolm D. Evans

Ethics and Authority in International Law
Alfred P. Rubin

Sovereignty Over Natural Resources
Balancing Rights and Duties
Nico Schrijver

The Polar Regions and the Development of International Law
Donald R. Rothwell

Fragmentation and the International Relations of Micro-States
Self-determination and Statehood
Jorri Duursma

Principles of the Institutional Law of International Organizations
C. F. Amerasinghe

Lightning Source UK Ltd.
Milton Keynes UK
UKHW02n2022120718
325645UK00011B/145/P